EVE'S SEED

EVE'S SEED

Biology, the Sexes, and the Course of History

ROBERT S. McELVAINE

McGraw-Hill

New York   San Francisco   Washington, D.C.   Auckland   Bogotá
Caracas   Lisbon   London   Madrid   Mexico City   Milan
Montreal   New Delhi   San Juan   Singapore
Sydney   Tokyo   Toronto

FOR

LAUREN,
SCOTT, and EVAN

Library of Congress Cataloging-in-Publication Data
McElvaine, Robert S., 1947–
  Eve's seed : biology, the sexes, and the course of history / Robert S. McElvaine.
    p. cm.
  Includes bibliographical references and index.
  ISBN 0-07-135528-6
   1. Sex role—History. I. Title.
  HQ1075 .M386 2000
  305.3'09—dc21   00-056634

McGraw-Hill

A Division of The **McGraw·Hill** Companies

1 2 3 4 5 6 7 8 9 0 DOC/DOC 0 9 8 7 6 5 4 3 2 1 0

ISBN 0-07-135528-6

Printed and bound by R. R. Donnelley & Sons Company.

McGraw-Hill books are available at special quantity discounts to use as premiums and sales promotions, or for use in corporate training programs. For more information, please write to the Director of Special Sales, Professional Publishing, McGraw-Hill, Two Penn Plaza, New York, NY 10121-2298. Or contact your local bookstore.

 This book is printed on recycled, acid-free paper containing a minimum of 50% recycled, de-inked fiber.

CONTENTS

ACKNOWLEDGMENTS

The minute specialization of academics in narrow subdivisions of knowledge is one of the pernicious manifestations of the atomization that plagues the modern, excessively mobile, marketplace world. Sociologist Robert Bellah and his colleagues have put it well: "When the world comes to us in pieces, in fragments, lacking any overall pattern, it is hard to see how it might be transformed" [*Habits of the Heart: Individualism and Commitment in American Life* (Berkeley and Los Angeles: University of California Press, 1985; New York: Harper & Row, 1986), p. 277]. If we are ever going to put our societies back together, we may well find that the place to start is in trying to put knowledge back together. This book attempts to contribute to that process.

Even so, one must draw on specialized knowledge in any attempt to take a more holistic view. We have to transcend dualism and realize that *both* the pieces *and* the whole are important. I have asked many specialists to read and criticize the portions of what I have written that deal with their areas of expertise. They have saved me from several potential embarrassments. I hasten to add that in a number of instances I have not followed their advice, and none of them should be held accountable for any errors of fact or oddities of interpretation that remain.

Among those who have read and commented upon portions of the manuscript as it has progressed are Sarah L. Armstrong, Robert Bergmark, George Bey, Kristen Brown, Cleta Ellington, Tracy Fessenden, Richard Freis, Michael Galchinsky, Paula Garrett, Dick Highfill, T. W. Lewis, Mark Lytle, Anne MacMaster, William H. McNeill, Debora L. Mann, Robert B. Nevins, Leanora Olivia, Judith Page, Darby Ray, Lisa Sigel, Elise L. Smith, Steven G. Smith, Elvin Sunds, Lionel Tiger, and Sanford Zale.

The ideas in this book were shaped in important ways by interaction with the students in my classes at Millsaps College over a period of several years.

Many students have broadened my understanding much more than they realize. Seth Holiday stands out as particularly deserving of thanks for his direct contributions to my thinking. My student assistants in the course on these ideas that I have taught for the last several years, Lynn Pohl, Ashley Phillips, Tara Chase, Erin Keller, and Sarah Casey, have been very helpful. Amanda Coody, Bridget Foss, Allison Harris, Christopher Hedglin, Colleen Graham, Jake Kidder, Tara McLellan, Sarah Katherine McNeil, Laurin Stennis, and Lee Anne Waskom are other students who helped to advance my thinking on certain points.

Among the others who helped me in a variety of ways are Mel Berger, Carol and Charles Boyle, David C. Davis, Patrick E. Delana, William D. Frazier, Betty Freidan, Catherine R. Freis, Michael Fuquay, Floreada Harmon, Clark Hultquist, Frank M. Laney, Anna and John Lee, Robert and Rose Lee, Laura E. Nym Mayhall and Michael Dunn, Charles and Joan Meehan, Tom and Mary Ellen Molokie, Fifi Oscard, James and Betty Parks, Linda and Michael Raff, Charles and Harrylyn Sallis, Michael B. Stoff, and Mary Jean Tully.

Louise Hetrick has assisted me in numerous ways throughout the time this book was in the making. Her help has been invaluable. I have also benefited from the assistance of Jeanne Bodron-Smith, Rajat Chaudhuri, Dixie Fontenot, Larry Horn, Carole Martin, Lynda McClendon, Carl McGehee, and Virginia Salter. Edward T. Chase has provided valuable guidance from the outset. My agent, David Hendin, has been enormously helpful.

Amy Murphy has gone beyond what might normally have been expected of an editor. Her interest and belief in this project has played a significant part in bringing it to completion.

As always, my greatest debts are owed to my family. My late parents, Edward and Ruth McElvaine, provided the largest part of the environment that shaped me and my thinking. They could not have done a better job. Our children, Kerri, Lauren, Allison, and Brett, are my inspiration. Brett was my companion during much of the writing. The latest additions to our family, Scott Itzkowitz and Joshua Evan Itzkowitz, have added immeasurably to my happiness.

None of it would have been possible without Anne, *the* love of my life.

Robert S. McElvaine
Clinton, Mississippi
May, 2000

A Man's World?

Hell hath no fury like a man devalued.

If the complex argument of this book had to be reduced to a single sentence, that would be it. More about that shortly. First, though, the outlines of the problem that led to the exploration that produced this argument and conclusion.

"Life Is Dramatically Unfair to Women"

"We hear and we say that life is unfair, but what this report shows is that life is dramatically unfair to women," declared the administrator of the United Nations Development Program, speaking of a 1995 worldwide survey of the status of women.[1]

Life is dramatically unfair to women.

If such a statement could still be made with accuracy as the second millennium was drawing to a close, certainly it has been applicable throughout the five millennia for which we have some written evidence of how people lived. Although there are still a few people who cling to the faith that there is a small culture here or there in which men are not dominant, it is now generally accepted, as feminist anthropologist Sherry Ortner said in her famous 1972 essay, "Is Female to Male as Nature Is to Culture?," that although the degree of male dominance varies, the subordination of women to men is something approaching a cross-cultural universal.[2]

But *why?* Are men just naturally dominant and it has always been so?

Despite the enormous gains women have made in the past few decades, one suspects that many men—and women—look at the long, unbroken history of male dominance and privately still harbor the suspicion (or firmly hold the conviction) that women are biologically inferior. Although I had completed most of the research and much of the writing of this book before Jared Diamond's *Guns, Germs, and Steel* appeared, when I read that book I was much struck by the parallel between what he saw as the major reason his analysis of the actual causes of world dominance by European-descended people was needed and my own view of a similar need for an adequate, historical explanation of the subordination of women:

> [W]e have to wonder. We keep seeing all those glaring, persistent differences in peoples' status. We're assured that the seemingly transparent biological explanation for the world's inequalities as of A.D. 1500 is wrong, but we're not told what the correct explanation is. Until we have some convincing, detailed, agreed-upon explanation for the broad pattern of history, most people will continue to suspect that the racist biological explanation is correct after all. That seems to me the strongest argument for writing this book.[3]

Similarly, continuing widespread suspicions that the *sexist* biological explanation of another broad pattern of history is correct after all seems to me the strongest reason for what I am undertaking with this book.

The broad pattern of history that is the subject of this book is, I believe, even more fundamental than that which Diamond explored. And the broad pattern for which he sought an explanation was one that has primarily been evident for "only" the last five hundred years. The pattern of domination by one sex over the other stretches over at least five thousand years.

If the matter is not so simple as that men are "naturally superior," several absorbing questions open up: *When* did men establish their control over human societies? *How* did they do so? *Why* did they find it desirable to do so? Most important of all, what has the subordination of women meant for society as a whole? Has history itself been shaped in fundamental ways by the belief in female inferiority?

A variety of possible answers to these questions has been offered.

Many people in the Judeo-Christian tradition still respond to the question of why women are treated unfairly by saying that it is *not* unfair, because women were subordinated by God as a punishment for Eve's sin. Although this argument cannot be taken seriously by educated people today, the story itself plays a crucial part in the interpretation I shall present in this book, as will be explained presently.

A second accounting for the domination of men over women is what might be termed the "because we can" argument.*

---

*I take the name from a line in the 1975 movie *The Stepford Wives,* in which the character Diz gives this answer to the question of why the men in Stepford are replacing their human wives with completely subservient artificial women.

The claim is simply that men have used their greater average size and upper body strength to impose their wills on women. Thomas Jefferson gave voice to this reasoning in 1785, when he wrote: "The stronger sex imposes on the weaker. It is civilization alone which replaces women in their natural equality."[4] Aside from the Eve-is-to-blame explanation, this belief that men have asserted control by sheer brute force and that male dominance has been lessened by civilization has probably been the most widely accepted answer to the question of why women have been subordinated. The notion that "cavemen" went around clubbing women over the head and mistreating them to a greater degree than have their more refined descendants remains a staple of the popular imagination.*

The explanation of why life has been dramatically unfair to women presented here begins with the converse of the "because we can" argument. I propose that the underlying source of male assertions of superiority is "because we *can't.*" It is the male inability to bear and nourish children that causes many men to feel insecure. Because of this relative incapacity, many men suffer, largely subconsciously, from what might be termed "womb envy" and "breast envy." So, while making the claim that women are "by nature" inferior, many men have actually harbored a fear that women are, in certain respects, by nature superior. Men's inability in this regard is a matter of circumstance, and many men seem to have felt as Yossarian did in *Catch-22:* they are "willing to be the victim of anything but circumstance."[5] Such men seek to make women "by culture" inferior and exclude them from certain roles.

In order to compensate for what men *can*not do, they tell women that they *may* not do other things.

Pregnancy, birthing, and nursing have always constituted a "no-man's land." In response to this circumstance, men have, throughout history and

---

*In the late nineteenth century the opposite of this "the memory of man runneth not to the contrary" picture of male dominance emerged. It persists in some quarters today. Thinkers as varied as Johann Jakob Bachofen, Friedrich Engels, and Sir James Frazer postulated a "prehistoric" period of matriarchy [Johann Jakob Bachofen, *Das Mutterrecht* (Stuttgart: Krais and Hoffman, 1861); Friedrich Engels *The Origin of the Family, Private Property, and the State* (1885; New York: International Publishers, 1942); Sir James Frazer, *The Golden Bough* (1890)]. Portions of their arguments were taken up by a group of wishful-thinking feminists a century later. Archeologist Marija Gimbutas insisted in the 1970s and 1980s that a peaceful, egalitarian society centered on worship of a Mother Goddess thrived in Neolithic Europe but was wiped out by violent, nomadic, patriarchal males from the steppes of central Eurasia [Marija Gimbutas, *Gods and Goddesses of Old Europe* (Berkeley and Los Angeles: University of California Press, 1974); Gimbutas, *The Language of the Goddess* (New York: Harper & Row, 1989)]. This idea was carried to more ridiculous extremes by Riane Eisler in her 1987 book, *The Chalice and the Blade* (New York: Harper & Row, 1987).

across cultures, set up a variety of "no-woman's lands": war, politics, clergy, business, men's clubs, and so forth. From which activities women are excluded varies from one culture to another, but some form of exclusion can be found in all societies. The underlying motivation for such practice in our own culture is reflected in a striking statement made by an American Catholic bishop in 1992: "A woman priest is as impossible as for me to have a baby."[6]

Because they cannot compete with women's capabilities in the crucial realms of reproduction and nourishing offspring, men generally seek to avoid a single standard of human behavior and achievement. They create separate definitions of "manliness" which are based on a false opposition to "womanliness." A "real man" has been seen in most cultures as "not-a-woman (*notawoman*)."

Although this fear of male biological inferiority and the resulting tendency to insist that the sexes are "opposite" is the essential starting point for exploring the ways in which women have been subordinated and what the wider consequences of that subordination have been, it is *just* the beginning. This factor has always been present, although the degree of its impact has varied as other circumstances have changed. It is in those changing circumstances—history—that we must seek more complete answers to questions about why, how, and when females were subordinated and how sex has shaped history.

Evolution as Protohistory

Until the last third of the twentieth century, our view of history was grossly distorted by a huge error: the omission of half of our species from the record of human experience. The exclusion of women from history was, in fact, one of the most important examples of men establishing their own ground, on which women were not permitted to tread: *You have the babies, because we can't; but you may not enter our exclusive club that we call history.*

Historians have now gone a long way toward rectifying this immense misreading of the past. (The exclusion of women from positions of power never meant that they were without influence in shaping history or were helpless objects only manipulated by men.) But that is just the first step in the needed expansion of our historical field of vision.

Although our understanding of the times that came before us has improved substantially with the restoration of women to our history, two other, closely related, fundamental mistakes continue to prevent us from reaching a proper understanding of the human past and present: the discounting of human nature and of "prehistory." It is these omissions that have left us without a convincing explanation of why women have been so long subordinated and how sex has shaped history. Such an explanation is needed to combat the idea that the received sexual hierarchy is based on biological superiority or inferiority.

This book brings together two modes of inquiry that have advanced our understanding in recent years but have remained separate (and largely hostile): history, especially women's history, and the neo-Darwinian perspective that has appeared in the field of evolutionary biology and has been adopted by some researchers in the social sciences.* Much recent work has shown that human evolution left us with a variety of proclivities (human nature) that were "designed" to adapt our ancestors to live in an environment that is vastly different from the one in which most of us live today.

But something very important is missing from these arguments: *history.* In jumping from evolution to the modern human experience, sociobiology and evolutionary psychology miss fundamentally important developments during the period when human-made changes first created a social environment for which the human biogram was not well adapted. This includes the critical last five thousand years of "prehistory," which, as we'll see shortly, historians conventionally shortchange, as well as most of the five thousand years traditionally called history. It is that gap—the last ten millennia—which the present book seeks to begin to fill.

If the practitioners of revamped evolutionary science have largely ignored history, historians have even more ignored evolution. Most historians, along with most people involved in all of the social sciences and humanities, have long been panicked at any suggestion of the possibility that anything in human beings might be innate.

Misled by a belief that has been dogma in many intellectual circles since the time of John Locke, that humans at birth are blank slates which are thereafter shaped solely by personal experience, and by its modern equivalent, faith in complete cultural determinism, we have generally ignored human biology. Many people today panic at the very mention of "human nature," fearing that if they so much as admit the possibility of its existence they will be castigated as social Darwinists—or worse. In recent years we have been reminded of where an apparently biological approach can lead by the racist ideas contained in Richard Herrnstein and Charles Murray's *The Bell Curve* (1994)[7] and by the argument put forth by Randy Thornhill and Craig Palmer in *A Natural History*

---

*A group of evolutionary feminists, such as Sarah Blaffer Hrdy, Patricia Adair Gowaty, and Barbara Smuts has emerged in recent years. [Sarah Blaffer Hrdy, *The Woman That Never Evolved* (Cambridge, Mass.: Harvard University Press, 1981); Patricia Adair Gowaty, ed., *Feminism and Evolutionary Biology* (New York: Chapman & Hall, 1997); and Barbara Smuts, "The Evolutionary Origins of Patriarchy," *Human Nature,* vol. 6 (1995), pp. 1–32; Sarah Blaffer Hrdy, *Mother Nature: A History of Mothers, Infants, and Natural Selection* (New York: Pantheon, 1999)]. But the findings and ideas of these women have yet to register with either historians or most more traditional feminists.

of Rape (2000) that rape is a behavior that evolution selected for.[8] But the genuinely scientific evidence that we are not, in fact, blank slates at birth, *wholly* shaped by culture, has become overwhelming. The time is past when historians or the general public can afford to ignore the valid findings of science because some researchers have abused this sort of investigation and reached outrageous conclusions. We must stop throwing out the Darwinian baby with the racist and sexist bathwater.[9] The attempt must be made to bring together neo-Darwinian evolutionary biology and history to form a new way of understanding the human experience: *biohistory.*

I believe in the unity of knowledge—what Edward O. Wilson terms *consilience:* that for all the variety of explanations that can be offered by different disciplines, all intersect and "there is intrinsically only one class of explanation."[10] This book attempts to make a contribution to beginning to blend history with other branches of knowledge by combining biology (and several other disciplines) with history to reach conclusions vastly different from those of Herrnstein and Murray, Thornhill and Palmer, or the social Darwinists.

My approach to utilizing biology to enhance our understanding of history differs radically from social Darwinism. That discredited creed held that natural selection is just "the way things are" and that we should—indeed, that we *must*—model society after its uncaring brutality and intense competition. My position is that natural selection and the human nature that it produced need to be understood so that we can devise ways to guide our innate proclivities into channels that we choose, on the basis of our own moral decisions. It is foolish to deny that natural selection has played a major part in making us the way we are. Our task as humans is not to dispute this notion, but to envision "the way things ought to be" and use our knowledge of the way natural selection has molded us to help us to find means by which we can move closer to that vision. The evolution of human nature must be seen as *protohistory,* the first history, the starting point for subsequent history.

Anyone who looks seriously and with an open mind (which should not be confused with a blank slate) at the findings of modern biology cannot doubt that there is such a thing as human nature. Our distant ancestors had adapted biologically to live in small bands of collector-hunters,* *the* hominid and human way of life for at least 98 percent of our evolution. It was this process that created the human nature—the mixed constellation of motivations that give human beings predispositions to respond in certain ways to certain cir-

---

*I use this terminology rather than the more familiar "hunter-gatherers" because it has been shown that more of the diet of these societies that have been studied in recent centuries comes from plants than animals and because "collecting" implies something more difficult than "gathering," and therefore better conveys the reality of this activity.

cumstances and to desire particular situations of living—that remains with us down to the present. Some understanding of this human biological inheritance (the *biogram*[11] of *Homo sapiens*) is essential to a proper comprehension of history. It seems to be common sense that the study of history, the unfolding of human life, should be grounded in knowledge of human biology, the science of that life. Yet for most people in the historical profession, that has rarely been the case.

History Does Not Begin with a Blank Slate

To an only somewhat lesser extent, historians have also ignored "prehistory." Understandably reluctant to draw many conclusions about life in times for which there are no written records, historians have for the most part acted as if human history began about the same time that writing was invented, shortly before 3000 B.C.E. (*Before Common Era*, what has traditionally been designated as "B.C."). If human history cannot be properly understood without an acquaintance with the innate biological predispositions with which evolution left us, neither can it be accurately fathomed without some knowledge of the effects of the monumental alterations in the human social environment that occurred during the approximately five thousand years preceding the conventional starting point for history. If hominid and human evolution through the Paleolithic Age are protohistory, the five thousand or so years from the development of agriculture to the invention of writing can be seen as *deuterohistory,* a second era of history that set the stage for the five thousand years conventionally called "history."

Although we have rarely, if ever, noticed the connection, historians have been applying Locke's tabula rasa concept to human history as well as to individual humans. To act as if "history" began with a blank slate five thousand years ago is as profoundly misleading as to see the human infant at birth that way. Indeed, it is basically the same mistake, because to say that humanity's slate was blank around 3000 B.C.E. is to discount completely not only all of "prehistorical" experience but also any biological influence on human behavior.

Ironically, historians have generally taken a view of the scope of the human story that is similar to that of biblical fundamentalists, because the latter customarily date Eden at about six thousand years ago. But humans and their direct ancestors had been around by that time for four to five million years. "Conventional history," Colin Tudge rightly observes in his 1996 book, *The Time Before History,* "starts almost at the end."[12]

It is easy to appreciate the hesitation of historians in saying much about the period before writing. In a literal sense, after all, prehistory *is* a blank slate. The methodological difficulties involved in considering such periods for which there are no written records are enormous. But there were people living in these vast eons, and they had lives—there is a "prehistoric history." Learning about this history is very difficult, and conclusions one reaches about it must be classified as tentative and in some cases even speculative. It involves borrowing from many other disciplines, including biology, archeology, anthropology, and the study of religion and mythology. Yet if we, as historians, believe that "what is past is prologue," we must face up to the difficulties, because we will understand that human history in the time when there was no or little writing has had substantial effects on the history that followed.

"History from the bottom up" came into vogue at the end of the 1960s. This perspective involves seeing history from the vantage point of the oppressed rather than the oppressors, the losers rather than the winners: slaves, peasants, industrial workers, immigrants, minorities. It has been a most worthwhile and edifying project, one which has meshed well with the expansion of women's history, since women have almost always been "on the bottom." (The significance of such sexual metaphors is enormous, as will be explained later.) The effort must now be made to give "history from the bottom up" a new meaning: to "get to the bottom of things," to find the roots, the source, the basis, of history.

What most of us in the historical profession have been doing is like trying to examine and understand the construction of the upper stories of a tall building without looking at the structure's foundation or its lower floors. To truly transform our conception of history, we need now to go beyond the new carpenters and building materials (women historians and historical women) that have come onto the construction site in the past few decades. We need a new blueprint, one that includes the lower stories, the foundation, and even an analysis of the bedrock on which they rest.

It will be argued in these pages that the bedrock on which the foundation of history stands is the set of innate characteristics and proclivities that developed over the unimaginably long evolution of hominids and humans, that the foundation is sex, including misunderstandings of it and metaphors based upon it, and that the lower stories are the roughly five thousand years between the development of agriculture and the invention of writing.

Sex and History

Feminist historians have done a good job of showing that, as Joan Wallach Scott has put it, "sexual difference cannot be understood apart from history."[13] But all sorts of previously obscured vistas open up when we comprehend that the converse is also, and even more importantly, true:

History cannot be understood apart from perceptions of sexual difference.

One of the primary objectives of this book is to explore how people's views of sexual difference have shaped history.

Karl Marx had it wrong. Class has, to be sure, been a major factor in history; but class itself is a derivative concept that is based on the ultimate causative power in history: sex. Marx's famous formulation must be revised: *The history of all hitherto existing society is the history of struggles based on the division of our species into two sexes, jealousies emanating from this division, exaggerations of the differences between the sexes, misunderstandings about sexual reproductive power, and metaphors derived from sex.* Together, these closely related matters constitute the most important, but largely neglected, set of motive forces in human history. Control—or the claim of control—over the means of *re*production has been even more fundamental to history than has control of the means of production.

The implications of the questions about the sources and development of male dominance and female subordination go far beyond the treatment of women. It will be contended here that male subordination of females is at the very base of how our society operates and how we view the world. An understanding of when, how, and why men asserted complete dominion over women will begin to provide us with answers to many other questions about why human societies operate as they do.

Taking sex seriously as the basic underlying force in history throws *everything* into question; it obliges us to rethink all of history and see it from a new perspective, one that places primary emphasis on areas that have been almost completely ignored by most historians. It does not simply change the cast of characters; it totally revises the plot line. From this perspective, the most significant historical events took place before or outside the usual field of vision of historians. The climax of the drama, as we shall see, took place in what might be considered Act I, scene 2, at a time when conventional history has not yet raised the curtain. Historical directors have, in fact, simply dropped the whole of Act I from their productions. But the action taking place in the scene we are playing out at the beginning of the third millennium cannot be comprehended, by either the cast or the critics, without a serious examination of that long-ignored opening act.

A Distant Mirror

It is an age in which dramatic social and economic changes have disrupted previously existing sex roles. The traditional roles of one sex have been devalued, and members of that sex have begun to move into roles and occupations previously defined as appropriate only for the other sex. Changes are underway in the sex-linked roles of provider and caregiver. All these alterations are leading to inevitable resentments. Our whole way of life seems to be changing in radical ways. Traditional religious beliefs and family structures are being altered. Many people fear that the world as we know it may be coming to an end.

The time described in the preceding paragraph is a vast era that was, in terms of changing sex roles, the mirror image of the last century. That period continues to hold sway over our lives today. It began about ten thousand years ago, when the invention of agriculture started to disrupt long-established ways of life, finally devaluing the traditional male roles of hunting and group defense. The result was what may be termed a "masculinist movement" by which men gradually took over roles previously defined as female, ultimately changing the human understanding of procreation and religion in ways that have influenced all of recorded history and continue to affect us profoundly in our own time.

The invention of agriculture (including the keeping of animals as well as the purposeful growing of plant food) reshaped human life in such essential ways that it should be seen as the first of two "megarevolutions" in human history. It "*dis*-placed" (took away their place in society) men by undermining the value of what they had traditionally done, especially hunting. At the same time it "*re*-placed" (put into a new position in society) women by fundamentally altering the relationship between resources and population. It did so in such a way that substantial population growth became desirable and women were obliged to give up most of their previous role in production and concentrate much more on reproduction. Men, in need of new roles, sought to take over roles previously identified as female. Today, some five centuries into a second megarevolution based on increasing mobility (both social and spatial) and a consequent reconceptualization of the world as a marketplace, it is women who are seeing a traditional role undermined. Extraordinary advances in productivity and medicine have so increased population that we now find ourselves, in one important respect, returning to a situation similar to that before agriculture: the environment's capacity to support human population has nearly been saturated. This development means that women are no longer called upon to spend so much of their lives in child-bearing and child-raising. "There is no longer a single country in Europe where people are having enough children to replace themselves," the *New York Times* reported in 1998.[14] Women, in short, have now been "dis-placed," albeit to a lesser degree than was the case with men in the wake of the development of agriculture. As men did thousands of years ago, women today are seeking new roles by entering occupations that had been reserved for the other sex. This, in turn, has once again threatened the status of men, many of whom are reacting in ways similar to those of their very distant forefathers.

The Genesis of History

The most important account of the "prehistoric" devaluation of roles for which men had been biologically "designed" and the consequences it had for men and women is well known to almost everyone in the Western world and hundreds of millions of people beyond, but it has not been recognized as such. The key to that recognition is the view that came to be widely accepted among anthropologists and others only in the last two decades of the twentieth century, that it is highly likely that women invented agriculture. The reasons for this conclusion will be discussed in Chapter 4 of this book, but the best-known version of the story is in a very familiar Chapter 3.

The story in Chapter 3 of the Book of Genesis which Christians came to call "the Fall of Man" actually does describe a "prehistoric" fall of men, but in a very different way from what has been thought. As I shall explain in detail, the story in Genesis is an allegorical representation of the "fall" that men experienced as a result of women's invention of agriculture (Eve eating from

The Genesis of History
The story of Adam and Eve in the Book of Genesis is an allegory for women inventing agriculture and dramatically changing the situations of both sexes. The results are evident in this illustration from a fifteenth-century Flemish manuscript of the *Speculum Humanae Salvationis:* Adam digs in the fields as Eve devotes herself to caring for children and spinning. (Musée Condé, Chantilly/Giraudon/Art Resource)

the Tree of Knowledge): once food could be intentionally produced, the traditional male roles, particularly as hunters, were greatly devalued. This story (like many other ancient myths in a variety of cultures) blames women for the loss of the collector-hunter way of life, which from a distance came to look like paradise to men obliged to go "forth from the Garden of Eden, to till the ground" and earn their bread by the sweat of their brows doing the "woman's work" of supplying plant food, and punishes women by declaring them henceforth to be totally subordinate to men. The low esteem in which the "women's work" of agriculture was held is shown dramatically in Chapter 4 of Genesis, when the male God shows no regard for the produce brought to Him by the farmer Cain but is pleased by the "manly" offering of meat from Abel.

It will further be argued in this book that the early chapters of Genesis contain the very basis of history. In the second chapter men attempt to overcome their feelings of inferiority by asserting complete superiority over women through a drastic rearrangement of the order of creation that is given in Chapter 1, where men and women are created simultaneously on the sixth day. The contrast of the account in Chapter 2 could not be sharper: in this version, man is created on the first day, then all other living things, and last of all, woman. Even more important, men claim creative power in Genesis' second chapter through the literally incredible story of the birth of a woman out of a man. In Chapter 3, womb envy is stood on its head when the blessing of the power to give birth is redefined as a curse. The Fall of Man has been transmuted into the Fall of Woman.

Read this way (and there is much more to it, as we'll see later), the first four chapters of Genesis are restored to their place at the beginning of history, but in a markedly different way from that in which they long held that place in the Judeo-Christian tradition. These chapters become a mythologized synopsis of the real Act I of human history, told from the very slanted viewpoint of men who saw themselves as victims of the events in that Act.

Biology + Environment = History

A basic argument of this book is that human history consists of the interplay of our innate proclivities with changing, human-altered social environments. I believe that most of the largest problems we face today—and most of the greatest difficulties throughout the recorded portion of human history—stem from a mismatch between the human nature that evolved over millions of years of human evolution and the human-made social environments that have existed for about ten thousand years, since the invention of agriculture radically altered the circumstances in which *Homo sapiens* lives. That mismatch has grown much greater in the modern world, as the social environment we have manufactured has departed ever farther from the conditions for which humans are biologically adapted.

The development of agriculture, causing people to become sedentary, live in much larger societies, and deal with such new issues as surplus, property in land, and impersonal relationships, generated social conditions for which humans were not biologically adapted. Because there was insufficient time for much biological adaptation to the rapidly changing social environment, it was necessary to create more complex values, which amount to cultural adaptations to circumstances for which our biological inheritance does not suit us. The invention of agriculture proved to be mother to the necessity of establishing complex values to mediate between human nature and the transformed social environment.

Metaphors Make History

Another of the major beliefs that informs the arguments presented here is that how we *live* in the world affects how we *perceive* the world.[15] Changes in the social environment bring about changes in the selection of ideas and worldviews that will be deemed acceptable. This is to say that the principles of Darwinian biology apply to human thought and scientific understanding itself. In much the same way that organisms that are better adapted to a new physical environment are the ones that will survive and thrive, *ideas* that are better suited to a particular social environment are the ones that will become accepted.

Metaphors are one of the primary means through which the outlook shaped by the social environment is transmitted to science and the thinking of people at large. Metaphors are wonderful devices; writers would be at a loss without them. But the unfortunate tendency to take metaphors literally can lead to gross errors in understanding. Metaphors do not represent reality; to think they do is almost sure to be misleading. Certain metaphors have become so powerful that they have shaped (and often *mis*shaped) in fundamental ways for thousands of years how we have seen the universe and ourselves. A principal focus of this volume is on what I believe are the two most important of the metaphors that have led us astray, the two master metaphors through most of human existence. The first of these is that such concepts as *manhood* mean superiority, power, and dominance, and terms like *womanly* equate with inferiority, weakness, and submission. This is literally the Master metaphor, since it is used as the basis and model for all power relationships, all situations in which one man claims to be "master" over another. The use of this Master metaphor can be termed *pseudosexing:* the classification of an individual of one sex as the other. Plainly this metaphor developed in part as a means of combating male fears of inferiority and is a manifestation of the "notawoman" definition of manhood.

But this metaphor is so fundamental that its deeper origins must be sought not simply in "prehistory" but in prehominid evolution. The idea that other animals use metaphorical behavior may be surprising, but it is clear that this is what is going on when a dominant male among several species mounts a subordinated male and simulates intercourse with him. The former is, in effect, "saying" to the latter: "I am so dominant over you that I can treat you like a female."

Symbolic mounting is, as Chapters 13 and 14 will explain, an unexplored but highly significant aspect of human male behavior. Sometimes the practice is as direct and literal among humans as it is among other primates—in male prisons, for instance. But human males generally do not have to act out intercourse in order to pseudosex other men and indicate that they are dominant over them, as they assume themselves to be over women. The capacity for language has given humans a much wider range of symbols and metaphors than is available to other primates. Men can and do use *words* in place of symbolic actions. One man saying "Fuck you!" to another carries exactly the same symbolism as does the mounting of a subordinated male macaque by a dominant one. Such language of domination and subordination can accurately be called *verbal mounting.*

The second master metaphor that has shaped the human experience since before recorded history began is one that proved to be all but irresistible after plow agriculture began. The apparent analogy of a seed being planted in furrowed soil to a male's "planting" of semen in the vulva of a female led to the conclusion that men provide the seed of new life and women constitute the soil in which that seed grows. This metaphor is a central part of what was the most consequential and far-reaching mistake in human history: the idea that men are solely responsible for procreation. This monumental error, which I call the "Conception Misconception," has had profound effects on all of recorded history and continues to plague us today, centuries after we learned for sure that it *is* an error. The seed metaphor reversed the apparent positions of the sexes in regard to procreative power. What had always appeared to be a principally female power was transformed into an entirely male power. No longer apparent bystanders in reproduction, men now claimed to be the reproducers, while women were reduced from the seeming creators to the soil in which men's creations grow: not to put too fine a point on it, women were equated with *dirt.* Women were left with all the work of procreation, but men now took all the credit.

During the Neolithic Age, then, women both ceased to be major producers (as men took over the production of plant food along with continuing their traditional responsibility for providing animal food) and ceased to be seen as having reproductive power. The woman-made world of agriculture had, paradoxically, become a man's world to a degree unprecedented in human existence. Hell hath no fury like a man devalued.

Neither, apparently, hath heaven.

The belief that men have procreative power led inevitably to the conclusion that the supreme Creative Power must also be male. The toxic fruit that grew from the seed metaphor was male monotheism.

The combination of the belief that God (or the god who is the ultimate creator) is male with the notion that humans are created in God's image yielded the inescapable conclusion that men are closer than women to godly perfection. Thus the line from the misconceptions about conception emanating from the seed metaphor to the belief, given its classic expressions by Aristotle, Aquinas, and Freud, that women are deformed or "incomplete" men is clear and direct. There is no telling how much evil throughout history might have been averted or eased had the growth of this vine of thinking somehow been nipped in the bud.

Even this brief introduction to the arguments that will be made in this book should be sufficient to show how completely inadequate the usual scope of history is. By the time humans began to record history, what in some respects were the most meaningful changes—the most important *history*—had already taken place. As a result of the development of agriculture, before the conventional starting point of history, humans had already moved into a new reproductive situation in which population expansion was possible and desirable, women had been largely consigned to reproduction, men had seen their traditional roles devalued and claimed procreative power, and women had come to be seen as inferior. Goddesses were in decline and the ultimate Creative Power was beginning to be seen as belonging to a male deity. By starting near the end, we historians have put ourselves in the same situation as almost all of the other people who lived during the last five thousand years. We have taken all these changes as givens, a constant—the way things are—rather than as the products of historical development that they in fact are.

Asking the Right Questions

The seed that "Eve" showed people how to use for their own benefit changed the world in ways wholly beyond anything "she" could have imagined. We have been living with the consequences throughout the recorded period of history, but with, at best, only the dimmest perception of their genesis. This book constitutes an attempt to begin to bring that genesis into sharper focus and to explore the different understandings of history and present-day life that a greater comprehension of their deep bases opens to us.

I believe that the underlying forces of human nature, male jealousy, exaggeration of sexual difference, devaluation of male roles, mistaken belief in exclusive male reproductive power, and seeing the ultimate Creative Force as male have shaped history throughout the world, at least in all the areas where agriculture developed. But the focus of the book will become increasingly narrow as we move through time, coming in recent centuries to be almost exclusively on the Western world and especially the United States. There are two basic reasons for this: It is in the West and particularly in the United States that the forces of the modern world which are increasingly spreading around the globe have largely taken shape, and this is the portion of the world about which my knowledge is sufficient to make the sort of analysis I am undertaking.

The research and thinking that I have done on the vast questions addressed in this book have substantially changed the way I look at the world; it is my hope that the book might begin to do the same for others. If human beings do not change some of the fundamental ways that we have been looking at the world, our troubles are surely going to become worse, especially since we now find ourselves in an environment in which the roles that have traditionally been assigned to women are declining in value and the roles for which men evolved but were devalued thousands of years ago have still not been adequately replaced.

I do not claim that I have all the answers—or even very many of them. But one cannot hope to find the right answers until one begins to ask the right questions. That is what I have tried to do in the pages that follow.

CHAPTER 1

90 Percent Nature; 90 Percent Nurture?

Biology, Culture, and History

We must, however, acknowledge, as it seems to me, that man with all his noble qualities . . . still bears in his bodily frame the indelible stamp of his lowly origin.

CHARLES DARWIN (1882)[1]

The beings who constitute the subject matter of history are members of a biological species called *Homo sapiens,* a species that reproduces sexually and so takes two forms, female and male. I begin with the modest proposition that these facts matter for the study of history.

It appears that most people, at least in the United States, do not think that they do. Although they reach the conclusion by traversing very different paths, two large groups of people, together making up a substantial majority of the population, do not think that we are biological creatures. One is the Biblical Creationists. An opinion poll in 1999 found that fully half of all Americans at the end of the twentieth century believed the biblical account of creation to "actually be the explanation for the origin of human life on Earth," three times as many as believed "the theory of evolution as outlined by Darwin and other scientists" to be the explanation (the rest favored some combination of the two or had no opinion).[2]

Such results, like the vote by the Kansas State Board of Education the same year to de-emphasize the teaching of evolution, leave most sophisticated, liberal people aghast and feeling smugly superior as they smirk about how stupid and backward such a large percentage of the "hicks" in the country must be to

17

have such ridiculous beliefs. Yet, for practical purposes, many educated, liberal people are as afraid of the implications of evolution as are the "hicks" they look upon with contempt.

The accepted position in much of the academic world—in many quarters, the *only* position that will be countenanced—is that all characteristics of people are culturally "constructed," which is to say that humans may be the consequence *of* biological evolution, but that process no longer has any consequences *for* us. It says that humans are *from* nature; that we may still be *in* it; but that we are no longer *of* it. The communicants of this faith (most academics in the humanities and social sciences and most feminists, along with most liberal intellectuals in general) can accurately be classified as Cultural Creationists. To them, culture is as fundamental as *the* basis of human existence as the Bible is to those who see it as the unerring source of knowledge. Much as the biblical fundamentalists believe that God created people out of a formless lump of clay, cultural fundamentalists believe that cultures create people from blank paper.

Both of these groups shrink from accepting the logic of evolution, and for somewhat similar reasons. Both base their opposition to evolution on the assumption that accepting it would prevent them from achieving their goals. In other words, neither group bases its rejection of the idea that biology has shaped us on an analysis of the evidence supporting that argument. Rather, both groups start with the premise that evolution will undermine their objectives and so it must be rejected, irrespective of the evidence. Conservatives fear that evolution leaves no place for divine purpose; liberals fear that it leaves no place for human purpose. Both are afraid that evolution means that we are at the mercy of biological forces and can do nothing to improve ourselves or change conditions.

Although neither group is likely to acknowledge it, both groups are occupying a common ground. Conservatives and fundamentalists reject evolution straightforwardly; they simply deny that it happened. Liberals, humanists, and feminists are generally too well-educated to deny that evolution occurred; they just insist that it has no effect on us now. The end result is the same, though: evolution doesn't matter; it doesn't affect our lives today. To insist that it has no effect on us is to put one's head in the sand almost as far as those who deny it happened.

Feminists fear that admitting that evolutionary biology shaped us means that we have no control over our destiny and cannot change such things as the subordination of women. Fundamentalists fear that admitting that evolutionary biology shaped us means that we have no control over ourselves and so are going to act "like animals." John Morris, president of the Institute for Creation Research in Santee, California, for example, complains that the belief that humans are descended from animals destroys human purpose and morality. "The teaching of evolution is doing damage," he says. "If you have animal instincts and animal desires, why not have sex, or give in to any other desire?"[3]

The similar fears of both groups are misplaced. To say that evolution shaped us is not to say that we have no control over our destiny. In fact, understanding *how* evolution shaped us is the starting point for establishing some control over our destiny.

Biology and History: A Sad History

Sigmund Freud's oft-quoted declaration, "anatomy is destiny," is wrong. But that does not mean that its converse, "biology has no effect on us," is right. Such dualistic, either/or thinking ("if not *x,* then *−x*") has, in fact, played an important role in the ways in which misperceptions of sexual division have shaped history.

Freud made the comment in reference to difference between the sexes and to support the view that there are things that, because of biology, women cannot or should not do. That he did so points to one of the reasons why arguments connected with biology have long been suspect among most people who consider themselves liberal and enlightened: such arguments have often been employed for purposes of maintaining the subordination of women and racial minorities. Accordingly, the enterprise of attempting to utilize biology in understanding human society and history has been ceded to those who have misstated, misinterpreted, and misused the scientific approach.

One of my purposes in this book is to help reclaim Darwin and the concept of human nature for the humanities and social sciences and for liberal-minded people in general by connecting history with biology. I believe that the long-standing article of faith among liberal intellectuals that there is no such thing as human nature is both wrong and highly counterproductive.

In order to discuss human history in a meaningful way, it is necessary to begin with an exploration of what human beings are. British philosopher Mary Midgley opened her 1978 book, *Beast and Man,* with this simple declaration: "We are not just rather like animals; we *are* animals."[4] Confronted with such a statement, most of us would say, "Well, of course." Under our breaths, though, we would be likely to add, "What of it?" That we are animals is a proposition that educated people now generally accept, but one that we still tend to ignore when it comes to drawing conclusions from it.

Attempting to speak of human nature can be dangerous. An historian or anyone else in the humanities or social sciences who becomes interested in pursuing this concept through some acquaintance with evolutionary biology is likely to be greeted by his or her colleagues with a shocked, disgusted look and a muttered, "You haven't become one of *them,* have you?" Reactions to any attempt to link biology to history or society are reflexive. Horrified critics pay little or no attention to the arguments presented in a new study; instead, they react to past, discredited attempts to employ evolutionary thinking in these fields.[5] When I was in the early stages of working on this book, I sent a summary of my arguments to a friend who is a prominent historian and a feminist. She became so apoplectic at my suggestion that there are innate qualities in human beings ("All this return to biology is misguided"* was one of her gentler comments) that she ignored all the other points I was making and concluded that my argument fits "nicely into these reactionary times." Whatever else I may be accused of, I am confident that no one who reads these pages with an open mind will conclude that my ideas are reactionary.

It is worth reiterating that the main reason for the hostile attitude toward connecting biology with history is that the practice does not have a distinguished pedigree. The form of most previous efforts at applying Darwinian thinking to history has been analogy—to see historical developments as part of a Darwinian struggle for survival in which the most "fit" (nations, races, individuals, corporations, etc.) succeed and the less "fit" fall by the wayside, resulting in historical "progress." This "social Darwinism," which dominated American thought in the late nineteenth and early twentieth century, was used to justify extreme nationalism, racism, war, gross economic inequality, and a total lack of concern for those in need. Small wonder, then, that the mere mention of trying to ground an examination of history on an understanding of evolutionary biology sets off alarms in so many quarters.

Yet it is difficult to disagree with Theodore Roosevelt's 1910 contention that "he who would fully treat of man must know at least something of biology, of the science that treats of living, breathing things, and especially of that science of evolution which is inseparably connected with the great name of Darwin."[6] Like so many of his contemporaries, Roosevelt was heavily influenced by social Darwinism. He and the other social Darwinists of his day misapplied evolutionary science to the study of history, but it does not follow that his insistence that historians need to know something about biology was mistaken.

Given the historian's concern with the influence of past developments on present conditions, it would appear natural that she or he would employ an evolutionary perspective. This seems to carry the concerns of the study of his-

---

*Actually I agree that a good deal of the return to biology has been misguided; but that does not mean that a careful, sensible return to biology that does not claim more than it can back up is misguided.

tory back an additional and very large, but entirely logical, step. Evolutionary biology should provide historians with a means of assessing how changes over much longer periods of "prehistory" affect the times that they study. History that ignores biology and human evolution is ahistorical, because it omits the events and effects of the longest period of human existence.

But most written history *has* ignored the results of human evolution. Despite the evident need for beginning any historical inquiry with an understanding of the nature of the creatures being studied, after most historians had properly rejected social Darwinism, they jumped to the conclusion that biology has nothing important to say to them. I disagree. Historians should see their role as beginning where that of biologists leaves off, perhaps with archeologists and anthropologists helping to bridge the gap. Yet throughout most of the last century historians have gone about their studies in blissful ignorance of the findings of biology. So have most other humanists and social scientists.

Sociobiologist Edward O. Wilson was not far from the mark when he wrote in 1978 that "astonishingly, the high culture of Western civilization exists largely apart from the natural sciences. In the United States intellectuals are virtually defined as those who work in the prevailing mode of the social sciences and humanities. Their reflections are devoid of the idioms of chemistry and biology, as though humankind were still in some sense a numinous spectator of physical reality."[7]

A Whiter Shade of Pale: The Tabula Rasa Today

Wilson's implicit challenge, which he made explicit two decades later in *Consilience*,[8] has been taken up by a growing number of social scientists. Since I began work on this project in 1989, Darwinism has made a comeback among some in the social sciences. A growing number of evolutionary psychologists and evolutionary ecologists have made an effort at rehabilitating the reputation of applying Darwinian thinking to human behavior. This effort is generally to be applauded. It should after all, be clear that "behavior evolves through natural selection, just as anatomy does."[9] But many of the practitioners in these new fields have been much too quick in claiming that this or that aspect of current society is the direct, simple result of biological evolution. It has often proved too tempting when examining evolutionary effects on human behavior to jump to conclusions that may be unwarranted. Much of evolutionary psychology (and almost all of its most controversial claims) has concentrated on differences between the males and females in their sexual proclivities. I'll defer this question to Chapter 3, where it will be more appropriate to discuss it in the context of addressing the whole issue of sexual difference.

In his 1991 book, *In Search of Human Nature,* Carl Degler wrote of numerous psychologists, sociologists, anthropologists, and political scientists who
have in the past three decades accepted the existence of innate proclivities in
humans. But the distinguished Stanford University historian was unable to
point to a single prominent practitioner of his own discipline who has
employed a recognition of innate human tendencies in his or her work.[10] The
years since have not filled this void and it is high time that historians joined in
the understanding that the people who are their subject matter are, at the most
basic level, animals and that human nature has to be taken into account in the
study of history. I hope that this book will become a starting point in that effort.

The fear of the taint of the implications of social Darwinism (and, worse,
Nazism, which was also based in part upon a gross misapplication of biology
to society) has to be overcome so that historians may benefit from the important findings of modern biology. Efforts at overcoming the stigma have
remained difficult in recent years for at least two important reasons. One has
to do with some of those people who took up sociobiology in its early years.
Their claims have seemed (and not without reason) extravagant. Some of them
appeared to be preaching a rigid determinism—for all practical purposes,
fatalism. Wilson himself boldly stated his views in terms that seemed to indicate the ultimate insignificance of human beings:

> [I]n evolutionary time the individual organism counts for almost nothing. In a
> Darwinian sense the organism does not live for itself. Its primary function is
> not even to reproduce other organisms; it reproduces genes, and it serves as
> their temporary carrier. . . . [T]he organism is only DNA's way of making more
> DNA.[11]

On one level, of course, this statement is true, but it sounds too much like
a total rejection of human dignity and significance.

More important in causing humane people to condemn sociobiologists is
the fact that their ideas have been used to support egoism, and their doctrines,
like those of Darwin a century before them, were quickly taken up by racists,
misogynists, jingoists, and xenophobes. The most notorious example of this
was the racist argument made by Richard Herrnstein and Charles Murray in
their 1994 book, *The Bell Curve,*[12] that blacks are intellectually inferior to
other races. This book seemingly confirmed the fears of "decent" people in
the humanities and the social sciences that any contact with the idea of human
nature or evolutionary biology would contaminate them with unacceptable
ideas. The only sensible response was to quarantine the infected and keep
inoculating everyone else against the plague of "human nature" by insisting,
regardless of the evidence, that it does not exist. The best way for people who
consider themselves to be guided by reason (and therefore susceptible to hav-

ing their minds changed by evidence) to maintain their belief that there is no such thing as human nature is to try to keep themselves ignorant of the evidence.

Cultural determinism is a modern version of John Locke's tabula rasa. Locke's meaning has frequently been misinterpreted, particularly by liberal social scientists in the past century. When he wrote in 1690 that the human mind at birth is like "white Paper, void of all Characters, without any *Ideas*," he was referring to knowledge, all of which he contended comes from experience. It does not appear to have been Locke's intention to imply that people are not predisposed to act in certain ways; only that they *know* nothing specific until experience teaches them.[13] This concept became part of modern liberal dogma, and in time Locke's white paper became even cleaner, as twentieth-century social scientists argued that the newborn human mind is absolutely blank and that it is *only* environmental conditioning that determines what a person will become.

This view did not arise full grown. Franz Boas, the most prominent American anthropologist of the early twentieth century, forcefully rejected the then-prevalent belief that there are innate differences in the mental capacities of different races. In doing so, Boas was actually clearing the way for the proper use of biology in studying humans. He was not rejecting human nature, but seeing it as something indivisible, a constellation of inbred tendencies that unifies humanity.[14] The concept of what we might term the Union of Human Beings was based on fundamental shared human characteristics that are biological.

Boas was right, but many of his followers got carried away with his emphasis on culture as the explanation for differences among groups of humans, coming quickly to the extreme and wholly unwarranted conclusion that there is no shared human nature. In 1917, Boas student Alfred L. Kroeber completely dismissed biology as having anything to do with history: "For the historian—him who wishes to understand any sort of social phenomena—it is an unavoidable necessity, today, to disregard the organic as such and to deal only with the social."[15]

Here, in effect, was a Declaration of Human Independence from the animal world, an act of secession from biology and so from the Union of Human Beings to establish an artificial world of human self-creation, a Confederacy of Culture—or, rather, a large number of separate and equal confederacies of culture. This was an early part of a trend that was correctly summarized by political scientist Steven Peterson in 1978 when he said "for half a century, most social scientists have taught and conducted their research on the assumption that human behavior is almost totally learned and that our genetic make-up contributes little, if anything, to our behavior."[16]

In fact, though, the argument that human beings are entirely the creatures of culture is merely the latest link in a chain that stretches back for thousands of years, into prehistory—a chain that provides important insights into the whole of human history and is the main subject of this book. As I shall explain in detail later, humans originally understood themselves to be a part of nature, the products of a creative force that was believed to be female and natural. After the invention of agriculture showed that human intervention could influence the processes of nature, that view began to change, with creation eventually being attributed to a power that was outside of and above nature—a *super*natural force that came to be seen as a male God who is not *in* but *above* nature, ruling over it (or her).

This was an early stage of a process that has continued ever since of transforming what were once seen as female functions into male functions. In the modern world this trend has gone much farther. To see people as wholly the products of culture is essentially to say that we are artificial, not natural—the offspring of varying cultures that have usually been thought of as largely the creations of men. Not Mother Nature (or even a Father God), but something man-made is now said to be the ultimate source of what we are. In the modern social science view, a man-made culture replaces God as the supernatural force. Cultural determinism is the completion of the millennia-long masculinization of creation.

The viewpoint of the cultural creationists was popularized in the 1920s by American psychologist John B. Watson. His book *Behaviorism* was first published in 1914, but its hyper-Lockean ideas did not captivate the public until the volume's third edition in 1925. By this time many social scientists, reacting sharply against the excesses of those in their professions who had appropriated the name of Darwin, were eagerly embracing the odd notion that human events can be understood completely on their own terms, without reference to any innate predispositions that evolution may have left in humankind—in fact that evolution left *no* such innate motivations, that people are utterly devoid of inborn behavioral characteristics. Watson left no question about how completely blank he believed the human tablet was at birth when he boldly proclaimed: "Give me a dozen healthy infants, well-formed, and my own specified world to bring them up in and I'll guarantee to take any one at random and train him to become any type of specialist I might select—doctor, lawyer, artist, merchant-chief, and, yes, beggar-man and thief, regardless of his talents, penchants, tendencies, abilities, vocations, and race of his ancestors."[17] Watson had carried John Locke to his logical, but incredible, conclusion. His arguments were taken up and spread even more widely by B. F. Skinner in later decades.

In 1930, anthropologist Margaret Mead weighed in with the assertion that human nature is "the rawest, most undifferentiated of raw material, which must be molded into shape by its society, which will have no form worthy of recognition unless it is shaped and formed by cultural tradition."[18] And in her 1934 anthropological classic, *Patterns of Culture,* Ruth Benedict assured her readers that, whatever biology might have to do with insect societies, it has nothing to do with human social systems.[19]

Such beliefs—or articles of faith—became ever more pervasive in the social sciences during the middle decades of the twentieth century. Anthropologist Ashley Montagu put the human secession from nature in the most uncompromising terms in 1968, when he wrote that the human "has no instincts, because *everything* he is and has become he has learned, acquired, from his culture, from the *man-made* part of his environment, from other human beings."[20] Several of those attending a 1976 meeting of the American Association for the Advancement of Science argued that "human brains were 'uncoupled' from any genetic influences whatsoever—that, like computers built to a standard design, their relative levels of performance were completely determined by programming,"[21]* which is to say that culture is entirely responsible for constructing the human mind.

Locke's metaphorical paper of the mind had by this time been made even whiter than today's television commercials promise us the right bleach will make our stained clothing. A human, the social science consensus has held, is an "empty organism."[22] Only the experiences of life fill in the void that is said to be there at birth. Just how an evolutionary process that had been filling organisms with increasingly complex behaviors suddenly produced one species that is empty is a question that cultural creationists have left unaddressed.

Since the 1920s most social scientists—and, sad to say, historians—have marched along in what might be called Lockestep, insisting not just that humans are very adaptable (which, plainly, we are), but that we are, as the extreme statements by Watson and Montagu indicate, *infinitely* adaptable. In 1972 Lucien Malson proclaimed that "the idea that man has no nature is now beyond dispute." He declared that the belief that man "has or rather is history," nothing more, "is now the explicit assumption of all the main currents of contemporary thought."[23] This extreme view can be characterized in a single word: absurd. Humans have evolutionary history and "prehistory" as well as history. We are all of these things.

While most practitioners in these fields continue to assume and act upon the premise that a human begins life as a tabula rasa, no reputable biologist

---

*The now extremely common use of such computer-related language as metaphors for the characteristics of the human brain is a modern example of how metaphors can come to be taken literally and dramatically distort truth. Two such master metaphors that have misguided people over the entire course of what is usually considered history are a major focus of this book.

would agree. Most biologists now sensibly reject the whole nature/nurture dualism, contending that the characteristics of a human result from the interaction of genes *and* environment, not one *or* the other.

"One is not born, but rather becomes, a woman," Simone de Beauvoir declared in *The Second Sex* in 1952.[24] In her 1999 book *The First Sex,* anthropologist Helen Fisher takes the opposite position: "A woman is born a woman."[25] Both statements are too absolute. One is *both* born a woman *and* becomes a woman—as well as anything else she is.

What could be more obvious than that *both* innate characteristics *and* the social environment play major roles in shaping human behavior? Fisher herself quickly backs away from her absolute statement and offers a powerful image for the actual relationship of the forces that shape us: "Environment and heredity are eternally intertwined, locked in a pas de deux."[26] Many of the combatants on both sides pay lip service to this point, perfunctorily mentioning that "of course" the other set of factors has some influence, but they quickly return to raising their side's flag over almost all of the territory. The only notable exceptions to arise in recent years are some evolutionary psychologists who sensibly contend that "the supposed dichotomy between nature and nurture is a meaningless one.... [G]enes and environment are not separate, conflicting influences on the development of the human mind. Rather, they work in concert, and are designed to be that way."[27] But many of the practitioners in this field have gotten carried away with what they think can be attributed to the biological portion of the human makeup, as I shall discuss later.

Many years ago my father made what should be the final, winning argument in the nature versus nurture debate. We were talking about a boy in the neighborhood who was a chronic liar and petty thief. My father commented that, in view of the circumstances in which he knew the boy to have been brought up, the cause of his behavior must have been "ninety percent environment." After someone reminded my father of what the boy's parents were like, he revised his assessment: "In his case, I think it's ninety percent nature and ninety percent nurture."

And so, for those of us who are not unduly troubled by mathematical impossibility, it is with humans in general.

A Map of Blank Paper

Despite the fears of one side in the nature/nurture struggle, the idea of human nature poses no threat to most liberal goals. On the contrary, it is essential to them.

The insistence that people are utterly plastic and shaped only by the particular culture in which they find themselves negates many of the goals toward which the liberals who take this position aspire. If all humanity had nothing in common beyond some basic physical characteristics and the capability of interbreeding, but was otherwise blank paper upon which vastly different scripts could be written by various cultures, what could bring diverse cultures together? And what of those who fear that accepting the existence of innate traits would promote racism and xenophobia? Would not these maladies be more difficult to deal with if there were no human nature? Under the crude assumptions of cultural determinism, people brought up in the ways of one society would have *nothing* in common with those brought up differently in another society. The extreme multiculturalism that is an outgrowth of cultural creationism espouses, as Jonathan Zimmerman of New York University has said, "the insidious idea that there is no single Truth; there is only your truth and my truth, both of which usually reflect our different races, ethnicities, and genders."[28] For practical purposes under cultural creationism these categories become like separate species. If culture were the only thing that determined what people are, what reason would those entirely formed by one culture have for cooperating with those "created" by another?

One after another of the liberal objectives is undermined if one accepts the extreme tabula rasa view. On what grounds could people in one culture complain of human rights abuses in another? Unless there is something common to all of humanity, there is no basis for people in one culture to assess the actions of those in another. "Gee, Herr Hitler, we in our culture don't believe in killing innocent people by the millions, but I guess that's the way your German society shaped you. Isn't that *interesting?*" This may seem extreme, but what other position could a person who maintains that culture is the *sole* determinant of values and behavior take?

There is, in any case, no need to rely on such imagined responses to prove the point. Reality, unfortunately, provides genuine instances of similar statements. In 1989 a New York judge sentenced a man named Don Lu Chen to a mere five years of probation for beating his wife to death with a hammer. The wife had cheated on her husband, the judge said, and the killer was Chinese. "He was a product of his culture," the understanding jurist proclaimed in explaining the light sentence.[29]

Where the denial of human nature leads was shown clearly at the 1993 World Conference on Human Rights in Vienna. A group of repressive regimes made the argument that "any definition of human rights should take account of 'national and regional particularities and various historical, cultural and religious backgrounds.' "[30] A major contention was made that the concept of women's rights should not be considered universal, because different cultures define women's roles differently.

Such complete cultural relativism is where the belief that there is no underlying human nature leaves us. We wind up saying, "Nazis will be Nazis," "Chinese will be Chinese," and "misogynist cultures will be misogynist."

The concept of human rights is dependent on the existence of human beings who share a common humanity.[31] If cultures determine everything, there can be no human rights, since there would then be little meaning to the term *human*. How can an empty organism have rights other than those filled in by his or her culture? Nor can there be women's rights. There can only be things like "Saudi Arabian rights," and if the Saudis choose to confine their rights to men . . . well, that's how their culture constructed them and it should be of no concern to people from other cultures. If men in India throw widows on their husbands' funeral pyres because their culture has decided such women are useless, "inauspicious persons,"[32] if some African societies demand that girls have clitoridectomies because their culture doesn't think females should have sexual pleasure, if Americans of European ancestry in the seventeenth, eighteenth, and nineteenth centuries enslaved people of African ancestry because the culture of the former taught that black people are inferior . . . well, you get the point.

Tabula rasa devotees have painted themselves into an intellectual corner in which any common genetic inheritance cannot be of any significance. Different cultures in the world quite obviously are different, so if they are all that matters, it follows that different nationalities and races *are* different—which is what racists and xenophobes have maintained all along.

If we were actually blank paper, governments could make of us anything they wanted.[33]* Many of the horrors of the twentieth century were perpetrated by people acting upon the extreme cultural determinist assumption that there is no such thing as human nature and therefore people can be reshaped into anything. The most notorious examples of ideologues who thought they could make "new" people in an image that they chose are Mao Zedong and Pol Pot. The results were a far cry from Skinner's vision of a paradise engineered by behaviorism in *Walden Two*. Each political figure killed millions of his own countrymen and -women trying to write a new script on what he took to be the blank paper of humanity. Both proved instead that there was something on the paper that could be removed only by an erasure of such force that it destroys the paper itself.

One of the chief fears of liberals concerning the acceptance of innate predispositions is that it would somehow curtail freedom. Actually, though,

---

*Noam Chomsky has made this point well: "If in fact humans are indefinitely malleable, completely plastic beings, with no innate structures of mind and no intrinsic needs of a cultural or social character, then they are fit subjects for the 'shaping of behavior' by the state authority, the corporate manager, the technocrat, or the central committee." [Chomsky, "Language and Freedom," (1970), in James Peck, ed., *The Chomsky Reader* (New York: Pantheon, 1987), p. 154.] Or: "The principle that human nature, in its psychological aspects, is nothing more than a product of history and given social relations removes all barriers to coercion and manipulation by the powerful." [Chomsky, *Reflections on Language* (New York: Pantheon, 1975), p. 132.]

human nature is essential to the possibility of freedom. Were there not something that made a person human in the first place, and gave him or her some tools with which to work—a basis on which to act—there could be no way for the individual to resist being made into anything the people running society wished. If there were nothing innate, there would not really be an individual person at all; just society and its creations.

If there were nothing "natural" and sex roles, for instance, were *entirely* the result of conditioning, how would any woman, shaped by society to fit and accept her role, ever come to question her status?

A substantial amount of human malleability is essential for reform to take place, and obviously there is a large degree of malleability. But there are limits. *Infinite* malleability is not only unnecessary for the achievement of liberal ends but would also make such achievement impossible.[34]

It is nothing short of astonishing that liberal thought has gone along since early in the twentieth century following a road map that made it certain that it could never reach its destination. A map of blank paper is not of much use.

The reason that so many liberals have clung to their insistence that human nature should be ignored is, I believe, a fundamental misapprehension concerning the implications of human nature. They have feared that the admission of the existence of innate characteristics will lead to findings on how people *differ.* In fact, the real meaning of human nature, as Boas understood, is to be found in showing the ways in which people are *alike.* As Robert Wright has said, unlike the old social Darwinists, "today's Darwinian anthropologists, in scanning the world's peoples, focus less on surface differences among cultures than on deep unities."[35]

Biology unifies the people of the world; culture divides them.

Complete plasticity and cultural determinism is, in any case, a notion that makes no sense. Mary Midgley has put the central point succinctly: "Not everybody can always be on the receiving end of culture."[36] If culture determines everything about people, but people create culture, how did culture first come into being?

None of this argument is to deny for a moment that there are immense cultural variations in human practices. But this diversity is plainly not without limits. And it is our biology that imposes those limits.[37]

The modern desire to deny all limits has, in fact, been one of the main bases for the rejection of human nature. When confronted with a characteristic that appears to be a cross-cultural universal, many social scientists will go to extraordinary lengths to show that it *could,* just possibly, have a cultural cause. Most anthropologists have, for example, accepted that subordination of women exists to some degree in all human societies[38] (although that degree and its expression vary enormously). Rather than accept that this indicates an innate male proclivity to seek dominance (it has nothing to do with actual "superiority"; it is just that the drive to dominate is one of those characteristics that is, on average, more powerful in males), many social scientists have sought some "cultural universal"* that could account for it.[39] They find a cultural universal preferable to anything biological because they assume that anything cultural is more susceptible to alteration and so does not impose the limitations that accepting anything as innate would. The fear of limitation is evident in the opening lines of a 1995 nature/nurture article in *Newsweek:* "Every day, science seems to chip away at our autonomy."[40] It can also be seen in psychologist Nancy Chodorow's equation of "biologically derived" with "inescapable."[41] In fact, the only hope for modifying and controlling those factors that *are* innate is to recognize them as such.

Ignoring the existence of natural, genetic predispositions is not "liberal" or "feminist"; it is foolish.

Biological Determinism

But the fact that one side in a debate is wrong does not mean that the other extreme is right. If many liberals and feminists got caught up in cultural determinism for political reasons, a similar connection is to be found between right-wingers and social Darwinism and evolutionary psychology. Those who want to keep social arrangements as they are and to maintain racial, sexual, national, religious, and socioeconomic divisions have found it convenient and expedient to argue that these features of human life are "natural." The conservatives' motive in choosing a side in the nature/nurture debate was no more based on science than was the liberals' identification with the other side.†

---

*This is not to say that there cannot be culturally based characteristics that approach universality, at least in certain social environments. I shall be discussing some of these in this book. But what makes these phenomena universal is the interaction of particular sorts of human-induced changes in the social environment (such as the development of agriculture) with the biological universals of human nature.

†That ideological and political factors often determine positions in biology/culture debates is clear in another oddity that has emerged in our public discourse. On issues such as the effect of excessive sex and violence in the media, liberals and conservatives often reverse their nature/nurture positions. Conservatives, usually more likely to accept biological determinism, insist that cultural influences play a large role in our social problems. Liberals, who habitually argue that environment [culture] is almost wholly responsible for what we become, are prone to contend that a saturation of sex and violence in popular culture has no influence on the behavior of young people. The same political basis for positions and inconsistency is evident in explanations of homosexuality. Once again, liberals and conservatives switch their positions from what they usually say in general about biology vs. culture. Liberals usually argue that sexual orientation is innate, while conservatives maintain that homosexuality is learned and can be "unlearned."

There is every bit as much wrong with the extreme, conservative, biological determinist viewpoint as with the extreme, liberal, cultural determinist approach. Those on the "nature" side can be just as dogmatic as their rivals. The individual has no more freedom, dignity, or responsibility in their system. The all-powerful creator god Culture of the tabula rasa school is replaced by a lord named Gene in the biodeterminists' cosmology. The latter have established a new religion of Natural Selection with the Gene as its God and Darwin as its Prophet. Its catechism goes something like: "Why did the Gene make me? The Gene made me for Its own purposes, to experiment with, to reproduce Itself, to serve It, and to pass DNA to future Genes."

If this seems absurd, consider some of the statements the biodeterminists have made. The following are from Richard Dawkins's (literally) incredible book, *The Selfish Gene:* "The argument of this book is that we, and all other animals, are machines created by our genes." Or: "Genetically speaking, individuals and groups are like clouds in the sky or dust-storms in the desert. They are temporary aggregations or federations. They are not stable through evolutionary time. . . . [But the gene] leaps from body to body in its own way and for its own ends. . . . The genes are the immortals."[42] Like diamonds, it seems, genes are forever. We organisms correspond to a necklace made of those diamonds: we are subject to being broken up so that the really important items can be rearranged and passed on to our heirs.

And in his early years as the father of sociobiology, Edward Wilson was prone to such statements as: "Human behavior . . . is the circuitous technique by which human genetic material has been and will be kept intact. Morality has no other demonstrable ultimate function." (It is interesting that Wilson entitled the brief first chapter of *Sociobiology* "The Morality of the Gene," but said nothing in it about morality in any recognizable sense. This was perhaps inevitable, since a gene is as utterly incapable of morality as it is of selfishness[43].) Wilson has since moderated his biodeterminism, and he now points the way toward a useful and necessary reconciliation among the natural sciences, social sciences, and humanities.

As Darwinism had been a century and more ago, sociobiology has been latched onto by people who seek to justify the unjustifiable. Conservatives seize on the principle of natural selection to maintain that everything that exists should be left alone, because it was made that way by the god of adaptation. But this is not so. It ignores genetic drift, whereby characteristics come into being that provide no evolutionary advantage, but also no disadvantage, and so survive despite Darwinian selection, not because of it. The actual essence of the Darwinian principle of selection is not that a trait must be well adapted in order to survive, but that it not be *poorly* adapted relative to other traits. It is possible for some features to continue to develop after they have fulfilled their original evolutionary function. Human intellectual ability is probably an example of this. It grew far beyond what was necessary for human survival in the eons during which it was physically developing (although perhaps not beyond or even up to what is necessary for survival in the nuclear age; indeed it may yet prove to be ultimately maladaptive by destroying the species).

Another point must be made about the complacent conservative faith that whatever *is,* ought to be. Even those traits that were selected in a Darwinian sense can have more than one consequence. In particular environmental circumstances, a trait may have provided advantages that led it to be selected for, even though it produced other, undesirable results. It is probable that this is how sickle-cell anemia spread through a significant portion of the African population. The sickle-cell trait provides immunity against malaria and so was beneficial in many regions of Africa, but it also produces another, less immediately debilitating, disease, sickle-cell anemia. When malaria is not a serious threat, the trait that was once on balance helpful becomes clearly maladaptive. There are, as we shall see, other examples of multiple-effect traits, some of them affecting behavior, that have become more harmful than helpful in human environments that emerged over the last ten thousand years.[44]

We Are Our Histories—All Three of Them

Each side in the classic nature/nurture debate has useful contributions to make, so long as they are kept within reasonable bounds. The nonsense that each side preaches when it goes to the extreme of its interpretation serves as a useful reminder that *anything*—pointedly including our innate predispositions—carried to excess is likely to be harmful.

Where extremism can lead is evident in the fact that the individual human being virtually disappears in the schemes of both sides. The biodeterminists see the person as "like a cloud in the sky," the "vehicle" for DNA; the cultural determinists see her or him as the mere creation of society. One side sees the person as an insignificant mass made up of all-important constituents, the other as an insignificant constituent part of an all-important mass. Whether putty in the hands of a selfish gene* or clay in the hands of an omnipotent soci-

---

*The vogue of "selfish determination" is a good example of one of the major themes that will be explored in this book: that the socioeconomic environment at a given time shapes the worldview of people living in that environment. Darwin saw brutal competition among individuals as the motivational force of evolution at least in part because he lived in a society based upon such competition. Some sociobiologists of the late twentieth-century Western world were prone to believe that all creatures are motivated solely by self-interest because they lived in a society whose mottos were "Look out for Number One" and "What's in it for *me?*"

ety, the particular human being fades into insignificance. We need to see humans where we are, on a level between the micro and macro.

In fact many of the past combatants in the nature/nurture war came eventually to retreat from their more extreme positions. Late in his career, erstwhile culture-is-everything proponent Alfred Kroeber accepted the biological basis of human nature. Similarly, in the later part of her career Margaret Mead recognized that some parts of human nature are not so malleable as she had once believed. From the other side, by the 1980s Edward Wilson was ready to acknowledge a greater role for culture interacting with biology. But for all their talk of interaction of biology and culture, most scholars still come down heavily on one side or the other.[45]

And, although some social scientists have begun to rediscover human nature, many humanists have been moving in the other direction for the past few decades. The continuing ascendancy of the "everything-is-constructed-out-of-nothing" version of cultural determinism in many academic circles (particularly in literary criticism) shows how far we have to go to reach a sensible blending of biology and culture.

Much of the environment in which we live does consist of cultural constructs, and they can vary enormously—but not infinitely—in superficial yet meaningful ways; but underneath these differences is a deep structure of human universals that is common to all people. We usually call this universal set of innate properties, this "species character,"[46] human nature. It is true enough that culture has constructed much of the environment that we experience and that it plays a very large role in shaping us. But every edifice needs a foundation and is made from building materials. Biology provides both the foundation on which our cultural systems have been raised and the building materials used in their construction. Cultures are constrained in what they can construct by what building materials are available in the deep structure of the human biogram. People acknowledge this fact when they refer to a culturally induced characteristic as having become "second nature." This implies the existence of an underlying, biologically based "first nature."

Notwithstanding the talk of interaction in some quarters, the largest part of the problem with both sides in the debate has been their steadfastly dualistic approach. In fact nature and culture are no more polar opposites than are women and men. One is not superior to the other; they can and must work together. As female and male must be combined to be creative, so must nature and culture.

We must expand our understanding of the environmental forces that shape us. Nature and culture are actually much more closely connected than the combatants on either side perceive. In truth, both "sides" see the environment as what molds us. But, contrary to what the cultural determinists believe, it is not just the medium-term cultural environment and short-term individual environment in which we have lived that affect us. The (very) long-term, collective (species) environment in which our distant ancestors lived—what is technically termed "the environment of evolutionary adaptation (EEA)" or the "ancestral environment"[47]—also shapes us. Put another way, three types of history mold us: evolutionary history, cultural history, and our personal history. None of these can operate independently.

Locke's metaphor needs revision. Humans at birth may seem to be blank tablets, but they are better viewed as *apparently* blank sheets that have been beneath other sheets on a pad. Evolution pressed hard in writing on those preceding sheets, leaving imprints on the seemingly blank page that we are at birth. Our experiences, many of them specific to the culture into which we are born, then write on this sheet, but with a very soft-lead pencil. The tendency is for some of the loose lead or graphite to slip into the indentations left by evolution.

What this image reflects is that there is no absolute genetic or biological determinism, but there most certainly is a strong genetic influence on human actions—and not only individual actions. Human history is not guided by evolutionary prehistory, but there can be no question that history is affected by biology in ways subtle and not-so-subtle. What biology does determine is how various environments will affect us.[48] History is the record of the interaction between biological human nature and changing environments. Geneticist Theodosius Dobzhansky summarized the interaction well in 1963: "In a sense, human genes have surrendered their primacy in human evolution to an entirely new, nonbiological or superorganic agent, culture. However, it should not be forgotten that this agent is entirely dependent on the human genotype."[49]

"There are," as science journalist Natalie Angier has said, "plenty of evolutionary biologists who know that their effort to understand human nature is far, far from over, is a neonate who has yet to find his way to his mother's teat."[50] But, while we must be much more careful than some hardcore evolutionary psychologists have been to distinguish that neonate from the dirty liquid remnants from the washings of social Darwinism, racism, and sexism in which we find it, we must recognize that the infant is in there and breathing. The united attempts by the fundamentalist and feminist doctors to abort him or her have failed, and their attempts at infanticide must be defeated.

CHAPTER 2

The Way We Were (And Are)

Human Nature

Try with a pitchfork to drive out human
nature, she always returns

HORACE[1]

"He acts like an animal, has an animal's habits! Eats like one, moves like one, talks like one," Blanche DuBois says of Stanley Kowalski in Tennessee Williams's 1947 play, *A Streetcar Named Desire*. "There's even something—sub-human—something not quite to the stage of humanity yet," she continues,

> Yes, something—ape-like about him, like one of those pictures I've seen in—anthropological studies! Thousands and thousands of years have passed him right by, and there he is—Stanley Kowalski—survivor of the Stone Age! Bearing the raw meat home from the kill in the jungle! . . . Maybe we are a long way from being made in God's image, but Stella—my sister—there has been *some* progress since then! Such things as art—as poetry and music—such kinds of new light have come into the world since then! In some kinds of people some tenderer feelings have had some little beginning! That we have got to make *grow!* And *cling* to, and hold as our flag! In this dark march toward whatever it is we're approaching. . . . *Don't—don't hang back with the brutes![2]*

Blanche's statement sums up the views many of us hold of both animal behavior and early humans. We classify the former as "brutish" and assume the latter to have been closer to that "brutal" way of life than we are now. Most modern people have an image of "cavemen" with clubs beating each other over the head and dragging women off by the hair.[3] These assumptions are mistaken; but Blanche's further point that we must cultivate the "tenderer feelings" if we are to survive the "dark march towards whatever it is we are approaching" (a comment written, significantly, just after revelation of the Nazi Holocaust and the dawn of the nuclear age) is on the mark.

The "tenderer feelings" are not, however, qualities that have been developed since "the Stone Age." They are as much a part of the human nature that had evolved by the time the Paleolithic gave way to the Neolithic era some ten thousand years ago as is the capacity for what we misleadingly term "brutality."

Animals do not generally "act like animals" in the pejorative sense in which that phrase is usually employed with reference to human behavior. The activities in which humans are most often said to be "acting like animals" are those involving sexual indulgence and violence toward other people. The inappropriateness of the "animal" terminology in these areas is particularly striking.

Rape, for example, is *not* "animal behavior" in the way the phrase is usually used. With few exceptions, forced intercourse is not part of the experience of other animals.[4]* Tellingly, though, when the environment in which animals live is drastically altered, especially through overcrowding, such forcing of females begins to occur fairly frequently among creatures in whom it had been virtually unknown. This brings up a larger point. Experiments in which animals are placed in unusual circumstances in order to learn something about their "true nature" are off base. The same distortion enters into the study of "primitive" people, a favorite example being the Ik people of Uganda, who, after being driven from their hunting area and severely mistreated, showed great callousness toward one another. The assertions of some anthropologists to the contrary notwithstanding, this behavior tells us nothing about human nature. These were not whole, "natural" people, but broken, no-longer-natural ones.[5] Their callousness in these conditions is of importance to us because their worst behavior may reflect what happens to people—or other animals— when they have to face an environment substantially different from that for which they evolved.

In terms of frequency of sexual encounter, the almost universally accepted idea that people with large appetites are "acting like animals" is absolutely wrong—well, perhaps not *absolutely*. People who are said to be acting like animals in regard to frequent sexual indulgence actually are acting like an[†]

---

*Randy Thornhill and Craig Palmer [*A Natural History of Rape: Biological Bases of Sexual Coercion* (Cambridge, MA.: MIT Press, 2000)] make the argument that males in a few species, such as scorpion flies, have evolved mechanisms for forced copulation and that this has direct relevance to human behavior. This absurd contention deserves less attention than it has received.

†There are a few others. The bonobo actually outdoes the human in this regard.

animal: *Homo sapiens.*[6] Most other species confine their sexual activities to a short mating season and generally appear to derive no great joy from them. The difference is that in most other species the sole purpose of sexual intercourse is procreation. While that is obviously *a* purpose with humans, with us sexual contact also serves as a device for bonding between a male and female. Were this not the case, there would have been no need for human females, unlike the females of most other primate species, to become receptive throughout their cycles. Nor would there be any purpose in us enjoying "it" as much as we do, or stretching it out with foreplay. For most other animals, sexual intercourse is a matter to be gotten over with as quickly as possible, and only at times when it is likely to result in offspring.[7]

Nor is wanton attack on fellow members of one's species a normal behavior among other animals. Reference to the modern city as a "jungle" is ubiquitous. Cities are indeed dangerous and impersonal. But are these conditions really junglelike? If by the "jungle" we mean a primitive form of human society, the image is inaccurate. Jungles certainly can be dangerous, but the source of the danger is other species and occasionally other bands of humans, not fellow members of the community. And on the central question of impersonality, the modern city is at the opposite end of the scale from most primitive human societies. People in the latter lived (and in a few scattered places still live) in small, tightly knit communities. It appears that humans evolved to live in just such small, highly personal groups. If so, the major trouble with modern urban life may be that it is *not* sufficiently like a jungle. And, in a larger sense, the modern human predicament may to a significant extent lie not in the fact that some of us "act like animals," but in the circumstance that we no longer live in settings in which we *can* act like animals—that is, like the particular sort of animals that we are.

Deep History: Human Evolution

The first step in the study of history, it seems to me, must be to take account of what Edward Wilson accurately terms "deep history"[8]—the evolution of the particular sort of animals we are. Given the purposes of this book, there is space here to do this only very briefly, after which I shall explore some of the traits that this evolutionary process left in us.[9]

The degree of difference in the DNA of the two species indicates that the branch of the primate order that ultimately produced modern humans diverged from that leading to chimpanzees between 6 and 10 million—probably about 7.5 million—years ago.[10] The evolution of hominids (the primate family of which humans are the only surviving member) centered on three factors: bipedalism, which had developed by 4 million years ago and enabled our ancestors to carry and throw things while on the move; later, rapid growth of the brain, particularly those portions thereof that made language possible; and the fact that much of that brain development came to occur after birth, which vastly increased adaptability and demanded a very long period of infant dependency.

Evolution works in unpredictable ways. Sometimes an apparently maladaptive mutation can become an advantage, if it leads to changes needed to overcome its disadvantages and those changes prove to be beneficial. A couple of seemingly maladaptive mutations in early hominids may have been transformed into a major advance. Unlike other primates, hominids have toes that are not suitable for effective grasping. And, at some point in hominid evolution, our ancestors came to have far less hair than do other large primates. (It has not yet been determined when the latter change occurred, but the absence of grasping toes is a feature of all hominids.) A young chimpanzee, for instance, can easily hold on to its mother's body hair. This leaves the mother's hands available for knuckle walking. The hominid had to find ways to deal with her offspring's poorly constructed toes and, perhaps, her own lack of hair. Bipedalism may well have been stimulated by a nearly hairless creature's need to be able to carry infants without grasping toes.[11] An alternate (or perhaps complementary) explanation of bipedalism is that it proved adaptive when global cooling and the creation of the Great Rift Valley (resulting from the separation of tectonic plates) caused the thinning of the forest cover in East Africa and presented an opportunity for a primate that could follow first a dual life, partly arboreal and partly terrestrial, in the thinned woodlands and then a wholly terrestrial lifestyle in grasslands.[12]

It is, in any event, now clear that bipedalism developed long before there was any significant expansion in brain size. The 1992 discovery in Ethiopia of a nearly complete, 3-million-year-old skull of an *Australopithecus afarensis* male (the same species as the famous "Lucy" skeleton that had been discovered nearby in 1974[13]) left no doubt that this early hominid, which lived between 4 and 3 million years ago and walked on its hind limbs, had a brain far too small for complex thought.[14] The subsequent presentation in 1998 by a team of anthropologists led by Meave Leakey of the National Museum of Kenya of evidence that *Australopithecus anamensis,* a hominid dated at 4.07 million years ago, walked on two feet expanded the gap between bipedalism and a larger brain. At this writing it remains uncertain whether the earlier *Australopithecus ramidus,* which dates to 4.4 million years ago, was bipedal.[15]

Around 2.5 million years ago the genus to which modern humans belong, *Homo,* originated. The earliest fossils of a species in this genus are of *Homo habilis,* which had a brain about 40 percent larger than those of the later australopithecines, but barely more than half the size of the brain of modern *Homo sapiens.* They appear to have eaten more meat than the australopithecines, although they probably obtained most it by scavenging. *Homo habilis* derives its name, meaning "human with ability," or "handy man," from the fact that this species began using crude stone tools for cutting, butchering, and other tasks.[16] Members of the new *Homo* genus also had the advantage of an anatomy that allowed much faster and more efficient bipedal locomotion: running.[17] Surely this provided a significant advantage over the plodding australopithecines.

Then, about 1.7 million years ago, *Homo erectus* emerged.[18] This appearance was a major event. This species' brain was much larger (about 80 percent greater than that of the later australopithecines), but its importance lay as much in an adaptation to the larger brain size as in the size itself, as we shall see in a moment. The more intelligent and adaptable *Homo erectus* was able to spread out from Africa to most of the Eastern Hemisphere. Over a period of several hundred thousand years, this species used cultural adaptation to develop methods for hunting, to discover how to make controlled use of fire, and to make better tools and weapons than their predecessors. These were very important changes, but the pace of cultural change was extremely slow.[19]

Very slow cultural change continued to be the norm for a long period after archaic *Homo sapiens* appeared, approximately 500,000 years ago. There does not seem to have been another major advance until the development of much better tools, the manufacture of which required considerable foresight and planning, about 200,000 years ago.[20] Even after the anatomically fully modern *Homo sapiens sapiens* came on the scene in Africa, perhaps 125,000 years ago, the pace of progress remained slow.* Growing evidence supports the belief that a single speciation produced the *Homo sapiens sapiens* group in Africa and it gradually dispersed to displace other forms, with all modern humans coming from a common ancestry, and all "racial" differences having arisen only in the last 100,000 or so years.[21]

---

*The terminology *Paleolithic Age* (Old Stone Age) is used to designate the vast period of the history (conventionally designated as part of "prehistory") of anatomically modern humans' existence prior to the development of agriculture. Thus the Paleolithic's ending point is generally agreed upon as about 8000 B.C.E., although some anthropologists favor the insertion of an intermediate Mesolithic Age between the Paleolithic and the Neolithic. Its start is more vague, sometimes being set as early as the apparent emergence of *Homo sapiens sapiens* around 125,000 years ago and sometimes as late as 50,000 years ago. I shall use Paleolithic in the broader sense; but either way, the Paleolithic encompasses by far the largest part of human history. I shall use only the Paleolithic/Neolithic periodization, without classifying an intermediate Mesolithic.

During the unimaginably long period of hominid and human evolution, there were remarkable continuities. The lives of hominids were based first on collecting and scavenging, and later on collecting and hunting as a means of subsistence.[22] This remained the case until about 10,000 years ago, when rudimentary agriculture* and herding began to replace collecting and hunting in several regions around the globe. So more than 99.99 percent of hominid biological evolution (and 98 percent of *Homo sapiens'* evolution) took place in an environment and for a way of life radically different from that in which most humans live today—and from that in which people have lived throughout recorded history. Put another way, there have been no more than five hundred generations since the first humans began to pursue an agricultural way of life. This is a mere blip on the scale of evolutionary time.

Although some physical evolution has occurred over the past ten thousand years, almost all of the selective pressures that made humans what we are today operated under constraints that were likely to shape creatures to succeed as collector-scavengers or collector-hunters.[23] No other point is of more importance in seeking to understand some of the fundamental problems men and women have confronted throughout the recorded portion of history.

The situations in which humans found themselves after the development of agriculture were in important respects very different from those in which their ancestors had evolved. There was insufficient time for physical evolution to have much significant effect on adapting *Homo sapiens* to this new environment. Some of the mixture of inbred traits that biological evolution left in humans were well-suited for a larger, more complex and settled society; others were not. The functions for which some of our innate traits evolved may no longer exist; but the traits themselves remain, the behavioral counterparts of the human appendix.[24]

The Hand We Are Dealt

Before we can sensibly discuss how the circumstances of the sexes and their reactions to those circumstances have shaped the last ten thousand years of history, we need to assess the lasting effects of evolution on women and men. An examination of the composition of our inborn foundation, the human "biogram," on which all subsequent history has necessarily had to be con-

---

*Anthropologists distinguish between *horticulture* (farming that uses only hand tools, such as hoes) and *agriculture* (farming that utilizes machinery, beginning with plows). I will use the term *agriculture* in the more common way, to refer to all forms of intentionally growing crops. Technically, the rudimentary form to which I am referring here is horticulture. Agriculture in the anthropological meaning of the word did not arise until between 6000 and 5000 years ago.

structed, will provide a base for our discourse throughout the book. The set of human characteristics I shall discuss in the remainder of this chapter is not meant to be an exhaustive inventory of human nature. Rather, I seek to focus on those innate tendencies that have the most relevance to our subject matter of how changes in the situations and perceptions of the sexes from the time of the invention of agriculture onward have shaped and misshaped history.

These include a remarkable degree of adaptability; the fact that humans are social animals but also have strong selfish motivations (that is, both co-operativeness and competitiveness); an inclination towards pair bonding and family formation; identification with a small, personally known group of other humans; pseudospeciation with regard to other humans; and anger and aggression. A few other innate tendencies that will have some relevance to our subject, such as acquisitiveness, will be left to discuss when the occasion to do so arises.

As we look in greater detail at these significant portions of our biological inheritance, it should be kept in mind that these are predispositions, not fatalistic determinants of what we *must* do. They cannot be eliminated (save perhaps by neuropharmacology or genetic engineering,[25] yet even then we would be likely to discover that we still need aspects of most of our apparently ill-adapted traits), and they can be ignored only at our great peril. But we are not slaves to our biological inheritance. If we discover what our inbred tendencies are and take them into account, they can be directed into channels that are better suited to modern human life. That is the primary function of cultural values. This managing of our innate motivations can never be done, however, without an understanding of how we are "preprogrammed"*; and it cannot be done without cost, completely, finally, or in any way that may strike our fancy. Our biological inheritance does not determine our destiny; it does restrict our choices.

Our human nature is the hand that is dealt to us; what we do with that hand is still up to us. The cards we receive place certain limits on what we can do, and if we hope to do well, we had better look at the cards. One can win at poker with almost any hand, but winning is unlikely to happen without one knowing what cards are held.[26]

Premature Birth

Paradoxical though it sounds, the most important innate characteristic of our species is its extraordinary adaptability. It is this quality that causes much of

---

*I am here employing one of the metaphors that has so misled people by implying that we are similar to machines or computers. On the few occasions when the use of such a metaphor seems unavoidable, I shall enclose it in quotation marks to indicate that it is not to be taken literally.

the confusion in the nature/nurture debates. Cultural determinists recognize this trait and mistakenly conclude that it completely supercedes all others, leaving us blank slates on which culture can write *any* story. For their part, evolutionary psychologists and others who emphasize the power of our biological inheritance often fail to give this fundamental human characteristic its due and so overestimate the degree to which other evolutionary legacies affect our behavior.

The adaptability of *Homo sapiens* is so much greater than that of any other species that it might well be considered *the* fundamental human trait. "Perhaps our greatest distinction as a species," as Jared Diamond has said, "is our capacity, unique among animals, to make counter-evolutionary choices."[27] It is not that humans are so well adapted, but that we adapt so well. The basic cause of this adaptability has to do with large brains, but not as straightforwardly as it might seem at first. We do, indeed, as Robert Wright has noted, "have huge brains whose whole reason for being is deft adjustment to variable conditions."[28] But there is more to it: we have big heads. Because hominids had adopted bipedal walking before their brains increased significantly in size, when heads became substantially bigger, anatomical adaptation had to try to find a way to reconcile them with upright posture. As the size of the hominid brain expanded from *Australopithecus* to *Homo,* so did the female's pelvic opening or birth canal. But the pelvis could only be so large if bipedal locomotion was to be efficiently maintained. As the head became too large for the mother's pelvic opening to accommodate at birth, the evolutionary solution that emerged was for birth to occur well before brain development (and so head size) was completed. Thus our forebears began to be born "undone" or "half-baked," with much head growth and brain development left to occur after birth. All human births are literally premature. This appears to have already been the case with *Homo erectus,* which is believed to have been born with a brain only one-third its adult size (which was about two-thirds the size of our brains) and it is very clearly the circumstance with *Homo sapiens.*[29] The after-birth growth of the brain provided hominids and humans a huge asset by allowing for far-greater cultural adaptation, since so much of what a human becomes is shaped when the outside environment can interact with (but not eliminate) the genotype. The consequent very long (and very pronounced) period of infant dependency also served to make protohumans more social and interdependent. It is probably the source, as well, of the family, since long infant dependency placed a survival advantage on having two parents to protect and instruct the offspring.

The extraordinary amount of postnatal brain development in humans (and our immediate *Homo* predecessors) is totally without precedent in other animals and, along with brain size itself, it gives us an immense advantage in adapting to changing environments. The ability to adapt is the most adaptive trait an organism can possess. Great though human malleability is in comparison with other species, however, it is not unlimited. Other aspects of the human biogram impose limits on how far our flexibility can be taken.

Born Unfree

The second key component of the human biogram is that we are social animals. Two factors, the long period of infant dependency, and the fact that they came eventually to depend upon hunting large game for a significant portion of their nutrition, obliged our ancestors to become increasingly social and cooperative. Food sharing, however, appears to have become a way of life among members of the *Homo* genus before they started to engage in much big-game hunting.[30] Humans share food to a degree far beyond what other primates do, and even beyond other group hunters, such as wolves. Some other primates (chimpanzees and baboons) will share food with fellows who beg it from them, but usually they do so with considerably more reluctance than is the rule among wolves and, more so, among humans.[31] Beyond brain size and the species' extraordinary adaptability (both of which were themselves almost certainly advanced by social activity), the capacity for a remarkable level of social cooperation probably provides humans with our greatest advantage over other species.[32]

Social animals instinctively crave and enjoy companionship and a degree of cooperation with others of their species, even when such actions have no apparent direct survival value for the individual (or for her or his genes, in that the help is given to nonrelatives). Thomas Jefferson put the point well, albeit necessarily in pre-Darwinian terms, when he wrote in an 1814 letter: "The creator would indeed have been a bungling artist, had he intended man for a social animal, without planting in him social dispositions."[33]

Being social animals does not mean that humans do not also have innate self-centered motivations. The simultaneous existence of conflicting characteristics contributes to the difficulty in sorting out human nature, but it is a fact that must be accepted.

Despite the claims of some very influential seventeenth- and eighteenth-century thinkers such as Hobbes, Locke, and Rousseau about "mankind in a state of nature,"* humans are not—and never were—independent. I'll leave it to others to determine whether lions are "born free," but it is obvious that people are not. The human infant may be the most dependent creature on the

---

*This will be discussed in Chapter 10.

planet. Paradoxically, the long period of infant dependence helps to provide humans with the means of achieving a degree of self-sufficiency in adulthood. But the natural state of humans, even when full-grown, is one not of independence but *inter*dependence. We and our hominid ancestors have always been social animals, living from the earliest times in interdependent groups, first as bands of collector-scavengers and collector-hunters and subsequently in increasingly complex agricultural and then urban societies. The solitary, self-sufficient egoist, far from being an approximation of humankind in a State of Nature, actually amounts to humanity in a State of *Un*nature.

The very concept of the human self has meaning only in relation to others, that is, in the context of society. There is no *choice* between self and society; the two are reciprocal. One cannot properly exist without the other.

Presumably the mixture of selfish and social motivations in humans has been a substantial evolutionary advantage over creatures that were almost solely one or the other. If so, a balance between the selfish and the social is not only biologically necessary for us, but in all likelihood it is also still beneficial to the overall interests of the human species. Many, if not most, of our problems in the modern world come from systems that emphasize either the selfish or the social side of the human biogram to the virtual exclusion of the other.

We Are Family

A tendency toward lasting pair bonding between a male and female, both of whom live with and provide some degree of care for the female's offspring, is a characteristic of humans* that is not shared with most other primates. Among gibbons and a very few other primate species, fathers as well as mothers participate in raising the young; but among the apes that are closest to humans in the evolutionary chain, this is not the case.[34] Chimpanzee societies are based upon females who care for their young and continue to have close ties with their offspring even as the latter reach adulthood. Males mate with many females and rarely show any great interest in the infants, with whom they seem to be aware of no connection to themselves.[35]

Because all human infants are essentially helpless for a period of at least a few years, and require nearly constant attention, their needs take up a substantial amount of their mothers' time. Hence there is a great advantage to having a second parent help provide food and protection. This fact would have

---

*Obviously this desire to bond with someone from the other sex does not apply to a significant minority of individual humans. But it is generally the case that those who are attracted to members of their own sex also seek to form some sort of family. The fact that the vast majority of people in cultures around the world attempt to form some kind of families strongly suggests that there is a biological predisposition to do so.

selected for a growing degree of male parental investment, since offspring who are eaten before they are of an age to have offspring of their own cannot pass along their genes.[36]

Gibbons and humans, although far more different in other respects than chimpanzees and humans, share a few key characteristics. The females of both species have a menstrual, rather than an estrous, cycle. This means that they are receptive to intercourse at most times, not only around their ovulation (although the sexual desire of a woman usually increases near her time of ovulation[37]). It appears that it is because this quality makes it possible for males to satisfy their sexual urges with a single partner that the menstrual cycle moved these species toward pair bonding and a substantial degree of monogamy.[38] Unlike most other primates, human females do not advertise their time of ovulation. Although there are several theories about why human ovulation is concealed, it seems clear that "cryptic ovulation"[39] gives the male a greater incentive to stick around in order to assure that his genes will be passed along.[40]* The affection that frequent intercourse with the same partner helps to develop and sustain provides the male with an interest in his mate's offspring, even when he is unaware (as, it seems safe to assume, gibbons always have been and humans probably were through most of their evolutionary development) of his own role in procreation.

Obviously there is a vast array of practices in this area in different cultures, including many varieties of polygamy. As for possible differences between the sexes on matters related to pair bonding, sexual relations, and family life, those questions will be deferred to the next chapter, when the whole issue of biological sex differences is discussed.

Because having two adults intimately concerned with the well-being of the young provided an advantage to the species, the general trend in human evolution is undeniably toward pair bonding and lasting families.† Pair bonding (albeit often with some backsliding, especially by men) and the family are, the exceptions notwithstanding, among the traits that characterize the human species.

The Band Plays On

The family is the basic unit of human society, but our sociability extends well beyond close kin. Human nature clearly includes a predisposition to identify with a small group of people. It was in troops or bands of from perhaps thirty to a few hundred members that most of our progenitors lived and evolved.[41]

---

*This is not, of course, a conscious motivation in other species and rarely is in humans. The presumption is that evolution would tend to select for traits that led to such reproductive success.

†This, obviously, has not been the trend of cultural evolution in the Western world in recent decades. The ramifications of this divergence from human nature are discussed in later chapters.

Evolution "designed" us to live in *personal* societies of this size. For at least five thousand years (and in a few places perhaps as much as eight thousand years or more), some humans have been living in larger, increasingly unnatural circumstances, culminating in the immense modern city.

The social instincts that we humans certainly possess are not directed toward humanity as a whole but toward a small group such as those in which our distant ancestors lived. Our socially oriented traits are most readily triggered by personal recognition.

Cooperation within bands of collector-hunters was clearly adaptive in the Paleolithic environment, but there seem also to have been evolutionary advantages to developing a distrust of "strangers"—people outside the band. Unknown people could easily represent danger. Chimpanzees react with fear and aggressive actions when confronted with other members of the species they do not know, especially if the strangers are adult males.[42] Thus there is built into us a set of instincts that distinguish between the group with which we identify and all others. We have a natural tendency to be friendly and compassionate toward our fellows but fearful of "outsiders." By the time an infant is beyond nine months old, his or her reaction to seeing a stranger is likely to be freezing with fright, an increased pulse rate, and often crying.[43] In adults the "natural" reaction (often mitigated by learned cultural values) to strangers seems to be to distance oneself and prepare for a fight in case it should it become necessary.[44]

What our nature leads us to seek is a situation in which we can live with a substantial degree of security about the intentions of those around us. In personal groups, whether they be a Paleolithic collector-hunter band, a medieval manor, or a nineteenth-century American village, members of the community usually know what to expect from one another. They can "take each other for granted."

When we humans find ourselves living in societies much larger than those in which (and *for* which) our forebears evolved, the parts of our biograms that control responses connected with communities and outsiders cease to serve us well. That the social part of our natures operates on the basis of personal knowledge means that it was possible, without danger of our innate tendencies becoming nonadaptive, to expand a community beyond the normal numbers of the collector-hunter band, but only to a size at which one could recognize all or at least most other members of the group. The limit for such a community is probably about the size of a small town. Clearly it is possible for people to identify themselves with larger aggregates, but not in the same personal manner, and so not with quite the same powerful, inbred emotions operating in a normal fashion.

The desirability of living in communities small enough that members can know one another has been recognized by a variety of observers throughout

human history. Aristotle said the ideal size for a polis was such that every citizen could know every other by sight.[45] The Greek polis has been described as
"so *intimate* a union." And the accurate sense of Aristotle's famous dictum
about man being a political animal is better expressed as "Man is a creature
who lives in a polis."[46] Far from being the reflection of simple ethnocentrism,
this is a realistic assessment of a most important part of human nature.

Nineteenth-century German sociologist Ferdinand Tonnies pointed to the
same feature of the human biogram when he distinguished between what he
termed *Gemeinschaft,* a small, personal community, and *Gesellschaft,* a large,
impersonal society in which individuals lose their identities and become
anonymous[47]—a lifestyle for which some species, such as rats, are biologically suited, but humans are not.

Identification with the Band
After humans left the social environment for which we are adapted—that of a small
band of people who are known personally—and began living in much larger, impersonal societies, the innate need to identify with a group had to be met in artificial ways.
One way in which this sense of belonging has been found over the last century is by
identification with sports teams. Here Liverpool's football (soccer) fans "go wild" as
their team wins the English championship in 1977. Such fans sometimes entered into
violent physical clashes with the backers of other teams. (Wide World Photos)

The United States Census Bureau takes account of the same distinction by designating a town of more than 2,500 inhabitants as an "urban" area. On its face, this appears ridiculous. A town with a population of 3,000 hardly seems to belong in the same classification as New York City. But the distinction may be valid in a biological sense. Somewhere around 2,500 may be the limit on the number of people with which we can achieve a feeling of personal community. When that number is surpassed, we move from a personal to an anonymous environment, and we are not innately "programmed" for the latter situation.

As soon as substantial numbers of people started to live in larger societies—beginning at least as early as the late seventh millennium B.C.E. (c. 6250 B.C.E.) at Çatal Hüyük in Anatolia (modern Turkey), which is believed to have had a population of 6,000 or more—it became necessary to set about trying to devise cultural means of modifying the innate identification with a small band and distrust of those who were not readily recognizable.

It is necessary to address a related matter. If humans are biologically "programmed" to live in small groups and to distrust strangers, it might seem to follow that nationalism, racism, and ethnic hostility are both natural and inevitable. But this is a misunderstanding of the innate tendency to identify with a *personal* community. If our predisposition is for small communities, then identification with a Greek polis, a Chinese peasant village, a small town in Indiana, or a neighborhood in Brooklyn is "natural," but identification with Japan, the British Empire, or the United States, let alone "the free world," "the Aryan race," or "the international proletariat" is not. The difference is well exemplified by Sonny Corleone at the end of the film *The Godfather, Part II.* He says the people who enlisted in the army following Pearl Harbor are "a bunch of saps" because "they risk their lives for strangers." When his brother Michael counters that they are risking their lives for their country, Sonny snaps back with a response based upon innate human proclivities: "Your country ain't your blood—you remember that!"[48] Identification with "our family,"* which can be extended to the size of a personal community, is natural; identification with strangers, which nationalism requires, is not. The rise of fervent nationalism and of international class consciousness (to whatever extent the latter may ever in reality have existed) are cultural adaptations of innate traits, not themselves part of human nature.

---

*There can be little question that the concept of *la cosa nostra* ("our house" or "our family") against "others" or "strangers," which has been the basis of Sicilian organized crime, has deep roots in human evolution. That, of course, does not make it "right"; only those who make the error of equating *natural* with *good* would think that it did.

If humans were able to adapt culturally to the huge nation-state by developing emotional nationalism during the last five centuries, might we not further adapt to an identification with all humanity? Perhaps. But given our biological makeup it will not be easy.

Our social instincts, again, are triggered by personal contact. Our capacity for love, obviously, is greatest for those with whom we are closest. Our feelings for others can best be understood as a series of concentric circles surrounding us. The power of our emotions is strongest within the central circle, our family. The next larger circle, that of close personal friends, also readily elicits our compassion. Then there is the circle of the community in which we live, a neighborhood, a small town, or perhaps the people with whom we work, the closest modern approximations to the hominid band. As long as this community is small enough that its members can be known on a personal level, our natural inclinations lead us to identify strongly with it and we are willing to act altruistically toward its members.

The kinds of feelings that a person naturally develops toward her or his family and community, however, cannot be expected for the unknown multitudes of city, nation, or planet. We *cannot* "love everybody" equally. Love is personal; it is literally not humanly possible to love anonymous masses— "humanity"—in the innate way we do our family and friends.[49]

There is a further difficulty with trying to instill values that will lead us to identify with all humanity. It seems that part of the way in which we identify with others and so know "who we are" is by determining who we are *not,* as rats do by attacking those who do not have the "right" odor. Therefore, in addition to the major obstacle of overcoming our innate resistance to identification on a mass, impersonal level, which had to be done to establish nationalism, an identification with all humanity would also require us to overcome the apparently natural desire to classify some people as "others." National identification seems, in fact, to be achieved principally through the definition of "others" who are said to be different from "us." Many people of French descent in Quebec, to cite one of the many such examples, refer to those who do not speak French as *les autres,* the others.[50]

This tendency to know who we are by who we are not may explain the discomfort felt in many quarters over the end of the Cold War. Americans seemed to cast about seeking someone to replace the Soviets as the "other": the Japanese, the Iraqis, *some*body. "The warrior," Sam Keen has rightly said of this predisposition that tends to be especially powerful in males but is also present in females, "is marked by a negative identity; his life is oriented against the enemy, the rival, the competition."[51]

If there is not a "them," does there cease to be an "us"? Is the predisposition to dislike as powerful as that to like? Do we need somebody to hate as much as somebody to love? We may not want to hear the correct answers to these questions, but as is the case with the rest of our biological makeup, what we don't know *can* hurt us.

As to the apprehension that the innate tendency to identify with the band might mean that racism is "natural," there are two answers. First, even if there were some degree of natural inclination toward racial identification, that would in no sense justify racism. Because many of our inbred tendencies are no longer adaptive, there is absolutely no reason to classify them as "good" or "right." Second, the key to identification with the band seems to be *personal* contact within a group small enough for that to take place, not the genetic similarity of its members. If our groups tend to be homogenous, this is probably not because we have a biological preference for people most genetically similar to us, but because the races have been and to a large extent continue to be segregated, thus making the formation of strong personal bonds between members of different races less likely.

"Kill the [Blankety-Blanks]!"

Humans kill far more of our own species (our *conspecifics,* in biological terminology) than do other creatures. But this does not mean that we lack inhibitions against doing so—*if we recognize another person as truly being human, "like us."* Rather, we seem better able than members of other species to turn off such inhibitions by an ingrained process called *pseudospeciation.* What this means is that we have a facility for seeing those outside the group with which we identify as if they were not really members of our species—to *dehumanize* them.[52] It is unlikely that any other innate human trait has been as harmful over the course of recorded as history as this one. Bill Clinton was on target when he warned of this predisposition in an address to gay and lesbian supporters in Los Angeles in 1999. "The biggest problem we've got is the primitive age-old fear and dehumanization of the other people who are not like us," Clinton said.[53]

That this predisposition to question the full humanity of people outside our group, which lies at the root of many of the most horrible acts in history, is innate is indicated by the fact that collector-hunter tribes often call themselves by names that mean "*the* people." Even the essentially peaceful bush people of the Kalahari, for example, refer to themselves as !Kung, which translates to "*the* human beings."[54]

During the vast ages in which our biogram was being developed, such a readiness to see humans not of one's own group, who might often represent danger, almost as if they were another species was apparently more conducive to survival than was not doing so. Indeed, this tendency seems to be an unpleasant side effect of human sociability. If strong bonding with the band provided an evolutionary advantage, then "outsiders" were likely to be looked upon with great wariness. The social nature of our distant ancestors led them to desire to protect those in their group. This necessarily meant protecting them not only from members of other species but also from other humans who did not belong to their band or tribe.[55]

The fact that our social instincts are not automatically "good" is also apparent if we realize how many of the worst actions engaged in by humans, from gang rape to genocide, are done in groups. What Goethe once noted about his fellow Germans, that they are "so estimable in the individual and so dastardly in the collective,"[56] could at one time or another be said of most of us.

The close relationship between the innate tendencies of identification with the band and pseudospeciation is evident in the fact that many of the most selfless, altruistic acts in which men engage occur during wars. A particular wartime act, viewed from one perspective, may constitute heroic self-sacrifice for one's group and be deserving of the medals for valor that it often brings. Yet that same act, viewed from another perspective, may appear to be the most barbarous slaughter of what are in fact fellow human beings; however, from the first perspective the act is not deemed to be murder because the slain victims have been "otherized." Viewed from the second perspective, the heroic act that brought a medal may become an act of cruelty deserving the most severe punishment a society inflicts.

The combination of strong ties with—even altruism for—those close to us and a tendency to mistrust strangers is a potent one. Without our capacity for pseudospeciation, humans would have great difficulty participating in wars or acts of discrimination, let alone those of genocide, such as were carried out by European-descended people in previous centuries against the native peoples of the Americas and Australia or, in the twentieth century, the Turkish annihilation of Armenians, the Nazi Holocaust against the Jews, the slaughter of Hutus by Tutsis and vice versa in Rwanda, or the "ethnic cleansing" by Serbs in Bosnia and Kosovo, to name a few.

It is only possible to kill "brutally" if we have identified the victim in the way a "brute" (that is, another animal) would: as a member of a different species. Killing "Redskins," "Niggers," "Honkies," or "Gooks" is compatible with our biological natures; killing human beings is not.

Winston Churchill made one of the baldest statements of pseudospeciation on record in his account of the British machine-gun slaughter of Muslim tribesmen at Omdurman in the Sudan in 1898. It was "like a pantomime scene," Churchill said. "These extraordinary *foreign* figures . . . march up one by one from the darkness of Barbarism to the footlights of civilization . . . and their conquerors, taking their possessions, forget even their names. Nor will history

Pseudospeciation
This San Francisco newspaper cartoon celebrating the Chinese Exclusion Act of 1882 vividly exemplifies the human capacity to "otherize" people different from ourselves, perceiving them as if they are not human. (Photo: Caroline Buckler)

record such trash."[57] In the same vein, social Darwinist Theodore Roosevelt hailed "the spread of the English-speaking peoples over the world's waste space" (by which he meant territory occupied by non-Anglo-Saxons).[58] Social Darwinism is, in fact, in large part an endorsement of pseudospeciation.

The perpetrators of the Nazi Holocaust employed euphemisms and dehumanizing terminology in separating themselves from their victims, in order to shut off their innate inhibitions against cruelty to and killing of their conspecifics—their fellow humans. The Hitlerian objective was to make the world *Judenrein,* "ridded of Jews." This is the sort of language used when we talk of ridding the world of bacteria, vermin, or pests. We were glad to rid the world of smallpox. When the same terminology is used for people, they cease to *be* people in the minds of those speaking this way. There was a requirement that the bodies of Jewish and other victims in the Nazi death camps never be referred to as "corpses"; instead they had to be called "sticks of wood" or "pieces of shit."

Like other traits produced by evolution, the tendency to question the humanity of outsiders can be ignored only at great peril. But the existence of a proclivity for pseudospeciation does not mean that racism, war, jingoism, xenophobia, and occasional outbreaks of genocide are the inevitable lot of humankind. Like other innate predispositions, this one cannot be eliminated, but it can be controlled. Because it begins with the inbred tendency to distrust strangers, the first step in controlling pseudospeciation is to make other people and their cultures better known to us, and so less "strange." The key is in finding ways to get us to recognize the humanity of others. That this goal is possible has been shown repeatedly. The outpouring of donations for African famine relief that followed the television images of starving Ethiopian children in the mid-1980s is but one such example. For all its faults, in fact, television has a distinct power for good in bringing a realization of common humanity to people around the globe. One might point also to the way in which television images of the Vietnam War undermined support for that war in the United States. This happened at least in part because television showed Americans the humanity of the suffering Vietnamese and so called forth the natural inhibitions against mistreatment of fellow humans.

Decency and compassion are "natural virtues." This fact is comforting, because it provides an innate base upon which human values can be (and, throughout history, have been) constructed. But we must remember that our biological drives are mixed. The application of our natural virtues is largely confined to those who are close to us, and it can actually lead us to be evil toward "others." It is only through culturally created values that take into account our biological natures that we can hope to extend these natural virtues to people beyond our families and communities.

Can We Make Love, Not War?

There has long been great controversy over whether humans have an innate proclivity for anger and aggression. Many well-meaning people fear that the existence of an evolution-constructed human predisposition to become angry and aggressive under certain conditions would mean that warfare is inevitable. Given the weapons of mass destruction that now exist, they believe that the only hope for human survival rests in proving that anger and aggression are the products of culture, not genes.

The best way to prove this assertion would be to show that some human cultures are completely nonaggressive. The second best proof would be showing that another species of primates closely related to humans has no tendency to become angry and aggressive.* Both claims have been made. Seemingly peaceful human cultures have been identified in the Eskimos, the !Kung, and the Zuni. Chimpanzees have been called the "peaceful primates."

---

*It is curious that many of those who pointed to the supposed peaceful nature of chimpanzees as an indication that humans are not predisposed to be violent simultaneously denied that humans have any nature, in which case it obviously would matter not a whit for human behavior what the nature of chimps is.

What these "discoveries" of putatively nonaggressive people and chimps amount to can best be characterized as wishful thinking. It is certainly true that some human societies have been much more successful than most at controlling anger and aggression. But that is hardly the same thing as saying that those traits do not exist in people of such cultures. If something is in need of being controlled, it must exist.

Anthropologist Ruth Benedict explained the many means whereby the Zuni sought to prevent aggressive behavior.[59] Several other anthropologists, including Elizabeth Marshall Thomas, have done the same with !Kung. But these cultures are *anti-aggressive,* not *non*aggressive.[60] To say that among Eskimos and other such societies "social codes stressed the importance of muting animosities and restraining jealousy and anger"[61] plainly indicates that these traits are innate and in need of cultural control.

Unlike Europeans, European-Americans, and most other modern societies, the anti-aggressive cultures are not warlike. Although many aspects of Western culture serve to encourage aggression, the Zuni, !Kung, and Eskimo societies do everything they can to discourage it. But the raw material with which both modern Western and so-called primitive types of cultures operate—human nature—is the same, and the evidence is overwhelming that a portion of that human nature is to be innately prone to anger and aggression.

The most striking evidence of this tendency toward aggression is to be found in changes over time among the peaceful peoples themselves. As recently as early in the twentieth century, the now "harmless" !Kung had a murder rate as high as that in many American cities today. The change from a society with a high murder rate to a peaceful one over a generation or two suggests that, under certain conditions, a dramatic cultural transformation can be achieved relatively rapidly, bringing the propensity in humans to be aggressive under some control. But the innate nature of aggressiveness is evident in the rapid transformation in the other direction undergone during the 1950s by some of the Semai people of Malaya. Among the most nonviolent people ever found (and usually cited to prove that men are not innately prone to aggression and violence[62]), some of the Semai changed dramatically when the British got them involved in a war against Communist guerrillas. The Semai soldiers became, as one of them put it, "drunk with blood." "We thought only of killing," he said.[63]

Those societies that have been most successful in controlling human aggression necessarily have understood that there is a propensity toward aggression that needs to be controlled. Their cultural values reinforce behaviors that counteract aggression.[64] The rest of us could learn much from the values and practices of the few peaceful human societies but only if we accepted, as they do, that anger and aggression can be controlled but never eliminated or "cured." In this effort all of us would be like a person afflicted with alcoholism. If we ever could manage, through the adoption of certain values, to bring our aggressive natures under control, we would forevermore be "recovering aggressives," never "former aggressives."

The notion that our cousins, the chimpanzees (*Pan troglodytes*), are naturally peaceful creatures, once widely accepted, is no more. Jane Goodall, the most famous observer of chimpanzee life in the wild, originally believed these creatures to be nonterritorial and basically peaceful. After further observation of the animals at Gombe, Tanzania, however, Goodall revised her conclusions. It now appears that, in this regard, chimps are pretty much like people. Like collector-hunters of our own species, they establish territories with somewhat flexible boundaries. Males bond closely into a group and react with hostility to conspecifics who are not members of their band; they are prone to become aggressive in a substantial number of situations.[65] The coup de grace (actually much more a *coup sans grace*) to the "peaceful primate" view of chimpanzees has been provided by the direct observation since 1974 of several instances in which raiding parties of male chimps attacked and brutally killed members of another chimp community. Some of these raids included such atrocities as "tearing off pieces of skin, . . . twisting limbs until they break, or drinking a victim's blood."[66] Because these findings do not conform to what many people want to believe about the "naturalness" of aggressive tendencies, many people continue to cling to Goodall's earlier beliefs like security blankets.

More recently a new candidate for the title of "peaceful primate" has arisen: the bonobo, or pygmy chimpanzee (*Pan paniscus*). As closely related to *Homo sapiens* as are chimpanzees, bonobos inhabit an area in the Congo Republic south of the Congo or Zaire River, separated from chimpanzees, whose territories are exclusively on the other side of the river. Bonobos have found that they can literally "make love, not war." When a bonobo gets into a potentially violent confrontation with another member of the species, he or she transforms it into a sexual encounter. The bonobo in an unpleasant situation readily converts it into a pleasant one by engaging in sexual relations with the potential enemy, regardless of the sex or age of the opponent/sex partner. Competition often becomes copulation as sex is used to reduce tension.[67] Bonobos are very different from their closest relatives in another, connected regard. Males do not rape or batter females or kill infants, as chimpanzee and human males sometimes do. This different behavior is apparently the result of females banding together to keep male aggressiveness under control. Female bonobos bond with one another by engaging in homosexual relations: using their large clitorises for genital rubbing that the local Mongandu people call *hoka-hoka*.[68]

Before we become overly excited about what the bonobos' employment of pansexuality as a displacement activity for violent competition might mean for humans, however, two points must be made. First, clearly this adaptation was needed because these cousins of ours, like the chimpanzees, had aggressive drives in their natures. The species has not been *non*aggressive; rather, it has developed a means of diverting its aggressive and competitive drive. Second, the bonobos' way of defusing a proclivity for violent confrontation cannot be a successful way for humans to defuse their own proclivities for violence because, unlike either chimpanzees or bonobos, the human biogram predisposes us toward pair bonding. Human females are unlikely to unite overcome male dominance by bonding through *hoka-hoka,* because they must compete with one another for desirable male partners. Humans, chimps, and bonobos share about 98.4 percent of the same DNA, but that still leaves 1.6 percent to account for differences. It is entirely plausible that the genes that incline humans toward aggressive behavior are among those we share with chimpanzees, while those that predispose us more or less toward pair bonding are among those that differ from those of the other animals.

What the bonobos' success in the displacement of violent confrontations means for humans is that it should be possible for us to find ways of diverting our aggressive tendencies into less dangerous channels.

Despite the wishful thinking, few of us really doubt that we have a natural tendency to become angry. That, plainly, is the implication of the oft-heard phrase "uncontrolled anger." To say this is to say that anger exists, innately, in all of us, so we must strive to control it.

The cause of the trouble, once again, is dualistic thinking. Some people argue that if anger and aggression were natural human traits we would so enjoy fighting that we would have destroyed ourselves; since we have not, we must be naturally social and cooperative, not aggressive and competitive.[69] Such thinking falls into a classic either/or fallacy. Humans are not *either* aggressive *or* cooperative; we have both proclivities in our biogram. In fact, the two are closely related. It is when we are cooperating with others in our group that we tend most readily to become aggressive toward others. "War," Desmond Morris has correctly said, "is more the result of male group cooperation than of male aggression."[70]

That we have an innate tendency to become angry not only *was* a good thing, but it still *is*—under some circumstances. Warfare with modern weapons is a result of anger and group cooperation that have become maladaptive. But other aspects of anger remain adaptive under modern circumstances. If we did not have the capacity to become angry over certain conditions, there would be no such thing as justice. It is part of our biological makeup to become outraged at what we see as injustice. As any parent can attest, nothing so upsets a child as a situation that she or he believes "isn't fair." If such situations did not anger us, we would never do anything to remedy them. Fortunately, injustice *does* get us angry. The very words we use in discussing movements for social justice indicate the connection between the biological mechanism that motivates them and anger/aggression. We call our efforts to right wrongs "struggles," "battles," or "campaigns."[71] To demur is human.

An angerless world clearly would not be human. People are not always nice. And they *shouldn't* be. If they were, the result would be a far cry from paradise. It would be a world of lobotomized people going around smiling and saying, "Have a nice day."

The problem with anger is not that it exists, but that it sometimes gets out of control. Any useful trait can become dangerous if carried to excess. Having a tendency to get angry does not oblige us to go to war any more than having teeth fatalistically determines that we must bite someone.[72]

Anger is a particularly good innate trait in which to notice how biology and culture interact. Anger is, in this respect, like sexual desire. Both are biological, but in both cases, culture shapes what will "turn you on." It is undeniable, though, that what gets "turned on" when we are either angered or sexually aroused is a physical, glandular apparatus. Biology gives us the tendency to be turned on in these regards, but culture and values have a very important effect in determining under just what circumstances these attributes will be activated.[73]

Speaking of sex, it is high time that we do so. Let us now focus directly on this division of our species and what it has meant for us and our history.

CHAPTER 3

Men Are from New York; Women Are from Philadelphia

Sex and the "Notawoman" Definition of Manhood

> She was goddess because of her force; she was
> the animated dynamo; she was reproduction—the greatest
> and most mysterious of all energies.
>
> HENRY ADAMS (1905)[1]

It all started with sex.

A basic premise of this book is that the division of humanity into sexes and the ways in which the significance of that division has been interpreted have been a central force—perhaps *the* central force—throughout history.

"A man would never get the notion of writing a book on the peculiar situation of the human male,"[2] Simone de Beauvoir wrote in *The Second Sex* (1952). Yet it is precisely "the peculiar situation of the human male"—and "his" reactions to it, especially since the advent of agriculture—that has shaped much of history. This volume is, in part, the book that de Beauvoir said a man would never think of writing.

"I never wanted to be a woman,"[3] the Arnold Schwarzenegger character in the 1994 movie *Junior* exclaims during the fifth week of his pregnancy.

Perhaps not. But the fact that women can do seemingly magical things that men cannot has had a deep but largely unexamined effect on all of human history.

Neither Opposite Nor "Apposite"

In the last chapter we discussed human nature, the innate characteristics that unite all humans. But there is one aspect of innate biological traits that seems to divide us: sex.

The question of biological differences between the sexes is a thicket that one hesitates to enter. But enter it we must if we are to analyze the roots from which the particular history that is the subject of the rest of this book grew. This issue is capable of instantly provoking heated debate. The extremes in the argument get most of the attention. Some feminist factions continue to insist that women and men are "just the same except for different plumbing." At the opposite extreme is the "anatomy is destiny" camp, ranging from Sigmund Freud to John Gray's extraordinarily popular and absurdly titled *Men Are from Mars, Women Are from Venus.*[4]

Both sides in this debate are wrong. The scientific evidence that there are genetic and hormone-based average differences in some behaviors and ways of thinking between the sexes has become so overwhelming in recent years that it can no longer be ignored.[5] These disparities are (with the obvious exception of certain reproductive functions) far from absolute; there is much more overlap than difference, and the distinctions are *much* more subtle than the Mars/Venus group believes. Males and females are far more alike than different; but the small average variations can have important consequences. We are neither "opposite" sexes nor "just the same except for different plumbing"—neither opposite nor "apposite." To be accurate, what we should say is not "the opposite sex," but "the somewhat different sex." Difference in no way implies inequality, and the overlap means that there is no justification for blocking an individual from any occupation on the basis of sex.

The argument that biological sex makes no difference is the ultimate of the tabula rasa idea: all humans at birth are cutout figures on blank paper, differing only in whether they have their genital organs showing or concealed. This conception is nonsense. Differences in brain structure are not meaningless. Hormones obviously affect behavior, and men and women differ, *on average,* in their hormones. *On average* is emphasized because the words are critical to a proper understanding of sexual difference.

But the idea that the sexes are radically different, like creatures from different planets, is even more ridiculous. The small, genuine differences often have been wildly exaggerated, for reasons that I shall address as the chapter unfolds. The Mars/Venus argument is merely the latest in a long line of gender extending.

Does Sex Matter?

Is sex an absolute difference? Yes and no. But much more no. Sexual division might seem to make all of us "half humans." In fact, however, both men and women are nearly complete humans, each lacking just a bit, principally in each case an essential part of the ability to reproduce.

It has become normal practice among scientists to refer to females as the "default sex"[6] since every embryo starts out as female and stays that way unless male hormones make it male. This usage can easily become a modern version of Aristotle and Freud, classifying females as "incomplete males." Alternatively, it can become an argument that females are the "true humans" (or whatever species) and that males are "misshapen females" who were perfect until their brains were damaged by a bath of testosterone before birth. (This conception is not fanciful. Feminist philosopher Mary Daly has referred to men as "mutants."[7]) Both such views are unwarranted.[8] Female and male are simply two different forms that a sexually divided species takes; neither is deformed; neither is superior nor the ideal version of the species. In fact, *both* sexes are incomplete in the important sense that they are incapable of replicating themselves without combining with a member of the other sex.

But, beyond the obvious differences related to reproduction,* all differences based on sex are only on average and so far from absolute that they are quite flexible. With intensive weight training, for example, some women can become very masculine in body structure. Women who build their bodies to resemble those of men often cease to menstruate, indicating that they have gone a long way toward altering their sex.[9] From the other side of the supposed vacuum of interplanetary space, male lactation is a very unusual but not unheard-of occurrence.[10] Any categorization that is sufficiently flexible for this degree of change and border incursion to occur is not properly seen as one of opposites. Significant average biological differences between the sexes, other than those directly involved with reproduction, are in many cases real, but it is worth emphasizing again and again that the sexes are *far* more alike than different. A large part of the difficulty in this area probably stems from the mistaken assumption that if the biological difference between the sexes in reproductive roles is absolute, so must be any other biological differences.

---

*These differences, while obvious, have had great significance in shaping attitudes that in turn have shaped history in ways that are not at all obvious.

This false reasoning leads some greatly to exaggerate and universalize small average differences and leads others to deny that any average biological differences exist.

The truth is much more complex. "The genetic differences between males and females," as Jared Diamond has noted, ". . . turn out to be slight and labile." Hormones clearly play a large part in sexual difference. Although most of the Mars/Venus sorts completely ignore the fact, "male/female differences in hormones aren't absolute but a matter of degree."[11] And that degree varies from individual to individual.

In addition to variations in the fetal brain's hormone exposure, another biological basis for the average, but not nearly absolute, difference between the sexes in many tendencies is that there are some sex-linked genes that are quite unevenly distributed between women and men, but which are not exclusive to one sex.[12]

There are also average differences between the sexes in brain operation and structure. Most brain functions tend to be diffused through both hemispheres in women and more concentrated in one hemisphere in men. Women appear to have stronger connections between the two sides of their brain.[13] This could predispose the average woman to a more blending approach and the average man to a more dualistic, binary, either/or approach (possibly because making quick decisions on such questions as "friend or foe?" and "fight or flight?" proved to be adaptive for ancestral male hominids engaged in hunting and defense). Research indicates that the corpus callosum, the brain's message exchange center, is more developed in the typical female brain. A 1991 study of cadaver brains found that the rear portion of the callosum was up to 23 percent larger in women than men.[14] This finding may mean that a woman's brain has, on average, the capacity to make more connections by shuttling more information back and forth between the hemispheres. Female brains appear, on average, to be better equipped for blending, integrating, connecting, seeing relationships, and accepting ambiguity, while male brains tend to be better at separating, differentiating, and distinguishing—making distinctions.[15] Both are useful and necessary functions, and both are obviously present in both sexes. But there may be a structurally based *average* difference between men and women in the degree to which they typically engage in each of these modes of thinking.[16]

Several recent studies of the brains of women and men, conducted by a variety of methods, including brain scans, anatomical studies, psychological tests, and functional magnetic resonance imaging, have found subtle, but significant, differences. A 1995 study, for example, found that while men and women did equally well at a mental task, they used their brains in "very different" ways to do so. Men used only a small section of the left brain, while women used diffuse sections of both the left and right brain.[17] Another study found that men at rest have, on average, more activity in the older parts of the brain's limbic system, which are connected with action. The average woman at rest in this study had a higher rate of activity in the newer, more complex regions of the limbic system, which are connected with symbolic activity. "These results," the researchers concluded, "are consistent with the hypothesis that differences in cognitive and emotional processing" have a biological basis.[18]

There is, of course, a huge danger of overinterpreting these scientific findings. An obvious example is the simple-minded argument that, since the average woman's brain, corresponding to the smaller average size of her body, is smaller than the average man's brain, men are more intelligent. In fact, one study indicates that the smaller female brains actually have 11 percent more neurons than the larger male brains.[19]

Unlike their social Darwinist predecessors of the late nineteenth and early twentieth century, the researchers at work in recent years on brain differences between women and men consistently emphasize that "different" does not mean "better" or "worse."[20] Neither sex is "superior" to the other; they are just a little different, on average, in certain capacities. Evolution has "customized" the brain to meet particular environmental situations. If some circumstances were encountered more often by one sex than the other, subtle differences in the behavior of women and men in those areas would result.[21] Each sex is "a living archive of its distinctive past."[22] It is, however, essential to realize both that the pasts of the sexes were far from completely different and that the distinctiveness has been cultural as well as biological.

Paleolithic Sex Roles

Differentiation between the roles of the sexes exists in all complex species that reproduce sexually, including the primates closest to humans such as chimpanzees and gorillas, and there is no reason to think that it was not the practice among Paleolithic collector-hunters. But difference need not imply great dominance of one category over the other. The distinction between women and men is not apt to be great in groups that do not produce surpluses. Such is the case in most modern collector-hunter societies that have been studied. Tasks are divided on the basis of sex, but the contributions of the two kinds of people are recognized to be of essentially equal worth to the group as a whole.

The fact that the males of our biological forebears of the Paleolithic age became hunters is of great importance; but that importance is easily misinterpreted. In the first place, important though it certainly was, hunting has been overemphasized by such anthropologists as William Laughlin, Lionel Tiger, and Robin Fox into an interpretation of human evolution that sees males as the only significant actors in the advance of the species.[23]

Hunting

One of the two major roles played by men in Paleolithic collector-hunter cultures was providing meat for the band, often by group hunting, which placed a premium on cooperative behavior. This cave painting from eastern Spain depicts a group of men using bows to hunt. (Musée de l'Homme/Robert Harding)

The second possible misinterpretation of the importance of hunting stems from the fact that in our own experience we tend to think of it as a rather solitary pursuit—a view that would lend support to the belief that human nature is basically self-centered and individualistic. This is a serious mistake. The type of hunting that hominids eventually adopted was of large animals that could be successfully undertaken only by cooperative efforts among a group of hunters. In this, humans differ from all other primates except for chimpanzees who occasionally perform such activities. That our omnivorous branch of the primate order developed a large brain and the capacity to speak made it possible for them to engage in cooperative hunting. But it is a mistake to think that it was hunting that initiated these developments and made humans social.

Hominid hunting of large animals apparently began about one-and-a-half million years ago. No projectiles have been found dating from before that period.[24]* Because hominids had already been around and living socially for a few million years prior to this time, the basis of hominid and human society

---

*Hunting can occur without such weapons; slingshots, for instance, can be used to hurl unmodified rocks. But the development of projectiles probably serves as a fairly good rough approximation of the time when serious hunting of large animals began.

must be sought elsewhere. The foundation of group living among human fore-runners can reasonably be assumed to be the same as it is among other mammals, particularly primates: a mother and her offspring.[25] Because mammals must nourish live young, females of this animal class necessarily form bonds with their offspring. The longer the period of dependency, the stronger those bonds will be, and they are longest in humans.[26] Primate societies are, as sociologist Jessie Bernard has put it, "matrifocal almost by definition."[27] They move beyond a mother and her offspring when females come to cooperate with one another.[28] The model for food sharing on a wider scale presumably was that of a mother feeding the young from her body.[29] As feminist Eliza Burt Gamble said in 1894, "the maternal instinct is the root whence sympathy has sprung and that is the source whence the cohesive quality of the tribe originated."[30]

Males are not the focal point of the kinship groups that form the basis of primate social organization, both because their relationship to offspring is not apparent and because they do not form the same strong bonds with infants that females do. Their roles are to help provide food for the group, through collecting plant food and capturing small animals (tasks in which both sexes engage), and to provide protection. Certainly, females also play a protective role, especially when their own offspring are threatened, but protection of the group became more of a male role.[31] Males presumably became responsible for these duties because they were physically unable to carry out the functions of bearing and nourishing children, and so had the "free time" to take up another essential responsibility.

The differing roles of males and females among early hominids led to significant differences, *on average,* between the sexes in certain characteristics. It is beyond doubt that males are *usually* more aggressive than females. This is true among other primates and across human cultures. Furthermore, it seems that members of both sexes become more aggressive when they are subjected to increased levels of testosterone and less aggressive when given greater amounts of estrogen, although some recent research throws this simple equation into question.[32]

Women are generally better than men at verbal ability and are more discerning than men in most of the senses. These capabilities were connected to communicating with, caring for, and protecting the young during evolution. Men, on the other hand, developed a superiority in visual-spatial ability, which was adaptive in their more wide-ranging activities. Particularly after hunting developed, these abilities helped men in finding their way around and in aiming projectiles at their prey.[33]

As they became terrestrial, rather than arboreal, early hominids' vulnerability to predators increased and so did their need for protection. This was already an area of male responsibility; their hormones made them generally more aggressive than females.[34] The original purpose of this aggressiveness was defensive. The adoption of a terrestrial life encouraged the already existing aggressiveness in male hominids. It also required them to cooperate more for purposes of protecting the band. It seems likely that it was the defensive killing of large predators that led early humans to begin hunting. After a threatening beast had been killed, the humans might as well eat it. (Stone butchering tools appear to antedate projectiles used in hunting by as much as two hundred thousand years.[35]) This practice probably led them eventually to realize that they could use the same techniques for offensive purposes: killing other animals not only when they threatened humans, but seeking them out so that they could be killed and eaten. Such hunting of large, fast, and powerful animals required even more cooperation than did the provision of group defense, and it seems clear that it created selective pressures favoring bonding traits (as well as additional aggressiveness) in male humans.[36]

Hunting was not the wellspring of human society; extended infant dependence had already created a society based upon the mother-child unit. But if those factors made hominids increasingly gregarious, males too had to find ways of bonding and creating associations. It was inherently more difficult for males to form such close connections on the basis of kinship because of the uncertainty of their relationship to offspring. So men met their human need for social ties through bonding with one or more females and through association with other males for the purpose of group defense.[37]

Hunting expanded upon the foundation of group defense to make males more cooperative. What this development suggests is that both female and male humans have strong social motivations, but the basis of their bonding differs. The two kinds of bonding are complementary in human social organization. The female type focuses "upon the continuity of the community through the nurturing and socialization of the next generation," while male bonding is "directed toward the preservation of the community from external threat."[38]

The difference in type of bonding may be one of the most significant distinctions (as always, on average) between women and men. The attachment of a woman who becomes a mother to another human being is more lasting, intimate, and intense than any experienced by an adult man. (Of course, all of us start out with that experience of attachment, but for males it is not repeated later in life.) As radical feminist Shulamith Firestone has put it, "a basic mother/child interdependency has existed in some form in every society, past or present, and thus has shaped the psychology of every mature female and every infant."[39]

The usual male contribution to the community is, as anthropologist David Gilmore has said, "less direct, less immediate, more involved with externals;

the 'other' involved may be society in general rather than specific persons."[40] This is to say that male support for others tends to be somewhat more impersonal than that given by females.

The starkest difference between the ways in which the sexes contributed to the hominid and early human community is that males often did so through violence (killing prey and fighting when necessary to defend the group against other animals or, perhaps, other groups of their own species), while females helped the group through nurturing (bearing, nourishing, and caring for the young).

The different roles for men and women as earlier hominids evolved into *Homo sapiens* meant that somewhat different traits were selected for. The tasks of men through most of human evolution have been best served by dualistic thinking, the rapid distinguishing of "us" from "them," and the taking of immediate action on that basis. This has resulted in male rites of passage involving "win-or-lose contests" and manhood being seen as "an either/or condition"[41]—"separate the men from the boys," and so forth. The tasks of women were based much more upon connections among people. Both had their versions of "us" and "them," with women tending to think more in terms of their family[42] while men, less sure of their kinship, depended more upon other men in the context of group defense and, later, hunting. This difference may have given women, on average, a somewhat narrower conception of "us" but at the same time a stronger, more intimate bond than that of the defender or hunter with his comrades.[43]

The sense of community among males is created through initiation rites (including such modern versions as military boot camps and gang initiations). These rites emphasize to the maturing male that he is part of the group and owes allegiance to it. He is shown that he must subordinate his personal interests to those of the community.[44] Although a greater average desire for group membership among males appears to be innate, the male communities themselves are artificial (man-made); they must be learned and are usually enforced by authority.

The Sexual Spectrum(s)

There appears, then, to be an average difference between women and men in many characteristics. To summarize: Men, to begin with the obvious, *tend* to be larger and have greater upper-body strength. Women have an *average* superiority in verbal ability, men in visual/spatial perception.[45] Men *generally* have a greater affinity for risk taking and stronger proclivity for group allegiance. Women *tend* to have better developed senses of smell, touch, and hearing. More men than women are likely to make quick yes-or-no decisions, while more women than men are apt to take a longer-term, contextual view, considering nuances and alternatives. The average woman has a greater proclivity for nurturing than the average man. Both sexes are very capable of anger and aggression, but these traits seem to be more frequently expressed in men.[46] All of these average differences appear to have some biological basis that was adaptive for the somewhat different tasks of the sexes as humans evolved. All of these average differences have, however, been exaggerated by the imposition of cultural demands for distinct, opposite male and female roles.

It must be re-emphasized that we are not speaking of anything approaching absolute differences. (Even Sigmund Freud, who often treated sexual differences as extreme, recognized that "in human beings pure masculinity or femininity is not to be found in either a physiological or biological sense." "Every individual," Freud properly said, "on the contrary displays a mixture of the character-traits belonging to his own and to the opposite [sic] sex."[47] The modes of thinking and other characteristics of men and women are on a continuum, not in two distinct groupings. Women and men are not A and Z; they are distributed on what might be depicted as a femininity-to-masculinity scale, from F to M. On such a scale, most women would be found in the G-H-I-J range and most men in the I-J-K-L range, but with some of each sex in all categories, save perhaps men in F and women in M. The distribution might look something like this graph, which depicts a concept, not particular data.

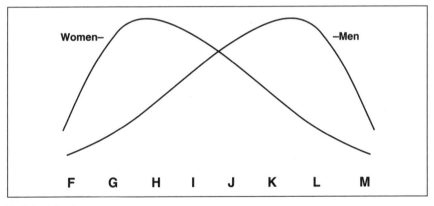

The Sexual Spectrums

Yet even this image of a continuum or spectrum greatly oversimplifies the reality. A particular individual may have some characteristics that are more common in a female and others that are more common in a male. "Tides of powerful sex hormones can masculinize one part of the brain while they leave another region untouched."[48] So there are a whole series of female-male spectrums for different characteristics and the same person is likely to occupy a different relative position on each of them—perhaps an H in one trait and a K in another. And there is, as biologist Roger Gorski has rightly said, "so much overlap that if you take any individual man and woman, they might show differences in the opposite direction" from the statistical norms.[49] But, since on each of these scales far more members of one sex than the other will be found toward one end of the spectrum, it is appropriate to label them, although very cautiously, "female" and "male."

"Darwin Made Me Do It"

The temptation to ignore the complications and claim greater, clearer, and more consistent differences between the sexes than the evidence supports has been a problem for many of those who have taken up the banner of evolutionary psychology in recent years.

One of the principal arguments of evolutionary psychologists has been that men have a strong proclivity for having sexual intercourse with many different partners and without commitment, while women are much more concerned with long-term commitment.[50]

What evolutionary psychologists have been saying on this issue reinforces conventional wisdom. Comedian Lenny Bruce appears to have been a pioneering evolutionary psychologist when he declared: "Let's face it: guys are different." Bruce contended that women usually "have to at least *like* somebody" before they will have sexual intercourse with him. "But with guys, that doesn't even enter into it, man, because guys are *detached;* they're different. You put a guy on a desert island and he'll do it to the mud, a chicken, a sparrow, *any*thing—a knothole."[51]

Of course Bruce, like many men who make arguments like this, was attempting to justify male (and particularly his own) philandering. The biological argument made by evolutionary psychologists was hinted at it when Bruce said that men are "detached." The argument is that during the evolutionary process male and female humans developed (or, more accurately, *retained,* since they were carried over from our forebears in other species) differing reproductive tendencies. The reason is that men have the potential to reproduce hundreds, even thousands, of offspring during their lifetimes—if they can find enough different women who are willing to join with them in the endeavor. (One thinks of the Saudi royal family, Pablo Picasso, Wilt Chamberlain, and assorted Kennedy men as examples of this apparent evolutionary predisposition in males. Moulay Ismail the Bloodthirsty of Morocco [1646–1727] is said to have fathered 888 offspring, including forty sons born in a three-month period in 1704.[52]) Women, on the other hand, have the potential for at most about twenty offspring during their reproductive years—and that, to be sure, would be stretching it. (The apparent woman's record is held by Brazilian Madalena Carnauba, who gave birth to twenty-two children.[53])

The result of these differing capabilities, anthropologist Donald Symons asserted in 1979, is that, "with respect to sexuality, there is a female human nature and a male human nature, and these natures are extraordinarily different, though the differences are to some extent masked by the compromises heterosexual relations entail and by moral injunctions."[54] Symons was pursuing a line of reasoning about sexual selection that had been outlined by Robert Trivers in 1972.[55] Symons and a host of evolutionary psychologists who have followed[56] argue that evolution has left men and women with distinct tendencies in terms of sexual liaisons because throughout most of "human evolutionary history the sexual desires and dispositions that were adaptive for either sex were for the other tickets to reproductive oblivion."[57]

From the standpoint of passing his genes along, the argument goes, a man just does not have to be very choosy about whom he mates with. For him, a "mistake" (which in Darwinian terms would mean combining with someone whose genes were not well suited to provide for the offspring's survival) is not very costly, because he can (at least in theory) just "try again" (and again and again . . .) with other women. "Don't put all your eggs in one basket" is, it would seem, an adage that confuses its gametes. It is males who don't have to "put all their sperm in one basket." For this reason, evolutionary psychologists argue, it would seem likely that evolution would have selected for a tendency in men to be attracted to many females. This inclination would probably, over the eons, result in the largest number of surviving descendants carrying their genes.

As the maxim from Lenny Bruce suggests, the consequences of this putative aspect of our evolutionary heritage have long been a part of popular wisdom. A few more examples: A poster for the film version of *Madame Butterfly* proclaimed:

For Her, Love Meant Forever.
For Him, Love Meant Until His Ship Sets Sail.[58]

In 1960 the Shirelles, seemingly speaking for their sex in general, sang: "Tonight you're mine, completely / You give your soul so sweetly / Tonight the light of love is in your eyes / But will you love me tomorrow?" A few months later, in 1961, Rick Nelson seemed to provide the male answer: "I'm a travelin' man / Make a lot of stops all over the world / And in every port I own the heart of at least one lovely girl."[59]

Nora Ephron summed it up in her screenplay for the 1989 film *When Harry Met Sally*. Harry declares that no man can be just friends "with a woman he finds attractive—he *always* wants to have sex with her."

"So you're saying that a man *can* be friends with a woman he finds unattractive?" Sally asks.

"No, you pretty much wanna nail them, too," Harry honestly responds as a spokesman for human males as evolutionary psychology sees them.[60]

With a woman the matter is seemingly otherwise. Given a very limited number of opportunities to reproduce, she cannot afford to be undiscriminating in her selection of mates if she wants to assure the survival of her genes into future generations. (Of course all of this sort of talk is very loose and misleading; virtually no one actually *thinks* this way and makes conscious decisions on such a basis—and no genes think at all. What is meant is that evolutionary pressures selected for genes that give us predispositions to think and act in such ways.) The woman has to be much more concerned about what kind of man joins with her in any of her relatively few opportunities to have children. She also has to try to find a man who will stay with her and help to protect and provide for their offspring. Concern for offspring is a consideration for men, too, but many evolutionary psychologists have argued that because males have so many chances for offspring, they can, evolutionarily speaking, get away with being more casual about looking after any particular child they may father.[61] Jimmy Carter, it seems, need not have felt obliged to confess to a *Playboy* interviewer in 1976 that he "looked on a lot of women with lust" and had "committed adultery in my heart many times."[62] That, evolutionary psychologists tell us, is just the way men are.

All this speculation makes for a very damning case against men but one with which many men seem rather pleased, because they think it explains and excuses their unfaithfulness. "Darwin made me do it" has become a handy rationalization for male infidelity.[63] But is it accurate? The efforts at providing an evolutionary explanation of the apparent male proclivity for philandering and the double sexual standard has, understandably, drawn fire from many critics, most of them women. Science journalist Natalie Angier, herself not at all unsympathetic to the idea that evolutionary biology can be helpful in understanding human behavior, has pointed out many of the self-serving exaggerations of sexual difference that hardcore male evolutionary psychologists have made.[64]

There can be little question that male evolutionary psychologists have created caricatures of male and female sexual behavior. Philandering men, after all, have to have women with whom to philander, so an immense imbalance between the sexes in this activity is a mathematical impossibility.[65]

Natural selection is a complicated process, and there are always many pressures, often operating at cross-purposes, at work. As most evolutionary psychologists acknowledge, other selective pressures served to narrow the gap between the sexual appetites and strategies of males and females that would be expected from the divergence in potential number of offspring. The male's prospect for fathering a large number of descendants is dependent on more than just his ability to produce gametes. Obviously, a male can reproduce only if he can persuade a female to join with him in the enterprise. This requirement means that the evolutionary considerations that guide the female in her reproductive strategy have an important effect on which males succeed in reproducing. If the female's limited opportunities for procreation have selected for a genetic predisposition toward lasting attachments, this tendency must have created an indirect selective pressure in favor of males who are disposed to stick around and help bring up junior.[66]

There is also the near certainty that during human evolution—as today—having two parents to provide for and protect an infant greatly enhanced the offspring's chances for survival. As historian Linda Pollock has noted, "good parental care is adaptive."[67] Among humans, with our prolonged period of infant dependency, the evolutionary principle might be altered to "survival of those with the fittest parents."[68] This consideration, too, would have provided a selective pressure in favor of men who had a capacity for forming lasting ties with a particular woman.

When they contend that virtually all men are alike, all women are alike, and that they are radically different in their attitudes toward sexual intercourse without commitment, evolutionary psychologists slip back into rigid biological determinism and complete sexual opposition. As is the case with so many other characteristics that differ on average between the sexes, in this area many people have leaped from an observed average difference to the false conclusion that there is something approaching an absolute difference. There is no single male or female human reproductive strategy. In fact, as evolutionary biologist Barbara Smuts notes, "the variation is tremendous, and is rooted in biology. Flexibility itself is the adaptation."[69]

For our subject, the significance of the debate over a wide, naturally selected gap in sexual behavior between men and women is that it is one of the latest examples of a long-standing defensive practice by men. When they "argue in favor of a yawning chasm that separates the innate desires of women and men,"[70] evolutionary psychologists and their mostly male followers are imposing a dichotomy on the continuum of behavior by the sexes.[71] Just how wide and deep they have tried to make what they see as the Grand Canyon of Sex can be seen in the words of the man who started it all. "One can, in effect, treat the sexes as if they were different species," Robert Trivers wrote in his "seminal"* 1972 paper, "the opposite sex being a resource relevant to producing maximum sur-

---

*The reason for the quotation marks will become evident in Chapter 6.

viving offspring."[72] It would be hard to imagine a way to say the sexes are more absolutely different than to assert that they are like different species—unless, of course, someone were willing to go even further into realm of the sex war theater of the absurd by asserting that women and men are from different planets.

But *why* has the desire to pretend that the sexes are opposite been so strong among men?

The Non-Menstrual Syndrome

"What do women want?" a puzzled Sigmund Freud asked, speaking for many members of his sex. His answer—that women want a penis—is as unsatisfactory as it is revealing. He never found a satisfactory answer, perhaps because he was asking the wrong question. The question with the greatest significance for history is, "What do men want?" The reason that this is the more important question is not because men are superior or inherently more important, but because their attempts at finding an answer have had such an impact on the course of history as it has unfolded for both sexes.

The question "What do men want?" is actually a corollary to a more fundamental question about species that reproduce sexually: "What do males do?" The most basic purpose of males in species that reproduce sexually is to provide a means of remixing genes to create genetic diversity as a hedge against future environmental changes. In the simplest terms, males' function is to serve as living storehouses for alternate genes and to provide them when needed for remixing, which in mammals takes place inside a female's body. These tasks do not provide full-time work. Humans took a major step toward a solution to the problem of male unemployment when their relatively huge brains led to their infants having a very prolonged period of dependency. The premium that this dependency placed on a high level of male parental investment (fathers devoting considerable time, effort, and resources to assisting their offspring) led to the major Paleolithic male roles in provision and protection. But proper male roles remained less clear than female roles.

Each sex can find reason to be jealous of the other. Freud made a great deal out of the consequences of penis envy, but it seems likely that a larger percentage of men are more envious of women's apparent powers than women are of men's. The psychological difficulty for men has its origins in the continuum of traits that differ on average by sex. The fact that the sexes are not opposites means that women and men can generally do almost all of the same things, but an average woman can perform better in some areas and an average man can perform better in others. Women can do just about anything important that men can, albeit, on average, less well in some areas. But there are some important things that women can do that men simply cannot: carrying, giving birth to, and nourishing babies from their bodies.

"Be a man!" is an exhortation heard frequently in almost all human cultures. But who is ever urged to "be a woman!"? The implication seems to be that being a man is "a precarious or artificial state" that must be won through severe tests.[73] Part of this difference, plainly, stems from the lack of a physical event, as with the onset of menstruation in females, that signals manhood. Throughout human existence, many men have suffered from what might accurately be called NMS—Non-Menstrual Syndrome.

Let me give readers of both sexes a moment to get over their skeptical, derisive laugh at this seemingly outlandish statement.

After you have regained your composure, consider that menstrual bleeding both clearly demonstrates that a girl has become a woman and symbolizes the life-giving potential of women. Accordingly, it is a logical focus for male jealousy. In many so-called primitive cultures, initiation rites for males include circumcision at puberty, which plainly is meant to mimic the onset of menstruation by creating artificial genital bleeding in males at the same point in life that it begins in females.[74]

But there is also a deeper purpose in male initiation rites. Masculinity always seems to be in doubt; the role of men is uncertain, not something that comes naturally.[75] Being a woman is thought to be a straightforward, obviously useful role, but being a man has had to be culturally defined.

Men have always been challenged by the creative powers of women (especially because it seems likely, as we'll discuss later, that people through most of human existence did not understand that there is a significant male role in procreation), and so have sought roles that would be similarly important.[76] As Margaret Mead pointed out, women gain an identity from maternity, but "the male needs to reassert, to reattempt, to redefine maleness."[77] A woman would have been less likely to experience the sort of doubt that led René Descartes to formulate his famous first principle of knowledge: *Cogito ergo sum* [I think, therefore I am]. A woman usually has less reason than a man to doubt her purpose or existence: "I (have the capacity to) give birth, therefore I am." Men have found it necessary throughout history to try to find other activities on which to rest the proof of their existence, worth, or "manhood." Later in the book, we shall be seeing some opening clauses men have, in effect, substituted for the opening *I think* part of Descartes's logical declaration, as they attempt to convince themselves that they have a reason for being equivalent to women.

The "Notawoman" Definition of Manhood

There is something in—or, rather, *not* something in—the male sex that makes men desire to be dominant in some areas of life.[78] Many men throughout the ages have insisted that women must be excluded from various activities and roles because something is "lacking" in females. However that may be, it is undeniable that something is lacking in males: the ability to carry, give birth to, and nourish offspring.[79] An extremely significant factor throughout history has been men's susceptibility to what, reversing Freud, can be termed, along with the "Non-Menstrual Syndrome," "womb envy" and "breast envy." Psychoanalyst Karen Horney introduced this idea in her 1926 paper, "The Flight from Womanhood." Horney did to Freud what Engels had said Marx did to Hegel: found him standing on his head and set him upright. Horney argued that motherhood provides women with "a quite indisputable and by no means negligible physiological superiority." When she began analyzing men after long experience analyzing women, Horney said, she got "a most surprising impression of the intensity of this envy of pregnancy, childbirth, and motherhood, as well as of breasts and of the act of suckling."[80]

Anthropologist Ashley Montagu later expanded on the concept of "womb envy" in his 1953 book, *The Natural Superiority of Women,*[81] but the importance of this phenomenon for broadening our understanding of history has generally been overlooked.

Probably the best example of womb envy is that many collector-hunter groups practice a ritual called *couvade* (from the French *couver,* "to hatch"), in which the husband simulates labor pains while his wife gives birth.[82] In some cultures, fathers take on the full child-bearing actions. Fathers go into "laboring huts," where they thrash about in pain while the mother is giving birth in another location. A modern version of men seeking to take center stage from women in the drama of childbirth may be the male obstetrician using his skill to "deliver" the baby.[83]

One of the most striking renditions of these male jealousies clearly shows its source in male envy of female biological functions. The men of the Sambia tribe of the Papua New Guinea Highlands are fierce warriors. Like the men of many other cultures, they stage raids on their own villages, taking boys away from the softening influences of their mothers and putting them through a variety of manhood tests. But the men of this tribe are so fearful of what they take to be the power of all things female to weaken males and so determined to be the opposite of women that they believe that true masculinity can only be acquired by replacing mother's milk with the ingestion of semen. In a poignant attempt to do one of the things women do, but they cannot, these men "feed" young boys "masculine milk" from their bodies by having the boys engage in fellatio with them. They do their best to imitate womanly functions while insisting that their purpose is to make their boys masculine. Tribal elders instruct boys that they should "ingest semen every night, as if it were breast milk or food." The Sambia men go so far in taking credit for what females do and they cannot that they claim that it is their semen placed in a woman that not only makes her pregnant but also that produces her breast milk: "We cop-

Breast Envy
The fact that women are physically equipped to do things that men cannot do has been a source of male insecurity and envy of women throughout history. Men have sought redress for their biological exclusion from some activities by using cultural restrictions to exclude women from other activities. (Horace Bristol, "Rose of Sharon," 1938)

ulate with a woman and she produces breast milk; then she feeds the infant."[84] The Sambia also exhibit NMS in an unmistakable way: young men take part in ritual nose bleeding that mimics menstruation.

While the extreme practices of Sambia males are unusual, the envy of female powers is not. Many men around the world and throughout history have been deeply troubled, consciously or otherwise, by "the deficiencies of male equipment."[85] Like pregnancy and childbirth, breast feeding can be seen as a "bastion of female privilege."[86] Although it remains a challenge to find men who will admit it, many men feel left out because of their incapacity in this regard. Men who are envious of women's abilities have sought something exclusive to males to counter the things women can do that the men cannot.

On the institutions—whether located in a tree house or an exclusive sky-scraper—that they establish for themselves, males put up signs, actual or implicit, with messages similar to one in an old New York ale house: "McSorley's, Where Men Are Men and Women Are Not Allowed."[87]

To put it directly, men tell women that they *may* not do certain things as a way of compensating for the things that men *cannot* do. Biology has established a no-man's land; men retaliate by using culture to establish a variety of no-woman's lands.

Examples are legion. One particularly telling one is that in medieval Europe it was said that if a woman entered a wine cellar, all the wine would go sour, so wine cellars were kept as all-male preserves.[88]

Given their apparently greater average proclivity for thinking in dualistic terms, men were especially prone to see the sexes as polar opposites. But that tendency has been augmented by other reasons men have for polarizing the sexes.

The unstated fear of inferiority that many men have leads them to tend to exaggerate the difference between the sexes. Because men cannot compete with women in certain areas (a man's "carrying capacity," for instance, is nil), a single standard of human accomplishment might put men at a disadvantage. They have, therefore, had an additional reason for emphasizing and greatly overstating differences between the sexes. The less similar "being a man" was made to seem to "being a woman," the better the prospects for men to feel that they were superior. So men have generally sought to define male roles in terms of opposition to what women do; "being a man" has usually been seen as being as different as possible from "being a woman." What a woman is seemed clear; so what a man should be has most often been seen as the opposite. Freud was on the right track when he said that male identity is based on a boy's separation from his mother and identification with his father, but it is actually motherhood itself (and hence "womanhood"), rather than their own mothers, that threatens men, since motherhood is a power that they can never achieve. The "father" with which boys are called upon to identify is a misconception of masculinity that is based on complete opposition to femininity.

This process greatly magnifies and intensifies the small genuine differences between the sexes, often to the point where it transforms small divergences of degree into huge disparities of kind, causing us to think in the very misleading terms of "opposite sexes."

Under this way of thinking, *woman* is established as the thesis and *man* is seen as its antithesis: *female* is the standard, and *male* is the negative of *female:*

$$\male = -\female$$

From this viewpoint, the name for man could be *notawoman* or *anti-woman*. (Something like this negative understanding of the male as the one incapable of giving birth and nourishment was suggested in the early 1990s ABC television show, *Dinosaurs,* in which the baby called his father "Not-the-Momma."[89] This conception is, again, a serious error, inasmuch as the sexes are not opposite, just a little different.

Few people like to think of themselves in negative terms, so to compensate for their inability to compete with women's abilities in certain areas, men established opposing criteria under which *they* would be superior. To make the negative *notawoman* positive, men had to turn *woman* into a negative. This would make *man* the negative of a negative, and so positive:

$$♂ = -(-♀)$$

One unfortunate result of men's attempt to turn their deficiency into something positive was to define maternity as a handicap. Karen Horney pointed out how this "sour grapes" (or should we say "sour eggs" and "sour milk"?) attitude toward motherhood is expressed in male argument: "[I]n reality women do simply desire the penis; when all is said and done motherhood is only a burden . . . and men may be glad that they do not have to bear it."[90] We shall see a bit later how this argument was made most effectively in the Bible.

The most tragic consequence of the notawoman definition of manhood is that, since womanliness is understood in terms of the capacity to give life, manliness has often come to be seen as the capacity to give death—a willingness to kill or be killed. If *woman* is defined as the "giver of life," seeing *man* as its antonym makes the word mean "taker of life." This definition of being a man comes down (usually not consciously) to something like: *We may not be able to create life; but surely we can risk and destroy it.**

The definition of *man* in opposition to *woman* may not be universal, but it is evident in all parts of the world. Among the Ibo of Nigeria, for example, the word *agbala* means "woman," but it is also used to designate a man who has taken no titles—that is, one who has not proved his manhood by such a feat as bringing home the head of an enemy.[91] This sort of "proof" of manhood makes clear its association with taking life.

The Non-Menstrual Syndrome is intertwined with the woman/life, man/death dichotomy of the notawoman conception of true manhood. Menstrual blood shed from women's bodies is a sign of their ability to give life. In taking life, through hunting or war, men shed blood of other animals or peo-

---

*This view never changed after men began to claim that they "give life." (See Chapter 6.)

ple (not infrequently including their own), thus producing an apparent symmetry that confirms the putative opposition in function between the sexes and, perhaps, eases the effects of NMS. The "red badge of courage" that young males have traditionally sought to attain by shedding blood in battle with other animals or humans[92] is their artificial substitute for the "red badge of womanhood" that young females attain naturally through the onset of menstruation. "We didn't say to ourselves," Phillip Caputo recalled of his group of Marines' first firefight in Vietnam, "We've been under fire, we've shed blood, now we're men. We were simply aware, in a way that we could not express, that something significant had happened to us."[93]

We often hear the proud comment, "he died like a man." Has anyone ever heard someone say, "she died like a woman"? A question that is likely to arise for girls as they mature is: "Am I a woman? Could I give birth?" In cultures around the world, the corresponding question that often forms in the minds of boys as they approach manhood is: "Am I a man? Could I kill?"[94] Although this lamentable conception of what it means to be a man probably arose from our innate tendency to think dualistically, it was substantially reinforced by the erroneous belief that men have nothing to do with giving life. The negative-woman idea of manhood became so ingrained that it persisted long after it was learned that men *do* participate in giving life. Indeed, it endures even today.

Yet, even under the notawoman notion that sees the proper role for men in serving their families and communities in terms of killing, there is no requirement that the killing be of other people. Through most of human existence the male role usually involved the killing of other animals for purposes of protection and food provision. This gave men something useful to do, and the provisioning aspect tended to somewhat lessen the extreme notawoman concept of manliness, because it meant that men, too, were participating in nourishing others.

This notawoman way of defining manhood was seriously flawed, but it worked well enough over the eons of collector-hunter societies. Because the roles assigned to men were somewhat contrived, however, the meaning that they provided for men's lives was precarious. Any radical change in the importance the traditional male roles of hunting and protecting against predators was likely to leave men adrift and make the desire to see themselves as not-women more ominous.

The Denial of New Jersey

The problem is not that men are inherently evil or even that the qualities found more commonly in men are necessarily bad. Rather, it is that men have so often been, not gender-benders, but gender-extenders. They have in most cultures throughout most of history constructed a hypermasculine ideal that rejects everything considered feminine and grossly exaggerates those characteristics that are in reality only somewhat more common in men than in women, turning the "macho" into the ultimate good and everything considered feminine into the definition of undesirable and inferior—particularly, of course, in men. Male initiation rites almost invariably teach boys "to value what is tough and to despise what is 'feminine' and tenderhearted."[95]

Making *masculine* and *feminine* into polar opposites, rather than just tendencies on a continuum, has obscured the vast middle ground. On questions of gender, we have been taught that the hottest places in hell are reserved for those who maintain their neutrality—or seek any sort of moderate position. Along with Archie Bunker, many men yearn for a world where "girls were girls and men were men"[96]—and where the sexes are so different that they seem to come from different planets. The men who have defined the battle lines in the putative war between the sexes—those who have, in truth, been the ones who declared that war—have drawn those battle lines so sharply that the middle ground is a minefield.

This is a way of thinking that is, literally, a bi-polar disorder.

Examples of gender extending range from menstrual taboos, which in many cultures separate menstruating women and their reminders of female reproductive power from men, through such arbitrary rules as the Mosaic law's declaration: "A woman shall not wear anything that pertains to a man, nor shall a man put on a woman's garment; for whoever does these things is an abomination to the Lord your God,"[97] and the practice of the Dogon people of West Africa of attempting to eradicate from a man any appearance of femaleness in his prepuce through circumcision and from a woman the seeming vestige of maleness in her clitoris through excision,[98] to the 1996 proclamation of the Taliban rulers in Afghanistan, not only that women must be completely veiled but also that all men must grow beards. *Let there be no mistake!* anxious men seem to be saying through their edicts. *The separation must be clear and complete. We cannot let ourselves be grouped with them!*

The problem, again, is not masculinity per se, but the hypermasculinity that has been constructed by men as a means of compensation for womb envy and similar fears of male inadequacy. Of course all men do not suffer from such jealousy to an extreme degree. As PMS does with women, NMS and womb envy affect some men severely, others slightly, and still others seemingly not at all. The reason that it has been such a powerful force throughout history is that the men who have been most insecure have so often been the ones most driven to seek power. As leaders they have been able to mold opinion by pushing definitions of manhood in notawoman terms and ostracizing men who failed sufficiently to exaggerate masculinity and deprecate things and actions classified as feminine.

Gender extending seems to exist in most cultures, but it is clearly worse in some. The degree and expression of the notawoman formulation varies not only between cultures but also over time. When men feel particularly threatened, whether by advances in the status of women or declines in the status of men (or both simultaneously), they are likely to seek ways to widen the perceived gap between the definitions of femininity and masculinity—to try to establish a full-blown gender apartheid.

Two such eras that are of particular importance to us are the long transition in the Neolithic Age, as the consequences of the development of agriculture radically altered the situations of both sexes, and the period in which we live today, when population pressures, higher living standards, greatly increased life spans, democratic beliefs, and technological advances have significantly changed the circumstances of women. In terms of the situations of the sexes, the present period is the Neolithic as seen in a looking glass.

The actual differences between men and women might better be suggested by saying "Men Are from New York, Women Are from Philadelphia." The sexes are fundamentally similar, but not identical. Culture has magnified the differences that do exist (and conjured some other differences out of thin air). What many men have attempted to do is deny the existence of New Jersey.

In fact, though, New Jersey is the most densely populated state in the United States. Individual women and men are to be found at various exits along the New Jersey Turnpike—but even that image does not suffice. The same individual might be at the Camden exit for one trait, the New Brunswick exit for a second, and the George Washington Bridge for a third.

The Master Metaphor and the Mother Metaphor

The notawoman definition of manhood and gender extending are intertwined with one of the most powerful metaphors humans have ever employed. As some men sought dominance over others, they had but one model upon which to base their system of hierarchy: the claimed superiority of men over women and all things defined as masculine over all things defined as feminine.[99]

Much of human history has been built on this supposed fundamental power relationship. All other forms of authority were variants of the male domination of females. Dominant men claimed to have the male role and placed subordinated men in the female position. This symbolism of man equals power and domination, woman equals submission and subordination is one of the master metaphors that have been at the base of human history and continue to shape our thinking today. It can, in fact, be called "the Master metaphor," because it provides the rationale for men who claim to be masters of others. It was only with the move to agriculture that a much wider system of power differentiation began to be elaborated, but the use of sexual metaphor for relations of domination and subordination is not simply a construct of human culture. In fact, it is not even a human invention. It may be hard to believe that other animals employ metaphors, but in this case it is clear that they do. Dominant males in many species mount subordinate males and simulate intercourse as a means of signifying their dominant position.* (The power of this metaphor through history and down to the present will be explored in Chapters 13 and 14.) This is an act of symbolism among the males; the fact that they take the ability to treat another male as if he were a female to be a sign of dominance does not mean that the males of the species are *actually* dominant over the females in any objective sense. Indeed, men are likely to imagine themselves to be in power even when they are not.

The notawoman conception of manhood and the Master metaphor have always been harmful, but the harm was kept within reasonable bounds in collector-hunter societies. It seems likely that the most important metaphors in the Paleolithic Age largely counteracted and balanced one another. At the same time that the Master metaphor was reflecting and promoting the argument of male superiority, another metaphor was pointing in the opposite direction. In every culture anthropologists have examined, women have been considered closer to nature than are men.[100] The belief that creative power and nature itself are female—what might be termed the mother metaphor, as in "Mother Nature"—reinforced the idea of female power and worth.

As long as the mother metaphor retained its persuasiveness, it could serve as a check on the worst potential ill effects of the notawoman idea and the Master metaphor. But about ten thousand years ago there began a series of revolutionary developments that would eventually produce a new, all-conquering metaphor that would nullify the mother metaphor and leave women and everything associated with them much more subordinated.

---

*This is a good example of the sort of insight that a biological perspective on history can provide. I am indebted to Gerda Lerner's provocative book, *The Creation of Patriarchy,* for stimulating some of the thinking that produced this book. But the lack of a biological perspective led Lerner to conclude that the use of sexual symbolism for other forms of domination was a development that occurred in the Bronze Age. In fact, as the symbolic mounting that takes place among many other animal species shows, its origins antedate human existence.

CHAPTER 4

Paradise Lost

Agriculture and the Genesis of "History"

Do I dare
Disturb the universe?

T. S. ELIOT (1915)[1]

We know the story well. Indeed, it is probably the most widely known story in the Western world, perhaps the entire world. Most Jews and Christians long accepted the early chapters of the Book of Genesis as an accurate record of the beginning of history and believed that the events recounted in them shaped the course of all subsequent history. Many religious people still accept this narrative as literal fact, but scientific discoveries in the last few centuries (not to mention glaring internal contradictions in the Genesis story) have made it impossible for most educated pto take the story of Adam and Eve and the Garden of Eden seriously. It has been dismissed in intellectual circles as just another myth, meaningful only in terms of how belief in it shaped the views and actions of people in later history.

But there is a difference between taking a story literally and taking it seriously. I shall argue in this chapter that the story of the loss of Paradise in Genesis should be taken seriously, although certainly not literally, as a reflection of key developments in "prehistory" that actually are the foundation upon which much of recorded history rests. Myths can sometimes be almost as revealing about the topics they discuss as a straightforward historical account would be.

We shall see later in this chapter that the Genesis story can usefully be read as a mythologized summary of the most important events of "prehistory," as those happenings were seen in distant retrospect from the highly biased perspective of men who believed themselves to be the injured parties in the after-

82

math of the events to which Genesis refers: the development of methods by which food could be intentionally produced and the enormous transformations in human life that flowed from this understanding.

The Book of Genesis is, then, fundamental to a proper understanding of the genesis of the period of human existence customarily termed "history," but not in the way biblical fundamentalists believe it to be. The missing link between the Genesis story and the actual genesis of "history" is the realization that women probably invented agriculture. But before we get into that, let us take a look at just how important the events that transpired in the five thousand or so years before the point at which historians routinely begin their accounts actually were.

Extended History

A generally unnoticed parallel between the Genesis story accepted by biblical fundamentalists and the accounts presented by most modern historians is that both begin at about the same time. Seventeenth-century Anglican Archbishop James Ussher used the chronology of the Bible to calculate that the world began on October 23, 4004 B.C.[2] Although most modern advocates of biblical inerrancy are probably not that precise, they continue to date the beginning of history from about six thousand years ago. This time, ironically, is rather close to the point from which, for practical purposes, most of us in the historical profession still tend to begin our accounts.

A major problem with historical interpretation is that historians have usually spoken of the time a few centuries before 3000 B.C.E. when writing was invented as "the dawn of history,"[3] and then proceeded to act as if it were also the dawn of human existence. Of course we all know that this is not true, but rarely have historians given much consideration to the time before writing, which was actually the vast majority of human existence. Most textbooks in world or Western civilization, for example, devote a page or so to the hundreds of thousands of years of the Paleolithic Age and perhaps three or four pages to the Neolithic, which itself was as long as all of subsequent history.

The reluctance of historians to say much about history before writing is understandable. The problems in trying to reach conclusions about "prehistory" are huge. But ignoring what came before the time of writing is more dangerous than trying to come to some comprehension of "prehistoric history" on the basis of scanty evidence. One of the principal arguments of this book is that developments occurring in the five thousand years before the invention of writing and the two thousand or so years after that advance very profoundly affected human beings and their outlook on the world. In fact, they have so affected humans that no proper understanding of history is possible without an exploration of the enormous changes that took place in this period before historians conventionally begin their examination.

Thus, we must begin to develop an "extended history."[4]

The first step toward a comprehension of history is an exploration of the human nature that was shaped over the eons of the Paleolithic Age, what sociobiologist Edward O. Wilson has termed "deep history."[5] The preceding chapters attempted that task. The second step in historical understanding is an examination of the impact on that human nature of the monumental transformations that took place in the millennia of the Neolithic and Bronze Ages, from about 8000 B.C.E. to nearly 1000 B.C.E. Those changes and what they have meant for us throughout later history are the subject of this and the following three chapters.

Invention Is the Mother of Necessity

As we have already seen, one of the qualities that most distinguishes humans from other species is our amazing adaptability. But *Homo sapiens* also has a unique ability to alter the other side of the equation between organisms and their environment. Not only can we adapt ourselves to changes in the environment; we can also make significant changes in the environment in which we live.* Surely the most important such alteration of the environment was the intentional growing of larger quantities of edible plants and animals. That discovery lifted the ecological constraint that the size of the naturally occurring food supply imposes on all animals.

Any serious change in a species' environment necessitates adaptation. The cause of the environmental change matters not at all in this regard. Human-made transformations require adaptations as much as "natural" changes do. Once human intervention had significantly altered the environment in which people lived, further intervention became necessary. Hominids began to intervene in the environment long before the invention of agriculture. The development of tools, containers, simple weapons, and hunting were all human alterations of their situation. These early hominid developments certainly affected the social environment, but they were extensions of things that our ancestors were already doing, did not drastically change the characteristics that were adaptive, and took a very long time to develop.

---

*Although humans have learned how to change our environment in some important ways, this development by no means indicates that we have escaped from nature and become "supernatural" beings. Anyone who doubts this need only ask the victims of the latest hurricane, tornado, earthquake, or drought whether they believe we humans have fully become masters of our environment.

About forty thousand years ago there began the first cluster of dramatic changes in human life, which has been called "our Great Leap Forward,"[6] or "the creative explosion." It was in this era that much more elaborate tools and carefully crafted weapons, made of bone and ivory as well as stone, appeared. There is evidence for the first time of people constructing sturdy houses. People conducted rituals as they buried their dead, indicating a religious belief. Most significantly, humans began to produce art, including jewelry, small stone sculptures, and, ultimately, by about twenty thousand years ago, the magnificent cave paintings of southern France and northern Spain.[7]

As important as were the changes between about forty thousand and ten thousand years ago, the intentional production of food was a much more pivotal human-made transformation. This development, too, was an outgrowth of what people were already doing. It would not have arisen otherwise. But intentional food production changed the way people live in a much more radical way than had the earlier human-made changes, and it came too rapidly for there to be sufficient time for much biological adaptation to the new circumstances. Cultural adaptation would have to be used to try to bridge the widening chasm between a human nature shaped to adapt people to live in small collector-hunter bands and a new, dramatically different environment.

Because the necessity for new, broader human intervention was created by other human intervention, it can accurately be said that this is a case of invention (of new ways of life) being the mother of necessity (for new, more complex cultural values to adapt people biologically designed for an anachronistic mode of existence to their new situation). And "mother" is a particularly appropriate term for the most important source of the necessity for immense cultural adaptation.

Human history is, in its essence, the interaction of human intention with the environment, including the human biological heritage. This is what *culture* is. A look at the etymology of that word is useful in understanding the ways in which culture interacts with the human biological inheritance.

The word *culture* is derived from the Latin word *cultus,* meaning *cultivation.* Cultivation refers to a human practice that intervenes in nature in order to promote certain ends. This points toward one of the early forms of human culture, *agriculture.* What techniques of agriculture do is to encourage the growth of certain plants that are deemed beneficial to people and to discourage others, usually classified as weeds, that get in the way of the human intention of improving the supply and quality of food. The human actions involved in this earliest meaning of cultivation do not create something from nothing. Cultivation in this basic case refers to working with the materials that nature provides, trying to enhance some and diminish others.

Culture intervenes in human nature in exactly the same way that agriculture intervenes in the larger natural environment: it *cultivates* already existing characteristics, stimulating those believed to be useful and weakening those that have come to seem dangerous or detrimental. This process is much the same as plowing the ground, planting seed, irrigating, weeding, and killing insects that are harmful to plants.

For example, a farmer can use one part of the natural environment to control another, by, say, introducing birds or other animals that are natural enemies of the insects that harm the crops. Similarly, people can employ values to make use of some portions of the mixture of traits contained in human nature to counteract others. In the human-made environments in which people have lived throughout recorded history, some inborn predispositions are the equivalent in the biogram of weeds or pests in the biosphere. In order to reach the ends desired, ways must be found to "pull the weeds" and "control the vermin." One way to accomplish this result is by using other parts of the innate motivational system to check the undesirable ones.

But the analogy goes still farther. This should not be surprising, because it is not simply a metaphor. The relationship between cultural values and human nature is not merely *like* that between agricultural cultivation and the natural environment; it is in fact the *same* process: humans intervene to manipulate the givens of nature in order to achieve goals people have deemed to be desirable.

We know that under different circumstances there are changes in what people consider to be beneficial crops and what they judge to be undesirable organisms that must be rooted out. What one time and place classifies as weeds another may list as a delicacy. Ralph Waldo Emerson defined a weed as "a plant whose virtues have not been discovered."[8] In a similar fashion, the innate qualities determined to be worthy of cultivation and those in need of suppression have not remained constant throughout human history. Alterations in the human environment have modified the mix of characteristics that will work best for people.

Then—and most importantly—there is the effect of human intervention itself upon the environment. In the case of the larger environment, this point hardly needs elaboration today. The consequences of human intervention on the biosphere have become huge, and those earlier human inventions have very clearly become mother to the necessity of developing new methods of counteracting them.

It may not at first be as clear, but the impact of human intervention on the biogram has been as dramatic as that on the biosphere. The biogram of *Homo sapiens* is the foundation of all human culture and provides the raw material out of which all cultures and values must be constructed. But once human intention intervenes and creates a culture, that culture becomes an additional part of the environment in which people find themselves. Subsequent attempts at creating new values are constrained not only by the materials of human nature but also by pre-existing culture.

Extensive remodeling can (and sometimes must) take place, but it is likely to be based upon at least the shell of the old structure (culture) as well as the foundation and raw materials of biological human nature. Culture, in short, is not a fixed condition but a process responsive to new situations. Environmental policymakers must take into account not only the natural circumstances of the planet and of the locale in which they are working but also the effects of previous human intervention. (For example, they must deal with human-introduced pollutants as well as with the natural ecology.) Likewise, those who seek to develop appropriate values for changing conditions have to concern themselves with the values people hold at a given time as well as with innate human qualities. Old values neither disappear nor survive as new ones emerge; they evolve: they are transformed in attempts to meet new situations.[9]

The Agricultural Megarevolution

It would be difficult to overstate the importance of the earliest substantial human interventions in the environment. Their impact on human life was enormous. What has often been called the "agricultural revolution" or "food-producing revolution" (either of which should be understood to include the domestication of animals for food) occurred over several thousand years, and so that event does not seem to fit the usual definition of a revolution as an abrupt break with the past.[10] In fact, though, truly fundamental changes in human society never take place quickly. The apocalyptic visions of political and religious revolutionaries never come to pass. The people in charge and even the surface structures of society can be changed overnight; but cultures need time to adapt to altered circumstances. Revolutions do occur, but only over long periods of time. The genuinely massive changes in human life can be seen only by viewing what historian Fernand Braudel has termed the *longue durée*.[11]

Agriculture and other means of intentionally producing food took thousands of years fully to "take root." But the development was utterly revolutionary with respect to the degree of change in many different aspects of human life that it finally brought in its wake. In fact, the impact of this change was greater than that of any other in human history. The consequences were so vast that this series of developments demands a name signifying change far more fundamental and widespread than has been the case with the political events commonly referred to as revolutions. The development of agriculture and animal herding and breeding deserves to be seen as the first of two massive transformations in human life—the first of two "megarevolutions."

No more than a brief outline of the results of the first of these megarevolutions can be given here. I shall focus on the areas of Southwest Asia, Northeast Africa, and Southeast Europe, from which what came to be called "Western" civilization arose, but similar developments seem to have occurred in other areas as agriculture came into widespread practice. The impact of this first megarevolution touched most areas of human life. It ultimately amounted to the sort of "disturbing of the universe" contemplated in T. S. Eliot's words quoted as this chapter's epigraph.

The Agricultural Megarevolution came in two phases: the intentional production of foodstuffs through planting and the use of hand tools (horticulture), and then the dramatic increase in this intentional production that came with the development of the plow. The first phase may have begun on an occasional and isolated basis as early as 16,500 B.C.E.[12]; it came into extensive use in the Fertile Crescent from the Nile to the Tigris and Euphrates valleys after 8000 B.C.E. The second began late in the fifth millennium B.C.E, which marks the beginning of agriculture in the narrower, anthropological sense of the word. Dramatic changes in the social environment began with the introduction of horticulture, but their impact accelerated greatly in the megarevolution's second phase. It was only after the introduction of the plow that many of the massive effects stemming from this human alteration of the social environment became fully apparent. Interestingly, the introduction of the plow took place at almost exactly the time that biblical chronology dates as the beginning of the world.

Human life was changing in dramatic ways. The inbred characteristics and motivations of men and women that had evolved over the preceding hundreds of thousands of years were placed in vastly different circumstances, for which they had not been "designed" and to which some portions of the human biological inheritance were not well adapted.

The Agricultural Megarevolution spawned many major changes in human life, among which were the following:

- A more settled existence
- The creation of substantial surplus
- Vastly increased population
- The concept of land ownership
- Undermining of the roles males had held in collector-hunter societies
- The creation of cities with too many people for personal identification with the community
- The rise of larger states, large-scale war, class hierarchies, slavery, writing, and urban life
- The complete subordination of women

- A "scientific revolution" that reversed the understanding of which sex is responsible for procreation
- A religious reversal of the view of the creative force(s) to which we now refer as God
- A new concept of the relationship between humans and nature

In short, this early act in the human drama provided the stage directions, typecast the leading characters and those who would be consigned to supporting roles, established the major themes, and defined the general plot line for the remainder of the production called *History.*

Women Revolutionized Human Life

Women invented agriculture. This viewpoint has come to be widely accepted in recent years. It cannot be proven conclusively, but anthropological, archeological, mythological, and religious evidence combine to show that it is far more likely than that men were responsible for this world-transforming development. Indeed, the only reason that men had long been assumed to have been the inventors of agriculture is that most people have reflexively believed that men have done everything important in human history.

Plant food was an area of female responsibility in the collector-hunter bands' sexual division of labor. So it is reasonable to think that it would have been women who first undertook the intentional and systematic growing of edible plants, possibly when climatic changes reduced the quantity of naturally growing plants. Women knew plants; plants were their business. Because women were also the primary preparers of food, they would have been more likely to notice the results of seeds falling onto the ground. In horticultural societies in our own times, cultivation is usually considered "woman's work," as it was among the indigenous people of the forest regions of eastern North America, such as the Iroquois, who were in a relatively early stage of horticulture at the time Europeans arrived in the area.[13] When an anthropologist in the 1970s asked women of a horticultural/hunting people in the remote Amazon jungle of eastern Ecuador whether the men could do the gardening, they laughed and said, "They couldn't; they only know how to chop [trees]."[14] (Of course today's collector-hunters cannot be equated with our distant ancestors and their actions and views in themselves prove nothing; but when added to other sorts of evidence they strengthen the case for women having developed horticulture.)

Many ancient religions and myths attribute the invention of agriculture to a goddess. Tablets found in Mesopotamia, for example, thank the Goddess Ninlil for teaching her people how to farm. Other Mesopotamian myths

named the goddess Nisaba as both the grower of grain and the founder of civilization and knowledge. Egyptians credited the Goddess Isis, known as "the
Lady of Bread" and "the inventress of all," with the beginning of farming.[15]
Many Greeks said that it was the goddess Demeter who had first taught people to farm. And then there is the serpent in the Garden of Eden—but we're
not quite ready to get to that yet. All these myths are further support for the
belief that women invented agriculture. Other ancient myths and religious stories reinforce this belief, as we shall see shortly.

"Be Fruitful and Multiply"

Agriculture provided a much larger and more dependable food supply than had
previously been available. Farming also made it necessary for people to settle
in one place for considerably longer periods than most collector-hunters had in
earlier times. The combination of a more settled existence (making it less difficult for a woman to have a new baby while a previous child was still in need of
extensive care) and a more dependable food supply made possible an unprecedented growth in population. It has also been argued that the movement to agriculture put a premium on population growth and family size, because large
families would mean that more workers would be available.[16] But this argument, by itself, makes little sense. Surely children in pre-agricultural groups
could begin to help with collecting at as young an age as—or even younger
than—they could provide substantial help in agriculture. Yet it seems that the
rise of agriculture did in fact result in a desire for larger families.

This puzzle points to another basic transformation wrought by the development of agriculture. There was no benefit from larger families in collector-
hunter bands, not because the children would not soon be able to contribute to
their own upkeep, but because such societies usually operate on the principle
of balance. The animal and plant resources upon which they depend for survival are limited in quantity and, so long as they know of no way to increase
the supply of food, the benefit of the additional hands provided by more children is outweighed by the danger posed by their additional stomachs to be
filled. There can be no premium on extra laborers in a situation in which no
surplus is produced. Each person is approximately able to provide for her- or
himself and in that sense represents neither gain nor loss for others. But if
resources are scarce, additional people may consume food needed by those
already there. In such cases, population growth constitutes a threat.

Ecologists refer to animals in a situation such as that in which humans
lived prior to the invention of agriculture as following a K-selected strategy of
reproduction (determined by population density having reached the carrying
capacity of the environment). Their population is near the level that the

resources in their habitat can sustain, and the best strategy is "to produce a few high-quality offspring and protect them until they are self-sufficient." The dramatic change in the human environment brought by agriculture moved humans toward an r-selected reproductive strategy, in which more abundant resources lead to prolific reproduction seeking to utilize the plenty that is available. This shift substantially altered the ways in which women spent much of their lives, as will be discussed more fully in the next chapter.[17] (It is intriguing that the new r-selected strategy is explicitly endorsed in the first chapter of Genesis: "Be fruitful and multiply, and fill the earth. . . ."[18] Prior to the development of agriculture and herding, such a directive would have been a prescription for disaster—as indeed it is in today's overpopulated world.) So, throughout human existence prior to the development of agriculture and animal husbandry, limited resources meant that people lived in a steady-state existence. Their goal was subsistence, to have *enough*. The possibility of creating a surplus was probably not thought of, because the forces that produced the flora and fauna would not have been thought to be amenable to human control. With no surplus of goods to be had, distinctions among the members of a group were presumably not great.

In addition to a division of labor and roles between the sexes, struggles over potential mates and for the admiration of others must also have gone on among early humans, as they do in other animal species. Such criteria as strength and particular skills presumably led to some degree of status differentiation within each sex. But for people living without surplus and with essential roles being performed by both sexes, a high degree of equality is likely to prevail, and distinctions that do exist are usually less pronounced than they are in societies that produce surpluses. Without surplus there are fewer ways of making and showing distinctions. If there is just about enough for everyone and everyone must have enough in order to survive, major inequality of possessions is incompatible with group survival.

Agriculture made feasible the establishment of much greater distinctions among men. By making a sedentary way of life both possible and necessary, agriculture made accumulation of goods physically possible (it was not practical for nomadic people to carry many possessions with them, even if surplus goods had been available) at the same time that its increased production provided the surplus to be accumulated. (The huge houses with numerous closets and vast attic and basement space, supplemented by rented self-storage units, that are so common in the United States today, as we seek to store all the surplus we have amassed, are the end result of a process set in motion by the development of agriculture and a sedentary way of life.) This development made possible increased leisure for some, increased labor for others, and gradations among property ownership throughout the society.

An Environment for Which Humans Are Not Adapted

The Agricultural Megarevolution altered human existence in many other ways. Larger populations and surplus mixed with aspects of the human biogram to give rise to writing, laws, money, greed, and full-scale warfare.

People desire a degree of predictability in their lives. Attaining this goal becomes more difficult when they leave small, personal communities and enter larger groups, where "strangers" abound. Because it is difficult to know "what to make of" a stranger, having a record of agreements comes to be desirable. Writing, therefore, is developed, in part, to supplement speech with those whose trustworthiness is unknown, and laws displace handshakes or similar gestures.

In a similar fashion, money also becomes necessary as a medium of exchange in larger groups. The "cash nexus," like the "legal nexus," is a substitute for personal ties. "Unnecessary in the village climate of mutual obligations," as historian Kevin Reilly has said, "money was essential in the city society of strangers."[19] It would not be far from the truth to say that the potential for evil (when dealing with strangers) is the root of all money.

A part of the human biogram, as I explained earlier, is self-centered, and one of our innate characteristics is anger, which can readily lead into aggressiveness. These predispositions had clear adaptive advantages in the environment in which humans evolved. Aggression is, it seems, a specifically *economic* form of behavior. It is not practiced by animals that generally do not face shortages of essential resources, but is engaged in by those that at least at times confront scarcity.[20] Although the life of collector-hunters in areas with bountiful food supplies often includes much leisure time, hominids apparently confronted scarcity often enough for an aggressive tendency to develop.

Here, then, we have a splendid example of what can happen when a motivation that was well adapted for a particular set of circumstances is plunged into a new situation. Evolution does not produce traits that are harmful to the organism in the current environment, but neither does it check predelictions that carry no current danger. Another example of such a no-longer adaptive predisposition is the appetite humans have for sugar. In the wild this craving was useful, and there was no danger of getting too much of it. But, as our dental bills in the prefluoridation era attested, that is no longer the case in our current civilization. Our once-adaptive appetite became dangerous when something that had been scarce became abundantly available.[21] Indeed, "a fast-food restaurant is a little monument to the diet of our ancient ancestors," as evolutionary psychologist Leda Cosmides has said. "Fast food has all the things that were very hard to get for our ancestors—such as salt, sugar, and fat—and so having an appetite for these things was very important back then. . . . But since our ancestors could never get enough of this stuff, we don't have an evolved mental mechanism that says, 'Aha, I've had enough sugar and fat.' "[22] In the ancestral environment, salt, sugar, and fat were "slow food"; humans could not obtain them quickly, or in large quantities. So we have no innate means of resisting them now that what was once slow food has become fast.

Much the same thing happened on a broader scale after agricultural practices produced a surplus of foodstuffs. People were accustomed to confronting conditions of scarcity from time to time, and reacting to them by being self-centered and aggressive, behavior that was necessary for survival in such circumstances. With the invention of agriculture, and the surpluses and large societies it produced, humans found themselves in a situation in which self-centeredness and aggressiveness/acquisitiveness with regard to resources were no longer appropriate.[23] But these were ingrained biological predispositions; like our cravings for sugar and fat, they did not instantly vanish simply because they had lost their adaptiveness. With a surplus available, these once-adaptive traits were transformed into the unpleasant characteristic we call greed. What is good and useful in one environment (and when practiced in moderation) can become evil and dangerous in another environment—and when carried to excess. Biologists use the term *hypertrophy* to designate such excessive development of an organ or trait.

Horses and dogs in nature face conditions under which struggle is necessary in order to obtain sufficient food; when they are put in the presence of a superabundance of prepared food, they eat themselves to death. Humans do not, as a rule, do this; but our previously useful acquisitive proclivities can be transformed into gluttony. (It may, in fact, be the case that most of the seven cardinal sins are the result of the hypertrophying in an altered environment of traits that had been adaptive in the ancestral environment.)

An Offer They Couldn't Refuse

The benefits that intentional production of food promised and produced were irresistible for most humans who were introduced to the new technology. It seemed the proverbial "offer they couldn't refuse." But as time went by, some downsides of the new way of life became apparent. Sociologist Elise Boulding has raised an interesting question about the effects of the adoption of agriculture: "If any one band of nomads could have anticipated what lay in store for humankind as a result of that fateful decision . . . , would they after all have moved on?"[24] Many people in later millennia must have asked themselves a question like this as they weighed the benefits against the negatives of their altered lives.

Perhaps the most important of the negatives, the fact that the two princi-pal male roles, hunting and group defense, declined substantially in impor-tance, will be dealt with extensively in the next chapter. Suffice it to say for the moment that as adequate, sometimes abundant, food was being made available through planted crops and kept animals, the stature men enjoyed as hunters declined, and eventually they began to take over the "woman's work" of supplying plant food. It also became apparent that farming required harder, more consistent work than did hunting. Men in collector-hunter soci-eties that continued to exist into the twentieth century, such as the !Kung of the Kalahari Desert in southern Africa, often hunted no more than four days each week, while women collected sufficient plant food to feed their families for a week in two-and-a-half days.[25] Farming, particularly using early, very labor intensive methods, can demand all-day work almost every day for long stretches in growing and harvesting seasons. Moreover, swelling populations were dependent on increasing crop yields. Bad weather, insect infestations, or plant diseases could produce famine much more rapidly in relatively heav-ily populated farming societies than such problems had in the sparse popula-tions of collector-hunter bands.

People who had taken up agriculture found that they had, as Boulding has said, "exchanged a life of relative ease, with enough to eat and few posses-sions, for a life of hard work, enough to eat, and economic surplus."[26]

As hard-working farmers listened to tales handed down in oral traditions of a collector-hunter way of life of seeming ease, plenty without hard work, and prestigious roles for men, it must have sounded like a lost paradise. But when the bargain that had initially been irresistible came to look less than per-fect, people discovered that it was also irreversible. Returning to a life that depended on nature's unaided bounty was simply not an option once popula-tions had swelled far beyond a size that could subsist on naturally occurring food sources. The realization that there was no turning back surely added to the green glow of the grass in the natural garden on the other side of the hill.

None of this, of course, is meant to indicate that the invention of agricul-ture was *actually* such a bad step. But its seemingly detrimental results were bound to be emphasized by men who were unhappy with those aspects of their lives. If stories in the oral traditions of groups that had long ago moved from collecting and hunting into agriculture informed men that women were responsible for developing the new way of life, men unhappy with their lot in farming were provided with an inviting target for their anger.

Stories that combine accounts of women having invented agriculture with the argument that this development proved to be detrimental to the interests of men are, in fact, common among the ancient myths of many cultures around the world. They have not previously been recognized as such, in part because the idea that women invented agriculture had been virtually "unthinkable" in the male-dominated societies that have existed through almost all of recorded history.

It may seem hard to believe that stories about a way of life abandoned thousands of years before could survive in an oral tradition over all that time, but there are clear examples of folk memories among nonliterate people having been passed down over periods as long as eight thousand years. Indigenous people in Australia, for instance, have given descriptions of landmarks

An Offer He Couldn't Refuse

Women attained the knowledge of how to produce food. Men embraced the new way of life, but eventually came to see the long-gone collector-hunter way of life as a lost paradise. The third and fourth chapters of The Book of Genesis constitute an allegory for the invention of agriculture by women. The knowledge that Eve picked from the tree was how to produce food, which men later came to see as what destroyed the "paradise" in which food could be obtained without the "sweat of their brows" in tilling the soil. (Albrecht Durer, *Adam and Eve,* 1504. Museum of Fine Arts, Boston) that were submerged after the last ice age. Modern divers have found these formations to be just as the folk stories depicted them.[27] And Plato told of an Egyptian sage who related stories that appear to date back some six thousand years and have been shown by modern scholars to be correct.[28] So it is quite possible for myths in various cultures to represent allegorical accounts of the effects of the invention of agriculture thousands of years earlier.

The Seductive Farmer's Daughter

One striking allegory for how men came to blame women for the changes that followed the commitment to agriculture is to be found in the world's first known major work of literature, the mythic poem *The Epic of Gilgamesh* (third millennium B.C.E.). The heroic ruler Gilgamesh becomes excessively arrogant and aggressive, upsetting both his subjects and the gods. "The onslaught of his weapons has no equal," we are told. When the people of the city of Uruk can take Gilgamesh's horrors no longer, they implore Aruru, the Goddess of Creation, to help them. She obliges by creating a double of him. The double, Enkidu, starts out as a wild "man of nature," living with and like the beasts, sucking the milk of wild animals. We are told, in a most significant phrase, that as a natural man Enkidu "knew nothing of cultivated land."

What civilizes this man of nature is (and again this is of vital importance) a woman. Enkidu spends six days having intercourse with a courtesan. She is said to be teaching him "the womans' art," or to be doing "a woman's task," which has generally been taken simply to mean having sex. It does mean having sex, but not *just* that. I believe the image is one that actually employs intercourse as a metaphor for using her wisdom to tame the natural man and lead him away from his wildness and into civilization (that is, the settled life of agriculture, which, along with sex, is considered "the woman's art")*:

> He listened to her words and accepted her advice;
> The counsel of the woman
> He took to heart.[29]

As a result, "Enkidu was grown weak, for wisdom was in him." He sits at the woman's feet and she tells him, "You are wise, Enkidu, and now you have become like a god." Enkidu then becomes Gilgamesh's best friend and tames him.

Afterwards, however, Enkidu comes to regret having been civilized. He blames the woman (the inventor of agriculture) for having caused him to lose

---

*A woman teaching a man to have intercourse is itself a symbol for women teaching men how to plant crops, as I shall explain in Chapter 6.

his free, natural paradise (collecting and hunting). Speaking of the "gate" between the natural life of the wilderness and the civilization of the city of Uruk, he declares:

"O gate, had I known that this was thy purpose,
And that thy beauty would bring on this disaster,
I would have lifted an ax and shattered thee all

. . .

May the hunter not obtain the desire of his heart."
His heart prompted him to curse also the prostitute.[30]

Reflecting the impossibility of returning to the life of collector-hunters after agriculture has been established, Enkidu finds that he can no longer communicate with the animals and commune with nature. Despite his desire to go back, he must stay in the way of life to which the woman has enticed him and make the best of it.

This story can be read as a remarkable mythical account of the effects of the invention of agriculture as they were seen several millennia after the fact. Women, the inventors of agriculture, are blamed for the loss of what seems, in retrospect, to have been paradise. Women's "sin" seems to have been the imparting of this "wisdom" to "natural" men.

Losing Eden

Since *The Epic of Gilgamesh* is not central to the lives of most Western people today, few readers are likely to be startled by the assertion that it is an allegory for the invention of agriculture. But the similarity of this account to the story of Eve and the Fall in Genesis should not be missed. In both cases it is wisdom (or the desire for wisdom) that is said to have caused the loss of paradise. The argument that the third and fourth chapters of the Book of Genesis constitute an early assessment of the mammoth consequences that altering the human environment through the knowledge of breeding and agriculture had brought is likely to raise a few eyebrows. But I am convinced that this is just what those chapters are about.[31]

The first chapters of Genesis tell of the creation of a self-propagating pre-agricultural paradise in which humans had everything they needed, without work. There was no need for human intervention to produce food in Eden: "And out of the ground, *the Lord God made to grow* every tree that is pleasant to the sight and good for food."[32] This natural bounty was available for the picking—that is, gathering or collecting: "You may freely eat of every tree of the garden."[33] But this paradise was to be lost if the man were to eat the one fruit that is forbidden, that from the Tree of Knowledge—the fruit that is produced through knowledge humans have obtained.[34] The "sin" of acquiring the knowledge of how to produce food is what obliges man to work by the sweat of his brow in order to obtain food:

> cursed is the ground because of you;
> in toil you shall eat of it all the days of your
> life; thorns and thistles it shall bring forth
> to you; and you shall eat the plants of the field.
> In the sweat of your face you shall eat bread.[35]

This translates quite clearly into a lament that there is need to labor under a system of agriculture (knowledge), while it is supposed at this late date that the long-gone life of the collector-hunters (now made into a lost Eden) was one of bounty without work, where people lived well merely by picking the fruit from trees whenever they so desired. This certainly was an idealization, but the fact is that agriculture *did* require far greater discipline and harder and more consistent work than collecting and hunting.[36]

Then, most significantly, there is the fact that it is the woman who is blamed for having eaten from the Tree of Knowledge: "So when *the woman saw* that the tree was *good for food* . . . and that the tree was to be desired to make one wise, *she took of its fruit* and ate; and she also gave some to her husband, and he ate."[37] One way to look at this is that it was men who were telling the story (which I am convinced it was; I do not accept Harold Bloom's contention that "J," who wrote the oldest strand of Genesis, the one with which we are primarily concerned here, was a woman[38]) and they were simply following the innate tendency to cast the blame for any evil away from themselves. Surely this must have played an important role in the onus for having lost Paradise being placed on Eve and so women in general. But if women actually did invent and develop agriculture and were associated with it in the minds of men, then for the men who wrote Genesis to castigate Eve for having gained the wisdom that lost Eden fits perfectly with an understanding of that wisdom as agriculture.*

That being cast out of Paradise means the beginnings of agriculture is made even more explicit at the end of the third chapter of Genesis: "Therefore the Lord God *sent him forth from the garden of Eden to till the ground* from which he was taken."[39]

Genesis 3:16 reflects the fact that the alteration in human life caused by women's invention of agriculture had led eventually both to a switch to an *r*-selected reproductive strategy and to the greater subordination of women.

---

*Once again, as in *Gilgamesh,* the knowledge that the woman imparted to the man has often been interpreted as sexual intercourse, since it is only after they eat the fruit that that the couple realize that they are naked. The significance of this association will be discussed in Chapter 6.

Duke religious studies professor Carol Meyers has suggested that this passage should be translated in a somewhat different way than it is usually rendered:

> To the woman he said,
> "I will greatly increase your toil and your pregnancies;
> (Along) with travail shall you beget children.
> For to your man is your desire,
> And he shall predominate over you."[40]

This passage attempts to overcome womb envy. Female creative power is redefined as a punishment. Ashley Montagu has nicely described this process. "If one happens to be lacking in certain capacities with which the opposite [*sic*] sex is naturally endowed, and those capacities happen to be highly, if unacknowledgedly, valued," the renowned anthropologist wrote, "then one can compensate for one's own deficiency by devaluating the capacities of others. By turning capacities into handicaps, not only can one make their possessors feel inferior, but anyone lacking such capacities can then feel superior for the very lack of them."[41]

It was, as we shall see in detail in succeeding chapters, the(ir) development of agriculture that made women "the second sex." This is just what the story in Genesis says.

There is more. The Fall, the loss of innocence, the gaining of knowledge, is said in Genesis to be the cause of people having to choose between good and evil ("your eyes will be opened, and you will be like God, knowing good

Going Forth from Eden to Till the Soil
The new roles for men and women after "Eve" had discovered agriculture are well represented in this segment of an illustration of the story of Adam and Eve from the Moutier-Grandval Bible, Tours, ninth century. God banishes the woman and man from Eden, after which the woman is fully occupied with a child and the man earns their bread by hard labor tilling the soil. (Bridgeman Art Library)

and evil"; "Behold, the man is become like one of us, knowing good and evil. . . ."[42]). Prior to eating from the tree of knowledge, people's natural "innocence" is presumed to have sufficed. That innocence amounts to human nature, the biogram I partially outlined in Chapter 2. The assumption by the compilers of Genesis is that before the Fall (the development of agriculture), being "innocent"—doing what was natural—worked. The contention is that there had then been no need for cultural values to help people choose between good and evil. But with the changes instigated by the knowledge of agriculture, the environment was so altered that simple reliance on "doing what comes naturally" was no longer fully adaptive.

Just as Enkidu finds that the route shown by women into the world of agriculture is a one-way street, Adam is prevented from returning to Eden when God places "the cherubim, and a flaming sword which turned every way" to guard the way back to paradise.[43] You can't go home again.

The story of Cain and Abel in the fourth chapter of Genesis is a further allegorical representation of the consequences of the Agricultural Megarevolution, as I shall explain in the next chapter. For now, let us note that it is Cain, the man who has taken up the "womanly" occupation of farmer, who brings murder (probably representing as well excessive violence and warfare) into the world, eliciting a curse from God. The curse on Cain, the farmer, is the second instance in Genesis of the male God condemning a man who takes up the "female" way of life, farming. Cain, the introducer of violence, is, moreover, identified as the father—or grandfather—of sedentary culture or "civilization": "Cain knew his wife, and she conceived and bore Enoch; and he built a city." And the harmony and cooperation that are assumed to have existed in the golden past before agriculture are no longer to be found in the tiller of the soil, as Cain indicates when he asks rhetorically, "Am I my brother's keeper?"[44] This story corresponds neatly with the understanding that agricultural surplus eventually led to an increase in individualism, aggression, warfare, and greed.

The serpent who entices Eve represents a goddess. Snakes were frequently linked with female deities in "prehistoric" and ancient times, perhaps because the reptiles' shedding of skin was associated with menstruation.* Thus the serpent has a role, albeit an unrecognized one, in the Judeo-Christian tradition similar to that of Nisaba, Isis, and Demeter, as a goddess who introduced farming. The tree itself probably also represents a goddess as the source of the

---

*It should also be noticed that Yahweh attempts to divide women from the serpent/goddess: "I will put enmity between you and the woman," He tells the serpent. And it is said to be as a punishment for their acquisition of (agricultural) knowledge that women are to be subordinated to men. (Genesis 3:15–16)

A Goddess Teaching People How to Farm
Many ancient myths attribute the teaching of farming to people to a goddess, such as the Mesopotamian Nisba or the Greek Demeter. The serpent in the Genesis story also represents a goddess, as Michelangelo hints by placing a woman's head and torso at the top of the snake. (*Fall and Expulsion,* 1509–10. Bridgeman Art Library)

knowledge of agriculture, since a tree was also often a symbol of a Goddess with creative power.[45]

It would be expected that Adam would curse Eve and the serpent as Enkidu did the prostitute who seduced him away from his natural paradise, but the authors of the Genesis version of the story left it to the male God to do the cursing of both the serpent/goddess and the woman. The wording of the curse on the serpent is noteworthy:

> The Lord God said to the serpent,
> "Because you have done this,
> cursed are you above all cattle,
> and above all wild animals;
> upon your belly you shall go,
> and dust shall you eat
> all the days of your life. . . ."[46]

To place the serpent/goddess below all other animals was to put her in a similar position at the bottom of the hierarchy to that assigned to women. The line about eating dust also has significance, as we shall see later (in Chapter 6).

Good story-telling leaves spaces for the listener or reader to fill in the gaps from the context of what has been told. The authors of Genesis left it to the reader to figure out what Eve said to Adam as she gave him the fruit to eat. Once we see the likelihood that the story is about women developing intentional means of growing food, it seems likely that Eve's words would have been something like this: *Try this; it's good. . . . And, believe it or not, I grew it myself! The tree [goddess] taught me how!*

These chapters in Genesis are an early description of how the changes started by the development of agriculture had so transformed the human environment that the natural characteristics of people had to be restrained by the elaboration of more complex values. This account, as it was held in the collective memory, assumed that people prior to the advent of agriculture had lived in an Eden in which they could satisfy their needs by eating fruit from the trees (that is, collecting), without significant labor, and without need for any restraints on their actions.

The Genesis story says that the acquisition of the knowledge of how to grow crops destroyed that paradise and made necessary hard labor, introduced greed and large-scale violence, and obliged people to develop a new system of values to govern human behavior.

Another way to put the message being related by the compilers of Genesis is: Ignorance was bliss.

Pandora's Bread Box

A similar oral history of the transformation from a pre-agricultural time in which people acted naturally and thereby did "good" without the need of values or laws, to a troubled present is to be found in Greek mythology. The Greeks and Romans referred to the lost Paradise as the "Golden Age." "The fruitful earth poured forth her fruits unbidden in boundless plenty," Hesiod wrote of this primordial time.[47]

> First was the Golden Age. Then rectitude
> Spontaneous in the heart prevailed, and faith,

said the Roman Ovid.

> Avengers were not seen, for laws unframed
> Were all unknown and needless. . . .
> . . . they dwelt
> Without a judge in peace. . . .
> . . . secure
> A happy multitude enjoyed repose.

Ovid made it explicit that the lost Paradise being described was prior to humans gaining the knowledge of agriculture:

> Then of her own accord the earth produced
> A store of every fruit. The harrow touched

Her not, nor did the plowshare wound
Her fields. And man content with given food,
And none compelling, gathered arbute fruits.[48]

Conditions worsened in the succeeding Silver Age, which unmistakably refers to the rise of agriculture: "Crops would no longer grow without planting. The farmer was obliged to sow the seed, and the toiling ox to draw the plough."[49] Or, in Ovid's version:

Then were the cereals planted in long rows,
And bullocks groaned beneath the heavy yoke.[50]

But worse was to come, as human intervention further altered conditions from those for which people had been "made." More deadly weapons in the Bronze Age led into the horrors of the Iron Age. Here the effects not only of iron weapons but much more of how the creation of surplus perverted formerly adaptive human traits are abundantly evident:

... And last of all
The ruthless and hard Age of Iron prevailed,
From which malignant vein great evil sprung;
And modesty and faith and truth took flight,
And in their stead deceits and snares and frauds
And violence and wicked love of gain
Succeeded. ...[51]

"The earth, which till now had been cultivated in common, began to be divided off into possessions. *Men were not satisfied* with what the surface produced, but must dig into its bowels and draw forth from thence the ores of metals. Mischievous *iron* and more mischievous *gold,* were produced. War sprang up, using both as weapons. ..."[52] In the Iron Age, Hesiod said, "men shall give their praise to violence and the doer of evil. Right will be in the arm."[53]

And by what means were all these horrors unleashed upon men? "Zeus, of the towering thunders," angered by Prometheus' stealing of fire, created woman (Pandora) and had each of the gods of Olympus give her a gift "to be a sorrow to men who eat bread." Before Pandora and her gifts from the gods arrived, Hesiod relates, "the races of men had been living on earth free from all evils, free from laborious work."[54] Hesiod refers to Pandora as "this beautiful evil thing" and says that women "are accomplished in bringing hard labors."[55] Epimetheus, the man to whom Zeus sent Pandora, "took the evil, and only perceived it when he possessed her."[56] The woman proceeded to lift "away the lid from the great jar" she brought with her, "scattering its contents, and her design was sad troubles for mankind."[57] A gift from the gods to "men who eat bread" that is scattered (like seeds), causes men to have to work hard and bring them sad troubles, and is perceived as evil only after it has been possessed, sounds a lot like the secret of food production. Once again it is a woman whose apparent gifts from the gods, like the knowledge found by Eve, cause the imagined pre-agricultural paradise to be lost.* Like the Hebrews, the Greeks were saying: *Beware of women bearing gifts.*

Ovid's description of the final result of what we can now recognize as the changes unleashed by the invention of agriculture is particularly significant:

> . . . Piety was slain:
> And last of all the virgin deity,
> Astraea vanished from the blood-stained earth.[58]

Astraea, the goddess of justice, left the earth because she became weary of the iniquities of men in the evil days after the knowledge of farming had transformed the environment and forfeited the supposed paradise of the Golden Age of collecting and hunting. But this can be read as mother earth "her" self having lost her virginity when people began to plow her body, leaving her blood-stained.

Like other cultures, the Greeks (and thence the Romans) knew a great deal about human prehistory and what agriculture and surplus had wrought. So did the Hebrews, but their account was less straightforward and more symbolic than that of the Greeks. Unfortunately the Bible's allegory of the transformation from the imagined natural "paradise" of the collector-hunter to the troubled surplus of the agricultural warrior has been taken literally by most people who have read it. If one understands the meaning of the images, Genesis is, like its Greco-Roman counterpart, a metaphorical, exaggerated, and sexist, but not wholly inaccurate, account of the key developments in "prehistory."

"The discovery of agriculture, which at the beginning of the Neolithic had been such a positive step by women," anthropologist Margaret Ehrenberg has

---

*Stories of human decline from a lost golden age have been prevalent in cultures around the world. The *Tao Te Ching,* written in China in the sixth century B.C.E., for instance, parallels the Genesis and Greek stories of how attaining knowledge (presumably agricultural) caused the loss of Paradise ("the Great Way") and necessitated the introduction of human-made ("artificial") values ("human kindness and morality"):

> It was when the Great Way declined
> That human kindness and morality arose;
> It was when intelligence and knowledge appeared
> That the Great Artifice began.
> —*Tao Te Ching,* chap. XVIII.

accurately said, "was by the end of the period to have unforeseen, and unfortunate, consequences for them."[59]

Thus far, we have only begun to scratch the surface of just how unfortunate some of the consequences of the invention of agriculture were to be for women—and society as a whole. The remainder of the book will detail their extent and impact, from the Neolithic Age to today.

CHAPTER 5

Hell Hath No Fury Like a Man Devalued

The Neolithic "Backlash"

It is impossible to strip [the woman's] life of meaning
as completely as the life of the man can be stripped.

MARGARET MEAD[1]

For a few decades in the middle of the twentieth century, the most prominent theory of human evolution centered on "Man the Hunter" as the font of human progress.[2] "Hunting is the master behavior pattern of the human species," William S. Laughlin flatly declared in 1966. "Hunting has placed a premium upon inventiveness, upon problem-solving."[3] "In a very real sense our intellect, interests, emotions, and basic social life," wrote Sherwood L. Washburn and C. S. Lancaster the same year, "all are evolutionary products of the success of the hunting adaptation."[4] "The complexities of human social life in the hunting phase required bonded male groups that were much more complex than those found in vegetarian groups," maintained Lionel Tiger and Robin Fox in 1971.[5]

That interpretation is now largely discredited.[6] Surely some characteristics that evolved more noticeably in men were selected because they were adaptive for hunting. But other claims that used to be made for hunting as "the master behavior pattern of the human species" must be rejected. One reason is that, since they began with the assumption that men did almost all of the hunting, the Man the Hunter theorists were excluding females from the evolutionary process as totally as historians before the last third of the twentieth century had left women out of the telling of history. Such statements as Laughlin's betray an equation of *man* with "the human species." In any event, many of the Man the Hunter claims just will not hold up. An example: In light of the clear average superiority that modern women have over men in verbal ability,[7] the argument that men on the hunt were the inventors of language borders on the absurd. That claim also seems odd when it is combined with the usual reasoning that women were especially poorly suited for hunting expeditions because the small children they would have to carry with them would be apt to make noise and quiet was essential in sneaking up on prey. An activity for which silence is best suited would not seem a likely candidate for the source of language.

The argument in this book might well be termed the "Woman the Farmer" theory. Even more critical, though, is the fact that one major result of the development of agriculture and herding was that the need for hunting declined dramatically. Thus the argument presented here might better be termed the "Man the Hunter-No-More" thesis.

The Neolithic Male Unemployment Crisis

The beginnings of the problems of the sexes are rooted in biology, not so much in the sense of innate differences themselves, but in the cultural reactions to those differences. As we have seen, the basic problem lies in the apparent unequal distribution of procreative power and the actual unequal distribution of reproductive and nourishing capacities between the sexes. This circumstance presumably has led many men in almost all cultures throughout human existence to suffer from a degree of womb and breast envy. In reaction, they established a variety of definitions of manhood on the common basis of opposition to womanhood. But specific historical (and "prehistorical") developments greatly exacerbated the problem.

"The economic roles of men and women are differentiated in all surviving hunter-gatherer societies, a category that encompassed all human societies until the rise of agriculture ten thousand years ago," as Jared Diamond has summarized. "Men invariably spend more time hunting large animals, while women spend more time gathering plant foods and small animals and caring for children."[8] During the enormously long eons in which humans existed as collector-hunters, then, the sexes both had fairly clear and obviously useful roles. Women seemingly produced and actually fed and cared for offspring. They also provided much (probably a majority) of the food for the group through collecting. Men did the bulk of the hunting, providing highly valued meat.* Men also had the primary responsibility for defending their band from predators. Since women could do things that men could not, men had proba-

---

*Meat protein is of much better quality in terms of essential amino acids than protein found in most plants, a fact that apparently gives humans an innate taste for meat as a relatively small but highly significant fraction of their diet. [Colin Tudge, *The Time Before History* (New York: Scribner's, 1996), p. 197].

bly already devised their own culture-specific definitions of manhood and based them on separation from and opposition to womanhood, allowing men to consider themselves to be superior. But there was an essential modus vivendi, an acceptable division of labor, a rough equality between the sexes.

Agriculture greatly changed the lives of both sexes. In the early stages of horticulture, it is likely that the prestige of women increased. They were, before they moved more fully into larger-scale reproduction, providing a substantial amount of the food for the group and they were responsible for dramatic changes in the way people lived. But men, always at least subconsciously jealous of women's apparent procreative power, would not long tolerate a feeling of reduced importance. The first male "backlash" was brewing.

What Have We Done?
Masaccio's *Expulsion from Eden* (Fresco. ca. 1425. Brancacci Chapel, Sta. Maria del Carmine, Florence) captures the way some people, with the benefit of hindsight, came to look on the development of agriculture and the loss of what they imagined to have been a Paleolithic Paradise. Roles of both women and men were dramatically affected.

Because farming placed a premium on a growing population, one of women's traditional roles (reproduction) came to be even more valued than it had been. Gradually, they were called upon to become nearly full-time producers of children and ceased to be significant producers of food.* The status of women, which had presumably risen somewhat after their development of agriculture, began to decline as they were obliged to spend more of their time in reproduction and less in production of foodstuffs for their families and community.[9] Put another way, when men began to cultivate fields, they also started to cultivate women as never before. (Just how appropriate this terminology would come to seem after the development of plow agriculture will become apparent in the next chapter.)

As much as agriculture altered women's way of life, largely removing them from one of their two traditional roles, the new system had an even more devastating impact on the lives of men.

Robert Bly and Sam Keen, prophets of the "men's movement" that emerged at the beginning of the 1990s, have argued that the industrial revolution undermined the roles for which men are biologically designed.[10] They are one megarevolution and between five and ten thousand years off in their analysis. As the advent of agriculture enhanced the value of one of the traditional roles of women and left them with less time to participate in production, the new way of life simultaneously devalued both of the traditional male roles. Agriculture altered the human social environment in a way that fundamentally degraded the importance of both hunting and defense against other species. It is true that industrialism has in some ways made matters worse for men, but that modern system is in fact part of a multifaceted male response to agriculture's destruction of the roles for which evolution shaped men's innate characteristics.

A statement that British historian Eric Hobsbawm made about the impact of the industrial revolution precisely captures the impact of the Agricultural Megarevolution: "It transformed the lives of men beyond recognition. Or, to be more exact, in its initial stages it destroyed their old ways of living and left them free to discover or make for themselves new ones, if they could and knew how."[11]

As the intentional production of food (including meat from kept animals) came to supply almost all of a society's nutritional needs, hunting lost importance. By making possible larger populations in a relatively constricted area, moreover, early agriculture encouraged the overhunting of game. Thus, hunting became not only less necessary but also less feasible. Simultaneously, the need for protection from predators of other species also declined. In settled

---

*Of course, women performed many other important roles in most agricultural societies, including spinning, weaving, and pottery-making.

agricultural communities, dangerous beasts were few and far between. Men were being "*dis*-placed" from both of their traditional roles as women were being "*re*-placed" from the dual role of reproducer and provider of plant food into the role of nearly full-time reproducer.

Shrines dating from the late seventh and sixth millennia B.C.E. in Çatal Hüyük center on a goddess. What is most intriguing about this Anatolian site (in modern-day Turkey) is that at first there were also shrines dedicated to hunting, but around 5800 B.C.E. they seem to have been completely displaced by worship of a goddess. A hunting mural in one shrine was covered with white plaster at about this time, and male cultic statues disappeared. The supposition is that the full triumph of agriculture led for a time to a greater emphasis both on the women who had invented and continued to practice it, and on a female deity.[12]

Where did this leave the men? The symbolism of the hunt scene being obliterated is highly suggestive. The need to seek supernatural assistance in the hunt had evaporated. Men's sense of value and importance was likely to follow. Men had seemingly been made redundant. They faced massive unemployment and, as the adoption of the double-edged term used for modern unemployment crises, *depression,* suggests, this situation was likely also to be a huge psychological problem.

Male redundancy does not mean, however, that early agricultural societies were "matriarchies."[13] There is no evidence whatsoever for a time of women dominating men.[14] This is a convenient point at which to make plain that, despite the importance of women in collector-hunter cultures, there is no reason to think that women were dominant in those pre-agricultural societies. Prehistoric matriarchies are a figment of the imaginations of nineteenth-century Swiss anthropologist J. J. Bachofen,[15] Friedrich Engels,[16] and some modern feminists.[17] Men, after all, have always had the advantage (on average) of superior size and upper body strength and it is unreasonable to suppose that they would ever have let women physically dominate them. It is entirely reasonable, though, to believe that in these societies in which women were seen as having creative power, and in which they provided much of the food, women enjoyed a much greater degree of equality than members of their sex have had in most of recorded history.

Women must have gained in prominence and prestige during the period after they had invented farming. In fact, among the Iroquois, the compensation to the family of a murdered woman was twice that for a murdered man.[18] But women did not attempt to "rule" over men, perhaps because many do not have the advantages in physical strength that men have and because most females do not have a strong biological drive to dominate. They compete, as we have seen, in other ways. Nor were these early agricultural societies (or the collector-hunter ones that preceded them) the seats of female "independence," "autonomy," and sexual freedom* that some feminists have sought to make them.[19] Feminists who search for autonomous women in "primitive" cultures are making the same fundamental mistake that so many male thinkers have made since the seventeenth century: they are grafting the modern notions of independence, autonomy, and individualism onto societies that were to some extent communal and to a great extent interdependent. Neither men nor women were "autonomous" in these societies.

Surely, though, the changes in the relative prestige of female and male activities that followed the early development of agriculture increased male insecurity. We can see from modern cases that insecure, threatened men are apt to take out their frustrations on women and to try to dominate them.[20] What happens in such individual cases today seems to have taken place on a collective scale in the Neolithic Age.

"You Got to Invent *All* the Difficulties"

What agriculture did was to exacerbate a problem inherent in the condition of men: their uncertain role. We have already seen that men often establish exclusive roles for themselves to compensate for the things that women can do but men cannot. Because the activities reserved for males are largely artificial, however, the purpose that they give to men's lives is constantly endangered. "It is impossible," Margaret Mead correctly contended, "to strip [the woman's] life of meaning as completely as the life of the man can be stripped."[21]

The rise of agriculture accomplished the first and most important such stripping of meaning from men's lives. Women's invention of ways intentionally to produce food created a severe identity crisis for the male sex—and eventually led to the results of the notawoman concept of manliness becoming far more harmful. Defense and hunting had provided suitable worthwhile roles for men and had helped to shape their biology. Agriculture made men much more dependent on new, artificial (culturally created and defined) roles. Anthropologists who have studied societies that recently moved from collecting and hunting to agriculture have found that the adoption of a sedentary lifestyle leads to a much stronger male insistence on rigid, segregated sex roles,[22] indicating that men whose positions have been thrown into question are likely to fall back defensively on gender-extending notawomanhood. Mead neatly captured the resulting central issue of subsequent history. "The recurrent problem of civilization is to define the male role satisfactorily enough," she wrote, that a man

---

*Although there almost certainly was never a culture in which utter promiscuity for women was accepted, there may have been a *somewhat* less restrictive environment for female sexuality in the period before agriculture, as will be discussed in the next chapter.

may "reach a solid sense of irreversible achievement, of which his childhood knowledge of the satisfactions of child-bearing have given him a glimpse."[23] But this persistent problem for males was probably never put better than in the words Mark Twain placed in the mouth of Tom Sawyer in *Huckleberry Finn:* "You got to invent *all* the difficulties. Well, we can't help it, we got to do the best we can with the materials we've got."[24]

One of the most significant facts for human history is that many of the new roles that men established for themselves after the invention of agriculture were appropriated from women. In recent decades many men have complained that women have entered what were formerly considered to be male occupations. But much of early human history (as usually defined) and late "prehistory" entailed this process operating in the other direction: as their own roles were devalued, men took over functions that had previously been defined as "female." What this amounted to was a Late Neolithic–Bronze Age "Masculinist Movement" in which men asserted, in effect, "We can do important things, too."

The first of the female roles that men appropriated was agriculture itself. A process that has continued into modern times and been labeled the "masculinization of agriculture"[25] actually began in the Neolithic Age. Men started to engage in farming. After the development of plows brought the animals that had traditionally been men's responsibility into the fields and made greater physical strength seem to be necessary for the work, men took over farming and redefined it as "man's work."[26] But it really was not, insofar as it did not satisfy some of the proclivities, such as competition and conquest, that had been selected for in males when their main roles had been as defenders and hunters. Those male traits found little useful outlet in the largely woman-made social environment of agriculture, where people met their needs not by conquering animals, but by nurturing them (albeit ultimately to kill and eat them), much as they did plants. Men might come to call themselves "breadwinners," but, unlike hunted meat, bread is not really something to be *won.* Raising plants and kept animals is not a matter of winners and losers, but of growers and nurturers.

The agricultural way of life is, in fact, one that is essentially feminine. Hunting involves the securing of food through subduing and conquering other creatures. This activity was in keeping with traits more common in males, characteristics that presumably developed for defense and were expanded by hunting. Growing plants and domesticating animals, on the other hand, involve not conquest but nurturing; in both cases what is required is caring for young, fragile organisms during their periods of greatest vulnerability. (We use the same word, *nursery,* for places in which young children and young plants are cared for.) To put it directly, agriculture and the domestication of animals are "mothering" activities.

If it is true both that women invented agriculture and that the agricultural way of life is one that operates on practices and values that are at least somewhat more congenial to women than men, it is ironic in the extreme that this development seems ultimately to have led to a much greater subordination of women. To see how this outcome of the Agricultural Megarevolution was reached, we must look further at some of the immense changes it brought about.

Because agriculture is based upon traits more common in females, as it became the focal point of human society, men came eventually to feel left out. This feeling was accentuated by the gender extending in which so many men engage, which led them to repress their own nurturing tendencies, because those qualities were classified as *only* feminine and so disgraceful in men.

Additionally, because men had "always" dealt with animals, herders as well as hunters were likely to look upon men who farmed as "not real men" ("wimps," in our current terminology): *"Real men" don't fool around with plants.* Here again the symbolic story can be found in Genesis. God is not pleased with the offering of agricultural produce that Cain, the "tiller of the ground," brings Him. Growing plants is seen as lowly "women's work," and the product of farming is an unworthy offering to God. The male God seems to be saying to Cain something like: *How dare you bring me the sort of food women produce? You* wimp! In contrast, God "has regard" for Abel and his "manly" offering of meat from a sheep.[27]

The men who did take up farming were bound to have some of these same feelings about themselves (much as many women who are career-oriented today are susceptible to feelings of not being "real women"). Men who had such doubts would be likely to blame—at least subconsciously—women, the inventors of agriculture, for creating a situation in which they had to engage in an "unmanly" occupation.*

Women had discovered—or created—a New World (which is to say, a vastly altered environment), and men would have to make a place for themselves within it. Men's ultimate reaction to the devaluing of their previous roles constituted an early male "backlash," next to which the backlash against feminism detected by Susan Faludi in the early 1990s pales in comparison.[28] This apparent link between aspects of our current situation and that which followed the invention of agriculture is important. Many analysts believe that they detect today developments that actually took place between ten thousand and five thousand years ago. For example, George Gilder has declared:

---

*If we really were blank slates, becoming farmers would rapidly have "feminized" men, and there would have been no need to find new outlets for proclivities "designed" for hunting and defense. That agriculture did not feminize men or eliminate some of their no-longer adaptive traits is another firm indication that biology has written something indelible—though malleable—on our slates before culture writes more.

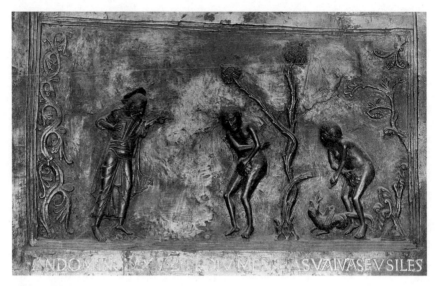

It Was _Her_ Idea!
As the Lord reproaches Adam for gaining the knowledge (how to produce food) that loses Paradise, Adam blames the woman. Eve casts the blame on the serpent, representing the earlier goddess-centered religions. As men came to resent the devaluation of their roles as hunters and defenders, they tended to blame women for having developed agriculture. (Detail from the bronze doors of the Cathedral of Hildesheim. ca. 1015)

"When our social institutions deny or disrespect the basic terms of male nature, masculinity makes men enemies of family and society."[29] He was speaking of the late twentieth century, but his comment better describes what happened as a result of the Agricultural Megarevolution.

The Immoral Equivalent of Hunting

"No Men Needed" said signs in front of factories and businesses during the Great Depression of the 1930s. The same message seemed to confront men in the new world of agriculture during the Neolithic Age. After the Agricultural Megarevolution had devalued their traditional roles, men began to see themselves as "losers." The development of ways intentionally to produce food did to Neolithic men what some recent observers have said the modern economy has done to modern men: "[T]hey have been pushed by forces they don't understand into roles in which their masculinity has nothing to do but roil and fester."[30] When there is no legitimate outlet for the traits associated with masculinity, a defensive, exaggerated hypermasculinity emerges, particularly among those males who are most insecure about their manhood.

The Plow and the "Masculinization" of Agriculture
This cylinder seal from late third millennium B.C.E. Mesopotamia shows men leading and guiding a two-handled plow. Beginning in the fourth millennium B.C.E., men found that one of the formerly female roles that they could redefine as "men's work" was the provision of plant food. But farming did not satisfy some of the characteristics that evolution had developed in men to adapt them to their earlier roles as hunters and defenders.

Once again, it is Cain who best illustrates the consequences. After God has, in the modern parlance, "dissed him" as a wimp, Cain strikes out violently. So did devalued men in general as they sought to prove their manhood in a "No Men Needed" society.

Men, stuck with increasingly maladaptive proclivities as part of their biograms, had to employ cultural adaptation to mediate between their natural inclinations and the altered social environment. They would, in short, have to create new uses or outlets for those portions of their biological makeups that agriculture made superfluous: new "manly" roles. The roles taken from women, precisely because they were originally developed to coincide with the more female proclivities, could not fully satisfy male motivations. So men changed their practices in other ways. The most obvious redirection of traits more common in males was large-scale war which, although it resulted from a group of causes related to the invention of agriculture, can most basically be seen as the substitution of hunting men for hunting beasts. "As hunting was ceasing to be a viable way of life," Barbara Ehrenreich has said, "what men did at that point was pretty scary. They invented war. They found something for themselves to do. It was glorious, it flattered their egos."[31]

I would paraphrase William James by saying that war arose as the immoral equivalent of hunting.

Men had been protectors and partial providers in pre-agricultural societies. The traits that they had used for the provision of meat were no longer especially needed under agriculture, so it is plausible that they may have turned them exclusively to protection. This adaptation may have led to a hypertrophying of aggressiveness and the desire for conquest. The increased competition became a self-fulfilling cultural adaptation, by increasing the need for protection from other men who were now more likely to pose a threat. Characteristics that in a more natural environment had been used both for hunting other animals and for defense against other species and other men came eventually to be used under agriculture for offensive actions against other humans. "Murder and hunting may be more closely tied together than we are used to thinking," suggest Richard Wrangham and Dale Peterson in their 1996 book, *Demonic Males*.[32] Defensive characteristics used for offensive purposes created a greater need for defense and so made the more male qualities that had lost their adaptiveness "useful" once more. Here was a classic, although most unfortunate, case of cultural adaptation.

But a few other of the traits that had developed to a more pronounced degree in men than women may have proved to be even more instrumental in producing wars than was aggressiveness. With their generally greater penchant for establishing lines of command and hierarchical structures, and their desire for a feeling of belonging to a group, many men were as well suited for organization into the newer form of hunting parties, armies, as they had been for the original. "The soldier kills more to conform, and to support his buddies, than because of his personal hatred of the enemy," as Desmond Morris has said.[33]

The way in which hunting was converted into warfare may have been by means of groups of men "hunting" the domesticated herds of other groups, the latter seeking to defend "their" animals, and the former then attacking the men as well as their animals.[34]

By late in the fourth millennium B.C.E., the consequences of mixing certain of the innate human characteristics with the surpluses and other ramifications of agriculture and animal breeding were becoming clear. The need to settle in one place that these practices forced upon people, combined with the population growth made simultaneously possible and desirable by the availability of surplus, had caused the creation of towns of considerable size. These trends were substantially accelerated by the introduction of the plow. This development brought more and more people into societies larger than the "personal" size for which we had been biologically developed. The desire for property and status—and for security in them—led to the formation of states, with governments exercising substantial authority over large numbers of people.

Humans had never been above fighting with one another, including conflicts between groups or bands. Cave paintings of groups of men shooting arrows at one another date back to at least 15,000 B.C.E.[35] But in times when men still had important roles as hunters, there was nothing (save, perhaps, some attractive women) worth taking from another band, there was no concept of land ownership, there were not enough people to oblige groups to live in close proximity to one another, and there was not much cause for war. The rise of agriculture, with its diminution of traditional male roles and its creation of surplus, eventually changed this situation. It did so both by providing something that might be seen as worth fighting over (the products of surplus, good land on which to farm, and a greater value in women to produce more laborers) and by establishing organizations of people (states) large enough to engage in conflict of sufficient magnitude to merit the name *war.*

The larger aggregations of people probably played another part in producing warfare. The wrenching of people from the personal-sized communities for which their biograms prepared them meant that their need to identify had to be transferred to an impersonal entity—the state—for which it was not designed. This further disruption of the sort of life for which human nature was adapted may well have facilitated other mutations in behavior. The hypertrophying of identification with the band may have been instrumental in the hypertrophying of aggression.

By the third millennium B.C.E. there were horrible wars of conquest taking place in Mesopotamia. The horror was due not only to the size of the states in conflict and the greed that inspired them, but also to another technological advance, metal making. This development eventually brought better farming implements (especially plows), but first it produced better weapons.

In these early agricultural/warrior societies, the somewhat more male traits of dualism, dominance, aggressiveness, and self-centeredness were fashioned into the "masculine" values of patriotism, hierarchy, military virtues, and ownership. In the conditions of this time, these "masculine" values "worked." This is not to say that they were "good," but merely that they fit well enough with the combined natural and human-made environmental conditions to permit survival.

A useful example of the changes that had occurred and the qualities that now dominated is to be found in the world's first known major work of literature, the aforementioned mythic poem *The Epic of Gilgamesh* (third millennium B.C.E.). As so many other men had in the altered environment of agricultural/warrior societies, the heroic ruler Gilgamesh becomes excessively arrogant and aggressive, upsetting both his subjects and the gods. "The onslaught of his weapons has no equal," we are told.[36]

Or this, from Assurnasirpal, the Assyrian ruler from the ninth century B.C.E.:

> with vigorous assault the city I besieged and took; their many houses I burned; many soldiers I took alive; their spoil in abundance I carried off; the city I overthrew, razed and burned with fire; . . . their soldiers I slew; their booty in cattle and sheep I carried off; their boys, their maidens I dishonoured. . . .[37]

The "dishonouring" of the maidens suggests the underlying motivation for such behavior, which has been all too common throughout recorded history. The dishonouring of the boys is an expression of the Master metaphor by which men treat other males as women to indicate their dominance over them.*

Hell hath no fury like a man devalued. But the full impact of that fury has yet to be addressed.

---

*This practice will be examined in detail in Chapter 13.

CHAPTER 6

Going to Seed

The Metaphor that (Mis)shaped History

The mother is no parent of that which is called
her child, but only nurse of the new-planted seed
that grows. The parent is he who mounts.

"APOLLO"[1]

"It isn't what we don't know that kills us," Mark Twain pointed out, "it's everything we do know that ain't so."[2] This chapter's focus is on the most important and influential thing that people have known throughout most of history that "ain't so."

All of the extraordinary consequences of the invention of agriculture that were discussed in the last two chapters pale in comparison with the seizure of another, decidedly biological, female role that men accomplished several millennia into the Agricultural Megarevolution—probably at about the time that the plow completed the transformation of horticulture into full agriculture, beginning around 4000 B.C.E.

No one can say with any certainty when humans first perceived the male role in procreation. It is hard to believe that later Paleolithic humans, whose brains were equal to ours today, had not noticed a connection between copulation and pregnancy. But that relationship is far from one-to-one, so the connection probably remained mysterious. It is likely that it was understood that a woman had to "be with a man" before she could conceive,* but the creative

---

*There is evidence from fairly early Neolithic art of some understanding that men played a part in the process: a Çatal Hüyük stone plaque dating from prior to 5000 B.C.E. depicts a man and woman intertwined, followed by a mother with a child. James Mellaart, *Çatal Hüyük* (New York: McGraw-Hill, 1967), pp. 148 (Plate 83), 184.

act was something that the woman seemed then to do herself. Accordingly, the ability to create new life was a mystical power associated with females. One indication of this is that it appears that most early societies were matrilineal.[3] In any society in which the male role in procreation was not understood, this practice would be a matter of necessity. People who did not fully recognize the existence of fathers could hardly trace descent through a male line.

A striking example of the difficulty of understanding the male role in pro-creation can be seen in an anthropologist's discussion of the topic with Australian aboriginal women in the first third of the twentieth century. The entire continent of Australia was without agriculture prior to the arrival of English colonists near the end of the eighteenth century of the Common Era (C.E., the equivalent of A.D.); thus, this land mass can serve as a most unusual window

"Out of Woman"
When procreation was seen as a female act, it was thought of as a natural process and this female power that males could not match was the source of male "womb envy." Here the Aztec Goddess Tlazolteotl, the "Mother of Gods" and goddess of childbirth, cre-ates in the natural way. (Dumberton Oaks Research Library, Washington, DC.)

through which to view how people without benefit of the seeming insights provided by the process of planting seeds may have viewed reproduction.* These Australian women believed that it was necessary for a man to "open a road" for the child, but that men played no other role in procreation. They refused to believe the actual part played by semen when they were told. One woman cited as conclusive proof that men have nothing to do with reproduction the fact that she had had a child several months after her husband's death. Another succinctly stated the reproductive philosophy of these aboriginal women (and, quite possibly, of most pre-agricultural people) by declaring: "Him nothing."[4]

Many people in modern societies are likely to laugh at, or at best look condescendingly at, the ignorance of such "primitive" people. They obviously had a great misconception about conception. Yet most "civilized" people throughout most of recorded history have accepted an equally erroneous view of conception. One of the most important consequences of the development of agriculture was to reverse the sort of misunderstanding expressed by the Australian women and replace it with the opposite misunderstanding.

The female-invented and female-oriented system of agriculture at length provided insecure men with a way to seize primacy by claiming for themselves the role in procreation (and, as we shall see in the next chapter, Creation) that had for so long ("always," insofar as the word has practical meaning for humans) been assigned to females. Thus what might be called Conception Misconception I, that females hold all the reproductive power, was inverted and replaced by its antithesis, the opposite and equally wrong Conception Misconception II, that males have all the reproductive power. No mistake has been more important than the latter in shaping the history of the sexes—or, consequently, history in many other areas. Because it is this second misconception about procreative power that has held sway throughout almost all of recorded history, it is for our purposes here *the* Conception Misconception, and I shall refer to it by that name

"Born Again"

The apparent lack of a major male role in the creation of new life had led men in much earlier times to devise ways in which they could play a part in the creation of new people—or at least of new *men*. Boys as well as girls are originally "of woman born," and most societies have allowed them to remain for several

---

*Of course the way one nonagricultural society viewed reproduction is not necessarily the same as others did, but this example at least demonstrates that some people who were not familiar with the process of planting seeds were unaware of the male role in procreation.

years in the woman's world into which they were first born. In collector-hunter cultures (and, in different ways, in agricultural societies, as well), however, around the time boys reach puberty the men of the group take them and place them in what is in effect a collective "male womb."[5] Initiation rites conducted by the adult males transform the boy into a man and amount to a second birth. What happens in the initiation rites varies from culture to culture, but as we have seen, they frequently involve activities such as genital bleeding or the Sambia feeding of "male milk" to the boys that are unmistakably based on envy of women. Through such rites the young male is "born again," but this time artificially, not naturally, and now he is "of man born."

Prior to agriculture's devaluing of other male roles, this sort of male creation—or re-creation—of new men was sufficient to provide men with a feeling of worth and accomplishment. But after the rise of early agriculture stripped them of other functions, men felt the need for something more.

The Conception Misconception

Revolutions in social and economic arrangements lead eventually but certainly to revolutions in scientific understanding. When people begin to *live* in the world in different ways, they are bound to come to *look* at the world in different ways.[6] This process parallels evolutionary biology. Certain ideas become acceptable as the social environment changes, much as certain organisms are better adapted for a changed natural environment. These revolutions in understanding always disturb the currently accepted religious beliefs. Such, we all know, was the case with the Copernican and Darwinian revolutions (both of which were stimulated by radical changes in the socioeconomic situation). What made Darwinism so unsettling in particular was that it dealt with the fundamental question of how we came to be—an essentially religious question.

Although it is not generally realized, a far earlier scientific revolution, dealing with much the same question, overturned the basic religious beliefs of early humans to an extent at least as great as the Darwinian revolution has upset religious beliefs in the past century-and-a-half.

At some point during the development of agriculture and animal husbandry, probably as a result of observation of kept animals,* people began more fully to perceive the male role in procreation—to comprehend that the sum of 1 plus 1 could sometimes be 3. (Stories told in historical times suggest

---

*The direct connection is easier to observe in animals that have an estrous cycle than in humans, since in these other species the ratio between mating and pregnancy is much closer to one-to-one.

that this recognition had occurred at a time recent enough to remain in the collective memory. The Athenians, for instance, credited an early king, Cecrops, with the discovery: "On account of him men first learned that they were begotten from two."[7]) Although this may seem like a simple enough matter, it eventually produced a scientific revolution with dramatic consequences in religion, society, and values. The magnitude of the revolution was increased because men, whose function as hunters had been devalued by the development of agriculture and who therefore felt a need for re-establishing their importance, had in their somewhat greater average proclivity for dualistic thinking, a ready means to invert their understanding of the roles of the sexes in reproduction.

This reversal did not happen quickly. Much as the knowledge that seeds produce plants appears to have existed for thousands of years before a whole new way of life based upon that understanding was instituted, knowledge of a greater male role in procreation probably existed for a long time before a whole new way of life based upon this (mis)understanding was instituted. The change probably did not happen until after the development of the plow produced a far greater surplus and completed the displacing of the old male role, which lends support to the thesis that the reversal was in substantial part caused by the male need to establish a new place in the drastically changed society.

One indication that the transition from female emphasis to male emphasis in procreation was underway, but was still a matter of contention, in the third millennium B.C.E. is the Sumerian Myth of Enki and Ninhursag. According to this story Ninhursag, who had once been seen as the great mother, the creator goddess, took the semen of the god Enki out of the womb of another goddess and placed it in the ground, where it grew and produced plants. Apparently seeking full creative power, Enki ate the plants and the power of the semen in them (his own) was so great that it made *him* pregnant. Because he had no womb in which to carry the offspring, Enki became ill and Ninhursag placed him inside her so that the "seeds" could develop and be born.[8]

Although the seeds have come to be seen as semen (a change with huge implications), in this third-millennium story they are still said to have been planted by a goddess. This rendering probably reflects agriculture having been originated by women. Enki is plainly making an attempt to seize procreative power (along with agriculture) for males, but at this early point he is not yet entirely successful. The Myth of Enki and Ninhursag says that the interaction of father and mother is necessary for procreation. But it is clear that the greater power has already shifted to the man—it is his semen that procreates. The woman seems necessary only to provide an environment in which that creative power can reach fruition.

The transition from female to male procreation continued during the later third and second millennia. In the Myth of Enki and Ninmah, a god and goddess have an argument over which of them is more important in procreation. Enki is partially successful in his attempt to create a being on his own. He releases semen, but he does not place it in a woman. The result is a horribly deformed and helpless creature. Enki realizes that the woman is still needed, but he has come close to achieving male-only creation. Enki says people should praise phallic power but should also remember the role of women in procreation. Yet a major power shift has occurred. The myth ends with the statement that the power of Enki was clearly greater than that of the goddess Ninmah.[9]

By the middle of the second millennium, women had come to be seen as little more than containers in which the child, wholly created by the male, had been deposited and grew to the point at which he or she could emerge into what could by now accurately be termed "the world of men." We have been living with the consequences of this world-shaking and world-shaping error—the Conception Misconception—ever since. Had dualism not misled people into thinking in an "if not A, then the opposite of A" manner—if instead the fact that elements from *both* parents are *blended* to create a new life had been understood and accepted—much of human history might have been markedly different than it has been.

But after it was comprehended that the male had something important to do with procreation, it was easy enough to reach, over a period of time for the transition, the conclusion that he had almost everything to do with it. His contribution, semen, was readily visible. But what did the woman contribute? Little more, it could be argued, than an environment in which the potential child, deposited by the man, could develop. The tiny human ovum was not discovered until William Harvey did so in the seventeenth century C.E., following the invention of the microscope.[10] The belief in male-only creation had become so deep-seated that the first scientists who examined sperm under a microscope "believed that they 'saw' the little man (*homunculus*) in the sperm."[11]

"My Vulva Is a Well-Watered Field"

The way in which the Agricultural Megarevolution led to this first revolution in scientific understanding was through a metaphor that was used as the basis of the new explanation. The transition from the misunderstanding of the reproductive process as being solely a female function to the misunderstanding of reproduction as a solely male function was enormously facilitated, if not totally caused, by the emergence of this virtually irresistible metaphor. Once it developed, the metaphor drove the misconception and assured its acceptance.

Those of us who write are very familiar with the problem of mangling metaphors; but the metaphor that emerged after the invention of agriculture mangled us, especially women, and it mangled all of subsequent history.

It seems likely that it was only after men themselves took over the task of planting seeds and began to place them in plowed furrows that the seed metaphor arose. The planting procedure seemed to be exactly analogous to the man "planting" semen in the "furrowed" vulva of the woman. (The power of this metaphor is evident in the fact that the Latin word *semen* means seed.) In an early second-millennium Mesopotamian literary composition entitled "Plow My Vulva," the goddess Inanna (Ishtar) sings: "My vulva is a well-watered field—who will plough it?" The all-too-eager response of Dumuzi, the king of Uruk, is: "Dumuzi will plough it for you."[12]

In *The Eumenides* (458 B.C.E.), Aeschylus made the complete male seizure of procreative power and the agricultural metaphor on which it was based explicit by placing in the mouth of Apollo the words used for this chapter's epigraph: "The mother is no parent of that which is called her child, but only nurse of the new-planted seed that grows. The parent is he who mounts. A stranger she preserves a stranger's seed."[13] Here is a complete reversal of the view of the pre-agricultural Australian woman quoted earlier. Through Apollo, Aeschylus is in effect saying: "*Her* nothing."

"I will show proof of what I have explained," Aeschylus' Apollo goes on. "There can be a father without any mother." He points to Athena, daughter of Zeus, who himself was the grandson of the original creator Earth Mother, Gaia. Zeus is said to have swallowed his wife to prevent her from creating a child and then to have given birth *himself* to Athena, who sprang full-grown from his head. Athena herself endorses this revolution in authority. "There is no mother anywhere who gave me birth," she declares.[14] A more powerful portrayal of the male taking of the creative force from the female would be difficult to imagine.*

Marilyn French has stated the logical progression of this thinking as follows: "Suddenly they [men] were aware that they were part of the process. It may have even seemed that they caused it, since no one could see the active physiological processes occurring within women's bodies. Men planted the seed: who knew that it took two seeds to make a baby? Women were indeed . . . like the earth—rich, fertile, but empty unless a seed took root in it."[15]

Images based on men planting seeds in women have been ubiquitous since the changes of the Agricultural Megarevolution took hold. Included in the

---

*It should be noted that these words are placed in Athena's mouth by a male playwright. *Genesis* and the rest of the stories that provide accounts of the great reversal were, of course, also written by men.

ancient Egyptian "Instruction of Ptahhotep" is the statement: "She is a fertile field for her lord."[16] In "The Hymn to Aten," written during the reign of the Egyptian pharaoh Akhenaten in the fourteenth century B.C.E., the Sun God is praised as "You who have placed seed in woman."[17] In Sophocles' *Antigone* (443 B.C.E.), Creon declares: "there are other fields [women] for him to plow."[18] "After her father had crammed her with his seed," wrote the Roman poet Ovid, "[h]er womb satisfied/With its prize:/A child conceived in evil."[19] Early in the second century C.E., Plutarch wrote in his *Life of Lycurgus* that it had been lawful in Sparta "for an honest man that loved another man's wife . . . to entreat her husband to suffer him to lie with her, and that he might also plough in that lusty ground, and cast abroad the seed of well favored children."[20] In the Koran, Allah tells His people (that is, men): "Women are like fields for you; so seed them as you intend" (or, as another translation puts the same lines: "Your women are your tilth, so come into your tillage how you choose").[21]

The seed metaphor is readily apparent in both Jewish and Christian writings as well. A few examples will suffice. The use of *seed* for offspring is ubiquitous in the Hebrew Bible. "And, behold, I establish my covenant with you, and with your seed after you," God says to Noah, and subsequently to Abram.[22] In chapter 38 of Genesis, God condemns Onan for "spilling seed" that He had commanded him to plant in Tamar.[23] In the laws of Leviticus, there is frequent use of the seed metaphor, for example: "If a woman have conceived seed, and born a man child . . . ,"[24] and specifically of the phrase "seed of copulation."[25] If a wife "puts out her hand and seizes him [a man who is beating her husband] by the private parts," the law in Deuteronomy declares, "then you shall cut off her hand; your eye shall have no pity."[26] A footnote in *The New Oxford Annotated Bible* explains that "this exceptionally severe law" stems from the belief that the male sexual organs are "the spring of fertility and should not be blemished."[27] In the New Testament, Paul refers several times to "the seed of Abraham."[28] The reference to "the fruit of thy womb" in the Catholic "Hail Mary" prayer can be taken as another example of the seed metaphor, although the idea of a virgin woman giving birth can, as we shall see in detail later, be seen as the ultimate undermining of the seed metaphor and implicitly a throwback to the earlier idea of female creation.

The echoes of the Conception Misconception's guiding metaphor reverberate in Thomas Aquinas's thirteenth-century *Summa Theologica,* in which he pronounced that an infant "receives its form only by means of the power which is contained in the father's seed."[29] "Among perfect animals," the leading Catholic theologian proclaimed, "the active power of generation belongs to the male sex, and the passive power to the female." "Woman is defective and misbegotten," Aquinas continued, "for the active power in the male seed tends to the production of a perfect likeness according to the masculine sex; while the production of woman comes from defect in the active power, or some material indisposition."[30]

Nor is the seed metaphor confined to the Western world. A woman in an isolated, polyandrous society in the Himalayas of Nepal, for example, made the following remark to an anthropologist in the 1980s: "I am like the field. I must be ready for all my husbands. They will care for me and I will bring them all a good harvest."[31]

Greek or Roman, Pagan, Jew, Muslim, Christian, or atheist, ancient, medieval, modern, contemporary—the same image is used in agricultural (and postagricultural) societies the world over. The seed metaphor appears to be something approaching a cultural universal—or, rather, an *agri*cultural universal. The metaphor is so powerful that it seems to have been accepted almost everywhere that plow agriculture developed. The analogy was readily adopted both because it seemed so obvious and persuasive and because it so well served the objectives of dis-placed men. This erroneous belief and the Conception Misconception it symbolizes provided males with some reassurance about their own importance in this critical area of human life and it served to bolster their claims of male supremacy.

That this extremely misleading metaphor is still with us can be seen often in popular culture. Consider, for example, a striking bit of dialogue in the 1983 movie *The Big Chill*. The Mary Kay Place character, Meg, declares: "I've been taking my temperature and I know I'm ovulating right now. The ground is ready; I just need someone to plant the seed." "Yeah, but who's going to be the lucky farmer?" Sarah (Glenn Close) responds.[32] Here, separated by nearly four thousand years and coming at a time when we have known for centuries about the reproductive significance of the ovulation to which the character refers, is an almost exact repetition of "Plow My Vulva," with all of the seed metaphor's erroneous implications about male-only procreation.

In an episode of the television comedy *Cheers* in the late 1980s, Lilith, a pregnant woman, said to her husband, Frasier: "I am the warm soil in which you planted your seed. Let's go and sleep nude on the roof and let the rain fall on this soil and its crop." And in the 1987 film *Raising Arizona,* the Nicolas Cage character refers to his wife's "barrenness" (a word used, significantly, interchangeably for unproductive soil and unproductive women) with these words: "The doctor explained that her insides were a rocky place where my seeds could find no purchase."[33]

And on it goes. After one has become cognizant of the significance of the seed metaphor and has attuned his or her ears to it, hardly a day passes when it is not heard somewhere, often from people who would presumably be taken aback if they were aware of the implications of the figure of speech they so casually employ. In the course of normal reading in the period of a few weeks in mid-1999, I ran across—without looking for them—the following examples: social and political critic Barbara Ehrenreich, writing in *Harper's Magazine:* "A human male has never known for sure whether he's planting a seed in fertile ground"[34]; Margaret Talbot writing in *The New Republic,* criticizing the favorite argument of evolutionary psychologists, which she says is: "Men always have been, and always will be, . . . helplessly programmed to spread their seed far and wide"[35]; and anthropologist Helen Fisher, writing in her book *The First Sex,* referring several times to the efforts of men to "spread their seed."[36] All three of these writers are feminists. That even they do not realize the large role the metaphor they so casually and reflexively used has played in leading women to be treated as "the second sex" shows just how deeply ingrained in our consciousness it is.

Just what is the significance of this gross scientific error? The Conception Misconception and seed metaphor transformed man from little more than a bystander into the godlike creator of life and woman from the goddesslike creator into, well, *dirt*—that, after all, is what seeds are planted in.

Of course goddesses had long been associated with the earth and its life-giving powers but that "prehistoric" association had carried with it very different implications. Then the soil itself—*her*self—had been seen as having creative power. "Then *of her own accord the earth produced / A store of every fruit,*" Ovid wrote of the Golden Age before the discovery of agriculture, "And warmly cherished buds and blooms, produced / *Without a seed.*"[37] But the Conception Misconception transferred the creative powers from the soil to the seed/semen and the earth/woman was reduced to merely an environment in which it could grow. It is fascinating that this view of the female role is very similar to the Australian aboriginal women's image of the man's contribution. They contended that the semen left in the uterus after copulation serves as a sea on which the embryo floats "like a waterlily."[38]

In Genesis the soil has no creative power. Here, unlike in Ovid's Golden Age, Mother Earth produces nothing of her own accord. "She" is lifeless until a male (God) begins to dispense the life force—to plant seeds: "The Lord God *planted* a garden in Eden."[39] The earth or soil is merely the medium *in which* the male God causes life to grow: "And *out of the ground the Lord God made to grow* every tree. . . ."[40] And the earth or soil is the *material* out of which this male deity forms a being to whom *He* gives life: "[W]hen no plant of the field was yet in the earth and no herb of the field had yet sprung up . . . then the Lord God formed man *out of dust from the ground,* and breathed into his nostrils the breath of life; and man became a living being."[41]

The chorus in *The Eumenides,* representing the displaced goddesses and the whole concept of female creation, suggests just this result of the seed-planting argument by complaining: "That they could treat me so! I, the mind of the past, to be driven under the ground, out cast, like dirt!"[42]

"The Woman's Art"

Now that we have seen the meaning and power of the seed metaphor, let's return briefly to two of the ancient myths that I have contended are allegories for women inventing agriculture. The understanding of how the seed metaphor links agriculture and sexual intercourse opens up the way to deeper analysis of these stories.

As we saw in Chapter 4, both *The Epic of Gilgamesh* and the story of Adam and Eve in Genesis depict a woman imparting knowledge to a man and thus causing him to lose forever his natural paradise. An understanding of the seed metaphor adds another layer of support to the interpretation of the knowledge women conveyed to men as the way intentionally to produce food.

In both *Gilgamesh* and Genesis, the woman entices the man. In the former case it is made explicit that she is having sexual intercourse with him. This is not clearly stated in Genesis, but Eve's sharing of the fruit with Adam has often been interpreted as symbolic of introducing him to sexual relations (in part because it is at the moment that they eat the fruit that "the eyes of both were opened, and they knew that they were naked"[43]).

The seed metaphor thus brings together in these stories two interpretations: a woman teaching a man how to have intercourse with her becomes a perfect symbol for women teaching men how to plant crops in the ground. Both are seductions by woman, the temptress. This alters what Eve said to Adam to something like this: *You see, if you plant your seed in me* (*or the earth*), *you can control the production of new living things. Go ahead, try it! You'll like it!*

Control over reproduction—the creation of new life—whether new human life through "planting seeds" in women or new plant life through planting seeds in the ground, meant, as the serpent told Eve, that people "will be like God." And, as we have seen, it seems likely that it was women's invention of agriculture that had led to men learning that they could claim power over both types of reproduction.

So the common view that "the woman's art" or the knowledge that the women teach to Enkidu and Adam is sexual intercourse turns out not to be a competing interpretation to the one I am offering. It is actually completely compatible with seeing that knowledge as how to control the reproduction of new crops. The Genesis version is especially intricate and ingenious and so has been extremely difficult to unravel (particularly without the aid of the recently developed belief that women taught men how to grow plants for food). It is a metaphor wrapped within another metaphor. Eve's offering of the fruit to Adam *is* a metaphor for sexual intercourse. But sexual intercourse is, in turn, a metaphor for seed planting. Further complicating matters, the latter is a bidirectional metaphor: as seed planting had become a virtually universally understood image for intercourse, it was reasonable to reverse the symbolism and use intercourse as a metaphor for seed planting or agriculture. This, I believe, is the method used in telling the story in Genesis 3.

"Taken Out of Man"

The Conception Misconception and seed metaphor and the confusions that followed from them enabled men to stand womb envy on its head: *Sure, new life grows in you, but we create it; we are the sex with the power!* The reversal was given its most influential religious sanction in the Bible.

"Out of Man"
According to the second chapter of Genesis, the first birth of one human from another was completely different from any other that has ever occurred. Yahweh performed a Caesarian section on the Virgin Adam and a female was born of a male. This mythical event was so extraordinary that it resulted in women forever after being called by a name that means "out of man," although no other woman—or man—has ever been taken out of anyone other than a woman. (Michelangelo, *The Birth of Eve*, Sistine Ceiling, 1511. Sistine Chapel, Vatican City)

The stunning revolution in thought is most emphatically depicted in the Bible in the second chapter of Genesis. This representation of the reversal is well known to most of us, but not recognized as such. God places Adam—the *Virgin Adam,* it is worth mentioning—under anesthesia and performs a Caesarean section on him, pulling Eve out of his body: "So the Lord God caused a deep sleep to fall upon the man and while he slept took one of his ribs and closed up its place with flesh; and the rib which the Lord God had taken from the man he made into a woman and brought her to the man."[44] This, obviously, is not the way it happens in nature, but it perfectly symbolizes the new idea of male creation. It is a clear example of womb envy, because it asserts, in effect, that the first human "womb" was male. The Genesis account goes on to say that Eve "shall be called Woman [*ishshah*], because she was taken out of man [*ish*]."[45] Here we see just how pervasive are the effects of the mistaken belief that males do the creating: The very terms we use to designate women are derived from the literally incredible idea that woman was "taken out of man," when the obvious reality is that every man or woman who has ever existed was "taken out of woman." Paul later noted this discrepancy and tried—without much success—to account for it when he wrote to the Christians at Corinth: "as woman was made from man, so man is now born of woman."[46]

When the derivation and implications of the word *woman* are understood, it becomes apparent that, as a result of the Conception Misconception, the names we use for males and females are reversed. Since males are actually taken out of females, it would be more accurate to designate a female by a name, such as *man,* and then to call a male by a derivative of that term, such as *woman.*

Women as Real Estate

Men in pre-agricultural societies did, of course, find it desirable to "have" women, and one of the primary advantages of gaining ascendance among men in the group was the potential for mating with several women. In some cases men apparently offered women as "gifts" to secure friendship with other groups.[47] (A remarkable vestige of this practice survives to the present, in the outrageous but usually unconsidered custom of the father "giving away" the bride.) And because they were the source of reproduction, women were plainly valuable. While reproduction was essential, however, it was through most of human existence easy to get too much of a good thing, as there was a limit to how many people the collector-hunter way of life could support.

Under agriculture, with its creation of surplus and its need for more labor, women continued to produce the same "product" that they always had: children. But gradually a woman came to be seen as something besides a wondrous producer of life: she became a substantial asset to those who could "claim" her, because what she produced had become an unmixed advantage.

Birth control has always been a central determinant of women's lives. From the time of the development of agriculture into the twentieth century, *birth* was the subject, *control* the verb, and *woman* the object. *Birth controlled women,* because in the *r*-selected reproductive environment into which agriculture placed humans, women were obliged to devote most of their lives to giving birth and caring for children. In the twentieth century and beyond, as we have moved back into a *K*-selected reproductive situation, *birth control* has taken on a very different meaning. *Woman* is now the subject, *control* still the verb, and *birth* the object. *Women control birth,* a reversal that is a major part of actually transforming women from objects into subjects in the sense of people with options for a variety of actions.

Agriculture brought with it an economics of surplus, which in turn increased the incentive for holding certain types of property that could help to produce surplus goods, notably land and laborers. Most important of all, though, would finally be the only "resource" that could produce new laborers: women. They ultimately came to be seen as the equivalent of the machine tools of an industrial economy: capital goods that made other capital goods.*

As the development of agriculture led to the concept of land ownership, land became more than *a* form of property; it became the most important form, because it was *productive* property. This is why land came to be called *"real* estate," or "real property." As contrasted to personal possessions, land was real property because it was what was used to produce other things that people wanted. But agriculture had also made another form of "property" highly valuable to men. Although women were, so far as I am aware, never called by such a name, they too came often to be treated as *real* estate. The seed metaphor greatly facilitated the process by which women were equated

---

*A reflection of this view could be seen in the United States as late as the mid-nineteenth century. Slave women commanded higher prices than slave men because they performed this function of producing new productive "property." Nor had the idea vanished in the late twentieth century. At the infamous convention of the Tailhook Association in 1991, naval officers were seen wearing T-shirts reading "Women Are Property" [Anna Quindlen, "What About the Boys?" New York Times, May 2, 1993, p. E19]. And in many areas of the world today, women are explicitly treated as property. Just a couple of examples that were reported in the news media in 1999: A Guatemalan woman who was being tortured by her husband was informed that she was "his property and he could do what he liked [with her]," words echoed by the Guatemalan police when she sought protection." The position of the government was that it could not do anything to protect a wife from her husband, since he owned her. In Congo, similarly, women who were abused by their husbands could obtain no assistance from the government, because it is considered "a matter of *his authority.*" [Barbard Bradley, "Immigration's Asylum Ruling," "Morning Edition," National Public Radio, July 8, 1999, http://search.npr.org/cf/cmn/cmnpd01fm.cfm?PrgDate=07/8/1999&PrgID=3].

with land and became real estate. Young, fertile women, like rich land, now produced—no, under the Conception Misconception, they were seen, like soil, as being *used by men to produce*—something of value; in their case, future workers.

This new incentive for holding productive women existed even if the male role in procreation was not fully understood, because new workers were valuable to a man regardless of whether he believed that he had helped to create them. But as the male part in reproduction was perceived, men found additional reasons for wanting to control and subordinate women. Assuring that a woman had sexual relations exclusively with him was the only way a man could be certain that her children were also his. The sort of "prehistoric" complete sexual freedom for girls and women envisioned by some feminists, partly on the basis of mistaken information in Margaret Mead's *Coming of Age in Samoa*,[48] does not appear likely to have existed anywhere.[49] It does, however, seem likely that women's sexuality would have been less strictly controlled by men in the times before the male role in reproduction was fully understood.

As agriculture created conditions under which they were called upon to be pregnant and caring for children for most of their lives and so no longer much involved in food production, women became much more economically dependent on those who did produce the food, men. Women had, of course, always needed (or at least greatly benefitted from) assistance from a mate in raising children. But this need increased into much greater dependence when most women ceased to produce much food. At the risk of oversimplifying, this change in circumstance can be summarized as follows: Women in collector-hunter bands needed men as protectors and co-providers; in agricultural societies, women needed both protection and nearly full provision.

Women's increasing dependence appears to have come about during approximately the same time period when men were coming to understand their role in reproduction (and soon greatly to exaggerate that role). Thus, after agriculture was well established, a man would have two incentives for placing greater restrictions on "his" woman's sexual activity: to assure himself that her offspring were really his and to have more children to become workers on his land. Men's and women's altered roles meant that women were more than ever before placed in a position where they would be obliged "to exchange their sexual freedom for protection and provisioning from men."[50]

The Farmers Become the Farms

An ironic outgrowth of women's invention of farming, then, was that they came to be seen as farms—privately-owned productive real estate—themselves. As a result of the development of agriculture, the long-standing functions of men had become redundant. They had, as a common expression refers to such outdated things, "gone to seed." Among their responses was to "go to seed" in another sense: to assert that *they* produce the seed that creates new life. We now know, of course, that this analogy is wrong. Semen is not a seed; it is the equivalent of *half* of a seed. Neither a sperm nor an ovum gives life; rather, each provides a "half-life." Yet we continue to act in many ways on the basis of the erroneous seed metaphor.

What has formed the unspoken but pervasive basis of male authority throughout history? The mistaken idea that men are the "authors"—the creators. (Note that the root of the word *authority* is *author*.) A clear example of such misappropriated "authority" is the *patria potestas* that gave an ancient Roman man the power to "dispose of" his children. A father was thought to be the creator of "his" children and so he was granted the right to take away the life he was supposed to have given. Referring, as we still do, to highly original, productive ideas as *seminal* is yet another reflection of the mistaken belief that semen is *the* source of creation.

Prior to the Agricultural Megarevolution, women both did the work of procreation and got the credit for it. The Conception Misconception and its seed metaphor enabled men to leave women with all the work of reproduction while men took the credit for it. It's nice nonwork, if you can get it. And, throughout recorded history, men have been able to get it anytime.

The sort of thinking that resulted from the Conception Misconception was perfectly captured in a letter to the editor I saw in 1999. A man was reacting to a statement columnist Deborah Mathis had made that "the world is their [men's] oyster and pretty much always has been." "I could not agree more," the man wrote. "We deserve it. We made it all happen."[51]

The seed metaphor is the big poisonous weed that grew in the midst of the sustaining crops after women invented agriculture. Although attempts have been made from time to time to control its effects, this weed has never been pulled up roots and all. Until a complete extraction is accomplished, the weedy seed metaphor will continually sprout up in many areas of our lives, causing untold problems.

CHAPTER 7

"All Power and Glory Are Yours, Almighty Father"

Male Monotheism and Its Consequences

> He [a man] is the image and Glory of God;
> but woman is the glory of man. (For man was not made
> from woman, but woman from man. . . .)
>
> ST. PAUL[1]

By the third millennium B.C.E., men had succeeded in transforming the no-man's land produced by the New World of agriculture women had discovered into a man's world. The result, which is very much still with us four thousand years later, is well summarized in the concluding acclamation of the Catholic Eucharistic prayer:

All power and glory
Are yours, Almighty Father
Forever and ever.

Of course the "Almighty Father" referred to in that prayer is God, and this points to the connection between the Conception Misconception and the most consequential alteration in the history of religion.

For all the ill effects that the Conception Misconception produced, certainly the greatest harm flowing from it was that it led, virtually inevitably, to the assumption that *The* Creative Force—God—must also be male. That, in turn, particularly when combined with the belief that people are created in the image of God (for example, "Then God said, let us make man in our image, after our likeness"[2]), again almost necessarily, induced the conclusion that men are closer than women to godly perfection. Human history for thousands of years has been profoundly shaped by these mistaken impressions. Their impact continues to hold sway over us at the beginning of the third millennium C.E.

Paleolithic Religion

The mystery of the origins of new life probably provided the basis for early religious belief. If women created new human life, it would seem to follow

What Does God Look Like? A Woman
To Paleolithic collector-hunters, the logical conclusion was that, since creative power is something that female humans and animals possess, the Creative Force(s) in the universe must also be female. The numerous female figurines that have been discovered from this time *may* be representations of goddesses with creative power. (The "Venus" of Willendorf, ca. 25,000–23,000 B.C.E. (Naturhistorisches Museum, Vienna) (Corbis)

that *the* Creative Force that made the world—that which most societies during most of recorded history have thought of in male terms and which we now call God—was also female.

Much has been written in recent years about a prehistoric religion based on worship of an all-powerful Mother Goddess.[3] This contention has met strong resistance because it runs counter to assumptions that have been deeply ingrained for thousands of years—and because the conclusions of many of those who have claimed that there was a unified, widespread, monotheistic religion centered on a Mother Goddess in Paleolithic Europe have been based on copious quantities of wishful thinking leavened with a few dashes of uncertain evidence. In fact, one group of feminist anthropologists has followed a course similar to that of some sociobiologists and evolutionary psychologists: they start with a conclusion they want to believe and grasp at any "evidence" that seems to support that conclusion. The idea that the "original" human religion worshiped a Mother Goddess is as beguiling to some feminists as the ideas that men are naturally philanderers and that beautiful, nubile young women are biologically attracted to older, well-to-do men is to some older, well-to-do men. In truth, there simply is not sufficient credible evidence of a widespread religion based on the worship of a singular Goddess.

But, as is so often the case, rejecting one extreme argument does not mean that its opposite is true. The fact that some sociobiologists and evolutionary psychologists have leaped to conclusions they wanted to reach based on insufficient evidence does not mean that biology has no influence on human behavior and history; similarly, we can reject the wilder claims of the Mother Goddess faithful without denying that female deities with creative power played significant parts in the religious beliefs of many "prehistoric" cultures.

There is substantial reason to believe, as was discussed in preceding chapters, that women in many societies prior to the invention of agriculture enjoyed a greater degree of equality than have women through almost all of recorded history. It is also undeniable that powerful goddesses were worshiped (along with male gods) before the rise of male monotheism. The reasons for this practice are apparent. Women played very important roles in collector-hunter societies: producing children and collecting a large portion of the food needed to sustain the group. Because the male role in reproduction was not understood, procreation seemed to be a mystical power held by females. It would generally follow from the belief that females have procreative power that the highest creative power—the deity ultimately responsible for creation of the world—must also be female. Such views seem to be most common among collector-hunter cultures that have survived into modern times.

But such beliefs are not universal in extant societies that have not developed agriculture. These cultures differ greatly in their views of divinity, the relative positions of men and women, and creative power. As might be

expected, there is, as anthropologist Peggy Sanday has shown, a strong correlation between relative sexual equality in a society and the attribution of creation to female or combined female-male deities, while a high degree of male
dominance correlates directly with a belief in male creators. Cause and effect
in these correlations is not clear.[4]

There is, then, reason to think that many, but not all, early human religions,
while polytheistic, saw the ultimate creative deity or force as female. It is far
more plausible that people who associated procreative power with females
would conclude that the primal Creative Force was also female than that they
would think it male. There would have been no basis for the latter conclusion.

The strongest physical evidence of female-centered religions is the numerous Upper Paleolithic and Neolithic sculptures of female figures with
enlarged maternal attributes that have been found over wide areas of Europe
and Asia. (Similar depictions of females have been found at Paleolithic sites
in Africa and the Americas.[5]) Representations of the female form as Giver of
Life date back to at least 30,000 B.C.E., first as engravings of vulva and then,
by about 25,000 B.C.E., as full figures.[6] The latter "venuses," as they have usually but misleadingly been called, appear to have been something more than
the fertility symbols they have most often been classified as. Nor were they
the pornography of dirty *very* old men—"the characteristic products of unre-
generated male imagination," as one observer characterized them.[7] There are
a variety of possible explanations of these figurines, including that they might
have been used in sympathetic magic to bring about pregnancy, as models to
explain pregnancy to girls as they came of age, and that they were simply dolls
used as toys.[8] But if we can put aside our long-held assumption that the Creator is a male God, we can see the strong possibility that these statues were
representations of a creative deity as *she* was assumed to be by people in a
variety of collector-hunter societies for many thousands of years.

"Strong possibility" is as far as the "venus" figurines can take us, though.
Imagine what a future archeologist of the sixth millennium C.E. might conclude about Christianity if all she or he had to go on were several digs at the
sites of second-millennium Catholic cathedrals. Ornate rose windows honoring a female figure and below the window a dead man hanging from a cross to
which he had been nailed: *Obviously a matriarchal society that worshiped the
female deity depicted on the rose window and held men in such low regard that
the women literally crucified them . . .*

If we do accept the figurines as powerful female deities or creative forces,
that is certainly not to say that they represented a single Mother Goddess in a
monotheistic religion. It seems more likely that Paleolithic religion would
have centered on multiple spirits and forces,[9] but that those which were seen
as ultimately creative would have been represented as female.

It may also be significant that Paleolithic religious ceremonies appear often to have taken place in caves. This practice is open to many interpretations, the most common one being that difficult and perhaps frightening places deep in caves were used for male initiation rites. But another possibility is that, as womblike openings in the earth, caves were seen as appropriate places for worship of a life-giving goddess who was often associated with the earth. That association was presumably the basis for believing that life which was seen as emanating from the Earth Mother should be returned to Her at death, perhaps to be reborn. A surviving element of this extremely ancient Earth Goddess religion (by way of the distorting mirror of the Genesis story of man being created from dust or clay) is the "from earth to earth" line that is still used in many funeral rites.

Initially, the development of agriculture seems only to have enhanced the worship of a female deity or deities. If women invented agriculture and remained its primary practitioners in the early period of its systematic application, the cause for seeing a female as the major, creative deity would have become even greater in this period than it had been in earlier eras. This development is reflected in the previously discussed displacement of shrines for hunting gods by one to a goddess in Çatal Hüyük in the sixth millennium B.C.E.[10]*

Male Gods Seize Creative Power

There has been much less variety in views of the relative position of the sexes and in beliefs about procreative power and the sex of Creative deities in societies that have fully developed agriculture than there was and is among collector-hunters and early horticultural societies.

The two basic causes of this consistency in outlook are those discussed in the preceding chapters. First, the changes that agriculture produces have been similar everywhere it has arisen: it has greatly decreased the value of hunting, which had been the principal male activity, and it has made possible and desirable a significant increase in population, thereby escalating the demand on women to devote their lives almost entirely to bearing and raising children. Male dominance directed agricultural societies toward a belief in male creative deities, which in turn reinforced male dominance. Second, agriculture had provided a metaphor for procreative power that was so obvious and powerful that it was virtually irresistible. The common acceptance of this metaphor pointed agricultural societies toward similar conclusions about the sexes and about procreative and Creative power.

---

*See Chapter 5.

If many of the original religious beliefs were based upon the mistaken belief that procreation was accomplished primarily by females, the new (mis)understanding of reproduction had to lead to a new religious outlook. Male storm or thunder gods displaced the goddesses as the creative force, the source of life.[11] These gods clearly represented male power and the violence that was becoming so common among men, and they bore such names as Adad, Ramman, Thor, Rudra (Shiva), Yahweh, and Zeus (or Jupiter).

Signs of this reversal abound in ancient religions. In a careful, scholarly study of the role of goddesses in Mesopotamian religion, Tikva Frymer-Kensky found that a process of diminution of the powers of goddesses was already underway when the written record begins. The direction of takeover by gods of what had once been powers ascribed to goddesses occurred over a period of at least two thousand years. There are repeated "intimations that they [goddesses] had once been more prominent than they are in the classic Sumerian period [in the third millennium]."[12] These findings add major support to the belief that, at least in Mesopotamia and surrounding areas, female creative powers had held primacy in an earlier, "prehistoric" time but were slowly being supplanted by male gods after the full development of plow agriculture.

The process of gods displacing goddesses as the Creative Force had neared completion in some places by the second millennium. In the Babylonian creation epic *Enuma Elish,* written down around 1100 B.C.E. but reflecting changed religious views dating back at least five hundred years before that, the male god Marduk violently overthrows the primordial mother goddess, Tiamat, "she who gave birth to all." To establish his supremacy as king of the gods, Marduk "shot the arrow that split the belly, that pierced the gut and cut the womb [of Tiamat]. . . . [H]e straddled the legs and smashed her skull (for the mace was merciless), he severed the arteries and the blood streamed down the north wind to the unknown ends of the world."[13]

This reads like a scene from a David Lynch film. Little doubt is left as to who is in charge—or as to the apparent efficacy of brutality. By cutting Tiamat's womb, Marduk destroys her natural creative power. In essence, he "castrates" Tiamat, as this myth does to women in general. The idea of castrating a woman seems so odd to us today, and we have no word to denote it—facts that reflect the complete triumph of the Conception Misconception. It is not possible to take away from someone a power she is believed never to have had. But the story of Marduk and Tiamat is not an isolated instance in the ancient world. There are, as we shall see later in this chapter and the next, several similar stories of "female castration" in the mythology of ancient civilizations.

Marduk then "gazed at the huge body, pondering how to use it, what to create from the dead carcass. He split it apart like a cockle-shell."[14] He proceeds to make the heavens and the earth out of the two halves of the slain goddess's body. The Creative mother has been reduced to a "monster"; creation is now a male function, and it is seen as an "artful work" rather than a natural process. "We live in the body of the mother, but she has neither activity nor power," as Frymer-Kensky puts it.[15]

It is also significant that a male god is now said to create from dead matter. The earth is no longer a living, powerful, life-giving Mother. Rather, all the life is seen, in reflection of the Conception Misconception, as flowing from the all-powerful male. As theologian Rosemary Radford Ruether has pointed out, "dead matter, fashioned into artifacts, makes the cosmos the private possession of its 'creators.' "[16]

The revolution in creative power and consequent diminution of the social position of women is also apparent in other ancient religious traditions. In one Egyptian version of creation, for example, the male Sun God, Ra, says: "I conceived in my own heart . . . I it was who aroused desire with my fist; I masturbated with my hand, and I spat it out from my own mouth."[17] Creation by self-arousal and masturbation seemingly leaves no role whatsoever for a female deity, although the word for *hand* is feminine and may be seen as a kind of vestigial female, making this version of creation an intermediate one between female and male types but far along the spectrum toward the latter end.[18]

As in other locales, in Egypt the new, male version did not win out easily, quickly, or completely. Throughout the history of ancient Egypt, the creator goddess in the form of Isis held a major place. Although Isis came to be described as the daughter of Ra, She was also known as "Oldest of the old," "the goddess from whom all Becoming arose," "the Great Virgin," "the Great Isis, Mother of God," and "the Great Mother of all Nature."[19] These titles suggest that Isis had been seen as *the* Creator in "prehistoric" times (and still was by many of her devotees well into the era of writing). The powers that Egyptians believed Isis had to resurrect the dead were probably a carryover of her original life-giving creative powers.

In Greek mythology, in addition to the story of Zeus giving birth to Athena, creative goddesses are replaced by Aphrodite (Venus),* no longer a creator, but merely the goddess of love. Aphrodite means "Foamborn," which derives from the fact that, far from being the Creator, she is herself the creature of what is now seen as the source of life, semen (foam). Hesiod related that Aphrodite was born from the semen of the severed testicles of Ouranos, which his son Kronos threw into the sea after castrating his father.[20]† The procreation inversion is further evidenced when it is noticed that, because Aphrodite was

---

*A similar transformation had occurred earlier in Mesopotamia. There the remaining important goddess after the other, creative ones had been eclipsed was Inanna, or Ishtar, who like Venus was said to be the morning or evening star. She becomes a goddess of love (and war).

†It may also be that the sickle used in this deed symbolizes agriculture, which "castrated" men by devaluing their formerly useful occupations.

A Male-Made Goddess
Unlike earlier goddesses who had been seen as possessing creative power, Aphrodite (later the Roman Venus) was only the goddess of love. The stripping of creative power from females is indicated by the story of Aphrodite's creation. Her Greek name means "Foamborn," because she was said to have been created from the foamy semen of Ouranos' castrated testicles floating on the sea. This is one of many mythical accounts that arose after the establishment of agriculture in which creative power is said to belong entirely to males. (*Birth of Aphrodite,* from the *Ludovisi Throne,* early fifth century B.C.E. Museo Nazionale Romano, Rome)

born from semen (i.e., "seed") floating on water, she has no mother and is the result of creation from semen alone. [Another name for her is Philommedea "because," Hesiod says, "she appeared from *medea* (members)."[21]] Indeed, Aphrodite's birth does not even involve the earth (mother). She is *entirely* man- (or male-god-) made—even more so than Athena, because Zeus had had to swallow a female goddess to perform his creative feat.

In India the violent storm god called Rudra in the *Rig Veda,* but later known as Shiva, who takes precedence over the creator goddess (who persists as his wife, Shakti), is frequently depicted in a carving made in a stone phallus. This symbolism is at least as clear as that of the foam that creates Aphrodite. Shiva comes to be identified with both destruction and reproduction, thus representing two of the major outcomes of the megarevolution that began with the invention of agriculture and breeding. As a god of destruction, Shiva stands for the new level of violence and warfare resulting from agricultural surplus and the formation of states; as a god of reproduction, he embodies the erroneous scientific revolution that held males to be the creators.*

The same displacement can be seen in the Bible, although it requires a more careful look. Not only is it a male deity who creates "the heavens and the earth," but He also creates all forms of life, including humanity. The very name of the Hebrew God indicates the switch in views of the sex with creative power. One way to translate *Yahweh* is: "*He* who causes to be."[22] "The Lord God" is said to have "formed man of *dust from the ground,*" which can be read in the light of the all-conquering agricultural metaphor as "woman." But, as we have seen in the preceding chapter, the life-giving power is clearly and exclusively that of the male God, who "breathed into his [the man's] nostrils the breath of life; and man became a living being."[23] Humanity (*'adham*) is formed *from* the ground (*'adhamah*), but is given life *by* the male God. As in the *Enuma Elish,* the male God is creating life from lifeless matter, which, as dust or clay, refers to a Mother Earth now thought to be lifeless, not life-giving: without generative power: *Let earth receive her king.*

The chief difference from the story in the *Enuma Elish* is that in the Bible we are given no account of the male God having slain the earth mother, as Marduk did to Tiamat. Mother Earth is already dead when we come in on the story in the Bible. The violent slaying has occurred offstage before the opening scene and, because the playwrights were on the side of the male God, the crime is not mentioned. If the *Enuma Elish* is the R-rated David Lynch version, Genesis 1 is the G-rated Disney adaptation of the artful-male-god-seizes-creative-power-from-earth-goddess story, much as the fruit sharing in Genesis 3 is the G-rated symbolism for sexual seduction (and agriculture) that is shown in a PG-13 cut in *Gilgamesh.*

Yahweh is unmistakably another example of a thunder god replacing a creative goddess. He is sometimes explicitly referred to as *El Shaddai,* meaning "God, the One of the Mountains," or "Storm God" (usually rendered into English as "God Almighty"). And when Moses brought the people to meet God at Mount Sinai before receiving the Ten Commandments, we are told, "there were thunders and lightnings," and "God answered him in thunder."[24]

Then there is the curse on the serpent. The snake is portrayed, even more than the woman, as the first cause of the Fall. Given the long association of

---

*It is significant, however, that in some parts of southern India, Shiva was seen as androgynous. I shall have more to say about hermaphroditic deities later.

snakes with goddesses,* when Yahweh says to the serpent, "Because you have done this, cursed are you above all cattle, and above all wild animals," He is displacing the female deity and asserting His supremacy over her.[25]

Masculinist Oldspeak

Another example of the emerging idea of male primacy is the order of creation in the second chapter of Genesis, which completely contradicts that given in the first chapter. In chapter 1, God creates man and woman simultaneously and presumably as equals, after all other forms of life, on the sixth day. But in Genesis 2, God creates man on the *first* day: "In the day that the Lord God made the earth and the heavens . . . the Lord God formed man . . ."[26] Then, after man, God creates plants and "*out of the ground* the Lord God formed every beast of the field and every bird of the air."[27] [Notice again that, as in His creation of man, God uses the lifeless (Mother) earth or soil as the matter from which He creates life.] The last of all living things to be made, according to the Genesis 2 account, was woman, widely separated chronologically from the creation of man. If the order of creation outlined in the first chapter of Genesis is progressive, ascending, even evolutionary, with male *and* female humans at the apex, that given in the second chapter seems to be descending, with man as the supreme creation at the beginning and woman as the lowest of living things at the end.

One thing that heaven has in common with hell, it would seem, is that it hath no fury like a man devalued.

"Heaven's" fury continues to be exhibited when the male God gives man the power to name woman, as he has all the animals. This is another crystal-clear assertion being made by the men who were the authors of Genesis that men are to be considered vastly superior to women and to have dominion over them. Women are, in this sense, being placed in the same category with animals: subordinate creatures to be named by their master, man. And remember that the name the man chooses for the female animal of his species, *woman,* means "out of man."

Some today complain of "feminist Newspeak," such as unisex terms for God and supplanting the suffix -*man* with -*person*. They have cause to worry. Language is power. The best evidence for this is something these critics fail to realize: the male terms for God—and the very word *woman*—were part of what at a much earlier time could have been castigated as "masculinist Newspeak." The adoption of this now very Oldspeak was a central part of the

---

*As I pointed out in Chapter 4, the reason that snakes were associated with goddesses is thought to be that their shedding of skin seemed analogous to menstruation.

triumph of the late Neolithic/Bronze Age masculinist movement. Saying something does not make it so; but saying it often enough, for a long enough time, and with "authority" can make it *seem* to be so and be accepted as so. And this can have immense effects. The early revolution in worldview and the language that accompanied it have influenced us mightily throughout recorded history.

Man's Dominion over (Mother) Nature

The triumph of the male God was not only over the creative goddesses, but also over nature. Creative goddesses had always been associated with nature and natural processes. They had generally been seen as operating through nature, not dominating it from the outside (or "above"). That the *Enuma Elish* characterizes Marduk's creation as "artful work" hints at another major change in worldview that was part of the megarevolution begun by the invention of agriculture.

Women have usually been seen to create naturally; when men attempt to equal them through creations of their own, they must do so through artificial means. It was women who began to gain some control over nature by developing agriculture*, but it was only after this new system had dislodged men from their traditional (and natural) occupations and men had "masculinized" farming that a different outlook on the relationship between nature and humanity started to emerge.

When men took over the "woman's work" of growing plants, they did the best they could to transform the occupation into something that seemed to be appropriate for "masculine" approaches. Plants might have to be nurtured, but if nature could be viewed as something to be conquered, controlled, and dominated, men could see farming as a more appropriate occupation for them.

Previously, humans had seen themselves (as they still see themselves in collector-hunter and most horticultural societies) as in and of nature. Now men began to see themselves as over nature, dominating and ruling it (her) and women—and commanding the (re)productive capacities of both. And the male God was now said to have created Nature (which translates to having precedence over any goddess, as in Ra coming to be seen as the father of Isis).

The placement of a male God and men above nature is made explicit in the first chapter of Genesis. Yahweh creates by His word—His will ("And God

---

*Interestingly in light of the usual association of women with nature and men with culture, women probably began many of the early cultural innovations, the use of human intervention to alter the natural environment for human benefit: the making of slings in which infants could be carried, the cooking of food, the making of clothing, spinning and weaving, and agriculture.

said, . . . And it was so.")." He commands the earth (which can be read as "the late Earth Mother") to bring forth vegetation and living creatures. Then *He* directly creates man "in our image"—a phrase of monumental importance in shaping our history—and commands him to "subdue" the earth and "have dominion over the fish of the sea and over the birds of the air, and over every living thing that moves upon the earth."[28]*

The same contrast in outlooks toward nature—and its connection with the introduction of the plow—can be seen in much more recent times in the Western Hemisphere. At the time of their contact with Europeans, many of the indigenous peoples of North America still saw the earth as their mother, who became pregnant and gave birth to new life each spring. To people with such religious views, plowing the earth would be like raping their mother—or their goddess. "You ask me to plow the ground!" exclaimed a horrified Chief Smohalla of the Wanapun to white men. "Shall I take a knife and tear my mother's bosom?"[29] Once they had taken the fateful step of tearing the body of Mother Earth, men necessarily began to take a different view of their relationship with nature. No longer did "She" produce new life by Herself; now men took control by opening Her and planting seeds in Her furrowed vulva—not natural vulva, but labia that the men were cutting themselves.

No longer *a part of* nature, both the Creative Force and humans have come to be seen as *apart from* nature. When a goddess was seen as the Creator, creation was natural; with a God, creation becomes an "artful work," something that is *super*-natural. Less obvious, but of at least equal moment, is the fact that men, too, have come to be seen as super-natural, the rulers over nature, the earth, and "natural" women.

Clearly, it was the knowledge of agriculture that had given humans the arrogance to start thinking this way. But agriculture did oblige men to work *with* Nature, even as they were claiming dominion over Her. There remained room for further deterioration in the relationship between man and nature. That unhappy development would be one of the by-products of a second megarevolution in the second half of the second millennium C.E.

He Is the Image and Glory of God

Once the Conception Misconception had led to the view that God is male, the die was cast for relations between the sexes for most of subsequent history. If it is believed that God is male and that humans are created in *His* image, the

---

*All of this is from the Genesis 1 version in which men and women are created simultaneously and equally, but the idea of "man" having been created in God"s image and having dominion over nature has throughout most of subsequent history been conflated with the chapter 2 version to equate *man* with "human male" and place women among the subordinated animals and nature.

What Does God Look Like? A Man
The single most familiar image of God in the modern world is that which Michelangelo painted on the ceiling of the Sistine Chapel in 1511. This Judeo-Christian God bears a striking resemblance to the image of Zeus in the next illustration. The apparent basis for the similarity is that men created both gods in their own image.

conclusion seems necessarily to follow that men, who would under these circumstances more closely resemble God, must be closer to perfection than women are. (God = male ∴ man ~ God ∴ God > man > woman.) Too powerful to omit is one more example of the reasoning that flows from the Genesis 2 version of the Conception Misconception (the male God created man from lifeless soil and woman from man) and the consequent belief that God is male, all of which is based on the agricultural metaphor. In the sixth chapter of Genesis we are told: "When *men began to multiply on the face of the ground,* and daughters were born to them, the *sons of God* saw that the *daughters of men* were fair; and they took to wife such of them as they chose. . . . [T]he sons of God came into the daughters of men, and they bore children to them."[30] Men are the sons of God; women are the daughters of men. If so, there is no room for doubt about who is subordinate to whom.

This line of reasoning* is the basis of the pernicious arguments of Aristotle, Freud, and so many others that women are "incomplete" or "deformed men." St. Paul made explicit that this hierarchy from male God to male human to female human is based on the idea of male (pro)creative power and the male

---

*Of course in Aristotle's case the Conception Misconception is not derived from the Bible, but it is based on the same sort of reasoning.

God's creation of Eve from Adam: "[H]e [a man] is the image and Glory of God; but woman is the glory of man. (For man was not made from woman, but woman from man. Neither was man created for woman, but woman for man.)"[31] Paul's argument was that God is to man as man is to woman as master is to slave.[32] Aristotle would identify what women are missing as "soul" or "the spiritual." Freud would more directly name the missing piece in women as the penis. We can now see that what Aristotle and Freud were saying amounts to the same thing.* If God (or, among polytheists like the Greeks, the most powerful of the deities) is a male to whom humans are similar, presumably He must have a penis (a very large one, we may suppose) and testicles; so those malformed creatures made in His image (and *his* image) who lack these appendages must also be assumed to be farther removed from the spiritual and divine than are those who, like God, have these male organs. A striking example of this reasoning is to be found in the laws enumerated in Deuteronomy: "He whose testicles are crushed or whose male member is cut off shall not enter the assembly of the Lord."[33]

Nor is there any need for someone to be a religious believer in order to be infected by this idea, since it so permeates most cultures that everyone receives it through osmosis.

The Seed of Faith

A displacement of matriarchy never occurred, because what never existed cannot be displaced. But there does seem to have been a change from relative sexual equality in many "prehistoric" societies to complete male dominance in agricultural societies. And religious practices switched from the worship of a variety of deities of both sexes (which often included the idea that Creative power is uniquely female) to the worship of a single, all-powerful male God.

This metamorphosis may not seem as dramatic as the violent overthrow of a peaceful, matriarchal, monotheistic, Goddess-worshiping Eden by violent men, which was conjured up by such writers as Marija Gimbutas and Riane Eisler. But the actual story is, quite literally, every bit as *sexy*. The real fall of women was not quite as far as that imagined by the proponents of prehistoric matriarchy. It was a fall, not from female dominance, but from nonagricultural societies of essential sexual balance† to the severe sexual imbalance that has characterized virtually all agricultural societies. This transformation was, in fact, the most consequential in human history.

---

*The ideas of Aristotle and Freud on women will be explored more fully in later chapters.

†Although many men were trying to compensate for the feelings of inadequacy they felt in comparison with women's abilities by claiming superiority in some respects.

What Does a Man Look Like? A God

As the seed metaphor led most people finally to invert the ancient belief in female procreation and replace it with the doctrine of male procreation, the understanding of the sex of the Creative Force inevitably underwent a similar reversal. Beginning in the fourth millennium B.C.E. and gaining momentum into the first millennium B.C.E., the conception of the dominant, creative gods—or, later, the single God—as male arose and triumphed. This statue of Zeus, ca. 460 B.C.E., reflects what became the most common image of God, one that carried over to the monotheistic religions. If God or the dominant god looks like this, it is obvious what sort of sexual organs humans must have to be most similar to the Divine, and only men have such equipment. (Marburg/Art Resource, New York)

A fundamental operating principle throughout recorded history has been that, as Simone de Beauvoir put it in *The Second Sex,* "humanity is male and man defines woman not in herself but as relative to him."[34] The source of this extremely influential and damaging belief is the Conception Misconception, based on the seed metaphor, which grew out of the Agricultural Megarevolution after it had devalued male roles. The Conception Misconception led directly to the idea that God is male—and so to the notion, also made explicit by St. Paul, that men are little gods who can and should rule over women. This is the basic reason why women have been so subordinated for the last five to six thousand years.

This monumental misunderstanding has deeply influenced the lives of women and men ever since it first arose, and it continues to affect us today in profound, but generally unrealized, ways. As philosopher Mary Daly has said, "If God is male, then the male is God."[35] These contemporary consequences of the Conception Misconception are fully explored later in the book.

The words *seed* and *faith* have often been linked. Evangelist Oral Roberts was fond of preaching about what he termed "seed-faith living."[36] In the late twentieth century, books with titles or subtitles such as *Seed Faith, Nourishing the Seed of Faith,* and *Faith as a Seed* were published by Christians of various dominations.[37] This connection between seeds and religion is much more appropriate than those who make it realize. When an anthology of Thoreau's later writings on natural history was published in 1993, it was entitled *Faith in a Seed.*[38] The truth is that the major monotheistic religions that have formed the undergirding for much of civilization are faiths that are founded in a seed—or, rather, a seed metaphor.

The forbidden fruit of agriculture that Eve offered Adam was poisonous indeed. It first infected and debilitated men's traditional way of life and left their prestige severely weakened. Ultimately, though, the seeds from that fruit grew the tree of male monotheism from which subordinated women have been dangling ever since.

The rest, as they say, is *history.*

CHAPTER 8

"No Mother Gave Me Birth"

Women and Men in the First Millennium B.C.E.

If only we could have children without the help of women!
"HIPPOLYTUS"[1]

The first few millennia of what is usually termed "history" were shaped by the ways in which men adapted to the reduction of their earlier roles that the invention of agriculture had brought about. The first backlash had produced "a man's world." The result was a dramatic swing toward the "masculine" end of the values spectrum. But the violence, hierarchical domination, and competitiveness that were featured portions of the male accommodation with the changed environment became less adaptive as populations grew and warfare and its weapons became more terrible. The violent male gods that had emerged as the principal deities had not provided a solution. There was, then, a growing need for values more often associated with women to rein in the tendencies that were more common among men. Some way had to be found to reintegrate into society such "feminine" traits and values as nurturing, compassion, and blending, which had once been symbolized by important goddesses, most of whom had vanished or been strictly subordinated by this time.

The process of cultural development and value formation is not simple or linear. Like the human nature with which it must work, culture does not act as a unit moving steadily in one direction. There are conflicting cultural forces and values, designed to meet different needs, just as there are conflicting innate motivations, evolved to meet different situations. While the "masculine" ways were winning out and "working" (after a fashion) in the early historical period, they were also creating new problems and demonstrating the need for some curbs to be placed on them.

A useful image for what was taking place might be that of a wave. The turbulence that had been unleashed by the changes associated with the rise of agriculture created a large surface movement in one direction (the "masculine" direction), but the force of this wave created at the same time an undertow in the other ("feminine") direction.

So within the structure of early civilization, increasingly dominated on the surface not only by men but also by "masculine" traits and values, "feminine values" survived and were recognized by at least some men, as well as many women, as a needed check on the worst abuses resulting from male proclivities.

Without the once-powerful goddesses, what influence could be brought to bear on men to bring themselves under more control? It is my contention that the growing need for values more often associated with women to rein in the tendencies that were more common among men was met by a religious innovation that in effect constituted a return of goddesses in a variety of guises, most notably in the form of a group of male gods and prophets who appeared in and just after the first millennium B.C.E.

It has frequently been noted that the sixth century B.C.E.—often called the "Axial Age"—saw a remarkable array of religious innovators and prophets throughout what would later be called the Old World (principally across the southern half of Asia, extending into southeastern Europe), including Lao-tse, Confucius, the Buddha, Mahavira Jina, several of the Jewish prophets, and the early Greek philosophers. At the end of the fourth century B.C.E., Alexander the Great reversed this trend by raising the "masculine" militaristic and hierarchical values to a new level. The extremely male-oriented imperial settlements of the Hellenistic and Roman eras represented a system that was so weighted toward the "masculine" end of the values spectrum it ultimately increased the need for a resurrection of the values more associated with women. That hope would finally be accomplished when Jesus brought the constellation of values usually seen as feminine to the most complete and powerful form that the Western world has known.

The conditions occasioned by the rise of agriculture and its long-rippling disruptive aftershocks varied greatly in the disparate lands from which arose the teachers and prophets of the first millennium B.C.E. Their chronological proximity suggests, however, that they were responding to problems that were felt at this time throughout the civilizations stretching from China through India and the Middle East into northeastern Africa and southeastern Europe.

It would be foolish to suggest that these thinkers held their important beliefs in common; differences among them were large. Yet there is a thread that runs through these diverse seekers. All were, unlike the exponents of the thunder gods who had become dominant between one and two thousand years earlier, preachers of peace and reconciliation and opponents of acquisitiveness and selfishness. Some of them—the Buddha and, later, Jesus—also took the dramatic step of abandoning band or tribal identification and pseudospeciation by appealing to all people in the world. They argued that the values that had previously brought some degree of cooperation within groups must be extended to outsiders. This endeavor was going beyond both male and female biological propensities, since both sexes had formed bonds (although of somewhat different kinds) with "their own" and been wary of "strangers."

There is space here for only the briefest description of how the varied philosophies and religions of the era fit into the general attempt to bridge the divide that had opened between human nature (and especially the exaggerated "masculine" traits) and the environment after the invention of agriculture. Following extremely abbreviated looks at corresponding developments in China and India, somewhat more attention will be paid to the Hebrew, Greek, and Roman situations, because of their clear places in the direct line of ancestry of the modern Western world.

Jen-tle Men

In China there was, between the sixth and third centuries B.C.E., a period of remarkable inquiry that came to be called the Age of Philosophy. This development occurred, as might be expected, following the serious disruption of a previously existing balance. An ancient imperial system was replaced by a division of China into independent city-states. Perhaps more important was the introduction of increased specialization and wide-ranging trade. These changes brought with them growing disparities in wealth, as small numbers of men accumulated vast fortunes. Greed, which had presumably become a problem in China as elsewhere after agriculture had introduced surplus,* was worsened by the economic changes that began around the seventh century B.C.E.

The thinkers and teachers of the era that began in the sixth century B.C.E. were attempting to establish values that would allow the Chinese people to come to terms with the changed socioeconomic environment. In light of the fact that such maladaptive tendencies as greed and aggression were causing the problems these philosophers faced, it is significant that they called themselves the *Ju,* meaning "the gentle" or "the yielding." The name itself suggests a reaction against aggression, violence, and domination—and a move to check

---

*The Chinese agricultural system, however, differed from that of other areas in that it did not make extensive use of the plow until late in the first millennium B.C.E.

some of the more male behaviors that were producing undesirable results in the new environment.

Lao-tse, who is said to have lived in the sixth century B.C.E., viewed the universe in dualistic terms, but posited a "oneness" (*tao*) underlying the dichotomies that we find in the world. In this oneness, Taoists believed, harmony is created by the blending of opposites, the *yin* and *yang,* associated with the female and male.[2]

Taoism posited a completely good human nature that was corrupted by society. As one of the many ancient traditions that saw the acquisition of knowledge (which, again, I believe means the knowledge of how to produce food) as the beginning of human misery, Taoism prescribed a return to natural simplicity, without surplus and the evils it unleashed:

> Banish wisdom, discard knowledge,
> And the people will be benefitted a hundredfold.
> Banish human kindness, discard morality,
> And the people will be dutiful and compassionate.
> Banish skill, discard profit,
> And thieves and robbers will disappear
> . . .
> Give them selflessness and fewness of desires.[3]

Confucius (K'ung Fu-tse) (551–479 B.C.E.) and his followers saw themselves as the restorers of ancient values, but they were in fact the developers of new values to adapt to an altered social environment. Confucius took a set of ancient, mystical religious beliefs and converted them into a powerful ethical system. Most importantly, he transformed the concept of *jen,* which had previously been used to describe an accepted member of the tribe, into the idea of good. *Jen* came to mean following such values as gentle behavior, humanity, unselfishness, and showing deference to others.[4]

Etymology can shed important light on the development of values to control portions of human nature. The Indo-European root *gene* or *gen* (and hence the Latin *gens*), which refers to birth or family, underwent a metamorphosis parallel to that of the Chinese *jen.* It is the root of such words as *genealogy, genus, genre,* and *kin,* referring to family and groups based on close relation, but it came also to produce such words as *gentle* and *kind.* Thus to act as a "gentle-man" came finally to imply the curbing of some of the worst—and the least *jen,* or "gentle"—male tendencies, and so treating outsiders the way one would members of the family or tribe. Humans are naturally (as the common root of the words implies) kind to kin, but in the evolving social environment it became necessary to try to treat others as we would our kin. To call, as George Bush did in 1988 American presidential campaign, for "a kinder, gentler" nation is literally to ask people to treat each other as if they were kin.*

The essence of Confucius's expansion of the concept of *jen* can best be expressed as: *Do unto others as you would unto brothers.*

The widening of the meaning of these terms, in both China and the West, from family and tribe to practices toward others that are based upon the ways one acts within the family or group, is one of the clearest examples of how new values developed to meet the changed social environment and how those values had to make use of what was already present in human nature. Significantly, the terminology used in this instance is that which came to connote sorts of behavior often associated with women—particularly in their dealings with close "kin"—("gentle," "kind"), but was then employed to describe an ideal for men. "Gentle-men," whether in ancient China or the late medieval or modern West, have always been those who make an effort to control some of the less desirable portions of the more male biological inheritance and behave at least a bit more like women.

Confucius was the first to develop the concept of the "gentleman," which would also become an ideal among some in Greece and Rome, and would re-emerge in late medieval western Europe. In one of his more striking statements on the subject, Confucius said: "A gentleman takes as much trouble to discover what is right as lesser men take to discover what will pay."[5] In distinguishing gentlemen from those who simply follow their instincts, he declared: "Gentlemen never compete."[6] Confucius suggested that the basic rule for people to live in society is what came to be called the Golden Rule: "Never do to others what you would not like them to do to you."[7] And he believed that it is necessary to stick to the essentials, to be contented with what is sufficient, rather than always wanting more.[8] Confucius argued for rule by moral example rather than physical force.[9]

Lingams and Hermaphroditic Deities: Sex and Religion in India

In India, older religious beliefs were intertwined in the early centuries of the first millennium B.C.E. with a strict hierarchical system dominated by the priestly aristocracy, the *Brahmins*. This system, with its violent storm gods, such as Indra, corresponded to the "masculine" value accommodations that

---

*As Bush discovered to his dismay, given the male propensity for gender extending, a man who makes such pronouncements leaves himself open to being called womanly. Insecure men who find themselves in such a situation usually seek ways to demonstrate their manhood. The consequences in Bush's case as well as several others will be explored in Chapter 14.

had also been reached among the Mesopotamians, Hebrews, and Greeks. But the growing problems of an increasingly complex society and economy showed that the value system was in need of revision.

Around the middle of the first millennium B.C.E., there arose in India new values, which had been hinted at in the Upanishads several centuries earlier. Basically, they consisted of a revolt against hierarchy and dominance, a call for nonviolence (*ahimsa*), and a self-denying (ascetic) lifestyle. A more thoroughgoing challenge to the male-oriented system of the time would be hard to imagine.

One of the most important realizations in Indian religion had already come in the ninth century B.C.E., when it was said in the Upanishads that heaven and hell are within each of us. This concept represented an understanding that, in modern biological terms, we each have inbred tendencies within us, some of which are adaptive and some maladaptive—in short, human nature is mixed.

Asceticism came to be highly respected, but Hinduism provided lesser forms of denial and control for the majority of people who could not be expected to live up to the ascetic ideal. This modified set of beliefs and ethics furnished large numbers of Indians with a set of values at least somewhat at variance with those of their male-dominated, hierarchical, violent, and materialistic society.

Two major Indian religious reformers of the dramatic sixth century B.C.E. went particularly far in the direction of values usually associated with the "feminine" end of the spectrum. Mahavira Jina (ca. 540–477 B.C.E.), the founder of Jainism, directly repudiated the caste system and insisted upon the nonviolent doctrine of *ahimsa*. Like the other values-givers of the age, he saw an essential need to curb passions and the innate predispositions, such as greed, anger, pride, lying, envy, and lust.[10]*

Gautama Siddhartha, the Buddha (550?–480? B.C.E.), was a contemporary of both Mahavira Jina and Confucius. So the Indian "Awakened One" was facing essentially the same altered human environment that led to the promulga-

---

*The similarity of this list to the seven cardinal sins in the Catholic Church is not coincidental. These same problems are mentioned in one society after another, to the point where it becomes apparent that they represent the basic biological tendencies that can cause trouble in agricultural or urban societies. Some of them are even troublesome among collector-hunters. One observer of the !Kung bush people has said, "The most frequent accusations heard [among them] are of pride, arrogance, laziness [the seventh of the Catholics' deadly sins, sloth], and selfishness." [Richard B. Lee, "The !Kung Bushmen of Botswana," in M. G. Bicchieri, ed., *Hunters and Gathers Today: A Socioeconomic Study of Eleven Such Cultures in the Twentieth Century* (New York: Holt, Rinehart and Winston, 1972), pp. 327–368, as quoted in Edward O. Wilson, *On Human Nature* (Cambridge, MA: Harvard University Press, 1978), p. 85].

tion of new, more "feminine" values by the Jain and Chinese reformers. Along with many others of his time, Gautama was upset by the growth of large, impersonal states. He yearned (as the human biogram directs) for a personal community. Although he believed in the virtues of self-denial, the Buddha preached a "middle way" between self-indulgence and asceticism. He also opposed greed and demanded an order based upon social justice, in which no one would be either very rich or very poor.

Gautama said that people are possessed of an insatiable appetite for consumption, not only of material things but also of ideas and experience. What is necessary to overcome this innate appetite is to bring one's passions, such as greed, anger, and hatred, under control. The values adopted by the Buddha are very much in keeping with those of other systems emerging in this historical period. They called for the curtailing of predispositions that had become harmful in the new environment.

What the Buddha had discovered was the *Dharma,* the Eternal Truth—a set of values to guide life. The person who followed these values would be "thorough in the religious life, thorough in the peaceful life, thorough in good actions, thorough in meritorious conduct, thorough in harmlessness, thorough in kindness to all creatures."[11] All of this adds up to something very close to being thorough in the behaviors usually associated with women.

What may be most significant about Gautama is that he saw this truth and set of values as being for *all* people. He called upon his monks to be missionaries, bringing the Dharma to people of every nation.[12] This universalism constituted a major step in value development by attempting to get beyond the natural group or tribal identification and pseudospeciation inherent in the storm god religions.

Neighbors, Strangers, and Those without Male Genitals

Changes in Hebrew society and religion during the first millennium B.C.E. furnish an excellent example of the larger trend in that millennium. The middle of the first millennium B.C.E. was the period during which, in addition to the development of all the other momentous value systems, the Hebrew prophets began to transform Yahweh from a God of vengeance into a God of compassion. In the process, they were making their image of Yahweh less completely male. As they moved from a nomadic to an agricultural, and finally to an urban, social environment, subtle changes took place in the Hebrews' conception of their God and what He demanded of His people.

There was, to be sure, always a strong ethical basis in the religion, from the time of Moses onward. But in the early years those values were firmly rooted in such practices as retribution, pseudospeciation, dominance of men over women, and hierarchy. In its early centuries, Hebrew society was empathically a man's world.

The Torah, and most especially the Ten Commandments and the following Covenant Code, contains rules that were intended to control no-longer-adaptive portions of the human biogram. This purpose is indicated by their negative formulation. The emphasis is almost all on what, in the King James wording, "thou shalt *not*" do. The Commandments are prohibitions attempting to prevent behaviors that, though counterproductive in society, are inbred tendencies within people.

The other point that is most interesting about the Decalogue in the context of human nature and the development of values to adapt to the changed social environment is its emphasis on respecting the rights, well-being, and property of *neighbors:*

> You shall not bear false witness against your *neighbor.* You shall not covet your *neighbor's* house; you shall not covet your *neighbor's* wife, or his manservant, or his maidservant, or his ox, or his ass, or anything that is your *neighbor's.*[13]

Certain behaviors to which some people may be predisposed are being proscribed, but the focus is strongly on behavior toward other members of the group. The most powerful and oft-quoted such statement of values in the Torah is the injunction in Leviticus that is usually repeated simply as: "You shall love your neighbor as yourself." Any possible ambiguity concerning the meaning of "neighbor" dissolves if the entire passage is read: "You shall not take vengeance or bear any grudge *against the sons of your own people,* but you shall love your neighbor as yourself: I am the Lord."[14]

Trying to love one's neighbors as oneself might simply seem part of human nature. But it constitutes one of the most important steps in human attempts at bridging the gap that changes begun by agriculture had opened between the human biogram and the social environment. The attempt was revolutionary because *neighbors* meant the whole people of Israel, not just a personally known band. The natural circle of identification was being widened, and the rule sought to curb in a broader context some of the most destructive of the innate human traits. But at this point there was no attempt to overcome pseudospeciation. Identification with the band was merely being enlarged, not counteracted. Far from prohibiting some evil activities with regard to outsiders, the Torah explicitly endorsed actions against "strangers" that would not be tolerated if taken against members of the expanded group.

In Leviticus and Deuteronomy there are many examples of the distinctions between the treatment expected for fellow Israelites and that which is acceptable when dealing with "foreigners." This difference is to be seen in everything from money lending to slavery and conquest. Values of cooperation and compassion are evident—but only for members of the group. "If there is among you a poor man, one of your brethren," the Mosaic law says, ". . . you shall not harden your heart or shut your hand against your poor brother, but you shall open your hand to him, and lend him sufficient for his need, whatever it may be." Every seven years the debts of all fellow Hebrews are to be forgiven; but not those of outsiders: "Of a foreigner you may exact it; but whatever of yours is with your brother your hand shall release."[15] "To a foreigner," Hebrews were told, "you may lend upon interest, but to your brother you shall not lend upon interest."[16]

"Stealing"—enslaving—"brothers" or "neighbors" is considered an entirely different matter from doing so with "strangers" (or, in the King James wording, "the heathen"), as is clearly stated in Leviticus:

> As for your male and female slaves whom you may have: you may buy male and female slaves from among the nations that are round about you. You may also buy from among the *strangers* who sojourn with you and their families that are with you, who have been born in your land; and *they may be your property.* You may bequeath them to your sons after you, to inherit *as a possession for ever;* you may make slaves of them, *but over your brethren the people of Israel you shall not rule, one over another, with harshness.*[17]

It is important for our purposes to note that the references to "others" who may be made property include both males and females, while the references to those who may not be enslaved are to "your brother"[18] and "your brethren the people of Israel." The reason that these "brothers" could not be owned was that they were members of the "covenant community." That community explicitly excluded all women. The sign of inclusion in the covenant was circumcision: "This is My covenant, which ye shall keep, between Me and you and thy seed after thee: every male among you shall be circumcised. And ye shall be circumcised in the flesh of your foreskin; and it shall be a token of a covenant betwixt Me and you."[19]

In their early history, then, the Hebrews had succeeded in developing important values to mediate among some of the innate predispositions that had been thrust into a changed environment. There was even an occasional glimmer of the possibility of extending compassion beyond the bounds of the group. But the bulk of early Hebraic law makes sharp distinctions between "us" and "them." The very concept of "Gentile" is a classic formulation of the innate predisposition toward pseudospeciation. It is blanket term for "them," "the others," everybody who is not like "us."

This is entirely as would be expected from the perspective we are using here. As a shepherd folk just beginning to settle in larger communities, the early Hebrews did not yet face a situation that obliged them to make a concerted effort to move far beyond the identification with the band and pseudospeciation that came naturally to them, as to all humans. Serious modification of these instincts and the dominance relationships and violence that went with them in a society of surplus would not, in any case, have fit well with the religious outlook they and other people of the Middle East at this time had developed. A violent male thunder God who identified Himself with a particular group of men was hardly likely to command much restraint of aggressive and domineering proclivities, at least not so long as they were directed against "Gentiles."*

"As One Whom His Mother Comforts . . ."

By the time of the prophets in the mid-first millennium B.C.E., the Israelites had become not only a settled but also substantially an urban people. That the traditional ways were not working in this altered environment is evident from some of the comments of the prophets. Speaking of the city of Nineveh and foretelling its destruction, the late seventh-century prophet Nahum seemed to offer a sweeping condemnation of urban life: "Woe to the bloody city, all full of lies and booty—no end to the plunder!"[20] The view of city life taken by Nahum's contemporary, Zephaniah, was at least as harsh: "Woe to her that is rebellious and defiled, the oppressing city! She listens to no voice, she accepts no correction."[21] If people were to make it in this unnatural environment, a modification in values would be necessary.

The most significant change in the Hebrew outlook during the Axial Age was the reintroduction of female qualities into the Deity. The key person in this regard was the second prophet Isaiah (who wrote the portions of the Book of Isaiah beginning with Chapter 40). This Isaiah was yet another, albeit slightly older, contemporary of Confucius, the Buddha, and Mahavira Jina. (The dates of the second Isaiah's life are unknown, but his chapters were written just before the Persian conquest of Babylon in 539 B.C.E.) Like them, his call was essentially for a move toward characteristics usually associated with women. He insisted that what Yahweh wanted from His people was not fast-

---

*These statements are not intended to single out Judaism in a negative way. The tradition that began with this view of a jealous, violent, male, monotheistic God is the accepted foundation of modern Christianity and Islam as much as it is of modern Judaism. As Judaism developed in later years, it stressed precisely those passages in the Torah that repudiate pseudospeciation. In the Passover Seder, the emphasis is not at all on the many permissions to mistreat outsiders but on the words that underscore common humanity: "Remember that you were a slave in the land of Egypt" [Exodus 23:9; The same point is made in Exodus 22:21]; "When a stranger resides with you in your land, you shall not wrong him. . . . You shall love him as yourself, for you were strangers in the land of Egypt"; "You shall not oppress a stranger, for you know the feelings of the stranger."

ing, but helping others: "Is this not the fast that I choose: to loose the bonds of wickedness, to undo the thongs of the yoke, to let the oppressed go free, and to break every yoke? Is it not to share your bread with the hungry, and to bring the homeless poor into your house . . . ?"[22]

But the most remarkable innovation of the second Isaiah (building, as we shall see in a moment, on some hints by Jeremiah) was to speak of God in maternal images, using terms that are plainly and biologically female[23]:

> Hearken to me, O house of Jacob, all the remnant of the house of Israel,
> who have been borne by me from your birth,
> carried from the womb;
> even to your old age I am He, and to gray hairs I will carry you.
> I have made, and I will bear; I will carry and will save.[24]

A bit later, Isaiah's God declares: "As one whom his mother comforts, so I will comfort you."[25]

The Yahweh described by the second Isaiah remained very masculine in some respects, but it is evident that "He" had developed androgynous features. This transformation is a reflection (conscious or otherwise) of the need to revive the qualities more linked with females that had been denigrated and so suppressed in men who feared being seen as "unmanly."

Another way in which this need manifested itself in this period was in the rise to prominence, beginning with Jeremiah, of the figure of Rachel, the wife of Jacob, as a sort of heavenly mother:

> Rachel is weeping for her children;
> She refuses to be comforted for her children, because they are not.[26]

Yahweh's response to Rachel is intriguing. Usually translated "my heart yearns for him,"[27] the Hebrew verb that is used derives from *womb** and the passage can be translated as God saying, "my womb trembles for him; I will truly show motherly compassion upon him."[28] A few lines later, Jeremiah declares: "the Lord has created a new thing on the earth: a woman protects a man."[29]

Rachel Imenu—"Mother Rachel"—continued to occupy an important position in Judaism in the centuries that followed.[30] She came to play something of the role that the Virgin Mary would later among Christians. Together with the more androgynous view of God provided by Jeremiah and the second Isaiah, Mother Rachel (although not seen as a goddess herself) met some of the need for a female element in the divine.[31]

---

*It is significant that the words for *compassion* in both Sumerian and Hebrew were derived from the word for *womb*.

Perhaps one of the reasons for making Yahweh more androgynous and for the elevation of Rachel to such heavenly prominence was to counteract the renewed worship among the Hebrews of a goddess, referred to in Jeremiah as "the queen of heaven." It was not only women who were attracted to a female deity in the changed environment that the Hebrew people faced. This goddess worship appears to have been introduced to Judah in the seventh century B.C.E. by King Manasseh. The male adherents of Yahweh did not appreciate the attempt to restore a goddess. The worship of this goddess is referred to as an "abomination." About the time that the leading people of Judah were taken in captivity to Babylon, there was much dispute over whether so many horrors had befallen the people of Jerusalem because some of them had started to worship a goddess or because they had *stopped* doing so.[32]

Although Judaism remained a male-oriented religion, the humanitarian reforms pushed by the prophets, the attempt by some Hebrews to revive goddess worship, the subsequent introduction of more female qualities into their understanding of God, and the elevation of Rachel indicate that a "feminization" of Judaism was occurring. Like their contemporaries across the southern half of Asia, the followers of Yahweh were experiencing an incongruity between the largely "masculine" value system that had gained ascendancy in the latter part of the Agricultural Megarevolution and their transformed, increasingly urban social environment. They were attempting to revolutionize their values in a similar way.

Sleeping with the Enemy: Classical Greece

Ancient Greece provides fascinating insights into the interaction among human nature, sex, values, and the social environment altered by the invention of agriculture. There we find the place where the earlier ways of greater equality between the sexes had survived the longest, but also perhaps the sharpest, reaction against those views and against women. In Greece we can also see the dangers of a strict adherence to dualistic thinking and two of the most striking examples of the consequences of attempts to deal with portions of the disruptions growing out of the Agricultural Megarevolution without an understanding of other aspects of human nature and the changed environment.

On the island of Crete, a goddess appears to have reigned as the leading deity and Creator well into historical times, down to the middle of the second millennium B.C.E. There, as elsewhere, she was frequently depicted with snakes wrapped about her arms. The key point, again, is that she is not yet Aphrodite or Venus, not merely a goddess of love or fertility. She is the Creator.[33]

Women in Crete, like the island's goddess-centered religion, perpetuated the ways of an earlier age. There is considerable evidence that matrilineal

descent persisted there into the Minoan Period of the third and second millennia.[34] And females apparently continued to act as farmers in Crete. Women are
frequently shown tending fruit trees in Minoan art works.[35]

Another aspect of the society of Crete was highly unusual for a time so late
in the Agricultural Megarevolution. The state was not politically centralized;
instead, Minoan society was divided into clans based upon kinship ties.[36]
Human nature is, of course, far more compatible with such personal communities than with the larger aggregations that had emerged in many other areas.
This coexistence in Crete of small communities with apparent equality for
women suggests the possibility that men who have not been dislodged from
the personal communities for which humans are adapted are more willing to
accept larger roles for women in those communities.

The peaceful civilization of Crete was devastated by a series of natural dis-
asters in the fifteenth century B.C.E., and the island was subsequently taken
over by the Mycenaean Greeks, who substantially modified the ancient practices. Then, in the twelfth century B.C.E., Greece and Crete were conquered by
a Greek group with very male-oriented practices, the Dorians, and the whole
Aegean area fell into the period of decline that is often called the Greek Dark
Ages.

The civilization of classical Greece that arose from this era of general illit-
eracy maintained a few features of the Minoan culture, but it was radically different in its views of women. The roots of classical Greece are found in the
writings of Homer and Hesiod in the ninth and eighth centuries B.C.E. The attitude toward women expressed in these works is one of full-blown misogyny.
Agamemnon, to cite one instance from Homer, gives his wife, Clytemnestra,
an Eve-like role when he asserts that in plotting to kill him she "defiled herself and all her sex, all women yet to come, even those few who may be virtu-
ous."[37] Women are explicitly considered as property in *The Iliad,* where they
are listed among the spoils of war. "[A]nd still more hoards from here: gold,
ruddy bronze, women sashed and lovely, and gleaming gray iron, and I will
haul it home, all I won as plunder," Achilles complains, "All but my prize of
honor," which, of course, is another woman.[38]

Hesiod was even more extreme. He speaks of good being replaced by "this
beautiful evil": "women, for mortal men an evil thing."[39] To Hesiod, women
are not the bringers of evil into the world of men; they *are* that evil. They are
not humans, but "the breed of female women."[40] This was complete "otherization." Nor was this an idiosyncrasy of a lone, bitter misogynist. He was speaking for a culture.[41] In the classical period, Greek men often labeled women as
the *genes gynaikon,* the "race of women."[42] Here was literal pseudospeciation
of an extraordinary degree. Greek men were so dividing themselves from
women that they saw women as another species.

What could account for such extreme hostility to women? There is not a single, neat answer to this question. In Hesiod's case, there are hints what one source (although certainly not one unique to the Greeks) of male misogyny could be. Some men saw the birth of new humans as the reason that people have to die (to make room for the next generation), and so they blamed women, who give birth, for introducing death. The ultimate cause of death is birth—or conception, depending upon one's view of when life begins. (A similar suggestion is made in Genesis, which blames the woman's sin for making men mortal.*) In his *Theogony,* Hesiod recounts the attempts of the early generations of gods to prevent the births of their children because they know that a son will conspire with his mother to displace his father.[43]

There is another source of the extreme Greek misogyny that is more specific to the circumstances out of which classical Greece arose. Men of this society were competing with a preceding culture in which women had played a prominent role and in which the supreme divine power may still have been seen as female: Minoan Crete. This culture was much more recent than those of relative sexual equality in other areas and therefore potentially more influential.

The superceding of the relatively egalitarian culture of Minoan Crete by Greece is a major part of the reason why Greek men of the classical period saw their civilization as being the result of their triumph over woman and everything connected with them. The idea of a still-recent transfer of power is depicted in myth after myth: Zeus seizing (pro)creative capacity by swallowing Metis and then giving birth to Athena from his own head; Perseus severing the head of the gorgon Medusa; and the Athenians defeating the Amazons.

In these stories we can see the ramifications of the utter dualism upon which the Greek worldview (which, in turn, has been so influential ever since) was based. Pythagoras established a dualism that saw the male/female polarity as the basis of the universe. As he and subsequent Greeks divided the world into sets of polar opposites, they followed the familiar practice of identifying the "good" pole in each case with men and the "bad" pole with women.

---

*God warns Adam and Eve that eating from the Tree of Knowledge will result in their death. Because Adam eats, at Eve's behest, from that tree, they and their descendants are banished from Eden and its tree of life, the fruit of which would enable them to "live for ever" (Genesis 3:2–3, 22–23). This outcome is in keeping with the interpretation of Original Sin, the eating of the apple, being sexual intercourse, as a result of which women will be obliged to bear children. Looked at this way, the serpent was wrong: eating from the Tree of Knowledge (having sexual relations) *did* cause Adam and Eve to die, since that act would produce offspring, for whom they would have to die to make way. As I have pointed out earlier (in Chapter 6), seeing the apple as intercourse (the power of reproduction) is not inconsistent with seeing it as agriculture (knowledge of how to control the reproduction of plants and animals for food).

Whatever the role of sexual division in producing or encouraging dualistic thinking, it is certain that this relationship operated in the other direction: dualistic thinking has greatly encouraged the belief that there is a much greater degree of sexual division than there actually is.

One effect of strict dualism was that it limited the Greeks (and everyone else who has adopted it) to "two alternatives: rule by men or rule by women. No middle, or third, course was imaginable."[44] Particularly in light of the fact that there was a society in their not-too-distant past that had followed a middle course but which therefore appeared in their dualistic thinking to have been a matriarchy, Greek men of the mid-first millennium B.C.E. saw women as the enemy, the other, the thing that had to be subdued.

The belief that women are inferior but a constant threat to men was an oft-repeated theme in classical Greece. "Therefore, we must defend the men who live by the law, never let a woman triumph over us," Creon proclaimed in *Antigone*. "Better to fall from power, if fall we must, at the hands of a man— never be rated inferior to a woman, never."[45]

But what the men of ancient Greece were actually subduing was not a polar opposite, both because women are not anything approaching polar opposites of men and because the Minoan society had not been a matriarchy. What the misogynists of classical Greece were really battling was a more androgynous society, one that more closely resembled the actual, limited degree of difference between the sexes—a society, in short, that, unlike that of classical Greece, was *not* based upon dualistic gender extending.

That it was such an androgynous* society that the Greeks were fighting is evident in their myths. Part of the horror of Medusa and the other gorgons to those who think dualistically is that they are androgynes, females with many male attributes. The snakes that serve in lieu of hair on the gorgon head may represent the goddesses of earlier times, but they are also phallic. In any case, they indicate power, and the head of Medusa clearly symbolizes the *vagina dentata,* the "vagina with teeth."[46†] Perseus's severing of the head of Medusa therefore symbolizes the same thing as Marduk's cutting the womb of Tiamat in the *Enuma Elish.* Such actions plainly destroy the creative power of women and so might be called primitive, violent hysterectomies. In fact, however, they are, as we saw in the preceding chapter, more accurately termed female

---

*I do not use this word, as many people do today, to mean that there are no differences between the sexes, but to indicate a realization that the similarities are far greater than the differences, an acceptance of the need for the significant sexual differences that do exist, and an understanding that those differences do not imply any inequality.

†That the gorgon head with its curly hair represents a vagina is also suggested by the sexual connotations of the belief that when a man looks at it he turns to stone.

The Image of Woman as the Source of Evil

Greek men of the classical period used gorgons as symbols of unsubordinated women. They were an enemy that must be kept subdued. The head of a gorgon represented a "vagina dentata," a vagina with teeth. The snakes that form her belt represented the creative goddess. When Perseus severed the head of Medusa, he was in effect "castrating" her and women in general. The head of the gorgon Medusa that appeared on the shield of Athena, the subordinated goddess who served as a cheerleader for male domination and creative power, constituted a reminder that creative power had been separated from women. (Metope from the Temple of Selinunte with Perseus and the Gorgon. Museo Archeologico/Palermo, Palermo, Italy) (Art Resource) castration. This concept seems bizarre to us today because we associate castration with a loss of power and we have lived for so many centuries in a social environment in which women and power have not been linked. In our culture, vaginas are assumed to be toothless. But the idea of female castration was still meaningful to Mesopotamians in the third millennium B.C.E. and to Greeks of the classical era because they were not so far removed from a time when women had held a degree of power.

It is no accident that the severed head of Medusa appears on the shield or armor of Athena, the favorite goddess of the men of the city that bore her name. Athena's prominence does not indicate any importance for women; on the contrary, she symbolizes their complete subordination. She is a "non-woman."[47] Recall the words that Aeschylus placed in her mouth that provide this chapter's title: "There is no mother anywhere who gave me birth." Aeschylus made this lack of female creative power the clear basis for Athena's declaration: "I am always for the male with all my heart."[48] This statement clearly shows her to be just what Greek men had made her: Athena was a cheerleader.

Displaying the decapitated head of Medusa, however, was a more extreme statement than that made by the modern young women who wear school sweaters and jump up and down on the sidelines of a football game, hailing the males on the field of battle. The gorgon head on Athena shows that the *vagina dentata* has been defanged and women have been tamed and subordinated. The ultimate meaning of the Perseus myth, as classicist William Blake Tyrrell has said, "is the denial of birth from a female."[49] Placing Medusa's head on the shield of Athena, the cheerleader for male supremacy, symbolizes the removal of all power, including procreation, from women. Athena leads the cheers for the other team, for the people who have classified women as an alien, enemy species. Feminists seeking an equivalent of "Uncle Tom" as a rebuke for a woman who gladly plays the demeaning role assigned to her by her oppressors—and even roots for them—might try "Aunt Athena."

Nowhere is the concept of woman as representative of the other, the enemy, clearer than in the myth of the Amazons. The Amazons were said to be a nation of women who enslaved men, using them only for reproductive and related purposes, and were given to frequent warring. The Amazons were, in short, a complete inversion of the ordered world that Greek men had made for themselves. They were not at all the women represented by the earlier powerful goddesses and the Minoan civilization. They had *no* feminine ideals or practices; rather, they were the antithesis of the feminine. The Amazons were simply women who had taken on all the attributes usually associated with men.

Significantly Hippolytus, the product of a union of the Athenian hero-king Theseus with an Amazon (whom Theseus had raped and taken captive), was chosen by Euripides to sum up the feelings of Greek men toward women: "If

Men Defeat Women

Nowhere, perhaps, is the triumph of men over women more clearly portrayed than in the myth of the Greek defeat of the Amazons—powerful, manlike women who probably represented the greater degree of female equality that had existed in the Minoan civilization on Crete as late as the middle of the second millennium B.C.E. (Battle of Greeks and Amazons, from a frieze on the Mausoleum, Halikarnassos. Mid-fourth century. B.C.E. British Museum)

only we could have children without the help of women!"[50] Hippolytus goes on to declare: "I'll hate you women, hate and hate and hate you, and never have enough of hating. . . . [E]ternal, too, is woman's wickedness. . . . [S]uffer me to trample on them forever."[51] That a man whose mother was from a group the Athenians used to symbolize female power and had been raped by a Greek man (who subsequently defeated the Amazons as a whole) would make such a statement has similar meaning to the "motherless" Athena becoming a champion of male dominance.

Athenian Androcracy

The case against Classical Greece's attitudes toward women appears to be one in which the defendant might be hanged without the formality of a trial, but the matter of the Greeks and feminine values is, in fact, not nearly so simple. At the same time that Athenian men were expressing such misogyny,* some among them were actually attempting to refashion a balance of values between the supposed masculine and feminine extremes.

---

*One of the city's mythic heroes was Theseus, who was hailed for being a multiple rapist [Tyrrell, Amazons, pp. 4–5, 9]. Theseus was said to have raped Ariadne, Helen, and several other women as well as the Amazon who became the mother of Hippolytus.

The Athenians managed to develop principles that enabled them to adapt, for a time, to the new urban social environment. An essential feature of that value system was democracy. When Athenian democracy is being praised, it is often pointed out that it was a *direct* democracy. This political system is usually described in words like "the people themselves were the government." To a greater extent than was the case virtually anywhere at any time prior to the nineteenth century, this statement is in one sense true. But in another sense, it is completely false. The paradox between these two senses contains within it both the success and a large part of the ultimate failure of Athenian democracy.

By the end of the sixth century B.C.E., Athenian *citizens* did rule the polis, and directly. Not included in the citizenry, however, was a substantial majority of the polis's adult population: women, those not born to Athenian parents, and slaves. The exclusion of these three groups reveals the fatal flaws in Athens' otherwise commendable principles. Each of the disfranchised groups, in fact, represents a case of Athenian men's failure to come to grips with a portion of the human biological inheritance.

First, note a point that should be obvious but has not been to most observers throughout history: If there is, on average, a sexual division of values—and regardless of whether its source is attributed to biology or culture— "majority rule" when only men are permitted to be citizens will mean something quite different from majority rule when both sexes are given a voice. Rather than a true democracy, Athens was an *androcracy*. No matter how enlightened a society's men may be, if they are the only ones with any power in the government, the society will remain highly susceptible to an outbreak of overwrought male passions.* This imbalance is at least a partial explanation of what happened to Athens during its Golden Age in the fifth century B.C.E.

Greek (and especially Athenian) men were very community-minded. But, as has too often been the case in human history, they defined their community on the basis of who was *not* part of it.[52] Unquestionably, when Protagoras proclaimed that "*man* is the measure of all things," he meant males.[53] The public-spirited Greeks had no use for someone who was not concerned with public life. They called such a person an *idiot,* literally a "private person." But because women were completely excluded from public life in classical Athens (and almost all other societies for more than two thousand years thereafter), they were under this definition necessarily "idiots." The exclusion of women from public life in Athens meant their exclusion from *human* life, given the general acceptance of Aristotle's dictum that "man is by nature a political animal."[54]

---

*Something similar could be said of a "democracy" confined to women (*gynocracy*), whose particular passions surely can also be carried to excess; but such a female-only democracy is unknown to human history.

The Greek polis, one classicist has said, "was marked as a double exclusion: the exclusion of women, which made it a 'men's club'; and the exclusion of slaves, which made it a 'citizens' club."[55] This is true, but incomplete. These were not the only groups the Athenians otherized. The second category of people in Athens who were excluded from participating in this participatory democracy, the *metics* or "foreigners," demonstrates another major failure to bring a biological predisposition under control. This one, too, would play a large role in the downfall not only of Athens, but of the whole system of classical Greece. The part of the human biogram in question is, of course, the tendency toward identification with the band and the corresponding distrust of "strangers" or "others."

The third group excluded from Athenian democracy, the slaves, showed the Athenians' affinity for dominance, another of the usually more male traits, and one that also stood in the way of making democratic values fully balanced and truly effective.

Despite all of these very serious shortcomings, Athens in the late sixth and early fifth centuries made a strong effort at achieving a balance of values. That balance was embodied in a series of Greek concepts that can help us in our own pursuit of a better balance that will bridge the growing chasm between our biogram and our social environment. The first of these is *sophrosyne,* which refers to a quality of judgment that issues from one's understanding of his (we would add "or her") limited place in the world. Limitlessness terrified the Greeks,[56] who realized what too few of us do in the modern world: that a complete lack of limits causes everything to dissolve. The ideal, then, was "moderation in all things" and "nothing too much."

The Greeks believed that there is a "right order," which is fragile. Had they understood right order to mean the balance that values create between human nature and the social environment, they would have been correct; and certainly that right order is fragile. Their difficulties arose from their confusion of "right order" with the wrong order that they established on the basis of subordinating "inferiors," especially women and slaves. Although many Greek intellectuals practiced homosexuality, for instance, it was approved only if it was in keeping with their view of right order. It was acceptable for a mature male citizen to take the male sexual role in relations with "inferior" males as well as with women. The only males who could take on the female role were slaves, *metics,* and young males with an older man. Male citizens could take on the female role only until they began to grow beards. Anything else would upset right order of femaleness equaling inferiority.[57]

There were other violations of right order in addition to those that threatened the sexual hierarchy. Any attempt to exceed limitations endangered right order. Actions that threatened to destroy the right order were categorized as *hubris,* the most notable form of which was self-love and indifference to others, what Christians call the sin of pride.

As the fifth century B.C.E. progressed, Athenians became less public-spirited and more individualistic. The state turned to imperialism, collecting tribute or protection payments from lesser poleis in the Delian League. By the later years of the Peloponnesian War at the end of the fifth century B.C.E., Athenian individualism was approaching egoism. That long and horrible war also ended moderation by unleashing the inclinations to anger and violence that are present in most people and are, on average, stronger in men.

The level to which the Athenians had sunk by 416 B.C.E. was evident in their actions against the neutral polis of Melos. For their "crime" of neutrality, all the adult males of this polis were butchered and the women and children were sold into slavery. In the slightly longer run, the consequences of unleashing one part of human nature were devastating for the Athenians themselves and for the rest of Greece.

It would be ridiculous to suggest that such atrocities as those inflicted on the Melians could not have taken place if women had shared equally in the decision making of the Athenian polis. Certainly they *could.* But I do not hesitate to say that this sort of event would be *less likely* in a society in which the ideal of *sophrosyne* was enhanced by a balance of voices between the sexes and so between the values more associated with one sex or the other.[58]

Classical Athens plainly was not such a society. Much of what seems on the surface most admirable about Athenian life vanishes when the complete repression of women is entered into the equation. The well-known and often-praised practice of placing almost all of their efforts and resources into creating beautiful public buildings and places, while showing little concern for their private residences, for example, takes on a very different meaning when we consider that the public areas were defined as the world of men and the private ones were the places to which women were confined.

Whistling Past the Menstrual Hut

In the sixth century B.C.E., the same period in which so many of the religions and philosophies based on reintegrating more "feminine" values were emerging throughout the urbanized portions of the Old World, there was a sharp growth in the popularity of the Eleusinian mystery religion in Athens. The religion, focused on the worship of the Earth Mother Demeter, dates back at least to the beginning of the second millennium B.C.E. and presumably was a descendant of the earlier pervasive worship of creative goddesses. (Demeter was said to have come to Greece from Crete.[59]) But its resurgence, including the construction of a grand new telesterion (temple) in the 500s B.C.E., is suggestive of the same need for an infusion of more feminine values that was being felt in other regions at that time. Greek men, however, reacted with hostility to this development.

The worship of Demeter was centered in the town of Eleusis, a dozen miles northwest of Athens and under its political control. Greek tradition held that it was here that people had first learned to plant wheat. The myth upon which the religion was based said that Demeter's daughter Kore (or Persephone) was kidnapped and raped by Hades (Pluto), the god of the underworld. In her search for her daughter, Demeter was taken in by a king at Eleusis, where she taught the people agriculture. (Again it is the female who is said to have brought the knowledge of agriculture, corresponding to what we now

A Divine Mother and Child Image: Demeter and Kore
Demeter is one of the goddesses who is credited with the founding of agriculture, representing women actually having been the principal inventors of this new way of life. Her daughter, Kore, rises in the spring, much as Jesus would in a later religion. This stone statue is from Thebes, Boeotia. (Louvre)

believe to be the historical truth.) A deal was finally struck whereby Kore was returned to her mother for two-thirds of each year but had to go back underground for the other third. The symbolism of the growing season and the planting of seed in the ground is obvious. The Eleusinian Mystery used this as a metaphor for human rebirth, as well. Several of the religion's practices have their echoes in the later Christian mysteries, including resurrection (of what might be seen in the Eleusinian religion as "God the Daughter" by "God the Mother") and ritual cleansing and initiation by a sprinkling of water. But they were themselves echoes, in a culture that greatly subordinated women, of a much older and long-repressed principle of female divinity.[60]

It is in the light not only of the past power of goddesses and women in the Minoan period but also of the contemporary rise in popularity of the Eleusinian religion that Aeschylus' arguments against the importance of motherhood in 458 B.C.E. must be seen to be fully understood. The trilogy of which *The Eumenides* is the concluding play ends with the furies, representing the powerful goddesses of the past, being persuaded to accept their banishment to a place underground. The initial protest of the old goddesses perfectly captures what has happened to them, and women in general, as a result of the seed metaphor: "That they could treat me so! / I, the mind of the past, to be driven under the ground out cast, like dirt!" Yet, as Aeschylus tells it, the old goddesses finally accept their "new chambers" and "plunge beneath the ground" to "hold off what might hurt the land."[61] The urgency for Greek men of the argument Aeschylus was making was precisely that some women were, like the furies in his play, resisting consignment to the role of farm land—to being classified as "like dirt." The ideas of female divinity and some creative power for women were not yet dead, and some of the leading male minds of classical Greece were doing their best to finish them off.

About a century after Aeschylus, Aristotle took up the assignment with evident relish. Perpetuating and extending the fundamental error that had been made a few thousand years before in seeing the father as *the* procreator, Aristotle went about as far in arguing for male superiority as it is possible to go. He began with the classic dualistic error that had played a large part in producing the Conception Misconception. "It is impossible," he said, "that any creature should produce two seminal secretions at once."[62] In fact, of course, we now know that it is not only possible but actually the case for all sexually reproducing organisms to produce two types of "seminal" material, which must be combined in order to be productive. Completely endorsing the Conception Misconception and providing it with its most important scientific authority, Aristotle declared in *Generation of Animals* that "the semen produced by the male is the cause of the offspring."[63] He contended that semen is "spiritual," while the female contribution is little more than "primitive matter."[64]

Aristotle tried to invert womb envy by saying that the great defect in women is that they lack procreative power. Prior to the development of agriculture, when males were not thought to play a significant part in reproduction, men had seemed like "infertile women" or "deformed women," who were defined as male by their inability to reproduce. Now Aristotle asserted that it is the other way around. He argued that women provide the physical substance of the offspring ("primitive matter"), but that it is the father who gives life ("soul," "spirit") to this inanimate material. Aristotle declared that a female is essentially "a deformed male": "A woman is, as it were, an infertile male; the female, in fact, is female on account of inability."[65] What she lacks, the philosopher explained, is "the principle of Soul." He contended that females are a kind of "monstrosity."[66]

Aristotle also attempted to reverse the Non-Menstrual Syndrome. He classified menstrual fluid as a weak form of semen, lacking in the male fluid's life-giving powers. What Aristotle's claims about sexual secretions amount to is the avowal that it is men who have the good genital emission, while menstrual discharge is, as he delicately put it, similar to diarrhea and is just a diluted, sterile facsimile of semen (which the philosopher said is almost "divine").[67]

But one suspects that Aristotle was whistling past the menstrual hut.

In all of this, Aristotle was expressing deeply held assumptions of his culture. He and many other Greek thinkers saw man as the "form" of the ideal human. This conception, as I indicated at the end of the previous chapter, is a variant of seeing God—or the most powerful, creative god—as male. It means that males are closer to the ideal human and so females are lower, farther from the ideal. Such assumptions were at the base of the common instructions men gave to their pregnant wives: raise the baby if it is a boy; expose it and let it die if it is a girl.[68]

Nowhere is the dualistic basis of much human (and especially male) thought so evident as among the Greeks, and nowhere are the sexual associations of dualism more apparent than in Aristotle. As he saw it, the world is to be understood through opposing forces or principles. Aristotle did not doubt that in each dualistic pair there is a superior and an inferior. Form is superior to matter, good to evil, light to dark, soul to body, rationality to emotion, and so forth. In each case, Aristotle identified the superior side of the dichotomy with males and the inferior side with females. Since he took these inequalities to be natural, he had not the slightest doubt that it is right for men to rule over women. "The courage of a man," Aristotle declared, "is shown in commanding, of a woman in obeying."[69]

The assumption that everything in the world is divided into unequal opposites, the prototype for which is male and female, provided Aristotle with a justification for all other forms of dominance, such as masters over slaves and Greeks over "barbarians."[70] Thus an entire system of dominance and hierarchy was constructed on the foundation of dualism that was suggested by sexual differentiation and on the failure to understand that difference does not have to entail either polar opposition or inequality. This line of thinking long antedated Aristotle, of course. But the philosopher gave the dualistic, power-oriented, hierarchical masculine value system its classic expression—one which, although eventually diluted, persists in many quarters to the present day.

And yet . . .

Aristotle has become too easy a target. His role in our subject, like that of Athens, is not quite so simple as it appears on the surface. Plainly, Aristotle was a very important purveyor of ideas that are at the root of many of the troubles experienced throughout most of history. But he also expressed the basic *sophrosyne* idea of "moderation in all things" as the "golden mean," and made it the underlying theme of his system of values.[71] Aristotle let dualism and misogyny get the better of him, completely undermining the benefits that might have been derived from his values of moderation. But in expressing those values he made himself as important a figure in the potential solution as his misogyny made him in the problem.

The Proto-Modern Hellenistic Man's World

Following the conquests of Alexander "the Great,"* in the fourth century B.C.E., mass, impersonal societies arose, first in the Hellenistic kingdoms and then in the Roman Empire. Although the Hellenistic civilization was a blend of Greek and "Eastern" (mostly Persian) ways, the values that were dominant during the last three centuries B.C.E. were by no means a blend of opposites. Rather, they were far on the "masculine" side of the scale. There was consid-

---

*It is worth pointing out that "the Great" is a title that has only been appended to the names of leaders who exhibited "masculine" virtues or values in the extreme. (The only case of a woman who came to be known as "the Great," Catherine II of Russia, is no exception. It was her "masculine" qualities that led to the honorary title.) These virtues have invariably included excessive militarism, aggression, and love of power and dominance. It would, in fact, not be very far from the mark to suggest that a minimum qualification for being considered for the title "the Great" is responsibility for the killing of tens of thousands of humans and the oppression of millions. Excellence in adherence to "feminine" values has often led to sainthood, but never to anyone being called "the Great." That Mohandas Gandhi, one of the modern world's foremost practitioners of "feminine" values, was given the Indian title *mahatma,* which is partially derived from a Sanskrit word that translates to "great," simply confirms the point. The other part of the derivation of *mahatma* means "soul," so the title translates to "the Great Soul," which in practice implies almost the opposite of "the Great."

erably more mobility, both social and geographical, than there had been previously. Spatial mobility had, throughout the evolution of humans and their close relatives, characterized males more than females. It might not appear at first blush that mobility would be inconsistent with the human evolutionary heritage. If our ancestors evolved to live as collector-hunters, they must have moved about a good deal. But that was a very different kind of mobility. Hominids and Paleolithic humans moved around *in groups*. Their physical surroundings might change, but it was not a disorienting experience, because they remained with the people who provided their sense of identity and belonging—they took their "place" with them.

The mobility of the Hellenistic era—very significantly, like that of the modern world, which has experienced a megarevolution based on mobility similar to the one that had a false start in the centuries after Alexander—was sharply different from the sort in which human nature had developed. The Hellenistic world was a "new world"[72] in many of the same ways as the new world that arose after 1492 from Europeans' contact with what they called the "New World." People felt uprooted. Fierce economic competition became the norm. People began to relate to one another by contracts, rather than community customs. Although some grew very rich, the extremes of wealth and poverty became more pronounced. The possibility of upward mobility implied as well the prospect of downward mobility, creating increased feelings of insecurity.

The cosmopolitan* urban society was impersonal; it denied people an identification with a group of a size in which other members could be known. With this natural desire blocked, community feeling declined. Political interest lessened, not merely because there was no democracy, but because there was no polis, no community of which people felt a part, about which they cared, and which they felt cared about them.[73]

As social and political values declined, extreme individualism replaced them. Again and again the protomodern outlook of people in the Hellenistic era shows through: "Everything that limits freedom of personal choice [was] . . . considered with disfavor."[74] The source of the individualistic outlook that permeated the age was well stated by the philosopher Timon of Phlius:

> As the individual walked through the streets of the great cities, he was lost in the crowd, become a simple number in the midst of an infinity of human

---

*In this Alexander's new world order ran counter to human nature. Despite the meaning of *cosmopolitan,* the cosmos cannot be a polis; it is much too large and impersonal, and so cannot meet the human need for a personal community with which to identify. Given that human need, *cosmopolitan* is as contradictory as its modern counterpart, "the global village."

beings like himself, who knew nothing about him, of whom he knew nothing, a man who stood alone in bearing the weight of life without friends, without reason for living. . . .[75]

The modern sound of this indictment of Hellenistic society is unmistakable. This early period of urban cosmopolitanism showed the difficulty of reconciling human nature with the crowded, anonymous society of large, diverse cities. The same mobility, impersonality, extreme individualism, and dearth of community feeling, but in each case to an even greater excess, are among the major problems we face today.

On the positive side, the position of women improved noticeably in the Hellenistic era. One reason for the better treatment was that men retreated from the public life that Greek males had enjoyed in the polis. As they withdrew into the private realm that provided their only defense against the anonymous cosmopolitan world outside, men found themselves on the turf that had been designated as "female."

The Growing Need for "Feminine" Ways in a Paterfamilias Society

Roman society was firmly based upon values most often linked with men: authority, stability, order, hierarchy, militarism, and legalism. By the last century B.C.E. and the first centuries C.E., Rome was also turning increasingly to materialism, overconsumption, and self-absorption. Such characteristics were the products of biological predispositions that had been adaptive among collector-hunters but had hypertrophied in the impersonal urban-imperial Roman social environment.

The ways of early Rome were deeply rooted in the male-oriented values or virtues* that had grown out of the later part of the Agricultural Megarevolution: subordination of women, slavery, hierarchy, patriotism (pseudospeciation), loyalty, supremacy of the state over the individual, respect for tradition, war, and expansion.

Total male dominance in early Rome was evident in the position of the *paterfamilias,* the man who exercised thorough control over a family. The creation of families centered on a man who sent daughters off to become members of another family while accepting young women into his own. This situation was a complete reversal of the one among apes (and, perhaps, protohumans), in which mothers were the creators of social organizations, sent young males off at puberty to join another family, and decided whether to

---

*The word *virtue* itself is derived from the Latin root for "man" and literally means "manliness."

accept young males from other groups. This reversal was a significant part of the larger seizure of female roles by males that characterized the later period of the Agricultural Megarevolution. The switch to belief in male power over procreation was so sweeping that, until late in the Republic, Roman law recognized no relationship via women, not even that of a mother and her child.[76] The offspring was the father's, not the mother's, who, because of the Conception Misconception, was seen only as a vessel in which the man's seed could grow.

The absolute power of the Roman father was symbolized by the placing of each newborn infant at his feet for him to accept by picking it up or reject by leaving it. The unaccepted child was killed or abandoned.[77] The Roman view of abortion carried the same message. Romans were "pro-choice" on abortion, as they were on infanticide, but with the vitally important difference from the modern interpretation that for the Romans the choice was exclusively that of the man. A man was free to choose to order that "his" unborn child be aborted, or that his just-born child be exposed—or, for that matter, that his grown child be killed. The children were literally his; because it was accepted that *he* had created them, he *owned* them. But if a woman had an abortion without her husband's consent, she was subject to repudiation by the husband. And in the second century C.E., provision was made for a pregnant woman to be put under guard in order to prevent her from aborting the fetus. Her womb (the equivalent of her husband's farmland) was placed in custody to protect the property of her husband that it contained.[78]

Two points about the man's control over abortion and infanticide are of special interest for our subject. One is that the control would appear to have been a further outcome of the male seizure of the power of reproduction, a power that implies also the power *not* to reproduce. The other is that it represents the presumption that women should not make important decisions because they not rational. If women made these decisions, they would be influenced by emotion (which, of course, was considered to be bad). We can see from current practice that many women can make the decision to abort a fetus, but few mothers would choose to expose their babies after nine months of attachment. Men, feeling considerably less connection to the unborn or just-born child, could make these decisions on a "rational" (economic) basis, not an emotional one.

Nothing so fully indicated the position of women in the Roman Republic as the fact that they were literally anonymous. Women in Rome were not given first (personal, individual) names. Instead, they were usually known by the feminized name of their father. This practice indicated, as one scholar has put it, that Roman men believed that women were not "genuine individuals, but only fractions of a family."[79]

The set of "masculine" values worked well enough in Rome, as it did elsewhere, until further changes in the human environment made some of them considerably more maladaptive. Conquest—particularly Rome's ruthless triumph over Carthage in the three Punic Wars (264–146 B.C.E.)—brought with it growing centralization and imperialism, a rapid swelling of population and urbanization, excessive wealth, greed, an insatiable appetite for luxury, vastly increased class differentiation, the availability of many more slaves, and an extraordinary taste for violence and bloodshed.[80]

One of the most remarkable alterations in the Roman outlook and values that came in the wake of the Punic Wars and the establishment of the empire was, as had been the case following Alexander's imperialism, the rise of individualism. The lure of wealth and indulgence apparently led many of the formerly community-minded Romans to become self-centered. Divorce—always the "right" of a Roman man, for any reason or no reason—became common and available to women. Family life declined.[81] The positive side of the weakening of family was that it liberated women from some of the repression of the male-dominated Roman family; the negative side was that it "liberated" both sexes from the lasting personal bonds that human nature craves.

Among the many abuses that arose in Rome in the last two centuries B.C.E. and continued thereafter, the two most notable were self-indulgence and cruelty. Neither of these vices is rare among humans, but both reached their outer limits in Roman society. Never (not even in the United States today, although we seem to be getting uncomfortably close to it) has the innate desire for sustenance gone as far astray under conditions of surplus as it did among the Roman aristocracy. The infamous *vomitorium,* in which Romans who had gorged themselves would induce regurgitation in order to allow even more needless overconsumption, is unsurpassed in this type of self-indulgence.

Even more revolting, though, was the Roman liking for human carnage. And this abuse may be more indicative of the extreme imbalance of Roman society and thinking than the extraordinary overconsumption, because the latter was necessarily confined to the wealthy, but large portions of the population, across class lines, indulged their appetite for watching gore and killing. Earlier games and circuses had often been bloody affairs, but it was not until 29 B.C.E. that the first permanent amphitheater for gladiatorial contests was constructed in Rome. In these battles, men engaged in mortal combat for the amusement of large throngs that often shouted for the victor to thrust his sword into the heart of the loser. Nor was this the extent of the horror. The shows also featured mass butcherings of the defenseless and the exposure of unarmed people to lions and other beasts. Crowds roared their approval as the animals tore apart the flesh of living human beings. These shows became so popular that the massive Colosseum was built (80 C.E.) to permit more people to see the ghastly displays.[82]

As was the case in the Hellenistic kingdoms that preceded Roman dominion in the eastern Mediterranean, imperial Rome at its height was a huge, protomodern, cosmopolitan, impersonal society in which the more "masculine" values became stronger, but in which growing individualism led to some improvement in the treatment of women. There is no question that the position of women—at least those in the aristocracy—improved substantially during this period. It is often said that women were "emancipated" in the last years of the Republic and the first centuries of the Empire.[83] But this in no way detracts from the assessment that, in terms of dominant values, Rome had by the late first century B.C.E. become more of a male world than ever before. The "liberation" (and certainly it was only a partial liberation) of women did nothing to enhance feminine values. On the contrary, to the degree that women were emancipated in the Roman Empire, it was because such emancipation fit with the masculine values that were so completely triumphant.

The moral degeneration was not, of course, universally approved. Many Roman writers condemned the bloody spectacles and the unabashed promiscuity of the age. But most of them saw women as the source of the trouble. Many of the points that such men as Juvenal, Martial, and Tacitus made about the degradation of Roman society were valid. But their misogyny led them to blame women's immorality and desire for luxury for the problems.[84]* In fact, the lust and greed displayed by many members of both sexes in imperial Rome are more accurately seen as consequences of the victory of an impersonal society of disconnection that failed to fulfill some of the basic needs of human nature.

It also should be noted that the behavior of prominent women that was so righteously condemned by many male moralists stemmed from these women adopting male practices. Perhaps it is true that Augustus's wife, Livia, poisoned many members of his family, and that Claudius's wife, Messalina, was a shameless adulterer. But what was so horrifying to the men relating their acts was not the misdeeds which, at least in the case of shameless adultery, were not at all uncommon among the men of their time and class, but that they were engaged in by women.

---

*Juvenal's extremely bitter "Against Women" is an excellent example. He says that when people were poor, women were chaste, but when they become rich, "There's nothing a woman won't do, nothing she thinks is disgraceful." That the outrage is about women acting the way many men do is clear when Juvenal writes: "God help her husband / . . . To her lovers she comes with her skin washed clean. But at home / Why does she need to look pretty?" [Gloria K. Fiero, ed., *The Humanistic Tradition* (Dubuque, IA: Brown & Benchmark, 1992), vol. 1, p. 137].

The fact that a small number of women gained political power in the Empire in the first few centuries C.E. in no sense means that ideals classified as feminine were not suppressed. Two third-century empresses, Julia Domma and her sister Maesa, for example, had children of theirs killed to advance their ambitions.[85] Nothing could show more emphatically that the price women paid for power in Rome was the abandonment of values generally associated with women. Imperial Rome was a man's world that came to allow a few women to play its games—so long as they played by the men's rules.

One aspect of the man's world of Rome was the popularity, especially within the military, of the Persian religion of Mithraism, which was imported into Italy and other parts of the western Mediterranean in the first century B.C.E. This cult focused on the worship of a sun god, Mithras. The sun had generally been associated with male deities, as the moon had with goddesses (because of the correspondence of the length of menstrual cycles with lunar months). The religion promised salvation for initiates, through the power of a personal savior. Thus it met a need that was being increasingly felt in the mass, impersonal Roman society, but it did so only for men. Mithraism completely excluded women. Although this aspect of the religion apparently appealed to some men, especially those involved in government and the military, Mithraism's male exclusivity meant that it could not meet the greatest need of the time. It excluded not only women but also the values most often identified with them. Instead, Mithraism stressed the "manly virtues" that were in keeping with Roman practice.[86]

The horrors of the Roman world by the last century B.C.E. and the first centuries C.E. were for the most part grotesque extensions of biological predilections that are, on average, stronger in males. Conditions cried out for an infusion of approaches that had been condemned as "feminine." Whatever its other attractions, Mithraism obviously did not fit the bill in this regard. These circumstances seemed tailor-made for the introduction of a religion based upon the resurrected "feminine" values represented in the past by powerful goddesses.

The first way in which an attempt was made to meet this need was through the widespread popularity of the religion of Isis. Enthusiasm for this religion was particularly strong in the urban areas, where the incongruity between hypertrophied male tendencies and the altered social environment was greatest. The worship of the Egyptian goddess reached Italy as early as the second century B.C.E. There were notable similarities between the Isis religion as it had developed by this time and the Christianity that would emerge more than a century later. Isis had come to be seen as a supreme deity, *the* Creator. She incorporated even the powers over thunder that were associated with the male creator gods who had usurped the position of the creator goddesses a couple of thousand years before. Isis proclaimed her powers:

I gave and ordained laws for men which no one is able to change.
I am she that is called goddess by women.
I divided the earth from the heaven.
I brought together women and men.[87]

The Isis religion in Roman times clearly was the resurrection of the powerful goddesses who had been interred (or "castrated") in the ways we saw in the preceding chapter.

Isis's magical powers hinted that she was an hermaphrodite.[88] The Isis religion prefigured Christianity in holding out the promise of rebirth (based on Isis's reconstruction of Osiris); in stressing individual responsibility and salvation; in appealing to the downtrodden, including women and slaves; in providing an intimate, personal relationship between the initiate and the deity; and in seeing that Supreme Being as being merciful and compassionate—in short, as displaying "feminine" values. A second century B.C.E. papyrus thanks Isis "for having given women strength equal to men."[89]

Interestingly, it was said that when Isis rebuilt Osiris, she had to omit one part that she could not find: his phallus.[90] This story may indicate the perceived need to restructure men to fit the new environment by eliminating—or at least restraining—some of the no-longer-adaptive proclivities that are more common in males and so are associated with male sexuality.

The Isis religion met many of the needs of a large number of Romans who were dissatisfied with aspects of their society: its violent and degenerate practices, its class stratification, and its emphasis on relationships based upon dominance and subordination. It attracted many devotees in the last years of the Republic and through the first centuries C.E. The worship of Isis was considered sufficiently threatening to the male-oriented world of Rome that on numerous occasions in these years the authorities ordered that altars and temples to the goddess be destroyed.[91]

Yet the religion of Isis did not serve as well as that of Jesus would, especially during the years in which Rome was in its serious decline, for many reasons. The Isis religion might have satisfied the purely religious demands of people seeking salvation nearly as readily as Christianity did. But it did not place a sufficiently heavy emphasis upon personal adherence to the values that were needed to curb the excesses of the time. More importantly, a religion in which the deity was seen as female and in which many of the priests were women was at a severe disadvantage.

One of the powerful goddesses of old had to return, but she would have an easier time getting a hearing and having a chance for her values to be accepted by men if she appeared in male form.

Of the major religions that offered the Roman people salvation and personal immortality, Mithraism was all male and could not meet the value needs of the time. The worship of Isis came closer to providing what was needed in the way of values. It appealed to men as well as women, but its view of the Supreme Being as a female limited its potential among the group most in need of an infusion of more female values: men. The way was open for a religion that could in some way synthesize portions of Mithraism with much of the Isis religion—one that combined a more "feminine" value system with a view of God as a male.

CHAPTER 9

She Is Risen——And Fallen
The Sexes from Early Christianity Through the Middle Ages

Crist was a mayde, and shapen as a man*
"THE WIFE OF BATH"[1]

The need to restrain some of the more male proclivities increased as populations grew, societies became more urban and complex, and warfare became more dangerous (because of larger armies equipped with deadlier weapons). An increased emphasis on feminine values was needed in the ethical system under which people operated. But this need could be met only by men themselves preaching feminine values. There was little prospect that large numbers of men would listen to a bunch of women (or a female deity) telling them that they should try to suppress some of their innate (and culturally enhanced) male tendencies—a message they were likely to hear as: "You men need to start acting more like women." This item would not be an easy one to sell in the male market under the best of circumstances. If there was to be any chance of moving men in this direction, the more feminine values had to be re-emphasized by men—and commanded by an apparently male God.

This process can be seen, in effect, as the return of one of the powerful creative goddesses in male disguise. (The statement by Chaucer's "Wife of Bath" quoted at the head of this chapter seems to suggest something like this.) This effort reached its culmination in the teachings of Jesus. He had a tough enough time persuading a people anticipating a violent warrior savior that he, preaching peace and compassion, was the Messiah. There was no way that

---

*Christ was a maid, yet shaped like a man.

men in religions and cultures as dominated by males as were Judaism and the Greco-Roman world* at the beginning of the Christian era were going to listen to, let alone follow, a female Messiah.

Like Chaucer a half millennium before him, Henry Adams perceived much of what I believe to have been the actual role of Jesus and his religion. "The historian who studied the sources of Christianity," Adams wrote of himself early in the twentieth century, "felt sometimes convinced that the Church had been made by the woman chiefly as her protest against man." Adams went on to suggest what had happened to religion in his own male-dominated, scientific era: "At times, the historian would have been almost willing to maintain that the man had overthrown the Church chiefly because it was feminine."[2]

Jesus Christ Supergenderblender

The role of the teachings of Jesus in the man's world of Rome has been well summed up by historian Jo Ann McNamara: "The Roman tradition upheld the virtues associated with male virility; the developing Christian tradition consciously urged the feminine virtues of compassion and humility on both women and men."[3]

The essence of the new, more feminine and universal values that Jesus taught is to be found in the Sermon on the Mount. When Yahweh had called Moses to Mount Sinai more than a thousand years earlier, the emphasis had been on values governing behavior within the tribe. Now Jesus went to another mountain—at least in Matthew's version, which is clearly intended to indicate that this new message is replacing or modifying the one carried by Moses. There he told his disciples that the old values were no longer good enough. Although of course he did not use this terminology, he was saying that it was now necessary for men to move along the scale of values in the direction of what had been classified as female traits—and for both men and women to suppress their innate proclivity for pseudospeciation.

In the Sermon on the Mount, Jesus explicitly repudiated the tribalism of the old covenant law and extended and universalized the values that Moses had proclaimed as ethical standards within the group:

> You have heard that it was said, "An eye for an eye and a tooth for a tooth." But I say to you, Do not resist one who is evil. But if any one strikes you on the right cheek, turn to him the other also; and if any one would sue you and take

---

*In both Greece and Rome, numerous large stone carvings of male genitalia were objects of civic reverence (*Love in the Ancient World* [1996, produced and directed by Christopher Miles, Milesian Film Productions, Primetime, and A&E Network]).

your coat, let him have your cloak as well; and if any one forces you to go one mile, go with him two miles. Give to him who begs from you, and do not refuse him who would borrow from you.

You have heard that it was said, "You shall love your neighbor and hate your enemy." But I say to you, Love your enemies and pray for those who persecute you, so that you may be sons of your Father in heaven; for he makes his sun rise on the evil and on the good, and sends rain on the just and the unjust. For if you love those who love you, what reward have you? Do not even the tax collectors do the same? And if you salute only your brethren, what more are you doing than others? Do not even the Gentiles do the same? You, therefore, must be perfect, as your heavenly Father is perfect.[4]

The view of the "heavenly Father" that Jesus presented here is a substantially different one from that of Yahweh in the Torah (although not so different from the more androgynous God of the second Isaiah). He is no thunder god. What "He" is, in fact, seems more like a "heavenly Mother." But in a male form himself and referring to God as "Father," Jesus was legitimating—sanctifying—the idea that it is appropriate, indeed necessary, for men to take up values and practices that might not seem to them to be properly masculine.

Earlier in the Sermon on the Mount, in the Beatitudes, Jesus clearly outlined a set of values that run counter to those that had been practiced since the establishment of the supremacy of male storm gods late in the Agricultural Megarevolution:

Blessed are the poor in spirit, for theirs is the kingdom of heaven.
Blessed are those who mourn, for they shall be comforted.
Blessed are the meek, for they shall inherit the earth.
Blessed are those who hunger and thirst for righteousness, for they shall be satisfied.
Blessed are the merciful, for they shall obtain mercy.
Blessed are the pure in heart, for they shall see God.
Blessed are the peacemakers, for they shall be called sons of God.
Blessed are those who are persecuted for righteousness' sake, for theirs is the kingdom of heaven.[5]

It would be difficult to imagine a more radical break with the prevailing male storm god ways than that outlined in these words. There has never been, of course, any serious question that Jesus' teachings were revolutionary, but the particular *way* in which they were radically subversive has, I believe, rarely been properly understood.

The modus vivendi that had been reached between the altered environment and human nature during the last three millennia B.C.E. was one based, as we have seen, on male dominance, hierarchy, slavery, and such "masculine" values as competition, readiness to resort to violence (military virtues), and tribalism (patriotism). This value system had worked well enough in the agricultural societies in which and for which it had developed, but it was increasingly counterproductive in the heavily populated urban cosmopolitan world of Hellenistic and Roman times.

Jesus directly challenged one after another of the prevailing masculine virtues. To the idea that militarism was necessary for protection, he said: "When a strong man, fully armed, guards his own palace, his goods are in peace; but when one stronger than he assails him and overcomes him, he takes away his armor in which he trusted, and divides his spoil."[6] When Peter attempted to use violence to defend Jesus, the latter rebuked him: "Put your sword back into its place; for all who take the sword will perish by the sword."[7] Against the common male desire for power and domination, Jesus said: "My strength is made perfect in weakness."[8]

The Letter of James, echoing the values Jesus had espoused in the Sermon on the Mount, directly confronted the part of human nature, especially strong in males, that places a premium on quick anger and response. The author of this letter, like Jesus, understood that this innate predisposition must be brought under control: "Let every man be quick to hear, slow to speak, slow to anger, for the anger of man does not work the righteousness of God."[9] This message might be paraphrased as: *Ask questions first, then you may not have to shoot.* Here was a clear understanding of both the human biogram (particularly in its male incarnation) and its incongruity with the social environment.

The emphasis on excessive accumulation and consumption that had grown up since agriculture had begun to provide a surplus was a frequent target of Jesus and his followers. Attacks on this hypertrophied trait provide some of the most memorable Christian exhortations, including the following: "For what does it profit a man, to gain the whole world and forfeit his life?"[10]; "whoever exalts himself will be humbled, and whoever humbles himself will be exalted"[11]; "it is more blessed to give than to receive"[12]; "it is easier for a camel to go through the eye of a needle than for a rich man to enter the kingdom of God"[13]; and "those who desire to be rich fall into temptation, into a snare, into many senseless and hurtful desires that plunge men into ruin and destruction. For the love of money is the root of all evils."[14]

The early Christians urged people to distinguish between wants and needs, to seek enough, rather than everything. "But if we have food and clothing, with these we shall be content," Paul wrote to Timothy.[15] They sought to replace competition with cooperation. "We are members of one another," Paul wrote to the Ephesians.[16] "[I]f you bite and devour one another," Paul warned, "take heed that you are not consumed by one another."[17] Compassion and sharing were, of course, frequently emphasized by Jesus and his followers.

Most obvious is when Jesus declared that at the Judgment God will reward the good, saying "for I was hungry and you gave me food, I was thirsty and you gave me drink, I was a stranger and you welcomed me, I was naked and you clothed me, I was sick and you visited me, I was in prison and you came to me," then going on to explain, "as you did it to one of the least of my brethren, you did it to me."[18] The First Letter of John contains a good example of the call to compassion: "But if any one has the world's goods and sees his brother in need, yet closes his heart against him, how does God's love abide in him?"[19]

Paul dualistically summarized the distinction between the maladaptive biological predispositions, which he called "the works of the flesh," and the values preached by Jesus, which he called "the fruit of the Spirit." In the former category, he included "enmity, strife, jealousy, anger, selfishness, dissension, party spirit, [and] envy." The Christian values that Paul enumerated sound like a list of those often associated with femininity: "love, joy, peace, patience, kindness, goodness, faithfulness, gentleness, self-control." Paul nicely stated the way these more feminine values could control undesirable innate predispositions when he said that "those who belong to Christ Jesus have crucified the flesh with its passions and desires."[20]

The Son of Woman

When it is recalled that the subordination of women appears to have been the model upon which other forms of dominance (and hence slavery and the whole system of hierarchy) were based, it becomes clear that any attempt to overturn the existing structure had to include a rejection of the subordination of women. Therefore, even if the deity and teacher urging a move (especially by men) toward feminine values of necessity had to appear in male form, if the message was to succeed in undermining the system of values based on power and dominance, it had to include the repudiation of male dominance over females.

Since the Christian Church that was institutionalized in the early centuries C.E. plainly did not treat women as equals, it is easy to miss the critical point that, to a substantial extent, Jesus *did* so treat them. Despite the facts that the New Testament was written during a period in which church "fathers" were in the process of securing anew the subordination of women and that there are many attacks on women in it, no such negative statement about women is ever attributed to Jesus himself.

In fact, what most of us think of as the early Christian position on women could with more accuracy be called the "Pauline position" on women. It comes from a series of statements in Paul's epistles. When Paul sought to justify the subordination of women, he turned for his authority not to the Messiah he followed but to the Torah, especially the androcentric version of creation in

Genesis 2 and 3, which had long been a key part of the usurpation of female importance.[21] How central that reversal of nature has been in subsequent errors is evidenced by Paul buttressing his case for male domination by saying: "For man was not made from woman, but woman from man."[22] Using this classic Judeo-Christian version of the Conception Misconception as authority, Paul put the consequences of the assumption that God is male in the most unmistakable terms when he wrote: "For a man ought not to have his head veiled, since he is the image and reflection of God; but woman is the reflection of man."[23] Women should be veiled, Paul thought, because they are, unlike men (who are closer to the supposedly male God), too imperfect. Paul was, in short, agreeing with Aristotle that women are "monstrosities."

Attempts to Revive Feminine Values
Jesus was the most important of several male religious and philosophical leaders from the sixth century B.C.E. to the first century C.E. who attempted to reintegrate more feminine values into the "man's world" that had become so entrenched by that time. Women were originally prominent among the followers of Jesus, as is indicated in this illumination. (*The Women at the Tomb,* from the *Rabula Gospel,* Zagba on the Euphrates, Syria. ca. 586 C.E. Biblioteca Laurenziana, Florence)

Although it has generally been conveniently ignored, women were centrally involved in the birth of Christianity. They were disciples, prophets, missionaries, and, most important, the first to recognize Jesus as the Messiah and the essential witnesses to the events most basic to Christian belief: the death, burial, and resurrection of Jesus.[24]

The people who first accepted Jesus as the Christ were the sisters of Lazarus, Martha and Mary of Bethany. Martha said to Jesus, before the raising of Lazarus, "I believe that you are the Christ, the Son of God, he who is coming into the world."[25] And it was Mary of Bethany who subsequently anointed Jesus' head with expensive ointment, signifying her recognition of him as the Messiah, the Anointed. The male disciples reproached her for wasting the valuable ointment, but Jesus said, "She has done a beautiful thing to me." He told them, "And truly, I say to you, wherever the gospel is preached in the whole world, what she has done will be told in memory of her."[26]

But Mary of Bethany has not been much remembered. Mark tells the story of the anointing, but does not even include her name, referring only to "a woman." (Recall that literal anonymity for women was part of the Roman system of repressing women.) Like other women who played key roles in the founding of Christianity, this Mary was shunted aside by the men who took control of the religion after Jesus was crucified. Luke, one of the major agents in downplaying the role of the women around Christ, alters the story of the anointing to make the woman "a sinner." In Luke's account there is no indication that she has performed the act of a prophet, recognizing Jesus as the Messiah.[27] Jesus assumed that this woman would (and should) be remembered, but for the most part she has not been. This disparity suggests a great deal about the ways in which Jesus' attitudes toward women differed from those of many men who became prominent in the Christian movement after his death.

Not surprisingly, women recognized that this suffering and serving man, who taught that everyone should behave in accordance with values usually associated with females, was the Messiah. His message that the last would be first had a special appeal to those who really were treated as "last"—on the bottom.[28] But it was Jesus' values that had a particular resonance for women. The male disciples had a difficult time accepting his meekness. The men still expected a "king of glory." It was Peter who, *after* the anointing by Mary of Bethany, resorted to the sword and cut off a man's ear before being restrained by a warning from Jesus. And it was, of course, Peter who denied Jesus three times—this, too, after the anointing. Doubting Peter. While the male disciples were doubting, denying, and abandoning their peaceful leader, we are told that many women followed him to Jerusalem.[29] The first disciple to whom the risen Christ appeared was Mary Magdalene.[30] This appearance was another indication of his refusal to accept the subordination of women that was at the base of the value system against which he was rebelling.

The men who took control of the Christian Church in the first few centuries after Jesus did their best to obscure the role of women in its early years. Later exegetes have generally followed suit. One modern student, for instance, has concluded that Phoebe, a deaconess referred to in Romans 16, was a "charitable lady, who because of her feminine virtues worked in the service of the poor and sick and assisted in the baptism of women."[31] It is striking that what this statement describes as "feminine virtues" are said to have caused Phoebe to perform just the kinds of services to others that Jesus himself undertook and called upon his followers to emulate. The biblical scholar does not seem to notice this, but it is a good example of the way in which the teachings and practices of Jesus amounted to a reinvigoration of feminine values.

Viewed from the perspective being used here, the rebirth that Jesus' rising represented can be seen as the resurrection of feminine values. These qualities had been buried by the effects of the disruptions of the Agricultural Megarevolution, the attendant reinterpretation of the roles of the sexes in procreation, and the eventual displacement of the creative goddesses by variants of the male thunder God. There are several interesting sidelights worthy of noting. First, the claimed virgin birth of Jesus, like those of the prophets of several other Eastern "mystery religions" of the era, implies a return to the mother as the (pro)creator. She gives birth without having been penetrated by a male—she procreates by *her*self.* Second, when Jesus foretold his resurrection, he said that the "Son of man" must "be killed, and after three days rise again."[32] He never made clear his understanding of "Son of man," a term he used several times to describe himself.[33] A possible reading is that the now maladaptive characteristics that were stronger in males had to be suppressed and men rise again with values that were better suited to the social environment. Another interpretation might be that the set of values associated with the Conception Misconception (implied by "Son of man") and the triumph of the male God over the goddesses had to be replaced by others. What those other values were is suggested by the facts that dying and rising on the third day corresponds to the moon's disappearance in its "new" phase and reappearance, and the moon had generally been associated with goddesses. The occurrence of Easter in conjunction with the vernal equinox put it at the time of spring rebirth that had long been linked to worship of creative goddesses. Indeed, the very word *Easter* is derived from the name of a goddess who was called Eastre in Old English. And then there is the crucified Jesus being placed in a cave, which might be taken as symbolic of the womb of the Earth Mother, and emerging from it, reborn.

---

*Of course this is explained as an act of God in the form of the Holy Spirit, but the implication of female creativity remains. The idea of virgin birth is the ultimate undermining of the seed metaphor.

In many places, particularly in those served by the Eastern Orthodox Church, Christians greet one another on Easter morning by saying, "He is risen!" It might be more appropriate, given what Jesus and his resurrection symbolized, to proclaim: "*She* is risen!"*

The "Efemination" of Christianity

The essence of Jesus' message, like that of the Buddha, is one of inclusion and nonviolence. The repudiation of pseudospeciation, dominance, and hierarchy is put even more succinctly than in the Sermon on the Mount in the oft-quoted passage from Paul's Letter to the Galatians: "There is neither Jew nor Greek, there is neither slave nor free, there is neither male nor female; for you are all one in Christ Jesus."[34] If Christianity at its outset was so inclusive, and Jesus intended not only to revive feminine values but to undermine the basis of dominance and hierarchy by accepting the equality of women, it must be asked how the Church came to be ruled exclusively by men.

There was a significant struggle in the early years of the developing Christian Church over the role of women. Part of this centered on the importance of Mary Magdalene, as opposed to Peter. Luke and Paul abetted the largely successful attempt to ignore Mary Magdalene and pretend that events had occurred the way Peter wished they had.[35] Despite the facts that three of the canonical gospels plainly state that the risen Jesus first appeared to Mary Magdalene and that women are prominently mentioned throughout the gospel accounts of the crucifixion and resurrection, Paul gave the Christians in Corinth an account of the first Easter and its aftermath that sounds as if it took place in a men's club: "[H]e appeared to Cephas [Peter], then to the twelve. Then he appeared to more than five hundred *brethren* at one time. . . . Then he appeared to James, then to all the apostles. Last of all, as to one untimely born, he appeared also to me."[36] Paul simply ignores the women. Like good chil-

---

*The argument in this section should demonstrate just how mistaken is the longstanding contention that women are not eligible to join the clergy because they are not "like Jesus." Such fallacious arguments continue. In 1977, Pope Paul VI declared that women cannot be priests "because our Lord was a man." In a 1994 Apostolic Letter, "On Reserving Priestly Ordination to Men Alone," Pope John Paul II said that the ordination of women in the Roman Catholic Church is not even a matter open to discussion because all of Jesus' apostles were men. (The error in that specific claim will be addressed in the next section.) In 1998, the Church raised the doctrine that women cannot be priests to the level of canon law and threatened to excommunicate Catholics who oppose the ban. And in 2000, the Southern Baptist Convention decreed that "the office of pastor is limited to men as qualified by Scripture." Compensating for what men cannot do by telling women what they may not do is still very much alive, although it never has been well.

dren, they are not heard. But neither are they seen. Jesus had not put up the usual male "No Girls Allowed" sign on his clubhouse, but Peter and Paul pretended that he had.

Although some Christian groups continued as late as the fourth century to see Mary Magdalene as one with apostolic authority, as men gained more power in determining which of the early writings would be given canonical standing they excluded, by about 200 C.E., those books such as the Gospels of Thomas and Mary that gave her (and other women) a prominent place.[37] Significantly, the Apostolic Church Order uses Magdalene herself to argue that women, because they are weak, must be saved by those who are strong, and so the priesthood should be confined to males.[38] (Notice how this parallels Aeschylus' use of Athena to endorse male supremacy.) Eventually, as the Church became fully institutionalized in the fourth century, the idea that women could hold positions of religious leadership was flatly branded as heresy.[39]

The denial of a place in the Church leadership for women was one aspect of a pervasive re-establishment of male supremacy among Christians. At least as important was the exclusion of a feminine element from the deity itself. Many early Christians (especially some of the Gnostics, who were eventually labeled as heretics) held that there is a female element in God. The Gnostic gospels, which were excluded from the canon by early Church leaders, and most of which remained unknown until copies were accidentally found in Egypt in 1945, emphasized the account of creation in Genesis 1 ("in the image of God he created him; male and female he created them").[40] The Gnostics took this, quite sensibly, to indicate that *both* sexes equally reflect God's image and that God is metasexual, transcending sexual division. A divine voice in one of the Gnostic texts proclaims: "I am androgynous. [I am both Mother and] Father, since [I copulate] with myself. . . . I am the Womb [that gives shape] to All."[41] Another of the Gnostic books reverses the Egyptian story that attributes Creation to Ra's will and masturbation by telling of a female divinity who "desired herself alone in order to become androgynous. She fulfilled her desire, and became pregnant from her desire."[42]

Many early Christians saw the Trinity as Father, *Mother,* and Son. In the Apocryphon of John, the Trinity appears before John and says, "I [am the father]; I am the Mother; I am the Son."[43] The book goes on to say of the Spirit, "She became the Mother of everything, for she existed before them all, the mother-father [*matropater*]."[44] In the Gospel to the Hebrews, Jesus refers to "my Mother, the Spirit," and in the Gospel of Thomas, he speaks of his "divine Mother, the Holy Spirit."[45]

A major part of the process of what might be called the "efemination" (a word meant to indicate something equivalent to emasculation) of Christianity was the rejection of any idea that part of the Trinity is female. As late as 325

C.E., when the Council of Nicaea attempted to establish orthodoxy, it avoided the question of the sex of the Holy Spirit by including in its creed the simple statement, "And we believe in the Holy Spirit." By later in the same century, however, the modified Nicene Creed emanating from the Council of Constantinople (381 C.E.) referred to the Holy Spirit in masculine terms. The Creed recited today leaves no doubt that the third member of the Trinity is also male: "We believe in the Holy Spirit, the *Lord,* the giver of life, who proceeds from the Father and the Son. With the Father and the Son, *he* is worshiped and glorified. *He* has spoken through the prophets."

In this Creed "the giver of life" is seen as a male. The monumental scientific error of the Agricultural Megarevolution was reaffirmed when this Creed was established, and it is perpetuated by hundreds of millions of Christians reciting these words every week right down to the present day. Surely we ought to know better than to continue to act as if males "give life" all by themselves.

What sense can be made of the idea that we refer to a Father and a Son, but not to a Mother? But, many would respond, we *do* speak of a Mother, the Virgin Mary. The problem with this interpretation, however, is that it leaves Jesus with a divine father and a human mother. The implication is an even more extreme version of Aristotle's view that what the father provides to a child is spiritual and divine, while the mother's contribution is merely mundane and material. When the gross misunderstanding of the role of the sexes in procreation and the effects of the agricultural metaphor are comprehended, it can be seen that all of this is a further outgrowth of that colossal and omnipresent mistake. The "seed" that would produce Jesus had to be divine, and so came from a "heavenly Father." The mother, though, could be earthly; in fact, for people with this way of thinking ingrained in them, she *had to be* earthly, because the role of the woman was thought to be that of the earth: soil in which a seed could grow. "Virgin soil" in this case, perhaps, but soil all the same.

The source of thinking of the divine spiritual creator as male and the contributor of the earthly human material as female is clear enough, but it has interesting implications. If Jesus' divinity came entirely from a heavenly Father and his humanity entirely from an earthly mother, it would seem necessarily to follow that he was "made flesh"—united with humanity—through a woman. Where did this leave mortal men in the process? The question was eloquently answered by the American feminist and former slave Sojourner Truth in 1851: "Whar did your Christ come from? From God and a woman! Man had nothin' to do wid Him!"[46] It is one of the most essential elements of Christian belief that God "became man" in order to suffer and die and thereby redeem humans from sin. If the way he "became man" was through a woman, then salvation was entering the world by the same route that Genesis says that sin did—via a woman.

Yet even though this understanding necessarily grows out of men's own formula (enshrined by Aristotle) of male equaling the spiritual and female equaling material (male = divine; female = earthly), men did not follow their premises to their logical conclusion. They continued to blame *all* women for Eve's bringing of sin into the world, but they rarely credited *any* women for Mary's bringing of salvation into the world. Eve's act was taken to be typical of women, but Mary's act was said to be unique. Eve represented all women; of Mary Catholics say: "blessed art thou among women." She is held to be different from all others of her sex.

Born Again as Likeawoman

The message of Jesus and his depiction of God is radically different from that of the Superman God of Genesis. How much so is evident in the contrast between God's attitude toward the sacrifice of Cain and the sacrifices that Christians say are acceptable to God. The Christian sacrifice is one of bread and wine ("fruit of the vine and the work of human hands"), two products of plants. The macho God of Genesis 4 ridiculed a sacrifice of such "womanly" plant stuff. One version of the Catholic Eucharistic prayer explicitly compares the sacrifice of these products from plants with the animal sacrifice of Abel that had pleased God: "Look with favor on these offerings and accept them as once you accepted the gifts of your servant Abel." By equating the bread and wine made from plants with his own flesh and blood (meaty, animal, "manly" stuff), Jesus was saying that the produce of the farm is as acceptable to the God he called "Father" as the result of the hunt had been to the God of Genesis.

What Jesus offered humankind (and what is symbolized by the bread and wine of communion) has usually been called a new covenant, a "second chance" after the original law had been broken by eating from the Tree of Knowledge. Viewed from the perspective taken in this book, this covenant can be seen as a way in which people could adapt to an inhospitable world. The "sin" of their forebears in gaining the knowledge of how to alter the environment had made that world unsuitable for their physical natures. Jesus' insistence upon the necessity of a person being "born anew" is another way of saying that one's physical birth leaves him or her ill equipped for the human social environment that had come into existence. Because of the changes brought about by what had been classified as Original Sin, people had to undergo a second, spiritual birth to bring their behavior into line with the circumstances in which they found themselves.[47] This rebirth consisted of accepting the teachings of Jesus, a set of values that would, if followed, bring people back toward the situation that had been lost when they left "Paradise" to till the soil.

The rebirth that Jesus sought to achieve, especially in males, is radically different from that of most traditional male rebirths in initiation rites. Those rites are intended to separate males from the world and ways of women, to emphasize the differences between men and women—to extend gender and make a man very clearly notawoman. In contrast, Jesus' idea of rebirth involves lessening sexual difference, bringing men closer to the world and ways of women—to tell a man that it is acceptable to be likeawoman.

What Jesus was calling upon people to do was to follow a set of values that ran counter to portions of human nature; *not* to "do what comes naturally."[48] It is, obviously, a difficult task to persuade people to suppress part of their biological nature. In order for any set of values to be effective in channeling human behavior into "good" directions, those values must be sanctified.

William F. Buckley, Jr., has accurately summarized the role in restraining innate human proclivities played by the values that Jesus taught and the necessity for sanctification of those values if they are to be effective. "So there is the sense in which Christianity is a continuing revolution against the ways of man [*sic*], beginning when he fled paradise," Buckley has written. His explanation of the ethical function of Christianity is in fact one of values in a broader sense: "But the Christian religion is about how people ought to act, not how they do act." "Christianity has checked the movements of millions of men and women who but for the pull of dogma would know no vital brake upon their behavior," Buckley rightly says. "Sometimes the brake is effective, sometimes it is not."[49]

The Mithraization of Christianity

For the goal of restraining some of the more male proclivities to be approached, Jesus' religion of feminine values had to be run by men—priests who, in imitation of Jesus, would preach feminine values from male bodies. (A French maxim says "there are three sexes—men, women, and clergymen."[50]) The result was the Greek tragedy that was early Christianity. The tragedy lay in the shame that things *had* to turn out as they did: A religion of essentially feminine values had to take on male garb and be run by men if it was to have any prospect of achieving its ethical purpose. But this compromise, however necessary, undermined the very values that Jesus had sought to promote. An outstanding (and astounding) example of how accepting male supremacy destroyed Christian values is to be found in the writings of Tertullian, who converted to Christianity at the end of the second century and became the first major Christian theologian in the Latin West. Tertullian's misogyny was so extreme that, though it has often been matched, it has probably never been surpassed. Like most Christian males, he ignored the religion's belief that Mary brought salvation into the world and focused instead upon the claim that Eve had brought sin into it. Tertullian saw women as agents of the devil. He said that a woman must "affect meanness of appearance" in her style of dress, "in order that by every garb of penitence she might the more fully expiate that which she derives from Eve,—the ignominy, I mean, of the first sin, and the odium of human perdition." His condemnation of women dripped with unabashed hatred: "And do you not know that you are (each) an Eve? The sentence of God on this sex of yours lives in this age: the guilt must of necessity live too. *You* are the devil's gateway; *you* are the unsealer of that (forbidden) tree; . . . *You* destroyed so easily God's image, man. On account of *your* desert—that is, death*—even the Son of God had to die."[51]

Everything would be perfect, Tertullian apparently thought, if only those (in his view, literally) *damned women* had never been created. He blamed them for the crucifixion, as well as, among other evils, leading men into sin by being attractive to them and wearing enticing clothing—an eighteen-hundred-year-old version of the "it wasn't rape, because she dressed as if she wanted it" argument.

Extreme though these views were, they were held by the man who has often been called the greatest Christian theologian in the West before St. Augustine. It seems that having a male-run church, though necessary in order to attract men to that church's largely feminine values, led to acceptance of the society's belief in female inferiority and, quite rapidly, to people like Tertullian speaking for "Christianity." If Christ had remained in his grave, surely he would have been spinning in it by this time.

If turning the Church into a male-dominated institution was necessary in order for it to have influence over male behavior, it obviously carried with it a high price. Unquestionably, the teachings of Jesus were considerably diluted as the Church reached its accommodation with the remnants of Roman society during and following the age of Constantine in the fourth century. What has not often been recognized is that an important part of the cause of that dilution was the suppression of women within the Church. The completion of male dominance in Christianity, occurring at about the same time that the Roman government accepted and corrupted the Church, weakened the more feminine values that were at the core of the religion and allowed for the return of such "masculine" principles as hierarchy and militarism.

---

*Like that earlier supermisogynist, Hesiod, Tertullian blames women for introducing death into the world. And, as in the story of Pandora, Tertullian saw women not only as the way through which evil entered the world but also as evil themselves. Surely he would also have joined in the lament of Hippolytus.

By the fourth century, women had already been eliminated from positions of importance in the Church. They had been banned from the priesthood. The gospels that told of the prominent role of women at the time of Christ had been excluded from the canon of the New Testament. Diatribes against women such as that by Tertullian had been written by prominent Christian thinkers. But the Church's attitude against women was not fully solidified until Saints Ambrose and Augustine put their imprimatur on the "Pauline" (or "Tertulline") view of women.[52]

Despite all of this, Christianity's early acceptance of women had given the religion an advantage over such all-male cults as Mithraism. And the religion's values, though certainly diluted from those preached by Jesus, still retained considerably more feminine features than did those of the mainstream of Roman society.

The worsening conditions in the Roman Empire had led large numbers of people in the Mediterranean world to be attracted to the "feminine" values of the early Christians. Those values were particularly alluring to the downtrodden. But before a majority of people in the Roman Empire—especially those who were better off—would be willing to become followers of Jesus, the values of the religion would have to be compromised to a degree sufficient to allow the continuation of many of the "masculine" practices of the Romans. Ultimately, the Christian values of peace, love, and humility were mixed with the Roman ideas of war, authority, and domination. This odd combination was begun when the Emperor Constantine became favorably inclined toward the religion, putatively as a result of a dream he had the night before he engaged in the critical Battle of Mulvian Bridge (312 C.E.). In the dream Constantine is said to have seen the first Greek letters of "Christ" and the words "By this sign you will conquer." He believed this dream to be a message from the Christian God, and so had a Christian symbol painted on his soldiers' shields. When his men were victorious, Constantine was convinced that it was the result of the intervention of the Christian God.[53] From this time onward, Christianity became favored in the Empire. By late in the century it would be the official state religion. It was a century in which it can accurately be said that Christianity gained a world and went a long way toward losing its soul—its "feminine" soul.

Constantine's dream symbolized a new submersion in people's minds of the (now-disguised) powerful goddesses and the rise once more of the notion that the Supreme Being is a violent male thunder God. Military conquest was about as far removed from the values that Jesus had taught as one could get. Yet it was the apparent help of God in bringing a military victory that led a Roman emperor to favor the religion Jesus had founded. The masculine values that had been seeping into Christianity since shortly after the crucifixion now started to flood into the religion, engulfing the more feminine values that Jesus had promoted.

Two events are highly significant, I believe, in terms of the switch from more feminine to more masculine values. First, during the fourth century Christians established December 25 as the birthday of Jesus and began to celebrate Christmas as the religion's major holiday. (No one, of course, had the slightest idea of what his actual day of birth was.) Second, those early Christians firmly fixed Sunday as their Sabbath.[54] Both of these practices had long before been taken up by the militant male religion of Mithraism. The importance of these observances being appropriated by the Christians, however, goes beyond the fact that they were adopted from a male-only cult that glorified military virtues. The reason that Mithraism had celebrated these days was because they worshipped Mithras as the Sun God. December 25, then thought to be the winter solstice, was seen as the "birthday" of the sun, which at that time of the year stopped sinking lower in the sky over the Northern Hemisphere and began to get higher again. *Sun*day, obviously, is the day of the sun.

Traditionally, the sun has been linked with male gods. So the Christian decisions to celebrate the "birthday of the sun" as the birthday of Christ and the Day of the Sun as their religion's sacred day can be seen as another part of the Christian move away from the more feminine values and practices with which the religion began. Their God became more fully associated with the old male conception of God as the sun, as well as the carrier of the violence of storm and thunder.

Virgin Motherhood

Suddenly in the fourth century it had become fashionable to be a Christian. Droves of "Christians of convenience" joined the Church after Constantine began to look favorably upon it. These were men on the make who did not need a weatherman to know which way the wind was blowing. Those who did still firmly believe in the original Christian ideas had to find a way to distinguish themselves from those in the new wave, which they did by denying themselves indulgences and becoming ascetic. But this did not make them any more accepting of women. Many male ascetics in the fourth century—and on through the Middle Ages—saw women in terms not all that different from those outlined by Tertullian. To them, women were the ultimate worldly temptation, which must be avoided at all costs. The implication certainly was that the ascetic saw the woman—the temptress—as the source of evil in the world. Women were believed to be "impure," an idea that came from two sources: Genesis and menstruation. The latter was one of the reasons that "pure" males who took religious vows thought that they would be "soiled" by intimate contact with a woman. "Nothing is so unclean as a woman in her periods," proclaimed St. Jerome (during, one suspects, a periodic bout with NMS). "What she touches she causes to become unclean."[55]

In the Middle Ages female virginity achieved a level of admiration bordering on superstitious awe.[56] One aspect of the respect for virgins may have fallen less into the category of purity than that of independence. Because marriage, from one perspective, amounted to ownership of women, virginity meant that a woman was *not* owned, and therefore was more autonomous—like a man.[57] (The most celebrated European woman in the entire medieval period, Joan of Arc, was a virgin who won her fame by doing what men normally do.) Perhaps the autonomy associated with virginity was a reason (certainly not the only reason) why the "Mother of God" had to be seen as a virgin—she was not only a pure woman but also an *unowned* one. How, after all, could the Mother of God be the property of a mortal man? (The "eternal virginity" of Mary—the mortal brothers and sisters of Jesus mentioned in the gospels notwithstanding[58]—was made Church dogma at the Latern Council of 649, thus negating her apparent "ownership" by Joseph.[59])

It is telling that veneration of the Virgin Mary arose in the eastern Mediterranean region when it did. In 325, as a more male-oriented Christianity was being institutionalized at the Council of Nicaea called by Constantine, his mother Helena built the first Marian shrine, in Nazareth.[60] As the Christian notion of the Divinity was further efeminated in the fourth century, the cult of Mary spread. And as Christianity became the state religion and began to persecute the female-centered religion of Isis, particularly under Theodosius I at the end of the century, adoration for Mary, who is in many ways a Christian counterpart of Isis, took off.[61] It is likely that the "black Madonnas" that are venerated in various shrines in Europe are carryovers of the worship of Isis and other variants of the Earth Mother.[62] So as some people in the late Roman period were re-interring the powerful goddess Isis and removing most of the "goddesslike" features from the religion of Jesus, others were resurrecting a goddess in a new form.[63]

Christianity's Accommodation with "Masculinity"

The compromise of Christian values that was an integral part of the accommodation with the Roman Empire also involved a compromise of Roman values. What emerged by the fifth century was a new mix of values, a new modus vivendi between human nature and the social environment. It was one that was considerably farther from the feminine end of the values spectrum than what Jesus had proposed, but also somewhat farther from the masculine end of that continuum than were Roman values prior to the accommodation with the

Christians. The mix worked well enough that it carried western Europe through at least eight centuries without massive revision. It proved to be the final value structure to attempt to deal with the monumental changes of the Agricultural Megarevolution, and would last until a second megarevolution began to cause new disruptions and incongruities between the nature and environment of human beings.

Many people contributed to the blending of Christian and Roman values that would produce the medieval value system, but the most important reconciler of these sets of values was St. Augustine of Hippo (354–430). Augustine synthesized Christian values with Roman practice by contending that what is to be judged is not outward action, but inward motivation. The real evils, he said, are the traits that I have argued are the outgrowths of the mismatch between human nature and the social environment, including greed, the lust for domination or power, and the love of violence (not violence itself). This meant, Augustine said, that the Christian emphasis over the first three centuries on pacifism was mistaken. War in itself was not evil; it could be used against the real evils, as a means of punishing wrongdoers.[64] Augustine actually turned war—*just* war, that is—into a Christian value, by seeing it as a means of restraining evil (maladaptive proclivities). He basically said that the New Testament injunctions against violence, such as "Do not resist one who is evil" and "To him who strikes you on the cheek, offer the other also,"[65] should not be taken literally. Rather, they should be applied to inward intentions.[66] He was turning the Sermon on the Mount upside down. Historian Frederick H. Russell has accurately called Augustine's arguments in this area a "revaluation."[67] In effect, Augustine was efeminating the essential teaching of Jesus by saying that it did not prohibit actions to which males seem especially prone. This certainly made the religion more palatable to men.

Loving one's enemies, in Augustine's view, did not mean that one could not inflict violent punishment on them. Love for your enemy might entail killing him. "Tough love," indeed. Augustine even saw war, under the proper circumstances, as a charitable act. If one could stop someone from committing additional sin by punishing him, this amounted to an act of love. *War is love,* Augustine was saying in an Orwellian twist, but only if it was motivated by a spirit of charity, not if it was undertaken for the enjoyment of inflicting pain. This is an interesting concept, but one must wonder how many people have ever gone to war in a spirit of charity toward their enemies.

If Jesus had resurrected the goddesses of old, Augustine re-interred them and resurrected the male thunder God. It was not without reason that St. Jerome called Augustine the "second founder of the ancient faith." But the faith that he was refounding was considerably more ancient than that of Jesus; it was in many respects the faith of Moses. In accommodating Christ with

Rome, Augustine was actually trying to reconcile Christ with the early view of Yahweh. Nor is it without justification that those who guided the Church's settlement with Roman authority and militarism are called the Church *Fathers* and their ideas are called "*patristic* thought."

Augustine was, like the other Church Fathers, a clear believer in male supremacy and in male procreative power. He said God's statement in Genesis that, as a result of Eve's disobedience, women would be subject to their husbands,[68] demanded explanation, "because we must believe that even before her sin woman had been made to be ruled by her husband and to be subject to him."[69] Not content to see women's inferiority stemming from Eve's causing the fall, Augustine believed it necessary to assert that God had intended from the moment He created Eve that women were to be ruled by men.

Once again demonstrating the ubiquitous influence of the Conception Misconception, Augustine argued that the sole purpose for which God had made woman was to be man's helper in bearing children.[70] This implied that man could create offspring on his own, but needed an appropriate place for his seeds to be incubated. As Augustine saw it, woman's only purpose was to serve as that soil. This was not a man likely to give much weight to ways associated with females.

But the more feminine values that Jesus had preached left a residue. And Augustine's own influence on the medieval value system was not entirely in the direction of restoring masculine values. The reason that the accommodation between the Romans and Christians was able to survive so long was that it achieved a balance that fit well enough with social environment. That meant that it had to retain some feminine characteristics.

"All Woes Which Befall Men Come from Women": Islam

During the period that we call the Early Middle Ages in Europe, what is chronologically the last of the world's major religions, Islam, arose to the southeast.

St. Augustine had said that human beings were so constituted that submission to God's will is what is best for them. This was also the central theme of the new religion founded by Muhammad in seventh-century Arabia. Muhammad believed himself to be the final recipient of God's message, the last in a long line of prophets that included Abraham, Moses, and Jesus.

There is little that would be inconsistent in seeing Muhammad as a messenger from the God of Abraham and Moses. The God he called Allah is readily identifiable as the Yahweh depicted in the Torah. The image in both cases is clearly that of a male thunder God who loses His temper, holds grudges, and inflicts violent punishment on those who fail to obey Him. Thus while Muhammad seems to follow well in the line from the early Hebrews, his message does not correspond as closely with that of Jesus. (This is certainly not to say, however, that Muhammad's teaching was very different from actual Christian practice, particularly as it had evolved by his day.)

Although Muhammad explicitly said that he was not a messiah, he was actually much closer than Jesus to the sort of leader that most Hebrew men had expected the Messiah to be. When Muhammad moved his band of followers from Mecca to Yathrib (which he renamed Medina) in 622, he took absolute power. Almost from the start of his ministry Muhammad was a political and military, as well as a religious, leader. Accounts of his activities over the next several years are dotted with such terms as "warrior spirit," "conquest," "domination," "dominion," "power," "control," "militant," and "by the sword."

Muhammad also readily engaged in pseudospeciation. He stopped the tribal fighting that had plagued Yathrib by creating a new community (*ummah*) there. But he soon defined the *ummah* as including only Muslims and turned violently against the Jews of the city who refused to convert to the new religion, massacring several hundred of them.[71]

The way for the Prophet's return to Mecca was begun by a raid on a Meccan trade caravan during the holy month of Rajab, when by common consent among the Arab tribes fighting was banned. Muhammad won control of Mecca and the rest of the Arabian Peninsula through a combination of military conquest and diplomacy. By the time of his death in 632, Muhammad was clearly the most powerful chief in Arabia, with almost all of its territory under his command. His prestige was based largely upon his demonstration of military power.[72]

In all these ways, Muhammad's outlook was very different from that of Jesus. Plainly, he did not expect the meek to inherit the earth. To him, turning the other cheek was the way of losers.

Although there was little practical difference in the attitudes toward such issues as violence and domination taken by Muslims and Christians when the two came into conflict with each other, there was a significant difference in the positions taken on these questions by the founders of the religions. The compromises that Christianity made to bring itself in line with the old order did not fully take place until three centuries after Jesus' death, but Muhammad made his accommodation with the old ways during his own lifetime.

Islam, however, did make a serious attempt to bring some inappropriate natural proclivities under restraint. Much like the Hebrews of Moses' day or the Christians at the time of the Crusades, the Muslims under Muhammad directed their inbred tendencies toward violence against outsiders as a means of creating "brotherhood" within the group. According to Muslim tradition, in his last sermon before his death Muhammad preached: "O ye men! Harken unto my words and take ye them to heart! Know ye that every Muslim is a brother unto every other Muslim, and that ye are now one brotherhood."[73]

It is clear enough from the wording of that statement (as it would be from much else in the religion) that Islam, like early Judaism and the revised form of Christianity, was intended principally for men. The Islamic value system, again like those of the early Hebrews and the Christians from the fourth century onward, settled considerably farther toward the masculine side of the value spectrum than the system that had been proposed by Jesus. But this fact did not mean that there were no examples of the values usually associated with women in it. Throughout the Koran, the collection of messages Muhammad received from Allah, almost every chapter, or *surah,* begins with the words "*bismillah al-rahman al-rahim*" ("In the name of God the Compassionate, the Merciful!"). Many of the *surahs* close with "God is Forgiving. Merciful." Compassion, mercy, and forgiveness are, of course, qualities or values that have more often been associated with women than men.

Whatever the place of "feminine values" in Islam, the religion, like Judaism and what emerged as the accepted form of Christianity, held women to be decidedly inferior creatures. They were generally considered to be the property of men, who were allowed to have as many wives as they could afford, up to a maximum of four. (Remember that the Koran repeats the Conception Misconception's seed metaphor and refers to women as fields to be planted.*)

Leading Muslim religious thinkers matched the misogyny of their Greek and Christian counterparts. The voices of Hesiod, Tertullian, and so many others can be heard reverberating in the words of Ghazali, an eleventh-century Muslim theologian. "It is a fact," he declared, "that all the trials, misfortunes, and woes which befall men come from women."[74]

Ghazali, along with most of his coreligionists, saw Eve as the source of this evil, and believed that Allah had dealt justly with that half of her progeny who most resembled her:

> When Eve ate the fruit which He had forbidden to her from the tree in Paradise, the Lord, be He praised, punished women with eighteen things: (1) menstruation; (2) childbirth; (3) separation from mother and father and marriage to a stranger; (4) pregnancy; (5) not having control over her own person; . . . (9) the fact that she must stay secluded in the house; . . . (11) [the fact that] two women's testimony [has to be] set against the testimony of one man; (12) the fact that she must not go out of the house unless accompanied by a near relative; . . . (15) the fact that merit has one thousand components, [only] one of which is [attributable] to women, while nine hundred and ninety-nine are [attributable] to men. . . .[75]

---

*See above, Chapter 6, p. 126.

Obviously Muslim women enjoyed no Eighth Amendment protection against cruel and unusual punishment.* But, cruel though it was, there was nothing unusual about this view of women or about its obvious sources. Notice that three of the first four "punishments" are attempts to reverse the Non–Menstrual Syndrome and womb envy. And, just as in Genesis 3, Eve's "sin" is used as the rationale for transforming women's reproductive power into a curse. When we see Eve's action as the invention of agriculture, it becomes clear that Muslim misogyny has precisely the same origins as Hebrew and Christian misogyny: men's envy of women's powers and men's resentment at their devaluation resulting from the changes brought by agriculture.

Knights and Madonnas: The Sexes in the Middle Ages

The usual image of Europe in the Middle Ages as an unchanging time is one that is quite misleading, yet one that my brief treatment and generalizations about the values of the age will tend to perpetuate. I follow this course for two reasons: a large amount of generalization is unavoidable in a very brief examination of human nature and sex over such a vast period, and while there were important changes over the long run of the medieval period and significant variations from place to place, the era was one of far less significant or rapid change than what would succeed it.[76] It is, then, wrong in an absolute sense to view the medieval period as a static time but right in a comparative sense.

The status of women in medieval Europe was certainly not high, but it improved a bit as the era proceeded. Throughout the Middle Ages, as at most times in history, the women who were most likely to achieve prominence were those who adopted values and practices usually associated with men. The Byzantine historian Procopius expressed this truism when he described Amalasuntha, who acted as regent in the Ostrogothic Kingdom of Italy for several years in the 520s while her son was a child, as "displaying to a great extent the masculine temper."[77] From this example at the onset of the Middle Ages to that of Joan of Arc (who was charged at her trial with "acting against nature"[78]) at their end, this was a thousand-year period in which virtually the only women whose names made it into the traditional histories were those who displayed the "masculine temper."

---

*Speaking of the U.S. Constitution, Ghazali's eleventh punishment is as telling about the Muslim view of women as the three-fifths compromise was about the American view of blacks. As that infamous agreement that was placed in the Constitution demonstrated that the American founding fathers believed that a black man is equal to three-fifths of a white man, the Islamic equation of the testimony of one man with that of two women indicated that the Muslim fathers believed a woman is equal to half of a man.

Through most of the Middle Ages, there was not much improvement in the view leading church thinkers took of women. They were still the daughters of Eve, with all that implied. "Of the numberless snares that the crafty enemy [the devil] spreads before us," warned one eleventh-century bishop, "... the worst ... is woman, sad stem, evil root, vicious fount ... honey and poison."[79] In the following century, the Decree of Gratian (1140) stated that "the subordination of women to men is the natural order of things."[80] Gratian reinvigorated Aristotle's dualism, seeing polar oppositions, each associated with the sexes, as the basis of the universe.[81]

From Gratian's time in the mid-twelfth century onward, much of the thinking of the High Middle Ages was based upon Aristotelian sexual dualism.[82] Leading thirteenth-century scholastic theologian Albertus Magnus made something of a reversal in traditional thinking when he argued that women enjoy sexual intercourse more than men. The reason he cited for this conclusion was, however, entirely in keeping with tradition. Echoing Aristotle, Albertus said that women are imperfect and so desire union with the perfect male more than he does with the imperfect female. And in his *Summa Theologica* (c. 1273), Thomas Aquinas declared that polarities are the essence of the natural order and repeated Aristotle's ideas that "woman is defective and misbegotten" and that man is "the beginning and end of woman, as God is the beginning and end of every creature."[83]

Yet the High Middle Ages did see a reinfusion of some of the more feminine values through the rise of code of chivalry and the increased veneration of the Virgin Mary.

The need for reform in the ways of fighting men is evident in the following description by an historian of the practices of the very *un*gentle-men of early Middle Ages: "Widows, seized on the very field where their dead and defeated husbands lay, had to marry the victors. Daughters were dragged to the beds of their fathers' murderers."[84]

The ideal of knighthood was to serve God. This end was to be accomplished by blending some of the traditionally more feminine values with the masculine military virtues. Knights were expected not only to be courageous and expert fighters loyal to those above them in the feudal hierarchy but also to become more caring and compassionate, more generous, and more concerned about the poor.[85] These values were put together as a code of chivalry in the twelfth century. The purpose was at least in part to make the behavior of men somewhat more acceptable to women, that is, to make the men more "civilized."

The consequences of the rise of chivalry are usually referred to as a "softening" of the ways of the men of the medieval upper classes. *Soft* is a term always associated with behavior and values that are considered to be more female than male. Another such word with female associations is *gentle*. This, too, was prominently used to describe the values that were embodied in the code of chivalry. It was said that they would make a man more gentle; they would make him a "gentle-man." We have already seen how this ideal, as espoused by Confucius almost two millennia earlier, was a way of restraining some of the least adaptive male proclivities by extending attitudes that were natural toward "brothers" to "others."

The development of chivalry was an indication of some change in attitudes toward women and feminine values, but more significant was the rise of the veneration of the Virgin Mary (which itself became an aspect of what was expected of the chivalrous knight). Although she had been a figure of great importance in the Eastern Church (in areas with a long history of important goddesses) since the fourth century, Mary had not received a great deal of attention in the Roman Church prior to the twelfth century. Then, however, she became so important that many of the exquisite Gothic cathedrals that were being built were named Notre Dame in her honor.

When it is understood that by the end of the fourth century the Christian Church in the West had been shorn of most of the feminine values that Jesus had established, the rise in the West of the cult of Mary nearly eight hundred years later suggests that the need for those values was re-emerging. The Virgin was now described as a fount of mercy and the Mother of All, or the Blessed Mother. It is clear that she was the means by which the ancient worship of goddesses was being reintroduced, but within the constraints of Christian dogma, with its all-male conception of deity. In her newfound position as the mother who loves *all* people, even sinners, and is full of compassion and mercy, Mary was reprising the role once played by various goddesses and subsequently by Jesus. Unlike the impression of the goddesses of old or Jesus, though, Mary was supposed to be a distinctly junior partner in the Christian cosmology. According to accepted theology, all she could do was to intercede with her son, which gave her an important but less-than-divine power.

The adoration of the Blessed Virgin Mother became common among men. This practice was an important aspect of the softening that began in the twelfth century, because it raised feminine values to a position of considerably greater respect than had been the case for nearly a millennium. Feminine values were now being held up as ideals to be pursued—up to a point—by men as well as women.

Everything, it seemed, was becoming "softer" in the twelfth century. A substantial number of Cistercian and Benedictine monks began to practice a devotion to "Jesus our Mother."[86] There was a notable change in the subject matter of literature and the other arts. Prior to this period, such medieval literature as there was concentrated almost solely on the "heroic" deeds of fighting men. Now, though, women began to appear and to be idealized. Painters

An Old Theme with New Names: The Madonna and Child

The theme of a virgin mother with a divine child is a very old one. The medieval veneration of the "Blessed Virgin Mother" constituted yet another attempt to restore the more feminine values that had been devalued when women were fully subordinated after the Conception Misconception and a male God displaced the notion of a mother goddess as Creator. Although the Virgin Mary was never considered to be part of the Trinity, her prominence did place a female figure at a level close to the deity and it led to men and women alike praying to a very prominent female figure, albeit one whose only power was as intercessor or advocate. (Andrea della Robbia, *Madonna and Child*. Late 15th century. Firenze, Bargello) (Art Resource) and sculptors as well as writers started to portray the Virgin Mary, other women, and sometimes scenes of family life.

Even more significant are the depictions of the Madonna with the infant Jesus, which became ubiquitous in painting and sculpture from the High Middle Ages through the Renaissance. These works implicitly placed the mother in a superior position to that of her Son.* God the Father is nowhere to be seen in these works, which amounted to a revival of portrayals of a creative goddess and her son. Such works had been characteristic of the Minoan and other ancient civilizations in which the worship of goddesses survived into "historic" (i.e., beyond "prehistoric") times. The Madonna-with-Child icons also replicate the numerous depictions of Isis and her infant son Horus, which had made plain who the Creator in that religion was.[87] This suggests a less than fully conscious desire to regain the values represented by the powerful goddesses.

Depicting Jesus as an infant with the Madonna symbolically restored the female element in the deity that had been excluded with the rise of the thunder gods and again with the establishment of the all-male Trinity in the fourth and fifth centuries C.E. This reinstatement of a female presence in an ostensibly male divinity reflected a medieval society that, while totally male-dominated on the surface, had blended into its mix certain of the more feminine values.

The softening of the High Middle Ages is important, but certainly it did not result in the "feminization" of medieval society. Remember, for instance, that in this era prominent men placed "chastity belts" on their wives. The use of this device was another reflection of the Conception Misconception's seed metaphor. It amounted to seeing a wife as a man's personal plot of soil, in which only he could plant his seeds. The chastity belt was designed to prevent a passing seed from falling into the fertile, furrowed soil of an owned woman and sprouting an unwanted crop of weeds. This practice ensured that the "plants" (children) to which a man devoted his resources were in fact his in a genetic[†] sense.

Europe in this era was still very much a man's world; but some of its sharp edges had been smoothed out. Women and feminine values remained distinctly second class, but both were held in somewhat higher regard than they had been in the early medieval period.

---

*Michelangelo's magnificent *Pieta,* with Mary holding her executed son, has similar connotations.

†Of course no one in the Middle Ages knew anything about genes. They were, however, very much concerned with paternity, an anxiety that had an effect similar to genetic interest.

CHAPTER 10

Human Liberation Is Women's Liberation

Women and Men in a Marketplace World

> Say, are not women truly, then,
> Styl'd but the shadows of us men?
>
> **BEN JONSON (1616)**[1]

It's a man's world.

Some would argue that this statement has always been true, since men have used their generally greater size and physical power to dominate women.[2] Others, like St. Augustine, would agree that it has always been a man's world but would attribute this condition to God's intention to make it so. I have contended that, whatever advantages size and upper-body musculature gave men, women had a considerable degree of equality in many pre-agricultural societies; a real "man's world" emerged only as a result of agriculture's disruption of traditional sex roles and the ensuing Conception Misconception.

Over the centuries, however, there have been changes in the degree to which ours is a man's world and the particular ways in which it is. In many respects, the modern world that began to materialize five hundred years ago is even more of a man's world than was the medieval period that preceded it. The dawn of the modern world—and the beginning of a second megarevolution characterized by accelerating mobility, both geographic and social, and an emerging reconceptualization of the world as a marketplace—was marked by three major developments: the opening of the "New World" of the Western Hemisphere to European penetration, the Protestant Reformation, and the Scientific Revolution. All three had important impacts on women and the values usually associated with them. So did such subsequent developments in the second Megarevolution as democracy, free-market economics, individualism, the Industrial Revolution, Darwinism, and Marxism.

The full contours of the massive upheaval that I call the Mobility Megarevolution are much too extensive to be discussed in this book. The sixteenth century saw the beginning of the replacement of the comparatively static, organic society of the Middle Ages by the mobile, individualist one of the modern world. By the seventeenth century, the fate of the old order had been set. That order, which British political thinker James Harrington aptly termed "the Gothick ballance," fell apart under the impact of the events of accelerating geographic and social mobility.[3] Further developments in the eighteenth and nineteenth centuries left modern people with a vastly different worldview from that of their medieval forebears.

In the broadest terms, the second megarevolution reversed many of the tendencies of the first. With the invention of agriculture, people had to become sedentary; as they put down roots in the literal sense, they had also to "put down roots" figuratively. This necessity meant that the general propensity of the first megarevolution was toward stability—that is to say, toward *im*mobility.

The essence of the second megarevolution has been to reverse that disposition toward stasis. Mobility is what changed the world during the just-completed second millennium (for the most part during the second half of that millennium). People have been "uprooted," meaning not only that most of us have abandoned the agricultural way of life, but also that we have "pulled up roots" and been set in motion, both geographically and socially.

I have argued that the first (agricultural) megarevolution, which was in all likelihood begun by women, established a way of life more in keeping with female practices and so eventually devalued the traditional contributions of men. This development led men to seek alternative outlets for their innate predispositions. As a result, they established a much more hierarchical and male-dominated social system than those which had existed previously. The second (mobility) megarevolution, however, was launched by men and was based much more on practices that are congenial to the biological predispositions more commonly associated with men: "individualism," mobility, competition, conquest, and accumulation. An ironic result of the first megarevolution was that a way of life invented by and more congenial to women led finally to women being far more subordinated than they had been previously. It is possible that the reverse will ultimately be the outcome of the second megarevolution: a system created by and more agreeable to men* may eventuate in an improved status for women.

But it should not be forgotten that the greater ascendancy of men that was the eventual result of the first megarevolution came only after the new woman-made system had devalued male roles. Thus far in the man-made second megarevolution, we have seen much more devaluation of female roles than we have an improvement in the status of women.

In this chapter, I can do no more than touch on some prominent examples of the ways in which this new transformation of the human social environment affected the issues with which we are concerned here—the interaction between that environment and human nature, the roles of women and men, the male quest for creative power, and religious outlooks—between the end of the Middle Ages and the early twentieth century.

Deflowering a Virgin Land

In a letter to Ferdinand and Isabella on his voyage of 1498, Christopher Columbus wrote: "I am well assured in my own mind that there, where I have declared [in what would soon be called America], lies the Earthly Paradise."[4]

Although there were not very many people who agreed with the Genoese captain that the original Garden of Eden was in America, the notion that America was a "New Eden" soon became widespread. Here was an unspoiled "virgin land," a place where the evils of Europe could be left behind. To many Europeans, America was almost another Christ: the second chance, the new covenant, the way to escape Original Sin.

That the new territory was called a "virgin land" is not without deeper meaning for our subject. America, like Mary, was seen as having been conceived without sin. Columbus wrote during his first voyage that the people he saw "are a very gentle race, without knowledge of [evil]; they neither kill, nor steal, nor carry weapons, and are so timid that one of our men might put a hundred of them to flight."[5] The admiral, whose flagship was the *Santa Maria,* had already named the second American island that he visited *Santa Maria de la Concepción,*[6] indicating that he considered the Virgin's status to be second only to that of the Savior himself.

But what would Columbus and his fellows do with this Virgin Land and her unspoiled—perhaps in his view "un-Fallen"—people? Just after commenting

---

*As I shall discuss later, the marketplace world that has developed from the Mobility Megarevolution came to be based on greatly exaggerated versions of traits associated with males. In fact the hyperindividualism and extreme competition that characterize the modern marketplace world is not all that congenial to many men.

upon the natives' gentleness and innocence, Columbus said that he was "of the opinion that a very short space of time would suffice to gain to our holy faith multitudes of people, *and to Spain, great riches and immense dominions,* with all their inhabitants; there being, without doubt, in these countries *vast quantities of gold."*[7] On his very first day in the New Eden, Columbus had offered his view that the pristine natives "would be good servants."[8] *Show me a second Eden,* he seemed to be saying, *and I'll preside over a second Fall more quickly than you can say "Eve."*

From the first days of Columbus's arrival in the "New World," then, Europeans saw America as fruitful and her people as weak, gentle, and peace-loving: like a woman or anyone with feminine qualities—indeed like the Virgin or Jesus. What Columbus and so many other Europeans proposed to do with "her," from the very outset of their acquaintance, is suggested in the comments of a few other early European visitors to the Western Hemisphere. Speaking in 1550 of how the natives of the New World should be treated, Spanish aristocrat Juan Gines de Sepulveda made the analogy of America and its people to women explicit, demonstrating in the process the continuing effects of the man-over-woman basis for other forms of domination and echoing Aristotle's concept of women: "The man rules over the woman, . . . the father over his children. That is to say, the most powerful and most perfect rule over the weakest and most imperfect. The same relationship exists among men, there being some who by nature are masters and others who are by nature slaves."[9]

A nobleman from Savona, Michele de Cuneo, who accompanied Columbus on his second voyage (1495), proudly recounted some of his activities in the islands that Columbus had just named "Eleven Thousand Virgins." In a letter that began with the words, "In the name of Jesus and of His Glorious Mother Mary, from whom all blessings proceed," Cuneo matter-of-factly reported that he had "captured a very beautiful Carib woman, whom the said Lord Admiral [Columbus] gave to me." He "conceived desire to take pleasure" with her, "but she did not want it and treated me with her finger nails in such a manner that I wished I had never begun." But Cuneo was no quitter. He "took a rope and thrashed her well, for she raised such unheard of screams that you would not have believed your ears." All's well that ends well: "Finally we came to an agreement in such manner that I can tell you that she seemed to have been brought up in a school of harlots."[10]

What Europeans would do with the Virgin Land that Columbus found was to rape it—"in the name of Jesus and of his glorious mother Mary from whom all good things come."

Lest it be thought that this was an attitude peculiar to those sailing under the Spanish flag, it must be briefly noted that the same sort of image was commonly employed by English men involved with the exploration and colonization of the

New World a century after Columbus. Sir Walter Raleigh was most direct when he said in 1595 that Guiana was "a countrey that hath yet her maydenhead, never sackt, turned, nor wrought."[11]* It was a condition in which Raleigh and other English invaders did not intend to leave "her" or any of her New World "sisters" for long. In 1584 two English captains sent by Raleigh to America wrote to him of the indigenous people they found on Roanoke Island in words almost exactly echoing Columbus's description from nearly one hundred years before: "[The Indians were] such as live after the manner of the golden age. . . . A more kind and loving people there cannot be found in the world."[12]

A New Eden inhabited by un-Fallen people ("noble savages") who seemed to have values usually associated with women; a virgin—these images of America were held by Europeans of various nationalities. There were more reasons than honoring Queen Elizabeth I for calling England's first American colony "Virginia." (It may be suggestive of the true meaning of the pervasive image of America as a Virgin Land that Elizabeth, the Virgin Queen, suffered from syphilis, a disease that had been introduced to Europe from "Virgin" America.[13])

The Reformation and Unintended Consequences

A very significant aspect of the Mobility Megarevolution was the Protestant Reformation, begun by Martin Luther in 1517 as a protest against the perceived excesses of the Catholic Church. Our concern here with the Reformation is with its connection to the views of the sexes that had emerged from the Conception Misconception.

Consider John Calvin, whose doctrine of predestination said that human beings, from birth, were predestined for either salvation or damnation. Calvinism raises very troublesome questions: Why would a loving God decide to foredoom to damnation some souls, individually guilty of nothing but being the descendants of Eve and Adam? Or why did those occupants of Eden sin in the first place if God is the cause and predeterminor of everything? It is clear that in Calvinism we are once more dealing with a male thunder God. Calvin spoke of God's "judgment" against those He damned. But if God was responsible for everything and people have no free will, it must be wondered against whom the judgment was rendered. Calvin's was no God of compassion; He was an unjust, sadistic God who caused people to be sinners and then pun-

---

*Those parts of the Western Hemisphere where the indigenous people had not taken up agriculture constituted a Virgin Land in another sense: the Earth Mother had not yet been violated. It seems significant that Raleigh (among many other Europeans) used the same metaphor employed by many Indians, such as Chief Smohalla, whom I quoted in Chapter 7.

ished them for His own actions. The goddesses of old, Jesus, and feminine values would not have found a very hospitable environment in Calvin's Geneva.

Pointedly, not just the Calvinists but Protestants in general rejected the veneration of the Virgin Mary that had grown so much stronger among western Christians in the four centuries preceding the Reformation. Protestants took the Bible as the sole authority, and they found no biblical basis for the practice. (This is hardly surprising, inasmuch as the role of women in early Christianity had been systematically discounted by the writers whose accounts made it into the canonical New Testament.)

The deveneration of the Blessed Mother is only the most dramatic of the ways in which Protestantism reflected the move toward a more male-oriented world that the Mobility Megarevolution brought about. It is significant that many of the statues and paintings in Catholic churches that radical Protestant iconoclasts destroyed during the Reformation were images of the Virgin Mary. The rejection of the saints who had taken the place of the multiple deities (including goddesses) of paganism removed another manifestation of female religious power. The elimination of saints also halted the veneration of male saints, many of whom were men, such as St. Francis of Assisi, who followed more feminine values. The suppression of religious orders eliminated another official position in the church for women. That women were not necessarily enthralled by the changes is apparent in the fact that Martin Luther repeatedly found it necessary to instruct his wife, the former nun Katherine von Bora, to stop saying the Ave Maria.[14]

This is not to say that the status of women was lowered by the Reformation. Some of the more radical Protestant sects moved toward full equality among believers, regardless of sex. Luther himself, in contrast to Hippolytus, declared: "Even if we could beget children without women we could not get along without them."[15] It was the *values* associated with women that were suffering a further beating as the modern world dawned.

In the seventeenth century the great Puritan poet John Milton showed that the ancient resentments against women still thrived among Protestants. Echoing Euripides' Hippolytus, Aristotle, Tertullian, and so many other male voices of yore, Milton placed the following words in Adam's mouth:

O why did god
Creator wise, that peopl'd highest Heav'n
With Spirits Masculine, create at last
This noveltie on Earth, this fair defect
Of Nature, and not fill the World at once
With Men as Angels without Feminine,
Or find some other way to generate
Mankind?[16]

The World Turned Upside Down

A fear that was frequently expressed in art works of Renaissance and Early Modern Europe is that the "natural" order of men ruling over women might be overturned. This dread is evident here both in a man standing on his head and, even more dramatically, in a woman riding a man. The image of a woman mounting a man was the ultimate reversal of the supposed natural order, as we shall see clearly in Chapter 13. Master of Housebook, *Coat of Arms with the World Upside-down*, c. 1485. (Rijksprentenkabinet, Rijksmuseum, Amsterdam)

It would be unfair and inaccurate to link the renewed male emphasis of the modern era exclusively with Protestantism. The most decisive image of God as a male that we have was formulated in the early stages of this especially male-oriented system: Michelangelo's vision of God as a bearded man. This early sixteenth-century work was, of course, done on the ceiling of the Vatican's Sistine Chapel and was completed a few years before Luther launched the Reformation, so it can hardly be tied with Protestantism. Yet it is significant that this enduring conception of a male Creator was the product of the same time period as the Reformation and the other early expressions of the Mobility Megarevolution.

Along with the increased masculine orientation after the Reformation, reflected in such imagery as Michelangelo's, came an alarming emphasis on and hysteria about witchcraft. And Catholics in the sixteenth and seventeenth centuries were nearly as likely as Protestants to persecute women as witches. This concurrent development of witchcraft hysteria and male-only religious practices was hardly a coincidence. As with the deveneration of the Virgin Mary and the forceful depiction of God as a man, it is the timing of the surge in witchcraft hysteria that is interesting. The number of witch trials in Europe increased exponentially in the sixteenth century—during the same period in which the male-conceived system based on mobility took off. And, rather suddenly, the assumption came to be that most witches were women. Whether conducted in Protestant or Catholic areas, the tens of thousands of trials for witchcraft (of which a quarter to a third resulted in executions) were another outcropping of the new era's fear of and desire to repress women, especially those who were thought to exercise power.[17] So were the frequent depictions in art of such "inverted," "unnatural" scenes as a man pulling a cart while a woman swings a whip above him, a woman riding on the stooped back of a man, and a woman fighting with a man over a pair of pants.[18] Particularly notable in this regard is a story that had wide currency in Europe at that time. It said that Aristotle, after warning his pupil Alexander the Great of the danger of the latter's infatuation with a woman named Phyllis, had himself fallen under her spell. Phyllis was said to have saddled and bridled the philosopher and ridden on his back.[19] Given Aristotle's key role in providing pseudoscientific support for the Conception Misconception, male supremacy, and women being "deformed males," the widespread acceptance of the notion that even *he* could be dominated by a woman indicates just how insecure many men were at the dawn of the modern megarevolution.

The deep male anxiety over having a useful place in the world, a concern that had long before been greatly worsened by the consequences of the invention of agriculture, is evident both in these images and the witch hysteria. The fear was similar to that which the Greeks had expressed in the myth of the

Amazons: a world turned upside down with women somehow coming out "on top." Fear of such an inversion combined with determination to prevent that from happening is unmistakable in early modern Europe.

Yet there were important implications in the Protestant Reformation that would eventually lead to an improved position for women. In attacking the church hierarchy, Martin Luther was suggesting that all humans are equal in the sight of God. The logic of this argument had to lead, eventually, to acceptance of women as being equal to men. In this respect, the Reformation is a microcosm of the modern megarevolution as a whole: male-initiated and male-oriented, but creating a logic that ultimately led to some improvements for women.

Science: The Impersonal God

A world in motion is more interesting than one that is presumed to be unchanging. The Mobility Megarevolution led to a scientific revolution in much the same way that the Agricultural Megarevolution had. In both cases, observations of the changed environment made possible new understandings of scientific phenomena. The mind must be prepared to think in certain ways before it is able to see phenomena that have been there all along.

The alteration in scientific outlook brought about by mobility was not mistaken, unlike the one that grew out of agriculture, but its effects were almost as profound—and not always to the good.

The possibility that the earth itself was not terra firma, but was in motion, was simply inconceivable in a time when society was immobile. A society in motion was a prerequisite to imagining a universe in motion. It is sometimes said that Galileo Galilei was the first to see the connection between the motion of planets and motion on the earth. What those who make this assertion mean by motion on the earth is physical or mechanical motion, and in that regard they may be correct. But in fact it was a connection, albeit probably an unconscious one, with social and geographic motion on earth that led Galileo's predecessors to conceive of the whole planet on which they stood as being in motion.

Nicolaus Copernicus and his sixteenth-century heliocentric theory bore essentially the same relationship to the Mobility Megarevolution as the idea of all-male procreation did to the Agricultural Megarevolution. The medieval view of the universe, derived from Aristotle and the second-century C.E. Alexandrian astronomer Ptolemy, with a few dashes of Christian theology added in the Middle Ages, corresponded perfectly with the immobile medieval ideal for society. The earth was believed to be a stationary sphere at the center, surrounded by crystalline spheres in which the planets and stars were embedded. These were said to be moved by angelic spirits. Beyond these spheres was a motionless heaven containing the throne of God.

In the medieval worldview, then, what motion existed was attributed to the personal actions of spiritual beings. It was as inconceivable to the medieval mind living in a personal society as it had been to all people living in such societies in the past that *impersonal* forces could control events. Such forces had been postulated in some of the mass impersonal societies that had existed, such as that of the Hellenistic era, but not in the sort of personal-sized communities for which human biology is geared. It is neither mere coincidence nor ignorance that accounts for the belief such communities, from primitive tribal groups to medieval Europeans, have held in the intervention of personal spirits—what the Irish call the leprechauns or "little people"—in their daily lives. It is simply a reflection of their own experience, in which personal causes can usually be found for human occurrences. When they cannot be found, they are assumed.

That impersonal forces could be in control of the universe, of the society, of the economy, and of politics, through such impersonal "laws" as gravity, inertia, or supply and demand, was a notion that could arise only after the society in which the thinkers developing these concepts lived had itself become impersonal. This was another major consequence of the Mobility Megarevolution.

The impersonal forces that began to be found at the time of Copernicus and became the basic quarry of the hunters of the scientific revolution were powers that could be expressed mathematically. One of the great complaints of people in modern mass societies is that they are reduced to numbers. This is another way of saying that they have been depersonalized. Such was precisely the intention of the scientists from Copernicus onward. Impersonal forces that can be expressed in impersonal numbers were (and remain today) the Holy Grail of the new science. (And, as science replaced Catholicism as the "universal" modern religion, its language, mathematics, took the place of Latin as the universal language.) The hope of science came to be the building of laws of greater and greater generality until, perhaps, *one* law of universal comprehension could be found. This law would be the impersonal equivalent of God. Science, it might be said, has sought a "monologism" that would, like monotheism, provide a single explanation for everything in the universe.

Isaac Newton made the greatest strides toward establishing that the universe operates according to laws of motion that can be understood by human reason and expressed mathematically. The universe Newton described in the late seventeenth century was a smoothly running machine that was patterned on the clocks and other mechanical devices of the age. The machine became one of the guiding metaphors of the Mobility Megarevolution, as the seed had been of the Agricultural Megarevolution. First the universe, and then the human being, came to be seen as machines.

How Does Creation Occur? As a Work of Artifice

The birth of Eve from "the Virgin Adam" notwithstanding, males do not appear to create naturally. Indeed, when it comes to "unnatural acts," Adam giving birth ranks with similar stories of "male motherhood" among the most unnatural. Hence, when creation is seen as the work of a male god—a Father—it comes to be seen as an artificial, mechanical process. This viewpoint, which would become dominant with the rise of science, is perfectly expressed in this Gothic illumination. (*God the Father as Architect,* from the *Bible Moralisee.* Middle 13th century. Osterreichische Nationalbibliothek, Vienna)

The machine metaphor became the basis for the religion of many of the Enlightenment thinkers of the eighteenth century—deism. People putting their faith in universal laws could accept a lawgiving God, but they could not tolerate a personal God who might intervene and break the laws. So the deists saw God as the builder of the machine who established the laws, wound the clock, set it in motion, and then let it operate without interference. But in fact the laws themselves were supreme, because they were seen as inviolable, even by the putative Lawgiver.

The deists' view of the universe as a smoothly running machine was a religion based on Newtonian physics. The Watchmaker God is an impersonal deity, very different from the Gardener God of Genesis, let alone the Earth Mother.

And a mechanical universe seemed to imply that male artifice, rather than female nature, was responsible for the creation. Leading men in the Scientific Revolution and Enlightenment frequently boasted of their creative powers. "Give me extension and motion," René Descartes boldly proclaimed, "and I will construct the Universe."[20]

The belief that the world can be understood entirely in terms of impersonal mathematical forces has had effects almost as pervasive as those stemming from the earlier belief that males are the sole procreators and therefore that *the* Creator is male. In fact, one way of looking at what this more modern scientific revolution has done is to see it as having taken the personal male God, with whom people late in the Agricultural Megarevolution displaced the creative goddesses, and neutered and depersonalized Him. The history of human views of the supreme creative power in the universe can be stated succinctly: first a She (or a Them), then a He, now an It.

The forces that science has sought to identify and understand since the sixteenth and seventeenth centuries have all the attributes of deities but one. They are in control; they determine what happens and often decide the fate of humans. They are universal.* They have their prophets. As Alexander Pope put it,

Nature and Nature's laws lay hid in night
GOD said, Let Newton be! and all was light.[21]

In place of incantations there are mathematical formulae. What, then, makes the law of gravity different from a god of gravity? Principally that it is an impersonal force whereas the god was a personal one. Gods were well suited to the personal communities in which most humans lived through the vast majority of human existence. Scientific laws seem to be better fitted to modern, impersonal societies.

Yet an impersonal Force cannot satisfy the needs of the human biogram. As social creatures, we find the impersonal forces with which science replaced the personal gods of religion as unsatisfying as we do mass, impersonal society itself. We need one or more personal God(s)/Goddess(es) as much as we need personal communities. The God of Science cares about no one. It treats everyone (and everything) equally, as mere matter that doesn't matter very much.

---

*One of the marvels of Newton's laws was that they brought together the celestial and terrestrial realms. He said that objects in the farthest reaches of the universe were governed by the same laws as those that operate on earth.

Yet, while science does not satisfy some of the needs of human nature, it does provide us with the means of beginning to understand that nature and so, perhaps, to find ways consciously to adapt ourselves to our changed environment.

Locke's Attempt to Erase Womb Envy

One of the most significant ideas that arose as part of the modern megarevolution is what has come in the twentieth century to be called cultural "construction." This doctrine had its origins in the pre-Enlightenment thinking of John Locke, who contended that a human at birth is a tabula rasa, a blank slate upon which experience writes the entire script of who he or she is to become.

From the perspective presented in this book, the most interesting point about Locke's epistemology (and its descendent, the complete cultural determinism that has been so widely accepted in our own time) is one that seems to have been entirely overlooked:

To say a baby at birth is a blank slate is yet another way to deny that women have creative power.

The Lockean/cultural determinist position holds that the female (nature) produces a physical being lacking in anything we would recognize as human qualities. It is, according to this argument, culture (which has generally been classified as *man*-made) that shapes the formless bit of matter into a human being. The idea of complete cultural construction is, in fact, the ultimate attempt to vanquish womb envy. If everything that makes a person happens *after* he or she is born, the importance of giving birth, that primal source of female power and focus of male jealousy, is reduced to a virtual nonevent. The importance of the power to give birth was one of the main things erased from the blank slate that Locke presented to our thinking.

The claims of both John Locke and modern cultural determinists are another way of saying what Aristotle did: the mother provides the matter, but the "father" (now seen as male-created culture) provides the soul, the spirit, the animation—the *life.* So, as science began to undermine Aristotle's influence, Locke produced a subtle and probably unconscious restatement of the ancient philosopher's misogynist viewpoint. Locke's version sounds better to the modern ear and so it has succeeded in preserving Aristotle's basic argument down to the present.

The Marketplace Misconception

Even more than the machine, the fundamental, guiding metaphor of the modern world is the marketplace. Its influence can be seen in such seemingly disparate fields as politics and biology, as well as economics. Poet Edward Young clearly stated the view of the universe as a marketplace in 1730:

Planets are merchants; take, return,
Lustre and heat; by traffic burn:
The whole creation is one vast Exchange.[22]

Thomas Hobbes had played a major role in establishing this worldview. His starting point was to define life in terms of motion and then to assume that each person in a "state of nature" is an independent individual.[23] Given what we know about the social nature of humans, this viewpoint is plainly wrong. Where, then, did Hobbes get the idea that people are "naturally" independent, that their "natural" relationship with others is "that condition which is called war; and such a war as is of every man, against every man," and that life in this condition was "solitary, poor, nasty, brutish, and short"?[24] Where else but by looking about him at the environment of the increasingly mobile society of his own day? Because we are social animals who evolved in a state of interdependence, the view of human society as a natural marketplace in which each individual competes with everyone else is misleading. What we can term the Marketplace Misconception that grew out of the second megarevolution has led us astray almost as much as the Conception Misconception that was a product of the first megarevolution.

Although it began with mistaken assumptions about human nature, the new free-market economics that was developed in the eighteenth and early nineteenth centuries was said to be based on science. Adam Smith was very much concerned with questions of right and wrong and argued that an unfettered free market would produce the common good, but most of his followers insisted that morality has no place in economics. This discipline, they maintained, was a science—a dismal one, perhaps, but a science all the same. Economics, like other sciences, would concern itself only with what *is,* not with what *ought to be.*

By the time of Smith's successors in the early nineteenth century, an individualism that came out of the thinking of Descartes, Hobbes, Locke, and Smith and saw the basic relationship among people as that of a contract had turned the Western view of human nature into the idea of *Homo economicus,* an independent "individual" motivated only by "his" self-interest and connected with others only through contractual relations. Much of modern society and its political and economic institutions are based upon this conception of human nature.

The very fact that the name *Homo economicus* was coined to describe the behavior of "man" in the modern world is an indication that this "species" is an artificial one (that is, *man*-made—and in this case it indeed was males who made it), which does not match the genuine natural traits of humans. We are still *Homo sapiens,* but we live in a world designed for *Homo economicus.* We have a biological need for membership in a personal community, but "economic man spends his days with . . . strangers."[25] Therein lies much of what is so disconcerting about modern society.

The rise of the Marketplace Misconception posed new threats to male security and self-image. The view of the world as one of constant competitive struggle among individuals meant that it was "every man for himself." All the talk of rugged individualism notwithstanding, male biology is not well suited for such an environment. Men, as we have seen, often have a need for a sense of belonging—to be part of a group, sacrificing some of their individuality for an identity provided by the band. The Marketplace Misconception undermined male association. Other men were transformed from potential associates into potential economic rivals. Market competition displaced male camaraderie.[26] Men, biologically predisposed to seek affiliation, were told that they must rely only on themselves. The "real man," who is in fact by nature a joiner, was redefined by the Marketplace Misconception as not only notawoman but also notamember. He must stand alone. Men have been called upon in the modern Marketplace world to be what are actually unnatural, unreal men—the sort of solitary men imagined by Hobbes.

Hard Economics; Soft Politics: Capitalism and Democracy

There is significance in the desire of modern economists not only to be "scientific" but also to make their science a "hard" one. By this term they mean that they engage in precise measurement and quantification.[27] *Hard* is assumed to be "better" and "higher" than *soft*. The terms *hard* and *soft* have obvious sexual connotations. Moral philosophy, like literature, comes to be classified as "soft" and therefore "feminine" and inferior. Real men, defining themselves in the dualistic notawoman manner, must be hard and scientific and think mathematically. When it is realized how much this sort of thinking permeates the modern world, it becomes clear just how much the modern worldview is based upon a "masculine" value structure that has been substantially intensified by the assumption that men must be the opposite of women.

Yet, in a great irony, this very male-oriented economics also finally wound up promoting greater equality for women. Because it is based on numbers, free-market economics sees every "one" alike, as a potential consumer and producer. Ultimately, women, too, had to be seen in the same way.

Democratic thinking followed a similar course. Few of the men who argued during the Enlightenment and the revolutionary era of the late eighteenth century that "all men are created equal" and for the "rights of man" had any intention of including women in their ideals of human equality. But their assaults on hierarchy began to undermine the model upon which other relationships of domination and subordination had been based: the presumed superiority of men to women. Political equality proved to be the greatest advance for women since the first backlash had reduced their status.

The importance of democracy in providing a substantial degree of equality for women would be difficult to overstate. The establishment of legal guarantees of equality served—although obviously with only partial success—to restrain men from using the physical size and strength upon which they had always depended to provide them with an advantage over women. By considering everyone to be equal, democracy reduces the opportunities in politics for those who crave great power over others, the human counterparts of the "Alpha males" in other species. Under the democratic ideal, the Alpha male will have no more "say" than the Omega male—or the Omega female. Democracy gives to those on whom silence had been imposed voices theoretically equal to that of the loudest (strongest) man. A political system that sees power flowing "from the bottom up" was bound to be of great benefit to those who had always been on the bottom.*

Democracy and capitalism fit together, but not in the way that is often assumed. The democratic doctrine of each person having equal political strength means that the amount of political power that a man (or, possibly, a woman) can accumulate is limited. This fact leaves those who traditionally sought dominance looking for another arena. The free market provides that venue. Under capitalism, the ambitious can compete in a contest in which the score is easily kept (in monetary units) and in which there are no limits on accumulation. While the democratic principle is "one person, one vote," the capitalist principle is "one dollar (pound, franc, yen, etc.), one vote," and an ambitious man can accumulate vastly unequal power. Democracy is, ideally, a leveling system; capitalism, obviously, is not. That this economic system has arisen in tandem with political democracy should not be surprising.

The great paradox of the Marketplace worldview is that it promotes equality in some areas of life as a means of encouraging the pursuit of inequality in others.

When Better Men Are Made, Men Will Make Them

As agriculture had thousands of years before, the new machine industry of the late eighteenth and nineteenth centuries provided metaphors for the changes in human living and thinking that it brought about. "The earth is a great machine given to man to be fashioned to his purpose," gushed American Whig publisher Henry C. Carey in 1858.[28]

But it was not just the earth that was seen as a machine; increasingly, as I noted earlier, the machine became the metaphor as well for human beings. And,

---

*This example is yet another one in which the sexual connotations of commonly used terminology are both easily overlooked and highly significant.

just as had happened with the prehistoric seed-planted-in-soil metaphor, the human-as-machine metaphor soon came to be taken literally. Those working on "artificial intelligence" computer projects today hoping to show that a machine can be made to "think" just like a human (and hence that a human is not merely *like* a machine, but *is* a machine) have gone the farthest in treating this modern metaphor as reality. But the notion that we are machines has been developing since the early days of the industrial age. We have long said things like: "You could see the wheels turning in his head." But our heads contain no wheels. We are *not* machines. Computers may to some small extent be patterned after brains, but it is certain that brains are not patterned after computers. In the modern age it is necessary frequently to remind ourselves that we are animals, not machines. We are much more like chimpanzees than computers.

The consequences of the literalization of the modern human-as-machine metaphor may prove to be as devastating as those of the ancient literalization of the semen-as-seed metaphor.

It was a use of the human-machine theme early in the industrial era that revealed the most about where the later stages of the modern megarevolution are taking us. Mary Wollstonecraft Shelley's *Frankenstein* (1818) captured many aspects of the effects the new machine industry was having on human thought. Although Shelley's subtitle title for *Frankenstein* is *The Modern Prometheus,* the story is actually a modern version of Genesis. As I have argued, the early chapters of the biblical Genesis are part of a transformation in worldview, growing out of the Agricultural Megarevolution, that postulated a male Creator God. Shelley's story is an example (although surely a much less central one than Genesis became) of the modern transformation in worldview, produced by the Mobility Megarevolution, that sees men themselves as the ultimate creators and humans as machines.

The creature in *Frankenstein* is a reflection of the creator, much as Genesis says that man is created in God's image. The creator is displeased with what he sees in his creation, and rejects it, much as Yahweh did in banishing Adam and Eve from Eden.

But there are critical differences in the stories, since they are about two essentially different transformations in the human social environment. One is that when he plays God, Dr. Victor Frankenstein makes a creature with greater strength than his own. "Remember, thou hast made me more powerful than thyself," the "monster" cautions his creator. "You are my creator, but I am your master, obey!" he later proclaims.[29] This concept differs sharply from that of the writers of Genesis, reflecting the modern conviction that man has become the master, or his own god. That the creatures (machines) were "better" than their human creators was evident to anyone who tried to compete against a gun, outrun a train, or outweave a power loom.

That men could create "offspring" that were stronger than themselves also meant that, even as they were demonstrating their apparently great creative power, men were simultaneously undermining one of their principal advantages over women. In the first megarevolution, when women invented agriculture, they unintentionally devalued the chief male roles of hunter and protector. In the second megarevolution, the machines that men invented had the unintended consequence of reducing the value of muscle power. Among the ironies of history is that the machines of the ultra-male-oriented Industrial Revolution further reduced male claims to special usefulness, since those devices would eventually enable women to offset the edge that muscles had provided to men. In this sense, the "monster" created by scientific men, like the one created by the fictional Dr. Frankenstein, was a real threat to the male position.

In *Frankenstein,* the fall from the joy and harmony that young Victor had experienced ("No human being could have experienced a happier childhood than myself") is caused by his quest for ultimate knowledge. "It was the secrets of heaven and earth that I desired to learn," he recalls. But, whereas the knowledge that led to the Fall in Genesis was that of agriculture, in Shelley's modern version it is the knowledge of science and mathematics that causes Victor Frankenstein to lose paradise. He gravitates towards one side of human nature, desiring the firm knowledge that he believes only rationality can provide: "I betook myself to the mathematics and the branches of study appertaining to that science as being built upon secure foundations, and so worthy of my consideration." Shelley leaves no doubt that it was the abandonment of the emotional side of human nature in favor of the purely rational side that caused Frankenstein's problems: "[O]ften did my human nature turn with loathing from my occupation"; "I wished, as it were, to procrastinate all that related to my feelings of affection until the great object, which swallowed up every habit of my nature, should be completed."[30]

Other significant differences between Genesis and *Frankenstein* confirm that the latter is about a new sort of Fall. It is not an agricultural apple but industrial electricity that leads Victor astray. The electricity that first attracts Victor to seek ultimate knowledge is in natural form (lightning).* What he (symbolizing science, technology, and industrialism) does corresponds perfectly with what agriculture did so long before: it is in both cases the addition of human ingenuity to something that occurs naturally that drastically and

---

*It had also been a terrible thunderstorm that set Martin Luther on his course in an earlier phase of the Mobility Megarevolution, but the effects of the experience were very different on the real and fictional characters. Luther was mortally frightened and made a pact with God; Frankenstein was filled with "curiosity and delight" and made a Faustian pact with Science.

dangerously alters the environment. And, if the Agricultural Megarevolution was launched by women and the resulting first Fall blamed on them through the symbol of Eve, the male orientation of the individualistic, competitive Mobility Megarevolution was represented by a male scientist who causes his own (and implicitly humankind's second) Fall. Victor Frankenstein and the men he represents are no more evil men than Eve and the women she symbolized were evil women. Both simply allowed curiosity to lead them into realms different from those for which humans were biologically adapted, with consequences that neither could foresee.

The Genesis writers were men telling an allegory about what women had done to disturb the universe by inventing agriculture. The *Frankenstein* writer was a woman telling an allegory about what men were doing to disturb the universe by inventing machine industry. Dr. Frankenstein's workplace was a sort of "Laboratory of Eden."

The man-as-machine metaphor should also be seen as a continuation of the millennia-old male quest to appropriate the roles of women. In seeking (pro)creative power, Victor Frankenstein is attempting not only to play God but also to play woman. He is a man who aspires to create a new life *by himself.* Victor postpones his marriage to Elizabeth in order to work on his project, thus rejecting the natural route to procreation with a woman in favor of striving to fulfill the desire of Hippolytus to "have children without the help of women." But, in Shelley's account, Dr. Frankenstein is a modern version of the Mesopotamian god Enki, whose attempt to create a being on his own was partially successful, but resulted in a deformed creature.*

Darwin's New Adam (Smith)

The excessively mobile, highly competitive society of the nineteenth-century Western world created in its own image a new understanding of nature. In addition to its important role in leading men into the extreme arrogance of believing themselves to be individual gods, the rise of machine industry also destroyed the harmonious view of the world that had been provided, even in the context of early mobility, by Newtonian physics. Newton's well-balanced physical world was reflected in the dominant eighteenth-century view of nature, that of Swedish botanist Carolus Linnaeus. The natural economy postulated by Linnaeus was one of limits, balance, and harmony. His world was still one of basic unity, not the disintegrating world of harsh competition that came out of the Industrial Revolution. Linnaeus saw nature as an efficient, interdependent whole, not as a struggle among independent, conflicting fragments.[31]

---

*See Chapter 6.

In the areas most affected by the Marketplace view and industrialism, the ordered world of Newton and Linnaeus had fallen apart by the mid-nineteenth century. In the 1820s, it had still been possible for reforming industrialist Robert Owen to name his utopian community "New Harmony." But industrialism was rapidly creating cities that might with accuracy have been named "New Discord." Everything was perceived to be in flux. Darwin is often blamed for this perception. But his theory was more the consequence than the cause of the movement and disorder. It was no accident that the ideas of Charles Darwin were developed in the London described by Charles Dickens.

If, as I have argued, scientific views of the universe are generally reflective of the social circumstances in which they develop, the difference between Newton's conception of a universe in regular, harmonious motion and Darwin's view of a disordered, unpredictable, chaotic struggle for survival must indicate an important change in what was going on in society—at least British society—between the late seventeenth and mid-nineteenth centuries. There can be little question that that change was the result of the acceleration of mobility that accompanied the Industrial Revolution.

Friedrich Engels well described the London in which Darwin developed his view of the natural world. "Isolation of the individual—the narrow-minded egotism—is everywhere the fundamental principle of modern society," Engels wrote in the 1840s. "The disintegration of society into individuals, each guided by his private principles and each pursuing his own aims, has been pushed to its farthest limits in London. Here indeed human society has been split into its component atoms."[32]

The Darwinian view of an animal and plant world in constant struggle and strife could arise only when this image corresponded with people's social experience (as it did in the nineteenth century), just as the Copernican idea of a moving earth had come along and gained acceptance only after the rigid order of the Middle Ages had begun to become more mobile. Darwin's social environment, as historian Donald Worster has said, "placed him in a position to see what the human mind had previously missed." And once he had seen this, others of his time and place were in a position to accept it. "The emphasis Darwin gave to competitive scrambling for place simply could not have been so credible to people living in another place and time."[33]

The invention of agriculture had led to the first scientific revolution and provided the metaphor for it in seed planting. Similarly, the development of machine industry led to the Darwinian revolution in science and provided its metaphor in the struggle for survival (the marketplace). In both cases the old religious beliefs were severely disrupted by the conclusions about human origins drawn from these metaphors. The first scientific revolution led people to believe that a male God who was superior to nature, rather than a female goddess identified with nature, was the cause of their existence; the Darwinian scientific revolution led people to believe that a chaotic process of "brutal" struggle rather than any deity at all was the cause of their existence.

God had been said to have created order out of chaos. It might appear that Darwin created chaos out of the order of earlier views of nature. But that interpretation is misleading. It would be more accurate to say that the new chaos of free-market, industrial society created Darwin's view of nature. An appropriate name for Darwinism would be "marketplace biology." As Darwin banished the Adam of Genesis, he cast Adam Smith as the leading man in his new creation story.

One of the most significant accomplishments of Darwin is one of the least noted. He completed the male conquest of female roles that had begun six thousand or more years before with the "masculinization" of agriculture and the notion of male responsibility for procreation. The subsequent triumph of a supernatural male God, separated from and above an apparently female Nature, had seemingly finished that male conquest. Yet nature itself, while subdued and subordinated to a male supernatural power and bent to the will of men, continued to be seen as female—as it plainly still was by the Romantics of the early nineteenth century. (This is made explicit, for example, in Wordsworth's *The Prelude*.)

On the face of it, Darwin was restoring "Mother Nature" to supremacy by removing the supernatural God from His role in creation. But, on closer examination it becomes apparent that, by patterning his understanding of nature after the competitive Marketplace economy, Darwin finally masculinized nature "her"self. In effect, Darwin performed a sex change operation on nature, replacing a nurturing Mother Nature with a stern, uncaring "Father Nature." Darwin did to nature what the Reformation had done to the divine earlier in the Mobility Megarevolution: completely masculinized it.* Whatever he may have done to God, Darwin effectively killed Mother Nature. Another refuge for feminine values lay in ruins.

The masculinization of nature that resulted from the industrial phase of the Mobility Megarevolution and was enshrined by Darwin has had momentous consequences. While nature was seen as female, man might try to dominate and control "her," but he would also want to combine with "her"—to "marry" "her." But when Darwinian nature came to be seen as male, men took a very different attitude toward it from what they had when it seemed to be female. Rather than something to be courted and loved (and made "graciously sub-

---

*Examples of this transformed view of nature abound in our culture today. To cite one instance, a 1998 athletic shoe television commercial spoke of "a hard, uncaring physical world." Nothing motherly there.

missive" to man's leadership), a male nature became a rival, a competitor, an enemy: something to be conquered. Men would be more likely to make war, not love, with a male nature.

The consequences of that changed attitude toward nature are not difficult to find today.

Marx and the Masculinization of Socialism

Next to Darwin, Karl Marx was the most influential thinker of the nineteenth century. It is no more usual to see Marx's ideas in sexual terms than it is to view Darwin's from that perspective. But this vantage point can provide useful insights into Marx and where he went wrong.

The dialectic employed by Hegel and Marx is closely patterned after sexual division and reproduction. "Opposites" (ideas, classes or modes of production, corresponding to sexes) are brought together to "synthesize" (or give birth to) a new but somewhat different version of the old ones, containing within it the "best" (in Darwinian terms, most adaptive) parts or traits of its "ancestors." Yet the offspring or synthesis is not a successful combination of the parents (or ideas or classes) but another partial, imperfect form (a male or female child—or a partially correct idea or mode, a thesis) that will have again to combine with its opposite sex or antithesis.

But while the Hegelian dialectic and the dialectical materialism of Marx follow the sexual model for producing new ideas, modes, and classes, they contain a critical difference. In sexual reproduction, the "thesis" and "antithesis" (female and male) come together in an act of *love* and *combination* to create an offspring that will combine some aspects of each of them but be of one sex or the other. But in the male-oriented systems of Hegel and Marx, the offspring or synthesis is produced by *conflict* and *competition* between the "parents." Rather than calling the synthesis of Marx's dialectical clash between classes a "love child," it would seem more appropriate to term it a "hate child."

And what is to be made, in light of this understanding of the sexual basis of the dialectic, of the belief of both of these philosophers that the process was finite and would result in a final perfection? The implication is that the process of sexual reproduction will eventually somehow manage to create a synthesis or offspring that is *not* a new thesis or partial truth, not a new female or male, but a whole, a perfection that is above the division that has always existed. In short, Hegel and Marx seemed to be saying that the sexually based dialectic will finally re-produce or re-create what it came from: an undivided unity: God, the end of history, or the classless society. In Marx, this circular process takes the form of history beginning with primitive communism and ending in modern communism.

The earlier socialists, whom Marx disdainfully dismissed as unscientific "utopians," had based their beliefs on religion (usually Christianity) and feeling. They may have had the authority of the old religion behind their type of socialism, but Marx claimed the blessing of the new God of Science for his brand.

What Marx was trying to do, although he did not put it in these terms, was to establish a "male" form of socialism. He employed all the usual symbols for female and male ways, equating the former with "bad" and the latter with "good" to an extent that would have made Aristotle proud. Where the earlier socialists were soft and romantic, Marx said his methods would be hard and practical. Theirs was a system of the heart; his would be a system of the head. Theirs was emotional, his dispassionate.

"Scientific socialism" was ultimately unscientific: Marx's insistence that human nature does not exist was both unscientific and extremely misleading. Without an acceptance of innate tendencies it was possible for Marx, like other modern thinkers, to ignore the emotional component of human beings. This inevitably led to a structure with no foundation.

Marx was attempting to divorce socialism from social feeling and feminine values. This effort was nonsense. Without feeling, which is the means by which the social part of human nature manifests itself, there is nothing to hold people together but calculation; Marx was reducing social relations to a utilitarian basis. There can be no social concern without the *capacity* for concern, which is absent in a worldview based upon the belief that everything can be understood solely in terms of human reason.

The separation of socialism from its basic set of values led to the most fundamental error of Marx and his followers: their attempt (which continued in the communist nations of the twentieth century) to use "masculine" means to reach "feminine" ends. The exclusive reliance on science and reason and the rejection of emotion as "unscientific" is but one aspect of this pervasive Marxian contradiction. Another is the extreme dualism at the base of Marx's worldview. He saw all of history as a clash between two opposing classes, the exploiters and the exploited. Obviously evil was on one side, good on the other. As Marx saw it, the gulf between the classes was unbridgeable; they were irreconcilable and had to fight each other. And, Marx said, the gap would only grow larger. His was a vision of ultimate reconciliation, but it would be reached through strict polarization—class extending that parallels gender extending.

The supreme irony in Marx's adoption of the strict dualism that is more characteristic of male than female thinking was that in doing so he was accepting the either/or view of the world upon which capitalism is based: me *or* you. Socialism has to be based in substantial part on the inclusive, blending sort of thinking that is somewhat more commonly found to a larger degree in females; it cannot sensibly be based only on exclusive, dualistic thinking. A mathematical, scientific approach is appropriate for the economic system of calculation that Marx was analyzing, but it is foolhardy to try to build a system of cooperation and sharing exclusively on this approach. Marx's attempt to do so was doomed from the start, but it took more than a century for this to become clear. Surely the collapse of communism in 1989–1991 left no doubt on this point.

In removing the religious basis and feminine values of early socialism, insisting instead on pure rationality and "masculine" approaches, Marx was to socialism something like what some of the early Church "fathers" were to Christianity—one who, in the name of a worldview based on feminine values, attacked the source of those values. It is tempting to see Marx as socialism's Constantine—the man who used methods diametrically opposed to the values upon which the system he was purporting to adopt was based. Marx, after all, said he wanted a system of harmony, but he argued that it could be reached only through conflict. While calling for cooperation and what had in fact been a worldview rooted in feminine values, Marx accepted many of the rationalist, utilitarian, and competitive premises of those he sought to overthrow. His insistence upon dualism over blending was as alien to genuine socialism as Constantine's employment of Christian prayer to win a battle was alien to the values preached by Jesus. The making of competition, even between classes rather than individuals, the route to socialism was as incongruous as the placing of a symbol of Jesus on battle shields. "Scientific socialism" is nearly as oxymoronic as "military Christianity." Yet Marx and Constantine were so successful in redefining the philosophies they adopted that both systems came rapidly and generally to be identified with their severely mutated versions.

The second megarevolution has been as contradictory in its effects on the sexes as was the first. The marketplace is an impersonal mechanism. As such, its logic led eventually to seeing everyone, including women, impersonally, as independent "individuals." But this viewpoint in no way indicated a decline in the dominance of "masculine" values. As Marilyn Waring has pointed out in her book *If Women Counted* (1988),[34] the Marketplace measures all value numerically (usually in monetary units). This approach severely undervalues (or recognizes no value whatsoever in) much of the work, often unpaid, traditionally done by women. So, as women have gained greater equality, they have often had to do so in a world run almost entirely on "masculine" values.

CHAPTER 11

No Woman Is an Island

"Feminine Values" in a Land of Self-Made Men

Repeal all past history,
you still can not repeal human nature.

ABRAHAM LINCOLN (1854)[1]

America has played the leading role in the world of mobility that has emerged since the Western Hemisphere was opened to European penetration. For this reason, along with others that I mentioned in the prologue, the remainder of the book will focus mainly on developments in the United States. The gradual move away from the values of the Middle Ages (which a majority of Western people carried with them into the modern world) was well underway by the time the British established colonies in North America. Those colonies were, in fact, in substantial measure a result of the new expansive thinking and the new capitalist mentality that the Mobility Megarevolution produced. Accordingly, this sort of thinking formed a part of the American experience from the outset. All of the "modern" trends emerging in Europe developed more quickly in America, where there was little established tradition to block them (or, more accurately, where the Europeans nearly obliterated the long-established traditions of the indigenous peoples).

Yet the Europeans who came to America carried with them traditional values as well as the new mood of movement and individualism. The values that the people of what became the United States adopted were in some important respects premodern. This factor was one of several that mitigated the most extreme effects of mobility in America until the late nineteenth and twentieth centuries.

Paradise Re-Lost: The New East of Eden

"What, then, is the American, this new man?" asked J. Hector St. John de Crèvecoeur in his 1782 book, *Letters From an American Farmer.*[2] The association of

America with a "new" sort of human is one that was made frequently in the early centuries of Europe's acquaintance with the existence of a "New World." In fact the Mobility Megarevolution, which was closely tied to the effects the "discovery" and colonization of America had on Europeans, did seem to be producing a sort of "new man" in these centuries. America was in many respects the place where those effects and that "new man" were emerging most clearly.

The new man of America is readily recognizable in Crèvecoeur's description as *Homo economicus:* "We are all animated with the spirit of an industry which is unfettered and unrestrained," he declared. Crèvecoeur argued that the new man of America worked "on the basis of nature, *self-interest;* can it want a stronger allurement?"[3] The new American Adam had taken on a most appropriate surname for an aspiring Everyman: Smith.

The most important point to realize, however, is that what increasing mobility was bringing forth was not a new man at all but a new social environment to which the same old biological man and woman would have to adapt. As many people saw it, the "new" environment in America was essentially a return to the oldest circumstances in which humans were believed to have lived: Paradise. The ways in which America appeared to its second earliest European visitors in the 1490s and 1500s as a New Eden have already been pointed out. But such views were by no means confined to the early explorers. They have been an integral part of the image (self- and otherwise) of America for the past five hundred years.

I shall cite but a few examples from what (in true American fashion) appears to be a limitless supply. In the same year that Crèvecoeur wrote (1782), poet Philip Freneau declared that the riches of America would cause the renewal of "those days of felicity . . . which are so beautifully described by the prophetic sages of ancient times."[4] And in the middle of the nineteenth century Walt Whitman wrote of America enabling people to return to the primeval mental state:

> O soul, repressless, I with thee and thou with me
> They circumnavigation of the world begin,
> Of man, the voyage of his mind's return,
> To reason's early paradise,
> Back, back to wisdom's birth, to innocent institutions,
> Again with fair creation.[5]

Yet, if America was the New Eden, it could not be like the old one. The new Adams and Eves who came to it brought with them the experience of several thousand years of eating from the tree of knowledge. No matter how pristine the setting seemed to be, those who would be its new inhabitants could hardly be called innocent. Alexis de Tocqueville stated it well in the 1830s when he wrote that America "still presents, as it did in primeval time, rivers that rise from never failing sources, green and moist solitudes, and limitless fields which the plowshare of the husbandman has never turned. In this state," the French nobleman added, "it is offered to man, not barbarous, ignorant, and isolated, as he was in the early ages, but already in possession of the most important secrets of nature, united to his fellow men, and instructed by the experience of fifty centuries."[6]

People had, through the development of values, achieved a degree of balance with the social environment of medieval Europe; with the discovery of the New World, they found themselves in a situation that had a strong potential for leading them to abandon those values and unleash their basic biological proclivities. In America with its abundance there seemed to be less need for the social restraints on primal urges that had been built up in the Old World. In this respect, the European arrival in America could be seen as a new *departure* from Paradise, a second Fall. It had an effect somewhat like that of the original development of agriculture. By producing surplus, that first megarevolution had transformed previously adaptive traits, such as acquisitiveness, into maladaptive tendencies, such as greed. The newfound abundance of the newfound land in the west had much the same consequence.

In Europe—and, to be sure, in Asia and at least parts of Africa—it had long been necessary for people to accept limits and to act with some degree of prudence. Not so in America—or so it seemed to the newly arrived Europeans. "Every object that met the sight in this enchanting region seemed prepared to satisfy the wants or contribute to the pleasures of man. Almost all the trees were loaded with nourishing fruits," Tocqueville wrote of an America that he certainly made sound like another Eden. "[A]nd," he added significantly, "the air of these climates had an indefinably enervating influence, *which made man cling to the present, heedless of the future.*"[7] Since prudence is not innate in humans but, as Edmund Burke put it, the "first virtue," it was unable to survive in the face of apparently unlimited abundance. In his aptly named *Journey to the Land of Eden in the Year 1733*, William Byrd reported that the members of his expedition had come upon "several large chestnut trees very full of chestnuts. Our men were too lazy to climb the trees for the sake of the fruit but . . . chose rather to cut them down, *regardless of those that were to come after.*"[8] The italicized phrases in both the Tocqueville and Byrd passages capture the essence of natural imprudence, which has been all too common in American history.

James Fenimore Cooper neatly satirized this aspect of America's return to nature (for that is what being imprudent is) in *The Pioneers* (1823) by having settlers dredge lakes so that they could get all the fish at once.[9] It has truthfully been said that "for three hundred years, the American response to a tree was to cut it down."[10] (Ronald Reagan spoke for this American tradition when he said, "a tree is a tree, how many more do you need to look at?"[11]) It would be difficult to deny that wasting resources is as American as apple pie. Rather than just eat from the trees of knowledge in their New Eden, the European unsettlers who came to America cut down those trees with reckless abandon.

The cause of such widespread improvident action among Americans has been encapsulated by novelist Wallace Stegner: "That we could be so greedy was based on the fact that there was so much to be greedy about."[12] For a considerable time many European and Euro-American observers believed that the greed that was unleashed by America's bounty did little harm. Tocqueville contended in the 1830s that it was "the present good fortune of the New World that the vices of its inhabitants are scarcely less favorable to society than their virtues." The immensity of America's resources, the French count said, led to an outlook that differed from that of the Old World: "What we should call cupidity, the Americans frequently term a laudable industry; and they blame as faint-heartedness what we consider to be the virtue of moderate desires."[13]

The common belief through much of American history was that there was not much need in the American environment for moderation—or for prudence, conservation, or the acceptance of limits. This attitude seemed to be confirmed by American conditions in the nineteenth century and before. Its cause was the apparently boundless abundance of the New World, which seemed to remove the need for these traditional values. After a visit to the United States, English reformer and journalist William Cobbett commented in 1817, "[in this country] you are not much pressed to eat and drink, but such an abundance is spread before you . . . that you instantly lose all restraint."[14] The same could be said of the effects of American abundance in areas beyond the dinner table.

The long-term consequence of what was thought to be a return to Paradise was seriously to weaken the attachment of Americans to such traditional values as prudence and living within limits. When disregard for the future began to cause greater harm in the late nineteenth and twentieth centuries, Americans' imprudent and wasteful habits, which were simply the result of following biological proclivities without much restraint from values, were hard to overcome.

Making (It With) Yourself

It is often said that Benjamin Franklin is the prototypical American man. One of the chief features that makes him such is that he was a "self-made man." This concept is the most American of ideas. The term itself was the offspring of American politician Henry Clay in 1832,[15] but the idea antedated the name. Clearly the notion is a consequence of the modern megarevolution. An examination of the implications of this terminology can clarify much about how that transformation shaped the ways we see ourselves, members of the somewhat different sex, and the world around us.

A man who is said to have made himself owes nothing to anyone else, including his parents. The concept of the self-made man is obviously one that is compatible with an extreme individualism; that doctrine separates one from both contemporaries and ancestors, neither of whom can be seen as having made any significant contribution to an individual who has made himself. It also removes any responsibility toward future generations, including one's own children, because they, too, are supposed to "make something of themselves."

But the implications of the self-made man go much farther than this. It is another reflection of womb envy: men try to make themselves because they are incapable of making anyone else. A man who thinks he "made" or "created" himself is in essence saying that he "gave birth to himself."[16]* What is subconsciously being asserted is that no woman had anything to do with creating such a man. The concept of the self-made man is one of the modern megarevolution's versions of exclusive male creation: the counterpart of Yahweh pulling Eve from Adam's abdomen or Athena springing from the head of Zeus. Mary Shelley's account of Dr. Frankenstein's efforts constitutes the definitive modern version of the male-doing-it-all-by-himself story. The self-made man creates as Ra was said to have created the world; he doesn't "make it" with a woman; rather, he does it all by himself: he makes it with himself.

The egoism resulting from extreme mobility takes the modern variant of male creation a step farther; not only is a male doing the creating without the assistance of a female, it is the individual male who is seen as *his own* creator: autogenesis. He can say, like Athena, "no mother gave me birth." Thus the American and modern idea of the self-made man completes the belief that the individual self is the creator—is God. It also indicates that the man who claims to be self-made is pretending (of course without realizing it) to have regained the primal wholeness of asexually reproducing protists. An amoeba is, in a real sense, self-made. A man cannot be.

Echoes of Aristotle can be heard in the self-made man ideal. Again there is the assertion that the woman in the act of birth provides only the formless, soulless matter, which is then made into something by the individual male. Now, though, it is not the father, but the son himself who provides his own soul and life. What is especially curious is that the idea of the self-made man arose in a time and place in which Locke's tabula rasa was widely accepted. These beliefs do not fit together well: It is not clear how a blank slate goes about creating itself.

The idea of the self-made man, which arose so strongly in nineteenth-century America and has been with us ever since, is a cult of self-worship. In that new

---

*Here again, in the terminology self-made man, the word *man* has overwhelmingly been interpreted to mean male. In fact, until very recently there was no talk of a self-made woman—and it still remains a rarely heard construction.

religion, both the Other and others cease to have any meaningful existence. The cult of the self-made man is incompatible with traditional religious beliefs and with human nature, both of which are based upon connection with and obligation to that which is beyond the self.

The term *manhood* has frequently been associated with independence. "Society everywhere is in conspiracy against the manhood of every one of its members," Ralph Waldo Emerson wrote in 1841. "Society is a joint-stock company, in which the members agree, for the better securing of his bread to each shareholder, to surrender the liberty and culture of the eater. The virtue most in request is conformity. Self-reliance is its aversion. . . . Whoso would be a man must be a nonconformist." Emerson also expressed the hope that he would someday "have the manhood to withhold" charity from those who were not close to him. "Are they *my* poor?" he asked. "I grudge the dollar, the dime, the cent, I give to such men as do not belong to me and to whom I do not belong."[17] A more forthright reflection of the identification with the band—with those known personally—would be hard to find. Emerson clearly equated "manhood" with independence and lack of concern for others beyond those he knew personally.

Henry David Thoreau agreed. "Oh for a man who is a *man*," he wrote. "How many *men* are there to a square thousand miles in this country? Hardly one. Does not America offer any inducement for men to settle here?" He defined a *man* as someone who is "independent, intelligent, and respectable."[18]

But this sort of definition of manhood, which came to be the norm in the United States and, increasingly, in the modern world as a whole, is one that is based on the Marketplace Misconception. As we have seen, total independence is not congenial to the usual male proclivities. It is, instead, an artificial ideal established to adapt men to the state of unnature of the Marketplace world.

Americans, especially in the nation's early years, tended to look with disdain at inherited wealth and position. Aristocracy was considered "effeminate." It was based on birth, and so in a sense was power and position that were obtained through a woman (even though inherited, in theory, from a man). The "real man" did not depend on a inheritance—on a mother—to make him; he made himself.

If a real man in America was self-made, the same must be true of the nation. The United States prided itself on being a self-made nation. No mother gave us (or the U.S.) birth. There had been, of course, a "mother country," but Americans fought a war to establish their independence from that mother. "Independence transforms the son into his own parent," historian Jay Fliegelman has said of the young American nation.[19] It is significant that the statement could be applied interchangeably to the ideal for individual males. For the nation, the achievement of independence turned the Sons of Liberty into the Founding Fathers, who, according to American mythology, proceeded without the help of women to give birth to a new nation.

A nation composed of "real men," which is to say notwomen, must also strive to prove that it is notawomanlynation.

The Sexual Bi-Polar Disorder, American Style

The sexual bi-polar disorder spread on a massive scale in the nineteenth century. Most women remained outside the new mobile, individualistic economic system in eighteenth- and early nineteenth-century America. As long as agriculture and small-town life predominated in America, feminine values played an important part in shaping the society's practices. While men worked in close proximity to the home (and, if in farming, in a "nurturing" occupation) there was some integration of feminine with masculine values. This certainly does not mean that in a male-dominated society feminine values enjoyed equality; but they were still in a position to exert some influence. Alexis de Tocqueville was among those who argued that it was the influence of women that moderated the effects of extreme individualism in America. Religion had often played an important role in "restraining men," he said, but it was powerless "in the midst of innumerable temptations which fortune offers" in the New World. Religion, he said "cannot moderate their [men's] eagerness to enrich themselves, which everything [in America] contributes to arouse, but it reigns supreme in the souls of the women, and it is women who shape mores."[20]

Similar arguments on women performing a civilizing function on men were common. Journalist Sarah Josepha Hale declared women to be "God's appointed agent of MORALITY," who must improve man's "human affections and elevate his moral feelings."[21] Thomas Paine had suggested much the same thing in his "An Occasional Letter on the Female Sex" (1775). Placing words in the mouth of an imaginary woman defending her sex, Paine said, "We are the wives and mothers. 'T is we who form the union and the cordiality of families. 'T is we who soften the savage rudeness which considers everything as due to force, and which would involve man with man in eternal war. We cultivate in you that humanity which makes you feel for the misfortunes of others."*[22]

---

*Paine's idealization of women per se provides a good opportunity for me to re-emphasize what I mean by "feminine values." Those values are not anything remotely approaching an absolute difference between women and men. They are, to be sure, related to biological predispositions that are usually stronger in women than in men, but women do not automatically fulfill the functions Paine cited. Women are quite capable of being savage and not feeling for the misfortunes of others. What can help to restrain such behaviors is the values that we often associate with women, as they are more commonly found in that sex. Unfortunately, gender extending has recast those values as *exclusively* feminine and inappropriate for men. What if women were in a general social position from which they could exert some influence, as they could to an extent in the agricultural, small-town societies of early America? Most likely there would be some softening of "savage" behaviors. But placing any particular woman in a position of great influence would provide no such assurance.

During the nineteenth century, the effects of mobility began to undermine the sexually integrated environment that had given feminine values some influence and restraining power. As men moved ever more into the mobile world churning outside the home, women for the most part remained situated in what became islands of some stability in an increasingly fluid and impersonal society. The doctrine of "separate spheres" arose in reflection of the changing situation—or "unsituation," since a major feature of the excessive mobility of the modern world is that people lose their sense of place and belonging. Precisely because the outside sphere was becoming more dominated by competitive "masculine" values, the sphere of the home was emphasized as a place where "feminine" values would reign.

The influence of feminine values—and of women—in the home may actually have increased in the nineteenth century, but the separation of this sphere from what eventually came to be called "the real world" sharply reduced the sway of those values "where it counts" (another phrase laden with significance). The home became an almost complete contrast to the world of business. In the former, at least ideally, people were not constantly expected to prove themselves; they were accepted and loved; cooperation took precedence over competition. Women's occupations in the home continued to be *callings* (the call coming from and for the other)—work directed toward the common good rather than self-seeking.[23]

What was happening as separate spheres for the sexes were established was sexual bi-polarism on a massive scale: "[T]he workplace was masculinized, the home feminized."[24] As the mobile, individualistic public world, with its seemingly heavily masculine (but in fact in some respects nonhuman) ways, rapidly developed in the nineteenth century, people realized the need for finding some means of maintaining the values that had been labeled as feminine. This necessity led to the segregation of male and female worlds, so that the sphere of the latter could serve as a refuge from a "real world" that was increasingly heartless—devoid of feminine values. That those values were preserved somewhere was to the good, but it was not of very much use if they were separated from what people—or, at any rate, men—considered to be the real world.

There are two important implications of terming the highly competitive world outside the home the *real world*. One, clearly, is that the world of home and family is not real, and so must be artificial. (In fact, of course, it is much more the other way around.) The other, related but less obvious implication is that Hobbes was right and the "brutal" world of individual competition that was arising with capitalism and industry is "natural," while the world of cooperation and mutuality, now to be confined to the home, is not natural, but a human construct. This assessment, too, is wholly contrary to fact, but that shortcoming has never prevented a belief from assuming critical importance in the conduct of human affairs. We still refer to the "arena" of individual competition, which is actually an artificial turf constructed for playing the games of the Marketplace, as the real world.

The separation of the male and female spheres (and so of masculine and feminine values) was artificial and another clear example of gender extending. The doctrine of separate spheres for the sexes was "a male creation," an invention designed to "serve men's needs."[25] Its effect was to say that the mixture of traits and values that exists in all of us is even less acceptable than gender-extending men had previously made it. The establishment of separate spheres was one response to the new threat to men's self-esteem posed by the Marketplace world and its demand that a man "make something of himself." Men were to become completely mobile, individualistic, and competitive and to follow *only* exaggerated masculine values; women were to be more stationary, cooperative, and nurturing and follow *only* exaggerated feminine values. One result was to place virtually the whole burden for human morality on women. The nineteenth-century American man, as historian Barbara Welter has said, neglected the values of his forebears and "felt some guilt that he had turned this new land, this temple of the chosen people, into one vast countinghouse. But he could salve his conscience by reflecting that he had left behind a hostage . . . to all the values which he held so dear and treated so lightly."[26] Women were to be selfless, while the male world outside was one that was constructed on acquisitiveness and selfishness.[27] It was left to mothers to inculcate virtue in the next generation, "since the fathers, alas, were too busy chasing the dollar."[28] The "angel of the house" was meant to be the counterbalance to the devils operating out in the Marketplace.

This separation produced profound psychological stress for both sexes, because it demanded of both that they act against human nature by trying to become pure versions of what are in fact only differing degrees along a continuous scale. Biology may incline "the average woman" to be somewhat less selfish than "the average man." But this tendency does not mean that women are capable of becoming the completely self-sacrificing ideals (epitomized in fiction by Melanie Wilkes in *Gone with the Wind*) that the separate-spheres doctrine called upon them to be. And biology may incline "the average man" to be slightly more individualistic than "the average woman." But this tendency does not mean that men can, without serious damage to their psyches, adopt the full-blown egoism that the system expects of them.

Because the biological predispositions are mixed in all of us, they cannot be segregated. Any attempt to do so, as has been done in much of the last two centuries, is a prescription for calamity. What was (and is) needed was not to create a haven from the heartless world, but to put some heart (that is, feminine values) back into that Marketplace world which has been based almost exclusively on extreme masculine values.

Paradise Regained?—Escape to the Frontier

The nineteenth-century American middle-class home became, as historian Michael Kimmel has nicely put it, "a virtual feminine theme park."[29] Men who were constantly told that the sexes are wholly opposite and that they must distance themselves completely from all things feminine could not feel at home when they were at home. To do so would be to admit to themselves that they liked some feminine things and so to jeopardize their standing as notwomen. Hence the home often failed to serve men as the haven from the inhuman Marketplace it was supposed to be. By defining the sexes as opposites, men obliged themselves not only to repress all of their own feelings and traits that had been classified as feminine but also to shun the entire side of life that had been categorized as the female sphere.

Small wonder, then, that escape was a dominant theme of American literature and mythology aimed at males. A man's home had become his prison— enemy terrain, since it had been defined as *her* domain, and *he* was told that he could not be a real *he* if he found such girl stuff even to be tolerable. The best way to avoid this threat was to "light out for the territory," as Huck Finn put it: Put as much distance as possible between your insecure manhood and the temptations of the feminine world.

The frontier's appeal—Horace Greeley's "Go West, young man"—was that of a double escape: from the Marketplace and from the world defined as woman's sphere. Here, it seemed, a man could "go home again"—home to a pre-agricultural Eden where he could still hope to put his natural inclinations to good use. He could be a hunter, like his distant ancestors. From this perspective, Crèvecoeur's complaint that men on the frontier "degenerated altogether into the hunting state"[30] had the matter backwards. The hope for many men fleeing the world of the Marketplace was that on the frontier they might be *re*generated altogether into the hunting state.

But this "Paradise Regained" ideal of finding on the frontier a way of returning to an environment for which male traits were well adapted was a forlorn hope. The reason was that the men who went West carried the Marketplace Misconception with them.

Men removing to the frontier sought an escape to a supposedly natural Hobbesian world: one of solitary individuals, of men separated from women and from one another. The frontier hero, as in James Fenimore Cooper's Natty Bumppo, was, as Christopher Lasch said, "the solitary hunter, unencumbered by social responsibilities, utterly self-sufficient."[31] He was, in short, a man

Paradise Regained?
The ideal of the solitary frontiersman as the new American Adam and the prototype of the "real man" is among the strongest of American myths. The problem with this attempt to escape from the threats presented by the Marketplace world and the sphere that had been designated as "female" was that it grafted the modern notion of individualism onto the man-the-hunter ideal. "Real men" in the pre-agricultural "Eden" had hunted in groups and been interdependent with women. Here Theodore Roosevelt poses in a studio as the mythical frontiersman. (Corbis)

adapted to Hobbes's State of Unnature, the Marketplace, not to the actual ancestral environment of humans, where the hunters were not solitary, where social responsibilities were paramount, and where no one was utterly self-sufficient. Nor was the ancestral environment in which men had found useful outlets for their innate predispositions one without women. It had been one of interdependence of the sexes.

The mythologized Daniel Boone who became, along with the wholly fictional Bumppo, the prototypical "real American man," was an ultimate loner, a man who rejected society and belonging to a group. In this important sense Boone, Bumppo, and other mythical frontier heroes were very different from what real men had usually been. The myth of the frontier held out to insecure men the hope of escape, but the promised land was not the paradise for genuine male ways that it seemed to be.

The frontier, then, proved to be no more of an effective refuge for men from the ravages of the Marketplace world than was the home. The latter had been defined as women's sphere and so already insecure men were afraid to utilize it; the former had been seen as a natural sphere for men, but it was defined in such an unnatural way, as a womanless world of total male self-reliance, that it was of use only as a forest of dreams for insecure males caught in a world for which they were not well adapted, never as a real male alternative to that world. The frontier was as much a masculine theme park as the house was a feminine theme park: Frontierland and Fantasyland. Both were separated from the real world for which humans were adapted.

Sex and Race: Civilization Penetrating "Savagery"

The connections between the status and treatment of women and blacks in America have long been speculated upon, but they continue to be a source of deep insights into the way we are. First of all, remember that the subordination of females had served for thousands of years* as the prototype for the subordination of others, including slaves. In this context it is hardly surprising that in both the mid-nineteenth and mid-twentieth centuries it was American women involved in struggles for the freedom and civil rights of blacks who began to see links between their own condition and that of a race held in subjugation. Those links were both very ancient and very real.

The ties between the subordination of women and of blacks (and others), however, were obscured by other symbolism. Women had become the representatives of civilization—a role they had held at least since the rise of chivalry. This role grew as the mobile male world of "brutal" competition came to seem ever less civilized and more like what Hobbes had imagined to be the state of nature. There had appeared to be a special need for this role in America, where the preservation of civilization in the "wilderness" was long

---

Millions of years if we take into account the use of symbolic mounting of subordinate males among other species. This subject will be fully discussed in Chapter 13.

thought to be in doubt. Blacks (as well as other races, such as the indigenous peoples of the Western Hemisphere), on the other hand, were made into symbols of savagery.

Tocqueville unquestioningly accepted these symbols as reality when he wrote of the benefits accruing from the presence of mixed-race people among the Indians of the United States. "Deriving intelligence from the father's side without entirely losing the savage customs of the mother, the half-blood forms the natural link between civilization and barbarism," Tocqueville proclaimed.[32] The blatant racism of assuming that intelligence was to be derived only from the white side of the union speaks for itself. But the fascinating aspect of this statement is the absolute assumption that the only way that a "half-blood" might be produced would be by a white father and a "savage" mother. Tocqueville made the same automatic assumption with regard to sexual relations between whites and blacks. "It is true that in the North of the Union marriages may be legally contracted between Negroes and whites; but public opinion would stigmatize as infamous a *man* who should connect *him*self with a *Negress* and it would be difficult to cite a single instance of such a union."[33]

In both these cases, it appears that a sexual connection in the other direction, between a red or black man and a white woman, was simply beyond the realm of consideration—literally unthinkable. Part of the reason for this was the desire to maintain an "appropriate" or "natural" order. If men were assumed to be superior to women and white people to black or red people, then it was thought proper and natural for one who was on the superior side in both categorizations to "have" one who was on the inferior side in both reckonings. Under such circumstances, there would be no question as to who was "on top." But for one who was on top in one vertical categorization but on the bottom in another (such as a man who was black) to form a sexual union with someone in the reverse situation (a woman who was white) would invert and disrupt all order. That was more fluidity than even the mobile European-American males of the eighteenth and nineteenth centuries were prepared to accept.

A white man could be on top of any woman and a black woman could be underneath any man without upsetting the accepted sense of order and propriety; others had to be more discriminating in their "choice" of partners. (I place choice in quotation marks because often for black women and sometimes for other women there was no choice involved.)

But I believe there was still something more to the assumption that in any liaison between members of different races the male would be white. Because the white woman had come to represent civilization itself, it was inconceivable that she could be *penetrated* by someone who was taken to represent savagery. It was, however, quite proper for civilization to penetrate savagery—that was supposed to be what the European conquest of America was all about.* (And this is just the sort of language that was used, as in a pioneer "penetrating the wilderness.") Then there was also the residue of the idea that males do the creating, or at least provide the important "spiritual" part of what goes into a new life. Under this assumption, it would be permissible for a "superior," "civilized" male to deposit his seed in the "ground" of a "savage" female. Some would even argue that it might be beneficial for that seed to draw some reinvigoration from the nutrients in the "unspoiled soil." But for a savage seed to be planted in civilized ground would be letting the barbarian within the gates—the sort of gates that men had sometimes locked with chastity belts.

Slave "Real Estate"

Because they were denied freedom, black slaves were the least mobile people in the New World of accelerating motion. Or, rather, they had little or no self-determined mobility. If white men often equated mobility with opportunity, to black slaves mobility almost always represented danger. (The one exception was the slim hope that mobility might take the form of escape.) For those brought to America from Africa, their first taste of involuntary mobility had been their enslavement and transport through the infamous Middle Passage. Slaves, whether African- or American-born, could be moved at any time, away from family, friends, and familiar surroundings. In all of this, they revealed in the starkest terms the downside of mobility. For them it clearly made for insecurity and threatened to break up families. In fact, however, mobility—if permitted to become excessive—carried similar threats for Europeans and European-Americans. But the threats were not so obvious in their cases.

That the acquisitive individualism emanating from the second megarevolution would destroy traditional values and cause social and family disintegration was first shown in what it sometimes did to African-American families. Cooperative, feminine values and family ties were especially important to black slaves, because they were sources of security in a world of insecurity. Well before the white family came to be seen as a refuge in the heartless world of modern competition, the black family served that function in the more heartless world of slavery.

Whites, including slaveowners, professed to believe in such virtues as chastity, marriage, and the family, but many of them demonstrated that they believed in profits more than they did in those values. Fertility in slave women

---

*This interpretation creates an apparent contradiction, because for civilization to penetrate savagery, civilization would have to be seen as male. But, while white women were the *symbols* of civilization, white men had no doubt that they (white men) were far more civilized than non-whites of either sex.

was held in higher esteem by most slaveholders than was any traditional virtue—and the slaveholders were usually not very particular about whose seed was planted in the fertile ground. Often they contributed their own. Historians who have studied plantation records have found that slave women gave birth to their first children at an average age of four to seven years younger than did contemporary European women.[34]

What was going on here is an excellent example of how America was the New East of Eden, the place where Paradise was re-lost. Recall that when the invention of agriculture made it possible for a person to produce a considerable surplus beyond what she or he consumed, fertility in women had become highly prized—and men had asserted ownership over women as well as land, the two forms of "productive property." As the ratio of land to population decreased in Europe (a process that took place very inconsistently, with epidemics and wars often reducing the population), large families had become somewhat less desirable. But in the seemingly boundless, virgin land of America, the ratio of land to people was huge, and the more hands a landowner could put to work, the greater his income was likely to be. Slave women in particular came to be seen in America as the kind of assets that women in general had become during the Agricultural Megarevolution. Slave women were seen as "real estate"—productive property—although they were not so termed. Nonslave women were also often used to produce large numbers of children to work the apparently limitless land of the New World. The persistence of the Conception Misconception's seed metaphor can be seen here yet again. Although the supply of women in early America was far more limited than that of land appeared to be, many men employed "their" women in just the same way they did "their" land: they used them up quickly by growing crops without caring for the "soil" or allowing it to lie fallow long enough to replenish itself. When this practice resulted in the woman's death, the man would then move on to the "virgin soil" of a younger wife in whom he could plant his seeds and raise another crop.

In addition to encouraging pre- and extramarital sexual relations by "their" slave women, slaveholders frequently broke up families by selling some members and retaining others, or by selling close relatives to plantations in different locales. One student of slave life has calculated that the average slave was likely during her or his lifetime to have eleven close relatives sold away.[35] This horrible reality of the way in which the quest for maximum profit undermined any respect for traditional values was well captured by an old Gullah preacher who completed a slave marriage ceremony by saying, "Till death or burkra [the white man] part you."[36]

It would take a while longer before the Mobility Megarevolution would fully become the threat to free families that it already was to slave families in the eighteenth and nineteenth centuries. In the meantime, those black families that were able to withstand the ravages of imposed disruption remained oases of stability and traditional values in a slowly disintegrating world. The mobile forces of disintegration would catch the black family and douse it with their solvents only in the second half of the twentieth century. By that time, many families of all ethnicities were succumbing to those same forces.

CHAPTER 12

"I Can't Be Satisfied"
The Sexes and Twentieth-Century Consumerculture

On or about December 1910,
Human character changed.
VIRGINIA WOOLF (1924)[1]

The remainder of this book will deal principally with various aspects of the twentieth century and the contemporary world, with the focus almost entirely on the Western world and principally the United States.* This sketch of the interplay of the sexes and perceptions of them during the last hundred or so years can be done with a few more detailed lines than has been possible for the preceding ten thousand years. But there is no way that a comprehensive portrait of this subject can be presented in the space of a few chapters. The treatment here necessarily must be highly selective. In this chapter a few important intellectual, cultural, and social markers of the period from the end of the nineteenth century to the 1960s will be used as windows into the larger questions that have been our focus throughout the book. The choices are eclectic, but not arbitrary. The topics and examples were chosen because they seem to provide particularly illuminating reflections of the most important developments of the era.

The remarkable statement of Virginia Woolf that stands as this chapter's epigraph captures, as Irving Howe has said, a "frightening discontinuity between the traditional past and the shaken present," a sense that "the line of history has been bent, perhaps broken."[2] The image of a "shaken" present is

---

*There are two main reasons for this focus, as I have indicated before, one practical and one historical: First, these are the places about which I know enough to analyze with some degree of "authority" (the practical reason). Second, these are the regions in which the trends that have increasingly taken hold in much of the rest of the world have proceeded the farthest (the historical reason).

precisely the right one, since what has so upset the modern world and broken its ties with the traditional past is excessive mobility. But, significant as it certainly is, Woolf's statement is very misleading. Human nature has *not* changed; for practical purposes, it can be taken as a constant.* What made it seem as though the human character or nature had changed was the drastic alteration in the social environment in which that nature had to operate. Such changes had been ongoing since the invention of agriculture some ten millennia earlier. The particular sorts of mobility-induced changes that produced the "shaken present" had been underway for nearly a half millennium. But by far the most drastic effects of human-made alterations in the social environment have been felt since the beginning of the twentieth century.

Beyond a doubt the twentieth century saw more dramatic changes in the ways people live than any other that preceded it. Obviously there were immense alterations in the way we communicate, transport ourselves, produce and preserve food, kill each other, cure diseases, store and process information, and influence the environment. At least as important as any of them has been a less discussed but deeper transformation: the mutation of the free market economy from an emphasis on production to a preoccupation with consumption. Few of the massive changes of the last century had effects as pervasive as those of the rise of an economy and culture built on mass consumption: what can be termed the Consumerculture.

Thus Spake an Insecure Man

Friedrich Nietzsche had seen himself as a man ahead of his time. "Only the day after tomorrow belongs to me," he wrote in 1888. "Some men are born posthumously."[3] If Hegel and Marx took German philosophy away from individualism in the nineteenth century, the apparent opposite of their collectivism was to be found in the thought of Nietzsche. His hyperindividualism made him a prophet of the side of the Mobility Megarevolution that came to be known as modernism and even postmodernism, which dominated much of Western culture in the twentieth century.

Nietzsche was the culmination of much of the thinking that had arisen since the early days of the modern megarevolution. Like Hobbes and Locke, he believed that humans are naturally independent. But Nietzsche went far beyond these earlier theorists of independence: he wanted people to *remain*

---

*Of course human nature *can* change—and *has* changed—through biological evolution; but that process is too slow to have much practical meaning in historical time, much less in a single century. We may now be on the verge of rapid change in human nature through genetic engineering, but that is a phenomenon of import for the future, not the past.

independent. "[A]ll contact between man and man—'in society'—involves inevitable uncleanliness," he declared. "All community makes men—somehow, somewhere, sometime 'common.' " Nietzsche's goal was "not to remain stuck to a person—not even the most loved—every person is a prison."[4] The Darwinian-influenced arguments that have over the past century completed the subversion of traditional values fully emerged in Nietzsche. He put into its most extreme form the idea of abandoning the values of the Judeo-Christian tradition in favor of a return to the primitive, no-holds-barred struggle that he and so many others believed to have existed before society and its values developed. He wanted to reverse the cultural evolution that had enabled human beings partially to counteract the effects of the biologically inbred proclivities that were not adaptive in human-made social environments. Nietzsche understood the role of values in controlling innate tendencies. He called moralities "recipes against his [the individual's] passions and declared that every morality is "a bit of tyranny against 'nature.' "[5]

Nietzsche's idea was the antithesis to the rational thesis represented by the science worshipers of the modern era. He perceived that it was the rise of commerce (mobility), with its uprooting of people and removal from their historical ties to the soil, that had destroyed tradition and replaced it with rational calculation. He also understood that this new scientific order would not—*could* not—satisfy human emotional needs. So he rebelled against rationality. But he rebelled also against traditional values and what he saw as the weak "slave morality" of religions, particularly Christianity with its emphasis on meekness. The "slave morality" for which Nietzsche had such contempt has obvious connections with the values usually associated with women. He preferred what he called "master morality," which has equally apparent ties to the "male virtues." (The very German term he used, *Herren-Moral,* indicates that he meant "man's morality"; it was a morality, he said, that demands "hardness."[6]) Nietzsche sought the emergence of an *Übermensch,* a "superman" with a "will to power"—a man, in short, similar to a silverback gorilla.

Like so many other major thinkers, Nietzsche was a virulent misogynist. He expressed contempt for women and everything he associated with them: compassion, softness, Christianity (with its "unmanly tenderness" and "almost feminine inability [of its adherents] to remain spectators, to *let* someone suffer"), "sentimental weakness," selflessness, a "warm heart," pity, love, and faith.[7]

For all his apparent breaking with the past, Nietzsche fully embraced the traditional male view of women: "Woman is by nature a snake," he proclaimed. " 'From woman comes all calamity in the world'—every priest knows that, too. 'Consequently, it is from her too that *science* comes.' Only from woman did man learn to taste of the tree of knowledge."[8]

In blaming women for introducing science into the world by eating from the Tree of Knowledge, Nietzsche came close to the argument I have made that this story actually refers to women inventing agriculture. He was renewing the ancient charge that women had lost Paradise. Science had killed God, Nietzsche said, and that, too, was the doing of women. For all his modernity, Nietzsche was filling his new bottles with very old vinegar indeed.

Thus spake an insecure man on the eve of the twentieth century, attempting in his own way, as have so many others throughout history, to show that he was notawoman.

"Man Is Nothing Else But What He Makes of Himself"

What Nietzsche sought was absolute individual freedom. This notion of "liberation" or complete liberty is the end result of the disintegrative forces of excessive mobility, and it was *the* belief of the twentieth century. It became the rallying cry of a disparate group of people, ranging across the political spectrum, from Ayn Rand to Jean-Paul Sartre, from the American Civil Liberties Union to the National Association of Manufacturers. Rand, the creator of fictional megalomaniacs, was a believer in the most extreme form of the "self-made man." She contended that the individual owed absolutely nothing to anyone else—a belief about as far to the political right as one can get. Sartre was often classified as a leftist, but he and other existentialists insisted that each person is *totally* free.

Freedom is a good, to be sure, but not an absolute good; freedom is good, but absolute freedom is not. Because we are social animals, only so much individual freedom is compatible with human nature. And that's just the problem. The belief that there is no such thing as human nature is the underlying assumption upon which so much of twentieth century thought and action rested. It is the essence of both economic modernism (capitalism) and cultural modernism, that each person makes him- or herself. (Such commonality might be surprising to most adherents to these movements who believe themselves to be in radically opposing groups.) That erroneous belief in self-making is the source of much of our trouble.

Sartre stated the existentialist belief as follows: "Man is nothing else but what he makes of himself."[9] This is very similar to the Rand argument. It is the absolute denial of human nature; it is Locke's tabula rasa run wild. We are, quite simply, not *that* free. There are constraints on what we can make of ourselves; the possibilities may be great, but they are not unlimited.[10] It was among the great tragedies of the twentieth century that so many people refused to recognize this seemingly obvious truth.

The belief that "man is nothing else but what he makes of himself" is, of course, yet another expression of the modern variant of male self-creation. It is to say, albeit subconsciously: "*Woman* sure didn't make me anything." On this point, existentialists and cultural radicals are on unacknowledged common ground with exponents of totally unfettered free market capitalism. Both contend that a man makes himself, through his will. "No mother gave me birth," many of the most advanced thinkers of the twentieth century sang in harmony with the male vocalists of nineteenth-century economics, whose voices still remain so strong today.

In rejecting this modern belief in absolute autonomy, philosopher Mary Midgley has summarized it as the contention that individuals are "purely mental entities, radically isolated, independent, self-creating and alien, perhaps hostile, to everything around them." The individual will, as Nietzsche had insisted in the face of a disintegrating world, is all there is.[11] That doctrine is the destination toward which the modern megarevolution has been moving.

As John Dewey pointed out in 1927, liberty isolated from life in a community is seen as "independence of social ties, and ends in dissolution and anarchy." Dewey said liberty should properly be understood as "that secure release and fulfillment of personal potentialities which take place only in rich and manifold association with others."[12] (Sartre, in contrast, said he had discovered what Hell is: "it's other people.") A definition such as Dewey's reflects the mixed nature of human motivation that has been all too rare among thinkers of the last century.

Also beginning from the tabula rasa assumption and so denying any meaningful human nature, but not accepting the power of the individual will and so reaching very different conclusions, were the behaviorists John B. Watson and B. F. Skinner. To the behaviorists the determining factor in human existence is just the opposite of what it is to the existentialists. Rather than an all-powerful individual will placed in a malleable environment, Watson and his followers postulated an almost infinitely malleable individual in an all-powerful environment. Arising in the first quarter of the century and reaching a peak of influence in its second and third quarters, behaviorism adopted the man-as-machine model that had become popular with the Industrial Revolution.

While the worldviews of the existentialists and the behaviorists seem to be in nearly total opposition, they share some basic assumptions that were taken as axiomatic by most thinkers of the twentieth century. One is disconnection from the past. Whether the blank sheet is to be written upon by an omnipotent will or an omnipotent environment, it is still assumed to start out blank. There is, then, no need to worry about what came before. The past—both evolutionary and historical—is superseded by the present, either the present will or the present environment.

Modern theories either eliminate the individual by dissolving her or him into a mass society (as Marx and his successors and, to a lesser extent, the behaviorists have done) or—much more commonly—separate the individual entirely from a social context (as Nietzsche, Rand, and other libertarians, champions of unregulated free-market economics, and the existentialists have done). The balanced notion expressed by Dewey, that of the individual *in* society, has nearly vanished in our excessively mobile age. If we are ever to cope successfully with the modern predicament, some way must be found to get beyond the strict dualism of self *or* society and regain a sense of blended wholeness.

Woman's Just Another Word for "Nothing Left to Lose"

No one did more to shape (and misshape) twentieth-century views of sex and the sexes than Sigmund Freud. Freud's thinking was very much a product of the modern social environment. He found the competition that had become so prevalent in modern society occurring within the mind, as well, in the form of the superego struggling with the id. He was also a man of his times in being so self-centered that he used himself as his sole reference point. "I always find it uncanny when I can't understand someone in terms of myself," he revealingly said.[13]

Most significantly, Freud saw people in purely physical, chemical terms—as machines. Like machines, humans had to get their energy from somewhere, Freud thought. This led him to develop such concepts as *cathexes* and *libido*, which postulated as the source of mental energy something like electrical charges coming from a power source based on sexual desire.

Although Freud was well schooled in the mechanistic worldview that had developed out of the later stages of the second megarevolution, his principal argument was that much of human behavior is based upon irrational motivations. As this emphasis on the irrational indicates, Freud, unlike so many modern thinkers, did not deny the existence of human nature. "[O]ur bodily organism, itself a part of that nature, will always remain a transient structure with a limited capacity for adaptation and achievement," he wrote in 1930.[14]

His acceptance of human nature allowed Freud to achieve a better understanding of the relationship between innate proclivities and the social environment than have most modern observers. The deep, primordial, instinctual drives and appetites that Freud labeled the id can readily be seen as the rough equivalent of the human biogram. (The concept of the id is a direct refutation of the tabula rasa; the id is a slate with writing on it from the beginning.) Freud perceived that the unrestrained following of these proclivities is incompatible with modern civilization. The restraints imposed by society and inculcated into a person in the form of conscience—Freud's superego or ego ideal—are what we usually call values. Freud said that the superego perpetuates the past. This, I believe, is precisely right. Values and traditions are based upon the experience of humanity; they connect us to our ancestors. But the modern movement toward complete "freedom" leads us to cut ourselves off from the past—and so from values or the superego.*

Although part of Freud's analysis was much more accurate than that of many modern thinkers, his influence has not, for the most part, been beneficial. There are two causes (only one of which was of his own doing) for Freud's failure to be more helpful in combating the modern predicament, despite his understanding of a substantial part of the source of the difficulty.

The part of the problem that was Freud's responsibility was his view of women. He sometimes admitted that he did not understand women, whose adult sexual life he once called "a dark continent."[15] But Freud never let this lack of understanding deter him from commenting extensively on the "opposite sex." Freud's view of women was based upon what might be termed a "phallusy." Like Aristotle, Freud believed that a woman is an incomplete man, *"un homme manqué."* Freud stated directly what the Bible and Aristotle had said more obliquely: What a woman is missing is a penis. A female is, Freud maintained, a "mutilated creature."[16] Although Freud complained that he had never found an answer to the question "what does woman want?,"[17] he had tried to answer that what a woman wants is a penis.

It should be obvious that a male "lacks" a vagina as much as a female "lacks" a penis, but Freud said that the latter is a vastly superior organ and so its absence is what produces envy. His message was clear: a vagina is nothing much, anyway, so no one would worry about not having one. He spoke of a girl's "discovery of her castration," indicating that he took it as axiomatic that the normal or complete human being has a penis and that anyone who does not must have lost it. (The deep source of this notion is, of course, the assumption, emanating from the Conception Misconception, that God is male and created men in His image.) Girls, Freud said, come to view themselves as inferior when they discover that they are "so insufficiently equipped."[18] To Freud, if I may paraphrase Kris Kristofferson, *woman* was just another word for "nothing left to lose."

In truth, of course, there is no basis for saying that males are *better* equipped; rather, the two sexes are *differently* equipped. Aristotle and Freud were not wrong in seeing women as imperfect, incomplete, "half-baked" forms. They are.

---

*There is, however, a far more distant past from which we cannot escape so easily: the evolutionary forces reflected in the human biogram, or Freud's id. So the more we elude the comparatively recent past of values/superego, the more we leave ourselves under the unchecked control of innate tendencies, many of which are no longer suited for living in our social environment.

But so are men. The gross mistake of these extremely influential men (and millions of others through most of history) was in thinking that females are "mutilated" males. Inasmuch as we now know that all embryos start out as female, with some being changed by a dousing of male hormones,[19] it could as easily be argued that women are the "normal" humans and men are "deformed women." It makes far more sense to see *both* males and females as incomplete versions of a perfection that is above sexual division.

Freud made many large errors in his analysis of women. The most basic was his underlying assumption that women are inferior to men. Firmly believing that the sexes are different, Freud was so indoctrinated in the concepts of hierarchy and dominance that (like most other people, including many of those who believe in sexual equality today) he could not imagine different categories to be equal. Given this assumption, Freud's acceptance of difference led him to assume inequality. Starting from the same assumption that there can be no difference without inequality, modern feminists' acceptance of equality leads some of them to assume that there can be no difference. Both are mistaken; the sexes are simultaneously (a little) different *and* equal.

Anatomy plainly is not destiny in any deterministic sense; but anatomy does have an effect, if not on destiny, then at least on some traits and attitudes.

One hesitates to try to psychoanalyze Freud, and I claim no qualifications in the field. But the strong possibility must be raised that Freud's idea of penis envy was the offspring of his own womb envy. His emphasis on female inadequacy and "organ inferiority"[20] may have been the result of his own repressed fear of male inadequacy and the inferiority of male organs when it comes to carrying, giving birth to, and nourishing new life.[21] Freud said that the only two possible views of a man toward women are "horror" or "triumphant contempt for her."[22] It is well known that a surface bravado—*acting* superior, claiming superiority—is often the cover for a feeling of inferiority. The concept of penis envy looks suspiciously like a classic reversal based on the negative image of man as notawoman, followed by the need to define *woman* negatively in order to make *man* a double negative and so positive.

That Freud's ideas on women were motivated by the deep causes I have presented in these pages is suggested by some of his statements on the subject. In asserting that girls blame their mothers for sending them into the world "so pathetically incomplete,"[23] Freud revealed an underlying assumption of female creation. But he then declared that "the penis owes its extraordinarily high narcissistic cathexis to its organic significance for the propagation of the species."[24] This argument is clearly based on the Conception Misconception. It assumes that female genital organs have little to do with reproduction: the penis is the propagator that "seeds" the woman's "soil." Combining these two statements by Freud points to the conclusion that he, like so many other men throughout history, really believed that women have creative power but displaced the inadequacy he felt as a result of that belief by insisting that the male organs are superior and the source of life. He also argued that, while women had "in the beginning, laid the foundations for civilization by the claims of their love," men had taken it over. "The work of civilization has become increasingly the business of men," he proclaimed in 1930.[25]

The concept of penis envy seems to have been Freud's version of whistling past the birthing room.

Freud made his own blunders in attempting to explain women, but most of the difficulties with Freudianism have resulted from its misapplication by popularizers. In this there is a striking parallel to the vogue of what were purported to be the lessons of Darwinism for human behavior. What might be dubbed *social Freudianism* was often as contrary to the actual meaning of Freud's theories as social Darwinism was to that of Darwin's findings. Nor was it mere happenstance that it was in the United States, the cutting edge of the effects of the Mobility Megarevolution and the Marketplace Misconception, that both of these distortions were most eagerly embraced. Social Freudianism, like social Darwinism, was well suited for the American (and modern) environment. Freud contended that neuroses are caused by the repression of the desires of the id. The popular notion that those restraints should be thrown off and the innate urges liberated seemed to be made for a land and an age of social mobility, freedom, individualism, and limitlessness. Many "advanced" thinkers in the United States in the second and third decades of the twentieth century believed that the cure for all ills was the release of repressed sexual impulses. They were right in thinking that this is a route to complete freedom, but because we are social animals, complete freedom is not what humans actually desire. This route is also one that leads away from the community and personal bonds that are necessary for human happiness and satisfaction. It is the road on the map of the Marketplace world that goes to perpetual discontent.

Psychoanalysis itself was especially attractive in such a society, since mobility and extreme individualism are inevitably anxiety-producing and since the very idea of limitlessness means that no one can ever be satisfied. The reality remains that no one can "have it all," yet the economy and culture encourage people to think that they can and to keep reaching for the unreachable. Paradoxically, this need for Freudian therapy resulted from social practices which were encouraged by misinterpretations of Freud's ideas. He had never been in favor of the complete "liberation" of the innate urges, because he realized that without some degree of social repression these unchecked urges would cause the destruction of society.

Freud has been credited—even by Betty Friedan, while she was condemning as pernicious his view of women—with helping "to free man from the tyranny of the 'shoulds,' the tyranny of the past."[26] Friedan's complaint was that Freudianism had been used to create a new tyranny of "shoulds" for women. The clear implication of such an argument (which is by no means exclusive to Friedan or feminists; it sometimes seems ubiquitous in modern society) is that the solution to our difficulties lies in liberating everyone from shoulds and the tyranny of the past. This liberation would constitute the abolition of values, tradition, and history. Freud's suggestion that it was necessary for a man to "kill" his father in order to become "autonomous" both lent unfortunate credence to this prescription and summed up many of the effects of the modern megarevolution. In his better moments Freud realized that such a course would destroy society, but some of his statements have allowed those who have advocated the abolition of values to invoke his name as the high priest of hedonism and virtual solipsism.

Lifting the Lid from the Id

"Consumption is the frontier of the future," declared economist Alvin Hansen in 1940.[27] He was right, and the implications of this alteration in the economy for life and the situations of the sexes have been enormous.

In its earlier stages, capitalism's logic meshed with traditional values. Accumulation was to be achieved by self-denial, saving, deferred gratification, and the work ethic—keeping a lid on the id. In the twentieth century, however, the productive capacity of industry expanded to such an extent that, even while Marxists continued to focus on productive relations, it was "consumptive relations" that were becoming central.

In the twentieth century the extraordinary success of the Marketplace economy in increasing production created a need for reversing many of the values that had been inculcated in people for the purpose of boosting production. It had become necessary to focus on the other side of the economic equation. The need to stimulate consumption so that it could keep up with production required the promotion of a consumption ethic.[28] Beginning in the 1920s, the new "industry" of advertising was given the mission of destroying the old values associated with the work ethic and encouraging the spread of self-indulgence through greater portions of the society. One result of this effort, as Thorstein Veblen perceived as early as 1899, is to "retard the adaptation of human nature to the exigencies of modern industrial life."[29] Leading corporate consultant Ernest Dichter drove home the point in the 1950s when he proclaimed that one of the basic requirements for modern business is "to demonstrate that the hedonistic approach to [a person's] life is a moral and not an immoral one."[30]

During the last century, businesses and their advertisers have almost completely lifted off the lid that the work ethic and other traditional values had placed on the id. The repercussions have been similar to those attributed to the lid-lifting performed by Pandora.

As advertising destroyed traditional values it promoted the new "lifestyle" of the twentieth century. People were no longer to define themselves on the basis of their occupations but on how they spent their leisure time—and on what they spent their money for. As the consumption ethic displaced the work ethic, consumption replaced work as the central activity of people's lives. Whether or not "you are what you eat," people in the last century have to a significant extent been considered to be what they buy. In this later stage of the modern megarevolution, Descartes has been modified. Now the disconnected person seeking assurance of being says:

I consume; therefore I am.[31]

For a man, adopting the consumption ethic could seem to be a surrender of manhood. Being caught up in accumulating things (which often obliges one to work under others and leaves him in debt) prevents him from being a "man." A man was supposed to provide, not consume. Fred Mertz perfectly summed up this conception of proper roles for the sexes in a classic episode of the television comedy *I Love Lucy:* "There are two kinds of people, earners and spenders—or, as they're more popularly known, husbands and wives."[32] The Consumerculture undermined this distinction. Its effects on men have been similar to what happened to their forefathers when agriculture first made accumulation (that is, consumption) possible and took away men's original provisioning role. The consumption ethic is as unfulfilling for male self-esteem as farming had been: *What, we're supposed to derive satisfaction from filling up shopping carts like a bunch of, of . . . gatherers, for God's sake?*

Yet as twentieth-century America progressed, the demand for mass consumption more and more required men to become consumers. To a man, this modern means of self-definition could become:

I consume, therefore I am not a real man.

While the consumption ethic was creating new problems for men's self-image, the 1920s saw the emergence of the "New Woman." Traditionalists continued to see women as different from—and more moral than—men. Women must be prepared to assume "the entire responsibility of the human race," a 1920 article in the *Atlantic Monthly* declared.[33] But the New Woman did not seem to be prepared to accept such responsibility. Old-line feminist Charlotte Perkins Gilman hit on some of the effects of the lifting of traditional values from biological predilections when she complained that the youth of the age practiced "unchecked indulgence in appetite and impulse."[34]

Epitomized by the "flapper," the New Woman of the twenties considered herself to be a rebel. In a sense she was, but she was a rebel in unconscious league with the economic radicals of the new consumption ethic capitalism, which was based firmly on a greatly exaggerated view of masculine values. The unfortunate truth is that in some respects the New Woman was all too similar to the "old boy."

The modern megarevolution had reached a stage at which the logic of its separation of society into free, individual consuming units required that women begin to be treated more like other such units. "The new woman," as historian William Leuchtenburg has written, "wanted the same freedom of movement that men had and the same economic and political rights."[35] The modern young women of the twenties eagerly "rebelled" into playing the role assigned to them, adopting a number of practices that had previously been considered male.

There is revealing symbolism in the fact that the new young women of the twenties actually attempted in some important respects to hide their female attributes and make themselves look more like males. The "boyish look" was in the highest style. Women favored short, bobbed hair and clothing styles that would hide the size and contour of their breasts and hips—if possible, to make it appear that they had neither. The flat-chested look was all the rage.[36]

Whether much of this was a significant advance for women or more a triumph of a system heavily weighted toward a hypermasculine competition is at least open to question.

"Remember My Forgotten Man"

What happened to many men during the Great Depression of the 1930s was similar, albeit on a far smaller scale, to what had happened to men after the development of agriculture. They had defined their manhood on the basis of opposition to womanhood and in terms of being the provider and protector. As they lost jobs and could not find new ones, men faced a situation that was rather like what had happened to their distant forefathers when hunting was devalued: the role that gave their lives purpose was lost. Margaret Mead's comment on the perpetually insecure situation of men is worth repeating: "it is impossible to strip [the woman's] life of meaning as completely as the life of a man can be stripped."

Since men have no clear roles and have had to make them up, their self-definition and security are especially fragile. Men can quite easily "break," as John Steinbeck put it in *The Grapes of Wrath*.[37] Not so a woman. "Woman can change better'n a man," as Ma Joad says. "Woman got all her life in her arms. Man got it all in his head."[38] What she (that is, Steinbeck) is saying here is that a woman can change better because she has an underlying continuity and security in her role. A man, on the other hand, has the meaning of his life "in his head"— it has been made up and so is constantly vulnerable. It cannot easily bend.

This male vulnerability to instant deflation is well represented in Zora Neale Hurston's 1937 novel *Their Eyes Were Watching God*. Joe Starks, the husband of the novel's protagonist, Janie, is the well-established Alpha male of the all-African-American town of Eatonville, Florida. His favorite interjection, significantly, is "I god amighty." One day while Starks and the other men are on the front porch having their usual "good-natured laughter at the expense of women," Janie strikes back: "Talkin' 'bout *me* lookin' old! When you pull down yo' britches, you look lak de change uh life.' The crushing "put down" emasculates Joe on the spot: "[H]is vanity bled like a flood," Hurston wrote. "Janie had robbed him of his illusion of irresistible maleness that all men cherish." Here was a classic case of saying that the emperor has no clothes—or, worse, that he has nothing *under* his clothes. Hurston then gave an excellent summary of where men are left if their carefully constructed roles and claims to authority are taken from them: "There was nothing left to do in life anymore. Ambition was useless."[39] Starks' health declines rapidly and he soon dies.

Janie's cutting comment symbolizes what happened to so many men who lost their jobs during the Depression: their fragile sense of manhood was shattered. Janie "broke" Jodie, as the experience of eviction and dashed hopes broke Pa Joad and many other Okie (and other) men in the 1930s. Ma says it all when she tells Pa, "But you ain't a-doin' your job, either a-thinkin' or a-workin'. If you was, why, you could use your stick, an' women folks'd sniffle their nose an' creep-mouse aroun'. But you jus' get you a stick now and you ain't lickin' no woman; you're a-fightin', cause I got a stick all laid out, too."[40] The Depression and an unfathomable economic system in which, as Steinbeck shows, a victim doesn't know who to shoot have taken away the man's "stick," much as Janie did by telling others that Jodie's "stick" looks "lak de change uh life." What is worse, Ma says that women are getting sticks of their own. A man who can't "lick no woman" has been transformed into a nonman. No longer can he persuasively claim to be notawoman.

Not only, then, did many men lose their roles in the Depression, they also saw the culturally erected limitations on what women were allowed to do, which had been built up over thousands of years as a way of compensating for man's inability in reproductive matters, begin to fall as women had to step into the breach and become providers. The women in *The Grapes of Wrath* watch their men carefully, waiting to see if they have broken yet so the women would know whether they should take over. "Women and children knew deep in themselves that no misfortune was too great to bear if their men were whole." The proof that Pa Joad has finally been broken is his acceptance of female leadership: "Funny! Woman takin' over the fambly. Woman sayin' we'll do this here, an' we'll go there. An' I don' even care."[41]

The situation was memorably illustrated by Steinbeck with the end of *The Grapes of Wrath,* when a helpless, starving man is being breast-fed by Rose of

Sharon.[42] There is no question about who is the provider and who is dependent in that scene. A more powerful symbol of men's reduction to dependence would be difficult to imagine.

The longing many men in the Depression had for a restoration of their proper place was perfectly captured in the song "Remember My Forgotten Man," from the movie *Golddiggers of 1933:* "Ever since the world began, every woman needs a man."[43]

The 1930s was, plainly, not a good time to be an insecure man, a category that multiplied rapidly under the impact of unemployment. When presidential candidate Franklin D. Roosevelt referred in 1932 to "the forgotten man at the bottom of the economic pyramid," he was speaking in terms to which vast numbers of men could relate.[44] As always seems to happen when men find their made-up roles threatened and they feel forgotten, a backlash set in. One manifestation of this was a sudden vogue in Hollywood in the thirties of men hitting women. This began with a famous scene in *Public Enemy* (1931) in which Jimmy Cagney hit Mae Clark in the eye with a grapefruit. The celluloid violence toward women escalated from there to the point where a film analyst wrote in 1938, "today a star scarcely qualifies for the higher spheres unless she has been slugged by her leading man, rolled on the floor, kicked downstairs."[45] Clearly, as critic Gilbert Seldes said at the time, the popularity of this trend stemmed from its meeting of a need for a reassertion of masculinity felt by men whose sense of manhood was threatened by unemployment.[46]

Snow White, a woman in a deep, deathlike sleep, who needs to be given life by a man, is the embodiment of the male reaction to the gender role reversal commonly found in the Depression. Threatened, emasculated men wanted to restore women to a situation similar to what Aristotle had said is the female contribution to procreation: lifeless matter until given animation and soul—life—by the man.

This is not only an attempt to reverse what was going on in the thirties; it is also a reversal of the reality of the Depression situation of the sexes: many men were more or less paralyzed (broken, as Steinbeck puts it), and had to be re-energized by the "kiss" (Disney's family-friendly metaphor for sexual relations) of a woman. The reality, then, was often that it was the man who was Snow White, in a sleeping death, who needed to be brought back to life by the woman's "kiss."[47]

What, after all, is a man to do to reassure himself of his manhood if he is denied the opportunity to obtain self-respect through the expected roles of provider and protector? "You don't know what it's like when your husband's out of work," a woman in California told a federal relief investigator in 1934. "He's gloomy and unhappy all the time. Life is terrible. You must try all the time to keep him from going crazy. And many times—that's the only way."[48]

The "that" to which the woman alluded was sexual intercourse: the last refuge of the unsuccessful man.* This opens up an important line of analysis, one that I believe can help to explain the actions of many men throughout history and especially in our own time. But before we go on to that, we need to take a brief look at the combined effects of the decade-and-a-half disruption of established roles for the sexes that was produced by the Depression and World War II.

The Not-a-Man in the Gray Flannel Suit

World War II provided men with means to restore some of their feelings of manhood. It opened up to large numbers of males the "manly" occupation of fighting for a cause. They could, for a time, once again clearly be of use. Moreover, in military units men could feel the sort of association with others that had become increasingly hard to find in the modern, individualistic world of the Marketplace. Here a man had a place; he could belong. He could even escape for the duration from some of the fetters of the unfettered Marketplace economy and Consumer-culture. "You had fifteen guys who for the first time in their lives were not living in a competitive society," a World War II veteran recalled while talking with Studs Terkel. "For the first time in their lives, they could help each other without fear of losing a commercial advantage."[49] Yet the war also continued the disruption of "normal family life," since so many men were overseas and the need for war production opened to women many occupations from which they had previously been excluded. Women were literally "wearing (the) pants" in jobs that required such masculine attire and in films depicting powerful women, such as Katharine Hepburn's character in *Woman of the Year* (1942).[50] The war was physically separating the male and female spheres to an extraordinary degree; millions of American men were thousands of miles away from "their women" and living in a virtually all-male environment. Paradoxically, it was simultaneously breeching the carefully constructed wall between the sexes back home. The world the soldiers left behind became one in which women successfully took on many of the responsibilities that men had long insisted were exclusively male. If they were crossing the line in occupational terms, many men wondered whether the women back home might also be "acting like men" sexually. Such fears of unfaithful wives and girlfriends by men who were themselves unfaithful is a major theme of

---

*Obviously sexual intercourse is much more than *just* this; it serves many other purposes for men and women. The point here is that this important, essential, central portion of life for secure people of both sexes can become all that is left for a man who feels he cannot fulfill any of the other roles that have defined *manhood.*

Norman Mailer's 1948 novel, *The Naked and the Dead.*[51] But perhaps the clearest example of how widespread this concern was is the extraordinary popularity of the Mills Brothers' 1943 record "Paper Doll." The song's message is that women are so untrustworthy that a man is better off with a paper doll: "I'm gonna buy a paper doll that I can call my own / a doll that other fellows cannot steal. . . . When I come home at night, she'll be waiting. . . . I'd rather have a paper doll to call my own, than have a fickle-minded real live girl."[52] This is much the same sentiment as that of the men in Ira Levin's 1972 novel, *The Stepford Wives:* real women are no good; they are a lot of trouble. Men would be better off with man-made women. What makes "Paper Doll" so important as a reflection of the thinking of the war years is its immense popularity: it was the second-largest-selling nonholiday song of the first half of the twentieth century.[53]

After the war American men faced what has been called a "crisis in masculinity." While they were successfully piercing the defenses of the Axis powers abroad, the bulwarks of male preserves and dominance at home had begun to crack. The fifteen years after 1945 can usefully be seen as a period of postwar sexual Redemption in which a great attempt was made to rebuild the sexual order that had been upset in the preceding fifteen years of depression and war. With the return of prosperity it appeared that men would have an opportunity to "set the (sexual) world right again." They could find employment, become providers, establish father-headed families, and return to "normalcy." Being able to have his wife stay home was a sign of success for a man in the 1950s. The housewife was a trophy that said *I'm a real man* as loudly as did the stuffed head of a big game animal on the den wall. It showed that a man was succeeding in his role as provider:

She consumes; therefore I am (a man).

But the economy after the war was increasingly dominated by huge corporations, and the society that was restored was that of the Consumerculture that had emerged in the years before the Depression. There was little room for "manhood" in the corporate world. The situation described in Sloan Wilson's 1955 novel, *The Man in the Gray Flannel Suit* was a challenge to masculinity.[54] A real man, especially in America, was supposed to be an individualist. Conforming, blending in, was not "manly." But even if one did not accept the individualist definition of manhood, being a cog in a huge corporate machine was not satisfying to the male biogram. Humans and particularly men, as we have seen, tend to have an affinity for membership in a band, a *personal* group in which they have a personal relationship to the leader. The mass, impersonal organization that is the modern corporation does not provide this sense of belonging.

A military uniform implied masculinity. A man in a gray flannel suit implied emasculation—being an underling, not your own man, being "soft," and so in a sense not a man at all. C. Wright Mills found the perfect econo-sexual image for this new "Little Man" in his 1951 book, *White Collar:* "he is seen as *the man who does not rise.*"[55] Corporate men had to find another way to prove (to themselves and others) their manhood—their notawomanhood. They felt emasculated by corporations almost as much as many men who were unable to provide for their families had in the Depression.

Women entering male fields during the war had signaled the danger of the emergence of a single standard of measurement. In response, the postwar period saw strongly renewed attempts at gender extending. Efforts by men to show that they were notwomen increased. One form these attempts took was the emergence of widely divergent "ideal bodies" for women and men. Christian Dior fashions designed to emphasize and exaggerate distinctly female

Gender Extending, Fifties Style
It was particularly important to men in the post–World War II period to avoid any confusion of the sexes. Women's fashions in the 1950s extended gender to an extraordinary degree, using every available means to amplify female characteristics. (Corbis)

anatomical features—tight tops, small waists, expanded hips with flared skirts, and very high heels—were introduced in 1947 and became the trend-setters. The "baby doll" look of the fifties took this cultural accentuation of sexual difference even farther. "Women's fashions," as historian James Patterson has noted, "largely prescribed by men who had an image of how the opposite sex should look, had hardly been so confining since the nineteenth century."[56] Worried men wanted to be sure they could tell at a glance who was who. Let there be no mistake—there must be no doubt. Only those with doubts, of course, insist on finding ways to eliminate doubt. The Christian Dior view of the female body was carried to greater extremes with the introduction of Barbie in 1959. It was during this same period that magazines with male readerships were advertising ways to stop being a "97-pound weakling" who gets sand kicked in his face and so does not "get the girl."

Gender Extending, Fifties Style

These winners in a "Mr. Muscle Beach" competition in 1954 display the sort of male bodies into which Charles Atlas promised to transform "97-pound weaklings." Significantly, the ads promised to make "HE-MEN—REAL SPECIMENS OF HANDSOME, MUSCULAR MANHOOD." The clear implication was that those who did not look this way (as radically different from female bodies as possible) were "she-men." (David Chapman)

In many ways the 1950s seemed a repeat of the 1920s, the decade in which social Freudianism took hold in the United States, but some aspects of the twenties were rejected in the fifties. The earlier decade had seen an emphasis upon liberation; the latter sought security more than freedom. This difference was most evident in the wide variance between the two decades' views of the proper role for women. The men and women of the fifties saw no need for a New Woman. What they wanted was a return of what they thought the women of old to have been: subservient housewives and mothers. The "Feminine Mystique" identified by Betty Friedan was a major aspect of the postwar attempt to regain normalcy. It can also be viewed as one of the ways in which Hitler "won" the World War II. The Nazis' slogan for women's proper role, "Kinder, Kirche, Küche" (children, church, kitchen), is hard to distinguish from the Feminine Mystique that gripped a majority of Americans after the war.

What tied the very different images of women in the twenties and fifties together was that both suited the requirements of the new economic system. The more independent woman of the twenties was part of the rise in self-indulgence that the new consumption-oriented economy of that decade demanded. For her part, the housewife of the fifties was playing a vastly different economic role from that of her mother. She usually worked very hard but produced little in the household economy. Instead, she used "store-bought" products for most of her work and activities. The woman of the Feminine Mystique was a full-time consumer. This role seemed perfectly to fit the needs of a consumption-oriented economy. The one "product" that women of the fifties were supposed to turn out was children, who were themselves new full-time consumers. Men trying to reassert their positions sought to make up for lost opportunities during the Depression and war. They did so by re-seeding their farmland (wives) that they had been obliged to lie fallow for a decade and a half and making it clear that the men were the breadwinners and the women were to bear and take care of their children. But this Baby Boom was an anachronism. The revival of an r-selected reproduction strategy in the K-selected environment of the twentieth century could not last long.

Male insecurity permeated many aspects of the 1950s. The hysteria over communist subversion provides an interesting perspective on this connection. Like so many other hysterias into which men have fallen throughout history, this behavior may aptly be named *hysteria:* "madness caused by the womb." The word, of course, derives from the idea that the womb causes madness in women; but the deep source of various hysterias among men may well be the threat that the power of the womb posed to insecure men. Referring to McCarthyism as a "witch-hunt" is particularly appropriate: as a "hunt" it seemingly provided an opportunity to utilize some of the traits that had evolved in men, and it was said to be undertaken to *protect* the nation. As had witch-hunts in the early modern period, it also was clearly related to male insecurity. One of the favorite charges of politicians who were prominent in this pursuit was that their opponents were "soft on communism." Liberals in general were called soft-hearted and soft-headed. Such qualities are not acceptable for a man (especially one who is insecure about his masculinity), because they imply he is soft elsewhere. The charge of being "soft on communism" had clear sexual meaning. There were similar innuendos in references to alleged communist sympathizers as "pink." Calling someone a "parlor pink" was even more clearly a way to insinuate that he was womanish and probably homosexual. Speaking in support of Dwight Eisenhower in 1952, Joe McCarthy said the nation would be better with a "khaki-clad President than one clothed in State Department pinks."[57] Similarly, Richard Nixon's statement in his 1950 Senate race that his opponent, Helen Gahagan Douglas, "is pink down to her underwear"[58] was a way to paint all of his opponents in soft tones with a broad brush dipped in pink paint. More important, perhaps, it allowed Nixon to remind voters (and himself) that his opponent was a woman, his enemies in general were "womanish," and hence he, on the opposite side, must be notawoman.*

The associations were so threatening that leading liberals felt it necessary to voice similar charges about communists in an effort to keep themselves from being painted in pink hues. Arthur Schlesinger, Jr., wrote in *The Vital Center* (1949) that communism was "like nothing so much . . . as homosexuals in a boys' school."[59] The fact that some of the leading witch-hunters, such as J. Edgar Hoover and Roy Cohn, were apparently homosexuals themselves, but greatly ashamed of their sexuality, adds support to the argument that McCarthyism was substantially an outgrowth of sexual insecurity. Joe McCarthy frequently described those he accused of being subversives as "homos" and "pretty boys" and spoke in the same breath of "communists and queers." He strove above all to be thought of as "a man's man."[60]

The rebellion from the right in the fifties was rooted in male insecurity and directed against an elite that was castigated as "effete." On another level, it may have been a reaction against a corporate economy in which men who had been taught that the real man is the one who makes himself found that there was little opportunity to do so. American men had just won a war and felt that they should now be able to feel like real men; but for many this was not happening. *Something* was wrong; *somebody* must be responsible for blocking the path to real manhood. The enemy had been clear in the war, but it was not in the postwar war. Now there apparently were enemies within. Whoever they were, they looked like everybody else.

---

*Nixon's apparent sexual insecurities, along with those of several other political leaders, will be discussed in more detail in Chapter 14.

Such is the theme of the 1956 movie *Invasion of the Body Snatchers.* Aliens who are patent stand-ins for communists replace people in a small California town. They look exactly like the neighbors, spouses, and girlfriends they replaced, but they are really enemies who are subverting small-town life. The greatest reason for terror is that one cannot tell "us" from "them." From the perspective of this book, this fear can be read as a reflection of many men's anxiety that the line between men and women had been blurred and must be firmly redrawn. (In a sense, women during World War II had been snatching the bodies of men by taking jobs that had previously been defined as male.) *We can't tell the body-snatchers from the humans or the commies from the real Americans, but we'll make sure we can tell the men from the women.*

But that was not enough. In fact, of course, the ideal of the self-made man had always been a dangerous illusion, and it was actually the hypermasculine economic system that was the source of much of their discontent. But anxious men generally find it easier to blame women and things classified as feminine for their problems than to take a hard look at the definitions of manhood. Since socialism and communism, at least in theory, go against the competitive male struggle, they provided a seemingly logical target for men who were anxious about their own manhood.

The idea that the anticommunist hysteria of the post–World War II years was tied up with male insecurity may be more readily accepted than the argument I am about to make concerning the other side of the cultural spectrum.

Fuckito Ergo Sum

Although it has rarely been noticed, the youth rebellion of the post–World War II era was in large measure a reaction to men losing their dominance and definition and a call for the restoration of men to their positions of power.

Consider first that both of the classic movies of youth rebellion in fifties, *Rebel Without a Cause* and *The Wild One,* strongly emphasized the need for a man to be notawoman. In the former, James Dean as Jim Stark is disgusted with his father who won't act like a man. Mr. Stark allows both his wife and mother to dominate him; he's on the bottom. He even wears a frilly apron. The one thing that Jim absolutely cannot tolerate is being called a "chicken." He agrees to a "chicky race" with another teenage male, Buzz, to see who will stay longer in a car heading toward a cliff. This is all about "being a man." Such competitions are obviously contests for dominance; they determine who the top male is. This is very apparent in *Rebel:* Buzz is the leader of the group—until he is dethroned by going over the cliff. The Natalie Wood character, Judy, acting like a female gorilla, instantly shifts her allegiance to Jim, the new Alpha male.

"Why do we do it?" Jim asks before they start the chicky race. "You gotta do something," Buzz replies.[61] That four-word sentence succinctly captures the male dilemma since agriculture devalued men's roles.

In *The Wild One,* the sheriff is "womanly." He wants to talk, reason with people. "If it looks like anything might develop into trouble, folks can just sit down and talk it over," he says. He won't *act.* "What am I supposed to do, *shoot* somebody?" he asks. Both his daughter and Johnny (Marlon Brando) are disgusted with his lack of manliness.[62]

It is in the soundtrack of the youth rebellion, its music, that the cry for manhood is most apparent. Early rock and the rhythm and blues whence it sprang were as much men's clubs as is the Catholic priesthood. The Founding Fathers of rock music had the same sexual composition as the Founding Fathers of the United States—or the Early Church Fathers. It is important to ask why this was the case. Surely it was not mere coincidence.

The "revolution" consisted in substantial measure of young whites patterning themselves on the lifestyles of some African-Americans. (The name of Marlon Brando's white motorcycle gang in *The Wild One* is the Black Rebels.) Those with the most experience in dealing with a situation are turned to as the experts. This is a major reason why black men have been seen as the role models for white men. Black men have certainly had the most experience with cultural and economic emasculation.

Norman Mailer accurately spoke in his 1957 essay, "The White Negro," of the rebellion's birth among "hipsters" in the postwar years as a "wedding of the white and the black [in which] it was the Negro who brought the cultural dowry."[63] A "language of Hip"[64] was an important component of that dowry, and one of its most enduring usages is *man* as a term of respect that is interjected into, it often seems, every other sentence spoken by those who utilize Hip language, as in, "Hey, man, what's up?"

The centerpiece of the putative revolution, which began in the fifties and spread so widely in the sixties that it came to be called the Counterculture, was sex. "For to him sex was the one and only holy and important thing in life,"[65] Jack Kerouac wrote of Dean Moriarty,* a fictionalization of his friend Neal Cassady and the central figure in *On the Road,* the *seminal* literary work of the Beat movement that served as one of the two main tubes through which black culture was tranfused into young whites. Music was the other. It began with jazz, which Mailer called "the music of orgasm."[66] That description applies even more to the music that soon displaced jazz as the medium of the rebellion, rock 'n' roll. The

---

*It seems significant that on the very first page of the novel, Kerouac relates that Dean wanted to learn "all about Nietzsche."

very name of this music is a euphemism for sexual intercourse, and sexual brag-gadocio has been one of its most prominent features throughout its history. A few examples from the early years: Billy Ward and the Dominoes singing "If your man ain't treating you right / Come up and see ol' Dan / I rock 'em, roll 'em all night long / I'm a sixty-minute man" (1951); Slim Harpo's classic statement in "I'm a King Bee"* (1957): "Well, I'm a king bee, buzzin' around your hive / I can make honey, baby—let me come inside / I'm young and able, to buzz all night long"; and Fats Domino boasting, "I'm ready, I'm willing, and I'm able to rock and roll all night" (1959).[67] Elvis Presley and a growing horde of other white rock 'n' rollers brought the music's message of sexual liberation to a huge audience of young whites.

That the revolution was about sex is clear. *Why* it was about sex and whether this was really revolutionary in terms of opposition to the Consumer-culture may not be.

Society today defines people on the basis of what they consume. (In fact, marketing specialists divide the population into "consumption communities."), Those, such as African-Americans, who are denied a place in the self-made-man/consumption ethic milieu and so are unable to achieve the definition of being expected of middle-class people—*I consume, therefore I am*—must turn to other means of asserting their existence. "To tell a man that work is the only way to achieve dignity, and then deny him that chance for dignity [is] immoral in the extreme," U.S. Senator Fred Harris declared in 1970.[68] One could add that to tell a man that in order to "be a man" he must be a provider of ever-increasing amounts of material things and deny him a reasonable opportunity to do so is to emasculate him. If consumption of things is defined as the sine qua non of exis-tence, those who cannot afford to buy things are likely to turn to consuming what is within their reach. The Consumerculture teaches everyone to be narrowly self-centered and so to see others as objects to be manipulated to advance one's own selfish desires. Hence those who cannot consume material things often consume people. If middle America consumes, then the men of lower America are left to find others they can exploit, whether male or female. Those Ralph Ellison termed invisible men will do *something* to become visible, to prove their own existence and their manhood: *I AM somebody; I AM a MAN*! Often such men have fallen back on a more basic definition of life (and manhood):

   I fuck, therefore I am (a man).†

---

*A king bee is, of course, another name for an Alpha male.

†Certainly a substantial number of women have also adopted this means of self-definition, espe-cially since the 1960s. But, as we have seen throughout history (and as Ma Joad indicated with her comment about women changing more easily than men), dramatic socioeconomic changes gen-erally are less threatening to women's sense of self. A woman usually has less reason to doubt her existence or that she can do something useful: *I (have the capacity to) give birth, therefore I am.*

This reformulation of Cartesian philosophy has been at the base of the actions of numerous marginalized or insecure men throughout history. It is especially illuminating, however, when applied to those on the outside of the modern consumption-centered society. For example, one of Ellison's characters in *Invisible Man* put the concept in this way: "And what will be his or any man's most easily accessible symbol of freedom? Why, a woman, of course. In twenty minutes he can inflate that symbol with all the freedom he'll be too busy working to enjoy the rest of the time."[69] As the lyrics quoted above demonstrate, it is very common in music, from rhythm and blues, through rock, to rap and hip-hop. The two 1955 versions of a Muddy Waters song, his own "Mannish Boy" and Bo Diddley's "I'm a Man," expressed the neo-Cartesian* philosophy in unmistakable terms. "I'm a Man / I'm a full grown *Man* / I'm a *Man* / I'm a rollin' stone / I'm a hoochie-coochie man," Waters sang.[†] The definition of manhood solely in terms of sexual prowess is even more apparent in Bo Diddley's rendition: "I'm a man, I spelled M-A-N, Man / All you pretty women, stand in line / I can make love to you, baby, in a hour's time / I'm a man, spelled M-A-N, Man . . . The line I shoot, will never miss / The way I make love to 'em, they can't resist / I'm a man, I spelled M-A-N."[70][¶]

It is not difficult to see why many African-American men found it expedient to fall back on this basic sense of self and manhood. Under slavery they had been classified as property, which meant they were considered like women. In a nation that came to emphasize the ideal of the self-made man, black men had been denied any opportunity to achieve manhood in the accepted way. They, had, moreover, been unable to protect "their" women from white masters. In the post-slavery period there was still scant opportunity for African-American men to "make themselves." What feminists and minority advocates would later call "the white male world of work"[71] was another of those critical areas of life that men had reserved for themselves to extend gender and compensate for their incapacity to give birth. To exclude black men from the same sort of "manly" activities from which women were excluded was to classify black men with (and so like) women. And while black women were often still subject to sexual exploitation by white men, black men were subject to lynching for alleged sexual overtures toward white women. Lynching commonly involved castration, the most unambiguous denial of manhood. And black women frequently found employment

---

*In reality this is clearly a much more ancient means of self-definition and reassurance of manhood than is Descartes' *Cogito ergo sum,* but our interest in it here is its powerful emergence as a modern response to the Marketplace world's *I consume, therefore I am.*

†*Hoochie-coochie* is, of course, a euphemism for sexual relations.

¶I point out the meaning behind this music not to condemn it or its creators, but to seek to understand its source in the marketplace definition of manhood and the exclusion of many men from access to that definition.

when men could not, leaving many black men in a persistent situation similar to that in which many white men found themselves during the Depression. Beyond all this, as the Consumerculture took hold, most African-Americans were left without the sort of education and employment that would provide sufficient income to achieve the lifestyle expected of a modern American man. Welfare provisions requiring "no man in the house" further said to African-American (and other poor) men: *You can't be a man; you can't provide for a family; you can't even have a family.* African-American men, then, were denied access to both of the traditional definitions of manhood: many had insufficient income to provide for their families, and a racist system often prevented them from protecting "their women." And they were generally left on the outside of the modern Consumerculture's definition of being. About all that was available to them to declare *I exist!* and *I'm a MAN!* was the one male function that is even more basic than providing and protecting—the one that is unquestionably biological and does not have to be artificially reserved for men, the one that no woman can duplicate and so most loudly proclaims: *You've denied me access to all the other marks of manhood and tried to classify me as notaman—and so as a woman. You won't let me be a provider or protector, so I'll be a penetrator. THIS will prove that I'm a MAN!*

Lo-men and Women

But why would middle- and upper-class whites follow blacks down this path? If the black rebels have clearly had a cause, have the whites been genuine rebels without a cause? I think the answers are to be found in comparing what the Consumerculture and the corporate economy did to those who were encouraged to participate in it with what it did to those who were denied access to it.

It is fitting that Arthur Miller's *Death of a Salesman* (1949) has become *the* American play. It brilliantly shows what the Marketplace world's definition of manhood on the basis of individual economic success can do to those who "walked into the jungle" and do not walk out rich.[72] Willy Loman, the archetypal modern antihero, is that failed man: the "Little Man" who, as Mills pointed out, "does not rise." He is obsessed with individual success, self-centered and self-destructive. After Willy has killed himself, his son Happy tries to defend him by saying that he "had a good dream. It's the only dream you can have—to come out number-one man."[73]* Of course that is the only dream that one is supposed to have in a modern, mobile, every-man-for-himself society.† But this obsession with success left Willy feeling that he was not a real man.

---

*More will be said about the specifics of what Happy said as well as the larger implications of this very important phenomenon in the next chapter.

†An athletic shoe commercial during the 1996 Olympics well expressed this modern winner-take-all philosophy: "You don't win silver; you lose gold."

Significantly, Willy, who symbolizes the human being in the modern consumption ethic environment, is engaged in the primary activity of the new, consumption ethic economy: marketing. He is so detached that he does not really know his own children; all he has thought of as a way to relate to them is to be successful. He keeps claiming to have friends and respect all over his sales territory: "I am known!"[74] But in fact, he is completely disconnected; he had attempted to prove his own existence and manhood by having an affair with a woman in Boston,[75] but in the end he has no one left to lose. Willy is "free."

Willy Loman is the representative low-man in a culture that only considers a high-man to be a real man. Notice how similar *Loman* is to *Woman*. A low-man is susceptible to great doubts about his manhood. He is likely to feel the pressing need to demonstrate his manhood to others so as to prove it to himself. Willy's son Happy is a practitioner of the philosophy we have been discussing. He has sexual intercourse with the fiancées of business executives:

I fuck "the Man's" woman; therefore I am a man.

This is his way of declaring: *I am somebody!* Having sex with a woman from the dominant group has often been used by subordinated men as a means of demonstrating freedom and manhood. By penetrating the high-man's woman, the low-man gets to act like a high-man and thereby reassures himself that he is not a low man—notalowman—notawoman.

So it becomes clear why those, like Willy, who had tried to play the game of extreme competition and self-creation but failed were prone to try to find their missing manhood and their very feeling of existence in sexual encounters. But what of all the middle-class youth who, before they had even tried to succeed, set out on the *free*way constructed by downtrodden, psychologically emasculated African-American road-builders?

"The crises of capitalism in the twentieth century would yet be understood as the unconscious adaptations of a society to solve its economic imbalance at the expense of a new mass psychological imbalance," Mailer wrote. The result, he said, was "the divorce of man from his values, the liberation of the self from the Super-Ego of society." Mailer saw that those outside the Consumerculture—African-Americans who had been excluded from it and hipsters who had seceded from it—were in fact the avant-garde of this modern world. He contended that they had become like psychopaths, thinking only of themselves and their immediate pleasure. Like children, he said, they were unable to accept the delay of the gratification of any desire.[76]

The psychological imbalance infects the whole consumption-ethic society. Perhaps the critical difference between the modern, mass-consumption world and all societies that have gone before it is that those in power now encourage those below them (everyone) to be discontented with their situation. In the past, it had always been in the interests of those dominating a society to preach contentment to the masses. In terms of maintaining social "order," it still is. But the need to sell more to more people leads to the constant preaching of revolution (or pseudorevolution), through advertising, media depictions of desirable lifestyles, and so forth. The person who is content with his or her condition has no reason to buy more. So people are led to feel powerless and unhappy and told that power and happiness are to be found by consuming more. Corporations now promulgate the feelings once urged by revolutionaries. Thus the economic imperative of the consumption-based market economy contradicts and undermines the social and political interests of elites. This situation is the basis of the irony that there are so many similarities between those who see themselves as the most radical opponents of the Consumerculture and those who dominate that culture.

Insatiability constitutes the common currency of the Consumerculture and the rebellion by those who were seemingly outside it. At least since the 1920s the principal message of the consumption ethic, conveyed through advertising, has been: *There's no such thing as _enough_*. Those who were trying to prove their existence and manhood by consuming (and abusing) women rather than material things adopted the same consumption ethic. "I can get more women than a passenger train can haul," boasted Jimmie Rodgers, the "father of country music" and one of the accepted ancestors of rock, in 1927.[77] A decade later, bluesman Robert Johnson, widely acknowledged as a primary forefather of what would become rock 'n' roll, sang: "I'm going to beat my woman, until I get satisfied."[78] Even in the twentieth century, it seems, hell still had no fury like a man devalued—not permitted to meet his society's definition of manhood. Because it centers on threats to a man's sexual identity, such fury is often directed against women.

Examples of such attitudes in popular culture abound. "Well, babe, I just can't be satisfied. . . . Well, I feel like snappin' a pistol in your face, I'm gonna let some graveyard be her restin' place—Woman . . . ," Muddy Waters sang in 1948. "Well, honey, I could *never* be satisfied . . . ain't no way in the world for me to be satisfied."[79] That song, "I Can't Be Satisfied," which is one of the primary founding documents (a seeming Declaration of Independence that is actually more a Declaration of Dependence) of the youth revolution that eventually came to be called the Counterculture, expresses exactly the same outlook as that preached in the Consumerculture. There is, in short, much less that is "counter" about the Counterculture than meets the eye.

In 1965, when the Rolling Stones composed their anthem of the youth revolution based on Waters's original, they made explicit that "Satisfaction" refers to both consumption and sex (or the consumption of both material things and women), and the modern man "can't get no(ne)"—or at least not enough—

in either category. The early verses are about advertising, the consumption ethic, and its basic message of insatiability:

> . . . the man come on the radio
> He's tellin' me more and more about some useless information
> Supposed to fire my imagination.
>
> I can't get no. Oh, no, no, no. Hey, hey, hey
> That's what I say
> I can't get no satisfaction, I can't get no satisfaction
> 'Cause I try and I try and I try and I try
> I can't get no, I can't get no
> No satisfaction, no satisfaction.
>
> When I'm watchin' my TV and a man comes on and tell me
> How white my shirts can be
> But, he can't be a man 'cause he doesn't smoke
> The same cigarettes as me.

Following this keen observation of the way in which the Consumerculture seeks to define manhood through the products one consumes (you can't be a man if you don't smoke Marlboros), the focus shifts to sexual satisfaction, with the suggestion that women tease men into a quest for unattainable satisfaction in the same way that corporate advertisers do:

> When I'm ridin' round the world
> And I'm doin' this and I'm signin' that
> And I'm tryin' to make some girl, who tells me
> Baby, better come back maybe next week
> 'Cause you see I'm on a losing streak
> I can't get no. Oh, no, no, no. Hey, hey, hey
> That's what I say. I can't get no, I can't get no
> I can't get no satisfaction, no satisfaction[80]*

In fact, the lament of Muddy Waters and the Rolling Stones, that men can't attain satisfaction in the way that women can, is among the most fundamental biological circumstances that form the basis on which history has been constructed. These musicians were addressing (presumably without realizing it)

---

*It is possible, in light of the ultimate sources of male insecurity we have been examining, to take this analysis to a deeper level. The "girl's" . . . "losing streak" is her menstrual period, during which she loses blood in streaks. It is said to be this that prevents the song's speaker from achieving satisfaction. Could it be that Jagger and Richards were suffering from a periodic bout with NMS when they wrote the song?

the same "recurrent problem of civilization" that Margaret Mead had identified: "If men are ever to be at peace," she wrote, each culture must develop "forms that will make men satisfied in their constructive activities without distorting their sure sense of their masculinity."[81]

The male quest for satisfaction has been a major factor throughout history, but in some respects it has become more troublesome and generalized in recent decades. Satisfaction is always beyond reach in the Consumerculture. This doctrine of insatiability has been so powerful that it was internalized even by those who were excluded from the Marketplace world, did not succeed in it, or thought they were rejecting its values. What those legions of men, both black and white, have actually been trying to say as they sought refuge from doubts about their manhood in sexual exploits is best stated by further revising Bo Diddley's paraphrase of Muddy Waters:

"I'm a man, I spelled N-O-T-A-W-O-M-A-N."

Insecure or threatened men have other interesting ways of delivering this message to others and themselves, as we shall see in the next chapter.

CHAPTER 13

Verbal Mounting

Pseudosexing, the Notawoman Definition, and Obscenity

Don't Be a Pussy!
BUMPERSTICKER SEEN ON PICKUP TRUCK, 1997

Fuck you!

This may not be an opening line of a chapter well designed to induce readers to continue, but this brief sentence, which has in recent years become one of the most common expressions in the English language, has much deeper meanings than most people recognize. An exploration of what this and similar profane epithets actually signify can open new vistas on some common male behaviors and the motivations behind them.

An inquiry into the meaning of *Fuck you!* might begin with a diagraming of the sentence. When we attempt to do so, two significant facts that are easily overlooked become apparent:

| Fuck | you

The first important point is that *fuck* is a transitive verb. It takes a direct object, and the identity of that object matters a great deal.

Consider, for instance, the object of the verb in the following declaration I saw on the men's room wall in a Fellini's restaurant in Atlanta during the 1996 Olympics:

FUCK THE MAN

Is there any difference in the meaning of this verb when its object is a man from what it means when its object is a woman?

Even more significant is the other point about this vulgar sentence that becomes evident when it is diagramed: there seems to be no subject. Yet the question of who is doing the fucking is at least as important as that of whom is being fucked. We all recall from our grade school days sentences in which the subject is an understood, but unstated, *you,* such as:

(You) | Sit down

But it would make little sense for you to be the understood subject of the sentence with which this chapter began, since it would then read: *You fuck you!* In fact, the only possible understood subject of this sentence is *I:*

(I) | Fuck you

This realization—particularly when it is combined with a man as the object of the verb—leads to some remarkable implications, to which we shall return shortly.

"Dick Fear" and Womb Envy

"War," declared comedian George Carlin in a 1992 routine overflowing with his trademark obscenities, "is a whole lot of men standing out in a field waving their pricks at one another. Men are insecure about the size of their dicks, and so they have to kill one another over the idea."

When I heard Carlin make these statements, I was struck by their at least superficial similarity to the thesis on which I had been working for several years. "It's called 'dick fear,' " Carlin continued,

> Men are *terrified* that their pricks are inadequate, and so they have to compete with one another to feel better about themselves. And, since war is the ultimate competition, basically men are killing each other in order to improve their self-esteem. You don't have to be a historian or political scientist to see the "bigger dick foreign policy theory" at work. It sounds like this: "What? They have bigger dicks? Bomb them!" And, of course, the bombs and the rockets and the bullets are all shaped like dicks. It's a subconscious need to project the penis into other people's affairs. It's called "fucking with people."[1]

I believe that Carlin was on to something very important, but the problem is not quite what he described—and it goes far beyond the dimensions he outlined. There are definite links between sex and war. And there is, as we have seen, an uncertainty inherent in the male condition. This insecurity is a factor in male competitiveness and, in cases where it becomes great, it can lead to war. But male insecurity is not simply a matter of penis size or fears concerning sexual inadequacy. The deeper problem is the one I described earlier: dualistic thinking leads men to conclude that if they cannot compete with women in child bearing and related activities, they must set up an opposing definition of manhood—they must define themselves as "the opposite sex." What Carlin calls dick fear is, in short, a subspecies of womb envy. What apprehensive men fear is that they will not be seen as sufficiently *manly,* which they take to mean the antonym of *womanly.* Hence, an insecure man will do things that he hopes will prove him to be notawoman. In the extreme, these things include rape and war.

It is often said that rape should not be confused with sex. Rather, this argument holds, it is an act of violence and dominance: "Rape is not sex but violence."[2] I believe this misses one of the most important aspects of the human condition. Rape *does* have something to do with sex. What it has nothing whatsoever to do with is love. There is an enormous (and, I believe, highly significant) amount of confusion among the words *love, sex,* and *rape.* A male sociologist and self-professed feminist once declared in my presence that "rape is an act of love." That is an inexcusable degree of confusion. If we are ever to understand ourselves, we must realize that love is connected with sex and sex is connected with rape, but these are not the same kinds of sex and so love has no connection with rape. Rape is a conjunction between sex, dominance, sexual insecurity, violence, and hate.*

Rape is *a* conjunction among these elements, but not the only one. War is another; and seeing how sex, dominance, violence, and war are related—and how they are connected with the notawoman definition of manhood—can provide some of the most important insights into the way we are.

The way in which rape and other forms of violence are linked to the notawoman ideal of manhood was made clear in testimony that Deborah Meier, the principal of an East Harlem high school, gave before a congressional hearing following the infamous 1989 "wilding" attack on a female jogger in Central Park. "The boys will acknowledge that their ideal of manliness exudes violence," Ms. Meier reported. "To be a man is to sneer in the face of the weak. To let your guard down is an invitation to danger or cruel jests, at the very least. Weakness [is] equated with sissiness. To be a thoughtful person is to invite a rep for being a homosexual."[3]

Such connections, fears, and insecurities are most extreme among men who have been denied opportunities to achieve a sense of manhood in the ways the society defines as proper. But they are not confined to the ghetto, as the remainder of this chapter and the next will make clear.

---

*The argument of Randy Thornhill and Craig Palmer that men might resort to rape when they are socially disfranchised [*A Natural History of Rape: Biological Bases of Sexual Coercion* (Cambridge, MA: MIT Press, 2000), p. 67–68)] would be correct, had they not gone on to contend that this is an evolved reproductive strategy. Rather, it is an attempt by such threatened, insecure men to assert their manhood by violently attacking women, whose powers they envy.

"Sissy, Wimp, . . ."

Given the general acceptance of the negative, notawoman definition of what it means to be a man, nothing is more threatening to a man's self-image than to suggest that he is acting like a woman. The slurs begin in boyhood with that stinging rebuke, *You throw like a girl,* and range from the relatively mild *sissy,* through *wimp,* to the vulgar *pussy* and *cunt.* The last two leave no doubt as to what is being suggested about the male against whom the taunt is used: that he is not a man at all; he lacks the sexual equipment that differentiates males from females and has been thought throughout recorded history, from before Aristotle to after Freud, to be the basis of male superiority. Recall that such a deficiency was considered to be literally damning in Mosaic law: "He whose testicles are crushed or whose male member is cut off shall not enter the assembly of the Lord."[4] The same point is made more directly today when one male says another is "dickless" or "lacking in balls."

Having "big balls" has long been a metaphor for power and dominance. The ultimate compliment to a man in Mediterranean cultures is to say that he is "a man with big testicles." An especially powerful man is sometimes said to be one "with testicles reaching the ground."[5] But this symbolism is by no means confined to Mediterranean societies. Witness the adoption of the Spanish word *cojones* into English, as a means of asserting one's putative masculinity. Such language and the use of the profane words for female sexual organs to denigrate men have become very common. It all comes down to a simple formula based on male wishful thinking and envy of female powers: male genital organs = power; female genital organs = weakness.

A few years ago, I saw the following manly advice on a bumpersticker on a pickup truck:

DON'T BE A PUSSY

The effect was completed by the vanity license plate, which read:

USEN U

On the walls of college men's rooms, I have observed the following fraternal graffiti:

When KA's get
bullied
by the
other frats
They call security
and cry about it!
Waaah, pussies!

And this exchange:

Fuck KΣ Pussies
  Oh yeah! You're really a big man
  writing shit on bathroom walls.
  You're a fucking loser; get a life
  dick sucker & come and say it
  to our face. You know where
  our house is, you little pussy.

This kind of language is all too familiar these days, but its significance is generally overlooked. On the principle that the best defense is a good offense, one of the ways for a male to fend off questions about his own masculinity is to suggest that another man is like a woman, and so, in the view of most men, inferior.

This is what one man saying *Fuck you!* to another is really all about.

Pseudosexing

"Looks like we got us a sow here, instead of a boar," one of the mountain men in the 1972 film *Deliverance* says of Bobby, the Ned Beatty character, whom he has just been literally riding. The "cracker" then tells Bobby to pull down his "panties" and proceeds to rape him. The plainly unwelcomed anal intercourse, along with the words *sow* and *panties,* are clearly intended by the character to demonstrate his dominance over another man by symbolically treating him as a woman.[6] (The same point had been made with only slightly more subtlety in James Dickey's 1970 novel.)

Sexual metaphors have been used throughout human history as a means of asserting dominance. As we shall see in a moment, the practice goes far beyond physical metaphors such as that just described. These metaphors are all unmistakably based on the notawoman conception of manhood. Collectively, the various permutations of male-is-superior-to-female symbolism constitute the *Master metaphor* of human history, the one that has been used as the basis of and model for all relations of dominance and subservience among people. Essentially, they all say: *Whatever is designated as male is superior to anything that is designated as female.* Or, more simply: male = master; female = subordinate.

During the legal battle over the sexual integration of the military college the Citadel, a remarkable statement on the prevalence of this metaphor was given in the testimony of the school's top-ranked scholar from the class of 1991. Asked how many times he had heard "the word 'woman' used as a way of tearing a cadet down," Ron Vergnolle replied that "it was an everyday part, every-minute, every-hour part of life" on the South Carolina campus. But he said that *woman* was not the term that cadets used when they wanted to denigrate a fellow male student by indicating that he was like a female. "[T]he large majority of the terms you were called were gutter slang for women. And it goes all the way down to the genitalia, and that's where the criticism was." Vergnolle made plain that this practice is a direct manifestation of what I have termed the notawoman definition of manhood: "And the point was, if you are not doing what you're supposed to do, you are not a man, you are a woman, and that is the way you are disciplined in the barracks every day, every hour."[7] "They called you a 'pussy' all the time," another former student said, or "a fucking little girl."[8] Virtually every taunt upperclassmen used against a freshman "equated him with a woman," still another former cadet said. One such insult he remembered seems particularly significant in light of the arguments in this book: "Bryant, are you menstruating this month?"[9] (Bobby Knight, the famed University of Indiana basketball coach, uses the same symbolism. When he wants to shame his players, Knight "puts sanitary napkins in the[ir] lockers."[10]) Instructors at the Citadel use the Master metaphor as a pedagogical tool. "Never use the passive voice," an English professor proclaimed to his class, "it leads to effeminacy and homosexuality." He derided those who make errors as "pansies."[11]

The proximate causes of the pervasiveness of this metaphor in recent years are particular to our history and culture—especially the growing insecurity of men in the extremely competitive Marketplace and Consumerculture that I outlined in the preceding chapter. But the ultimate sources of the metaphor must be sought deep in our past: beyond what is usually called "history"—in fact, back beyond what is generally thought of as human "prehistory." The origins of the Master metaphor predate the evolution of *Homo sapiens;* indeed, they predate the emergence of hominids. The idea that other animals use metaphorical behavior may be surprising, but it is plain that this is what is going on when a dominant male among several primate species, such as macaques, and a number of other mammals, mounts a subordinated male and simulates intercourse with him. The former is, in effect, "saying" to the latter: *I am so dominant over you that I can treat you like a female.* Such male animals apparently have some concept of "malehood" in terms of being "notafemale."

Such symbolic mounting is an unexplored but highly significant aspect of human male behavior. It is, obviously, a means of asserting a vertical distinction between individuals; it provides an answer to the question: *Who's on top?* Accordingly, it is similar to another practice we use to categorize people.

One of the more consequential human tendencies that we have explored in these pages is that toward pseudospeciation: falsely treating another member of our species as if he or she were a member of a different species. It is this capacity that allows us to turn off our natural identification with other members of our species and so be able to kill them. Its power and consequences

The Mounting Metaphor
Dominant males in many animal species, such as these Rocky Mountain sheep, use a metaphor to symbolize their superiority to a subordinated male: the dominant male mounts the subordinated one, as he would a female, and simulates intercourse. Human males frequently employ the same basic metaphor, although in our species it is more often done through language. (Corbis)

have been very evident in recent years in a variety of locales, from the Balkans to Rwanda. It is difficult to brutalize and kill human beings, but it is not so hard to commit atrocities against "Gooks," "Niggers," "Honkies," "Spics," "Micks," "Nips," "Krauts," or other creatures we have used language to dehumanize. Clearly this ability to engage in pseudospeciation is a major part of the basis for warfare.

The Master metaphor is based on a similar, but generally unnoticed, process that can usefully be termed *pseudosexing*—falsely treating another member of the same sex as if he were a member of the other sex. This is what men do when they subordinate other men by symbolically treating them as women. This tendency may be as important a factor in war and other forms of violence between humans as pseudospeciation so clearly is. The reason for pseudosexing is the same as that for pseudospeciation: to "otherize," to dichotomize, to distinguish in a dualistic manner of "us" and "them," so that dominance or hierarchy can be established. Sometimes the human practice of pseudosexing is as direct and literal as it is among some animal species.

The Physical Mounting Metaphor

Many readers, I imagine, are saying to themselves at this point, "I don't recall ever seeing a man mount another man and simulate intercourse in order to show the dominance of the first over the second." Indeed it is not a common occurrence, but in certain specialized realms it does happen. There are, for example, some practices in sports that bear a striking resemblance to mounting as a means of showing dominance: a wrestler pinning an opponent beneath him and, in American football, the practice of "piling on" a tackled opponent.

A more direct form of mounting of subordinated men by dominant men is the type depicted in the scene from *Deliverance*. This sort of symbolic mounting takes place commonly in prisons. In this male subculture, "everyone is tested," as one inmate said in 1987. "The weak—of personality, personal power, willingness to fight, physical frailty, timidity—are especially susceptible. . . . Respect is given to one who can control the life of another."[12] In male prisons, those who dominate are defined as males and those who surrender are reclassified as females (*girls, non-men*).[13] In prison, as Inez Cardozo-Freeman has said in her book, *The Joint*, "the supreme act of humiliation is to be reduced to the status of a woman."[14] Through the act of mounting subordinated males, men in prison are proclaiming their superior "manhood."

In 1997, five New York police officers were charged with "sodomizing" Haitian immigrant Abner Louima by ramming a broom handle into his rectum while he was in custody in a Brooklyn police station.[15] What was done to Mr. Louima was similar in its symbolism to what happens in prisons and to the victorious male primate mounting the subordinated male and simulating intercourse with him. The cops were asserting their dominance over the prisoner in the most obvious way: by demonstrating that they could penetrate him—"treat him like a woman."

And then, once again, there is the Citadel, where upperclassmen torment freshmen in the showers by knocking soap from their hands and, when the freshmen bend over, shouting, "Don't pick it up. We'll use you like we used those girls." And one company of upperclass cadets reportedly put sophomores through an ordeal called "Bananarama," which concluded with a banana being shoved into the younger boy's anus.[16]

Although this sort of symbolism became ubiquitous in the late twentieth-century Western world, it is by no means unique to our culture. A "real man" in ancient Rome, for example, was defined as a penetrator. "He did not have to restrict his sexual behavior to relations with women," Cambridge classicist Mary Beard notes. "What was crucial was that he did not allow himself to become penetrated. To *be* penetrated as a Roman man was a sign of effeminacy. . . . The Roman man had an image of himself as someone who must live up to that penetrative ideal."[17] To put it bluntly, it was acceptable in ancient Rome, as it is in modern prisons, for a man to fuck men as well as women and still be a "real man." What he could not do if he wanted to maintain his manly (notawomanly) status was to *be* fucked.

Making Hate

If the actual physical mounting of one man by another is not a common sight in the wider world outside prison walls, police stations, and military schools, that is because the capacity for language has given humans a much wider range of symbols and metaphors than is available to other primates. Human males do not have to act out symbolic (or, in prison, actual) intercourse in order to pseudosex other men and indicate that they are dominant over them, as they assert themselves to be over females. Humans can use *words* in place of (or, sometimes, in conjunction with) actions to symbolize precisely the same thing that the ceremonial mounting by a dominant male macaque of a subordinate male macaque (or the actual penetration of a subordinated prisoner by a dominant one) does.

We *do* use words for this purpose. Sometimes it is obvious. Former world heavyweight boxing champion Mike Tyson used to taunt an opponent before a bout by saying to him: "I'll make you into my girlfriend."[18] Almost all of our language of dominance and subordination among men is based upon pseudosexing. In 1979 historian Christopher Lasch commented upon the use of "vulgar terms for sexual intercourse" to mean "getting the better of someone, working him over, taking him in, imposing your will through guile, deception, or superior force." He viewed with some alarm what he saw as the phenomenon of "verbs associated with sexual pleasure" coming to be identified with violence and exploitation.[19] Lasch was pointing to a most important area of inquiry, but he made two mistakes that most others who have discussed this subject have also made.

One of these errors was also at the center of comedian Lenny Bruce's puzzlement at why people say *Fuck you!* to those they dislike. Bruce said that "fucking" is something nice, so it should not be wished upon one's enemies. He suggested instead that what we should say to those we do not like is: "*Un–fuck* you, mister!"[20] Both Lasch and Bruce confused *fucking* with *making love*. The former is *not* a "verb associated with sexual pleasure" if sexual pleasure is taken to involve affection; it is a verb associated with domination, subordination, and sexual violence.[21] The almost opposite connotations of the word have been put well by humorist Roy Blount, Jr.: "It's one of the best things we can do *with* someone, one of the worst *to* someone."[22] When Nigerian novelist Chinua Achebe wrote of one of his characters, "He trembled with the desire to conquer and subdue. It was like the desire for a woman,"[23] he was referring to a desire to fuck, not to love. Carlin used the word in the correct sense when he said: "What did we do wrong in Vietnam? We *pulled out*—not a very manly thing to do, is it? When you're fucking people, you gotta stay in there and fuck them good—fuck them all the way; fuck 'em to the end; *fuck 'em to death!* Stay in there and keep fucking them until *they're all* dead!"[24]

Fuck you! actually holds a meaning in direct opposition to *I want to make love to you. Fuck you!* could accurately be rephrased as: *I'd like to make hate to you!*

Lasch's other mistake on this matter was his assumption that this connection of vulgar terms for sexual intercourse with dominating someone else is a recent development. Actually the symbolic link of which this language is but a variant is older than the human species. It is a linguistic equivalent of ceremonial mounting.

Verbal mounting is an accurate way to describe the language men use to express domination and subordination.[25]

We can begin to see this by returning to the most obvious example of verbal aggression, the two-word insult with which this chapter began and that Bruce

Verbal Mounting
When one man says *Fuck you!* to another man, he is using the same metaphor that dominant male animals use when they mount a subordinated male. The metaphor is based on the male assumption that females are inferior and indicating that a man is like—or can be treated like—a female is the ultimate statement that he is inferior and subordinate. (© Wally McNamee/CORBIS)

found so "weird." *Fuck you!* is generally considered to be about the worst thing that one man can say to another. This statement has become so common in recent years that it is often used in jest among friends. But when not said among friends, and when it is realized that "I" is the understood subject of the sentence, "them's fightin' words." This verbal aggression can be gotten away with only by a male who is dominant* over the one to whom he says it.

The etymology of this vulgar term supports this understanding. *Fuck you!* is used as a form of verbal aggression based upon a symbolic linking of subordination with sexual dominance. The word *fuck* is Germanic in origin. It is derived from the Middle English *fucken,* "to strike, move quickly, penetrate," which was probably taken from the Middle Dutch *fokken,* "to strike" or "to copulate with."[26] In several different Germanic languages, variants of the word have both sexual and aggressive meanings, such as "to hit" or "to thrust."[27] The popularity in recent years of the expression "hitting on" as a synonym for "trying to pick up" a woman is an echo of this connection. This terminology shows that the connection of aggression and dominance among men with symbolic mounting goes back at least a thousand years. In fact, however, it goes back millions of years into evolution.

A good example of verbal mounting can be seen in the 1994 movie *Pulp Fiction.* The Samuel L. Jackson character, Jules, asks another male, "Do you think Marsellus Wallace is a bitch?" When he replies, "No, of course not," Jules fires back: "Well, then why are you fucking him like a bitch?"[28]

The fact that this language and behavior are among the most widespread manifestations of misogyny is obscured because men play the parts of both sexes, much as they did in Greek or Elizabethan theater. As happens physically in prisons, the language of verbal mounting consists of the dominant males taking the roles of men and casting subordinated males as women.

One man saying *Fuck you!* to another no more means that the speaker actually desires to have sexual relations with the man at whom the words are directed than ceremonial mounting by a dominant male in another species does.† What it does mean is something like: *I am sufficiently dominant over you that I can symbolically treat you as if you were a woman.* It means *I am a real man (notawoman); you're not.* It becomes a statement of logic: *I am to you as man is to woman. We (men) all know that man is superior to woman. Therefore I am superior to you.*

---

*Usually he is dominant in terms of physical strength and fighting ability, but in the modern world sometimes he is in other respects, such as property relations or social hierarchy.

†A human practice that is closer to the nonverbal symbolism used by other animals mounting subordinate males is "giving someone the finger." This symbolic act carries the same message of *I am dominant and can treat you like a woman* as the verbal equivalent of the gesture.

Putting a Man Down

Exactly the same pseudosexing message is at the base of virtually all of our language of domination and subordination.* "Fighting words" *are* verbal mounting. Almost every expression that men employ to "put down" other men amounts to "putting them down"—treating them as women. Some words that have become very common means for one man to taunt another are especially direct in this regard. As I have already pointed out, there can be little doubt about the implication of calling a man a *pussy* or a *cunt.* But consider the following examples: *Stick it up your ass; I really stuck it to him; Sit on it; Rotate on it; Up yours; You suck.*

To say that something or someone "sucks" has become a very common expression in the last decade. What it means is that the person or thing being so castigated is being linked with those who perform fellatio and have been classified as inferior: women or homosexual men. Why don't we say instead, *It gets sucked*? The reason, of course, is that reversing the metaphor would indicate that the antecedent of *it* is male and saying that someone is male is almost always considered to be a compliment, not an insult. It would be a *put-up,* not a *put-down.* Similarly, no man says *Fuck me!* to someone he wants to denigrate, because that would be to say: *You are to me like a man is to a woman,* and the assumption is deeply ingrained in almost everyone that this would mean that the other person is the superior.

Why, other than the mounting metaphor, would a man who seeks to dominate others be referred to as a *prick* or a *shmuck?* Such a man is alternatively classified as *a real pain in the ass.* To see how this familiar expression is another instance of verbal mounting, think about what might be causing a pain in that part of the anatomy. (Such a pain in the ass is likely to call a man he is degrading an *asshole.*) And what image but that of symbolic mounting is created by the man who has the misfortune of having such a domineering man as his boss and complains to friends or family, *the boss was really riding my ass today?* Other ways to put the same complaint would be: *He really screwed me, He was really on me today, He stiffed me,* or *He gave me the shaft.*

Ours is not an age given to subtlety, and any doubt as to the meaning of verbal mounting disappears in another, increasingly common expression for having

---

*I am familiar with this vulgar terminology mainly in the English language. Given several examples with which I have become acquainted in other languages, it is my assumption that the connections of words of domination with mounting symbolism are present in other languages as well. There are, however, languages in which the vulgar equivalents of *fuck* are only used literally. See Jesse Sheidlower, ed., *The F Word* (New York: Random House, 1995), pp. 227–232.

been "screwed" by someone: "He fucked me—*up the ass!*" Larry Ellison, the cofounder and CEO of Oracle, who achieved the title of "world's richest man" in the spring of 2000, indicated the underlying sexual meaning in the competitive arena of modern capitalism when he sent out instructions to his employees on how to deal with competitors. Word was passed down the chain of command that "Larry wants us to shove this up their ass."[29] As one scholarly compilation of the usage of such terms puts it, *butt-fuck* has a meaning "to victimize." "Males in particular . . . who have been denied promotion, given low grades . . . been fired, jilted [etc.] . . . commonly relate that they have been *screwed, fucked, . . . butt-fucked . . .* and so on."[30]

If one man gets carried away in "putting down" another, his colleagues are likely to urge that he *lay off of him.* The implication is that when one man is dominating another he is "laying" (on) him, treating him like a woman, simulating intercourse. The suggestion that there is a time to "lay off" also fits this analysis, since it is usually said after the subordinated male has given a sign of submission. Other male animals often give such a sign by assuming a position like a female "presenting" or offering herself for mating. This is what is meant when we say someone, such as a politician, has "rolled over" for someone else, such as a lobbyist or a special interest group, as in this 1999 example: "Then no harm will befall [Texas Governor George W.] Bush for rolling over for the gun lobby."[31] To "roll over for" is to assume a female position and present oneself to be penetrated by a male to whom one has been subordinated.

And, speaking of assuming positions, what does it mean when a policeman or another man in a position of authority commands someone to *assume the position?* Snoop Doggy Dogg clarifies this for us in one his songs, "Horny": "Assume the position so I can fuck you."[32] *Assuming the position* is precisely what subordinated male animals do when they present themselves to the dominant male to be symbolically mounted. The implications of being in a *position* of authority or dominance should be clear. It means to be in a position *on top.* Those who are in positions of command are usually concerned about "staying on top." As a television commercial for Chevrolet trucks put it: "They say the one on top has all the power."*

---

*Like the physical symbolism, the misogynistic notawoman definition of manhood carried over in ancient Rome as it does now into the language of verbal mounting. This fact is evident in such examples as the following lines from the Roman poet Catullus: "I'll fuck you both right up the ass, / Gay Furius, Aurelius, / For saying I'm not chaste, what brass!" [Catullus, *Catullus: The Complete Poems for American Readers,* Reney Myers and Robert J. Ormsby, trans. (New York: E. P. Dutton, 1970), p. 213]. And in the first century B.C.E., Marcus Terentius Varro used the Latin words *dicite labadeae,* meaning "to tell someone to suck," and is based on the vulgar Greek verb for "to fellate," *laikazein* [Jesse Sheidflower, ed. *The F Word* (New York, Random House, 1975), p. xxix–xxx].

The way to avoid vulnerability to being subordinated is often called *covering your ass*. This phrase is a clear reference to not being in a position where you can be "mounted." Our litigious society leads people to assume such *defensive postures*. Lawyers are always warning their clients not to put themselves in an *exposed position,* which means leaving yourself open to being dominated. Although being *caught with your pants down* could refer to other activities, it is likely that this common expression carries the same sexually symbolic message of warning about leaving yourself open to being "had," as in a man *having* a woman.

It is very clear that all this language is rooted in the notawoman definition of manhood. But attempts to prove masculinity by demonstrating that one is notawoman can get more extreme than *saying* "Fuck you!" They can result in many forms of "fucking" that go beyond words, including the real thing.

Penetrating Enemy Territory

Men assert dominance over other men through action as well as language, both by fucking them metaphorically and by actually fucking "their" women. Aside from the sort of actual mounting that takes place in prisons and, less often, elsewhere, one of the clearest examples of a metaphorical action based on the Master metaphor is slavery. For one man to enslave another is a very powerful way to say *(I) Fuck you!*

It is plain, as I discussed earlier, that rape is fucking, not loving. What may not always be so clear is who it is being fucked.

The world was shocked in the early 1990s as the stories of Bosnian Serb rape camps were told by some of the Muslim women who were assaulted in them. Words such as *unprecedented* were coupled with many reactions to these atrocities.

But there was, alas, nothing unprecedented about the apparently massive number of rapes committed by the Serbian soldiers. Before we single out the Bosnian Serbs for exclusive condemnation, we should recall that it is to that great American war hero, General George Patton, that the dictum, "Them that does the fighting does the fucking" is attributed.[33] And Patton was right; from the earliest times of warfare it appears that members of invading armies have engaged in rape as they "penetrated enemy territory."[34]

The sad truth is that the planting of the victors' penises in the women of the vanquished has often been as much a symbol of victory as the planting of the winners' flag in the soil of the defeated. "It is," the authors of a recently published world history text say, "a time-honored battle strategy: one hurts men by hurting their [sic] women."[35] As we have seen, at the time when Columbus was inserting the Spanish flag into various lands in the New World five centuries ago some of his men were, with his blessing, tying up indigenous women and inserting themselves into them. Again, this is connected to the fact that throughout most of recorded history men have generally viewed women as "property"—soil in which men plant their seeds. Given this belief, raping the women, the "property" of the enemy men, has been taken as the same as claiming the land of the enemy men. Both involve inserting "sticks" in what had been the enemy's property.

To the victors go the spoils—and the "right" to despoil the women who are counted among the possessions of the losers. Japanese authorities engaged in a variant of this practice when they forced Korean, Filipina, and other women to become "comfort women"—a euphemism for sex slaves—to provide pleasure for Japanese military men. These women were listed on shipping ledgers as "military supplies."[36]

Another way for men to emasculate other men and so assert their notawomanhood is the practice, discussed in the last chapter, of having sex with the wives, girlfriends, or daughters of those who are one's superiors in a social order. Happy Loman's description of his activities in this regard is especially revealing: "That girl Charlotte I was with tonight is engaged to be married in five weeks. . . . I don't know what gets into me, maybe I just have an overdeveloped sense of competition or something, but I went and ruined her. . . . And *he's the third executive I've done that to.* . . . And *to top it all,* I go to their weddings! . . . *I don't want the girl,* and, still, *I take it—and love it!*"[37] The words I emphasized are key. They make clear that the person he is fucking is the male executive, not "his girl." He says he loves *it,* but we need to be clear about what the antecedent to that pronoun is. Since he doesn't want the girl, what he loves cannot be making love to her; rather, *it* is making hate to the man to whom she is supposed to "belong." He loves it because it gives him the feeling of being on top of it all: him as well as her. Fucking her is merely a means by which to fuck him. If what Happy (and nonfictional low-men like him) are doing by having intercourse with the women of the high-men were classified as a crime, it would be a crime against property, much as the rape of a virgin was considered in ancient Mesopotamia and Israel.[38] Breaking a hymen that has been classified as the property of a high-man is a serious crime and therefore a way to "fuck *him.*"

A Culture Awash in Verbal Mounting

That masculinity has become particularly uncertain, not just for the low-men, but for many men in our society, is evidenced not only by the explosion in the use of such mounting language, but also in the use of mounting metaphors in popular culture. This is a major example of the growing desire among many men, in the face of recent gains by women, to reassert a wide, vertical difference between the sexes.

In roughly the same time period as that during which the epithet *Fuck you!* has proliferated, there has been a startling growth of violent misogyny in some forms of popular culture. In music, this ranges from these relatively mild sentiments from the late Tupac Shakur in "All Eyez on Me," which, except for the explicit language, do not go far beyond the sexual bravado of 1950s rhythm and blues and early rock: "Bitches I fuck with a passion, livin' rough and raw / Catchin' cases at a fast rate, ballin' in the fast lane"[39] through Snoop Doggy Dogg's "Ain't No Fun (If the Homies Cant Have None)": "I know the pussy's mine, / So I'm gonna fuck it a couple more times, / . . . Because she's nothing but a bitch to me."[40] Such tender sentiments are not limited, as some critics unfamiliar with contemporary music wrongly assume, to rap and hip-hop. A new category of music emerged in the last decade or so of the twentieth century. Love songs have presumably been with us since the beginning of music. In the 1990s what can accurately be classified as "hate songs" became very popular. Snoop Doggy Dogg was considered "the fastest-rising star in the music world" in the mid-nineties.[41]

The misogyny in such lyrics is incontestable. More important may be the apparent source of that fear and hatred of women. An unmistakable insecurity about the manhood of the composer-performers permeates this music, and questions about the meaning of manhood are at the root of the larger questions opened by an exploration of the meaning of such language as *Fuck you!*

Beyond the total contempt for all things female and the obvious insecurity about their own manhood suffered by the composer-singers of the violent misogyny in some forms of popular music—particularly, but by no means exclusively, in "gangsta rap"—another important point stands out. They frequently make references to intercourse from the rear and anal intercourse.

A few examples will suffice. The clearest may be Snoop Doggy Dogg's "Doggystyle" (1993): "We travel in packs / And we do it from the back / . . . / We do it doggystyle."[42] The album cover informs us that "Snoop is always on top of things."

Another case in this genre is Guns n' Roses' "It's So Easy" (1987): "Turn around bitch I got a use for you." Or, from the same album's "Anything Goes": "Panties round your knees, with your ass in debris. / Tied up, tied down, up against the wall."[43]

Such woman hating can be seen in recent music videos. Patently insecure males who want to dominate other men through mounting metaphors portray the "artist" engaged in anal intercourse with a subordinated man.

The most extreme misogyny takes the form of fascination with the mutilation of female genitalia, for example in 2 Live Crew's "Dick Almighty": "He'll tear the pussy open 'cause it's satisfaction / The bitch won't leave, it's fatal attraction."[44] This goes beyond the earlier *I fuck, therefore I am* philosophy. "Satisfaction" here is associated not just with consuming women, or even beating them, but specifically with violence aimed at women's sexual organs. It seems likely that male womb envy is at work. 2 Live Crew's "Put Her in the Buck" sounds almost like a modern version of Marduk cutting Tiamat's womb in the *Enuma Elish:* "A big stinkin' pussy can't do it all / So we try real hard just to bust the walls."[45] The conversion in some subcultures in recent decades of the term *motherfucker* into one almost of endearment[46] has similar implications of misogyny rooted in jealousy of maternal power.

When the phenomenon of verbal mounting is comprehended, it becomes apparent that what is unstated in the simple sentence *Fuck you!* is far more than the understood subject, *I.* What the expression actually means is something like:

> (I see my position relative to yours as being such that you are like a woman and I am a man, so I could) fuck you (if I had any desire to do so)!

The sorts of fears and insecurities evident in the music that began among inner-city youth are by no means confined to the ghetto or to low-men. The Bush family compound in Kennebunkport, like the Kennedy family compound in Hyannis Port, are, to cite two examples, rather far removed from the ghetto. But the quality of life in these luxurious locales provided their inhabitants with no protection against male insecurity. In fact, some of the highest men in society appear to have been driven by this sort of insecurity, as we shall see in the next chapter.

CHAPTER 14

"I Am *Not*awoman; Hear Me Roar"

Male Insecurity, the Drive for Power, and War

*"Politics gives guys so much power and such big egos they tend to behave badly towards women. . . .
I hope I never get into that."*

BILL CLINTON, 1970[1]

"But he was a man!" a trembling Richard Nixon affirmed of Theodore Roosevelt as Nixon concluded his rambling talk to the White House staff at the time of his resignation in 1974.[2] There can be little doubt that the disgraced president had himself in mind as he referred to his predecessor. The analogy was most appropriate. Theodore Roosevelt and Richard Nixon are two notable examples of political leaders who constantly sought reassurance of their own manhood.

Sexually insecure men often seek validation of their manhood by pursuing power. This is one of the reasons that the notawoman definition of manhood has had such an impact throughout history. It is certainly not the case that all men think this way, but those who do have frequently made their way into positions of power and so have had a disproportionate influence on the shaping of cultures and institutions. The insecurities of these high men have the potential to cause far more trouble than do those of the low men who seek ways to proclaim their masculinity. The greatest danger of all can come from sexually insecure men who reach the top by appealing to the fears of the anxious men in the lower ranks of the society. Adolf Hitler and his Nazi movement constitute Exhibit A of what this volatile mix can produce.

The deep association between sexual metaphors and establishing dominance among males that is explored in the preceding chapter leads into the connections many men make among sex, power, and war. This chapter uses a series of men who achieved power in the twentieth century to explore those connections in specific cases in a modern context. Aside from Hitler, the other examples are taken from the ranks of United States presidents: Theodore Roosevelt, John F. Kennedy, Lyndon Johnson, Richard Nixon, George Bush, and Bill Clinton. It should be understood that these examples are peculiar to the social environment of the time and place that have been the cutting edge of the Marketplace Misconception and the ideal of the self-made man. But, while this has caused the influence of male insecurity to play out in particular, supercharged ways in these men, such doubts have played major roles in the lives of many men who rose to power throughout history, from King Solomon and Alexander the Great (and before) to Bill Clinton (and, it is, unfortunately, safe to predict, after).

Four important caveats: First, although many leaders have suffered from a notably high level of sexual insecurity, this trait is not a prerequisite for achieving high political or governmental position. Even in the second half of the twentieth century, some leaders who appear to have been relatively secure in their sexuality did manage to rise to the top. (Jimmy Carter, for example, apparently confined his lusting to his heart.) Second, there is no intent to suggest that insecurity about masculinity was the sole determinant of the character or behavior of the men discussed in this chapter. Rather, the argument is that such self-doubts were important factors in shaping all these men who won power. Nor is what follows meant to indicate that all the men discussed here were alike. Far from it. Each was a very distinct individual, but each was misshaped in a particular way by internal questions about what it means to be a man, whether he was up to that standard, and how he should react to and relate to what they all mistakenly thought to be "the opposite sex." Finally, the focus in what follows on the shortcomings of these men in connection with sexual matters and attitudes and actions related to them should not be taken to deny that some of them had significant redeeming qualities. I see none, to be sure, in Hitler, and few in Nixon, but the others had significant positive attributes that, to varying degrees, provided some balance to the negatives stimulated by their insecure masculinity.

Wimp Rhymes with *Limp*

"You're talking to the wimp," a still-seething President George Bush said to reporters two and a half months after the end of the Persian Gulf War in 1991. "You're talking to the guy that had a cover of a national magazine, that I'll never forgive, put that label on me."[3]

"That label" so upset Bush for the same reason that it is such a powerful insult to almost any man: it throws his manhood into question. (*"Wimp,"* George Carlin reminds us, "rhymes with *limp.*"[4]) At the conclusion of the war with Iraq, there was some question about just what sign of submission and humiliation from Saddam Hussein would be acceptable to the American president. An understanding of the relationship between sex and domination suggests the most likely answer. The one symbol that really would have satisfied President Bush would have been for the Iraqi dictator to assume a position in which the American president could mount him and simulate intercourse.

President Bush's outburst—the unspoken subtext of which is very similar to those of the vulgar bumpersticker and the men's room stall literature discussed in the preceding chapter *(Now you can see that I am notawoman!)*—makes it reasonable to ask whether the desire to prove his manhood may have been Bush's principal motive for engaging in war. The perspective of biohistory that we have been developing in this book can help to answer that question and assist in explaining a good deal more about the actions and motivations of many political leaders. We shall return to the question about Bush after looking at similar issues concerning some other twentieth-century leaders.

A Big Stick

An understanding of the deep association between sexual metaphors and establishing dominance among males sheds a great deal of light on the connection many men make between sex and war. It is clear that some males seek to dominate others as a means of compensating for sexual insecurity.

Theodore Roosevelt provides a classic example. He was preoccupied with the necessity of war as an arena for the display of "manly virtues." For Roosevelt, as for so many men throughout history, the principal value of war was as a means of proving one's manhood. He once condensed his understanding of "man's mission in life" into three words: "work, fight, breed."[5] "All the great masterful races have been fighting races," he declared.[6] "He would like above all things to go to war with someone," a college friend wrote of Roosevelt in 1885. "He has just walked out of the hotel with a rifle over his shoulder. . . . He . . . wants to be killing something all the time."[7]

Plainly, Theodore Roosevelt was among those who defined manhood in the double-negative notawoman manner, including the inference that, because women give birth, a real man's proper role is giving death. "Every man who has in him any real power of joy in battle knows that he feels it when the wolf begins to rise in his heart," he said. "He does not then shrink from blood or sweat, or deem that they mar the fight; he revels in them, in the toil, the pain,

"I'm A Man, Yes I Am"
This painting of his highly publicized heroism in the Spanish-American War is the image Theodore Roosevelt wanted to present to the public—and himself: the warrior, the hunter, the self-made man, the *real* man, the *he*-man. His obsession with masculinity strongly suggests that Roosevelt's greatest anxiety was that he might actually be a "she-man." (Library of Congress)

the danger, as but setting off the triumph."[8] "I killed a Spaniard with my own hand, like a Jack-rabbit," the Rough Rider wrote to his friend Henry Cabot Lodge with the sort of pride a woman might take in relating to a friend that she had given birth. "Look at those damned Spanish dead," he had declared with great satisfaction when the battle was over.[9]

The strong suspicion must be that Roosevelt suffered from some sexual insecurity. He persistently spoke not only of war but also of practically everything in terms of sex. He always sought desperately to identify himself with masculinity and to avoid any hint of femininity. *Manly* and *masterful* were two of the words he most commonly used in his writing.[10] "An advanced state of intellectual development," he complained, "is too often associated with a certain effeminacy of character."[11] Roosevelt encouraged press coverage of his hunting trips, but would not allow photographs to be taken of him in his tennis clothing, because he considered tennis and its apparel to be "effete."[12] (One can almost imagine Roosevelt repeating a mantra: *I am not a woman; I am NOT a woman; I am Notawoman!*) He referred to those who opposed his orchestration of the so-called revolution in Panama in 1903 as "a small body of shrill eunuchs,"[13] which is the equivalent of shouting *Pussies!* or *Fuck you!*

at all of them—or of telling them they are barred from the house of God, since they do not have balls like God.

In his 1904 "Roosevelt Corollary" to the Monroe Doctrine, Roosevelt spoke of the "impotence" of some Latin American governments as the cause of the need for United States intervention.[14] Impotence was among Roosevelt's favorite images, one he used to show disdain for anyone he disliked. Woodrow Wilson's reluctance to take the United States into World War I led Roosevelt to indict him for doing "more to emasculate American manhood and weaken its fiber than anyone else I can think of."[15]

Anyone who persistently makes such associations would appear to be one who sees sex as a form of aggression—or aggression as a form of sex. It does not take an especially large (or Freudian) imagination to understand why Roosevelt used the "Big Stick" as his metaphor for military might. It was acceptable to him to *speak* softly (although he was in fact often very loud himself), so long as he had the reassurance that his stick was big and that *it* was not soft.

One reason for Roosevelt's concern about proving his manhood seems to have been his feeling of shame that his father had paid for a substitute rather than fight himself during the Civil War. Although he does not appear ever to have spoken directly of this matter, Roosevelt did make his torment over his father's "unmanly" behavior clear. "I had always felt that if there were a serious war I wished to be in a position to explain to my children why I did take part in it, and not why I did not take part in it," he wrote in his autobiography. And when he did make allusions to the issue, Roosevelt often used sexually laden images. In a speech while he was president in 1907, he declared: "I did not intend to have to hire somebody to *do my shooting* for me." The following year he spoke of his own participation in the Spanish-American War as having been "my one chance to cut my little notch on *the stick* that stands as a *measuring rod* in every family."[16] Much like Jim Stark in the later movie *Rebel Without a Cause,* it seems, Teddy Roosevelt was terribly embarrassed that his father was "not a man" and so was constantly trying to prove his own manhood. Theodore Roosevelt, like the James Dean character, felt it necessary to keep engaging in "chicky races" of one sort or another. He couldn't stand the equivalent of being called a "chicken" anymore than Jim could.

What Roosevelt, like so many other leaders throughout history, feared was the sort of fate that had befallen the notoriously unsuccessful King John of England: having his stick or sword become to object of ridicule. John experienced the ultimate indignity of being called "Softsword" (*Mollegladium*).[17]

"This Is My Rifle, This Is My Gun"

Theodore Roosevelt's case was extreme, but many sexually insecure men have risen to political power. It may be that the association of sex with dominance leads some such men to seek power over others precisely because they are concerned about their sexual identity and believe that gaining political dominance will prove their "manhood"—and silence the inner demons that keep questioning that status.

It is, of course, a commonplace observation that guns often serve men as substitute sexual organs. Marines are reported to have a "manhood" ritual which involves "alternately stroking the rifle and the penis while singing the Marine hymn: 'This is my rifle, this is my gun. This is for business, this is for fun.' "[18] The equation of penis and gun provides the most obvious link between (often insecure) "masculinity" and violence, as John Milfull has noted in his article on fascism as a "compensation for male inadequacies," aptly named "My Sex the Revolver."[19]

In many locales, particularly in the United States, the possession of a gun in good working order has long been as much associated with manhood as has the possession of properly functioning male sexual organs. The National Rifle Association's absolutist position against any sort of gun control can be understood only when the link between guns and the perception of manhood is taken into account. What gun control means to many NRA members is emasculation. That word is always used to mean the taking away of power; it is a clear indication that power and dominance have long been associated with male sexuality.

A seeming problem with the gun-as-penis analogy is that the natural device shoots life, but the artificial one shoots death. This paradox dissolves, however, if it is realized that the penile function for which the gun is substituting is not that of participating in the creation of life. This analogy is, instead, a good demonstration of the symbolic link that many men make between sexual intercourse and domination. If guns are metaphorical penises—cylindrically shaped devices that shoot—then using a gun on a man to subordinate him is analogous to symbolic mounting by primates. More striking is the similarity between threatening a man with a gun (or a whole country with massive firepower of all sorts) and the primate's display of his sexual organ as a means of intimidating and subordinating other males.

Men who have difficulty with their natural equipment are sometimes tempted to use mechanical guns to dominate others. An artificial potency can be used to subordinate men (and women) when a man's real organs do not permit him either to love or dominate a woman. This is a central theme in Warren Beatty's 1967 film, *Bonnie and Clyde*. Bonnie Parker is portrayed as being fascinated with guns. Clyde Barrow is very proud of his artificial guns, but his biological male "gun" will not fire. Bonnie always gets hot when there is shooting, and all his gunpower gives Clyde the appearance of great potency. But it is illusory. It is only when Bonnie "makes him somebody" by publishing a poem about his exploits that Clyde feels he has become a man and is finally able to perform sexually.

A Stiff Arm Means a Stiff . . .

Sexually linked motivations have been evident in men engaging in war since the earliest times. Adolf Hitler presents a remarkable example of a man whose sexual insecurity may have played an important role in leading him to lust after power, desire to dominate others, and seek war.* A 1945 Soviet autopsy on a body later confirmed by dental records to be that of Hitler showed that the Nazi dictator had only one testicle.[20] Some have contended that this may have been a primary source of his insecurity. From 1919 onward, Hitler carried a Walther pistol in a special pocket he had sewn into all his trousers. This enabled him to "feel its barrel pressed reassuringly against his thigh."[21] The Führer's fear of sexual inadequacy presumably played a part in his decision to take injections that included an extract from bull testicles.[22] Certainly the stiff-arm Nazi salute was a symbol of sexual potency. Hitler was known to brag in his younger days that his ability to hold his arm erect proved his masculine power.[23] (That Hitler as dictator of Germany often returned the stiff arm salute to him with a limp wave of his arm may be meaningful.)

Hitler's case is one of the most excessive in history. But male leaders who were far more mainstream than he was have allowed sexual thinking to influence their military decisions. President Kennedy's 1962 confrontation with Nikita Khrushchev over the latter's placing of Soviet missiles in Cuba is an exemplary case of a who-will-mount-whom contest. Kennedy had failed to keep up his support for the Bay of Pigs invasion of Cuba in April of 1961. Less than two months later Khrushchev had tried to dominate the younger Kennedy at their meeting in Vienna.[†] All of this seemed to challenge Kennedy's manhood. Now would he allow the Soviet dictator to stick missiles in the American President's "backyard"? Given the phallic shape of the missiles, the symbolic mounting that this act would constitute is apparent.

"He's Like God, Fucking Anybody He Wants To"

Many sexually insecure males try to develop reputations as "studs" who "conquer" many women. Several of the sons of Joseph P. Kennedy (as well as the

---

*This is not to suggest that Hitler's monumental evil can be "explained" in some simple way by his insecurity about his manhood, or that his quest for domination was merely a more extreme version of that found in other political leaders discussed in this chapter. What I *am* saying is that it is highly likely that sexual torment contributed to a significant degree to the making of the monster that Hitler became.

†That meeting was aptly described, in a telling phrase often used for such situations, as one at which the two leaders could "take each other's measure" [Arthur S. Link, *American Epoch: A History of the United States since the 1890's* (New York: Knopf, 1966), p. 877].

Hitler's Stiff-Arm Salute
had obvious phallic symbolism. His arm was
one appendage that he could get to rise up. His
sexual insecurities appear to have played an
important part in the mix of motivations that
produced one of the twentieth century's most
evil men. (Hulton-Deutsch Collection/Corbis)

father himself) come to mind as examples of males who have sought to "prove themselves" by treating women as playthings to be "had." Far from contradicting the idea that such men seek power over other men because of their sexual insecurity, this sort of behavior is based on the same motivation. When sexual relations with women are seen as conquests ("scoring"), they are fucking, not loving, and are scarcely different from the power-oriented symbolic mounting of males. And, as we have discussed, to men who view women as property, fucking another man's woman shows dominance over him as well as her.

John F. Kennedy's sexual exploits have become legendary in the years since his death. Washington insiders referred to him as "Mattress Jack."[24] "It was a revolving door over there [at the White House]," a member of the Kennedy Administration recalled. "A woman had to fight to get in that line."[25] While he was president, Kennedy apparently had sexual liaisons almost every day, with literally scores of women,[26] sometimes more than one in the same night—indeed, sometimes with two at the same time. "He loved threesomes—himself and two girls," one of his lovers* said. Many names of Kennedy's women have become widely known. "More alarming," as historian James N. Giglio has rightly said, "Kennedy occasionally had affairs with casual acquaintances and virtual strangers . . . as the result of solicitations of friends and aides."[27]

He seems to have been intent on increasing the risk he was taking. "The sheer number of Kennedy's sexual partners, and the recklessness of his use of them, escalated throughout his presidency," as journalist Seymour Hersh has noted.[28] He "reveled in personal excess and recklessness."[29]

Our concern here is not with yet another recapitulation of Kennedy's notorious behavior, but with how it may fit into the larger pattern of thought and action of men who are insecure about their manhood and seek power over others, often including the reassurance of fucking† as many women as possible.¶

The motivations behind Kennedy's behavior appear to have been multiple. It is obvious that he held women in low regard. Political scientist Barbara Ward correctly concluded that Kennedy "had little sympathy for the trained, intelligent woman."[30] "He didn't have any value for women, except for a particular purpose," Jewel Reed, the wife of one of Kennedy's Navy buddies, has said.[31] An unmistakable reflection of the fact that he was fucking, not loving, the women he collected was that he frequently could not remember their names, even when he wanted to "have" them again. "You, of course, as a young girl were of no importance whatsoever. Jack always called you kid, because he couldn't remember women's names," writer Gloria Emerson has said.[32] "I was just another girl. There was a compartment for girls, and once you were in the sex compartment, you weren't a person anymore," one of the women with whom JFK had an extended affair recalls.[33] Kennedy himself summed up his attitude toward women as anonymous playthings who existed

---

*This euphemism may be an appropriate term for how many of the women felt toward Kennedy. Surely, however, it would be entirely inaccurate to call him a lover of most of the women with whom he "slept."

†This is plainly the appropriate term here, since such men clearly do not love the women.

¶He was also quite willing to demonstrate his manly power by figuratively fucking men who opposed him. One example of Kennedy's use of verbal mounting came when he said he would retaliate against a man who tried to expose Kennedy's philandering. "I'm going to give it to him up to there," he said, indicating his neck. Later, when he was asked to name the same man as an ambassador, Kennedy said: "I'm going to fuck him. I'm going to send him to one of those boogie republics in central Africa." [Seymour M. Hersh, The *Dark Side of Camelot* (Boston: Little, Brown, 1997), p. 10].

for his amusement when he boasted in a note he wrote* on his 1960 campaign plane, the *Caroline:* "I got into the blonde last night."[34]

This attitude and behavior toward women is very different from and much more troubling than that of the powerful man who has a long-term relationship with a mistress, as such leaders as Franklin D. Roosevelt and Dwight Eisenhower did. Such a man may—in most cases probably does—have high regard for the other woman as a person. He loves her. Love plays no part in the Kennedy modus operandi. The other women are not seen as persons at all, much less highly regarded ones.

Kennedy's attitude toward women is clear from his actions and statements. The important question is why he felt as he did.

As is so often the case with men who seek power, Kennedy's concern was almost entirely with proving his own manhood to himself and to other men (especially his father). Women were merely a means to that end. "Kennedy's most significant attachments were not to women, but to men," one of his mistresses has said in what appears to be a very accurate assessment.[35] Like family friend Joe McCarthy, Kennedy was intent on being a "man's man." Fucking was about conquest, a modern version of the hunt. Kennedy liked to chase women with male friends he insisted accompany him on his expeditions.[†] Women were the animals to be pursued and "shot": *Vidi, vici, veni.* He had photographs taken of many of "his women," naked in bed, sometimes with him, and framed by a distinguished Washington gallery.[36] These pictures were his hunting trophies, which he could show to other men to impress them with what a powerful man he was and could admire himself, reassuring himself that he was a real man.

"The women . . . were symbols and rewards of aggressive privilege," as Kennedy biographer Richard Reeves has said.[37] The male secretary to Kennedy's Cabinet captured the effect that Kennedy's sexual adventures had on the men around him: "And he's like God, fucking anybody he wants to anytime he feels like it."[38]

I do not think that that's an accurate portrayal of God, but it certainly sounds like a silverback gorilla. The following description nicely states John F. Kennedy's charisma: "He throve on adoration and surrounded himself with starstruck friends and colleagues. Women swooned. Men stood in awe of his

---

*His voice had given out from extensive speaking while campaigning.

†This form of male bonding by going out together on woman-hunting expeditions is a Kennedy family tradition that is passed down from generation to generation, as was evident in a story that emerged in William Kennedy Smith's 1991 rape trial. Smith said that his uncle, Senator Edward M. Kennedy, then nearly sixty years of age, had awakened him to join him in a quest for women they could bed.

easy success with women, and were grateful for his attentions to them."[39] Kennedy's power over men was extraordinary. The men around him, those David Halberstam dubbed "the best and the brightest," were subservient to the leader. They got "tangled up in competing for his favor and his time. They wanted to hang out" with Kennedy.[40]

"He didn't have to lift a finger to attract women," Gloria Emerson remembers, "they were drawn to him in the battalions, by the brigades."[41] Many women, in short, "presented" to Kennedy much the way female primates of other species do to the dominant males.

John Kennedy is one of the most obvious examples of a human version of the dominant male primate. Even decades after his death and after numerous revelations about his misbehavior, people still are enthralled by him. In a 1999 poll in the United States, Kennedy received a plurality of votes as "the greatest historical figure of the century" and, even more remarkable, he was named by the highest number of Americans as the greatest figure in politics or government in the world in the last thousand years![42] The thousand days of the Kennedy administration have somehow come to be seen as the greatest time in a thousand years.

The realization that Kennedy was much like a silverback gorilla is important, but biohistory only begins with the connections between human and animal behavior. We must avoid simplistic "explanations" that amount to biological determinism. Apparently an innate proclivity leads many women to

Much As Many Women Did with J.F.K. . . .
. . . females of other primate species, such as this macaque, "present" themselves to a dominant male to indicate their desire for intercourse with him. Kennedy was one of the clearest examples of a human equivalent of the Alpha male of a primate band. (Ernesto Rodriguez Luna)

be attracted to such a male and to be eager to mate with him. Similarly, there is a biological predisposition in men that inclines many of them to be attracted to and willing to defer to such a male, so that they can be part of his band. The similarities between these behavior patterns and those in some other primate species is undeniable. But while humans are like other primates in some ways, we are a distinct species. And two very important points we have already encountered counsel caution in going too far with the silverback analogy: First, *Homo sapiens* has thrived on diverse behavior patterns, so what attracts some females and males may well repel others. Second, humans seem to be evolving toward long-term pair bonding and away from the winner-take-all-the-females sort of pattern that is more the norm for gorillas. This trend suggests that the behavior exemplified by Kennedy is a carryover of prehuman practices. The behavior cannot yet be classified as vestigial, however, because both men and women obviously still have, to varying degrees, a tendency to respond favorably to the man who exhibits these Alpha characteristics.

How this all plays out in human history depends on many other factors. What causes some men to strive for the power associated with the position of dominant male? Are some men simply born to be such powerful leaders? Are those who have the obsession to attain a position of dominance truly the great specimens of masculinity? Or are they often those who are driven by insecurity and seek dominance as a means of compensation, a way to calm their self-doubt?

Some of the answers to these questions may begin to emerge from an examination of Kennedy's background and the similarities between his experience and problems and those of other leaders discussed in this chapter.

There are more than a few hints of uncertain masculinity in what we know about the Kennedy men. The very practice of collecting women is often a sign of insecurity. Other small indications exist that Kennedy may have been concerned about showing himself to be notawoman. He did not like to be photographed without a shirt because he didn't want what he called his "Fitzgerald breasts" (which he thought were too large for a man) to be seen.[43] (The similarity to Teddy Roosevelt's horror at the idea of being photographed in an "effete" tennis outfit should be noted.) And Kennedy was extremely sensitive to the slightest suggestion of any association with homosexuality. The president was outraged at a *Time* magazine story that he had posed for a photograph for the cover of *Gentlemen's Quarterly*, which was said to be a favorite of homosexual men. Robert Kennedy put it bluntly when he called GQ "a fag rag."[44] It may also be significant that on some occasions John Kennedy's chosen ménage à trois partners included another man, his friend Congressman Torby Macdonald, and one woman.[45]

Two factors appear to stand out above others in shaping Jack Kennedy and producing the insecurity he spent his life trying to subdue: his relationship with his parents and the serious, near fatal illnesses through which he suffered as a child and which continued to plague him as an adult. Both indicate that he bore the burden of insecurities about manhood similar to those that bedeviled Theodore Roosevelt.

Joseph P. Kennedy insisted that his sons be real men. "And he wanted them to be number one. . . . I remembered how intensely he had focused on winning," Jewel Reed said.[46] "Jack was always striving to be strong for his father; to finish first, to shape his life in ways that would please Joe," as Seymour Hersh has put it.[47] A major part of the proper "real man" lifestyle that Joe Kennedy taught his sons (and role-modeled for them) was to "sleep with any woman they could."[48] Once when Joe was in his mid-sixties, he came into his Palm Beach home with a girl of seventeen or eighteen while Rose was entertaining then-Senate Majority Leader Lyndon Johnson, his wife, Lady Bird, and Johnson's aide Bobby Baker. The senior Kennedy took the girl upstairs and proceeded to engage in loud intercourse with her while his own wife and the Johnsons and Baker were certain to hear what was happening.[49]

J.F.K. was *"never able to stand up* to his father."[50] Making himself stand up for an excessive number of women, as his father did, was likely one way that he sought to prove he was a man worthy of his father. But it was not entirely clear that Joe Kennedy's model really was one of manhood. Like Theodore Roosevelt's father, Joe Kennedy had avoided active duty in war (in his case, World War I). Later, the senior Kennedy had been "ridiculed for his perceived cowardice during the intensified Luftwaffe bombing of London in 1940, when he chose to spend his nights at a country estate well away from the targeted city centers."[51] So his son Jack had further reason to feel the need to prove his manhood, as he did in World War II in a way his father never did and as he thought he was by, like his father, bedding every attractive woman that he could lay hands on.

Jack Kennedy seems to have been bitter toward his mother, and it is plausible that a major reason for the contempt with which he regarded women was that he blamed his mother for letting his father mistreat her and dominate him and the other children.[52]

Adding to the insecurity that threatened Jack Kennedy was his physical condition. He had been gravely ill both as a child and an adult, to the point where he had been administered the last rites on at least four occasions.[53] "He was heartily ashamed" of his illnesses, according to Henry James, a Kennedy friend since 1940. "They were a mark of effeminacy, of weakness, which he wouldn't acknowledge. I think all that macho stuff was compensation—all that chasing after women—compensation for something that he hadn't got."[54] What Jack Kennedy said about his obsession with always having a deep suntan—"It gives me confidence. . . . It makes me feel strong, healthy, attractive"—applies as well to his use of women.[55]

Similar concern about their manliness and their very survival probably produced the corresponding need in Theodore Roosevelt and John Kennedy to always be active and not to be left too much to their own thoughts. "He couldn't stand solitude; he couldn't stand being alone," Under Secretary of State George Ball said of Kennedy. "I think that had something to do with why those tarts were around."[56] One of his long-time lovers said Kennedy "wanted to fill his life 'with adrenaline.' " "What are we going to do that's exciting?" he would ask. "What will he do that will keep his attention from being pulled into darker events or darker feelings? When you want excitement," she said, "when you want to be occupied and pulled out of yourself, you're saying in some way that you don't have to mull over things that are painful, things that could be very uncomfortable."[57] This is much the same fear that Teddy Roosevelt expressed when he said, "Get action, do things; be sane."[58]

John F. Kennedy got plenty of the action he needed to feel alive and sane. He "did" *things,* which is what he apparently considered most women to be, very often. There can be little doubt that Kennedy was an exponent of the I-fuck-therefore-I-am philosophy. "If I don't have a woman for three days, I get terrible headaches," the president told an astonished British Prime Minister Harold Macmillan in 1961.[59]

"Has Ho Chi Minh Got Anything Like That?"

Lyndon Johnson and the Kennedys never got along. Johnson took some satisfaction in his belief that FBI Director J. Edgar Hoover had evidence of Jack Kennedy's sexual adventures. "J. Edgar Hoover has Jack Kennedy by the balls," Johnson remarked in language that was as typical of him as it is suggestive of his associations of sex and power.[60] Their backgrounds were drastically different in terms of geography, class, education, and culture. Yet Johnson appears to have been bedeviled by some of the same sort of sexual insecurities that shaped Kennedy. "Why, I had more women by accident than he ever had by design," Johnson was fond of bragging if someone mentioned Kennedy's philandering.[61] It seems clear that this was not true, but not for the lack of trying on Johnson's part.

LBJ is, in fact, a prime example of a man whose desires to "have" women and dominate men and whose susceptibility to being drawn into military adventures were clearly related to sexual insecurities and the notawoman definition of man. Johnson's brother recalled that when the future president was in college he was in the habit of coming out of the shower into another room, holding his penis and saying: "Well, I've gotta take ol' Jumbo here and give him some exercise. I wonder who I'll fuck tonight."[62] (The similarity of these words to some of the chronologically later song lyrics quoted previously is evident.)

One of Johnson's biographers has written of this politician's need to "try to dominate people, to get them to defer to his opinion, to get his way with them by any and every means."[63] It should be noticed how similar "getting his way with" other men sounds to a man "having his way with" a woman. Indeed the latter euphemism for intercourse has become ubiquitous in referring to men, sports teams, and military forces (or their commanders-in-chief) that decisively defeat their opponents.

What Lyndon Johnson always seemed most to desire was that others would personally acknowledge his power—and their dependence upon him. While he was in college he gained great influence over which students received jobs from the deans. All he insisted upon was that students *ask* him for his help. He demanded, in the words of biographer Robert Caro, "the acknowledgment— the deferential, face-to-face acknowledgment—that he had the power."[64] What Johnson sought can readily be seen as the human equivalent of a sign of submission that many male animals give by assuming the position of a receptive female. "His competitiveness and need to be top dog were at the core of his being," biographer Robert Dallek has written.[65] Johnson desperately wanted to be "king of the hill," the dominant male—not, it seems, because he so clearly was one, but because he was in constant dread that he was not. "No amount of success or personal gain could salve his ego or ease his need for deference," Dallek has concluded.[66]

Dallek describes Johnson's childhood as "an object lesson in the formation of a narcissistic personality."[67] Johnson is reported by another biographer to have associated from an early age strength and power with males and weakness with females to a considerably greater degree than is the cultural norm. "He loved his mother and loved being close to her, but he feared he was becoming a sissy," Doris Kearns has written. Johnson equated "femininity, intellectuality, and paralysis," and so felt "compulsions to move, keep control, stay in charge."[68] (As with Theodore Roosevelt, one can almost hear Johnson's inner voice saying, *I am a man, not a woman; I am a man; I am not a woman, notawoman!*)

"For every politician who chases a skirt," Johnson said, "there are ten who seek the love of millions." This was an insightful statement, but the two motivations are not mutually exclusive. In fact, they usually go hand-in-hand, as they did in his case. When the insecurity that drives a man to desire the love of millions is sexual, "chasing skirts" is another way to try to ease the self-doubt.

Johnson hated being vice president. In the position he was totally powerless (and therefore, as he saw it, feminine—his greatest fear throughout his life) and subordinate to Kennedy. Indeed, to someone who thought the way Johnson did, being vice president was playing the role of a woman to the president's dominant man. The vice president's constitutional duty, as it were, was to "assume the position" before the president, to "present" to the Number One Male. "Sexual conquests," Dallek points out, "gave [Johnson] temporary respites from feeling unwanted, unloved, and unattended."[69] He took such respites often while he suffered through his vice presidency. They helped him make the case to himself that he was notawoman, even while he was required to be submissive to the president. Reporters referred to Johnson's office in the Senate during those years as "the nooky room," where he carried on simultaneous affairs with several different women. The purpose his conquests of women served for Johnson is further demonstrated by the fact that he flaunted them.[70]

Johnson's insecurities and the sexual associations he made with them were of great importance not only in his never-ending quest for power and dominance, but in his involvement in the Vietnam War. "More than a little insecure himself," Halberstam has said of Johnson, "he very much wanted to be seen as a man; it was a conscious thing."[71] This personal need to prove his manhood played a large role in Johnson's getting into a war that he knew was almost certain to prove disastrous for his country and himself. Johnson indicated this awareness in what he said to Sen. Richard Russell in a June 1964 telephone conversation. The president told Russell of comments a friend from Texas had made to him when Johnson raised the possibility of withdrawing before the United States got more deeply involved: "Goddamn, there's not anything that'll destroy you as quick as *pulling out.* . . . They'll forgive you anything except *being weak.*" Johnson showed that he made the sexual associations implicit in the words I italicized when he went on to say to Russell: "We've got to conduct ourselves like men."[72] Johnson wanted to pull out, but that would not be manly and his political opponents would call him weak. Like the fictional Jim Stark and Theodore Roosevelt (who might justly be classified as semifictional), Johnson could not stand being called a chicken—a woman. His sexual insecurity is certainly not the only reason that tens of thousands of Americans and hundreds of thousands of Vietnamese died in the war, but it played a major role.

When his vice president, Hubert Humphrey, began to have doubts about the wisdom of the war, Johnson said Humphrey "wasn't a real man, he cried as easily as a woman."[73] On another occasion, hearing that a man in his administration was "going soft" on the war, Johnson sneered: "Hell, he has to squat to piss."[74] Implicit in this sort of statement is a desperate attempt at self-reassurance: *He's a woman. Not me! I'm notawoman!*

In 1967 the president astounded several top aides and Interior Secretary Stewart Udall by launching into a tirade about *his* war. Who the hell was Ho Chi Minh to think "he could push America around"? Then Johnson showed in the most unmistakable manner imaginable just what the war meant to him—

and it was literally what Carlin insists that all war is about: "the bigger dick foreign policy theory" or, more politely, male penis envy (which, I would argue, is actually a displacement of womb envy). The president unzipped his pants, pulled out the member that he had named (presumably in an attempt to calm his doubts) "ol' Jumbo," and proclaimed: "Has Ho Chi Minh got anything like that?"[75]

Johnson made a habit of exhibiting his sex organs for others to see, taking a special delight in doing so before "gentlemen of culture."[76] Surely Johnson was an outlandish case, but many of the men who directed American policy in Vietnam had similar motivations. "They wanted," as Halberstam has put it, "to show who had bigger balls."[77] Johnson's notion of what it means to be a "big man" is one that has been widely shared by men, probably throughout history—and before. Genital display is a common means of symbolizing dominance among male primates.

All the President's Notwomen

Richard Nixon was in many respects a different sort of man from both John Kennedy and Lyndon Johnson. Despite the fact that Nixon was widely hated and his enemies searched for every instance of wrongdoing on his part, no one ever made a serious charge that he was a "womanizer." Nixon was, biographer Stephen Ambrose says, "simply uninterested in women, indeed uncomfortable around them. He had . . . no ability to flirt, no interest in making sexual conquests."[78] In terms of relations with females, Dick Nixon seems almost the antithesis of a dominant male. Yet the connections Nixon made between sex and power were very similar to those that seem to have driven his two immediate predecessors in the White House. He shared their need to calm his inner demons by reaching the top and being a man's man. Like Kennedy and Johnson, Nixon sought dominance over other men; women seem to have been such a threat to his masculinity that he simply tried to avoid them.

Nixon frequently spoke of his fear of the United States becoming "impotent." He and his advisers worried that either the nation or the president might be turned into a "pitiful, helpless giant."[79] Such fears were nothing new in the Vietnam era. In the period after World War II, for example, Time-Life magnate Henry Luce warned that the if the United States failed to use its power and virility to dominate the world, the nation would be infected by "the virus of isolationist sterility" and have to "confess a pitiful impotence."[80]

As the public learned when transcripts of some of the tape recordings that he had clandestinely had made were released, Nixon was given to the use of sexual vulgarity, presumably in large part to demonstrate his manhood. He was a great fan of Patton, with all that implies. And Nixon's "point man," Vice

President Spiro Agnew, often mouthed speeches in which, echoing the associations made by Theodore Roosevelt, he attacked opponents of the Vietnam War as "ideological eunuchs" and "effete intellectual snobs."[81] The linking of intellectuals with femininity (or lack of manliness) in the speeches prepared for Agnew was exactly the same as that which tormented both Theodore Roosevelt and Lyndon Johnson.

Those who became involved with Nixon in the Watergate scandal often employed verbal mounting and spoke of power and dominance in sexual terms. In a memorable 1971 memo, presidential counsel John Dean talked of using federal agencies "to screw our political enemies."[82] Then there was (and is) G. Gordon Liddy, a virtual caricature of the believer in the power-is-sex creed (although hardly more so than Lyndon Johnson). More than two decades later, Liddy had not changed. As his electronic mail address in the 1990s, he chose a version of the penis-as-gun analogy: potent357@aol. On one of his radio programs in 1995, Liddy proclaimed: "Virile, potent Republican men are born to impregnate nubile, fertile Democratic women. That's just the way it is."[83] Liddy has been well described as someone who "wanted to go back to the days when *men were men* and life was simpler." He is classic dualistic thinker: "He hates the other side."[84] This pseudospeciation was the basic approach of the Nixon administration. Pseudosexing went right along with it. Even the activities that Liddy and his fellow Nixon burglars engaged in were referred to in such sexual terms as *entries, penetrations,* and breaking into supposedly "impregnable" buildings and safes.[85] (In fact, one of the burglars, Bernard Barker, used the code name "Macho.") According to his comrade, E. Howard Hunt, engaging in any of these power-oriented secret affairs made Liddy "horny." Hunt has said that whenever they got on a plane to travel to the site of one of their surreptitious entries, the first thing Liddy would ask was: "Can you get me laid?"[86]

Vietnam and the Fear of National Impotence

The outcome of the Vietnam War left many Americans with a fear of national impotence. Some of the American troops in Vietnam had expressed greater concern that they would suffer what they called "the Wound"—the loss of their testicles—than that they would die. The latter, many said, was a preferable fate. In a real sense the whole country suffered "the Wound" in Vietnam. That's what the so-called Vietnam Syndrome was about—the fear of national castration or impotence.

The sexual symbolism ingrained in international relations and wars was perfectly captured in a comment Senator Barry Goldwater made about the May 1975 American attack on Cambodia in retaliation for the seizure of an

American vessel, the *Mayaguez*. "It was wonderful," Goldwater chortled. "It shows we've still got balls in this country."[87] The reason for the need Goldwater and many others perceived to demonstrate that the nation's gonads were still functioning was plain: the United States had made its final, hasty *withdrawal* from Vietnam a few weeks before. To put it in the crude terms in which so many political leaders seem to think, our big stick did not appear to be so big any more—and it was limp. But the *Mayaguez* affair was not much of a mounting for a country or its leaders who were afraid, to again put it in the vulgar manner in which they often seem to think, that they "couldn't get it up anymore." It was that dread of national impotence that was most responsible for Ronald Reagan's 1980 victory over Jimmy Carter. That year's election was held in the shadow of Carter's apparent inability to show the Iranians who's boss with the hostage situation at the American Embassy in Tehran. Carter had failed symbolically to mount the Ayatollah Khomeini—indeed, he had allowed himself in effect to be mounted by the Shiite cleric.

The fear of impotence was not fully mollified by the spending of some two trillion dollars on the military in the Reagan years. Impotence, after all, can be caused by psychological factors, even when a man's equipment is in top working order. Although President Reagan insisted that his 1984 "invasion" of Grenada showed that "Americans are now standing tall and firm" and he was praised for "stiffening our foreign policy,"[88] that skirmish was hardly enough proof of national virility to dissipate the fear that America was still not all that stiff. In fact that little exercise corresponded to the *Mayaguez* raid. It came in the wake of another withdrawal after a disaster, that of American Marines from Lebanon after 241 of them had been killed in a car bomb attack on their quarters. The Grenada operation was more successful in diverting attention from the preceding debacle than the Cambodian incident had been, but it provided little reassurance about the size or hardness of America's stick.

Both the Cambodia and Grenada affairs amounted more to symbolic masturbation than symbolic mounting.

Kicking Saddam Hussein's Ass

The fear of impotence was still present when George Bush became president. It is likely that removal of that fear was one of the reasons that he wanted to enter a war with Iraq. A careful examination of his actions before Iraq's invasion of Kuwait and during the half year between that point and the conclusion of the war leaves little doubt that Bush sought more than the liberation of Kuwait. What he wanted was a *war* to liberate Kuwait. (Or, more accurately, a war to liberate the United States from its insecurity over its virility.) "I'm not going to compromise *one* iota," Bush proudly said of dealing with Saddam

Hussein in November 1990.[89] *(Real [insecure] men—which is to say real not-women—don't compromise.)* It was arguable that Kuwait might have been liberated from Iraq without a war, but Bush apparently believed that the United States could not have been liberated from its fears of impotence without a war.

Yet this is not a sufficient explanation for President Bush's motivations. In light of what we have seen about the connections between sexual insecurity, the drive for power, and aggressiveness in other men who have reached the pinnacle of political power, it is fair to wonder whether George Bush had similar personal insecurities in this regard. Certainly he personalized the dispute with Iraq to an extraordinary degree, making it into a gladiatorial combat between himself and Saddam Hussein. A friend suggested to me during the buildup toward war that Bush was "measuring penises with the guy." George Carlin's interpretation after the fact was the same: "That whole thing in the Persian Gulf was nothing more than a prick-waving dick fight. In this particular case, Saddam Hussein had questioned the size of George Bush's dick." Carlin went on to charge that Bush "has to act out his manhood fantasies by sending other people's children to die."[90] At this point in the routine, many people stop laughing and realize that there are serious issues in what the comedian has been saying.

Is Carlin's characterization justified?

There are many indications that the demons of sexual insecurity that George Bush sought to expel through the medium of a splendid little war were personal as well as national. It is worth remembering that he often said that Teddy Roosevelt was the president he most wanted to emulate.

The problem was not so much a matter of Saddam Hussein questioning the size of George Bush's sexual organ, as it was one of Bush's fear that many Americans were questioning his manliness.

Bush's greatest political liability was what the 1987 *Newsweek* cover story that so troubled him termed the "Wimp Factor." He was said to suffer "from a potentially crippling handicap, a perception that he is not strong and forceful enough for the challenges of the Oval Office. That he is, in a single, mean word, a wimp."[91] (Again, it should be plain that to call a man a wimp is simply a more acceptable way to call him a pussy or cunt.) There can be no doubt, particularly in light of his postwar comment on the story, three-and-a-half years after it appeared, that these charges disturbed Bush greatly. And *Newsweek* was hardly alone. In *Doonesbury,* Garry Trudeau had begun calling Bush a wimp in 1987. Nationally syndicated cartoonist Pat Oliphant added to what must have been Bush's torment on this matter by persistently portraying him carrying a purse over his shoulder, often wearing high heels and a dress or skirt. "Them's fightin' *images.*" The purse-over-the-shoulder depiction is one that plainly indicates that being a real man is seen as being notawoman.

Are You *Sure* You're Notawoman, George?
Cartoonist Pat Oliphant's persistent depiction of George Bush carrying a purse, wearing a skirt and high heels was one among many direct challenges to his manhood. He was frequently referred to—even in a *Newsweek* cover story—as a wimp. Garry Trudeau said Bush had "placed his manhood in a blind trust." Such accusations obviously feed a man's self-doubt. As president, Bush sought a way to prove—at least as much to himself as to his critics—that he was notawoman. (Universal Press Syndicate)

Bush may have sought a fight to demonstrate his manhood, as well as America's, by so humiliating a foreign leader as to symbolically mount him—or worse.

Bush had already had his own little symbolic mounting when he sent American forces into Panama to depose and capture the nation's "strongman" leader, Manuel Noriega in 1990. Some in the media referred to this small event as Bush's "initiation rite," in which he had demonstrated his "willingness to shed blood."[92] The Panama affair, it appears, was symbolic male menstruation.

But a man who had been so castigated as womanly needed to show more than a willingness to shed enough blood to signify that he had reached puberty. Throughout the months preceding the war with Iraq, President Bush spoke of "kicking Saddam Hussein's ass." This now-ubiquitous terminology is another form of verbal mounting, but it differs a bit from the other types. The sexual connotations were clear enough when Bush had previously used this language—in a stage whisper the day after his 1984 vice presidential debate with Geraldine Ferraro, when he said, "We tried to kick a little ass last night." This incident is doubly interesting. Since it is apparent that it was intended to be overheard, but with the cover (for *his* "ass") that he had supposedly not meant it to become public ("Whoops, oh God, he heard me. Turn that thing off"), the conclusion is warranted that Bush was trying to use this language to show his manliness six years before he said the same thing about Saddam Hussein. Bush subsequently dismissed the 1984 ass-kicking statement as just "an old Texas football expression,"[93] a clear and almost pathetic attempt to associate himself with that "manly" game. (Bush, of course, was a Yale baseball player, not a Texas football player.)

The second interesting feature of the ass-kicking comment about Ferraro is that it was not true. It was anything but clear in the eyes of most observers that Bush had "come out on top" in that debate. He was accurately described as having taken "off like the caffeine-crazed businessman in a Federal Express ad."[94] For a man not to come out on top when his opponent is a woman is the ultimate challenge to his manhood: letting a woman get on top of him.* After that and all the wimp accusations, not even winning the presidency of the United States would be enough to reassure George Bush of his manhood—to prove that he was notawoman. He would have to find a man's ass to kick. In the second year of his presidency, a suitable one presented itself.

But just how does the phrase "kick ass" fit into the practice of verbal mounting? The image is one of ultimate humiliation. It implies that the opponent has been defeated and he has been obliged to assume the position of the female to show his submission and subordination. When he presents his posterior to the dominant male, however, the latter refuses even to mount him, instead showing the ultimate disrespect of kicking the ass that is proffered to him for simulated intercourse.

That seems to be what George Bush had in mind for Saddam Hussein. If so, it must have been especially painful for him to see the Iraqi dictator (who obviously has extreme sexual violence motivations himself) still in power after Bush left office.

The Second Time as Farce

"Hegel remarks somewhere that all facts and personages of great importance in world history occur, as it were, twice." Karl Marx wrote, "He forgot to add: the first time as tragedy, the second as farce."[95] Marx's reference was to

---

*There was a time not very long ago when several American states had laws—*man*made laws—in their statutes prohibiting the reality on which this metaphor is based. It was actually written into law that, even for married couples, only man-on-top copulation was legal.

Napoleon and Louis Napoleon. But the pudding that really provides the proof of Marx's aphorism is Bill Clinton as the second coming of Jack Kennedy.

During the scandal that led to Clinton's impeachment, there was speculation that he may suffer from something called "sex addiction." This sounds suspiciously like an attempt to classify him as the victim. A simpler explanation is that, like so many other men who have risen to political power, Clinton suffers from sexual insecurity.

Some commentators asked why someone in a position of such great power risked it all for sex. This may have the question backward.

As we have seen, at the most basic level, what power has been about for many males in species closely related to humans has been the opportunity to "accumulate" females or, more precisely, to maximize the number of their offspring. "Males have evolved to possess strong appetites for power because with extraordinary power males can achieve extraordinary reproduction," anthropologist Richard Wrangham and his co-author Dale Peterson declare in their 1996 book, *Demonic Males*.[96] Power, as Henry Kissinger once sagely observed, is the greatest aphrodisiac. Examples of the accuracy of this maxim are common throughout human history, from King Solomon to John Kennedy. When Hillary Rodham Clinton was upset at seeing her husband go off with a woman at a party for his first inauguration as governor, her friend Susan McDougal repeated to the state's new first lady what the wife of Congressman Jim Guy Tucker had told her about women offering themselves to political leaders: "Betty told me that it doesn't change from the local, to the state, to the federal level. The girls just get prettier."[97] "If a male wins power, he will tend to use it to mate as many females as possible," Wrangham and Peterson observe.[98]

Yet the matter is not so simple. As we have also seen, *Homo sapiens* appears to be a species evolving toward pair bonding, but that evolution is incomplete. Some individuals are farther along this evolutionary path than others, but those who seek great power tend to be those most like Alpha male apes. Most societies, however, have tried to encourage pair bonding through the one-person, one-mate system of marriage.

Apparently, most often it is men who are insecure about their own manhood who attempt to compensate by seeking to achieve power and "score" with large numbers of women. There is reason to believe that Bill Clinton fits the pattern of insecurity encouraging a drive for power and promiscuity. Throughout his life he has been lacking in appropriate male role models. His biological father died before he was born; his stepfather was an alcoholic and a "skirt chaser." Clinton eventually filled this void by adopting President Kennedy as his model of male behavior. Much as Kennedy followed the horrible example of manhood presented by his father, Clinton patterned his lifestyle on that of John Kennedy. Thus the baneful influence of old Joe Kennedy continued to plague the American republic decades after his death.* The principal difference in the reaction to the philandering of the two presidents has been that Clinton's occurred after the women's movement and in an era when reporters were no longer willing to cover up such behavior.

Bill Clinton is the first of the male leaders we have discussed who came of age in the era when women were beginning to be taken seriously as the intellectual equals of men. Outwardly, at least, he is far more comfortable around intelligent, assertive women than any of the other men we have examined in this chapter. Two of the others, Hitler and Nixon, were so uncomfortable around women that they avoided them to a considerable extent. The Kennedy men and Johnson, on the other hand, saw women as inferiors who exist to provide pleasure for men and in no case should be taken seriously. Living in the age he has and being of the political and social persuasion that he has been, Bill Clinton never had the option of ignoring women or denying them a place at the table of policy and power. Yet, when we see what Clinton has done with women in private, it appears that all the good things he says and does for women in general mask the fact that he, like Kennedy, sees women as playthings. He is intellectually committed to the idea of the equality of women (an issue that Kennedy never had to confront), but he is emotionally and physically tied to the belief that women exist to provide him pleasure and to be dominated by him as he tries to calm his insecurities.

It is obvious that the sort of sex (or, as he would have it, "nonsex") Clinton is said to favor, fellatio, will not spread his genes. But it certainly gives him a feeling of power and superiority over women, who serve his desires while literally on their knees before him. It may well be that he was willing to risk his power for this because being in such a position relative to women has been the subconscious objective of his quest for power all along. To the insecure male, power without access to and dominance over women is not worth having. "This is fun," Clinton told Susan McDougal after he was first elected governor. "Women are throwing themselves at me. All the while I was growing up, I was the fat boy in the Big Boy jeans."[99]

That Bill Clinton's worldview is greatly influenced by the longstanding notion that women and everything associated with them should be considered as inferior is evidenced by his fondness for the mounting metaphor. A few

---

*This influence has lived on through others, besides Clinton. A significant portion of a generation of aspiring Democratic politicians patterned themselves after John F. Kennedy. This emulation has sometimes included the pattern of "scoring" with as many women as possible. Gary Hart is an obvious example. See Robert S. McElvaine, "The Kennedy Complex," *New York Times,* September 27, 1987.

examples: In August 1980 the Carter administration reversed itself and announced that all Cuban refugees still housed at locations in other states would be consolidated at a camp in Arkansas. Then-Governor Clinton, already in trouble in his bid for re-election as governor of Arkansas, was outraged. "You're fucking me!" he shouted over the phone at a White House official.[100] After his defeat that November, Clinton said bitterly of President Carter: "The guy screwed me and never tried to make amends."[101] Most strikingly, Clinton spoke to Gennifer Flowers in one of the telephone conversations she taped about a lawsuit that had been brought against him during his 1990 reelection campaign. The lawsuit charged that Clinton had used a slush fund to entertain at least five different mistresses, including Flowers. The conversation took place after Clinton had won another term. "I stuck it up their ass," the governor told Flowers, referring to those who brought the suit. Of his Republican opponent, Clinton said: "I just wanted to make his asshole pucker."[102]

Clinton likes to brag about his conquests of women. Monica Lewinsky recounted to Linda Tripp that the president told Lewinsky that he had deep-seated sexual problems, was congenitally unfaithful to his wife, and had had "hundreds" of affairs—so many that he circled on a calendar the relatively few days on which he had been "good."[103] The quantitative claims appear to have been wishful thinking and the sort of boasting exaggeration that many men would be expected to make to other men. That Clinton made such a claim to a woman is odd. He seems to have been trying to convince himself that he was really a philanderer on Kennedy's level. Bad as he was, and large as were the number of his conquests, however, Clinton does not appear to have been quite in the same league with his role model in the quantity of women with whom he had sex. Yet Clinton's story is in reality very much a tragedy, too. A man of enormous intellect and ability, he never accomplished what he might have. His achievements have been large, but they have been undermined by his weaknesses, which seem clearly to be related to his own particular manifestation of male insecurity. It is, also likely, however, that Clinton would not have reached the places of power that he did had he not been driven by those insecurities. In this sense, Clinton's tragedy is but a variant of the historical dramas in which so many other men unsure of their masculinity have taken the roles of leading man. Indeed, *Clinton,* a tragicomedy in too many acts to count, can be seen as a microcosm of the historical drama as a whole, as it has been so largely fashioned by similarly insecure men intent on proving that they were notwomen for ten thousand years.

The main point that emerges from a look at the manhood anxieties of several men who attained positions of power in the last century is that many problems in history have been at least partly caused by men who have been driven by a terrible need to prove to themselves and others that they are real men. We must be clear about what the original culprit is in this phenomenon. It is the deeply ingrained belief that the sexes are and must be opposite, which is rooted initially in male resentment of female powers that produced the double negative notawoman definition of manhood. This is a misunderstanding of sex as a hierarchical opposition, constructed in order to sooth male anxiety by inverting what troubled males fear is the actual order of power in the sexes. The misunderstanding has been greatly intensified by the seed metaphor and the idea that God is male and so women and all things associated with them are inferior. Both beliefs have led many men to recoil in horror from anything in themselves that seemed to be feminine. The modern image of the world is as a marketplace in which men must "make themselves." Such a viewpoint has exacerbated the inner terror of males who fear that they may not be sufficiently opposite to the other sex to be able to "make it"—and to make themselves.

Men who can accept that the sexes are a continuum, not polar opposites, have no reason to be terrified at any "feminine" feelings or traits that they see in themselves. But that concept is often a difficult one to accept in a cultural milieu built on gender extension.

CHAPTER 15

The "Masculine"/Marketplace Mystique

To Be a Woman or to Be Notawoman

Why can't a woman be
more like a man?

"HENRY HIGGINS"[1]

We find ourselves today in a social environment that is in important respects the inverse of that which emerged in the wake of the invention of agriculture. The intentional production of food brought about a new relationship between resources and people that greatly enhanced one of women's traditional roles. Now, however, improved medicine and diet have allowed us to be so fruitful that our multiplication has virtually filled the earth; hence a return to a K-selected reproductive strategy is in order. This necessity means that one of the roles of women is being devalued (although certainly not as much as the male role of hunting was devalued after the development of agriculture). Much as the depreciation of hunting led to the rise of "prehistoric masculinism," the reduced emphasis on child-bearing has contributed to the rise of modern feminism. A consequence of this alteration in the human condition is that we now must seek new, appropriate roles for *both* women and men. Returning women to their traditional status, as such modern masculinists as Promise Keepers and the Nation of Islam seek to do in their quests to re-establish useful, responsible roles for men, is simply not an option.

As a result of our species' movement back to a K-selected reproductive strategy and a variety of other factors—including the logic of the Marketplace worldview and political democracy that each individual should be seen as equal for certain purposes—women in Western societies in recent decades have obtained a degree of equality. But they have done so largely on men's terms. This was the less difficult route. It required the rejection of two deeply ingrained beliefs—that men and women are very different and that men are superior. But it left unchallenged two other major entries on the list of accepted truths: that difference necessarily means inequality and that masculine ways are superior to feminine ways. The argument became something like this: *Hey, guys, you're right about all that. Don't trouble your dualistic big heads with the concept that things can be both different and equal. And don't worry, your ways of doing things really are superior. It's just that we women can do them your way as well as you can.*

The latter argument has been one that men, at least insecure men, have had a very hard time accepting, with consequences for them to which we shall turn in the next chapter. But if early feminism asked men to abandon their long-cherished faith that *male* is superior to *female,* it at least did not ask them also to give up the perhaps more critical dogma that *masculine* is superior to *feminine.* For their part, women who made this sort of argument escaped the Feminine Mystique by accepting in its stead a Masculine Mystique.[2] (Betty Friedan herself has named something similar to what I am talking about the "feminist mystique."[3]) It could even be argued that the equality women have gained is similar to the peace that is obtained by surrendering. In demanding equality in a male-created system, some women have run up the white flag and gone over to the other side. Many of the apparent victories that women have won have been accompanied by the defeat of the values traditionally associated with their sex. Diana Shaw, the class speaker at the 1980 Harvard commencement, summed up well what was happening: "Contemporary feminism has taught us to reject the values conventionally associated with our sex. We are expected to pursue the male standards of success."[4] The reason this change in values occurred is not hard to find. What have been classified as feminine values are incompatible with the dominant system of the modern Marketplace world, based as it is on dualism, separation, competition, consumption, and limitlessness.

If the masculine ideal has been constructed, as this book argues, on the basis of the reversal of everything associated with women, a woman who adopts the male way thereby strives, as so many men have throughout history, to become notawoman.

The Female Persuasion

Henry Higgins was not alone in the exasperated question he asked about Eliza Dolittle in *My Fair Lady* that stands as this chapter's epigraph. Through most of history men have found occasion to throw up their hands at the different behavior of women. Doubtless the same has been true of women wondering at the odd ways of men. But because men have dominated most cultures, we have heard somewhat less about women's frustrations with men's behavior than the other way around. Whatever one may have thought of the strange characteristics of the other sex, however, through most of history few people of either sex doubted that women and men *are* different.

As the mistaken belief that things cannot be simultaneously equal and different has spread in the later stages of the modern megarevolution, however, some people have asserted that there are *no* innate differences between the sexes. Indeed the word *sex* has become unacceptable in most feminist and academic circles. The word implies that there *is* a biological difference between males and females, and this is one of the issues upon which debate has been virtually closed. *Gender* has replaced *sex* on most educated (and other) lips.[5]

The word *gender* should mean what it sensibly ought to: cultural differences between male and female roles that *include,* but are by no means limited to, biological differences between the sexes. If one could take this interpretation, the concept would, like many another blended or mixed one, be most useful. All too often, however, those who insist upon speaking of gender and not sex take the position that gender is *entirely* a cultural construct. In other words, when it comes to behavior and outlook, there are no biological differences between female and male. All such apparent differences are said to be wholly invented and learned. The old one-liner to the effect, "Sally is of the female persuasion," is now taken seriously in many quarters.

Being female or male, however, is not only a matter of persuasion.

The taboo on using the word *sex* leads to some strange statements. What is to be made, for example, of the following statement about former British Prime Minister Margaret Thatcher: "She has experienced nothing but advantage from her gender"?[6] Her *gender?* The point the writer was making was that Thatcher was able to get ahead in her career because she is a woman. What had this to do with her acculturation? Indeed, the article pointed out the obvious: that Mrs. Thatcher's views were about as far removed from values usually classified as feminine as those of any woman (or man) on the planet. If Margaret Thatcher were feminine—caring and nurturing—she might well have attracted many Conservative Members of Parliament—but as suitors, not as men seeking a party leader.

Similar misuses of *gender* can be found almost daily in the media. One can turn on the radio and hear a respected newscaster reporting that researchers have found that different types of headaches "vary by gender."[7] Really? You can open the paper and read: "Women in India are at monumental risk to gender violence. In India, more than 5,000 women are burned to death each year by in-laws and husbands who want higher dowries for a second wife."[8] *Gen-*

der violence? These humans are killed because they are biologically women, not because they have been made feminine by culture. In the early 1990s the National Collegiate Athletic Association debated a controversial issue it termed "gender equity" in college sports programs. The call was said to be for equal participation in sports by each "gender." But if the issue were actually gender equality, how would a masculine woman athlete, such as Martina Navratilova, be classified? Again it should be obvious that the real concern is with the number of *women* athletes, not the number of *feminine* ones.

When President Clinton nominated Ruth Bader Ginsburg to the United States Supreme Court in 1993, the news media were filled with reports that she had specialized in "gender law" and argued "gender equity" cases before the Court. But the group that she had helped to found within the American Civil Liberties Union was named, correctly, the Women's Rights Project.[9] Ms. Ginsburg had been concerned with discrimination against a sex, not a gender.

The extreme version of gender is a creation of the modern megarevolution. Gender as a purely cultural construction is the ultimate of the Lockean view that experience is the sole determinant of what a person becomes. This position, which was widely accepted in the early years of modern feminism, was stated succinctly by radical feminist filmmaker Bonnie Kreps in 1972: "There shall be no characteristics, behaviour, or roles ascribed to any human being on the basis of sex."[10] "One is not born a woman," Simone de Beauvoir had earlier asserted, "one becomes one."*

Happily, there has in recent years been a trend among some feminists away from this strange notion of sexual congruence.[11] Yet the "same except for different plumbing" position is no straw woman. That contention continues to hold sway in many quarters. A Vatican official reported in 1992, for example, that some American Catholics were pressing the Church to declare "that merely thinking of women as different from men is sinful."[12]

To say that biological sex has no influence on behavior remains fashionable and safe. But both common sense and biological science so clearly indicate that that argument is wrong that one wonders whether those who recite it really believe it.

Why does saying that there are average natural differences in the proclivities of men and women raise so many hackles? One underlying assumption makes the concept of biological differences between the sexes unpalatable: the dualistic belief that difference must entail inequality and so the acceptance of difference will allow the perpetuation of the subordination of women. The

---

*This statement is, to be sure, in substantial measure true. What we think of as a woman is certainly greatly influenced by culture. But people *are* born to be women or men.

oppression of women, Bonnie Kreps once asserted, "is based on the corrupt notion of 'maleness vs. femaleness.' "[13] The key word in that contention is the seemingly innocuous abbreviation for *versus*. As I have argued throughout these pages, maleness and femaleness *are* different, but they are not polar opposites. The fundamental error is the failure to understand that different things can be equal. Many feminists have mistakenly assumed that if there are innate differences, one or the other category—one or the other sex—must always be "on top."

This is just not the case. Different things *can* be equal. In its famous 1954 school desegregation decision, the Supreme Court declared that categories that are "separate" are "inherently unequal," not that *different* categories or things are inherently unequal. The sexes, I reiterate, are not separate; they are just a little different. Women and men are equal, but they are not congruent. The simple truth of this matter can be depicted symbolically:

$$ ♀ = ♂ \; ; ♀ \neq ♂ $$

Feminists have long been divided over the issue of whether women and men are alike or different, and so they continue down to the present. Betty Friedan took Margaret Mead to task for her ambivalence on this question.[14] As Mead's ambiguity on the issue suggests, the division has often been not just between feminists, but within individual feminists. Yet those who see this as a feminist schizophrenia are mistaken; so are the feminists who insist on taking sides on the issue. Their mistake is the product of a more basic error that many in the women's movement have made, an error that will be the major concern of this chapter. This is the fallacious assumption that because men have been dominant throughout recorded history, their ways must be the right ways.

It is, to be sure, true that sexual differentiation (and the resulting roles that were considered proper for women) have been used for at least six thousand years to degrade and subordinate women: to keep them in their place (actually, of course, to keep them in the place to which men had assigned them). But to assume on this basis that all female roles are bad and should be rejected—or that feminine values are inferior and should be repudiated—is to commit a classic dualistic error.

Women in His-story, or Her-story = His-story?

One of the bases for the modern women's movement is that, because of machinery and technology, there is now less reason for a sexual division of labor than there had been assumed to be in earlier times. There is also less reason for a division of values. This meant that the "values gap" was going to be closed. The major question, though, was *how* it would be closed: which sex would move toward the other's values?

"It is obvious," Virginia Woolf wrote, "that the values of women differ very often from the values which have been made by the other sex. . . . [Yet] it is the masculine values that prevail."[15] As Woolf's pronouncement suggests, there has been gender discrimination as well as sex discrimination; both values classified as feminine and women have been discriminated against. But gender bias and sex bias are not the same thing, and most of those who speak today of the former actually mean the latter. Equality between feminine and masculine values is as important as equality between women and men. Women should demand more than just equality; they should also examine the terms upon which "equality" is offered and gained. Are they "masculine" terms or terms of equality of values?

Feminists who adopt the Masculine Mystique (this is only one portion of what has become a feminist movement that is divided along several fault lines) and accept that masculine ways are best are misnamed. The sex they champion is women, but the gender that see as superior is masculine. Logically, then, they should be called masculinists.

The basic philosophy of modern individualism is that each person should be judged on his or her merits. This concept sounds good, but it leaves a critical question unasked: *Whose* merits? Whose scale of measurement is to be used? "Women have been largely man-made," Eva Figes wrote in her 1970 book, *Patriarchal Attitudes.*[16] She meant, presumably, that the concept of what is feminine was a creation of men, and that was substantially, but never completely, true. Women have always been able to exert some power over their own definitions and activities, even within a largely man-made system, much as African-American slaves were able to create a culture of their own and even exercise limited autonomy within a system designed to subordinate them totally.[17] The feminist movement of which Figes's book was an important part sought to help women take over the making of themselves. But if women who started making themselves followed a blueprint that was man-made, they would become different from what men had made them, but they still would not be shaping their own destiny. Historian Gerda Lerner has put this often disregarded issue well: "[Women must] understand that getting 'equal' parts will not make them equal, as long as the script, the props, the stage setting, and the direction are firmly held by men."[18]

If women gain "equality," but only on the basis of accepting the male script, they will not really have succeeded. They will have left intact the fundamental error that has been at the base of so many of our troubles for thousands of years:

the assumption that the male is the "normal human." This would repeat the error of prominent late nineteenth- and early twentieth-century feminist theorist Charlotte Perkins Gilman. In her 1898 classic, *Women and Economics,* Gilman assumed that *humanity* and *femininity* are opposites. All "human progress has been accomplished by men," she flatly declared. *"Man is the human creature."*[19] A better five-word summary of the Masculine Mystique has never been made, by man or woman. Equality for women without equality for feminine values will provide us with more women who are successful when judged by masculine standards. We will see more like the few women whose names used to appear in history books. But do we really need more Cleopatras, Joans of Arc, and Catherines the Great? Or would we be better served by more Francises of Assisi, Albert Schweitzers, Mohandas Gandhis, and Martin Luther Kings—more men who are successful when judged by feminine standards?

Indeed, if men and women were "just the same except for different plumbing," because men have dominated throughout recorded history, it would follow that the script that men have written is the proper one, and their history is the *real* history. The sexual congruence fallacy puts us back to the old belief that women should appear in recorded history only when they do the things men consider important. The logical conclusion of the assumption of congruence would be that real history should become once more almost completely *his*-story, although future history may contain many more "shes" playing significant roles in his-story.

A Third Great Irony in the History of the Sexes?

In the course of our look at the interaction of human nature and the changing social environment during the last ten thousand years, we have seen some great ironies involving the sexes. The invention of agriculture was in all likelihood the doing of women and it established a way of life more oriented toward the nurturing ways that are commonly found to a somewhat greater degree among females than males. The Agricultural Megarevolution, however, ultimately led to a markedly increased subordination of women and a substantial increase in violent conflict as men turned to other purposes innate traits that had lost some of their usefulness.

A second irony involving the sexes developed in the Mobility Megarevolution. "Individualism may be bourgeois," as one radical feminist noted in the 1980s, "but it is precisely the breakdown of a familial orientation and the development of individualism which gave birth to feminism."[20] This is just the irony. Individualism is a phenomenon that is the product of the modern megarevolution and its Marketplace Misconception of the world; it is somewhat more in keeping with the ways and values more commonly found in men than women. Yet its disintegration of the old society finally produced women's liberation along with other forms of liberation.

Once the effects of increasing mobility began to undermine the concept of hierarchy, the movement had to be toward the opposite pole, equality. Throughout the course of the Mobility Megarevolution, the "freeing" of one group of people has led to the discovery that another is bound up in the system of dominance and subordination. Abolitionist Abby Kelly provided a good example of the making of these connections when she said that women "have good cause to be grateful to the slave," because by "striving to strike his irons off, we found most surely, that we were manacled *ourselves.*"[21]

Certainly this movement has been mostly to the good. But it is well to remember that evil often consists of excess—of getting too much of what in moderation is a good thing.

The third great irony in the history of relations between the sexes could turn out to be the triumph of feminine values in a masculine world. The agricultural system, designed by women and based on ways more often found to a greater degree in women, devalued male roles and characteristics more commonly found in men, but eventually produced a triumph of masculine values. Similarly, the Marketplace system, designed by men and based on exaggerated masculine values, downgraded female ways and feminine values, yet might finally produce equality not only for females who follow the masculine script but also for feminine values. But that has not happened yet. We are still in a period of degradation of the more feminine values.

In the male-conceived world that has been with us since the Agricultural Megarevolution, woman's role has been said to be to serve man. ("I will make a helper for him," the male God says in Genesis as He decides to create a woman.[22]) The women's liberation movement was based upon legitimate resentment at this role, one that women in the movement often said is degrading, unnecessary, and unimportant.[23] But what was legitimate about the resentment was that the role was *exclusively* assigned to women, not that serving "man" (in the generic sense of humanity) is degrading, unnecessary, or unimportant. Looked at objectively, serving other humans is better and more "really necessary and important" than "screwing" them, as men (and women who have accepted the Masculine Mystique) are expected to do in the modern world.

Unquestionably, women deserve as many rights and opportunities as men. But do men not also deserve to be expected to have as many responsibilities to others as women have been expected to have?

But before we despair, recall that when men took up farming and appropriated other formerly female roles, they did not in the process become like women and lose their male predispositions. As I have already noted, if we were really blank slates and if gender were actually entirely constructed, men's taking up of female roles presumably would have completely "feminized" them. That it did not is another indication that human nature exists and that the relatively small average differences between women and men have a biological base. This being the case, we should have some confidence that women now entering male institutions will not lose their more female predispositions. They will not, in the end, be fully "masculinized."

Less reassuring is the realization that when traditional male roles were devalued in the Agricultural Megarevolution, male traits ultimately reasserted themselves in unexpected and often unfortunate ways. If the modern megarevolution and the Masculine Mystique continue to devalue traditional female roles, there is no way to know in what form the more female characteristics will eventually re-emerge.

"No ~~Girls~~ Girlish Ways Allowed"

"You don't build a company like this with lace on your underwear," a 1989 full-page ad for *Fortune* magazine in the *New York Times* proclaimed in huge letters.[24] The quote was said to be from one of "America's toughest bosses." It would be easy to dismiss the statement as the ranting of someone from the lunatic fringe of the machismo movement in business. But I believe that the boast says a great deal about the economic system that has developed during the modern megarevolution and the relationship of that system to traditionally masculine and feminine values.

The hope of many in the early years of the modern women's movement was that as women entered the traditionally male worlds, such as business, law, and politics, they would be able to "feminize" them. Perhaps these institutions that had been established on the basis of the more masculine values could be infused with a dose of feminine values. This effort was bound to be difficult. The attempt would mean "struggling to get into the system while questioning it," trying to be accepted as "one of the boys" while wanting to change the rules by which the boys play their game.[25]

At a 1989 conference at the Kennedy School at Harvard, Governor Madeleine Kunin of Vermont gave a superb assessment of the difficulties and internal conflicts facing women entering these spheres. "We would like to change the rules of the game," Kunin declared. "But then we find if we don't play by the rules, we don't play at all." Kunin directly addressed the conflict between feminine values and the systems built on male ways when she said that women entering politics hoped to construct "a less adversarial and more consensus-built system . . . that is what we are more comfortable with." The trouble, she pointed out, is that in politics, "it's win or lose. Nothing in between."[26]

Nothing in between. That sums up the essence of the dualistic thinking upon which our modern institutions and practices are based. Most women are not comfortable with such thinking. But as they have entered (individually or with a very few other women) institutions that operate on masculine values, women usually have little choice but to go along with dualism and all that flows out of it. Perhaps for a while they retain the hope that they will change the way things are done "later."

In a system that was created by males and is still based largely upon male thinking and masculine ways—indeed, on hypermasculinity—those women who are most likely to succeed are those who think and act most like men. Women have a tough enough time "making it" in areas that were until recently male preserves; they have a much tougher time if they adhere to feminine values. Three of the most prominent female political leaders of the second half of the twentieth century were Golda Meir of Israel, Indira Gandhi of India, and Margaret Thatcher of the United Kingdom. All oversaw their nations' involvement in wars. That fact may not prove anything, but it certainly suggests that women who reach the top in male-made institutions are pressured to act like men.

A major purpose of man-made institutions has always been to extend gender by creating artificial male preserves where men could reassure themselves that they are notwomen. Recognizing this fact, one can easily understand why women entering these preserves would also be expected to show that they are notwomen. If the *No Girls Allowed* signs had to be taken down, they would be replaced with new billboards proclaiming: *No Girlish Ways Allowed.*

If we can't make you check your ovaries at the clubhouse door and exchange them for testicles, at least we can make you check your girly thinking and feminine values before you enter our masculine, if no longer entirely male, sanctuary. There's nobody in here but us notwomen!

Since the differences in values between men and women are only on average, prejudgment on the basis of sex is unwarranted. It is difficult to see how anyone who looked at the policies of Margaret Thatcher could think otherwise. Her example shows the absurdity of the idea that there are absolute differences between men and women. Where did Thatcherism, with its total opposition to policies of compassion, leave women who fell into the dualistic trap by arguing that women are naturally good and so their coming to power would bring the millennium? "Gone," says journalist Polly Toynbee, "is the idea that sisters are essentially, genetically, spiritually better than men."[27]

That simple-minded, dualistic idea should be gone. But one of the troubles with dualism is that it tosses out the good ideas that are thought to be on the same side as the discredited ones. Margaret Thatcher—and any number of other women—can be used as conclusive proof that a woman is not, by virtue of her sex, automatically "better" than a man. That fact is meaningful to the argument that there is on average a difference, caused in part by biology, between the motivations and values of females and males only if the dualistic mode of thinking is accepted. All Thatcher shows is that putting women in positions of power in institutions should not be confused with infusing those establishments with feminine values. Feminine values can be held, in varying degrees, by women and men. There is no reason to think that any particular woman—especially one who has gotten to the top in a masculine-oriented organization—will hold them.

Getting Ahead

The woman who gets ahead in a male-oriented system is expected by the men in that system to act as if she, in the vulgar slang terminology, has gotten "a head." But women often find themselves in a no-win situation when they enter the winner-take-all world of business. They must act like men in order to succeed, but then they will be condemned for being masculine.

A prime example in popular culture is the Signourey Weaver character, Katharine, in Mike Nichols' 1988 film *Working Girl*. She is readily recognizable as a classic example of a "bitch."[28] But what is it that makes her a bitch? It is that she acts the way most ruthless, self-seeking, success-driven men do. Yet does anyone ever a call such a man a bitch?*

The masculine success model is intertwined with the acquisitive individualism of the Marketplace economy. When women began to accept these attitudes, the last defenses against the Marketplace mentality started to crumble. As columnist Joan Beck has said, in order to succeed women were expected to "compete assertively with men, [and] either have no children or act as if they didn't."[29] Women on the make are not supposed to share; like their male coun-

---

*A brief aside in light of our exploration of the sexual meanings in vulgar language: When men given to the use of profanity want to derogate a woman, they often call her a *bitch*. The first important point to realize is that a bitch is a woman who acts like a man, either sexually or, as in the Weaver character, in other ways. A bitch is a woman who screws other people, either literally or figuratively (or both). But what do men call a man to derogate him? In addition to all the synonyms for *woman* we saw in Chapter 13, the usual terms are *son of a bitch* or *bastard*. It is highly significant that both of these are in fact slurs on the *mother* of the person at whom they are aimed, not at the person himself. The popular African-American epithet, *Your mamma* is similar. All of them imply that the failing of the man being insulted is that "his women" are not under control. A woman can be attacked directly, but a man, as we have seen, can be put down only by "putting him down": treating him like a woman. Implying that a man's women—mother, wife, girlfriend, sister—are out of control is yet another way to say that he is not a "real man."

terparts, they try to get their share—or more than their share. (It is not acci-
dental, I believe, that the phrases *on the make* and *making it* have sexual as
well as business- or success-related meanings.)

So, for the most part, the women's movement has followed an approach
similar to that Booker T. Washington advocated for blacks in the late nineteenth and early twentieth centuries: Accept the structured society as it is,
accommodate yourself to the ways of the dominant group, and try to win a
place within that framework. Feminists have certainly not been as reticent as
Washington found it necessary to be. Their very militancy, however, has
served to mask the fact that while they are not content with the "pull yourself
up by your bootstraps" gradualism that Washington advocated (pulling yourself up by your bra straps would defy the laws of physics as much as pulling
yourself up by your bootstraps), many feminists have nevertheless accepted
the necessity of following the male path toward the male-determined concept
of success, just as the Washingtonians tried to pattern themselves after whites.

As anthropologist Ashley Montagu has said, "the greatest victory one can
yield to one's traditional enemy is to become like him."[30] Wendell Berry has
perfectly described what happened with women's (and others') liberation:
"The aims and standards of the oppressors become the aims and standards of
the oppressed, and so our ills and evils survive our successive 'liberations.' "[31]

Are things associated with men still considered to be superior? Anyone
who doubts that the bias continues should consider whether the reaction is the
same to the man who enters a traditionally female occupation as to the woman
who enters a traditionally male occupation. Of course not. It is much more
acceptable for women to enter "male" occupations than for men to enter
"female" occupations. This bias indicates the persistence of the assumption
that what men have usually done is more important than what women have
customarily done. Similarly, calling a young girl a "tomboy" is not quite a
compliment, but it is not especially derogatory. The same idea in reverse, however, is quite another matter. As we have discussed, calling a boy a "sissy," or
an adult man a "wimp"—or more vulgar synonyms—remains one of the worst
insults in our verbal arsenal.

The point is even more apparent in apparel. It is now quite acceptable for
women to wear most men's clothes, but it is entirely unacceptable for men to
wear most women's clothing, so much so that the mere raising of the question simultaneously raises eyebrows. Women are accepted into the male
world of business to just the degree that they are prepared to act like one of
the boys. This behavior entails "dressing for success": wearing women's
clothing patterned after male styles, such as suits and ties (a classic phallic
symbol). The "Annie Hall look" of the late seventies was one variant of this
practice.

Cross-Dressing Is a One-Way Street
Gender-extending men had proclaimed in the Bible that either sex wearing a garment that pertains to the other "is an abomination to the Lord your God" (Deuteronomy 22:5). In recent years, however, it has become totally acceptable for women to wear men's clothing. The "Annie Hall Look" that became popular in the late 1970s is a notable example. Yet it generally remains unacceptable for men to wear women's clothing. This is one reflection of the Masculine Mystique's assumption that masculine ways are superior. (Corbis)

Women dressing like men shows that the thrust of the Masculine Mystique is just the opposite of what the reformers of the Axial Age and beyond were attempting. Such men as Confucius and Jesus were trying to get men to act more like women. Today's reformers are attempting to get women to act more like men—and gender-extended men, at that. Women are encouraged to be more competitive, power-hungry, aggressive, and assertive. Compare the clergymen of old, representing a religion that sought to move men a bit more toward feminine values, wearing clothing that was reminiscent of female garb, with women of today who have accepted the male-way-is-the-right-way idea, wearing clothing that has been associated with men. The contrast is telling.

Many women in recent years have so much bought into (or surrendered to) the extreme male Marketplace philosophy that they have come to value work only if it is part of the gross domestic product. The quest for success accepts money as the only measure of value, which is simply to deny traditional feminine values. What makes working as a secretary, selling real estate, or any other job a more rewarding activity than raising children? Only that one is paid for it. To put a finer point on it, why is working in a child care center better than caring for one's own children? It would seem that the only answer is that one is paid for the former.

Of course, there are genuinely rewarding (in other ways than monetary) careers outside the home, and these—like all other jobs—must be open to women and men on an equal basis. Among these are various intellectual pursuits, medicine, nursing, teaching, social work, and several other fields. But there are relatively few such careers available for either sex. What most men (and now most women, too) do outside the home is intrinsically no more valuable and rewarding (and, in truth, often considerably less so) than traditional "women's work" inside the home. What is so rewarding about manufacturing or selling a variety of products for which there is no particular need in the first place?

But while we try to guard against devaluing the important roles women have traditionally held in nurturing and teaching children, we also have to recognize two other points. First, even if most mothers continue to engage in a larger amount of childcare than most fathers, precisely because these duties *are* so important, men should share in them to a much greater extent than they have in the past. This sharing will give women more time to do other (not more important, but different) things. Second, responsibilities related to motherhood are not lifetime careers, especially with longer life spans and population pressures leading to couples having fewer children. This fact, too, means that all or virtually all occupations must be open to both women and men. We can and should remove the culturally created and legal restrictions and let anyone enter any field she or he wants to. But that does not mean that we should ever expect to see equal numbers of the sexes in some occupations. Some types of work are always—or at least until genetic engineering may make alterations in our biograms—going to be more appealing to a larger percentage of one sex than the other.

"Hooking Up"

The acceptance by women of male ways also seems to have been the essence of the sexual revolution. Who benefitted most from the switch (in part—but only in part—the result of effective oral contraceptives) from a double standard to no standard at all? The abandonment of the old double standard meant that women could "act like men" in sexual, as well as other, affairs. In the process it made women more sex objects (albeit also sex subjects) than they had ever been before. If the double standard is wrong (and it is, although there appear to be biological as well as "who has the power" reasons why it has existed), then it was right to change it. But ending the double standard could have been accomplished in one of three ways: a new, common standard that was a compromise between the old, separate expectations for men and women could have been adopted; men could have adopted the old standard of women; or women could have adopted the old standard of men. It is apparent that what happened was closest to the third alternative. As in the business world, so in the sexual realm, women adopted the male model. Surely some women saw themselves as being better off as a result of this new freedom, but the principal beneficiaries have been men—especially powerful men.[32]

The basic argument of the sexual revolution of recent decades has been succinctly stated as: "(1) Sex is fun; (2) Lots of sex will be lots of fun."[33] Most people of both sexes would readily agree with the former proposition. Fewer women than men, however, have found the latter to be valid, especially if it was taken (as it almost always has been during the sexual revolution) to mean "lots of sex with lots of partners." There seem to be reasons other than cultural constraints for this unacceptability.

The males of most primates closely related to humans take no responsibility for offspring. Because of the high male parental investment that human infants need, human males have evolved *toward* lasting attachment and responsibility, but they still have a way to go. It is not *entirely* unnatural for men to brag about how many children they have sired by different women. This is why it is necessary to have values, usually expressed in religious teachings and often written into laws, designed to control male inclinations toward irresponsibility and encourage those toward responsibility. We do not permit men to go about deserting their wives and children and "taking" other women whenever lust arises in them.

Or at least we *did* not until the sexual revolution. That phenomenon of the last third of the twentieth century is another consequence of the constellation of modern conditions and beliefs that are the legacy of the second megarevolution: mobility, independence ("liberation"), solipsism, turning other people into objects, boundlessness, live-for-today, self-indulgence (the motto of the movement should have been "Whatever turns *me* on"), and instant gratification. Seen in this light, the sexual revolution is another manifestation of the Marketplace Misconception and particularly the consumption ethic. Advertising constantly urges people to think only of themselves and their personal enjoyment. Other people are to be seen as objects to be manipulated to increase *my* pleasure.

Marriage, like democracy, is a leveling institution. It amounts almost to sexual socialism. "One man, one woman" is the parallel to "one person, one vote." Marriage laws, like democracy, place some constraints (obviously far from fully effective) on those men among us who retain proclivities similar to those of gorillas. Lifting those restraints and establishing a sexual free market increases the opportunity of the man who accumulates power and money also to accumulate women.

The idea that women should be free to have intercourse with whomever they want, whenever they want, is a prime example of the consequences of the adoption of the Masculine Mystique by many women. It assumes that men have been thus free all along and that whatever men have done is what everyone *should* do: the "right" thing. The Masculine Mystique in this regard can be stated simply: *If he does it, why shouldn't she?*[34] The extent to which the male view has won out is indicated by the fact that hardly anyone seems to consider that this question can be reversed: If she doesn't do it, why should he? Although, as we discussed in Chapter 3, the difference is not nearly as extreme as some evolutionary psychologists believe it to be, it seems clear that men tend, on average, to be somewhat more comfortable than women with sex without emotional involvement.[35]

Adolescent and young adult males are given to talking among themselves in terminology that makes the greater male predilection for sex without commitment unmistakable. The talk is often indicative of anonymous action. When a young male says to his friends, *I wanna get laid,* it is evident that by whom is not the paramount consideration. Saying that he desires *a piece of ass* may not mean that the woman of whom that sector of the anatomy is a part is of no concern to him. But it surely does indicate that the qualifications for acceptance can be met by a large number of females. *Let's go out and find some pussy* hardly indicates a quest for lasting attachment. Males interested in "scoring" are keeping score: they count sexual conquests, figuratively collecting scalps or cutting notches in their guns.[36] Many Americans were horrified in the spring of 1993 to learn that a group of boys in the Los Angeles suburb of Lakewood had literally turned intercourse into a competitive sport. They kept score of the number of different girls (some as young as ten) with whom each of them had "hooked up," as they put it in terminology that became widespread among young people in the nineties. The leader of this self-styled "Spur Posse" at the time was a nineteen-year-old with 66 points.[37]

Such extreme behavior should not be taken to be normal for males. Like the similar activity by Kennedy men and other political leaders, such a desire to make as many conquests as possible is indicative of males who are insecure in their manhood. As will be discussed in the next chapter (when the Spur Posse will be reintroduced as one of several windows into contemporary male problems), the social environment in which men have found themselves during the last half century has heightened such male insecurity.

There is an innate tendency that is more pronounced in males than females on which insecurity can work. Few women take a similar attitude toward anonymous sex. A young woman might well say to her friends, *I want to make love with Bill.* Given our liberation of language, she might say *I want to fuck Bill.* But she would not be likely to put it in the impersonal, *I wanna get laid.* Many men admit to fantasies involving having sex with two or more women at the same time (some, like John F. Kennedy, have the power to make the fantasy real); very few women tell researchers of fantasizing about being in bed with more than one man. And the idea of a woman suggesting to her female friends, *Let's go out and find some cock,* seems quite far-fetched for most women, in part because it would be unnecessary to engage in such a search. Women who are choosy about with whom they will have sex may have to work at making a conquest of the man they want, but a woman who simply wants to have a sex with any man can usually find one who is willing almost instantly. There are, of course, women who have adopted ultramale ways by self-consciously embracing cold, impersonal, purely physical sex and turning men into objects. Singer-actress Madonna built a highly profitable career on promoting herself as the embodiment of the extreme form of the new woman. That new woman is indistinguishable from the new man of the Marketplace world: disconnected, existential, narcissistic, mobile, greedy, completely self-seeking, engaging in impersonal sex, and treating all others as objects. Writer Anselma Dell'Olio suggested the degree to which the sexual revolution was a triumph for men when she said in the early 1970s: "According to most men, a liberated woman was one who put out sexually at the drop of a suggestive comment, who didn't demand marriage, and who "took care of herself" in terms of contraceptives."[38] Men could (and quickly did) learn to adapt quite nicely to this environment of women's liberation. It is a truism that "any sexual revolution will tend to liberate more men than women."[39]

The beginnings of a sexual revolution have even hit China as marketplace economic reform has taken hold. It has liberated men there, too. "Men like to see women as objects," an editor at *China Women's News* said in 1995. "Chinese men need other women," claimed thirty-two-year-old Shanghai man who began having affairs about six months after his marriage. "Family life is one thing; life outside is another. You don't have to hide it; everyone at work knows who my girlfriend is."[40]

The sexual revolution is yet another step in the disintegration of the bonds that tie people together, which has been a major feature of the modern megarevolution's Marketplace Misconception. It results in women and men alike being "freed"—loosed of any lasting ties to another person and left as "autonomous individuals": liberated and isolated.

The concept of interdependence traditionally has been more associated with women than men, but prior to the modern megarevolution, it was associated in a somewhat different way with men as well. The women's movement has moved away from that concept, attempting to steer women toward the Marketplace concepts of independence and the "sovereign self."[41] But the self is not sovereign.

Free love is the supreme oxymoron. Someone who is genuinely in love *cannot* be free; to be in love is to be connected, tied, bound to another. It necessitates the acceptance of responsibility and mutual obligation. Totally free people can have sex, but never love, because to have love is to give up freedom. Liberation breaks bonds; love creates bonds. "Liberated sex" is pure *self*-indulgence; what is liberated is the self, which then treats all other people as objects—things to be used for the pleasure of the self.

Asked in the late sixties how her vacation in the Virgin Islands (an unlikely locale for her) had been, drug-rock queen Janis Joplin replied: "It was just like anywhere else; I fucked a lot of strangers."[42] *Fucking* strangers—literally or figuratively—poses no great problem for the human biogram. But *loving* strangers is an impossibility; human nature simply is not equipped for it.

Free love is likely to degenerate into "free hate." Since loving everybody is a biological impossibility, the attempt to do so can be diverted into a biological emotion that is more readily spread to large numbers of people: "otherization," and the hatred that goes with it. "My music isn't supposed to make you riot," Joplin declared. "It's supposed to make you fuck."[43] She failed to see the link between the two. As we have seen, *fuck* is a transitive verb; if its object is a stranger, the action in the verb cannot be one based on love, and so it is readily converted into hate.

The main reason why free love (or, more accurately, *liberated sex,* which, unlike free love, is not in an oxymoron) proves unsatisfying is that it ignores another biologically based predisposition: to settle down and have lasting, special (that is, loving) ties to another human being. This predisposition for lasting connection is, as we have seen, somewhat stronger (statistically) among women than men, but it is a powerful force—a *need*—in both sexes. Hopping from sexual partner to sexual partner will never provide human beings of either sex with lasting happiness. A comment Barbra Streisand made in 1991 says much about where the Marketplace worldview has taken us. "Even though my feminist side says people should be independent and not need to be taken care of by another person," she said, "that doesn't necessarily work that way. There's the human factor, you know."[44] The human factor. That is another way to say *human nature.* It would be well for all of us to remember that it precludes the complete independence the Marketplace Misconception has led us to see as natural and desirable and assures that the attempt to achieve it, including the pursuit of impersonal sex, will not produce satisfaction.

I do not mean to sound overly prudish. I am certainly not suggesting that people of either sex are horrible sinners if they have more than one sexual partner in a lifetime. But something very important and fundamentally human for both sexes is lost when sexual relations become casual and separated from any sort of personal commitment. Columnist Mona Charen has said it well: "When we demean sex, we demean our humanity."[45]

One faction of what has become a highly splintered feminist movement came to see the sexual revolution for what it has been. "In going back into new sexual values," Kathleen Barry wrote in 1979, "we are really going back to the values women have always attached to sexuality, values that have been robbed from us, and destroyed as we have been colonized through both sexual violence and so-called liberation."[46]

The linking of sexual violence and sexual liberation is an important one. As the expectation arose during the sexual revolution that women had taken on the same sexual standards as men, the difficulty facing a woman wishing to avoid casual intercourse greatly expanded. So did the prospect of being raped.

During the 1980s reported rape increased four times faster than the overall crime rate in the United States, reaching the astonishing pace of one rape every six minutes.[47] By the end of that decade estimates were that one of every ten American women would be raped at some point during her lifetime.[48] Two major reasons for this outrageous development are the sexual revolution's contention that women "want it"—with many different partners—as much as men do and its objectification of sex partners as "some*thing* to give *me* pleasure."

Our culture in recent years has led us to think that most women say *Yes* frequently, to many different men. Being told that women are just like they are, men come to believe that all women are just as desirous as many men are of sexual intercourse with almost anyone of the "opposite sex" that they find at least mildly attractive. This belief makes date or acquaintance rape far more likely. It puts the male in the position of thinking that if he does not "make it" with a particular female, she has rejected *him,* but would gladly do "it" with any number of other males. When she says *No* to him it becomes an affront not just to his hormones but also to his ego—his manhood. The typical male, in fact, feels almost obligated to "do it" with any willing female—and to try to persuade any female he finds attractive to be willing. In a nearly direct reversal of the situation prior to the sexual revolution, he is now likely to believe that *not* to try is a personal insult to a particular female: *I'd try to screw almost anything; but not you*!

Affronts to men's egos and their sense of manhood have become more numerous in recent decades.* In the next chapter we shall turn to a slightly different sort of the Masculine Mystique: the one that has grown increasingly more powerful in misleading men. If, after all, an exaggerated form of masculinity came to be seen as what women must pursue to be successful in the modern world of the Marketplace, how were men to react? When women are striving to become notwomen, what happens to men who have relied on the notawoman definition of manhood?

---

*One of the clearest threats to the fragile doctrine of manhood based on superiority and dominance is another victory won by the modern women's movement: a woman's right to choose an abortion. The perspective offered in this book can shed some light on this very controversial issue. When we realize how powerfully the seed metaphor that grew out of the Agricultural Megarevolution has shaped our thinking, it becomes apparent that a large part of the objection to women taking control of their reproduction is that it amounts to the farm land seizing decision-making power from the farmer. A woman's choice on pregnancy effectively undercuts the man's *authority*—his claimed position as the creator or author of the child. To the extent that the seed metaphor and Conception Misconception are at the base of all male claims to superiority, a woman's assertion of the right to choose is a direct challenge to that whole structure. Note that abortion itself does not pose this threat to the basis of male domination; rather, it is who makes the choice. In ancient Rome, as we have seen, abortion was totally compatible with male domination, since the choice was entirely the man's. As long as the seed planter can decide whether to allow the crop to grow until it is ready to be harvested or to plow it under, the sexual hierarchy is maintained. It is all about who controls the means of reproduction. But when the soil starts making decisions on the crop, the metaphor begins to unravel and so the whole structure on which male superiority is based is thrown into question: *Thou shalt not uproot what men have planted.*

CHAPTER 16

"I've Got to Be a Macho Man"

The Bi-Polar Sex Disorder
in the Last Half Century

"And we do exist.
I swear to God, we do exist!"
BILLY SHEHAN (1993)[1]

Our entire society is, to a very significant and largely unrecognized extent, built on sexual bi-polarism and the misogyny that goes with it. This fact should be apparent from the discussion in the preceding chapters. That such a situation exists does not, however, mean that fear and repression of women have been constant in degree. During the long periods of history in which women have seemed to know and accept "their place," misogyny has not reached its ugliest levels. It is in the times—among them the Neolithic Age and the last few decades—when men's roles have been threatened, women have seemed to be rising out of the place men have designated for them, and the sharp line between the sexes has been blurred, that insecure men have made their most desperate attempts to widen the closing gap between the sexes. It is in such periods that misogyny has become particularly virulent.

Clearly, women in Western societies today are closer to genuine equality than women have been in any major society since recorded history began some five thousand years ago. But, as happened when women's invention of agriculture increased their prestige and threatened male roles, many men are once again reacting harshly to the gains of women. "If establishing masculinity depends most of all on succeeding as the prime breadwinner," Susan Faludi wrote in *Backlash* in 1991, "then it is hard to imagine a force more directly threatening to fragile American manhood than the feminist drive for economic equality." At that time she concluded that the "free-floating anxiety over declining wages, insecure employment and overpriced housing" that many men felt in the 1980s had to be aimed somewhere, and "women, especially feminist women, became the all-purpose scapegoats."[2] Examples of these new attempts to reaffirm female subordination—and to reaffirm an endangered masculinity—have been all around us in recent decades. Antagonism toward women and all that is usually associated with them takes many forms, several of which are explored in this chapter.

My purpose is not simply to condemn men who lash out at women and take what are sometimes ridiculous or even pathetic actions intended to demonstrate that they are notwomen. Rather, as I have tried to do with other historical periods, it is my intention in examining our own era to seek to explain what has happened to men and how many of them perceive their situation, and to attempt to gain some understanding of why they react as they do. The ways in which many men react to their situation are wrong, but their problems are often genuine and deserving of respect.

Women have been, Faludi has said more recently, in her 1999 book, *Stiffed: The Betrayal of the American Man,* "just proxies for the real war—against a new economy and a new culture that could not be battled with obscenities and violence."[3] I believe she is right, but her statement has a vastly wider applicability than she gives it. As will be evident as this chapter progresses, I found Faludi's book extremely useful as a source of examples illustrating what is often termed the "male crisis." I also believe that she is very much on target in seeing the Marketplace economy as a major source of male insecurity. Where I differ with her, of course, is on the age and ultimate sources of the "crisis." Its particular manifestations in the period discussed in this chapter certainly have proximate causes in the post–World War II economy and culture. That era created new challenges for men insecure in their sense of manhood and so intensified misogyny and violence among some men. But what has been happening in recent decades is best understood as the latest battle in a proxy war that has gone on throughout recorded history, in which men have been using women as scapegoats for their grievances against an economy that was new around 8000 B.C.E.

This chapter's focus is this latest battle in the longest war in history; in fact as we have seen, it has been going on for longer than "history" as it is usually defined. The chapter's analysis begins—chronologically, socially, and culturally—where that in Chapter 12 left off: in the late 1950s and early 1960s. As I did in that chapter, I shall utilize in this one an eclectic but not random set of incidents and cultural markers as windows through which to see the situation of the sexes during roughly the past half century.

The All-Too-Credible Shrinking Man

The changes in the economy with the rise of the Consumerculture have been bringing the sexes together. Men in the 1950s strove mightily to return women to "their place" in the home and as fertile farmland in which male seeds could produce a bumper crop—and to steer women away from the roles and places men had reserved for themselves. But they did not have enough fingers to plug the proliferating holes in the dike they had constructed to hold back the sexual tide of the Marketplace economic system. By the sixties, women were being urged to become more like men in pursuing individual success and becoming breadwinners. Meanwhile, men were thrust ever more into a more "feminine" lifestyle of consumption. These developments led to many men reacting to the threat of gender integration by desperately seeking ways to demonstrate their masculinity (notawomanness) and trying to distinguish the sexes in every way possible.

The alternative to being a breadwinner that the new economy offered to men was, as Faludi has said, "to be a bread-spender; the 'New Man,' it turned out, was a shopper."[4] And the move from an industrial to a service economy represented "a shift from heavy-lifting 'masculine' labor to 'feminine' aid and assistance."[5] Increasingly men felt economically emasculated because they didn't make anything. They could, of course, "make" women—and, if they still believed in the ideas that had grown from the seed metaphor, they could make babies.

As the second half of the twentieth century progressed, growing numbers of men found it difficult to fulfill traditional masculine roles. The image of one-way dependence of a man providing for a dependent woman had been a large part of the masculinist reaction to the devaluation of male roles after agriculture was invented. The equations *man = independent* and *woman = dependent,* which had been constructed over thousands of years, were reinforced in the earlier stages of the modern megarevolution, especially in the American ideal of the totally independent self-made man. But the demands of the marketplace economy and the return to a K-selected reproductive situation that brought more and more women into the paid workforce posed a major threat to this millennia-old prop for masculine self-assurance.

Basing their definition of the appropriate relationship of man to woman on the idea that the former is the provider and the latter the dependent left men very susceptible to losing their women if they lost their jobs—or if the women started to provide for themselves. "Women have taken on a very masculine role in American society," a recently divorced California man complained in the mid-1990s. "The feminist movement has destroyed what was a perfect society with a few infractions. I'm just tired of being emasculated," he continued. "All of a sudden, my wife became—I don't want to say the breadwinner, but the focal point of earning our living. *She was serving both roles. And all of a sudden I'm trying to justify what my purpose is.*"[6] Such statements, which have become increasingly common among troubled men over recent decades, sound like remarkably clear echoes from an extremely distant past. The same words could be used to describe what had happened to men after women invented agriculture.

Even worse for men, the inheritors of millennia of recitations of male superiority, is when they find a woman has authority over them on the job. "Of course, the men working under me are resentful," a woman in such a position commented.[7] Of course. Men believe that "on top" is the proper male position, so for a man to "work under" a woman is to classify him as the woman.

The growing anxiety experienced by many men and their reaction to their perceived diminishment was represented in science fiction in the fifties in Richard Matheson's book *The Shrinking Man*[8] and the movie adaptation, *The Incredible Shrinking Man*. The protagonist, Scott Carey, begins to shrink after he is exposed to an atomic cloud, so the book and film bring together the fears of nuclear destruction with the idea that men are being diminished. As Matheson (and, one suspects, many other men, at least subconsciously) saw it, two developments that threatened to destroy the man's world that had emerged from World War II. One was obvious and applied in the generic sense of *man*. The invention of the atomic bomb had diminished humans to the point of possible self-inflicted extinction, raising the specter that we could become self un-made men. But males of the species faced the prospect of diminishment in the nuclear age even if the world was not destroyed. American men and those of the other Allies emerged victorious from this good war; they were "on top," as victors are supposed to be. Somehow, however, it did not seem quite the way it was supposed to be. The conjunction of the first public use of the Bomb with the end of the war cast a mushroom-shaped cloud over the triumph. In fact, it placed into serious question the prospects for the continued serviceability of war as a testing ground of masculinity.

Nuclear weapons mean that a war fought without limits would probably be one without winners; *all* would be losers. That fact is a commonplace, but I do not think that the full significance of this transformation has generally been perceived.

A war in which all are losers takes away the whole purpose of competition. If there are no winners, the very motive force of evolution—"survival of the fittest"—ceases to have any meaning. In a full-scale nuclear war, no one would be found to be "fit"; no one would survive. Natural selection would cease in such a nuclear war, because nothing would be selected *for*.

The nuclear age thus has brought us face to face with what one of the main motive forces, not only of human nature, but of nature in a wider sense, can do in an environment for which it was not designed. What agriculture and excessive mobility did to make some of our innate predispositions maladaptive has been central to human history. But all of that pales in comparison with something that has the potential to make the competition that has been central to biological evolution from the start of life utterly maladaptive.

Albert Einstein stated the central problem succinctly: "The atomic bomb has changed everything except the nature of man."[9] If human nature could not change quickly enough to adapt over a period of a few thousand years to the new environment created by agriculture, surely it has not been able to change in order to adapt to new circumstances that arose only a little more than a half century ago. The realization began to emerge—or perhaps to have effects even though it remained submerged, beneath the level of fully conscious understanding—among men after the end of World War II that there might never be another "good war" in which boys could become men and men could become heroes. That age-old male proving ground was in serious danger of being cordoned off with signs reading: CLOSED BY NUCLEAR CONTAMINATION.

But that was not the only threat to traditional masculinity that men faced after World War II. The blow to masculine self-image caused by losing their breadwinner status in the Depression had been compounded by the movement of women into male spheres of work during the war. "Men must work and women must spin," Ashley Montagu pointed out a few years after the war, "because if women stop spinning and start working, man's claim to 'creativity' and indispensability as breadwinner is undermined—and this he must resist."[10] Matheson has said that he thought women coming into the workforce in World War II "began the social diminishment of men."[11]

This threat to masculine security was wonderfully, if somewhat unintentionally, depicted in the 1946 movie *The Best Years of Our Lives*. The movie focuses on the changed world that veterans found when they returned home. The essence of the change was that it had become a woman's world. The wives seem to have been getting along very nicely while their protector-providers were thousands of miles away. The husbands' return disrupts their lives. Women and effeminate men who did not go to war (represented by a character named "Stinky") have taken jobs that should belong to the "real men." The situation of the returning veterans, as the movie portrays it, is nicely symbolized when one of them, Fred, awakens after a night of drinking to find himself alone in his friend's daughter's bed, with a frilly canopy over him. Clearly, the world has been turned upside down and the men will have to reassert their authority, as they are doing by the last reel.[12]

But male apprehensiveness was palpable in the postwar years, as we have seen from several vantage points in Chapter 12. "During this period," Matheson said of the fifties, "my stories were imbued with a sense of anxiety, of fear of the unknown, of a world too complicated which expected too much of individual males . . . the inability of others to understand the male protagonist, to give him proper recognition."[13] Distress caused by not being given what a man believes to be his proper recognition has long been a sore point for males who believe others are denigrating their manhood. This is the same grievance to which young black men now refer when they explain a verbal or physical attack on another male by saying, "He wouldn't give me my props."

Matheson's shrinking man is the embodiment of what many men have feared has been happening to them in the past half century. "What was I? Was I still a human being?" Scott Carey asks. "Or was I the man of the future?" He knows he is fighting a losing battle, that man's shrinking is irreversible: the Inevitable Shrinking Man. As he is further diminished, Scott becomes increasingly belligerent—a "caricature" of a man, as he says. The smaller he becomes, the more he wants to dominate someone, and of course a woman, his wife, becomes the target of his abuse: "Every day I become more tyrannical, more monstrous in my domination of Louise." (Here he echoes some of the statements we have heard from the vanguard of shrunken men, African-American males, such as Robert Johnson's "I'm going to beat my woman, until I get satisfied.") The film ends with Carey shrunk to nothingness and his voice heard shouting, "I meant something, too . . . I still exist!"[14]

Here in a 1950s science fiction book and movie was a vivid portrayal of the psychology of a growing number of men as the remainder of the century played out. To them, a shrinking man was all-too-credible.

The Radicalizing Question

Few of those who have canonized John F. Kennedy remember (or ever knew) the extraordinary extent to which his presidency was dedicated to making America safe for masculinity. Contending that affluence and overconsumption were making Americans flabby (and, implicitly, feminine), Kennedy was intent on restoring "vigor" through such expedients as school physical fitness programs and 50-mile hikes. He spoke in his acceptance speech in 1960 of "young men who are coming to power, men who are not bound by the traditions of the past, men who are not blinded by the old fears and hates and rivalries, young men who can cast off the old slogans and delusions and suspicions."[15] But when it came to the oldest and most pernicious of the fears, rivalries, delusions, and suspicions of men—those concerning women and their own manhood—the new young men who were coming to power in the sixties proved to be every bit as much blinded and bound by the traditions of the past as had been their forefathers throughout recorded history. The new young president, as we have already seen, led the way in being misguided by his own insecure masculinity. Kennedy's fondest hope was to pump up the shrinking man. And Kennedy's example reminds us of the sexual implications of a "shrinking man."

Norman Mailer did not hesitate to state the sexual subtext of Kennedy's presidency: "To keep America *up*. Virility is the unspoken salesman in American political programs today."[16] "What Kennedy was selling," Faludi rightly says, "was a government-backed program of man-making, of federal masculinity insurance."[17] The New Frontier was a fitting symbol for Kennedy's vision for a re-masculinized America. It was Teddy Roosevelt Redux.

The Kennedy administration is associated in the popular memory with the struggle against racial segregation, and it is true that some of the most important events in that effort took place during Kennedy's presidency. In fact, however, J.F.K.'s commitment to racial equality was less than firm. In his election-year biography of Kennedy, James MacGregor Burns entitled the chapter on civil rights "A Profile in Cowardice."[18] But that is another story. The early sixties also saw the rebirth of another struggle against an even more fundamental type of segregation. If the analysis I have offered in this book is correct, the maintenance of sexual inequality was the very foundation on which much of history had been constructed. Men had used sexual bipolarism to avoid the threat of a single human standard. This meant that sexual integration posed the greatest danger imaginable to insecure men. Sexual integration could show that the sexes were not opposite, which would mean that men could not sensibly continue to define manhood on the longstanding notawoman basis.

The peril to sexual segregation was not as evident in the early sixties as was that to racial segregation, but in retrospect it is clear that these were critical years in that struggle as well. The various structures that had been built to block sexual integration since it had reared its menacing head during World War II seemed to be holding as the decade began. But just beneath the surface the weaknesses in those bulwarks of male supremacy were being tested by probes from different flanks. From one angle, Betty Friedan was completing her indictment of the consignment of educated, middle-class women exclusively to the pursuits of motherhood and consumerism. From another, young women working in the civil rights movement were beginning to see the same connections between the oppression of minorities and their own situation that women abolitionists had perceived more than a century earlier.

Some of the women who worked with the Student Nonviolent Coordinating Committee (SNCC) in the Mississippi Freedom Summer of 1964 anonymously wrote a position paper that fall on "Women in the Movement." The paper is usually less remembered for its content than for SNCC leader Stokely Carmichael's infamous response to it: "The only position for women in SNCC is prone."[19] Carmichael was "just trying to be funny," but, as the authors of the position paper had already pointed out, "those who laugh the hardest are often those who need the crutch of male supremacy the most."[20] This is a key insight. The same point applies, as I have tried to show throughout this book, to those who bluster the most about their masculinity, brag the most about the number of their sexual conquests or the size and power of their sexual organs, insist the most loudly that women are inferior, and use most consistently the language of verbal mounting to "put down" other men. All of these common male actions are indications of insecurity and various forms of "the crutch of male supremacy."

Two of the women who had helped to compose the 1964 position paper, Casey Hayden and Mary King, carried their embryonic analysis of the sexual underpinnings of the entire system of dominance and subordination a large step farther in another brief document in 1965, "Sex and Caste: A Kind of Memo." In many respects this was to be of even more long-term importance in the undermining of the doctrine of male dominance than *The Feminine Mystique*, which had been published two years before. "Many people who are very hip to the implications of the racial caste system, even people in the movement, don't seem to be able to see the sexual caste system," Hayden and King pointed out, "and if the question is raised they respond with: 'That's the way it's supposed to be. There are biological differences.' Or with other statements which recall a white segregationist confronted with integration." The similarity in reactions should not have been surprising, because men who were challenged about "the sexual caste system" *were* (sexual) segregationists being confronted with integration. Hayden and King came very close to what I have argued in this book is the most fundamental truth about human history when they wrote: "All the problems between men and women and all the problems of women functioning in society as equal human beings are among the most basic that people face." If they removed the word *among*, this statement would be right on target. Similarly, they said that the issue they were raising "is a radicalizing question" that could take people beneath the surface problems.[21] Again the change of a single word would make this exactly right, as I see it: this is *the* radicalizing question, the key to everything else. Although Hayden and King said that "objectively, the chances seem nil that we could start a movement based on anything as distant to general American thought as a sex-caste system," that is just what flowed from their "kind of memo" and similar insights that women in the civil rights movement made.[22]

By the end of the 1960s, a small but growing number of radical feminists was beginning to put together a fairly coherent analysis of the subordination of women as the basis of history and the model for the oppression of other groups. Redstockings, a radical feminist group based in New York, for example, declared in its 1969 manifesto: "Male supremacy is the oldest, most basic form of domination. All other forms of exploitation and oppression (racism, capitalism, imperialism, etc.) are extensions of male supremacy; men dominate women, a few men dominate the rest."[23] The same document pointed out the immensely important practice I have called pseudosexing: "Any man is free to renounce his superior position provided that he is willing to be treated like a woman by other men."[24] A year later, Robin Morgan referred to the subordination of women as the "Primary Contradiction," which she described as follows: "when one half of the human species decided to subjugate the other half because it was 'different,' alien, the Other. From there it was an easy enough step to extend the Other to someone of different skin shade, different height or weight or language—or strength to resist." She spoke of "the suffering of more than half the human species for the past 5,000 years—due to a whim of the other half." She was, I believe, wrong in attributing this to "a whim" and to say that men's "decision" to subjugate women was caused by the fact that they were different. But the causal connection she perceived between this "Primary Contradiction" and all sorts of problems and evils stretching across all of recorded history was right on target. "All the way down this time," she declared at the end of her 1970 essay.[25] She and some of her "sisters" in the feminist movement at this time were getting quite close to "all the way down" with their analyses.

"Longer Hair and Other Flamboyant Affectations of Appearance"

One of the more remarkable developments of the sixties was the growing popularity of gender bending. The sort of blurring of the sexual dividing line that was done in the sixties was more radical than what had happened in the twenties. In the earlier period, avant garde women had adopted a boyish look, but in the sixties large numbers of men, the supposed superiors, started making themselves look more like women through such means as long hair, bright-colored clothing (often in floral prints), and jewelry—collectively referred to in the rock musical *Hair* as "longer hair and other flamboyant affectations of appearance."[26] This development seems significant. Why would a sizeable number of people choose to refashion themselves into facsimiles of a subordinated, supposedly inferior group? Why, in particular, would many males do this if, as I have been contending, manhood has almost always been defined on the basis of total difference from and superiority to women?

One answer may be that many privileged people in the civil rights and other reform and radical movements of the 1960s came almost to envy the oppressed. "But to become a true revolutionary one must first become one of the oppressed," Robin Morgan wrote, "(not organize or educate or manipulate them, but become one of them)—or realize that you *are* one of them already."[27] One of the reasons that some white males began to pattern themselves in some respects after women was probably their desire to become one of the oppressed. They could not become black, though they had readily adopted African-American slang, music, and so forth. Identifying with the civil rights struggle certainly exposed them to physical danger, but, as their black co-workers often reminded them, the whites could leave it all behind almost instantly and pass back into the safety and privilege provided by their white skin. As the argument that women were also an oppressed group gained wider currency, some white males semiconsciously sought to become more like women, as they had already tried to become more like blacks. If, as radical women were beginning to contend, woman is the prototype for all subordinated groups, and men based their domination on being the opposite of women, then men who voluntarily took on female attributes were challenging the whole structure of dominance/subordination at its most basic and vulnerable point. To say (and say especially forcefully through acts and lifestyle) that the sexes are not opposite is potentially the most radical position that anyone can take. "To take socially sanctioned 'women's wear' and flaunt it on a male body," as Faludi says, "was to send up society's most sternly guarded definitions of masculinity and femininity."[28]

Thus the riot that followed a police raid on the Stonewall Inn, a homosexual bar in Greenwich Village, in 1969 gave birth to a sixties rights movement that was in some ways an even more fundamental challenge to the very basis of the hierarchical "right order" than did the women's rights or African-American civil rights movement. One of the main reasons that insecure men are often so horrified by homosexual men, especially those who take on the female role, is that this orientation suggests that the sexes might not actually be opposite. If some men take on the female role in sexual acts—the ultimate area of sexual difference/opposition, it would seem—then the whole argument that the sexes are total opposites is thrown into question and the notawoman definition of manhood is seriously undermined. The reaction to the gay rights movement has, accordingly, often been even more hostile, violent, and widespread than the reactions against the movements seeking equality for women and African-Americans.

Of course most males who wore their hair long and went along with the styles of the second half of the sixties were neither homosexuals nor making a conscious statement about gender roles. But they were at the least exposing themselves to prejudice against "hippies, long-hairs, freaks, and fags," and so joining the category of the potentially oppressed. Yet for many males the idea of abandoning the traditional quest to demonstrate their own manhood was too great a leap into the abyss. Joining the oppressed is all well and good . . . but not if it exposes you to too much ridicule. Besides, the two model oppressed groups pointed in very different directions with regard to women. Many black men, including most of the musicians and many of the radical leaders of the freedom movement (as the Carmichael statement suggests), had accepted both the equations *man = free* and *woman = dominated* and the belief that subordinating women and treating them as sexual objects was a way to demonstrate manhood. Men who have been socially and economically emasculated are unlikely to take kindly to the suggestion that radical feminists were making that "cock privilege" be abandoned, since they see their "cocks" as their only hope of asserting any sort of privilege or manhood. So white males who tried to model themselves after black men would have a difficult time reconciling that effort with an identification with women.

Misogyny was, in fact, much more widespread among sixties radicals than is usually realized or acknowledged. This attitude was obvious and perhaps somewhat understandable among African-American men who so desperately felt the need to assert the manhood they had been denied. But the same attitudes were frequently expressed by white radicals. When a woman at the 1965 convention of Students for a Democratic Society, or SDS, tried to address the "women's issue," males in the audience screamed their ridicule (and insecurity). "She just needs a good screw!" was among the clever shouts. Another male member of SDS offered his assessment of women: They "made peanut butter, waited on tables, cleaned up, got laid. That was their role."[29] It only got worse as the movement degenerated in the later sixties. Some of the radical young males who emerged as media stars used their celebrity much as Kennedys and rock stars did, to "score" with as many women as possible. Some of the upwardly mobile males in the movement gained a following by "fucking a staff into existence," Marge Piercy noted.[30] As the fringes of the movement descended into infantile play-acting in the late sixties and early seventies, their macho posturing grew more extreme. Mao's famous maxim "political power grows out of the barrel of a gun,"[31] with its obvious phallic ostentation, was quoted frequently and approvingly. Black Panther Rufus "Chaka" Walls mocked women's liberation at the 1969 SDS convention by declaring: "We believe in pussy power." He went on to shout: "Superman was a punk because he never tried to fuck Lois Lane."[32] When a woman rose to speak at a 1969 antiwar rally, men in the audience shouted, "Take her off the stage and fuck her!"[33] Similar examples could be repeated almost endlessly.

One reason for all this blatant misogyny was clearly that many males in the movement, long hair notwithstanding, were just as likely to be sexually insecure as the next man. Moreover, some male opponents of the Vietnam War felt an additional need to assert their masculinity.

"We Lost. It's Over"

The war in Vietnam wreaked havoc with the idea of manhood for much of a generation of American males. Males were supposed to go to war; they had been brought up to think that it was often the key event in molding a boy into a man. Yet this war seemed very different from the "good war" their fathers had won a quarter century before. In many cases those who did not go (the overwhelming majority of the young men of the Baby Boom generation) had to live with the thought that they had failed to do what a man was supposed to do and so were not real men. But for most of those who did go to Vietnam, this war did not turn out to be the rite of passage to manhood that they expected, either.

Americans in Vietnam did not find a clear-cut enemy providing them with the opportunity for heroism. All too often they found that they could not distinguish between the enemy and the people they were supposed to be helping and protecting. Although this problem has often been discussed, I think it has a larger application that has gone unnoticed. What American servicemen found in Vietnam was a reflection of what men were concluding about their lives at home as well. In Vietnam women often turned out to be the enemy. When they came home, men returned to a changed society in which, as in Vietnam, they could no longer tell the women—those they had been taught it was their role to protect and provide for—from the "enemy" who was altering their world, taking their jobs and roles, and intensifying their doubts about their self-worth and manhood. The results of this equation of women with the enemy were horrifying in the war. At My Lai in 1968, to cite one example, a soldier forced a woman to perform oral sex on him while he held a gun to the head of her four-year-old child.[34] (We shall return to the significance of what happened at My Lai later in this chapter.) At times, the domestic results of that equation could be just as horrifying.

"We lost. It's over," Michael Bernhardt told his father when he returned from Vietnam. "And that was really unthinkable, that this was not going to be a war where you get 'em to sign a surrender on the USS *Missouri*."[35] In World War II, American men had won, but came home with the nagging fear that they really had not, because of the Bomb and the rise of women. (Women aren't supposed to *rise*.) But with Vietnam it was much worse for ideas of manhood. The implications of the simple sentence "We lost" were devastating for manhood. The losers surrender—like women; by losing and surrendering they show that they *are* women; they present themselves to be mounted by *us*, the winners, the dominators, the penetrators, the *real men*. But not in this war, this war that was so often against apparent civilians, often against women. Vietnam and the Vietnamese came to be explicitly identified with women. "Women," Doc in John Del Vecchio's 1982 novel, *The 13th Valley*, says contemptuously. "They all the time doin somethin jus so you can't expect why. They's like the dinks. If you expect them in the valleys they's gonna be on the hills and if you expects them on the hill they's gonna be in the valley. Women like that."[36] The enemy had been identified as womanlike; yet the United States could not win, could not come

A Rite Gone Wrong

War had traditionally been the ultimate rite of passage into manhood. But it didn't work out that way for American males in the Vietnam War. In this war, the enemy too often turned out to be women and children. This scene from early in period of major American involvement in Vietnam shows U.S. Marines apparently doing the right and "manly" thing—helping a wounded Vietnamese woman and child. But these casualties had been caught in a crossfire and their injuries may well have been caused by American weapons. That was increasingly the case as the war went on. American males involved in this war rarely had a feeling of manhood validated. The lost war was also a lost male rite of passage. It would be left in the years after the war for many American men to try to find elsewhere—for example, on movie screens—the feeling of achieved manhood this war had denied them. (Photo by Kyoichi Sawada ©Bettmann/Corbis)

out on top. The nation never exactly surrendered, but the images of helicopters "pulling out" in extreme haste with people dangling beneath was uncomfortably close to a picture of surrender. This was the ultimate shame for men. Recall Creon's declaration in *Antigone:* "Never let a woman triumph over us. . . . never be rated inferior to a woman, never."[37] Classify your opponents as women and then lose to them—what could be more humiliating to men who wanted to show that they were notwomen?

Young males had gone to what was supposed to be the proving ground for their manhood, but that ground had proved instead, in Tim O'Brien apt metaphor in *The Things They Carried,* to be "a shit field." The older men who sent them there had told them to set up camp in what turned out to be a latrine. "This little field, I thought, had swallowed so much," O'Brien wrote of the locale he used to represent the war. "My best friend. My pride. My belief in myself as a man of some small dignity and courage. . . . After that long night in the rain, I'd seemed to grow cold inside, all the illusions gone, all the old ambitions and hopes for myself sucked away into the mud."[38]

There were two manhood questions for those who fought in Vietnam. One—*How could we be real men and not be on top?*—concerned what did *not* happen there. The other, perhaps even more painful—*How could we be real men and have done some of the things we did or saw done in Vietnam?*—concerned what *did* happen there. These questions tore away at the hearts of many Americans in the years after the war.

"I'm Mad as Hell and I'm Not Going to Take It Anymore"

The remainder of the twentieth century was in substantial part shaped by the 1960s. Certainly that decade's effects on the questions we are concerned with in this book were more consequential than those of any similarly brief time period in history. In that tumultuous decade, the attempts to reestablish male dominance and sexual segregation that had been made after World War II came undone. Also the wall that had been constructed thousands of years ago to establish a bi-polar view of the sexes was breached to a greater extent than ever before. Although portions of the sixties quickly became passé, many of the developments regarding the sexes that had come together in that decade continued unabated in the years that followed. The Consumerculture, the sexual revolution, declining family size, the women's movement, abortion, homosexual rights, and male shame stemming from a lost war remained powerful forces. To these were added economic stagnation from the seventies into the early nineties.

As had the much more extreme economic crisis of the 1930s, the stagnation and loss of traditional jobs in the seventies and eighties posed a major threat to the masculine self-images of men who had rested their manhood on the role of provider. "I'm like the guy who's hanging from the cliff. I'm starting to lose my grip," said a laid-off McDonnell-Douglas planner in the nineties.[39] Susan Faludi has stated the contours of the situation well: "The American man" in these years had the "common experience of fear at losing the job . . . [and thus] any context in which to embed his life. If men are the masters of their fate, what do they do about the unspoken sense that they are being mastered, in the marketplace and at home, by forces that seem to be sweeping away the soil beneath their feet?"[40] Again, the applicability of such statements to what had happened to men and their roles after the invention of agriculture is apparent.

"The next thing you know, you're standing on the outside, looking in," another man who had lost his job in the aerospace industry said, echoing what his distant forefathers probably thought nearly ten thousand years before. "And you begin to ask, as a man, what is my role? What is it, really, that I *do?*"[41] The sexual implications of the loss of work are reflected in the language that is used to describe it. A *pink slip,* after all, is not something a real man gets. Since men have defined themselves by their work, as producers and providers, losing your job makes you womanly. And then there is that remarkably meaningful word *downsizing.* The term fits perfectly with the idea of "The Shrinking Man." "There's no way you can feel like a man," a California man said after losing his job in the early 1990s. "You can't. It's the fact that I'm not capable of supporting my family. . . . I'll be very frank with you," he continued slowly and deliberately. "I. Feel. I've. Been. Castrated."[42] Men who are the casualties of "downsizing" often feel that their manhood has been downsized, and this can become sexually very literal.

Men facing prospects such as these were likely to become desperate, angry, and sometimes violent. They were, as the Peter Finch character, Howard Beale, put it in the 1976 film, *Network,* "mad as hell" and they weren't "going to take it any more."[43] "As men's utilitarian qualities were dethroned, as their societal roles diminished," Faludi notes, "violence more and more came to serve as the gang leader for a host of rogue masculine traits."[44] There is space here to go into only a few aspects of this phenomenon, this search to find a lost masculinity, but it had myriad manifestations: spousal abuse, gay bashing, road rage, neo-Nazis, militias, gangs, soaring crime (particularly violent crime and most particularly rape), prison chic clothing, the popularity of fictional efforts to go back and win the lost war, the uproar against gays serving openly in the military, the large followings of G. Gordon Liddy, Rush Limbaugh, Oliver North, and David Duke, men's movements (both religious and secular), extreme sports, the vogue of professional wrestling and hockey, video games, ultimate-combat on pay-per-view . . . the list could go on. It includes all the accouterments of "power" so favored by some males: power ties, power lunches, pumped-up bodies, oversized tires on jacked-up trucks (the more grossly oversized, the better). Then there is the vogue in some quarters of the personal armored car, advertised as "Hummer—the ultimate power vehicle." Driving one of these monsters is the automotive equivalent of carrying an Uzi. An alternate advertising slogan might be: *Nothing says "Notawoman" like a Hummer.*

Of course those who actually *have* power and feel secure in their masculinity don't need the constant reassurance of such symbols. It is those who are heeding the call to "*act* like men" who are attracted to outward signs. Real men don't worry constantly about proving that they are real men. Real men don't have to put down others by saying those other men are *not* real men. Real men don't have to define themselves in terms of being the opposite of women.

Real men don't beat women. Real men don't rape. Real men, in short, don't worry about whether they're real men. Yet all too many men who want to believe themselves to be real men, but cannot convince themselves, have been engaging in just these sorts of actions in the last few decades.

Violent misogyny in popular music, from gangsta rap to such groups as Guns N' Roses and Nine Inch Nails, is an unmistakable example of the fears that give rise to actual physical violence against women. Axl Rose of Guns N' Roses has combined attacks on "immigrants and faggots" and "niggers" with complaints that women have all the power and "It's time to even the score."[45]

If the world needed to be reminded that hell hath no fury like a man devalued, the last few decades have provided a superabundance of memos containing that message in a variety of languages and codes—enough, in fact, to fill the newspaper headlines, television news broadcasts, and much of the popular culture.

Wayne's World Revisited

The ultramasculinity sought by so-called angry white males (but also by angry black males through their own separate-but-equal methods of attempting to assert manhood) sometimes looks like Frontierland or Adventureland, but it's actually a Fantasyland. Nor is it nearly as new as it is sometimes made to appear. Norman Mailer had outlined what was expected of the modern real man in 1963: "It was almost as if there were no peace unless one could fight well, kill well (if always with honor), love well and love many, be cool, be daring, be dashing, be wild, be wily, be resourceful, be a brave gun. And this myth, that each of us was born to be free, to wander, to have adventure and to grow on the waves of the violent. . . ."[46] In a world of endangered manhood, all a man can do to show that he is notawoman is to be violent and "love" well and many.

Many of the angry men yearn for the good old days when, as Archie Bunker put it in the theme song from *All in the Family,* "girls were girls and men were men."* The epitome of masculinity in the good old days was John Wayne. Wayne "had dominated surveys of the American men that were most admired for over thirty years" prior to 1980.[47] Wayne was a "man's man." He had been someone who knew how to act like a man. Just so. If this sort of masculinity was largely an act, who better to be its most admired exemplar than an actor? Wayne's wars were all celluloid. So were Ronald Reagan's, and when this actor-politician who knew how to act like a man won the presidency and

---

*Insecure men longing for the good old-fashioned "girls" from the good old days presumably explain why *submissive* appears to be among the most common words used on the cards London prostitutes post in phone booths to advertise their services.

became extraordinarily popular, especially among men, Wayne's World was seemingly restored.

During World War II, Reagan had gone "off to war," as his wife and Hollywood fan magazines put it. But his theater of war was especially theatrical: "Fort Hal Roach," the California movie studio where he was assigned to make propaganda films for the duration.[48] Similarly, the clearest examples of ultramasculinity during Reagan's presidency were in the realm of the imagination. An important aspect of the attempt to reassert masculinity has been to define the government as feminized and the enemy. The Vietnam War was lost, America is in decline, and men are not able to be real men, according to this viewpoint, because the government has been feminized: prone to emotion, weak, willing to compromise and negotiate, deceitful, maternal in trying to provide for people and make them dependent rather than obliging men to provide for themselves and "their women."[49] From this viewpoint, the feminized, maternal state is responsible for inverting the natural order, getting on top of men, denying opportunities for the achievement of manhood, enforcing sexual equality, and erasing the line of sexual opposition. If a feminized government has gotten on top of men, the way to reestablish masculinity and right order is for men to fight the government and get back on top of it. Reagan did this rhetorically, speaking with disdain of the "gub-mint," and declaring that government is the problem, not the solution.

Although the real sources of the problems troubling many men were to be found at much deeper levels of history, economics, society, and culture, there was a certain logic to seeing government as at least their proximate cause. Government, for instance, was taking away men's exclusive clubs and activities through such means as the enforcement of Title VII of the 1964 Civil Rights Act and Title IX in 1972, requiring equal opportunities in sports for women. The latter was especially galling to many men. Sports had constituted one of those realms that females had been told they *may not* enter. Sports were defined as a masculine arena, a substitute for war. Girls were supposed to watch guys perform and cheer for them—but now girls themselves were becoming athletes. "And the girls don't watch anymore," one California boys' coach complained. "The girls aren't interested," another agreed. "They're more into girls sports now."[50] And hadn't the government lost a war and failed to stand up to the Iranians? Wasn't the United States being pushed around by all sorts of minor countries? Hadn't the government failed to maintain the virility of the economy and to block foreign products from *penetrating* our markets and foreign people from *penetrating* our borders and so causing American men to lose their jobs? All of this and much more like it formed the subtext for Ronald Reagan's "vision" and popularity. He would put America back on top and put a stop to other countries treating the United States as if the nation were a woman.

All this was good politics and, if it could have been confined to Reagan's land of make-believe, its harm might have been kept within bounds (although the false analysis of the problems diverted attention away from the pursuit of the actual causes and possible solutions). But all of these attacks on a supposedly feminized government that was blamed for men's problems fueled the fantasies and paranoia of a substantial number of disturbed men who might seek vengeance against the governmental enemy. The antigovernment road Reagan helped to construct was a long and winding one, but the signs along its side pointed the way to Oklahoma City.

Aside from Reagan himself, the major figure in the reclamation project for American manhood during the eighties was another actor, Sylvester Stallone. In his film incarnations as Rocky and Rambo, Stallone revived Wayne's World and rechristened it Sly's World. The title of the first Rambo movie is intriguing. *First Blood* seems to be a reference to the onset of menstruation. In the male context shaped by the Non-Menstrual Syndrome, first blood refers, as we discussed in Chapter 3, to the "red badge of courage" that young males have desired as a seeming equivalent to the "red badge of womanhood" that young females' first blood provides. But the badge of manhood is denied to John Rambo and other American men in Vietnam. Somebody won't let them shed their first blood. "I do what I have to do to win, but somebody won't let us win," Rambo complains.[51] This statement readily translates to the generalized complaint of angry men (white or otherwise): *Somebody won't let us be men.* As always, that somebody is identified in a rapid regression as the Other, the enemy, the opposition, the opposite, the opposite sex, women, the feminine.

By the second installment in the film series, the feminine entity that won't let American males be men is clearly identified as the government. And "we get to win this time."[52]* *Time* magazine entitled its article on *Rambo: First Blood, Part II* most appropriately: "A Bloody Rite of Passage."[53] This time the boys would get to bleed; they would leave behind the woman's world into which they had been born and be reborn as men, triumphing over the feminized government that sought to prevent them from achieving their manhood. "The Viet Nam veteran," *Time* said, "has been given back his manhood."[54] The way in which manhood was supposedly restored was patently fantastic—essentially one "real man" going back and winning by himself a war against hordes of Vietnamese and Russians what the feminized American government had not been able to win with all its resources, manpower, money, and technology.[55] It was so far-fetched that it can better be seen as a measure of just how unattainable the old

---

*Rambo put these words in a question: "Do we get to win this time?" Colonel Trautman, his former mentor, replies: "This time, it's up to you." In other words: *This time you'll be given a chance to become a self-made man.*

notawoman conception of manhood has become. Sly's World for real not-women, like Wayne's and Reagan's, was a domain located in the imagination—a dream world fittingly headed by people from the Hollywood dream factory. It was no longer viable in the real world of the late twentieth century.

Being notawoman has always been a matter of image, but that fact has become much clearer in the last few decades. It is as if the Wizard has been exposed and we can see him manipulating the levers and smoke and mirrors. But many of us would prefer not to see how the tricks are performed so that we can maintain our illusions and continue to fight wicked witches as our enemies. By the end of the century this process of un-real men playing the parts of real notwomen and being elected to high office in the process had reached a new level of absurdity. Jesse Ventura, a "real" man from the make-believe world of professional wrestling, was elected governor of Minnesota and flirted with a run for the presidency. (And all the while he sold action figures of himself.)

"Woman Is the Nigger of the World"

As there is logic of a sort to blaming a putatively feminized government for men's problems, there is a similar sort of strained logic to violence against women and violence in general by dis-placed men. "If a man could not get the infrastructure to work for him, he could at least tear it down," as Fauldi says. "If the nation would not provide an enemy to fight, he could go to war at home."[56] It is not unusual or surprising that a man who feels he has been economically and socially emasculated and is being treated like a woman at work and in the outside world in general tries to come home and compensate there: *They may be fucking me out there, but I'll do the fucking here at home. The boss rides my ass at work, but I'll ride your ass and show you who's boss in my home!* And this attitude includes both senses of fucking, often with the emphasis on the making hate version.

This is part of the meaning of the 1972 John Lennon/Yoko Ono song, "Woman is the Nigger of the World":

Woman is the nigger of the world
Yes she is . . . think about it

. . .

We make her paint her face and dance
If she won't be a slave, we say that she don't love us
If she's real, we say she's trying to be a man
While we're putting her down we pretend that she's above us
Woman is the nigger of the world . . . yes she is

. . .

Woman is the slave of the slaves[57]

On one level the song reflects the fact that a woman has been likely to be at the bottom of the food chain—or, more accurately, the fucking chain, so let's just call it the *F-chain*. So she has been the scapegoat, the person on whom an insecure man can take out his frustrations through physical abuse. Given our assumptions that one must work, make things, and provide in order to be a real man, a man who has been *laid* off sees himself as having been treated as a woman. By *laying* his troubles on a woman, he temporarily regains a sense of manhood. "I was feeling good. I was in power, I was strong, I was in control. I felt like a *man*," a member of a domestic violence group said of the night he beat his girlfriend. "[But] that feeling of power didn't last long. Only until they put the cuffs on. Then I was feeling like I was no man at all."[58] Tony, the John Travolta character in the 1977 movie *Saturday Night Fever,* explained the way the F-chain operates: "Everybody's gotta dump on somebody, right? . . . My Pa goes to work and gets dumped on, so he comes home and he dumps on my mother, right?" He summed it up neatly: "Even the humpin's about dumpin'."[59]

There is more to the message in the Lennon-Ono song, however. It suggests, quite correctly, that woman is the model for all the "niggers" of the world: that the Master metaphor has allowed men who so desire to pseudosex anyone they seek to subordinate and treat him as they would what they consider to be the prototype for an inferior creature, a female. For the low-men, though, the bottom-feeders (and bottom-fuckers) in the social and economic F-chain, there's no one left to subordinate but the prototype herself, so woman becomes "the slave of the slaves." (And low-men are not confined to the actual lower ranks of society. Those who feel especially insecure in their manhood are likely to act in similar ways, even if they are financially well off.)

The Quest for the Holy Male

"You ever figure out who you are mad at?" a man at a Promise Keepers group meeting asked another. "I never figured it out. My wife says to me, 'You are angry *all* the time.' And I am! . . . But I don't know *who* I'm mad at—or *why?*"[60] This man gave voice to feelings that were shared to one degree or another by large numbers of dis-placed men in the closing decades of the twentieth century.

Several male movements have emerged to offer various paths troubled men might follow in reacting to their latest dis-placement. These range from the merely silly "wild men" who followed Robert Bly around carrying spears, through the more ominous Promise Keepers and Nation of Islam (largely parallel religiously based movements that seek to restore male responsibility by re-asserting divinely sanctioned male superiority), to the menacing militia and other right-wing groups that have arisen in the United States and several other nations, most of which combine misogyny with their racism, anti-Semitism, homophobia, and other affinities.

Novelist Paul Theroux was on the mark when he said in 1983 that the men's movement's quest for manliness is "fueled largely by a fear of women."[61] One prominent Promise Keepers preacher, Chuck Swindoll, liked to lead the throngs of men gathered at Promise Keepers' rallies in football stadiums in chants of "Power, power, we got the power."[62] But those who actually do have the power and are confident that they do have no need to engage in such rituals of mass reassurance. For all the surface bluster about wives submitting to their husbands, most of the men who participate in these movements are plainly insecure and searching for some meaningful form of masculinity with which they can identify and thus assert their manhood in a way that is convincing and satisfying to themselves.

When Nation of Islam leader Minister Louis Farrakhan held his "Million Man March" in Washington in 1995, bringing together hundreds of thousands of black men for a "day of atonement," the conventional wisdom was: "good message, bad messenger." This interpretation holds that the racist, anti-Semitic beliefs of Farrakhan and many of his associates tainted an otherwise admirable call for a reconstruction of a sense of responsible African-American manhood. In fact, however, the message left almost as much to be desired as did the chief messenger.

That there is a crisis among African-American males is beyond question. As I have indicated, in many ways black men have been the vanguard suffering the ill effects of the modern world before they reach others. But the crisis is by no means confined to black men, as is shown by the immense following that Promise Keepers attracted in the mid-1990s while preaching many themes similar to those of Farrakhan, without the racism. The vast numbers of men who were attracted to these organizations* is incontrovertible evidence that the feeling among men that there is something wrong in their lives is very widespread. The men's movement was tapping "into a deep current of malaise among American men."[63] Members of both movements pledge fidelity to their wives and children.[64] Organizers of the Million Man March called on African-American men to "take responsibility for their own lives and families, and to dedicate themselves to fighting the scourges of drugs, violence and unemployment."[65] All of these efforts are obviously praiseworthy.

Both Farrakhan and Promise Keepers founder Bill McCartney, the former University of Colorado football coach, called upon men to admit their failures

---

*The National Park Service estimated the crowd at the Million Man March at 875,000, and 1.1 million men attended Promise Keepers' stadium rallies in 1997 [http://www.igc.apc.org/africanam/hot/indexhtml; http://www.promisekeepers.org].

and make amends to those they've wronged, especially "their" women, and accept personal responsibility. That sounds good, but it turns out that what men have been wrong about in the view of these self-appointed restorers of manhood is giving up their power to women. Both defined the proper male role as that of head of the family. "We wanted to call our men to Washington to make a statement that we are ready to accept the responsibility of being the heads of our households, the providers, the maintainers and the protectors of our women and children," Farrakhan said.[66] That it is all about male identity is evident in his further comment: "No nation gets any respect if you go to war and you put your women in the trenches and the men stay home cooking." The same point was indicated by one of the other organizers of the march when he responded to criticism of Farrakhan's leadership by shouting: "We want to be led by a *man;* not some sissy or faggot!"

Basing its program on the Bible, Promise Keepers holds that men are the natural leaders over their wives and children. The group argues that it is time for males to stop acting like "feminized men" and to reassume their natural role of patriarch. Unless men take back the authority they have relinquished to women, Promise Keepers asserts, in language almost identical to that used by Farrakhan, the nation is lost.[67]

What both of these movements seek to restore is the same sexual order that men in the 1950s briefly reestablished. The Promise Keepers' counsel is exactly the same as the intended message of *Rebel Without a Cause.* Although kids of the fifties carried away different ideas, that movie was intended, as we have seen, to say that the trouble with society is men not fulfilling their proper roles as the authority in the family. This is obviously the problem in the family of Jim Stark (James Dean), but it is also what is wrong with Plato (Sal Mineo), whose father sends money for his support, but is absent, and Judy (Natalie Wood), whose father refuses to be affectionate. The Dean character says such things about his mother and father as: "Aw, she eats him alive, and he takes it. . . . If he had the guts to knock Mom cold once, then maybe she'd be happy and they'd stop pickin' on him. They [Jim's mother and grandmother] make *mush* outta him. I don't want to grow up to be like that." There is also the memorable scene of Jim's father, wearing an apron, on hands and knees, picking up a tray he had dropped while taking food to his wife. This, Farrakhan and McCartney would agree with Jim and the makers of *Rebel Without a Cause,* is the wrong men have done to women and for which they must atone. *Show the women who's boss, and our troubles will be over,* they contend.

At base what these movements are about is gender extending. Putting the Conception Misconception into his own terminology, McCartney maintains that men are the "initiators" and women "receptors," who are "brought to splendor" by men.[68] Like the authors of the Hebrew law in the Torah whom he likes to quote (and like Farrakhan and his lieutenants), McCartney is horrified by anything that tends to blur the line between the sexes, such as homosexuality: "You shall not lie with a man as with a woman; it is an abomination."[69]*

Most of McCartney's followers, however, do not appear to have been such extremists. They were in the market for a product that is always in high demand in periods of mass, impersonal, individualist society: a religion that promises a personal relationship with God.[70] This yearning for personal connection had been, as we have seen, a major factor in the spread of Christianity in the Roman era.

In order to attract men to religion, many of the entrepreneurs of right-wing Christianity have striven to masculinize Jesus. "Christ wasn't effeminate," Rev. Jerry Falwell has proclaimed. "The man who lived on this earth was a man with muscles. . . . Christ was a he-man!" "Christ was no wimp," agrees Christian former major league baseball player Brett Butler. "Jesus was a man's man," Christian bodybuilder John Jacobs maintains, apparently envisioning an incarnation of the Prince of Peace in a body like Arnold Schwarzenegger's.[71] The complaints of such men and many others about a "feminization of the church" and "sissified" pastors both ignore the fact that the church was efeminated or masculinized in its early centuries and point once more to the difficulty of selling more feminine values to men.[72]

Trying to Reclaim Their Golden Balls

For his part, poet Robert Bly, who struck a chord with many men with his 1990 best-seller, *Iron John,* saw the modern crisis in masculinity coming in large part from a dearth of "real man" role models and from modern men having become too close to women. Shepherd Bliss (who had changed his name from Walter when he became a Bly apostle; why he did not go whole hog and call himself *Hunter* is unclear) may have come closer to revealing the actual source of the men's movement's fears when he said: "Women aren't victims. We all know the power of women."[73]

Since the sixties peace movement (in which he had been prominent himself), Bly thought, "men had awakened their feminine principle only to be consumed by it. They had gone 'soft.' "[74] He was in some respects striking back at women from the movement who had told pacifist and radical males that they "*wanted* soft men": "We will sleep with you if you are not too

---

*It seems significant that both homosexuality and wearing garments appropriate to the other sex were classified as abominations in Hebrew law. What these practices have in common is that both tend to lessen sharp distinctions between the sexes, and so to suggest that the sexes are not opposite.

aggressive and macho."[75] But Bly seems to have concluded by the 1980s that, even if the women who said such things had thought they meant it, they were denying both their own and men's biological natures. Women would find themselves attracted to "wild men," even if they didn't want to be, and men would not find themselves attractive if they became soft. The equation *soft = female* is too ingrained in the natures of both sexes for either to find soft men acceptable. Whatever one may think of this analysis (and I think there is some merit to it, if it is not taken to extremes), the program Bly and his followers proposed to help "SNAGs" (Sensitive New Age Guys) recover "the wild man within" was ridiculous. At their weekend offensives,* for which participants paid hefty fees, men engaged in such activities as going around on all fours, howling, beating drums, and trying in a variety of other ways to "reclaim their golden balls"[76] (a reference to the fairy tale about "Iron John" that Bly used to illustrate what he thought men need to do).

Generally all the recent variations on the theme of restoring purpose to men's lives have been ineffectual because they are responding to the symptoms of the malady in masculinity but have misidentified or only partially identified its causes. Bly and his "mythopoetic" masculinist followers argue that the problem rests in men having failed adequately to separate from their mothers.[77] This analysis, as I see it, has the matter almost entirely backward. It is probably true that males need some sort of rite of passage into manhood to correspond to the females' menarche. But the need is not to separate maturing boys from women (which is what "separation from their mothers" actually means): That is the notawoman conception of manhood, "a relentless effort to repudiate femininity, a frantic effort to dissociate from women."[78] That idea reflects the very sexual bi-polarism that is the root of so many male problems. What that definition has long (very, *very* long) asked men to do is "to prove the unprovable"[79]: that they are the *opposite* of women. That assertion is and always has been nonsense,† but it is nonsense that has (mis)guided the thinking of men throughout recorded history. What is different in the modern world is that men have been told not only that they must be the opposite of women but also that, if they want to be real men, they must accomplish this impossible task by themselves: become *self-made* notwomen. This demand increases the personal stakes that are to be lost when a man places his bet on one of the numbers representing an accepted route

---

*I use that word *offensives* because it seems appropriate on many levels and the gatherings certainly were not supposed to be retreats.

†It is important to reemphasize, for the benefit of cultural determinists, that what makes the idea that men and women are or can be opposites nonsense is biology. Biology teaches us that men and women are very much alike (although with a few differences on average). Most cultures around the world have taught that the sexes are almost totally different.

to "real manhood" and watches the roulette wheel that is the modern Market-place world spin. The game is designed to put the gambling man at a great dis-advantage, and many of those who lose *are* lost. They desperately search for other ways to find themselves and define themselves as men in a way that fits with the accepted cultural conceptions.

"Girls Have All the Power"

A scarcely organized group of boys in Lakewood, California, calling them-selves the Spur Posse gained notoriety in 1993 when it became known that this club established its pecking order on the basis of how many different girls each one of the boys fucked.* Like so many males before them, these boys when they felt that their masculinity had been threatened sought reassurance by falling back on the most basic male biological function. And, like so many whites before them, they tried to model themselves after the American men with the most experience in social, economic, and psychological emascula-tion: blacks. They listened to rap music, used African-American slang, and idolized black basketball stars. Blacks were, in fact, the model for the "bad bad boy" who emerged in advertising and the culture, and these young Cali-fornia white males were very much shaped by that Consumerculture.

They did not even pretend to be rebelling against the dominant culture: they wanted in, they wanted to "make it big." Like Willy Loman, they sought to become known. "I just want to be up there with the big boys," one of them declared.[80] Another kept referring to their quest to get their "brand name" pub-licized. They were real-life[†] nineties' versions of low men.

Their analysis of the sources of their lowness and their attempts to deal with it were much closer to the thinking of other troubled men than was generally acknowledged. "Girls have all the power," complained one of the posse, reciting a basic male lament that reverberated over the millennia. They had fully adopted pseudosexing and the language of verbal mounting that expresses it. "He screwed us bad," one of them said of a Hollywood man who had supposedly said he would get a movie made about the boys. Another declared that a television host who had also "screwed" them "is a cock-sucking bitch." They even made their own contribution to the vocabulary of verbal mounting when they used the same term, *hooking,* both for "taking" someone while telemarketing and for "hooking" up with a girl.[81]

---

*This is clearly the appropriate word in this case.

†Or were they? They were so much into promoting themselves through the media that it might be more accurate to see them in the same category as Kris Kristofferson's "Pilgrim": "partly truth and partly fiction." ["The Pilgrim, Chapter 33," lyrics by Kris Kristofferson, Resaca Music, BMI.]

Females were purely objects to these boys, a raw material out of which they hoped to build their "brand name." "It doesn't count if you have, like, sex with a girl, like one hundred and fifty times, two hundred—that's only *one* point," Kevin Howard explained on *The Jenny Jones Show.*[82] The Spurs were playing the same game that Jack Kennedy did. They emulated Kennedy in another way, too. One of them had been sent to a juvenile detention center for having sex with a ten-year-old girl. "I didn't know how old she was," he said. "She had a body and everything. I just seen her at parties. I didn't even know her name." "These girls are *no-names,*" Spur Billy Shehan added. "We've got a *name.*"[83] Like the former president, the Spurs were more interested in females' bodies than their names. In fact, it seems that *no-names* was for both the insecure boys and the insecure president a synonym for *women.* (Recall that in ancient Rome it was common for females to be given no name of their own.) To have a name was to claim superiority, to "be a man." PUSSIES AREN'T HEROES was one of the signs adorning Billy Shehan's bedroom walls.[84] These boys desperately sought to "make a name for themselves" because on some level they realized that, under the winner-take-all criteria of the Marketplace worldview, they were in a regression away from manhood much like that in which Willy Loman had found himself—or, rather, *lost himself:* no-names, nobodies, low-men, no-men, wo-men. "We've got a *name*" was a way to say: *We're not women.*

All of this is apparent in the unsolicited declaration by Shehan that is this chapter's epigraph: "And we *do* exist, I swear to God, we do exist!"* Susan Faludi, who spent a good deal of time talking with members of the group, has identified Shehan as "the unofficial philosopher of the Spurs."[85] His statement leaves no doubt what that philosophy was. His outburst to Faludi is a remarkably straightforward declaration of the *I fuck, therefore I am* philosophy.

But even that behavior was not sufficient to prove to themselves their existence. By the late twentieth century, the notion had become widespread that if something is not captured by television cameras, it didn't really happen: *I am on television; therefore I exist.* These boys wanted this modern proof of their existence, too. What they really sought, it seems, was something like: *I fucked on TV, therefore I exist.* Then, perhaps, they would become "names," men who exist, who can say with conviction: *I am somebody! I'm a man!* They never achieved that, but some of them did at least get to talk about it on TV.

The game in which these boys were engaged, then, can accurately be called "the Name Game" (although played with no-names). But, their moment in the

---

*The degree to which the need to assert their existence and manhood has troubled men in recent decades is evident in how common such statements are. Shehan's declaration is almost identical to Scott Carey's at the end of *The Incredible Shrinking Man.* The same cry is heard from Willy Loman to Jesse Jackson's chant for young African-Americans: "I *am* somebody."

media spotlight notwithstanding, the boys of the Spur Posse never made much of a name for themselves. *Kennedy* had become the ultimate brand name; the Spurs, however, remained strictly generic.

Body Counts

The "scoring" in the Spur Posse's game (and Kennedy's) was the same as in that other game that took shape in the Kennedy administration, the Vietnam War. In both games, the score was tallied in body counts and the bodies were "no-names," inferior things to be fucked. "I got five!" "I got ten!" members of Charlie Company at My Lai shouted.[86] Shehan, the Spur Posse's leading scorer, was proud of his accomplishment, which he presumably would have been glad to express in the shout: *I got sixty-seven.* The number that John F. Kennedy got is unknown, but it is certain that it would dwarf Shehan's score to an extent similar to that by which Kennedy's brand name eclipses Shehan's generic version.

In Vietnam, keeping score by body counts meant that civilians, the elderly, women, and children could all be counted as points. Any-body counts. A similarly democratic principle of equality guides the scoring rules in the domestic Name Game of trying to prop up one's dubious masculinity by having sex with as many female bodies as possible. A ten-year-old girl shot in Vietnam could be used to inflate a soldier's body count much as the Spur Posse member tried to use a ten-year-old girl to add to his body count. They were all seen as nobodies, but they were no-bodies that counted in the quest to make a man believe what his circumstances had caused him to doubt: that *he* is somebody—a man.

The links among fucking, killing, and genital mutilation of females were revealed in the horrifying events in Vietnam, where "double veteran" was the slang for a GI who raped and murdered a woman. American soldiers mutilated many Vietnamese women by ripping open their vaginas with their bayonets or knives. What happened at My Lai must be seen in light of the associations that American men had made between the Vietnamese and women. It was a powerful combination of racism and misogyny that produced the horror there, in a place that was appropriately referred to by the Americans as "Pinkville" (because it was in a pink area on their maps). One member of Charlie Company found the ultimate way to say *Fuck you!* when he penetrated a woman's vagina with his rifle and pulled the trigger.[87] It is tempting to dismiss such atrocities as isolated acts by deranged, evil people. But, while the acts are certainly deranged and evil, it would be a mistake to dismiss them as unrepresentative.

What some of the American soldiers did to women in Vietnam (and of course such actions are by no means unique to Americans or that war) is very similar to Marduk's cutting of Tiamat's womb or Perseus's severing of the vagina/head of Medusa. The "double veteran" association of sexual inter-course and killing—"fuck 'em to death"—appears to be that very old form of male insecurity-bred misogyny: *We may not be able to give birth, but we can give death. One of my guns may not really shoot life, but the other one sure can shoot death.*

It is reasonable to think that such a recurring theme, over such a long period of time and variety of cultures says something about the male situation and a common response to it. As I have tried to show, female genital mutila-tion is an extreme, virulent manifestation of womb envy.

"One Pill Makes You Larger . . ."

Another manifestation of the increasingly desperate search for means of redraw-ing the fading line between the sexes emerged in the last third of the twentieth century. At precisely the same time that women began moving toward equality, what came to be called "anorexic chic" took off in the 1960s with the popularity of British model Twiggy. As the differences between men and women have nar-rowed in many respects, cultural ideals of female and male bodies have diverged to an extraordinary degree. Late twentieth-century culture created a vision of the ideal woman as a waif: the smaller the better. As women have grown toward equality in many areas of life, they have increasingly been encouraged to dimin-ish physically. Men, simultaneously, have been exhorted to build themselves up to phenomenal levels. (An attempt, obviously, to ease the "shrinking man" anx-iety: If my body is *this* big, I must be somebody.) A psychiatric disorder that is the virtual opposite of anorexia nervosa, called muscle dysmorphia (people with extremely muscular bodies who imagine themselves to be weaklings and con-tinually work at bulking up, often with the aid of steroids), has become increas-ingly common, mainly among men, since the early 1990s.[88] GI Joe and similar action figure toys aimed at boys have grown much bigger with ever-more-grossly exaggerated muscles in the last two decades. They form an impossible standard toward which boys are encouraged to aspire, as Barbie dolls do in the opposite direction with girls.[89] As women and men in the modern world seem less like opposite sexes, GI Joe and Barbie have preserved and extended the bi-polar ideals.

"One pill makes you larger, and one pill makes you small," Jefferson Air-plane sang in "White Rabbit."[90] Nowadays, with relatively few exceptions, it is males who are advised to take the pills that make you larger (steroids), while females are exhorted to take the pills that promise to make you small (diet pills). Go ask Alice, who—unlike Alex—is never even to think about being 10 feet tall (but who is advised to try to see if she can make her waist 10 inches small).

Turning women into facsimiles of famine victims has implications beyond mere reduction in size. Women whose weight falls to such extremes often cease to menstruate; thus they lose the great female power that has always been most threatening to many men. A woman without reproductive capacity ceases to be such a menace to the male ego. The same culture that warns men about the horrors of being a "97-pound weakling" (for "weakling," read "nonman") holds up for women the ideal of becoming a 75-pound "nonwoman" (in the sense of *woman* that many men have found so intimidating). That is a creature to which even the most insecure man can hope to convince himself he is superior.

For their part, males who attempt to become excessively large and muscular seem to be desperately seeking a way to prove themselves to be the opposite of women: *Here, at last, is something I can do that women can't!* They have been persuaded that in order to be real men they've got to be macho men.* "There is now an almost cartoonlike level of masculinity where aggression is as exaggerated as the idol's size," ABC News correspondent Kevin Newman noted in a 1999 report. "Boys [are] feeling this need to be big and powerful in order to feel good about themselves," says Dan Kindlon of the Harvard School of Public Health. "I don't think I'm big enough at all," an already excessively bulked-up sixteen-year-old boy told Newman. "I'd like to get a lot bigger. . . . I want to be as big as humanly possible."[91]

Or, perhaps, bigger than is *humanly* possible. The subconscious goal of excessive growth in men and excessive diminution in women seems to be to create in humans a sexual dimorphism similar to that of gorillas. In that primate species that is closely related to us, the males are as much as twice as large as the females; thus, dominant males are able to accumulate "harems" of several females—rather like many political leaders in our own species. If threatened male humans cannot succeed in the pretense that men and women are from different planets, perhaps they can reshape us into a species that will make the earth once again a Planet of the Apes, where drastic difference in body size leaves no doubt about who is the boss.

---

*The irony of using "I've Got to Be a Macho Man" for the title of this chapter is intentional. No doubt men who are struggling to prove their masculinity through the notawoman definition of manhood would generally be homophobic. And that song was intended by its performers, The Village People, to be a homosexual anthem.

CHAPTER 17

Fears of Our Fathers, Living Still

How Ancient Mistakes About Sex Continue to Affect Us

He can't do it, he can't change it
It's been going on for ten thousand years
PETER YARROW, MARY TRAVERS & ALBERT GROSSMAN (1967)[1]

In a 1997 *X-Files* episode on a modern Frankenstein theme entitled "The Post-modern Prometheus," a woman calls F.B.I. Agent Mulder and asks him to investigate her impregnation by a monster. She says that she was impregnated in the same way nearly two decades ago. "And now you're pregnant again?" Mulder's partner, Agent Scully, asks.

"Uh-huh. But, as I told Agent Mulder over the phone, that's what takes the cake."

Mulder explains to Scully: "Mrs. Berkowitz had a tubal ligation two years ago."

"You can't plant a seed in a barren field," Mrs. Berkowitz declares matter-of-factly.

As the third millennium dawns and we mark the approximate ten thousandth anniversary of the introduction of agriculture, the seed metaphor continues to be used routinely by people around the world. This metaphor is arguably the most destructive analogy ever devised by the human imagination. Of course we now *know,* and have known for centuries, that males do not have sole procreative power. Yet the Conception Misconception continues to affect our lives profoundly every day, because so much of our world for thousands of years has been constructed on the flawed foundation of believing females and the ways and values associated with them to be inferior.

371

We live in an era in which there has been dramatic change in the treatment of women, yet a 1995 United Nations study found that 70 percent of the world's poor are women and that, "despite two decades of advances in the education and health of women around the world, hundreds of millions of women in both rich and poor nations are still significantly undervalued economically, denied access to effective political power and kept down by crippling inequalities under the law."[2] A large part of the problem is that our outlook and our institutions have been so deeply influenced and shaped by the assumptions of exclusive male creative power, sexual opposition, and female inferiority that it is extremely difficult to bring about the sort of truly fundamental changes that are needed.

Men have de-valued women and classified them as inferior for two basic reasons: because many men feared that *they* are biologically inferior in their powers and because men were themselves de-valued by the development of agriculture. The fact that our very distant fathers did not have much faith in themselves is the fount of many of the most serious and persistent problems throughout recorded history. The fears of our fathers gave shape to the faith of our fathers and that in turn has misshaped us. Both the fears and the faith of our fathers are living still, and the effects of the mistakes made in such a distant past continue to be extremely pernicious.

Anyone who doubts that the misconception about conception that arose after "Eve" discovered the practical use of seeds still colors our religious views might consider the following incidents from the ten years preceding publication of this book:

In a 1991 Father's Day sermon, Cardinal John J. O'Connor of New York was reported to have "asserted the indisputable maleness of God."[3] The hostile reaction was sufficient that the prelate "clarified" his position a few days later, saying that he had not meant it the way it sounded.[4] A little more than a year later, in the space of an eight-day period in the fall of 1992, three things happened: the Church of England finally voted after a heated debate (and by a margin of only two votes) to permit the ordination of women priests; the Vatican announced that the decision constituted "a new and grave obstacle" to reconciling the Anglican and Roman churches; and the National Conference of Catholic Bishops in the United States admitted that it was so divided over the proper role of women in the church and society that it was abandoning a nine-year effort to come up with language on which its members could agree for a pastoral letter on the subject.[5]

In 1993 Catholic officials in Boston declared invalid baptisms that had been performed by a priest who used the inclusive "God, our Creator, through Jesus the Christ, in the power of the Holy Spirit" instead of the traditional, all-male "Father, Son, and Holy Spirit."[6]

In a 1994 Apostolic Letter entitled "On Reserving Priestly Ordination to Men Alone," Pope John Paul II reaffirmed the Catholic Church's position that the ordination of women is not even a matter open to discussion. The reason? The hoary argument that Jesus' apostles were all men.[7]

In 1997 the International Bible Society announced that it was aborting the publication of a gender-neutral translation of the New International Bible. "It's a victory for the word of God," proclaimed a Southern Baptist theology professor. "You don't compromise scripture just to make women feel included." No indeed; not when parts of "scripture" plainly were written as they were by men in the first place for the purpose of excluding or subordinating women—just to make men feel included.

In mid-1998, the Southern Baptist Convention, speaking for the largest Protestant denomination in the United States (and one that is growing rapidly in many areas around the world), altered its official statement of "Baptist Faith and Message" for the first time in thirty-five years in order to proclaim: "A wife is to submit graciously to the servant leadership of her husband."[8] A Catholic bishop in New Jersey promptly praised the Baptist Convention for its "perception, fidelity, and courage" in issuing "a contemporary and much desired statement in regard to the family." (This "contemporary" statement is, of course, based on St. Paul's reading of the Genesis version of the Conception Misconception. This sort of argument was contemporary during the first male backlash at least six thousand years ago. That so many men find it appealing to make such a claim today is a testament both to the power and durability of the Conception Misconception and to the similarities between men's perceived position today and that of their Neolithic forefathers.) A few weeks later, the Vatican raised its insistence that women cannot be priests to the level of canon law, thereby threatening with excommunication any Catholics who argue against this particular legacy of womb envy and belief in male procreative power.[9]

Then in 2000, the Southern Baptist Convention found unaccustomed common ground with the Church of Rome by proclaiming that "the office of pastor is limited to men as qualified by Scripture."[10]

Another Attempt at Adapting to the Human-Made Environment

My purpose here has been diagnostic, not prescriptive. It would be outrageously arrogant of me to suggest that I could provide the solutions to general problems that have been developing for ten thousand years. Even offering an analysis of what has caused those problems over the course of human history since the invention of agriculture is hardly an exercise in humility. I am persuaded that beginning to understand the deep underlying causes of the massive problems we confront is the essential first step in trying to do something about them. And I can do little more in these pages than to try to take that first step.

It would, however, be improper to end this reinterpretation of the human experience without making a few very preliminary suggestions about how we might begin to work toward the establishment of values that could provide effective means of reining in our maladaptive proclivities. That task will, in all probability, be more difficult than any other that human beings have ever faced. I make no pretense that taking the steps that I will outline in the remainder of this chapter would bring us anywhere near a cure for our present social ills. I merely believe that they might be helpful—a start on a long and arduous journey.

Our present circumstances are far from hopeless. We have moved a long way from the social environment for which human biology is adapted; we are not physically "designed" for the modern, mobile, urban world. But this mismatch does not mean that we need to return to a more primitive way of life in order to survive. A full realization of what the problem is can lead to the development of new cultural adaptations.

Past cultural adaptations, beginning with the values that were cultivated in response to the changes agriculture wrought in the social environment, have consisted of humans adapting themselves to an environment that the species itself had altered.[11] We need to do this again to meet the modern world crisis produced by the second megarevolution—and we need to do it better this time.

We can take some comfort from a couple of facts. One is that immunities to diseases can be acquired naturally, but we have also found ways to provide them artificially, through vaccines created by human ingenuity.[12] This development suggests, at least metaphorically (which we have seen to be a dangerous approach), that we might be able to devise means to inoculate ourselves against some of the ill effects of our innate motivations that now get us into trouble. These inbred proclivities that no longer operate to our advantage in an altered social environment can be seen as analogous to allergies or autoimmune disorders in which innate qualities that are supposed to aid us instead turn against us. These physical disorders are among the most difficult to treat or guard against, and the same is likely to be true of their social counterparts. But the analogy provides some hope—as long as we can avoid literalizing it.

More hope is to be found in the fact that humans have proven to be, through our intelligence, the most adaptive creatures in the planet's natural history. A species biologically designed to live in the savannas of East Africa has been able to adapt to life in arctic tundras and deserts—and even beneath the sea and in outer space. Creatures that have been able to use their wits to adapt to such drastically different physical environments should also to be able to devise ways to adapt through culture to radically altered social environments. If we can learn to live in the physical vacuum of space, we ought to be able to figure out how to live in the communal vacuum of large cities, too.

To do so, we have to realize just what the need is. It is to that end that the understanding of the way we are that I have presented in this book has attempted to make a contribution. It must further be understood that the adaptations that humans have made to physical environments that differ sharply from that for which we are biologically designed have been accomplished through artificial (human-made) means—devices that mediate between people, who remain basically unchanged, and the different environments. Such devices took the form, for example, of human-made clothing to protect a body that is biologically "unsuited" for extreme cold from the effects of such temperatures. We have not changed our natural capacity to withstand extreme cold or heat (we remain unable to do that); instead we have developed clothing, heating, and air conditioning. We did not, in short, change our natures to meet the difficulties presented by environments for which we were not biologically adapted; rather, we found ways to prevent those environments from affecting us too adversely.

Values, as I have tried to show, perform a similar function in mediating between a largely unchanged human nature and an altered (and altering) social environment. Over the millennia since the invention of agriculture began to change the social environment substantially, the success of our traditional values was not overwhelming, but those values got us by. Now, though, we find ourselves in a social environment that is vastly farther removed from that for which we are biologically suited than were those for which our traditional values were developed. The values necessitated by the development of agriculture were something like the making of clothing to mediate between the lightly haired, warm-blooded human body and the cold regions of the earth. But the changes in the social environment brought by the second megarevolution and the Marketplace Misconception have made the mismatch between our biogram and the environment much greater, and the values we now need to mediate between our natural inclinations and this hostile modern social environment would more resemble an astronaut's suit than a fur robe.

That our traditional values have been less successful in mediating between the human biogram and the highly unnatural social environment of the twentieth century has led many people to move toward abandoning them. This is like saying that since clothing of moderate weight does not provide sufficient protection from arctic cold, we should abandon all human-made garments and go naked into the Alaskan winter.

The abandonment of traditional values would leave us naked before the frigid winds blown up by the modern world. What we need is to reconstruct our values in such a way that they can provide effective protection from a social environment so different from the one for which *Homo sapiens* evolved that it can destroy a human without effective values almost as readily as sub-zero temperatures can destroy a human without effective clothing.

God Is an Hermaphrodite

What we need, above all else, is to achieve a genuine balance between feminine and masculine values. I doubt that this goal can be accomplished without undertaking what would be the most sweeping change in outlook of at least the last five millennia: ending the indefensible and extremely harmful view of God as a male—and even that would just be the first major step. We need also to go beneath that mistake and really accept that the sexes are co-reproducers. And beneath that to the ultimate problem: the mistaken belief that the sexes are opposite and so a "real man" has to be notawoman.

I have indicated why the mis-understanding about God being male arose and the deleterious consequences it brought about. We all know full well that procreation is not the work of males alone, but occurs only with the combining of female and male. Yet most of us continue religious practices and rituals based upon a long-outdated misconception about conception.

The first step in the salvation of our society is to stop thinking and talking in terms of "our *Father* who art in heaven" and start thinking and talking instead about "our *Creator*"—a unified Creative Force that is neither male nor female but combines both elements. This step is essential, because there is no way to see God as a male and simultaneously maintain a sincere belief in sexual equality. If one sex is closer to the Heavenly Perfection than the other, the former must be superior, the latter inferior. This outgrowth of the Conception Misconception, more than physical strength or any other attribute, has been the underlying, lasting basis for the subordination of women over the ages.

There have been some attempts to address the deeply ingrained view of God as male. The United Church of Christ has altered the language of the gospels to, for example, replace the words in Matthew 28, "in the name of the Father and of the Son and of the Holy Spirit" with "in the name of God the Father and Mother and of Jesus Christ the beloved Child and of the Holy Spirit."[13] A simpler form that has been suggested is: "Creator, Redeemer, Sustainer."[14]

Resistance to such a sensible revision in our understanding of Creative Power, to bring it into line with what we now know about procreative power, is enormous, however. The reaction to the inclusive description of the Trinity by Boston's Catholic hierarchy and the cancellation of the gender-neutral translation of the New International Bible mentioned earlier are among the many examples.

It is remarkable how mistakes become self-perpetuating. In the early centuries of Christianity, men wrote accounts of the life of Jesus that downplayed the role of his female followers. Then they excluded from the canon all reports that indicated that women played any major parts. Subsequently—and down to the present—male Church officials have used these distorted accounts to justify the continued barring of women from positions of importance in the Church.

Still, there are a few faint signs that even the Catholic Church may be beginning to be affected by the reality of women's gains in the modern world. In the summer of 1995, Pope John Paul II issued another apostolic letter, this one addressed to "the women of the world." In it he acknowledged the role the Church has played in "the global culture that exploits and dominates women," personally apologized for those in the Church who contributed to the oppression of women, praised many aims of the women's liberation movement, endorsed the equality of the sexes, and called for worldwide legislation outlawing sexual violence and economic and social inequality. The Pope said that, after centuries of discrimination, equality for women is a matter of necessity as well as justice.[15]

But the Pope maintained his unflinching opposition to birth control and the ordination of women.[16] These positions show that John Paul II still does not really understand the role his Church has played in what he very accurately terms a *global culture that has exploited and dominated women*. The opposition to birth control indicates that he does not understand that the Judeo-Christian-Islamic tradition's commitment to "fruitfulness" was based upon the r-selected circumstances of abundance that the invention of agriculture created. Nor, apparently, does he comprehend that we now live in a very different situation, one in which human well-being depends on switching to a K-selected reproductive strategy in which birth control *must* play a major role.*

Undoubtedly, the Pope was sincere in his apology to women. Nevertheless, he completely fails to appreciate that the supreme role that his Church and organized religion in general have played in the global culture of exploitation and domination of women is the perpetuation of the belief that God is male. That misogynist culture will survive as long as the idea that God is male does.

Religion has played a very positive role in promoting the more feminine values that have restrained some of the maladaptive portions of human nature.

---

*The same mistake is made by free-market extremists, such as George Gilder, who insist that the talk of an overpopulation crisis is "bogus" and attack what they term "the foolish notion that population growth hurts economic progress." [George Gilder, *Men and Marriage* (Gretna, LA: Pelican Publishing, 1989), pp. xi, 37, 98)]. Their desire to maintain traditional sex roles combines with their blind faith in the Marketplace to lead them into thinking we can just continue to multiply without concern for the size or resources of our planet.

It has, however, simultaneously been pushing in the other direction through its insistence that God is male and its general subordination of women.

To Be Fe-malformed

The injurious effects on women of the Conception Misconception and the resulting belief that God is male go far beyond the adoption by many women of the Masculine Mystique. The continuing consequences of these mistaken ideas can be literally lethal to females right down to the present. Until very recently (the early 1990s) virtually all medical experiments and surveys were conducted using male subjects (even to the point of using male rats in experiments), because maleness was (and is) still taken by so many people to be "normal." A National Institutes of Health study in the 1980s entitled "Normal Human Aging," for example, contained no data whatsoever on the more than half of the population that suffers from the "abnormality" of being female. Similarly, prior to the last decade, there had been little research funded for diseases that occur only in women, such as ovarian cancer.[17]

An even more detrimental aspect of the continuing ripples from the Conception Misconception is that a majority of couples the world over prefers having sons to having daughters. Under circumstances militating against large families, this bias can result in fates befalling female offspring ranging from abortion to infanticide. In China, where the government restricts couples in many areas to one child and practices forced sterilization, infant girls have an increasing tendency to turn up dead shortly after birth. Female babies are abandoned or killed in alarming numbers. Demographers warn that the combination of rigid population control with a general preference for sons over daughters may lead to social chaos in China by the second or third decade of the twenty-first century; at that time as much as 65 percent of the young adult population may be male and no wives will be available for literally millions of young men.[18] When we consider the social problems caused in the United States by unattached young men, the potential results of the prospective sexual imbalance in China are frightening.

Even in the United States there is a growing practice of sex selection by parents. Amniocentesis or ultrasound is used to determine the sex of the fetus, which is subsequently aborted if "it" is not of the desired sex. In a 1994 feature on National Public Radio, no physician with whom this practice was discussed could recall a case in which a boy had been aborted because the parents wanted a girl. In *all* of the cases of sex-selection abortion that were found in this unscientific survey, the "it" that was not of the desired sex was a "she."[19]

Some doctors question the ethics of aborting for sex selection, which they say is different from abortion because of a defect. This argument misses the point. As a consequence of the mistaken beliefs that have guided our thinking for thousands of years, in the minds of many people, being female *is* being defective. Those still under the spell of the Conception Misconception see being born without a penis as being malformed (or fe-malformed).

"*Woman* Is the Measure of All Things"

For all the seeming accomplishments of the women's movement, it has not succeeded in stopping the use of masculine terminology to refer to both men and women. It is still common, as a new millennium begins, to hear and see prominent people and publications that should know better speaking of everything from "mankind," "Neanderthal Man," and "the family of man" to "man's attack on his environment" and "man and his world."

The reasons that so many people (women as well as men) have slid back into using male words generically are that they find sexually inclusive terminology to be awkward and they just do not think it makes any difference. If questioned about it, they will say something like: *Everybody knows that when we call our species "man," that includes women, too.*

I used to accept that argument, because I found such constructions as "her and his" difficult to deal with, especially in speech. But I now believe that the way we use language in this regard is one of the most significant factors in the exclusion and subordination of women—and so, indirectly, in our failure to blend a sufficient helping of feminine values into our recipe for survival, success, and sanity in the modern environment.

The use of male terminology for humans of both sexes is another direct outgrowth of the Conception Misconception and its offspring, the belief that God is male. It is the presumption that men are the "true humans"—the model of what a human is really supposed to be—and its corollary, that women are imperfect approximations of that ideal, that leads (quite sensibly, if these suppositions were correct) to using male terms generically. A remarkable example of this way of thinking is that the full article on *women* in the *Encyclopaedia Britannica*'s first edition (1771) consisted of the following: "The Female of man. See *Homo*."[20]

This terminology is an instance in which the use of inversion can be usefully employed for the purpose of enhancing understanding. The subtle but extremely powerful effect that such language has in determining which portions of humankind we think are important can be brought home by asking men who think that *man* "of course" includes women how they would react to calling our species *woman* and saying that this term should just be considered to include men. How central to the species (or to evolution) would men feel if Darwin's 1871 book had been entitled *The Descent of Woman?* Engaging in this sort of substitution on a wide scale can be an enlightening experience. Replacing every male term that is being used generically with its female counterpart demonstrates just how central this type of language is to the way we look at ourselves and how great the practice's effects on women must be.

Would we be likely to view our position in the creation in another light if Chaucer had written: "Whan that the month in which the world bigan / That highte March, whan God first maked *woman*"? How might the world seem different if Protagoras had said "*Woman* is the measure of all things"? Would American males be as patriotic as most of them claim to be if the first truth that the Declaration of Independence had held to be self-evident had been that "all *women* are created equal"? How might American history be altered if the Jacksonian Era were known as the Age of the Common *Woman,* if William Jennings Bryan had declared "You shall not crucify *womankind* upon a cross of gold," or if Franklin Roosevelt had spoken of "the forgotten *woman* at the bottom of the economic pyramid" (which would, in fact, have been more accurate)? Would those of us who are men have felt as much of a thrill in 1969 if Neil Armstrong had called the first footstep on the moon "a great leap for *womankind*"?

Obviously, men would not feel truly included if female terminology were used in a putatively inclusive manner. The implication would be the same as it would be if we saw the Creator as "Our Mother, who art in heaven": that men are inferior and women (and, hence, feminine values) are superior.

Indeed, the inescapable connotation of using female terminology inclusively would be to reverse the conclusions of Aristotle, Freud, and the rest: it would indicate that women are the "true humans," more perfect than men, and that men are deformed or incomplete women, lacking in spirit, "soul," ovaries, a womb, breasts, menstruation, or whatever would then be considered to be the essence of full humanity. This, in turn, would point back to an underlying belief that the Creator in whose image humans were thought to be made was a Goddess—a Creator with female organs.

Although this inversion can unmask the reality of one of the principal things we have been doing wrong for thousands of years, actually carrying out the reversal would result not in a cure for the evil, but in the creation of its mirror image. Under these circumstances of assumed female superiority, men might not want to define manhood on the notawoman basis. Women might be inclined to define womanhood in a "notaman" manner, but probably not, since it is women's capabilities that have led men to the "opposite" definition.

While any sensible view of God must be as what humans would call an hermaphrodite, *we* are not. The use of words that refer to one half of humanity as synonyms for all people necessarily produces the feeling that only one half of humankind is truly human. So long as we continue to use *man* when what we mean is *human,* we shall have scant hope of reconstructing our values by giving genuine equality to those that are usually associated with women.*

Modern Notawoman: The Lost Sex

We frequently hear statements like these: "The black man is an endangered species."[21] "If we don't do anything about it, the black man is gone."[22] The more generalized fear that men are an endangered species is heard less often, but it, too, has gained currency in many quarters in recent decades. In one sense this fear might seem justified to readers of the preceding pages. The reality, as we have seen, is that black men are indeed on the front lines on the war over manhood in the modern world and so are the cutting edge of problems that are increasingly engulfing many other men—and the society as a whole. It could as easily have been said of men in the Neolithic—and, for that matter, at most any time in history—that they were an endangered species. But the changes that have taken place in the last few centuries, especially in the century just ended, have brought the ten thousand-year "crisis of masculinity" to a climax. Certainly most of the usual means for demonstrating manhood have become increasingly problematical since the mid-twentieth century.

But men are a sex, not a species, and referring to them as an endangered species is the sort of misleading metaphor that has produced so much trouble throughout history. It is, in fact, the sort of thinking by which a sex can be conceived of as a species that has led to much of the difficulty. In fact, *man* is not endangered. The "species" that is endangered is *notawoman.*

One of the major fusillades in the post–World War II battle to re-establish "right order" of male dominance and keep women out of roles that had been designated as male was a 1947 book written by psychologists Ferdinand Lundberg and Marynia Farnham entitled *Modern Woman: The Lost Sex.*[23] As has happened so often in history, these authors were displacing a men's problem onto women. The truly lost sex today is modern notawoman.

---

*Jacques Barzun has pointed out that *human* comes from the same Sanskrit *manu* and Latin *homo* root, which mean both "human being" and "man," as *man* does. But his conclusion that this makes a switch from words like *mankind* to *humankind* meaningless, if not ridiculous (New York Times, June 11, 1991), is mistaken. What Barzun's exercise in etymology does is to show just how pervasive the association of maleness with being "truly human" has been. Its derivation aside, *human* does not now carry the assumption of maleness that *man* does.

Men have tried all sorts of ways to maintain the idea that they are notwomen, the opposite sex, totally different, and better: they have made up metaphors, developed religions, created ideas of God in their own image, fought wars, set up exclusive realms for themselves, and so forth. But in the end, none of it has worked. All the means of proving that they are totally different from and superior to women have about run their course, as the various attempts to re-establish notawomanhood surveyed in the preceding chapter indicate. From the seed-planting creator to the warrior; from the warrior to the gang member; from the gang member to the Bly "wild man"; from the wild man to the militia man; from the militia man to the Promise Keeper; from the Promise Keeper to the fuck-'em-and-leave-'em body-counting stud with the big score; from the stud to the bulked-up pseudogorilla. Now there isn't any more.

We must go back and correct the original mistakes, and the most fundamental mistake of all is the idea that the sexes are polar opposites and real men must be totally different in every way from women. I have argued that the notawoman definition was an inversion based on the fear that there really is a hierarchical difference between the sexes and that women are superior. If we could finally accept what biology teaches us, that the sexes are not opposite and the differences that do exist are horizontal, not vertical, thousands of years of attempted inversion of something that was not actually a superior-inferior difference in the first place might be brought to an end—or at least brought under control.

Because the original assertion of male superiority was an outgrowth of the unstated fear many men had of female superiority in reproductive power, now that we know that both sexes contribute equally to the creation of an offspring (although, obviously, the degree of participation after the initial creation is vastly unequal), we ought to be able to get beyond both the Conception Misconception and the notawoman definition of manhood—and so the whole bipolar sex disorder.

We are *not* opposite sexes.

That point needs constant repetition and reinforcement.

There is not a "good sex" and a "bad sex." This book has concentrated on the ill effects throughout recorded history that have stemmed from the exclusion of women and feminine values from many important areas of human endeavor. But this focus on the detrimental effects of the repression of women does not mean that they are "the better half." Rather, women have been "the *repressed half.*" That is why it has been necessary to focus on women and the values associated with them as what has been largely missing from our decision making throughout recorded history.

Men are not "the bad sex," but by defining themselves as the opposite sex and seeing many necessary qualities, such as compassion and nurturing, as feminine, they have obliged themselves to strive to be the bad sex, even as they called it good, as in the African-American slang usage where *bad* means *good.* Men defining themselves as notwomen say: *We bad, man. We really* <u>*bad*</u>.

If men can fully realize that women are not all-powerful, then, just maybe, most men can begin to overcome the perceived need to feel all-powerful themselves: *If you're not so good, maybe we're not so bad, so we don't have to pretend that we're good and you're bad.*

The notawoman definition of manhood leads men to accentuate differences and carry to extremes some of the tendencies they usually have to a somewhat—but *only* somewhat—greater degree than women. It is in these more extreme forms that some of the male proclivities become especially dangerous. If we can finally get beyond the Conception Misconception and take full cognizance of the fact that men and women both participate in giving life, it could allow us to develop a different conception of manhood, one not based on "giving death." It could then be appreciated that *man* is not the negative or opposite of *woman,* but something quite similar. Men would then not have to prove their manhood by going around striving to do things as opposite from life-giving and nurturing as they can imagine.

Sexual Healing

What does it matter?

Obviously, it matters a great deal for the perception and treatment of women, and that is sufficient reason in itself to try every way possible to correct these age-old errors.

But the need to overcome the various ramifications of the bi-polar sex disorder exists for men as well as women, and for society at large. Although the Conception Misconception and the beliefs about male creative power that flowed from it have been extremely harmful to women and to society in general, they never really succeeded in easing male insecurity. All the claims of male procreative power amounted to whistling past the birthing room. The seed metaphor and male god ideas provided very functional rationales for subordinating women, but the deep, underlying fears remained. It is high time for men to abandon a way of thinking that is based on a belief that everyone now knows is wrong, that has caused untold problems throughout recorded history, and that never really achieved its purpose of overcoming womb envy.

Not only did this mistaken set of beliefs not heal the fundamental self-doubt experienced by many men, it also has been very harmful to them—as well as to women. The values and approaches that are often associated with women—compassion, cooperation, nurturing, self-sacrifice—are essential to human existence. Some of these qualities do seem to be found somewhat more commonly in women than in men. But in developing the notawoman definition of manhood, men have greatly exaggerated the difference and artificially polarized the sexes. They seek to deny in themselves, or at least in the image of the "real man," anything associated with women. Hence, there is a premium placed on suppressing tendencies in this direction that men have within themselves. Among the detrimental consequences of this denial by men of parts of themselves is widespread but mostly unacknowledged male depression. The very admission of depression is itself considered "unmanly" and so men often deny the depression that is itself the result of their denial of other tendencies classified as "feminine."[24] In this process, men lose a great deal, but they deny this as well, since what they have lost has been defined as "womanly" and so classified as inferior, if not utterly worthless.

So a result of the dichotomizing of gender roles is that some of the essential human characteristics that have been defined and denigrated as "womanly" have been shortchanged throughout recorded history—and they still are today. Since they were falsely made acceptable and proper only for women, who had also been barred from the public sphere in most societies, these indispensable values were excluded from areas of human endeavor where they were critically needed.

Women are essential in public realms, but it is perhaps even more true that values associated with women—feminine values—are needed in the public arena. Unfortunately, as we have seen, it often seems that insecure males are the ones most driven to seek power. So the men who have reached prominence in the public sphere have usually been those who most repressed their own "feminine" tendencies as improper for "real men."

A successful attempt to liberate men from the notawoman definition of manhood would have a most salutary effect on human life, for men and women alike.

"What Is It, Really, That I *Do*?"

Even if we could rectify the megamistakes that came out of the Agricultural Megarevolution and the misleading religious concepts and language that resulted from it, and beneath that, the erroneous idea of sexual opposition, we would still have something else to address. Indeed, if human beings fail to address this question, we shall never be able to overcome the errors that have plagued us throughout recorded history. Recall that the original reason for the Conception Misconception and the belief in a male Creator was the devaluing of traditional, biological male roles that resulted from the radical transformation of the social environment that the invention of agriculture brought about. We are unlikely to make much headway toward solving our problems unless we can find some proper (adaptive) outlet for those innate male proclivities that lost much of their purpose after the invention of agriculture. We must find an answer for the question asked by one of the dis-placed men quoted in the preceding chapter: "As a man, what is my role? What is it, really, that I *do?*"[25]

The most difficult task before us may be the one Margaret Mead identified: "If men are ever to be at peace, ever certain that their lives have been lived as they were meant to be, they must have, in addition to paternity, culturally elaborated forms of expression that are lasting and sure." Each culture must develop, Mead said, "forms that will make men satisfied in their constructive activities without distorting their sure sense of their masculinity."[26] Both the eventual male response to the invention of agriculture and the establishment of the various institutions of the second megarevolution were attempts to define such male roles.

But what the modern megarevolution has finally done in this regard during its late stages is another of the supreme ironies of history. The irony does not stop with this hypermasculine movement having finally led to women's liberation. In breaking down the artificial barriers that men had constructed to keep women out of most positions that had long been reserved for men, the second megarevolution has undermined not only one of its own major purposes but also much of what men had attempted to do in response to the first megarevolution's devaluing of their natural roles.

Men have resisted women entering "their" ["male"] occupations and institutions precisely because those careers and organizations were developed to give meaning to male lives that had lost much of their function after the triumph of agriculture. Mead pointed out that in most societies maleness "has to be underwritten by preventing women from entering some field or performing some feat."[27] This "dream of exclusion" has been a male quest throughout history. It has involved not only excluding women from certain occupations, roles, and organizations but also using pseudosexing to exclude many men from "real manhood."[28] William F. Buckley, Jr., summed up the dream in the thoughts of a fellow club member from his days at Yale: "Someday, damn it, we'll have a treehouse of our own. We'll build it out in the woods where Mother can't find us. And we'll eat when we want, what we want. We'll bring our friends. Have a secret club. And no girls."[29] That someday is not coming. The dream of exclusion has run its course. It needs to be replaced with a dream of inclusion. And one of the encouraging signs is that, while many insecure men have been resisting the idea of inclusion with all the might they can muster, many others seem to be becoming much more accepting. In this regard the most heartening indicator is the fairly rapid movement toward greater acceptance of homosexuals—the group that poses the greatest threat to men's long-cherished idea of sexual opposition.

Today, though, as what have been their roles lose their exclusively male definition, men are once again faced with the several-thousand-year-old question of what they can do that is *theirs*. There is a great need to develop satisfying, socially useful roles that employ the traits that are commonly part of the male biogram.

If modern men cannot find a role by appropriating the rituals of men from other times and cultures, as some in the men's movement of the 1990s advocated, neither can they solve their problem by trying to become just like women. Men do need to move *somewhat* toward more feminine values, but not all the way. Those feminine values are themselves an exaggeration, the result of gender extending, and so are not in their purest form fully congenial to most women. The utterly selfless woman is a creature of fiction, not the natural world. The greater infusion of more feminine values that we need should come from the acceptance by men of women and their values as equal to men and their values, not by men trying to become just like women. Men must find some way to be men that is not based on the notawoman definition.

What we need is to try to establish adaptive roles for men that are compatible with their innate predispositions. What men need is less a moral equivalent of war than a useful equivalent of hunting and group defense. We need to expend as much effort in "creating a world of work attractively male in spirit" as we do in opening access for women to formerly male occupations.[30]

Getting beyond the dualism of thinking we are "opposite sexes" would help us to get beyond double-negative definitions of manhood. We need to understand that there are many spectrums with female and male ends. Individuals of both sexes are distributed in somewhat different arrays along those spectrums, but the same person can be in different positions for different characteristics. There is no necessary link between being more toward the feminine side in one characteristic and another. If we can understand this concept, it may become more acceptable for men to take somewhat more "feminine" positions on some issues, without fear that this will result in them being thought of as "unmanly," "wimps," or "pussies."

We cannot, however, do without men or male ways and masculine values, either. William James overstated the case of war enthusiasts in 1910. He said that a world without the male virtues usually associated with war would be one of "clerks and teachers, of co-education and zo-ophily, of 'consumer's leagues' and 'associated charities,' of industrialism unlimited, and feminism unabashed. No scorn, no hardness, no valor any more! Fie upon such a cattleyard of a planet!"[31] The silliness of some of James's examples notwithstanding, a world without male ways and masculine values would not be desirable. Balance, once again, requires accepting both female and male ways and feminine and masculine values, with a recognition of their equality, not replacing the latter with the former.

But how to find proper, constructive outlets for male proclivities?

Part of the answer may be found in the fact that the original male roles were *socially* useful. Men hunted and defended not just for themselves but also to benefit their families and their communities. Manhood involved winning and losing, but competition and aggressiveness were instilled for social purposes. Men sacrificed for the common good.[32] The same was to a large extent true of most of the activities that men established (or appropriated) for themselves in response to agriculture's devaluing of their natural roles. War, for example, involves great sacrifice for what is believed to be the good of the warrior's community.

Although warfare has continued to be seen as a realm of male sacrifice for the common good, many of the new roles that have arisen out of the modern megarevolution have employed men's competitive and aggressive proclivities for individual, rather than group, purposes. As society has increasingly disintegrated into self-seeking individuals under the Marketplace worldview, this has come ever more to be the case. Aggressive competition among individuals in spheres such as business has given men something to do with their innate traits, but it does not satisfy the human need to be a useful part of a community. On the contrary, it undermines community by pitting citizens against one another, "exaggerating differences and exacerbating frictions," as political scientist Andrew Hacker has put it.[33]

The Marketplace worldview says every man is left *to rise* on his own merits; this vastly increases the pressure on men to "make something of themselves." When men were born into their socio-economic positions, they received their status from their mothers; now they are to make themselves. The insecurity increases. For every man who emerges as King of the Road in this extremely competitive environment, there are thousands of other men who are road kill.

When James called for a "moral equivalent of war," his intent was to find ways in which male biological predilections could be turned to socially useful purposes. His suggestion that young men be enlisted in an army to conduct "human warfare against nature"[34] would hardly be acceptable to us today, when we try to be environmentally conscious. But there remains a great need for social providing and protecting, and some form of social or community service that entails a degree of personal sacrifice for the common good is likely to be part of the solution to the problem.

Men will have to accept that most occupations and roles will be (and should be) open to both sexes. Whatever social provision and protection roles are established cannot be reserved exclusively for males; but they may be seen as somewhat more likely to be filled by males. And we should never expect (and certainly never mandate) equal numbers of men and women in those occupations that one sex or the other is likely to find more congenial. If men fully understand that their role in procreation is essential, but smaller, than that of women, then they may finally come to accept a similar division of other roles as equitable.

Overlapping Spheres

Obviously, attempting to solve what has been among the most basic problems throughout recorded history—the lack of useful roles that mesh with some of the more male inclinations—is a monumental job. But our task today goes beyond even this perplexity with which humans have never managed to deal in a wholly satisfactory manner.

Population growth now obliges us to move toward a *K*-selected reproductive strategy, thus reducing the importance—or at least the amount of time required for—the principal role that women have played in the past. Because of that fact, now not only must we re-invent male roles, we must also design new female roles that will provide useful outlets for *their* innate propensities, which are on average slightly different from those of males.

Women are joining men in the uncharted territory of "freedom" from the functions for which evolution molded us. In this sense, to be freed is to be made unnecessary[35]: *Freedom's just another word for nothing (important) left to do.* Men have been free in this regard for thousands of years. Now women are becoming freer in the same way.

Henry Adams had an interesting take at the beginning of the twentieth century on what was happening to the modern woman: "She was free; she had no illusions; she was sexless; she had discarded all that the male disliked; and although she secretly disliked the discard, she knew that she could not go backward. She must, like the man, marry machinery."[36]

So far what women have been doing in response to their changed circumstances is to enter traditionally male occupations, much as men did with farming after the invention of the plow some six-thousand years ago. But male-defined and -oriented occupations will no more provide fully satisfactory outlets for the more female predilections than female-defined and -oriented occupations did for the more male proclivities. (And it is, to say the least, doubtful that mothering can ever be reduced to a sport, as hunting has been.)

This shift in who fills the occupations is another way in which we are now experiencing a reversal of what happened following the invention of agriculture. In that distant period women moved from being co-providers and reproducers to becoming nearly full-time reproducers. Now population growth has combined with greater longevity to lead women back into being co-providers. Perhaps an appreciation of the fact that men are co-reproducers would make it easier for them to accept women as co-providers.

The useful roles we try to develop for the two sexes cannot be the fully distinct categories that have been designated in the past. Because men and women are not opposites, they need not, and should not, have wholly separate functions. Because the sexes are, on average, *a little* different, however, each of their roles has to be somewhat different. Because there is great overlap in the distribution of particular women and men on the scale of female and male characteristics, there should also be great overlap in the roles of the sexes. But maintaining small areas that do not overlap may be necessary.

Unless there is radical genetic engineering, men will never have babies or nourish the young from their bodies. Even if we can come fully to appreciate the fact that both sexes must participate in the creation of new life, the undeniable inequality of their participation in terms of time and effort will still leave men, however unconsciously, with some of the effects of womb envy, breast envy, and NMS. Therefore, no matter how knowledgeable we may become about the sources of our feelings and insecurities, there will probably remain a need for some compensating male roles.

Our need is not to switch from believing in male superiority to female superiority; not to switch from viewing the Creative Force as male to seeing "It" as female, but to understand "It" as being above sexual division; not to switch from seeing culture as the sole determinant of what we are to seeing biology that way, but to understand that both biology and culture (the evolutionary environment and the historical/social environment) make major contributions to what we are, and so we are both the same and different; not to switch from masculine values to feminine values, but to accept the latter as truly equal and so create an effective blend of the two; not to jump from defining men as opposite from and superior to women to seeing women as opposite from and superior to men, but to see the sexes as far more alike than different, and the differences to be only on average, of degree, not kind, and horizontal, not vertical.

If an overemphasis on dualism and sexual opposition is our most fundamental problem, and if that overemphasis was ingrained by the Conception Misconception leading to the subordination of women and the consequent efemination of society, it follows that anything that worked to bring about a greater respect and hearing for feminine values would serve also to advance ways of thinking that are alternatives to dualism. Because of this connection, a restoration of equality for feminine values would be valuable not only for what it might do to curb and rechannel some of the male proclivities that have become so dangerously maladaptive in the modern social environment, but also because it might serve to blunt the damaging effects of the excessive reliance on dualistic thinking that is at the very base of our afflictions.

Would the proposals mentioned above solve humanity's problems? Of course not. It will take a great deal of thinking on the part of a great many people to make any significant progress on our most fundamental problems. But before we can hope to find the right answers, we have to ask the right questions. My purpose in this book has not been to pretend that I have the answers, but to help us to begin to ask the right questions. Only then can we all, together, have any hope of coming up with workable solutions to the problems with which women and men have been grappling since "Eve's" discovery of the power of planting seeds removed our ancestors from the collector-hunter "paradise" for which we evolved.

Men's problems began with basic biological incapacities. But these problems have been made much worse by the most significant and extremely widespread way in which men have dealt with their sex's biological situation: the notawoman conception of manhood and gender extending. This development led to the creation of ideals of manhood that required men to strive to become artificial opposites of women. In the process, they repressed everything in themselves that had been classified as "feminine." Ultimately it led to the rejection of the biological need for identification with a personally known group in favor of the "independent" "self-made man" hyperindividualism that has characterized the modern Western world's (and especially the United States') definition of masculinity. That ideal—the dream Willy Loman and so many other modern men had been told is "the only dream you can have—to come out number-one man"[37]—is unattainable in our interdependent, social species. It cannot provide satisfaction and so it guarantees that men who accept it will be troubled.

Although we (probably) cannot change the biological foundation of male insecurity, we can and must change the cultural structures built on that foundation.

Ten thousand years should be long enough for women and men to figure out how to live harmoniously with the effects of the development of agriculture. We have yet to accomplish that, and now we must deal as well with the effects of the second megarevolution. We have been trying the opposite-sex, notawoman approach for those ten millennia. It hasn't worked all that well; indeed, it has produced what might be called the Ten Thousand Years War. Isn't it time for us to try a different way?

We need to get back, not to "the Garden" (the collector-hunter way of life), but to an acceptance of—indeed, a celebration of—the interdependence that characterized the sexes prior to the development of agriculture and has been the reality all along.

We *can't* go back to the "primitive"; nor can we go back to the *male = independent provider; female = dependent caregiver* model. We live in a human-altered environment to which we have to adapt. We have the enormous

They Had It Right

Although the modern women's movement split into many factions, some of which went off on odd tangents, the basic analysis of some radical feminists at the end of the 1960s and beginning of the 1970s was on target. The sign in this photo of a women's protest in 1970 has it just right, if we understand "Eve" to be women in general and the crime for which she was "framed" to be the invention of agriculture and the devaluing of traditional male roles. Eve has already served a sentence of thousands of years. Her case deserves to be re-opened. (UPI/Bettmann/Corbis)

advantage of being able to so consciously. *But we cannot take advantage of that ability if we ignore or deny our biology.* We have to create new adaptations of our biology to the new human-made environment.

In the past, we have let ignorance define us; it is time that we try to utilize the knowledge we possess to define our future. William Carlos Williams said it well: "Unless there is a new mind there cannot be a new line, the old will go on repeating itself with recurring deadliness,"[38] "What's past is prologue," Shakespeare wrote.[39] It is up to us, however, to determine what the past ten thousand years of errors about the sexes is a prologue to. Will it be a prologue to a future history that keeps recurring like an infinitely repeating decimal? Or will it be prologue to a future that finally recognizes the truth about and equality between the sexes and reconstructs our views, institutions, and values accordingly?

In light of the roles the Kennedy men have played, it is ironic to conclude this examination of the sexes in history by quoting one of them. But the lines from Robert Kennedy that his brother Edward used in his eulogy for him seem fitting: "Some men see things as they are and say why. I dream things that never were and say why not."[40] The fact is that if we want to have any hope of escaping from our predicament we have little choice but to try to create what never was—an understanding of the sexes as a little different and wholly equal. But to have a chance to create what never was, we have to do more than just say *Why not?* We have to take account of what always has been, what has always been influencing our history, even when we most vociferously deny its existence: our biological nature.

ENDNOTES

PROLOGUE: A MAN'S WORLD?

1. Barbra Crossette, "U.N. Documents Inequities for Women as World Forum Nears," *New York Times,* August 18, 1995.
2. Sherry B. Ortner, "Is Female to Male as Nature Is to Culture?" in Michelle Zimbalist Rosaldo and Louise Lamphere, eds., *Woman, Culture, and Society* (Stanford, CA: Stanford University Press, 1974).
3. Jared Diamond, *Guns, Germs, and Steel: The Fates of Human Societies* (New York: Norton, 1997), p. 25.
4. Thomas Jefferson, *Notes on the State of Virginia* (1785), in Saul Padover, ed., *The Complete Jefferson* (New York: Tudor, 1943), p. 607.
5. Joseph Heller, *Catch-22* (1961; New York: Scribner, 1994), p. 77.
6. Peter Steinfels, "Ordination of Women Puts New Fire in Bishops' Debate," *New York Times,* November 18, 1992.
7. Richard J. Herrnstein and Charles Murray, *The Bell Curve: Intelligence and Class Structure in American Life* (New York: Free Press, 1994).
8. Randy Thornhill and Craig Palmer, *A Natural History of Rape: Biological Bases of Sexual Coercion* (Cambridge, MA: MIT Press, 2000).
9. William F. Allman, *The Stone Age Present* (New York: Simon & Schuster, 1994), p. 29.
10. Edward O. Wilson, *Consilience: The Unity of Knowledge* (New York: Knopf, 1998), p. 266.
11. The term was coined by Earle W. Count [Count, "The Biological Basis of Human Sociality," *American Anthropologist,* vol. 60 (1958), pp. 1049–1085; Lionel Tiger and Robin Fox, *The Imperial Animal* (New York: Holt, Rinehart and Winston, 1971), p. 6].
12. Colin Tudge, *The Time Before History* (Simon & Schuster, 1996), p. 12.
13. Joan Wallach Scott, *Feminism and History* (New York: Oxford University Press, 1996).

14. Michael Specter, "Population Implosion Worries a Graying Europe," *New York Times,* July 10, 1998.

15. See Ludwik Fleck, *Genesis and Development of a Scientific Fact* (orig. German ed., 1935; Chicago: University of Chicago Press, 1979).

CHAPTER 1: 90 PERCENT NATURE; 90 PERCENT NURTURE?

1. Charles Darwin, *The Descent of Man and Selection in Relation to Sex* (1873; New York: P. F. Collier and Son, 1901), p. 797.

2. Fox News/Opinion Dynamics Poll, August 25–26, 1999; http://www.pollingreport.com/science.htm#Origin of Human Life.

3. ABC News, June 17, 1998; http://abcnews.go.com/sections/science/dailynews/evolution980617.html.

4. Mary Midgley, *Beast and Man: The Roots of Human Nature* (Ithaca, NY: Cornell University Press, 1978), p. xiii.

5. Robert Wright, *The Moral Animal: Evolutionary Psychology and Everyday Life* (New York: Pantheon, 1994), p. 7.

6. Theodore Roosevelt, "Biological Analogies in History," the Romanes Lecture for 1910, as quoted in Philip Appleman, *Darwin* (New York: Norton, 1970), pp. 512–513.

7. Edward O. Wilson, *On Human Nature* (Cambridge, MA: Harvard University Press, 1978), p. 203.

8. Edward O. Wilson, *Consilience: The Unity of Knowledge* (New York: Knopf, 1998).

9. Jared Diamond, *Why Is Sex Fun? The Evolution of Human Sexuality* (New York: Basic Books, 1997), p. 66.

10. Carl N. Degler, *In Search of Human Nature: The Decline and Revival of Darwinism in American Social Thought* (New York: Oxford University Press, 1991), p. 224 and *passim.*

11. Edward O. Wilson, *Sociobiology: The New Synthesis* (Cambridge, MA: Belknap Press of Harvard University Press, 1975), p. 3.

12. Richard Hernnstein and Charles Murray, *The Bell Curve: Intelligence and Class Structure in American Life* (New York: Free Press, 1994).

13. John Locke, *An Essay Concerning Human Understanding* (1690; Oxford: Clarendon Press, 1975), Bk. 2.1.2, p. 104. Emphasis in the original.

14. Degler, *In Search of Human Nature,* pp. 62–63, 80–82.

15. Alfred L. Kroeber, *The Nature of Culture* (Chicago: University of Chicago Press, 1952), p. 35.

16. Steven A. Peterson, "Biopolitics: Lessons from History," *Journal of the History of the Behavioral Sciences,* vol. 12 (October 1978), p. 19, as quoted in Degler, *In Search of Human Nature,* p. 234.

17. John B. Watson, *Behaviorism* (New York: W. W. Norton, 1924, 1925), pp. 103–104.

18. Margaret Mead, *Growing Up in New Guinea* [1930; reprinted in *From the South Seas* (New York: William Morrow, 1939)], p. 212.

19. Ruth Benedict, *Patterns of Culture* (Boston: Houghton Mifflin, 1934), as cited in Degler, *In Search of Human Nature,* p. 206.

20. Ashley Montagu, "The New Litany of 'Innate Depravity,' or Original Sin Revisited," in Montagu, ed., *Man and Aggression* (New York: Oxford University Press, 1968; 2d ed., 1973), p. 9. Emphasis added.

21. Walter Sullivan, "Scientists Debate Questions of Race and Intelligence," *New York Times,* February 23, 1976, as quoted in Noam Chomsky, "Language Development, Human Intelligence, and Social Organization," in James Peck, ed., *The Chomsky Reader* (New York: Pantheon, 1987), pp. 196–197.

22. Noam Chomsky, *Reflections on Language* (New York: Pantheon, 1975), p. 132.

23. Lucien Malson, as quoted in Chomsky, *Reflections on Language,* p. 128.

24. Simone de Beauvoir, *The Second Sex* (New York, Knopf, 1953 [c1952]).

25. Helen Fisher, *The First Sex* (New York: Random House, 1999), p. xv.

26. Fisher, *The First Sex,* p. xv.

27. William F. Allman, *The Stone Age Present* (New York: Simon & Schuster, 1994), pp. 176–177.

28. Jonathan Zimmerman, "Relatively Speaking," *New Republic,* September 6, 1999, p. 14.

29. Ellen Goodman, "Annual Equal Rites Awards Fete 12 Who Did the Most to Slow Women's Progress," *Clarion-Ledger* (Jackson, MS), August 22, 1989.

30. Alan Riding, "A Rights Meeting, But Don't Mention the Wronged," *New York Times,* June 14, 1993.

31. Francis Fukuyama, *The Great Disruption: Human Nature and the Reconstruction of Social Order* (New York: Free Press, 1999), p. 157.

32. "Morning Edition," National Public Radio, November 6, 1998.

33. Margaret Mead understood this and accepted it as an implication of her belief that human nature is "almost unbelievably malleable." Degler, *In Search of Human Nature,* p. 135.

34. Mary Midgley, *Wickedness: A Philosophical Essay* (London: Routledge & Kegan Paul, 1984), p. 106.

35. Wright, *The Moral Animal,* p. 7.

36. Midgley, *Beast and Man,* p. 9.

37. Irenaus Eibl-Eibesfeldt, *Love and Hate: The Natural History of Behavior Patterns* (New York: Holt, Rinehart and Winston, 1972), p. 13; E. O. Wilson, *On Human Nature,* p. 62.

38. Sherry B. Ortner, "Is Female to Male as Nature Is to Culture?" in Michelle Zimbalist Rosaldo and Louise Lamphere, eds., *Woman, Culture, and Society* (Stanford, CA: Stanford University Press, 1974), p. 70.

39. Nancy Chodorow, ["Family Structure and Feminine Personality," in Rosaldo and Lamphere, *Woman, Culture, and Society,* pp. 43–66] contends that it is the cultural fact that women have universally been responsible for early child care, rather than anything biological, that explains this phenomenon. Sherry Ortner, "Is Female to Male as Nature is to Culture?" in the same volume (pp. 67–87), offers a different cultural explanation: that women are seen as closer than men to nature and therefore inferior in status.

40. Geoffrey Cowley, "It's Time to Rethink Nature and Nurture," *Newsweek,* March 27, 1995, p. 52.

41. Nancy Chodorow, "Being and Doing: A Cross Cultural Examination of the Socialization of Males and Females," in Vivian Gornick and Barbara K. Moran, *Women in Sexist Society* (New York: New American Library, 1972), as quoted in Sarah Blaffer Hrdy, *The Woman That Never Evolved* (Cambridge, MA: Harvard University Press, 1981), p. 200*n.*

42. Richard Dawkins, *The Selfish Gene* (Oxford: Clarendon Press, 1976), pp. 2, 36.

43. E. O. Wilson, *On Human Nature,* p. 167; E. O. Wilson, *Sociobiology,* pp. 3–6.

44. Stephen R. L. Clark, *The Nature of the Beast: Are Animals Moral?* (Oxford, England: Oxford University Press, 1982), pp. 10–11, 58, 69.

45. Degler, *In Search of Human Nature,* pp. 221, 136–137, 310.

46. This term is used by Chomsky in *Reflections on Language,* p. 133.

47. Wright, *The Moral Animal,* p. 38.

48. Cowley, "It's Time to Rethink Nature and Nurture," pp. 52–53.

49. Theodosius Dobzhansky, "Anthropology and the Natural Sciences: The Problem of Human Evolution," *Current Anthropology,* vol. 4 (1963), pp. 138, 146–148, as quoted in Wilson, *On Human Nature,* p. 21.

50. Natalie Angier, *Woman: An Intimate Geography* (Boston: Houghton Mifflin, 1999), p. 346.

CHAPTER 2: THE WAY WE WERE (AND ARE)

1. Horace, *Epistles,* I.10, 24.

2. Tennessee Williams, *A Streetcar Named Desire* (1947), scene 4, in *The Theatre of Tennessee Williams* (New York: New Directions, 1971), vol. 1, p. 323.

3. Marilyn French, *Beyond Power: Of Women, Men, and Morals* (New York: Summit Books, 1985), p. 34.

4. Mariette Nowak, *Eve's Rib: A Revolutionary New View of Female Sex Roles* (New York: St. Martin's, 1980), pp. 73–78; Reay Tannahill, *Sex in History* (New York: Stein and Day, 1980; rev. ed., Chelsea, MI: Scarborough House, 1992), p. 17. Jane Goodall reports a very few cases of the "rape" of females by close male relatives among the chimpanzees she observed for a quarter century at Gombe, Tanzania. [Goodall, *The Chimpanzees of Gombe: Patterns of Behavior* (Cambridge, MA: Belknap Press of Harvard University Press, 1986), pp. 467–468.]

5. John B. Calhoun, "A 'Behavioral Sink,'" in Eugene L. Bliss, ed., *Roots of Behavior: Genetics, Instinct, and Socialization in Animal Behavior* (New York: Harper & Brothers, (Oxford, England: Oxford University Press, 1982), pp. 67, 13; Colin Turnbull, *The Mountain People* (New York: Simon & Schuster, 1972), pp. 265–295.

6. Jared Diamond, *Why Is Sex Fun? The Evolution of Human Sexuality* (New York: Basic Books, 1997), pp. 1–14.

7. Desmond Morris, *The Naked Ape* (London: Cape, 1967), pp. 73–83; Mary Midgley, *Beast and Man: The Roots of Human Nature* (Ithaca, NY: Cornell University Press, 1978), p. 39; Tannahill, *Sex in History,* pp. 16–21.

8. Edward O. Wilson, *Consilience: The Unity of Knowledge* (New York: Knopf, 1998), p. 12.

9. Readers interested in learning more about the evolution of modern humans should consult Göran Burenhult, ed., *The First Humans: Human Origins and History to 10,000 BC* (New York: HarperCollins, 1993), along with other books cited in the notes that follow.

10. C. G. Sibley, J. A. Comstock, and J. E. Ahlquist, "DNA Hybridization Evidence of Hominoid Phylogeny: A Reanalysis of the Data," *Journal of Molecular Evolution,* vol. 30 (1990), pp. 202–236, as cited in Jared Diamond, *The Third Chimpanzee: The Evolution and Future of the Human Animal* (New York: HarperCollins, 1992), pp. 18–24, 33.

11. Margaret Ehrenberg, *Women in Prehistory* (Norman: University of Oklahoma Press, 1989), pp. 42–46.

12. Richard Leakey and Roger Lewin, *Origins Reconsidered: In Search of What Makes Us Human* (New York: Doubleday, 1992), pp. 84–87, 164; Colin Tudge, *The Time Before History* (New York: Scribner, 1996), p. 192.

13. Donald C. Johanson and Maitland A. Edey, *Lucy: The Beginnings of Humankind* (New York: Simon & Schuster, 1981) pp. 16–24, 180–207.

14. William H. Kimbel, Donald C. Johanson, and Yoel Rak, "The First Skull and Other New Discoveries of *Australopithecus afarensis* at Hadar, Ethiopia," *Nature,* vol. 368 (March 31, 1994), pp. 449–451.

15. Meave G. Leakey, et al., "New Specimens and Confirmation of an Early Age for *Australopithicus anamensis,*" *Nature,* May 7, 1998, pp. 62–66; Tim D. White et al., "*Australopithecus ramidus,* A New Species of Early Hominid from Aramis, Ethiopia," *Nature,* September 22, 1992, pp. 306–312.

16. Leakey and Lewin, *Origins Reconsidered,* pp. 167–169.

17. Leakey and Lewin, *Origins Reconsidered,* pp. 194–198.

18. Diamond, *Third Chimpanzee,* pp. 34–36.

19. Diamond, *Third Chimpanzee,* p. 17.

20. Leakey and Lewin, *Origins Reconsidered,* pp. 226–28.

21. Diane M. Waddle, "Matrix Correlation Tests Support a Single Origin for Modern Humans," *Nature,* vol. 368 (March 31, 1994), pp. 452–454; A. M. Bowcock, A. Ruiz-Linares, J. Tomfohrde, E. Minch, J. R. Kidd, and L. L. Cavalli-Sfroza, "High Resolution of Human Evolutionary Trees with Polymorphic Microsattelites," *Nature,* vol. 368 (March 31, 1994), pp. 455–457; Leakey and Lewin, *Origins Reconsidered,* pp. 211–28.

22. M. Kay Martin and Barbara Voorhies, *Female of the Species* (New York: Columbia University Press, 1975), pp. 172–173.

23. George Edgin Pugh, *The Biological Origin of Human Values* (New York: Basic Books, 1977), p. 174.

24. Irenanus Eibl-Eibesfeldt, *The Biology of Peace and War: Men, Animals, and Aggression,* Eric Mosbacher, trans. (New York: Viking, 1979; orig. German ed., Munich: R. Piper & Co. Verlag, 1975), p. 166.

25. Francis Fukuyama, "Second Thoughts," *The National Interest,* No. 56, Summer 1999, p. 16.

26. Mary Midgley, *Wickedness: A Philosophical Essay* (London: Routledge & Kegan Paul, 1984), pp. 211–212*n*.

27. Diamond, *Why Is Sex Fun?*, p. 62.

28. Robert Wright, *The Moral Animal* (New York: Pantheon, 1994), p. 81.

29. Leakey and Lewin, *Origins Reconsidered*, pp. 159–162.

30. Leakey and Lewin, *Origins Reconsidered*, pp. 181–186, 198–199.

31. Goodall, *Chimpanzees of Gombe*, pp. 372–376; Pugh, *Biological Origin of Human Values*, p. 267; Edward O. Wilson, *On Human Nature* (Cambridge, MA: Harvard University Press, 1978), p. 29.

32. Francis Fukuyama, *The Great Disruption: Human Nature and the Reconstruction of Social Order* (New York: Free Press, 1999), p. 162.

33. Thomas Jefferson, letter to Thomas Law, June 13, 1814, in Merrill D. Peterson, ed., *Thomas Jefferson: Writings* (New York: Library of America, 1984), p. 1337.

34. Carl N. Degler, *In Search of Human Nature: The Decline and Revival of Darwinism in American Social Thought* (New York: Oxford University Press, 1991), p. 265.

35. Goodall, *Chimpanzees of Gombe*, pp. 149, 154, 450–466; Edward O. Wilson, *Sociobiology: The New Synthesis* (Cambridge, MA: Belknap Press of Harvard University Press, 1975), pp. 539–546.

36. Wright, *Moral Animal*, p. 58.

37. Sarah Blaffer Hrdy, *Mother Nature: A History of Mothers, Infants, and Natural Selection* (New York: Pantheon, 1999), pp. 220–222.

38. Tannahill, *Sex in History*, pp. 19–21.

39. Wright, *Moral Animal*, p. 68; Natalie Angier, *Woman: An Intimate Geography* (Boston: Houghton Mifflin, 1999), pp. 339–340; Diamond, *Why Is Sex Fun?*, pp. 70–88.

40. Tannahill, *Sex in History*, pp. 19–21; William F. Allman, *The Stone Age Present* (New York: Simon & Schuster, 1994), pp. 125–126. Sarah Hrdy has pointed out that the distinction in this regard between humans and other primates is not as great as has been thought, but she concludes that "there can be no doubt that the sexually sophisticated human species remains at the highly erotic end of the continuum, and our position there does indeed demand an explanation—but not necessarily a special explanation applicable *only* to humans. We are an extreme case, not a separate one." Sarah Blaffer Hrdy, *The Woman That Never Evolved* (Cambridge, MA: Harvard University Press, 1981), p. 138.

41. Chimpanzees have been observed living in groups of thirty to eighty, with some troops perhaps ranging up to 150 members [E. O. Wilson, *Sociobiology*, p. 539]. In itself, of course, this proves nothing about the size of hominid bands. But most groups of collector-hunters that survived into the nineteenth and twentieth centuries also live in bands in this size range.

42. Goodall, *Chimpanzees of Gombe*, pp. 330–332.

43. Hrdy, *Mother Nature*, p. 414.

44. Eibl-Eibesfeldt, *Biology of Peace and War*, pp. 105–107.

45. H. D. F. Kitto, *The Greeks* (Baltimore: Penguin, 1951, 1957), p. 65.

46. Kitto, *Greeks,* pp. 65, 74, 78. Emphasis added.

47. Ferdinand Tönnies, *Community and Society* (1887), Charles P. Loomis ed. and trans. (New York: Harper & Row, 1957).

48. *The Godfather, Part II* (1974, directed by Francis Ford Coppola, Paramount).

49. Midgley, *Beast and Man,* p. 81; Clark, *Nature of the Beast,* pp. 62–63.

50. Michael Wasser, letter, *New York Times,* August 28, 1991.

51. Sam Keen, *Fire in the Belly: On Being a Man* (New York: Bantam, 1991), p. 43.

52. Eibl-Eibesfeldt, *Biology of Peace and War,* pp. 122–125.

53. Associated Press dispatch, October 2, 1999.

54. Wilson, *On Human Nature,* p. 70.

55. Clark, *Nature of the Beast,* pp. 34–35, 42.

56. As quoted in Robert Maynard, "German Reunification: Inevitable?" *Clarion-Ledger* (Jackson, MS), February 9, 1990.

57. Winston Churchill, as quoted in John Ellis, *The Social History of the Machine Gun* (New York: Pantheon, 1975), p. 101. Emphasis added.

58. Theodore Roosevelt, as quoted in Richard Hofstadter, *The American Political Tradition—and the Men Who Made It* (1948: New York: Vintage, 1973), p. 274.

59. Ruth Benedict, *Patterns of Culture* (1935), chapter IV, as cited in Midgley, *Wickedness,* p. 90.

60. Midgley, *Wickedness,* pp. 90–91.

61. Eleanor Leacock, "Women in Egalitarian Societies," in Ranate Bridenthal, Claudia Koonz, and Susan Stuard, eds., *Becoming Visible: Women in European History* (Boston: Houghton Mifflin, 2d ed., 1987), p. 17.

62. See, for example, David D. Gilmore, *Manhood in the Making: Cultural Concepts of Masculinity* (New Haven, CT: Yale University Press, 1990), pp. 209–216, 230.

63. Wilson, *On Human Nature,* pp. 100–101. Semai life is, however, still notably lacking in violence. [Clayton A. Robarchek and Robert Knox Dentan, "Blood Drunkeness and the Bloodthirsty Semai: Unmaking Another Anthropological Myth," *American Anthropologist,* vol. 89, 1987, pp. 356–365.]

64. Eibl-Eibesfeldt, *Biology of Peace and War,* pp. 116–118.

65. Goodall, *Chimpanzees of Gombe,* pp. 488–534; Eibl-Eibesfeldt, *Biology of Peace and War,* pp. 60–69.

66. Richard Wrangham and Dale Peterson, *Demonic Males: Apes and the Origins of Human Violence* (Boston: Houghton Mifflin, 1996), pp. 5–21, 70.

67. Frans B. M. de Waal, *Peacemaking Among Primates* (Cambridge, MA: Harvard University Press, 1989).

68. Wrangham and Peterson, *Demonic Males,* pp. 205–210.

69. Leacock, "Women in Egalitarian Societies," p. 35, *n*2.

70. *Desmond Morris' The Human Sexes,* "Different But Equal" (Partridge Films, The Learning Channel, 1997).

71. Pugh, *Biological Origins of Human Values,* pp. 271, 398.

72. Midgley, *Beast and Man,* p. 81; Midgley, *Wickedness,* pp. 83, 90.

73. Midgley, *Wickedness,* p. 84.

CHAPTER 3: MEN ARE FROM NEW YORK; WOMEN ARE FROM PHILADELPHIA

1. Henry Adams, *The Education of Henry Adams* (1918; Boston: Houghton Mifflin, 1961), p. 384.
2. Simone de Beauvoir, *The Second Sex* (New York: Knopf, 1952; Modern Library, 1968), p. xv.
3. *Junior* (1994, directed by Ivan Reitman, Northern Lights/Universal).
4. John Gray, *Men Are from Mars, Women Are from Venus.* (New York: Harper-Collins, 1992).
5. Carol Gilligan, *In a Different Voice* (Cambridge, MA: Harvard University Press, 1982); Mary Field Belenky, et al., *Women's Ways of Knowing* (New York: Basic Books, 1986); Anne Moir and David Jessel, *Brain Sex: The Real Difference Between Men and Women* (1989; New York: Lyle Stuart, 1991); Laura S. Allen and Roger A. Gorski, "Sexual Dimorphism of the Anterior Commissure and the Massa Intermedia of the Human Brain," *Journal of Comparative Neurology,* no. 312 (1991), pp. 97–104; Doreen Kimura, "Sex Differences in the Brain," *Scientific American,* September 1992, pp. 118–125; Robert Wright, *The Moral Animal* (New York: Pantheon, 1994); Deborah Blum, *Sex on the Brain: The Biological Differences Between Men and Women* (New York: Viking, 1997; Penguin, 1998).
6. Helen Fisher, *The First Sex* (New York: Random House, 1999), p. xviii; Natalie Angier, *Woman: An Intimate Geography* (Boston: Houghton-Mifflin, 1999), pp. 39–42.
7. Mary Daly, in *Off Our Backs,* May 1979.
8. Jared Diamond, *Why Is Sex Fun? The Evolution of Human Sexuality* (New York: Basic Books, 1997), p. 44.
9. *Desmond Morris: The Human Sexes,* "Different But Equal" (Partridge Films, The Learning Channel, 1997).
10. Diamond, *Why Is Sex Fun?,* pp. 41–62.
11. Diamond, *Why Is Sex Fun?,* pp. 43, 49.
12. Eleanor Emmons Maccoby and Carol Nagy Jacklin, *The Psychology of Sex Differences* (Stanford, CA: Stanford University Press, 1974), pp. 360–362.
13. Christine Gorman, "How Gender May Bend Your Thinking," *Time,* July 1, 1995.
14. Sharon Begley, "Gray Matters," *Newsweek,* March 27, 1995, p. 51.
15. Deborah Tannen, *You Just Don't Understand: Women and Men in Conversation* (New York: Ballantine Books, 1990); Gilligan, *In a Different Voice;* Belenky et al., *Women's Ways of Knowing;* Fisher, *First Sex,* pp. 4–12.
16. Christine de Lacoste-Utamsing and Ralph L. Holloway, "Sexual Dimorphism in the Human Corpus Callosum," *Science,* vol. 216 (June 25, 1982), pp. 1431–1432; Christine de Lacoste-Utamsing and Ralph L. Holloway, "Sex Differences in the Fetal Human Corpus Callosum," *Human Neurobiology,* vol. 5 (1986), pp. 93–96; Sandra F. Witelson, "Hand and Sex Differences in the Isthmus and Genu of the Human Corpus Callosum," *Brain,* vol. 112 (1989), pp. 799–835; Sandra F. Witelson, "Structural Correlates of Cognition in the Human Brain," in Arnold B. Scheibel and Adam F. Welchsler, eds., *Neurobiology of*

Higher Cognitive Function (New York: Guilford Press, 1990), pp. 167–183; Moir and Jessel, *Brain Sex: The Real Difference Between Men and Women,* pp. 47–48, 193–196; Laura S. Allen, et al., "Sex Differences in the Corpus Callosum of the Living Human Being," *Journal of Neuroscience,* vol. 11, no. 4 (1991), pp. 933–944.

17. Bennett A. Shaywitz et al., "Sex Differences in the Functional Organization of the Brain for Language," *Nature,* vol. 373 (February 16, 1995), pp. 607–609.

18. Ruben C. Gur et al., "Sex Differences in Regional Cerebral Glucose Metabolism During a Resting State," *Science,* vol. 267 (January 27, 1995), pp. 528–531; Gina Kolata, "Man's World, Woman's World? Brain Studies Point to Differences," *New York Times,* February 28, 1995.

19. Kolata, "Man's World, Woman's World?"; Begley, "Gray Matters," p. 52.

20. Begley, "Gray Matters," p. 50.

21. William F. Allman, *The Stone Age Present* (New York: Simon and Schuster, 1994), pp. 46–47.

22. Fisher, *First Sex,* p. xvi.

23. William S. Laughlin, "Hunting: An Integrating Biobehavior System and Its Evolutionary Importance," in Richard B. Lee and Irven De Vore, eds., *Man the Hunter* (Chicago: Aldine, 1968); Lionel Tiger, *Men in Groups* (New York: Random House, 1969); Lionel Tiger and Robin Fox, *The Imperial Animal* (New York: Holt, Rinehart and Winston, 1971).

24. M. Kay Martin and Barbara Voorhies, *Female of the Species* (New York: Columbia University Press, 1975), p. 173.

25. Edward O. Wilson, *Sociobiology* (Cambridge, MA: Harvard University Press, 1980), p. 220.

26. Adrienne Rich, *Of Woman Born: Motherhood as Experience and Institution* (New York: Norton, 1976), p. 11.

27. Jessie Bernard, *The Female World* (New York: Free Press, 1981), p. 7.

28. Sarah Blaffer Hrdy, *The Woman That Never Evolved* (Cambridge, MA: Harvard University Press, 1981), p. 17.

29. Sally Linton, "Woman the Gatherer," paper presented at the American Anthropological Association Annual Meeting, 1970, San Diego, as quoted in Martin and Voorhies, *Female of the Species,* pp. 174–175; Marilyn French, *Beyond Power: Of Women, Men, and Morals* (New York: Summit Books, 1985), pp. 40–41.

30. Eliza Burt Gamble, *The Evolution of Woman: An Inquiry into the Dogma of Her Inferiority to Man* (New York: G. P. Putnam's Sons, 1894), p. 61, as quoted in Carl N. Degler, *In Search of Human Nature: The Decline and Revival of Darwinism in American Social Thought* (New York: Oxford University Press, 1991), pp. 109–110.

31. Male gorillas, for instance, act as sentries for their group. See Dian Fossey, *Gorillas in the Mist* (Boston: Houghton Mifflin, 1983), pp. 47–48, 199–200.

32. Maccoby and Jacklin, *Psychology of Sex Differences,* p. 368; Moir and Jessel, *Brain Sex,* pp. 75–82; Natalie Angier, "Does Testosterone Equal Aggression? Maybe Not," *New York Times,* June 20, 1995.

33. Moir and Jessel, *Brain Sex,* pp. 42–47; Maccoby and Jacklin, *Psychology of Sex Differences,* p. 361; Sandra Blakeslee, "Navigating Life's Maze: Styles Split the Sexes," *New York Times,* May 26, 1992.

34. Martin and Voorhies, *Female of the Species,* pp. 168–169; Melvin Konner, *The Tangled Wing: Constraints on the Human Spirit* (New York: Harper Colophon Books, 1982); John Archer and Barbara Lloyd, *Sex and Gender* (Cambridge, England: Cambridge University Press, 1985), pp. 138–139.

35. Nancy Makepeace Tanner, *On Becoming Human* (New York: Cambridge University Press, 1981), p. 240. French, *Beyond Power,* p. 37.

36. Tiger, *Men in Groups,* p. 58; Tiger and Fox, *Imperial Animal,* pp. 56–57, 86–89, 100.

37. Jonah Western and Shirley Strum, "Sex, Kinship and the Evolution of Social Manipulation," *Journal of Ethology and Sociobiology,* vol. 4, pp. 19–28, as cited in Lionel Tiger, "Ideology as Brain Disease," *Zygon,* vol. 20 (March 1985), pp. 31–39.

38. Martin and Voorhies, *Female of the Species,* p. 170.

39. Shulamith Firestone, *The Dialectic of Sex* (New York: Morrow, 1970), excerpted in Alison M. Jagger and Paula S. Rothenberg, *Feminist Frameworks* (New York: McGraw-Hill, 1978, 2d ed., 1984), p. 139.

40. David D. Gilmore, *Manhood in the Making: Cultural Concepts of Masculinity* (New Haven, CT: Yale University Press, 1990), p. 229.

41. Gilmore, *Manhood in the Making,* p. 12.

42. Bettyann Kevles, [*Female of the Species: Sex and Survival in the Animal Kingdom* (Cambridge, MA: Harvard University Press, 1986), p. 189] argues that in most animal species females are much more likely to cooperate with their kin than with others.

43. Tiger, "Ideology as Brain Disease," pp. 35–36.

44. Sam Keen, *Fire in the Belly: On Being a Man* (New York: Bantam Books, 1991), p. 31.

45. Sandra Blakeslee, ["Navigating Life's Maze: Styles Split the Sexes," *New York Times,* May 26, 1992] discusses experiments that showed that women and men typically find their way through a maze in different ways. Women tend to rely on "landmarks," while men are more likely to utilize vectors. It is possible that this difference is linked to the ancestral environment, in which there was a premium on an abstract sense of direction for men who were often hunting far from their home camps, while the ability to distinguish and remember edible plants would be advantageous to women engaged in collecting. "Tracking and killing animals entail different kinds of spatial problems than does foraging for edible plants," psychologists Irwin Silverman and Marion Eals have pointed out [Geoffrey Cowley, "It's Time to Rethink Nature and Nurture," *Newsweek,* March 27, 1995, p. 53].

46. Fisher, *First Sex,* p. xvi.

47. Sigmund Freud, *Three Essays on the Theory of Sexuality,* III: "The Transformations of Puberty," in James Strachey, ed., *Standard Edition* (London: Hogarth Press, 1975), p. 220, as quoted in Gilmore, *Manhood in the Making,* pp. vii, 22.

48. R. J. Nelson, *An Introduction to Behavioral Endocrinology* (Sunderland, MA: Sinauer Associates, Inc., 1995), as quoted in Fisher, *First Sex,* p. xviii.

49. Roger Gorski, as quoted in Kolata, "Man's World, Woman's World."

50. Wright, *Moral Animal,* pp. 33–92; Fisher, *First Sex,* pp. 197, 205–206.

51. *Lenny* (1974, directed by Bob Fosse, United Artists).

52. Sarah Blaffer Hrdy, *Mother Nature: A History of Mothers, Infants, and Natural Selection* (New York: Pantheon, 1999), p. 84.

53. Hrdy, *Mother Nature,* p. 84.

54. Donald Symons, *The Evolution of Human Sexuality* (Oxford, England: Oxford University Press, 1979), p. v.

55. Robert Trivers, "Parental Investment and Sexual Selection," in Bernard Campbell, ed., *Sexual Selection and the Descent of Man* (Chicago: Aldine de Gruyter, 1972).

56. Among the most noted is David Buss, *The Evolution of Desire* (New York: Basic Books, 1994). See also Buss, "Psychological Sex Differences," *American Psychologist,* March 1995, pp. 164–168.

57. Symons, *Evolution of Human Sexuality,* p. v.

58. *Madame Butterfly* (1932, directed by Marion Gering, Paramount).

59. "Will You Love Me Tomorrow?," written by Gerald Goffin and Carole King (Screen Gems-EMI Music, BMI, 1960), "A Travelin' Man," written by Jerry Fuller (Acuff Rose Music, BMI, 1961).

60. *When Harry Met Sally* (1989, directed by Rob Reiner, Castle Rock).

61. Robert Wright, "Why Men Are Still Beasts," *New Republic,* July 11, 1988, pp. 28–29.

62. Jimmy Carter, as quoted in Robert Scheer, "The Playboy Interview: Jimmy Carter," *Playboy,* November 1976, p. 86.

63. Fisher, *First Sex,* p. 267.

64. Angier, *Woman,* pp. 322–354.

65. Fisher, *First Sex,* p. 206.

66. Wright, "Why Men Are Still Beasts," p. 29.

67. Linda A. Pollock, *Forgotten Children: Parent-Child Relations from 1500 to 1900* (New York: Cambridge University Press, 1983), pp. 36–38, as quoted in Degler, *In Search of Human Nature,* p. 291.

68. Ellen Goodman, "The Motherhood Paradox," *Boston Globe,* May 10, 1992.

69. Barbara Smuts, as quoted in Angier, *Woman,* pp. 346–347.

70. Angier, *Woman,* p. 326.

71. I picked up the wonderful phrase "a dichotomy imposed on a continuum" from Wright, *Moral Animal,* p. 78.

72. Trivers, "Parental Investment and Sexual Selection," p. 153.

73. Gilmore, *Manhood in the Making,* pp. 2, 9, 11.

74. Keen, *Fire in the Belly,* p. 38; Bruno Bettelheim, *Symbolic Wounds: Puberty Rites and the Envious Male* (1954; rev. ed., New York: Collier, 1962), pp. 22–23, 45, 104–108.

75. Gilmore, *Manhood in the Making,* p. 20.

76. Keen, *Fire in the Belly,* pp. 17–18.

77. Margaret Mead, as quoted in Degler, *In Search of Human Nature,* pp. 136–137.

78. Sherry B. Ortner, "Is Female to Male as Nature Is to Culture?" in Michelle Zimbalist Rosaldo and Louise Lamphere, *Woman, Culture, and Society* (Stanford, CA: Stanford University Press, 1974), p. 71.

79. Margaret Mead, *Male and Female: A Study of the Sexes in a Changing World* (New York: William Morrow, 1949), pp. 159–160.

80. Karen Horney, "The Flight from Womanhood," *The International Journal of Psycho-Analysis,* vol. 7 (1926), as quoted in Susan Quinn, *A Mind of Her Own: The Life of Karen Horney* (New York: Summit Books, 1987), p. 223.

81. Ashley Montagu, *The Natural Superiority of Women* (New York, Macmillan, 1953).

82. Eva Cantarella, *Pandora's Daughters: The Role and Status of Women in Greek and Roman Antiquity* (Baltimore: Johns Hopkins University Press, 1987; orig, Italian ed., 1981), p. 105.

83. Raymond DeVries, "For New Fathers," *Lamaze Parents' Magazine,* 1998, p. 108.

84. Gilbert H. Herdt, *Guardians of the Flutes: Idioms of Masculinity* (New York: McGraw-Hill, 1981), pp. 210, 234–235.

85. Diamond, *Why Is Sex Fun?,* p. 43.

86. Diamond, *Why Is Sex Fun?,* p. 41.

87. Federal Writers' Project of the Works Progress Administration in New York City, *New York Panorama* (New York: Random House, 1938), as quoted in Christine Bold, *The WPA Guides: Mapping America* (Jackson: University Press of Mississippi, 1999), p. 104.

88. *Desmond Morris' The Human Sexes,* "Different But Equal" (Partridge Films, The Learning Channel, 1997).

89. *Dinosaurs* (ABC Television, April 1991–July 1994). Some critics complained that the show was sexist [Joanne Ostrow, "Sitcom Has Sexist Attitude," *Denver Post,* May 20, 1991].

90. Horney, "The Flight from Womanhood," as quoted in Quinn, *A Mind of Her Own,* p. 223.

91. Chinua Achebe, *Things Fall Apart* (New York: Astor-Honor, 1959), pp. 14–15, 11.

92. Keen, *Fire in the Belly,* p. 38.

93. Philip Caputo, *A Rumor of War* (New York: Holt, Rinehart and Winston, 1977), p. 127.

94. Keen, *Fire in the Belly,* p. 38.

95. Keen, *Fire in the Belly,* p. 37.

96. "Those Were the Days," written by Lee Adams and Charles Strouse (EMI Worldtrax Music, ASCAP, 1971).

97. Deuteronomy 22:5

98. "The First Words," Dogon creation story, in Barbara C. Sproul, ed., *Primal Myths: Creation Myths Around the World* (1979; San Francisco: HarperSanFrancisco, 1991), pp. 54–55. In parts of Africa female mutilation is still practiced. It includes clitoral excision, but often goes on to other tortures [A. M. Rosenthal, "Female

Genital Torture," *New York Times,* November 12, 1993]. This practice may have had its origin in such beliefs in primal androgyny, but other purposes of controlling women are clearly served by these practices today. It may also be that the far more common practice of male circumcision originated, at least in part, as a way to remove "femaleness" from males.

99. Gerda Lerner, *The Creation of Patriarchy* (New York: Oxford University Press, 1986), pp. 80, 89.

100. Ortner, "Is Female to Male as Nature Is to Culture?," pp. 71–74.

CHAPTER 4: PARADISE LOST

1. T. S. Eliot, "The Love Song of J. Alfred Prufrock," in Eliot, *The Waste Land and Other Poems* (New York: Harcourt, Brace & World, 1934), p. 5.

2. James Ussher, *The Annals of the World* (1658), p. 1, as quoted in *The Oxford Dictionary of Quotations* (Oxford, England: Oxford University Press, 1941; 3d ed., 1979), p. 554.

3. Such phrases are very common among historians. This particular formulation is even used by someone as up-to-date as Tikva Frymer-Kensky, *In the Wake of the Goddesses: Women, Culture, and the Biblical Transformation of Pagan Myth* (New York: Free Press, 1992), p. 62. Her historian's assumption that little can really be known about periods for which there are no written records prevented Frymer-Kensky from making full use of the implications of all the wonderful information she assembled and interpreted about the decline of goddesses in the third and second millennia B.C.E.

4. Colin Tudge, *The Time Before History* (New York: Scribner, 1996), p. 26.

5. Edward O. Wilson, *Consilience: The Unity of Knowledge* (New York: Knopf, 1998), p. 12.

6. Jared Diamond, *Guns, Germs, and Steel* (New York: Norton, 1997), p. 39.

7. William F. Allman, *The Stone Age Present* (New York: Simon and Schuster, 1994), pp. 186–219.

8. Ralph Waldo Emerson, "Fortune of the Republic," as quoted in *The Oxford Dictionary of Quotations,* p. 207.

9. Lawrence W. Levine, *Black Culture and Black Consciousness* (New York: Oxford University Press, 1977), p. 5.

10. Jack R. Harlan, "The Plants and Animals That Nourish Man," *Scientific American,* vol. 235 (September 1976), pp. 89–97.

11. Daniel Bell, *The Cultural Contradictions of Capitalism* (New York: Basic Books, 1976, 1978), p. 8; Fernand Braudel, "History and the Social Sciences: The *Longue Durée,*" from *Annales E.S.C.,* no. 4 (October–December 1958), in Fernand Braudel, *On History,* Sarah Matthews, trans. (Chicago: University of Chicago Press, 1980), pp. 25–54.

12. An article in *Science82* discusses the finding of evidence of horticulture being practiced at Wadi Kubbaniya on the upper Nile in southern Egypt between 18,500 and 17,000 years ago. [Fred Wendorf, Romuald Schild, and Angela E.

Close, "An Ancient Harvest on the Nile," *Science82,* vol. 3 (November 1982), pp. 68–73.]

13. Margaret Ehrenberg, *Women in Prehistory* (Norman: University of Oklahoma Press, 1989), pp. 77–78; Riane Eisler, *The Chalice and the Blade: Our History, Our Future* (San Francisco: Harper & Row, 1987), pp. 68–69; Ester Boserup, *Woman's Role in Economic Development* (London: Allen & Unwin, 1970); Barbara Rogers, *The Domestication of Women: Discrimination in Developing Societies* (New York: Columbia University Press, 1975), p. 283; Mary Beth Norton et al., *A People and a Nation: A History of the United States* (Boston: Houghton Mifflin, 1986, 2d ed.), p. 8; Judith K. Brown, "Iroquois Women: An Ethnohistoric Note," in Rayna R. Reiter, ed., *Toward an Anthropology of Women* (New York: Monthly Review Press, 1975), pp. 235–251; Eleanor Leacock, "Women in Egalitarian Societies," in Renate Bridenthal, Claudia Koonz, and Susan Stuard, eds., *Becoming Visible: Women in European History* (Boston: Houghton Mifflin, 2d ed., 1987), p. 27.

14. "Nomads of the Rain Forest," *Nova,* PBS, 1984; rebroadcast, September 3, 1991.

15. Merlin Stone, *When God Was a Woman* (New York: Dial Press, 1976), p. 3; Frymer-Kensky, *In the Wake of the Goddesses,* pp. 33, 40; Eisler, *The Chalice and the Blade,* p. 69; R. E. Witt, *Isis in the Graeco-Roman World* (Ithaca, NY: Cornell University Press, 1971), pp. 16, 23.

16. Gerda Lerner, *The Creation of Patriarchy* (New York: Oxford University Press, 1986), p. 212.

17. Sarah Blaffer Hrdy, *The Woman That Never Evolved* (Cambridge, MA: Harvard University Press, 1981), pp. 28–29, 40–41; Edward O. Wilson, *Sociobiology: The New Synthesis* (Cambridge, MA: Belknap Press of Harvard University Press, 1975), pp. 99–103.

18. Genesis 1:28.

19. Kevin Reilly, "City and Civilization," in Reilly, ed., *Readings in World Civilizations* (New York: St. Martin's Press, 2d ed., 1992), p. 21.

20. Edward O. Wilson, *On Human Nature* (Cambridge, MA: Harvard University Press, 1978), p. 103.

21. Stephen R. L. Clark, *The Nature of the Beast: Are Animals Moral?* (Oxford, England: Oxford University Press, 1982), pp. 94–95.

22. Leda Cosmides, as quoted in Allman, *Stone Age Present,* p. 50.

23. V. Gordon Childe's *The Dawn of European Civilization* [(London: Routledge & Kegan Paul, 1925, 5th ed., 1950), p. 109], offers a good description of how the changes wrought by agriculture led to increased competition and warfare in southeastern Europe.

24. Elise Boulding, "Women and the Agricultural Revolution," in Reilly, *Readings in World Civilizations,* p. 17.

25. Boulding, "Women and the Agricultural Revolution," p. 17.

26. Boulding, "Women and the Agricultural Revolution," p. 17.

27. Tudge, *Time Before History,* p. 251.

28. Mary Settegast, *Plato Prehistorian* (New York: Lindisfarne Press, 1990); Tudge, *Time Before History,* p. 17.

29. The Gilgamesh Epic, as quoted in Alexander Heidel, *The Gilgamesh Epic and Old Testament Parallels* (Chicago: University of Chicago Press, 1946, 2d ed., 1949), and in *The Epic of Gilgamesh,* N. K. Sandars, trans. (London: Penguin Books, 1974), reprinted in Reilly, *Readings in World Civilizations,* pp. 26–27.
30. The Gilgamesh Epic; Lerner, *Creation of Patriarchy,* pp. 132–133.
31. So far as I have been able to determine, the following interpretation of these chapters in Genesis is entirely new. The only hint of a small portion of it that I have seen is a few lines I found, long after I had first written this chapter, in Rosemary Radford Ruether, *Gaia and God: An Ecofeminist Theology of Earth Healing* (San Francisco: HarperSanFrancisco, 1992), p. 144.
32. Genesis 2:9. Emphasis added.
33. Genesis 2:16.
34. Genesis 2:17.
35. Genesis 3:17–19.
36. Charles B. Heiser, Jr., *Seed to Civilization; The Story of Civilization* (1973; Cambridge, MA: Harvard University Press, 1990), p. 1.
37. Genesis 3:6. Emphasis added.
38. Harold Bloom, *The Book of J,* David Rosenberg, trans. (New York: Grove Weidenfeld, 1990, interpreted by Harold Bloom), pp. 9–16; Ilana Pardes, *Countertraditions in the Bible: A Feminist Approach* (Cambridge, MA: Harvard University Press, 1992), pp. 33–37.
39. Genesis 3:23. Emphasis added.
40. Genesis 3:16; Carol Meyers, *Discovering Eve: Ancient Israelite Women in Context* (New York: Oxford University Press, 1988), p. 118.
41. Ashley Montagu, *The Natural Superiority of Women* (New York: Macmillan, 1952, rev. ed., 1968), p. 18.
42. Genesis 3:5, 22.
43. Genesis 3:24.
44. Genesis 4:2, 8–12, 17.
45. Frymer-Kensky, *In the Wake of the Goddesses,* pp. 155–158.
46. Genesis 3:14.
47. Hesiod, *Works and Days,* lns. 117–118, in Richard Lattimore, trans., *Hesiod* (Ann Arbor: University of Michigan Press, 1959), p. 31. The quotation here is a slightly different translation from Lattimore's.
48. Ovid, "The Four Ages," in *Ovid's Metamorphoses,* Brookes More, trans. (Boston: Cornhill Publishing Co., 1922), p. 7. I am grateful to Cleta Ellington for pointing out this version to me. Thomas Bullfinch, [*The Age of Fable* (1855; New York: Doubleday, 1968), p. 15] described the pre-agricultural status of the Golden Age in similar words: "The earth brought forth all things necessary for man, without his labor in ploughing or sowing."
49. Bullfinch, *Age of Fable,* p. 16.
50. Ovid, "The Four Ages," p. 8.
51. Ovid, "The Four Ages," pp. 8–9.
52. Bullfinch, *Age of Fable,* p. 16. First emphasis added; other two in original.

53. Hesiod, *Works and Days*, lns. 191–192, in Lattimore, *Hesiod*, p. 41.
54. Hesiod, *Works and Days*, lns. 8, 80–82, 90–91; pp. 19, 27, 29.
55. Hesiod, *Theogony*, lns. 585, 601, in Lattimore, *Hesiod*, pp. 158–159.
56. Hesiod, *Works and Days*, ln. 89, in Lattimore, *Hesiod*, p. 29.
57. Hesiod, *Works and Days*, lns. 94–95, p. 29.
58. Ovid, "Four Ages," p. 9.
59. Ehrenberg, *Women in Prehistory*, p. 107.

CHAPTER 5: HELL HATH NO FURY LIKE A MAN DEVALUED

1. Margaret Mead, *The Changing Culture of an Indian Tribe* (New York: Columbia University Press, 1932), p. 134.
2. Richard B. Lee and Irven DeVore, eds., *Man the Hunter* (Chicago: Aldine Publishing, 1969); Lionel Tiger, *Men in Groups* (New York: Random House, 1969); Lionel Tiger and Robin Fox, *The Imperial Animal* (New York, Holt, Rinehart and Winston, 1971).
3. William S. Laughlin, "Hunting: An Integrating Biobehavior System and Its Evolutionary Importance," in Lee and DeVore, eds., *Man the Hunter*, p. 304.
4. Sherwood L. Washburn and C. S. Lancaster, "The Evolution of Hunting," in Lee and DeVore, eds., *Man the Hunter*, p. 293.
5. Tiger and Fox, *Imperial Animal*, p. 88.
6. William F. Allman, *The Stone Age Present* (New York: Simon and Schuster, 1994), p. 203.
7. Helen Fisher, *The First Sex* (New York: Random House, 1999), pp. 57–65.
8. Jared Diamond, *Why Is Sex Fun?* (New York: Basic Books, 1997), p. 91.
9. Margaret Ehrenberg, *Women in Prehistory* (Norman: University of Oklahoma Press, 1989), pp. 105–106.
10. Robert Bly, *Iron John: A Book About Men* (New York: Addison-Wesley, 1990), p. x; Sam Keen, *Fire in The Belly: On Being a Man* (New York: Bantam, 1991), p. 54.
11. E. J. Hobsbawm, *Industry and Empire; An Economic History of Britain since 1750* (New York: Pantheon, 1968), p. 80.
12. James Mellaart, *Çatal Hüyük: A Neolithic Town in Anatolia* (London: Thames and Hudson; New York: McGraw-Hill, 1967), pp. 175–176.
13. Joan Bamberger, "The Myth of Matriarchy: Why Men Rule in Primitive Society," in Michelle Zimbalist Rosaldo and Louise Lamphere, eds., *Women, Culture and Society* (Stanford, CA: Stanford University Press, 1974), pp. 263–280.
14. Eva Cantarella, *Pandora's Daughters: The Role and Status of Women in Greek and Roman Antiquity* (Baltimore: Johns Hopkins University Press, 1987; orig. Italian ed., 1981), pp. 13–14; Ehrenberg, *Women in Prehistory*, pp. 63–66.
15. J. J. Bachofen, *Das Mutterrecht* (Stuttgart, Germany: Krais and Hoffman, 1861); Bachofen, *Myth, Religion and Mother Right: Selected Writings of J.J. Bachofen*, Ralph Manheim, trans. (Princeton, NJ: Princeton University Press, 1967).
16. Friedrich Engels, *The Origin of the Family, Private Property, and the State* (1885; New York: International publishers, 1942).

17. Elizabeth Gould Davis, *The First Sex* (Baltimore: Penguin, 1971); Marija Gimbutas, *Gods and Goddesses of Old Europe* (Berkeley and Los Angeles: University of California Press, 1974); Gimbutas, *The Language of the Goddess* (New York: Harper & Row, 1989); Riane Eisler, *The Chalice and the Blade* (New York: Harper & Row, 1987).

18. Eleanor Leacock, "Women in Egalitarian Societies," in Renate Bridenthal, Claudia Koonz, and Susan Stuard, eds., *Becoming Visible: Women in European History* (Boston: Houghton Mifflin, 2d ed., 1987), p. 28.

19. Leacock, in "Women in Egalitarian Societies," repeatedly makes such statements as "[a]ll told we have every reason to assume that autonomy and prestige for women obtained among early European hunters as they formerly did among other hunting and gathering people" (p. 26). Prestige, yes; "autonomy," certainly not. There is *no* reason for such an assumption, as Leacock herself indicates in several passages referring to the group interdependence that characterized these societies.

20. Barbara S. Lesko, "Women of Egypt and the Ancient Near East," in Bridenthal, Koonz, and Stuard, *Becoming Visible* (2d ed.), p. 43.

21. Mead, *Changing Culture of an Indian Tribe,* p. 134.

22. David Pilbeam, "The Fashionable View of Man as a Naked Ape Is: 1. An Insult to Apes; 2. Simplistic; 3. Male-oriented; 4. Rubbish," *New York Times Magazine,* September 3, 1972, p. 30, as cited in George Gilder, *Men and Marriage* (Gretna, LA: Pelican, 1986), p. 33.

23. Margaret Mead, *Male and Female: A Study of the Sexes in a Changing World* (New York: William Morrow, 1949), p. 160.

24. Mark Twain, *The Adventures of Huckleberry Finn* (1885: Franklin Center, PA: Franklin Library, 1979), p. 334.

25. Catherine McNichol Stock, *Main Street in Crisis: The Great Depression and the Old Middle Class on the Northern Plains* (Chapel Hill: University of North Carolina Press, 1992), p. 168.

26. A survey of sexual labor division in 104 horticultural and 93 agricultural societies found that while males are the cultivators in only 17 percent of the horticultural societies, they fill that position in 81 percent of the agricultural societies [M. Kay Martin and Barbara Voorhies, *Female of the Species* (New York: Columbia University Press, 1975), p. 283].

27. Genesis 4:2–5.

28. Susan Faludi, *Backlash: The Undeclared War Against American Women* (New York: Crown, 1991).

29. Gilder, *Men and Marriage,* p. x. Gilder has had some remarkable insights about sex roles and their origins, but he grossly misjudges what his own insights mean.

30. Judith Shulevitz, "The Fall of Man," *New York Times Book Review,* October 3, 1999 [review of Susan Faludi, *Stiffed: The Betrayal of the American Man* (New York: William Morrow, 1999)].

31. Barbara Ehrenreich, in "Who Needs Men?" *Harper's Magazine,* June 1999, p. 41.

32. Richard Wrangham and Dale Peterson, *Demonic Males: Apes and the Origins of Human Violence* (Boston: Houghton Mifflin, 1996), p. 219.

33. *Desmond Morris: The Human Sexes,* "Different But Equal" (Partridge Films, The Learning Channel, 1997).

34. Ehrenberg, *Women in Prehistory,* p. 105.

35. Irenaus Eibl-Eibesfeldt, *The Biology of Peace and War* (1975; New York: Viking Press, 1979), pp. 126–128.

36. *The Epic of Gilgamesh,* translated by N. K. Sandars (London: Penguin Books, 1974).

37. J. M. Rodwell, ed., *Babylonian and Assyrian Literature* (New York: Colonial Press, 1902), pp. 168–185.

CHAPTER 6: GOING TO SEED

1. Aeschylus, *The Eumenides,* lns. 658–661, in David Grene and Richard Lattimore, eds., *Aeschylus* (Chicago: University of Chicago Press, 1959), p. 158.

2. Mark Twain, as quoted in Mona Charen, "Early Childhood Not So 'Critical,' Says New Report," *Clarion-Ledger* (Jackson, MS), September 23, 1999.

3. Marija Gimbutas, *The Early Civilizations of Europe* (Monograph for Indo-European Studies 131, University of California at Los Angeles, 1980), pp. 33–34, as cited in Riane Eisler, *The Chalice and the Blade: Our History, Our Future* (San Francisco: Harper & Row, 1987), p. 14.

4. P. M. Kaberry, *Aboriginal Women, Sacred and Profane* (Philadelphia: Blakiston, 1939), p. 43, as quoted in Bruno Bettelheim, *Symbolic Wounds: Puberty Rites and the Envious Male* (1954; rev. ed., New York: Collier Books, 1962), p. 104.

5. Sam Keen, *Fire in the Belly: On Being a Man* (New York: Bantam, 1991), pp. 28, 31, 130.

6. Donald Worster, *Nature's Economy: A History of Ecological Ideas* (1977; Cambridge, England: Cambridge University Press, 1984), pp. viii, x.

7. Eusthathius, *Commentari ad Homeri Iliadium et Odyesseam, ad fidem exempli Romani* (Leipzig, 1825–1830), 18.483, as quoted in William Blake Tyrrell, *Amazons: A Study in Athenian Mythmaking* (Baltimore: Johns Hopkins University Press, 1984), p. 30.

8. Tikva Frymer-Kensky, *In the Wake of the Goddesses: Women, Culture, and the Biblical Transformation of Pagan Myth* (New York: Free Press, 1992), pp. 18–19, 48–49, 72.

9. Frymer-Kensky, *In the Wake of the Goddesses,* pp. 17–18, 73–74.

10. Frances and Joseph Gies, *Women in the Middle Ages* (New York: Thomas Y. Crowell, 1978), pp. 48–52.

11. Frymer-Kensky, *In the Wake of the Goddesses,* p. 236n.

12. "Plow My Vulva," as quoted in Frymer-Kensky, *In the Wake of the Goddesses,* p. 53; Iris Furlong, "The Mythology of the Ancient Near East," in Carolyne Larrington, ed., *The Feminist Companion to Mythology* (London: Pandora Press, 1992), pp. 16–20.

13. Aeschylus, *The Eumenides,* lns. 658–661, in Grene and Lattimore, eds., *Aeschylus,* p. 158.

14. Aeschylus, *The Eumenides,* lns. 662–663, 736, pp. 158, 161.

15. Marilyn French, *Beyond Power: Of Women, Men, and Morals* (New York: Summit Books, 1985) p. 64.

16. "The Instruction of Ptahhotep," verse 21, in Miriam Lichtheim, ed., *Ancient Egyptian Literature* (Berkeley and Los Angeles: University of California Press, 1975), vol. I, p. 69.

17. "The Hymn to Aten" (14th century B.C.E.), in Gloria K. Fiero, ed., *The Humanistic Tradition* (Dubuque, IA: Brown & Benchmark, 1992), vol. 1, p. 21.

18. Sophocles, *Antigone* (443 B.C.E.), ln. 642, in Sophocles, *The Three Theban Plays,* Robert Fagles, trans. (New York: Penguin, 1982), p. 89.

19. Ovid, *Metamorphoses,* Book 10, in *Tales from Ovid,* Ted Hughes, trans. (New York: Farrar, Strauss and Giroux, 1997), p. 116.

20. Plutarch, *Life of Lycurgus,* as quoted in Bertrand Russell, *A History of Western Philosophy* (New York: Simon & Schuster, 1945), p. 102.

21. *Al-Qur'an,* Sura II, line 223. The first translation is that of Ahmed Ali (Princeton, NJ: Princeton University Press, 1984), p. 39. The second is by E. H. Palmer (New York: Scribners, 1900), p. 33.

22. Genesis 9:9, 13:15 and *passim.*

23. Genesis 38:8–10.

24. Leviticus 12:2.

25. Leviticus 15:16–18.

26. Deuteronomy 25:11–12.

27. Herbert G. May and Bruce M. Metzger, eds., *The New Oxford Annotated Bible with the Apocrypha* (New York: Oxford University Press, 1973, 1977), p. 247*n*.

28. Romans 4:13, 9:7, 11:1.

29. As quoted in Alcuin Blamires, ed., *Woman Defamed and Woman Defended: An Anthology of Medieval Texts* (Oxford, England: Clarendon Press, 1992), p. 47.

30. St. Thomas Aquinas, *Summa Theologicae,* Part I, Q. 92, Art. 1, in Anton C. Pegis, ed., *Basic Writings of St. Thomas Aquinas* (New York: Random House, 1945), reprinted in Sheila Ruth, ed., *Issues in Feminism: An Introduction to Women's Studies* (Mountain View, CA: Mayfield Publishing Co., 4th ed., 1998), p. 121.

31. Dzoomkyet, as quoted in the PBS series, "Millennium," Part 2.

32. *The Big Chill* (1983, directed by Lawrence Kasdan, Columbia).

33. *Raising Arizona* (1987, directed by Joel Coen, Fox).

34. Barbara Ehrenreich, in "Who Needs Men?" *Harper's Magazine,* June 1999, p. 34.

35. Margaret Talbot, "The Female Misogynist," *The New Republic,* May 31, 1999, p. 36.

36. Helen Fisher, *The First Sex* (New York: Random House, 1999), pp. 39, 205, 209.

37. Ovid, "The Four Ages," in *Ovid's Metamorphoses,* Brookes More, trans. (Boston: Cornhill, 1922), pp. 7–8. Emphasis added.

38. Bettelheim, *Symbolic Wounds,* p. 104.

39. Genesis 2:8. Emphasis added.

40. Genesis 2:9. Emphasis added.
41. Genesis 2:5–7. Emphasis added.
42. Aeschylus, *Eumenides,* lns. 837–839, p. 164.
43. Genesis 3:7.
44. Genesis 2:21–22.
45. Genesis 2:23.
46. 1 Corinthians 11:12.
47. Claude Levi-Strauss, *The Elementary Structures of Kinship* (Boston: Beacon, 1969); Gayle Rubin, "The Traffic in Women: Notes on the 'Political Economy' of Sex," in Rayna R. Reiter, ed., *Toward an Anthropology of Women* (New York: Monthly Review Press, 1975), pp. 157–210.
48. Margaret Mead, *Coming of Age in Samoa* (1936; New York: New American Library, 1949).
49. Derek Freeman, *Margaret Mead and Samoa: The Making and Unmaking of an Anthropological Myth* (Cambridge, MA: Harvard University Press, 1983); Freeman, *The Fateful Hoaxing of Margaret Mead: A Historical Analysis of Her Samoan Research* (Boulder, CO: Westview Press, 1999).
50. Fisher, *First Sex,* p. 215.
51. Howard V. Blair, letter to the editor, *Clarion-Ledger* (Jackson, MS), August 29, 1999.

CHAPTER 7: "ALL POWER AND GLORY ARE YOURS, ALMIGHTY FATHER"

1. 1 Corinthians 11:7–9.
2. Genesis 1:26.
3. Marija Gimbutas, *Gods and Goddesses of Old Europe* (Berkeley and Los Angeles: University of California Press, 1974); Marija Gimbutas, *The Language of the Goddess* (San Francisco: Harper & Row, 1989); Merlin Stone, *When God Was a Woman* (New York: Dial Press, 1976); Carl Olson, ed., *The Book of the Goddess, Past and Present* (New York: Crossroad, 1983); Riane Eisler, *The Chalice and the Blade: Our History, Our Future* (San Francisco: Harper & Row, 1987).
4. Peggy Sanday, *Female Power and Male Dominance: On the Origins of Sexual Inequality* (New York: Cambridge University Press, 1981).
5. Marilyn French, *Beyond Power: On Women, Men, and Morals* (New York: Summit Books, 1985), pp. 51–54.
6. Alexander Marshack, *The Roots of Civilization: The Cognitive Beginnings of Man's First Art, Symbol and Notation* (New York: McGraw-Hill, 1972), pp. 281–340; Stone, *When God Was a Woman,* pp. 13–14; Anne L. Barstow, "The Prehistoric Goddess," in Olson, ed., *The Book of the Goddess,* pp. 7–15; Gimbutas, *The Language of the Goddess,* pp. xxii, 99, 141–144.
7. G. Clark, *Savagery to Civilization* (1946), as quoted in E. O. James, *Prehistoric Religion: A Study in Prehistoric Archaeology* (New York: Barnes and Noble, 1957), pp. 146–147.

8. Margaret Ehrenberg, *Women in Prehistory* (Norman: University of Oklahoma Press, 1989), pp. 75–76.

9. Ehrenberg, *Women in Prehistory,* pp. 73–74.

10. James Mellaart, *Çatal Hüyük: A Neolithic Town in Anatolia* (London: Thames and Hudson; New York: McGraw-Hill, 1967), pp. 175–76.

11. Gerda Lerner, *The Creation of Patriarchy* (New York: Oxford University Press, 1986), pp. 157–158.

12. Tikva Frymer-Kensky, *In the Wake of the Goddesses: Women, Culture, and the Biblical Transformation of Pagan Myth* (New York: Free Press, 1992), pp. 42–46, 70.

13. *Enuma Elish,* in Barbara C. Sproul, ed., *Primal Myths: Creation Myths around the World* (New York: HarperCollins, 1979), pp. 101–102.

14. *Enuma Elish,* in Sproul, *Primal Myths,* p. 102.

15. Frymer-Kensky, *In the Wake of the Goddesses,* p. 76.

16. Rosemary Radford Ruether, *Gaia and God: An Ecofeminist Theology of Earth Healing* (San Francisco: HarperSanFrancisco, 1992), p. 18.

17. "The Creation According to Ra," in Joseph Kastner, trans. and ed., *Wings of the Falcon: Life and Thought in Ancient Egypt* (New York: Holt, Rinehart, and Winston, 1968), p. 56.

18. I am grateful to Professor Tracy Fessenden for pointing out to me this interpretation of the Ra masturbation story.

19. R. E. Witt, *Isis in the Graeco-Roman World* (Ithaca, NY: Cornell University Press, 1971), pp. 14–20.

20. Hesiod, *Theogony,* lns. 175–198, in Richard Lattimore, trans., *Hesiod* (Ann Arbor: University of Michigan Press, 1959), pp. 133–135.

21. *Theogony,* ln. 200, p. 135.

22. Tikva Frymer-Kensky's contentions that the Israelites did not see God "as male in sexual terms" (*In the Wake of the Goddesses,* p. 144) and that "there is . . . in the Bible . . . no sense of gender differences" (p. 213) simply will not wash for the early period. It is obvious that Yahweh was seen as having male attributes; and the religion of the early Hebrews was plainly based on sharp distinctions between the sexes. (Frymer-Kensky does not even mention circumcision as the sign of covenant.)

23. Genesis 2:7.

24. Exodus 19:15–19.

25. Genesis 3:14; Lerner, *Creation of Patriarchy,* p. 196.

26. Genesis 2:4–7.

27. Genesis 2:19. Emphasis added.

28. Genesis 1:3, 6, 9, 11, 24–28.

29. As quoted in James S. Olson and Raymond Wilson, *Native Americans in the Twentieth Century* (Urbana and Chicago: University of Illinois Press, 1984), pp. 16–17. I am grateful to Professor Michael Stoff of the University of Texas for directing me to the source of this quotation.

30. Genesis 6:1–4. Emphasis added.

31. 1 Corinthians 11:7–9.

32. Ephesians 5:21–33, 6:1–9.

33. Deuteronomy 23:1.
34. Simone de Beauvoir, *The Second Sex* (New York: Knopf, 1952), p. xvi.
35. Mary Daly, *Beyond God the Father: Toward a Philosophy of Women's Liberation* (Boston: Beacon, 1973), p. 19.
36. For example, Oral Roberts, *Daily Blessing: A Guide to Seed-faith Living* (Old Tappan, NJ: Revell, 1978).
37. Don Pickney, *Seed Faith: God's Divine Master Plan to Greatness* (Malden, MO: Don Pickney Ministries, 1986); Bruce C. Hafen, *The Believing Heart: Nourishing the Seed of Faith* (Salt Lake City: Deseret Book Company, 1990); Beverly Capps Burgess, *Jack and the Beanstalk: Faith as a Seed* (Tulsa, OK: Harrison House, 1985).
38. Henry David Thoreau, *Faith in a Seed: The Dispersion of Seeds and Other Late Natural History Writings,* Bradley P. Dean, ed. (Washington, DC: Island Press, 1993).

CHAPTER 8: "NO MOTHER GAVE ME BIRTH"

1. Euripides, *Hippolytus* (428 B.C.E.), lns. 618–620, Eva Cantarella, trans., quoted in Cantarella, *Pandora's Daughters: The Role and Status of Women in Greek and Roman Antiquity* (Baltimore: Johns Hopkins University Press, 1987; orig. Italian ed., 1981), p. 170.
2. *Tao Te Ching,* Chapter 2; Arthur Waley, *The Way and Its Power: A Study of the Tao Te-Ching and its Place in Chinese Thought* (1934; New York: Grove Press, 1958), p. 143.
3. *Tao Te Ching,* Chapter XIX, in Waley, *The Way and Its Power,* p. 166.
4. Geoffrey Parrinder, ed., *World Religions: From Ancient History to the Present* (New York: Facts on File Publications, 1971, 1983), pp. 318–320.
5. Confucius, *Analects,* IV, 16; Arthur Waley, trans. (London: George Allen & Unwin, 1958).
6. Confucius, *Analects,* III, 7.
7. Confucius, *Analects,* XV, 23.
8. Confucius, *Analects,* XII, 7.
9. Confucius, *Analects,* XIII, 6; XIII, 11.
10. Padmanabh S. Jaini, *The Jaina Path of Purification* (Berkeley and Los Angeles: University of California Press, 1979), pp. 1–41.
11. Earl Henry Brewster, *Life of Gotama the Buddha* (New York: E. P. Dutton, 1926), as quoted in Kevin Reilly, ed., *Readings in World Civilizations* (New York: St. Martin's Press, 1988), p. 148.
12. Parrinder, *World Religions,* pp. 262–285.
13. Exodus 20:16–17. Emphasis added.
14. Leviticus 19:18. Emphasis added.
15. Deuteronomy 15:1–8.
16. Deuteronomy 23:20.
17. Leviticus 25:44–46. Emphasis added.
18. Leviticus 25:39.

19. Genesis 17:10–11.
20. Nahum 3:1.
21. Zephaniah 3:1–2.
22. Isaiah 58:6–7.
23. Tikva Frymer-Kensky, *In the Wake of the Goddesses: Women, Culture, and the Biblical Transformation of Pagan Myth* (New York: Free Press, 1992), p. 164. Some of the prophets in the mid-first millennium may indeed have understood the necessity that the Creator be *both* female and male, both mother and father. The second Isaiah appears to have been one of these.
24. Isaiah 46:3–4.
25. Isaiah 66:13.
26. Jeremiah 31:15.
27. Jeremiah 31:20.
28. Phyllis Trible, *God and the Rhetoric of Sexuality* (Philadelphia: Fortress Press, 1978), p. 50; Frymer-Kensky, *In the Wake of the Goddesses,* p. 267, *n.* 17.
29. Jeremiah 31:22.
30. Frymer-Kensky, *In the Wake of the Goddesses,* pp. 165–167, 268, *n.* 34.
31. Frymer-Kensky, *In the Wake of the Goddesses,* pp. 165–167, 268, *n.* 34.
32. 2 Kings 21:1–26, 23:4–14, 23:36–24:7; Jeremiah 7:16–20, 44:15–28.
33. R. F. Willets, *Cretan Cults and Festivals* (New York: Barnes and Noble, 1962), pp. 74–81; Cantarella, *Pandora's Daughters,* pp. 14–15.
34. Willets, *Cretan Cults and Festivals,* pp. 19–20.
35. Ruby Rohrlich-Leavitt, "Women in Transition: Crete and Sumer," in Rantae Bridenthal and Claudia Koonz, eds., *Becoming Visible: Women in European History* (Boston: Houghton Mifflin, 1977), p. 47. Margaret Ehrenberg notes that there is no evidence for matriarchy in Minoan Crete but that there is support for the beliefs that women in that society still practiced agriculture and oversaw religious activities. Ehrenberg, *Women in Prehistory* (Norman: University of Oklahoma Press, 1989), pp. 109–118.
36. Rohrlich-Leavitt, "Women in Transition," pp. 43–44.
37. Homer, *The Odyssey,* Book XI, lns. 430–440, Robert Fitzgerald, trans. (Garden City, NY: Anchor/Doubleday, 1961), p. 210.
38. Homer, *The Iliad,* Book IX, lns. 441–443, Robert Fagles, trans. (New York: Viking, 1990), p. 265.
39. Hesiod, *Theogony,* lns. 585, 600, in Richard Lattimore, trans., *Hesiod* (Ann Arbor: University of Michigan Press, 1959), pp. 158–159.
40. Hesiod, *Theogony,* ln. 590, p. 158.
41. Cantarella, *Pandora's Daughters,* p. 33.
42. Frymer-Kensky, *In the Wake of the Goddesses,* p. 203.
43. Marilyn Arthur, "From Medusa to Cleopatra: Women in the Ancient World," in Renate Bridenthal, Claudia Koonz, and Susan Stuard, eds., *Becoming Visible: Women in European History* (Boston: Houghton Mifflin, 2d ed., 1987), pp. 80–81.
44. William Blake Tyrrell, *Amazons: A Study in Athenian Mythmaking* (Baltimore: Johns Hopkins University Press, 1984), p. 28.

45. Sophocles, *Antigone* (443 B.C.E.), lns. 759–761 in Sophocles, *The Three Thebean Plays*, Robert Fagles, trans. (New York: Penguin, 1982), p. 94.

46. Frymer-Kensky, *In the Wake of the Goddesses*, p. 278, *n. 15*.

47. Cantarella, *Pandora's Daughters*, p. 28.

48. Aeschylus, *The Eumenides*, lns. 736–738, in David Grene and Richard Lattimore, eds., *Aeschylus* (Chicago: University of Chicago Press, 1959). p. 161.

49. Tyrrell, *Amazons*, p. 108.

50. Euripides, *Hippolytus* (428 B.C.E.), lns. 618–620, Eva Cantarella, trans., and quoted in Cantarella, *Pandora's Daughters*, p. 170.

51. Euripides, *Hippolytus*, lns. 664–668, trans. by David Grene, in David Grene and Richard Lattimore, eds., *Euripides* (Chicago: University of Chicago Press, 1955), vol. I, p. 190.

52. Cantarella, *Pandora's Daughters*, p. 38.

53. Plato, *Theaetetus*, 160d. Emphasis added.

54. Aristotle, *Politics*, Bk. 1, Ch. 2.

55. P. Vidal-Naquet, "Slavery and the Rule of Women in Tradition, Myth and Utopia," in R. L. Gordon, ed., *Myth, Religion, and Society* (Cambridge, England: Cambridge University Press, 1981), p. 188, as quoted in Cantarella, *Pandora's Daughters*, p. 194, *n. 2*.

56. Tyrrell, *Amazons*, p. xvii.

57. Martha Nussbaum, on Lynn Neary, "Homophobia," *All Things Considered*, National Public Radio, November 1, 1999; http://search.npr.org/cf/cmn/cmnpd01fm.cfm?PrgDate=11/01/1999&PrgID=2

58. F. A. Wright, *Feminism in Greek Literature: From Homer to Aristotle* (1923; reprint ed.: Port Washington, NY: Kennikat Press, 1969), p. 1.

59. Willets, *Cretan Cults and Festivals*, p. 20.

60. Allaire Chandor Brumfield, *The Attic Festivals of Demeter and Their Relation to the Agricultural Year* (New York: Arno Press, 1981), pp. 192–216; Robert Douglas Mead, ed., *Hellas and Rome: The Story of Greco-Roman Civilization* (New York: New American Library, 1972), pp. 303–304.

61. Aeschylus, *Eumenides*, lns. 837–839, 871–872, 1005–1008, Grene and Lattimore, eds., *Aeschylus*, pp. 164–165, 170.

62. Aristotle, *Generation of Animals*, Bk. I, Ch. 19, A. L. Peck, trans. (Cambridge, MA: Harvard University Press, 1943, 1953), p. 97.

63. Aristotle, *Generation of Animals*, Bk. 1, Ch. 21, p. 113.

64. Aristotle, *Generation of Animals*, Bk. 1, Ch. 21, pp. 113–119.

65. Aristotle, *Generation of Animals*, Bk. 1, Ch. 20, p. 103.

66. Aristotle, *Generation of Animals*, Bk. 1, Ch. 20; Bk. 2, Ch. 3; Bk. 4, Ch. 3; pp. 107, 175, 401.

67. Aristotle, *Generation of Animals*, Bk. 1, Ch. 20, pp. 103–119.

68. Cantarella, *Pandora's Daughters*, p. 92.

69. Aristotle, *Politics*, Bk. I, Ch. 13.

70. Maryanne Cline Horowitz, "Aristotle and Woman," *Journal of the History of Biology*, vol. 9, no. 2 (Fall 1976), pp. 183–213; Gerda Lerner, *The Creation of Patriarchy* (New York: Oxford University Press, 1986), pp. 208–210.

71. Aristotle, *The Nicomachean Ethics,* Bk. 2, Ch. 2, H. Rackham, trans. (Cambridge, MA: Harvard University Press, 1926, 1982), p. 77.

72. Cantarella, *Pandora's Daughters,* p. 90.

73. Cantarella, *Pandora's Daughters,* p. 93.

74. Cantarella, *Pandora's Daughters,* p. 95.

75. Timon of Phlius, as quoted in Mead, *Hellas and Rome,* p. 59.

76. Cantarella, *Pandora's Daughters,* p. 140.

77. Cantarella, *Pandora's Daughters,* p. 115.

78. Cantarella, *Pandora's Daughters,* pp. 119, 148–150.

79. Moses I. Finley, "The Silent Women of Rome," in Finley, *Aspects of Antiquity: Discoveries and Controversies* (1968; New York: Viking, 1968), p. 131; Cantarella, *Pandora's Daughters,* pp. 121, 124–126.

80. H. H. Scullard, *From the Gracchi to Nero: A History of Rome from 133 B.C. to A.D. 68* (London: Methuen, 1959; 2d ed. New York: University Paperbacks, 1963), pp. 13–16, 19–22.

81. Mead, *Hellas and Rome,* p. 78; Cantarella, *Pandora's Daughters,* p. 137.

82. Scullard, *From the Gracchi to Nero,* pp. 353–356.

83. Cantarella, *Pandora's Daughters,* pp. 140–143.

84. Arthur, "From Medusa to Cleopatra," pp. 101–103; Cantarella, *Pandora's Daughters,* pp. 143–148.

85. Jo Ann McNamara, "*Matres Patriae/Matres Ecclesiae:* Women of the Roman Empire," in Bridenthal, Koonz, and Stuard, *Becoming Visible* (2d ed.), p. 116.

86. A. D. Nock, *Conversion* (London: Oxford University Press, 1933, 1961), pp. 75, 132; Sarah B. Pomeroy, *Goddesses, Whores, Wives, and Slaves: Women in Classical Antiquity* (New York: Schocken Books, 1975), p. 225.

87. Frederick C. Grant, ed., *Hellenistic Religions: The Age of Syncretism* (New York: Macmillan, 1953), as quoted in Arthur, "From Medusa to Cleopatra," p. 95.

88. R. E. Witt, *Isis in the Graeco-Roman World* (Ithaca, NY: Cornell University Press, 1971), pp. 14–20.

89. Cantarella, *Pandora's Daughters,* p. 141.

90. Pomeroy, *Goddesses, Whores, Wives, and Slaves,* p. 220.

91. Pomeroy, *Goddesses, Whores, Wives, and Slaves,* pp. 217–226; Nock, *Conversion,* pp. 74, 150–152.

CHAPTER 9: SHE IS RISEN—AND FALLEN

1. Geoffrey Chaucer, *The Canterbury Tales* (1387–1400; New York: Modern Library, 1957), p. 310.

2. Henry Adams, *The Education of Henry Adams* (1918; Boston: Houghton Mifflin, 1961), p. 446.

3. Jo Ann McNamara, "*Matres Patriae/Matres Ecclesiae:* Women of the Roman Empire," in Renate Bridenthal, Claudia Koonz, and Susan Stuard, eds., *Becoming Visible: Women in European History* (Boston: Houghton Mifflin, 2d ed., 1987), p. 115.

4. Matthew 5:38–48.

5. Matthew 5:3–10.
6. Luke 11:21–22.
7. Matthew 26:52; John 18:11.
8. 1 Corinthians 13:9.
9. James 1:19.
10. Mark 8:36; Matthew 16:26.
11. Matthew 23:12.
12. Acts 20:35.
13. Matthew 19:24.
14. 1 Timothy 6:9–10.
15. 1 Timothy 6:8.
16. Ephesians 4:25.
17. Galatians 5:15.
18. Matthew 25:35–36, 40.
19. 1 John 3:17.
20. Galatians 5:19–24.
21. 1 Timothy 2:9–15; Elisabeth Schussler Fiorenza, "You Are Not to Be Called Father," *Cross Currents,* Fall 1979, p. 316.
22. 1 Corinthians 11:8.
23. 1 Corinthians 11:7.
24. Ben Witherington, III, *Women and the Genesis of Christianity* (Cambridge, England: Cambridge University Press, 1990), pp. 107–117.
25. John 11:27.
26. John 11:2, 12:3–8; Matthew 26:6–13; Mark 14:3–9.
27. Luke 7:36–50; Elisabeth Schussler Fiorenza, *In Memory of Her: A Feminist Theological Reconstruction of Christian Origins* (New York: Crossroad, 1983), pp. xiii–xiv.
28. McNamara, *"Matres Patriae/Matres Ecclesiae,"* p. 113.
29. Fiorenza, *In Memory of Her,* p. xiv; Matthew 26:51–52; John 18:10–11; Mark 14:66–72, 15:40–41.
30. Matthew 28:1–10; Mark 16:9; John 20:14–17.
31. Fiorenza, "You Are Not to Be Called Father," p. 304; Fiorenza, *In Memory of Her,* p. 170.
32. Mark 8:31.
33. There has been much discussion of the meaning of "Son of man" See Gerhard Kittel, *Theological Dictionary of the New Testament* (Grand Rapids, MI: Eerdmans, 1964–1976), abridged ed., pp. 1215 *ff.*
34. Galatians 3:28.
35. Evelyn Stagg and Frank Stagg, *Woman in the World of Jesus* (Philadelphia: Westminster Press, 1978), pp. 144–160.
36. 1 Corinthians 15:5–8. Emphasis added.
37. Elaine Pagels, *The Gnostic Gospels* (New York: Random House, 1979), p. 57.
38. Pagels, *The Gnostic Gospels,* p. 65.
39. Fiorenza, "You Are Not to Be Called Father," pp. 309, 312.

40. Genesis 1:27; Pagels, *Gnostic Gospels,* pp. 56, 66.

41. Trimorphic Protennoia, 45.2–10, in *The Nag Hammadi Library in English* (San Francisco: Harper & Row, 1977, 1981), p. 467; Pagels, *Gnostic Gospels,* p. 55.

42. Apocalypse of Adam, 81.2–9, in *Nag Hammadi Library,* p. 262; Pagels, *Gnostic Gospels,* p. 54.

43. Apocryphon of John 2.9–14, in *Nag Hammadi Library,* p. 99.

44. Apocryphon of John 4.34–5.7, in *Nag Hammadi Library,* p. 101; Pagels, *Gnostic Gospels,* p. 52.

45. Pagels, *Gnostic Gospels,* p. 52; Pagels, "What Became of God the Mother?" in Carol P. Christ and Judith Plaskow, eds., *Womanspirit Rising: A Feminist Reader in Religion* (San Francisco: HarperSanFrancisco, 1992), p. 110.

46. Sojourner Truth, as quoted in Alice Felt Tyler, *Freedom's Ferment: Phases of American Social History from the Colonial Period to the Outbreak of the Civil War* (1944; reprint: New York: Harper & Row, 1962), p. 458.

47. John 3:3–6.

48. Stephen R. L. Clark, *The Nature of the Beast: Are Animals Moral?* (Oxford, England: Oxford University Press, 1982), p. 117.

49. William F. Buckley, Jr., "Religion Taking a Beating," *Clarion-Ledger* (Jackson, MS), March 16, 1989.

50. Rev. Sydney Smith, Lady Holland, *Memoir* (1855), p. 262, as quoted in *The Oxford Dictionary of Quotations* (Oxford, England: Oxford University Press, 1941; 3d ed., 1979), p. 511.

51. Tertullian, "On the Apparel of Women," in Alexander Roberts and James Donaldson, eds., *The Ante-Nicene Fathers* (New York: Scribners, 1902), vol. 4, p. 14.

52. Norman F. Cantor, *The Meaning of the Middle Ages* (Boston: Allyn and Bacon, 1973), pp. 95–96.

53. Williston Walker, et al., *A History of the Christian Church* (New York: Scribners, 1985), p. 125.

54. Ernest Jones, "The Significance of Christmas," in Jones, *Psycho-Myth, Psycho-History* (New York: Hillstone, 1974), reprinted in Kevin Reilly, *Readings in World Civilizations* (New York: St. Martin's Press, 1988), vol. 1, pp. 131–139. A few references to Sunday as the day of Christian worship had been included in the New Testament, but the observation was not formalized until the fourth century. Stagg and Stagg, *Woman in the World of Jesus,* pp. 151–152.

55. As quoted in Bonnie S. Anderson and Judith P. Zinsser, *A History of Their Own: Women in Europe* (New York: Harper & Row, 1988), vol. 1, p. 80.

56. Morris Bishop, *The Horizon Book of the Middle Ages* (New York: American Heritage Publishing, 1968), p. 386.

57. Gerda Lerner, *The Creation of Patriarchy* (New York: Oxford University Press, 1986), p. 96; McNamara, *"Matres Patriae/Matres Ecclesiae,"* pp. 119, 123.

58. Matthew 12:46–50; 13:55–56; Mark 6:2–3.

59. Eva Cantarella, *Pandora's Daughters: The Role and Status of Women in Greek and Roman Antiquity* (Baltimore: Johns Hopkins University Press, 1987, orig. Italian ed., 1981), p. 168.

60. McNamara, *"Matres Patriae/Matres Ecclesiae,"* p. 121.
61. R. E. Witt, *Isis in the Graeco-Roman World* (Ithaca, NY: Cornell University Press, 1971), pp. 273–274.
62. Witt, *Isis in the Graeco-Roman World,* p. 274; Leonard W. Moss and Stephen C. Cappannari, "In Quest of the Black Virgin: She Is Black Because She Is Black," in James J. Preston, ed., *Mother Worship: Theme and Variations* (Chapel Hill: University of North Carolina Press, 1982), pp. 62, 65.
63. Naomi R. Goldenberg, *The Changing of the Gods: Feminism and the End of Traditional Religions* (Boston: Beacon, 1979), pp. 50–77, argues that the Virgin Mary constituted a reincarnation of a prehistoric mother goddess.
64. Frederick H. Russell, *The Just War in the Middle Ages* (Cambridge, England: Cambridge University Press, 1975), pp. 16–17.
65. Matthew 5:39; Luke 6:29.
66. Stanley Windass, *Christianity versus Violence: A Social and Historical Study of War and Christianity* (London: Sheed and Ward, 1964), pp. 24–29.
67. Russell, *Just War,* 17–18.
68. Genesis 3:16.
69. St. Augustine, *The Literal Meaning of Genesis,* XI.37, in Alcuin Blamires, ed., *Woman Defamed and Woman Defended: An Anthology of Medieval Texts* (New York: Oxford University Press, 1992), p. 79.
70. St. Augustine, *The Literal Meaning of Genesis,* IX.5, p. 79.
71. John B. Noss, *Man's Religions* (New York: Macmillan, 1949, 3d ed., 1963), pp. 725–729; Geoffrey Parrinder, ed., *World Religions: From Ancient History to the Present* (New York: Facts on File Publications, 1971, 1983), p. 468.
72. Parrinder, *World Religions,* pp. 468–469.
73. Philip K. Hitti, *History of the Arabs* (New York: Macmillan, 1937), p. 120.
74. *Ghazali's Book of Counsel for Kings* (*Nashihat al-Muluk*), F. R. C. Bagley, trans. (New York: Oxford University Press, 1964), p. 172, as quoted in Reay Tannahill, *Sex in History* (New York: Stein and Day, 1980; rev. ed., Chelsea, MI: Scarborough House, 1992), p. 234.
75. *Ghazali's Book of Counsel,* pp. 164–165, as quoted in Tannahill, *Sex in History,* pp. 233–234.
76. Robert S. Hoyt, *Europe in the Middle Ages* (New York: Harcourt, Brace & World, 1957), p. 286.
77. As quoted in Frances and Joseph Gies, *Women in the Middle Ages* (New York: Thomas Y. Crowell, 1978), p. 22.
78. Susan Stuard, "The Dominion of Gender: Women's Fortunes in the High Middle Ages," in Bridenthal et al., *Becoming Visible* (2d ed.), p. 168.
79. Gies and Gies, *Women in the Middle Ages,* p. 38.
80. Cantarella, *Pandora's Daughters,* p. 170.
81. Stuard, "Dominion of Gender," p. 164.
82. Stuard, "Dominion of Gender," pp. 164–165.
83. As quoted in Gies and Gies, *Women in the Middle Ages,* pp. 50–51, 41.
84. JoAnn McNamara and Suzanne F. Wemple, "Sanctity and Power: The Dual Pursuit of Medieval Women," in Bridenthal, et. al., *Becoming Visible* (2d ed.) p. 135.

85. Hoyt, *Europe in the Middle Ages,* p. 288.

86. Caroline Walker Bynam, *Jesus as Mother: Studies in the Spirituality of the High Middle Ages* (Berkeley & Los Angeles: University of California Press, 1982), pp. 110–169.

87. Witt, *Isis in the Graeco-Roman World,* p. 326, *n. 50.*

CHAPTER 10: HUMAN LIBERATION IS WOMEN'S LIBERATION

1. Ben Jonson, *The Forest* (1616), vii; "Song: That Women are but Men's Shadows," in *The Oxford Dictionary of Quotations* (New York: Oxford University Press, 3d ed., 1979), p. 284.

2. Ashley Montagu, *The Natural Superiority of Women* (1953; revised ed.: New York: Macmillan, 1968), pp. 34–35.

3. Michael Kammen, *People of Paradox: An Inquiry Concerning the Origins of American Civilization* (New York: Knopf, 1972; New York: Oxford University Press, 1980), p. 135.

4. Christopher Columbus, Letter to King Ferdinand and Queen Isabella, 1498, in A. W. Lawrence and Jean Young, eds., *Narratives of the Discovery of America* (New York: Cape and Smith, 1931), p. 300.

5. Lawrence and Young, *Narratives of the Discovery of America,* p. 137.

6. Lawrence and Young, *Narrative of the Discovery of America,* p. 102.

7. Lawrence and Young, *Narrative of the Discovery of America,* p. 137. Emphasis added.

8. Lawrence and Young, *Narrative of the Discovery of America,* p. 98.

9. Juan Gines de Sepulveda, *Democrates alter de justis belli causis apud Indios,* in Frederick B. Pike, ed., *Latin American History: Selected Problems—Identity, Integration and Nationhood* (New York: Harcourt Brace & World, 1969), p. 47.

10. Michele de Cuneo's Letter on Columbus's Second Voyage, October 28, 1495, in Samuel Eliot Morison, ed. and trans., *Journals and Other Documents on the Life and Voyages of Christopher Columbus* (New York: Heritage, 1963), pp. 210, 212.

11. Walter Raleigh, "Discovery of Guiana" (1595), as quoted in Annette Kolodny, *The Lay of the Land: Metaphor as Experience and History in American Life and Letters* (Chapel Hill: University of North Carolina Press, 1975), p. 11.

12. M. Arthur Barlowe, "The First Voyage Made to the Coasts of America," as quoted in Kolodny, *Lay of the Land,* p. 10.

13. Kammen, *People of Paradox,* p. 138.

14. William Monter, "Protestant Wives, Catholic Saints, and the Devil's Handmaid: Women in the Age of Reformations," in Renate Bridenthal, Claudia Koonz, and Susan Stuard, eds., *Becoming Visible: Women in European History* (Boston: Houghton Mifflin, 2d ed., 1987), p. 207.

15. Martin Luther, as quoted in Sherrin Marshall Wyntjes, "Women in the Reformation Era," in Renate Bridenthal and Claudia Koonz, *Becoming Visible: Women in European History* (Boston: Houghton Mifflin, 1977), p. 174.

16. John Milton, *Paradise Lost* (1667), Book X, in *The Complete Poetry and Selected Prose of John Milton* (New York: Modern Library, 1950), pp. 343–344.

17. Monter, "Protestant Wives, Catholic Saints, and the Devil's Handmaid," pp. 212–216.

18. Keith Moxey, *Peasant Warriors and Wives: Popular Imagery in the Reformation* (Chicago: University of Chicago Press, 1989), pp. 101–126; Chista Grössinger, *Picturing Women in Late Medieval and Renaissance Art* (Manchester, England, and New York: Manchester University Press, 1997), pp. 112–121.

19. H. Diane Russell, *Eva/Ave: Woman in Renaissance and Baroque Prints* (Washington, DC: National Gallery of Art, 1990), pp. 149–150; Grössinger, *Picturing Women in Late Medieval and Renaissance Art,* pp. 114–115.

20. Descartes, as quoted in John Herman Randall, Jr., *The Making of the Modern Mind* (Boston: Houghton Mifflin, 1926; rev. ed., 1940), pp. 241–242.

21. Alexander Pope, "Epitaphs. Intended for Sir Isaac Newton," in Louis Kronenberger, ed., *Alexander Pope: Selected Works* (New York: Modern Library, 1948), p. 330.

22. Edward Young, *Imperium Pelagi* (1730), as quoted in Milton L. Myers, *The Soul of Modern Economic Man: Ideas of Self-Interest, Thomas Hobbes to Adam Smith* (Chicago: University of Chicago Press, 1983), p. 17.

23. Thomas Hobbes, *Leviathan* (1651; London: J. M. Dent, 1973), Introduction, p. 1.

24. Hobbes, *Leviathan,* ch. 13, pp. 64–65.

25. Sam Keen, *Fire in the Belly: On Being a Man* (New York: Bantam, 1991), p. 54.

26. Michael Kimmel, *Manhood in America: A Cultural History* (New York: Free Press, 1996), pp. 55, 59.

27. Myers, *Soul of Modern Economic Man,* p. 6.

28. Henry C. Carey, "Of Wealth" (1858), reprinted in David A. Hollinger and Charles Capper, eds., *The American Intellectual Tradition* (New York: Oxford University Press, 1989), vol. 1, p. 247.

29. Mary Shelley, *Frankenstein Or, The Modern Prometheus* (1818; New York: Signet Classic, 1963), pp. 95, 160.

30. Shelley, *Frankenstein,* pp. 37, 41, 53, 54.

31. Donald Worster, *Nature's Economy: A History of Ecological Ideas* (1977; Cambridge, England: Cambridge University Press, 1984), p. 35.

32. Friedrich Engels, *The Condition of the Working Class in England in 1844* (1845), as quoted in Worster, *Nature's Economy,* p. 148.

33. Worster, *Nature's Economy,* p. 169.

34. Marilyn Waring, *If Women Counted: A New Feminist Economics* (San Francisco: Harper & Row, 1988.)

CHAPTER 11: NO WOMAN IS AN ISLAND

1. Abraham Lincoln, Speech at Peoria, Illinois, October 16, 1854.

2. J. Hector St. John de Crèvecoeur, *Letters From an American Farmer* (1782; New York: Penguin, 1981), p. 69.

3. Crèvecoeur, *Letters,* pp. 67, 70. Emphasis in the original.

4. Philip Freneau, in *The Freeman's Journal: or, The North American Intelligencer* (Philadelphia), January 9, 1782, as quoted in Henry Nash Smith, *Virgin Land:*

The American West as Symbol and Myth (Cambridge, MA: Harvard University Press, 1950, 1978), p. 11.

5. Walt Whitman, "Passage to India," in *Leaves of Grass,* 9th ed., 1892 (Franklin Center, PA: Franklin Library, 1979), p. 400.

6. Alexis de Tocqueville, *Democracy in America,* Thomas Bender, ed. (1835, 1840; New York: Random House, 1981), pp. 173–174.

7. Tocqueville, *Democracy in America,* pp. 20–21. Emphasis added.

8. William Byrd, *Journey to the Land of Eden in the Year 1733,* as quoted in Michael Kammen, *People of Paradox: An Inquiry Concerning the Origins of American Civilization* (New York: Knopf, 1972; Oxford University Press, 1980), p. 150. Emphasis added.

9. James Fenimore Cooper, *The Pioneers* (1823), cited in Kammen, *People of Paradox,* p. 151.

10. *Battle for the Wilderness,* film by Lawrence Hott and Diane Garey, "The American Experience," PBS, 1989.

11. Ronald Reagan, as quoted in Ronnie Dugger, *On Reagan: The Man and His Presidency* (New York: McGraw-Hill, 1983), p. 91.

12. Wallace Stegner, on *Battle for the Wilderness.*

13. Tocqueville, *Democracy in America,* p. 178.

14. William Cobbett, as quoted in David M. Potter, *People of Plenty: Economic Abundance and the American Character* (Chicago: University of Chicago, 1954), p. 79.

15. Irvin G. Wyllie, *The Self-Made Man in America* (New Brunswick, NJ: Rutgers University Press, 1954), p. 10.

16. Robert N. Bellah, et al., *Habits of the Heart: Individualism and Commitment in American Life* (Berkeley and Los Angeles: University of California Press, 1985; New York: Harper & Row, 1985), p. 82.

17. Ralph Waldo Emerson, "Self-Reliance" (1841), in Lewis Mumford, ed., *Ralph Waldo Emerson: Essays and Journals* (Garden City, NY: International Collectors Library, 1968), pp. 91–93. Emphasis in original.

18. Henry David Thoreau, "Civil Disobedience" (1849), in Thoreau, *Walden and Other Writings* (Garden City, NY: International Collectors Library, 1970), p. 285. Emphasis in original.

19. Jay Fliegelman, *Prodigals and Pilgrims: The American Revolution Against Patriarchal Authority, 1750–1800* (New York: Cambridge University Press, 1982), p. 224, as quoted in Michael Kimmel, *Manhood in America: A Cultural History* (New York: Free Press, 1996), p. 20.

20. Tocqueville, as quoted in Bellah, *Habits of the Heart,* p. 86.

21. Sarah Josepha Hale, as quoted in Carl N. Degler, *At Odds: Women and the Family in America from the Revolution to the Present* (New York: Oxford University Press, 1980), p. 27.

22. Thomas Paine, "An Occasional Letter on the Female Sex," *Pennsylvania Magazine,* August 1775, reprinted in Paul Lauter et al., *The Heath Anthology of American Literature* (Lexington, MA: D.C. Heath, 1990), vol. 1, p. 939.

23. Bellah, *Habits of the Heart,* pp. 40–41, 87–88.

24. Kimmel, *Manhood in America*, p. 53.
25. T. Walter Herbert, *Dearest Beloved: The Hawthornes and the Making of the Middle-Class Family* (Berkeley and Los Angeles: University of California Press, 1993), p. 187, as quoted in Kimmel, *Manhood in America*, p. 52.
26. Barbara Welter, "The Cult of True Womanhood: 1820–1860," *American Quarterly,* vol. 18 (Summer 1966), pp. 151–174, reprinted in Thomas R. Frazier, ed., *The Underside of American History* (New York: Harcourt Brace Jovanovich, 1971, 2d ed., 1974), vol. 1, p. 238.
27. Degler, *At Odds,* p. 55.
28. Welter, "Cult of True Womanhood," p. 257.
29. Kimmel, *Manhood in America,* p. 59.
30. Crèvecoeur, as quoted in Kimmel, *Manhood in America,* p. 61.
31. Christopher Lasch, *The True and Only Heaven* (New York: Norton, 1991), p. 94, as quoted in Kimmel, *Manhood in America,* p. 67.
32. Tocqueville, *Democracy in America,* p. 212.
33. Tocqueville, *Democracy in America,* p. 224. Emphasis added.
34. Herbert G. Gutman, *The Black Family in Slavery and Freedom,* 1750–1925 (New York: Pantheon, 1976), p. 50.
35. Paul A. David et al., *Reckoning with Slavery: A Critical Study in the Quantitative History of American Negro Slavery* (New York: Oxford University Press, 1976), p. 111.
36. Eugene D. Genovese, *Roll, Jordan Roll: The World the Slaves Made* (New York: Pantheon, 1974), p. 481.

CHAPTER 12: "I CAN'T BE SATISFIED"

1. Virginia Woolf, "Mr. Bennett and Mrs. Brown," a paper read to the Heretics, Cambridge, May 18, 1924, in Woolf, *The Captain's Death Bed and Other Essays* (New York: Harcourt, Brace, 1950), p. 96.
2. Irving Howe, as quoted in Daniel Bell, *The Cultural Contradictions of Capitalism* (New York: Basic Books, 1976, 1978), p. 48.
3. Friedrich Nietzsche, *The Antichrist* (written 1888; first published 1895), Preface, in Walter Kaufmann, ed., *The Portable Nietzsche* (New York: Viking, 1954, 1968), p. 568.
4. Nietzsche, *Beyond Good and Evil: Prelude to a Philosophy of the Future* (1886), sections 284, 41, in Walter Kaufmann, ed., *Basic Writings of Nietzsche* (New York: Modern Library, 1968), pp. 416, 242.
5. Nietzsche, *Beyond Good and Evil,* sections 198, 188, pp. 299, 290.
6. Nietzsche, *Beyond Good and Evil,* sections 260, 262, pp. 394, 400.
7. Nietzsche, *Beyond Good and Evil,* sections 202, 259, 260, 269, pp. 306, 393, 395, 409.
8. Nietzsche, *Antichrist,* section 49, pp. 628–629.
9. Jean-Paul Sartre, *Existentialism and Humanism* (London: Methuen, 1848), p. 28, as quoted in Mary Midgley, *Wickedness: A Philosophical Essay* (London: Routledge & Kegan Paul, 1984), p. 54.

10. Mary Midgley, *Beast and Man: The Roots of Human Nature* (Ithaca, NY: Cornell University Press, 1978), p. 71.

11. Midgley, *Wickedness,* p. 54.

12. John Dewey, *The Public and Its Problems* (1927), reprinted in David A. Hollinger and Charles Capper, eds., *The American Intellectual Tradition* (New York: Oxford University Press, 1989), pp. 135–136.

13. Sigmund Freud, as quoted in Betty Friedan, *The Feminine Mystique* (New York: Norton, 1963, Avon, 1983), p. 114.

14. Sigmund Freud, *Civilization and Its Discontents* (1930) in James Strachey, ed. and trans., *The Standard Edition of the Complete Psychological Works of Sigmund Freud* (London: Hogarth Press, 1953–1974), vol. 21, p. 86.

15. Freud, "The Question of Lay Analysis" (1926), in Strachey, *Standard Edition,* vol. 20, p. 212.

16. Freud, "Some Psychical Consequences of the Anatomical Distinction Between the Sexes" (1925), in Strachey, *Standard Edition,* vol. 19, p. 252.

17. Peter Gay, *Freud: A Life for Our Time* (New York: Norton, 1988), p. 501.

18. Freud, "Anatomical Sex Distinction," p. 254.

19. Helen Fisher, *The First Sex* (New York: Random House, 1999), p. xviii; Jared Diamond, *Why Is Sex Fun?* (New York: Basic Books, 1997), p. 44; Anne Moir and David Jessel, *Brain Sex: The Real Difference Between Men and Women* (New York: Lyle Stuart, 1991), p. 24.

20. Freud, "Anatomical Sex Distinction," p. 253*n*.

21. Gay, *Freud,* pp. 501, 522.

22. Freud, "Anatomical Sex Distinction," p. 252.

23. Freud, "Anatomical Sex Distinction," p. 254; Gay, *Freud,* p. 518.

24. Freud, "Anatomical Sex Distinction," p. 257.

25. Freud, *Civilization and Its Discontents,* p. 103.

26. Friedan, *Feminine Mystique,* p. 104.

27. Alvin Hansen, "Toward Full Employment," March 15, 1940, as quoted in Alan Brinkley, "The Idea of the State," in Steve Fraser and Gary Gerstele, eds., *The Rise and Fall of the New Deal Order, 1930–1980* (Princeton, NJ: Princeton University Press), p. 98.

28. Daniel Bell, *The Cultural Contradictions of Capitalism* (New York: Basic Books, 1976, 1978); Robert S. McElvaine, *What's Left?—A New Democratic Vision for America* (Holbrook, MA: Adams Media, 1996), pp. 47–49.

29. Thorstein Veblen, *The Theory of the Leisure Class* (New York: Macmillan, 1899), pp. 241–244.

30. Ernest Dichter, as quoted in Vance Packard, *The Hidden Persuaders* (New York: David McKay, 1957), p. 263.

31. Sam Keen, *Fire in the Belly: On Being a Man* (New York: Bantam, 1991), p. 134.

32. "Job Switching," *I Love Lucy,* episode first broadcast September 15, 1952.

33. "Mr. Grundy," "A Polite Society," *Atlantic Monthly,* vol. 125 (1920), p. 608, as quoted in Paula Fass, *The Damned and the Beautiful: American Youth in the 1920's* (New York: Oxford University Press), p. 37.

34. Charlotte Perkins Gilman, as quoted in Fass, *The Damned and the Beautiful,* p. 381*n.*

35. William E. Leuchtenburg, *The Perils of Prosperity,* 1914–32 (Chicago: University of Chicago Press, 1958), p. 159.

36. Leuchtenburg, *The Perils of Prosperity,* p. 172; Fass, *The Damned and the Beautiful,* pp. 21–22.

37. John Steinbeck, *The Grapes of Wrath* (New York: Viking, 1939, Penguin, 1976), p. 4.

38. Steinbeck, *The Grapes of Wrath,* p. 467.

39. Zora Neale Hurston, *Their Eyes Were Watching God* (1937; New York: Perennial, 1990), pp. 74–76.

40. Steinbeck, *Grapes of Wrath,* p. 388.

41. Steinbeck, *Grapes of Wrath,* pp. 4, 389, 467.

42. Steinbeck, *Grapes of Wrath,* pp. 500–502.

43. "Remember My Forgotten Man" (1933; lyrics by Al Dublin, music by Harry Warren; Warner Brothers).

44. Franklin D. Roosevelt, radio address, April 1932, in Samuel I. Rosenman, ed., *The Public Papers and Addresses of Franklin D. Roosevelt* (New York: Russell and Russell, 1938–1950), vol. 1, pp. 646.

45. Margaret Thorpe, *America at the Movies* (New Haven, CT: Yale University Press, 1939), p. 76, as quoted in Lois W. Banner, *Women in Modern America: A Brief History* (New York: Harcourt Brace Jovanovich, 1974), pp. 200–201.

46. Gilbert Seldes, "The Masculine Revolt," *Scribner's,* April 1934, pp. 279–282, as quoted in Banner, *Women in Modern America,* p. 200.

47. *Snow White* (1938, directed by David Hand, Walt Disney); Robert S. McElvaine, "One Depression, Two Remedies," in Richard B. Stolley, ed., *Life: Our Century in Pictures* (Boston: Little Brown, 1999), p. 115.

48. Lorena Hickok, Report to Harry Hopkins, from Salt Lake City, September 1, 1934, Lorena Hickok Papers, Box 11, Franklin D. Roosevelt Library, Hyde Park, NY. See Robert S. McElvaine, *The Great Depression: America, 1929–1941* (New York: Times Books, 1984, 1993), pp. 179–180.

49. Win Stracke, as quoted in Studs Terkel, *"The Good War": An Oral History of World War II* (New York: Pantheon, 1984; Ballantine, 1985), pp. 156–157.

50. *Woman of the Year* (1942, directed by George Stevens, MGM).

51. Norman Mailer, *The Naked and the Dead* (New York: Rinehart, 1948; New York: Henry Holt, 1981, 1998).

52. "Paper Doll," lyrics by Johnny S. Black, Edward M. Marks Music, BMI.

53. Joel Whitburn, *Pop Memories, 1890–1954* (Menomonee Falls, WI: Record Research, 1986), pp. 316, 631.

54. Sloan Wilson, *The Man in the Gray Flannel Suit* (New York: Simon & Schuster, 1955).

55. C. Wright Mills, *White Collar* (New York: Oxford University Press, 1951), p. xii. Emphasis added.

56. James T. Patterson, *Grand Expectations: The United States, 1945–1974* (New York: Oxford University Press, 1996), p. 362.

57. William E. Leuchtenburg, *A Troubled Feast: American Society Since 1945* (Boston: Little Brown, 1983), p. 34.

58. Patterson, *Grand Expectations,* p. 223.

59. Arthur Schlesinger, Jr., *The Vital Center: The Politics of Freedom* (Boston: Houghton Mifflin, 1949), p. 151.

60. Patterson, *Grand Expectations,* pp. 197–198.

61. *Rebel Without a Cause* (1955, directed by Nicholas Ray, Warner Brothers).

62. *The Wild One* (1953, directed by Laslo Bendek, Columbia).

63. Norman Mailer, "The White Negro" (1957), in Mailer, *Advertisements for Myself* (New York: Putnam, 1959), p. 340.

64. Mailer, "White Negro," p. 348.

65. Jack Kerouac, *On the Road* (1957; New York: Penguin, 1976), p. 2.

66. Mailer, "White Negro," p. 341.

67. "Sixty-Minute Man" (1951, lyrics by William E. Ward, Fort Knox Music and Trio Music, BMI); "I'm a King Bee" (1957, lyrics by James Moore, Embassy Music, BMI); "I'm Ready" (1959, lyrics and music by Al Lewis, Sylvester Bradford, and Antoine "Fats" Domino, BMI).

68. Fred R. Harris, Statement to National Manpower Policy Task Force, February 4, 1970, Harris Papers, 207/21, University of Oklahoma, Norman, OK.

69. Ralph Ellison, *Invisible Man* (New York: Random House, 1952; Vintage, 1995), p. 153.

70. "Mannish Boy"/"I'm a Man" (1955, lyrics and music by McKinley Morganfield, Mel London, Ellas McDaniel, Watertoons Music, Arc Music, BMI).

71. Susan Faludi, *Stiffed: The Betrayal of the American Man* (New York: William Morrow, 1999), p. 69.

72. Arthur Miller, *Death of a Salesman* (New York: Viking Press, 1949; Penguin, 1976), p. 48.

73. Miller, *Death of a Salesman,* p. 139.

74. Miller, *Death of a Salesman,* p. 126.

75. Miller, *Death of a Salesman,* pp. 116–121.

76. Mailer, "White Negro," pp. 358, 354.

77. "Blue Yodel No. 1 (T for Texas)" (1927, lyrics and music by Jimmie Rodgers APRS, BMI).

78. "Me and the Devil Blues" (1937, lyrics and music by Robert Johnson, King of Spades Music, BMI).

79. "I Can't Be Satisfied" (1948, lyrics and music by McKinley Morganfield, Watertoons Music, BMI).

80. "(I Can't Get No) Satisfaction" (1965, lyrics and music by Mick Jagger and Keith Richards; ABKCO Music, BMI).

81. Margaret Mead, *Male and Female: A Study of the Sexes in a Changing World* (New York: William Morrow, 1949), p. 160.

CHAPTER 13: VERBAL MOUNTING

1. HBO Comedy Hour: "George Carlin Live at the Paramount," 1992.

2. Jane C. Hood, "Why Our Society Is Rape-Prone," *New York Times,* May 16, 1989.

3. Deborah Meier, as quoted in William Raspberry, " 'Wilding': A Principal's View," *Washington Post,* May 19, 1989.

4. Deuteronomy 23:1.

5. Anton Blok, "Rams and Billy-Goats: A Key to the Mediterranean Code of Honor," *Man,* vol. 16 (1981), pp. 429, 437.

6. *Deliverance* (1972, directed John Boorman, Warner Brothers).

7. *Shannon Richey Faulkner et al. v. James E. Jones, Jr., Chairman, Board of Visitors of the Citadel et al.,* transcript of trial, volume 9, United States District Court for the District of South Carolina, Charleston Division, pp. 54–55, as quoted in Susan Faludi, *Stiffed: The Betrayal of the American Man* (New York: William Morrow, 1999), pp. 116–117.

8. Faludi, *Stiffed,* p. 145.

9. Faludi, *Stiffed,* p. 146.

10. Michael Kimmel, *Manhood in America: A Cultural History* (New York: Free Press, 1996), p. 298.

11. Faludi, *Stiffed,* p. 126.

12. Eugene Luetkemeyer, as quoted in John M. Coggeshall, "Those Who Surrender Are Female: Prison Gender Identities as Cultural Mirror," in John M. Coggeshall and Pamela R. Frese, eds., *Transcending Boundaries: Multi-disciplinary Approaches to the Study of Gender* (New York: Bergin & Garvey, 1991), pp. 90–91.

13. Coggeshall, "Those Who Surrender Are Female," pp. 81, 85, 88, 89, 91.

14. Inez Cardozo-Freeman, *The Joint: Language and Culture in a Maximum-Security Prison* (Springfield, IL: Charles R. Thomas, 1984), p. 400, as quoted in Coggeshall, "Those Who Surrender Are Female," p. 85.

15. "New York Officer Surrenders in Sexual Assault on Immigrant," *Los Angeles Times,* "4,000 in N.Y. Protest Police Torture Case," August 14, 1997, August 17, 1997; "The Louima Case: The Overview," *New York Times,* June 9, 1999, "Volpe Sentenced to a 30-Year Term in Louima Torture," December 14, 1999.

16. Faludi, *Stiffed,* p. 146.

17. Mary Beard, quoted in *Love in the Ancient World* (1996, produced and directed by Christopher Miles, Milesian Film Productions, Primetime, and A&E Network).

18. Joyce Carol Oates, "Rape and the Boxing Ring," *Newsweek,* February 24, 1992, p. 61.

19. Christopher Lasch, *The Culture of Narcissism: American Life in an Age of Diminishing Expectations* (New York: Norton, 1979), pp. 66–67.

20. *Lenny* (1974, directed by Bob Fosse, United Artists).

21. I am indebted to my friend and colleague, Professor Judith Page, for a conversation that pointed me toward this understanding.

22. Roy Blount, Jr., Foreword in Jesse Sheidlower, ed., *The F Word* (New York: Random House, 1995), p. ix.

23. Chinua Achebe, *Things Fall Apart* (New York: Astor-Honor, 1959), p. 45.

24. "George Carlin Live at the Paramount."

25. Although I developed the interpretation of the use of this sort of terminology as "verbal mounting" on my own, I have since learned that Carl Sagan briefly alluded to a similar point in *The Dragons of Eden: Speculations on the Evolu-*

tion of Human Intelligence (New York: Random House, 1977), p. 54. I have benefitted from reading Sagan's speculations on the matter. I am grateful to my former student Alex Bradshaw for directing me to this work.

26. *American Heritage Dictionary of the English Language* (New York: American Heritage Publishing, 1969), p. 531.

27. Sheidlower, *F Word,* p. xxiv.

28. *Pulp Fiction* (1994, directed by Quentin Tarantino, Jersey Films / Miramax).

29. Gary Rivlin, "One of a Kind," *New Republic,* May 15, 2000, p. 8.

30. Sheidlower, *F Word,* p. 47.

31. Kristen Rand, "Bush Has Made Sure that Gun Control Will Be an Issue" (Knight Ridder / Tribune News Service), *Clarion-Ledger* (Jackson, MS), November 28, 1999.

32. Snoop Doggy Dogg, "Horny," as quoted in Robert Bork, *Slouching Towards Gomorrah: Modern Liberalism and American Decline* (New York: ReganBooks, 1996), p. 123.

33. George S. Patton, as quoted in Sam Keen, *Fire in the Belly: On Being a Man* (New York: Bantam, 1991), p. 95.

34. Susan Brownmiller, *Against Our Will: Men, Women, and Rape* (New York: Simon & Schuster, 1975; Bantam ed., 1976), pp. 23–25.

35. Mark Kishlansky, Patrick Geary, Patricia O'Brien, and R. Bin Wong, *Societies and Cultures in World History* (New York: HarperCollins, 1995), p. 101.

36. Dai Sil Kim-Gibson, "Japanese Military Supplies: The Korean 'Comfort Women,' " paper delivered at the Annual Meeting of the American Historical Association, New York, January 5, 1997; Maria Rosa Henson, *Comfort Woman: A Filipina's Story of Prostitution and Slavery Under the Japanese Military* (Lanham, MD: Rowman & Littlefield, 1999).

37. Arthur Miller, *Death of a Salesman* (New York: Viking Press, 1949; Penguin, 1976), p. 25. Emphasis added.

38. Deuteronomy 22:28–29.

39. "All Eyez on Me" (Careers BMG Music/Joshua S. Dream Music/Songs of Universal, BMI).

40. "Aint No Fun (If the Homies Cant Have None)," (Suge Publishing/Ain't Nuthin' Goin' On But Fu-kin', ASCAP), on Snoop Doggy Dogg, *"Doggystyle"* (1993).

41. John Leland, "Criminal Records: Gangsta Rap and the Culture of Violence," *Newsweek,* November 29, 1993, p. 62.

42. "Doggystyle" (Suge Publishing/Ain't Nuthin' Goin' on but Fu-kin', ASCAP), on Snoop Doggy Dogg, *"Doggystyle"* (1993).

43. "It's So Easy" and "Anything Goes," both as quoted in Michael Medved, *Hollywood vs. America: Popular Culture and the War on Traditional Values* (New York: HarperCollins, 1992), p. 97.

44. 2 Live Crew, "Dick Almighty," on *As Nasty as They Wanna Be,* as quoted in Medved, *Hollywood vs. America,* p. 99.

45. 2 Live Crew, "Put Her in the Buck," on *As Nasty as They Wanna Be,* as quoted in Medved, *Hollywood vs. America,* p. 99.

46. Sheidlower, *F Word,* pp. 199–201.

CHAPTER 14: "I AM *NOT*A WOMAN; HEAR ME ROAR"

1. David Maraniss, *First in His Class: The Biography of Bill Clinton* (New York: Simon & Schuster, 1995), p. 218.
2. "Transcript of Nixon's Farewell Speech to Cabinet and Staff Members in the Capital," *New York Times,* August 10, 1974.
3. "Among Notables, Bush Plays One Tough Room," *New York Times,* June 17, 1991.
4. HBO Comedy Hour: "George Carlin Live at the Paramount: Jammin' in New York," 1992.
5. George E. Mowry, *The Era of Theodore Roosevelt and the Birth of Modern America, 1900–1912* (New York: Harper & Row, 1958, 1962), p. 110.
6. Richard Hofstadter, *The American Political Tradition: And the Men Who Made It* (New York: Knopf, 1948, Vintage, 1973), p. 276.
7. Charles G. Washburn, letter, April, 1885, as quoted in Howard K. Beale, *Theodore Roosevelt and the Rise of America to World Power* (Baltimore: Johns Hopkins Press, 1956), p. 36.
8. Theodore Roosevelt, as quoted in James T. Patterson, *America in the Twentieth Century* (New York: Harcourt Brace Jovanovich, 1976, 1983), p. 75.
9. Theodore Roosevelt, as quoted in Hofstadter, *American Political Tradition,* pp. 277–278.
10. Hofstadter, *American Political Tradition,* p. 273.
11. Hofstadter, *American Political Tradition,* p. 269.
12. John Milton Cooper, Jr., *The Warrior and the Priest: Woodrow Wilson and Theodore Roosevelt* (Cambridge, MA: Belknap Press, 1983), p. 70.
13. Cooper, *The Warrior and the Priest,* p. 71.
14. Cooper, *The Warrior and the Priest,* p. 72.
15. As quoted in Mark Gerzon, *A Choice of Heroes: The Changing Faces of American Manhood* (Boston: Houghton Mifflin, 1982), p. 52.
16. Theodore Roosevelt, as quoted in Cooper, *Warrior and Priest,* pp. 12–13. Emphasis added.
17. Ralph V. Turner, *King John* (London and New York: Longman, 1994), p. 14.
18. Sam Keen, *Fire in the Belly: On Being a Man* (New York: Bantam, 1991), p. 95. A variant of this "ditty" is quoted in Susan Brownmiller, *Against Our Will: Men, Women, and Rape* (New York: Simon & Schuster, 1975; Bantam ed., 1976), p. 23.
19. John Milfull, " 'My Sex the Revolver': Fascism as a Theatre for the Compensation of Male Inadequacies," in Milfull, ed., *The Attractions of Fascism: Social Psychology and the Aesthetics of the "Triumph of the Right"* (New York: Berg, 1990), pp. 176–185, esp. 182–183.
20. Some still question the accuracy of the Soviet autopsy report, arguing that the Soviets may have had political motives in derogating Hitler in this way. Distinguished Oxford historian and Hitler biographer Alan Bullock has declared in recent years, however, that "there's no question" that the autopsy's finding that Hitler had no left testicle is accurate. Ron Rosenbaum, "Explaining Hitler," *New Yorker,* May 1, 1995, p. 65.
21. Robert G. L. Waite, *The Psychopathic God: Adolf Hitler* (New York: Basic Books, 1977), pp. 150–152, 161.

22. Waite, *Psychopathic God,* pp. 160–161; Albert Speer, *Inside the Third Reich,* Richard and Clara Winston, trans. (1969; New York: Macmillan, 1970), p. 126.

23. Waite, *Psychopathic God,* pp. 157–158.

24. Editorial, "The Dish on Nancy," *Nation,* April 29, 1991, p. 544.

25. Thomas C. Reeves, *A Question of Character: A Life of John F. Kennedy* (New York: Free Press, 1991), p. 7.

26. Seymour M. Hersh, *The Dark Side of Camelot* (Boston: Little, Brown, 1997), p. 10.

27. James N. Giglio, *The Presidency of John F. Kennedy* (Lawrence: University Press of Kansas, 1991), p. 267.

28. Hersh, *Dark Side of Camelot,* p. 10.

29. Hersh, *Dark Side of Camelot,* p. 2.

30. Barbara Ward, as quoted in Herbert S. Parmet, *JFK: The Presidency of John F. Kennedy* (New York: Dial, 1983), p. 305.

31. Jewel Reed, as quoted in Hersh, *Dark Side of Camelot,* p. 26.

32. Gloria Emerson, as quoted in Hersh, *Dark Side of Camelot,* p. 22.

33. Hersh, *Dark Side of Camelot,* p. 23.

34. Janet Des Rosiers, the plane's stewardess, saved this note and others Kennedy wrote. *Washington Post,* May 29, 1987, as quoted in Richard Reeves, *President Kennedy: Profile of Power* (New York: Simon & Schuster, 1993), p. 707n.

35. Hersh, *Dark Side of Camelot,* p. 24.

36. Hersh, *Dark Side of Camelot,* p. 11.

37. Richard Reeves, *President Kennedy,* p. 291.

38. Fred Dutton, interview quoted in Reeves, *President Kennedy,* p. 291.

39. Hersh, *Dark Side of Camelot,* p. 13.

40. Hersh, *Dark Side of Camelot,* p. 30. See also pp. 26, 29, 32–33.

41. Gloria Emerson, as quoted in Hersh, *Dark Side of Camelot,* p. 22.

42. ABC News Poll, August 16–22, 1999. 506 adults nationwide. Margin of Error ±4.5%, conducted by TNS Intersearch. http://www.pollingreport.com/20th .htm#Greatest

43. Benjamin C. Bradlee, *Conversations with Kennedy* (New York: Norton, 1975), p. 29.

44. Richard Reeves, *President Kennedy,* pp. 287–288.

45. Parmet, *JFK,* p. 305.

46. Jewel Reed, as quoted in Hersh, *Dark Side of Camelot,* p. 17.

47. Hersh, *Dark Side of Camelot,* pp. 16–17.

48. Hersh, *Dark Side of Camelot,* p. 27.

49. Hersh, *Dark Side of Camelot,* p. 27n.

50. Hersh, *Dark Side of Camelot,* p. 41. Emphasis added.

51. Hersh, *Dark Side of Camelot,* pp. 44, 63.

52. Hersh, *Dark Side of Camelot,* pp. 17–18, 20.

53. Richard Reeves, *President Kennedy,* p. 24.

54. Henry James, as quoted in Hersh, *Dark Side of Camelot,* p. 15.

55. Hersh, *Dark Side of Camelot,* p. 15.

56. George Ball as quoted in Richard Reeves, *President Kennedy,* p. 671n.

57. Hersh, *Dark Side of Camelot,* p. 31.

58. Theodore Roosevelt, as quoted in Hofstadter, *American Political Tradition,* p. 272.

59. As quoted in Alistair Horne, *Macmillan, 1957–1986* (London: Macmillan, 1989), p. 290.

60. Lyndon Johnson, as quoted in Richard Reeves, *President Kennedy,* p. 288.

61. Robert Dallek, *Flawed Giant: Lyndon Johnson and His Times, 1961–1973* (New York: Oxford University Press, 1998), p. 408.

62. Sam Houston Johnson, on Lyndon Johnson, as quoted in Robert A. Caro, *The Years of Lyndon Johnson: The Path to Power* (New York: Knopf, 1982), p. 155.

63. Caro, *Years of Lyndon Johnson,* p. 111.

64. Caro, *Years of Lyndon Johnson,* p. 193.

65. Dallek, *Flawed Giant,* p. 278.

66. Dallek, *Flawed Giant,* p. 186.

67. Dallek, *Flawed Giant,* p. 4.

68. Doris Kearns, *Lyndon Johnson and the American Dream* (New York: Harper & Row, 1976; Signet, 1977), p. 35.

69. Dallek, *Flawed Giant,* p. 6.

70. Dallek, *Flawed Giant,* pp. 186–187.

71. David Halberstam, *The Best and the Brightest* (New York: Random House, 1972), p. 531.

72. Johnson telephone conversation with Richard Russell, June 11, 1964, in Michael R. Beschloss, ed., *Taking Charge: The Johnson White House Tapes, 1963–1964* (New York: Simon & Schuster, 1997), pp. 402–403. Emphasis added. The friend Johnson quoted was A. W. Moursand, a Texas insurance man and former judge.

73. Larry L. King, "Machismo in the White House: LBJ and Vietnam," *American Heritage,* vol. 27, August 1976, p. 99.

74. As quoted in Halberstam, *The Best and the Brightest,* p. 532.

75. King, "Machismo in the White House," p. 100.

76. Kearns, *Lyndon Johnson and the American Dream,* p. 44; Dallek, *Flawed Giant,* p. 186.

77. As quoted in Gerzon, *A Choice of Heroes,* p. 93.

78. Stephen A. Ambrose, *Nixon: The Education of a Politician, 1913–1962* (New York: Simon & Schuster, 1987), p. 585.

79. Jonathan Schell, *The Time of Illusion: An Historical and Reflective Account of the Nixon Era* (New York: Random House, 1975), p. 158.

80. Henry R. Luce, *The American Century* (New York: Farrar & Rinehart, 1941), as quoted in Susan Faludi, *Stiffed: The Betrayal of the American Man* (New York: William Morrow, 1999), p. 22.

81. Schell, *Time of Illusion,* pp. 57–58, 123.

82. John W. Dean, 3d, as quoted in Anthony Lukas, *Nightmare: The Underside of the Nixon Years* (New York: Viking, 1976; Penguin, 1988), p. 18.

83. "G. Gordon Liddy" Show," Westwood One Radio Network, July 19, 1995.

84. Lukas, *Nightmare,* p. 87. Emphasis added.

85. Lukas, *Nightmare,* pp. 93, 95.

86. Lukas, *Nightmare,* p. 175.

87. William Shawcross, *Sideshow: Kissinger, Nixon, and the Destruction of Cambodia* (New York: Simon & Schuster, 1979), p. 434.

88. Michael Kimmel, *Manhood in America: A Cultural History* (New York: Free Press, 1996), p. 291.

89. George Bush, CNN interview, November 15, 1990.

90. "George Carlin Live at the Paramount."

91. Margaret Garrard Warner, "Bush Battles the 'Wimp Factor,' " *Newsweek,* October 19, 1987, pp. 28–36.

92. Barbara Ehrenreich, "The Warrior Culture," *Time,* October 15, 1990, p. 88.

93. Walter Shapiro et al., "Shoot-Out at Gender Gap," *Newsweek,* October 22, 1984, p. 29.

94. Shapiro, "Shoot-Out at Gender Gap," p. 30.

95. Karl Marx, *The Eighteenth Brumaire of Louis Napoleon* (1852; New York: International Publishers, 1963), p. 15.

96. Richard Wrangham and Dale Peterson, *Demonic Males: Apes and the Origins of Human Violence* (Boston: Houghton Mifflin, 1996), p. 233.

97. James B. Stewart, *Blood Sport: The President and His Adversaries* (New York: Simon & Schuster, 1996), p. 71.

98. Wrangham and Peterson, *Demonic Males,* p. 234.

99. Stewart, *Blood Sport,* p. 70.

100. Maraniss, *First in His Class,* p. 379.

101. Maraniss, *First in His Class,* p. 388.

102. Michael Isikoff, *Uncovering Clinton: A Reporter's Story* (New York: Crown, 1999), p. 57.

103. Isikoff, *Uncovering Clinton,* p. 135.

CHAPTER 15: THE "MASCULINE"/MARKETPLACE MYSTIQUE

1. "Why Can't a Woman Be Like a Man?," music by Frederick Loewe, lyrics by Alan Jay Lerner, from the musical *My Fair Lady.*

2. I had been using this terminology for years and had written much of this book before I discovered that Myriam Miedzian uses "masculine mystique" to describe much the same problem that I am addressing here. Miedzian, *Boys Will Be Boys: Breaking the Link Between Masculinity and Violence* (New York: Doubleday, 1991), pp. xx, xxiii–xxvi, 10, 15–17. Her primary concern is the ill effects of the masculine mystique on males, but she also fully understands what it has done to some feminists: "Because the assumption that male is the norm was so deeply embedded in our culture, many women assumed that to be liberated meant to be like men" (p. 15).

3. Betty Friedan, *The Second Stage* (New York: Summit Books, 1981); Carol Gilligan, *In a Different Voice: Psychological Theory and Women's Development* (Cambridge, MA: Harvard University Press, 1982), p. 27.

4. Diana Shaw, as quoted in Friedan, *Second Stage,* p. 32.

5. I have discussed this topic in "What Ever Happened to S-x?" *Los Angeles Times,* July 22, 1993.

6. Polly Toynbee, "Is Margaret Thatcher a Woman?" *Washington Monthly,* May 1988, p. 34.

7. Bob Edwards, on "Morning Edition," National Public Radio, June 25, 1993.

8. Glenda Holste, "A Look at Headlines Highlights Issue of Women's Standing in Society," *Clarion-Ledger* (Jackson, MS), May 9, 1993.

9. *New York Times,* June 15, 1993.

10. Bonnie Kreps, "Radical Feminism 1," in Anne Koedt, Ellen Levine, and Anita Rapone, eds., *Radical Feminism* (New York: Quadrangle Books, 1973), p. 239.

11. See, for example, Friedan, *Second Stage;* Carol Gilligan, *In a Different Voice: Psychological Theory and Women's Development* (Cambridge, MA: Harvard University Press, 1982); Germaine Greer, *Sex and Destiny: The Politics of Human Fertility* (New York: Harper & Row, 1984); Suzanne Gordon, *Prisoners of Men's Dreams: Striking Out for a New Feminine Future* (Boston: Little, Brown, 1991); Deborah Tannen, *You Just Don't Understand: Women and Men in Conversation* (New York: Morrow, 1990); and Miedzian, *Boys Will Be Boys.*

12. As quoted in Richard N. Ostling, "The Second Reformation," *Time,* November 23, 1992, p. 58.

13. Kreps, "Radical Feminism 1," p. 239.

14. Betty Friedan, *The Feminine Mystique* (New York: Norton, 1963, Avon, 1983), pp. 135–149.

15. Virginia Woolf, *A Room of One's Own* (New York: Harcourt, Brace, and World, 1929), p. 76.

16. Eva Figes, *Patriarchal Attitudes* (Greenwich, CT: Fawcett, 1971), p. 12, as quoted in Susan Faludi, *Stiffed: The Betrayal of the American Man* (New York: Morrow, 1999), p. 13.

17. Lawrence W. Levine, *Black Culture and Black Consciousness* (New York: Oxford University Press, 1977).

18. Gerda Lerner, *The Creation of Patriarchy* (New York: Oxford University Press, 1986), p. 13.

19. Charlotte Perkins Gilman, *Women and Economics* (1898; New York: Harper & Row, 1966), pp. 74–75. Emphasis added.

20. Alice Echols, "The Taming of the Id: Feminist Sexual Politics, 1968–83," in Carole S. Vance, ed., *Pleasure and Danger: Exploring Female Sexuality* (Boston: Routledge & Kegan Paul, 1984), p. 63. See also Ellen Willis, *Beginning to See the Light* (New York: Knopf, 1981).

21. Abby Kelly, as quoted in James West Davidson et al., *Nation of Nations: A Narrative History of the American Republic* (New York: McGraw-Hill, 1990), p. 440.

22. Genesis 2:18.

23. Friedan, *Feminine Mystique,* p. 28.

24. *New York Times,* February 17, 1989.

25. Ellen Goodman, "Conference Gathers Women Who Are Moving Uninvited into 'His' Place," *Clarion-Ledger* (Jackson, MS) October 20, 1989.

26. Madeleine Kunin, as quoted in Goodman, "Conference Gathers Women."

27. Toynbee, "Is Margaret Thatcher a Woman?" p. 36.

28. *Working Girl* (1988, directed by Mike Nichols, 20th Century-Fox).

29. Joan Beck, "More Firms Must 'Make Room for Mom,' " *Clarion-Ledger* (Jackson, MS), April 10, 1991.

30. Ashley Montagu, *The Natural Superiority of Women* (New York: Macmillan, 1952, rev. ed., 1968), p. 10.

31. Wendell Berry, "True Integration," *Mother Jones,* June 1989, p. 17.

32. George Gilder, *Men and Marriage* (Gretna, LA: Pelican, 1986), p. 57.

33. Robert Wright, "Why Men Are Still Beasts," *New Republic,* July 11, 1988, p. 27.

34. Anne Moir and David Jessel, *Brain Sex: The Real Difference Between Men and Women* (New York: Carol Publishing Group, 1991), p. 109.

35. Robert Wright, *The Moral Animal* (New York: Pantheon, 1994), pp. 33–92; Helen Fisher, *The First Sex* (New York: Random House, 1999), pp. 197, 205–206, 222; Deborah Blum, *Sex on the Brain* (New York: Viking, 1997; Penguin, 1998), p. 140; Sarah Blaffer Hrdy, *Mother Nature: A History of Mothers, Infants, and Natural Selection* (New York: Pantheon, 1999), pp. 83–86.

36. Sam Keen, *Fire in the Belly: On Being a Man* (New York: Bantam, 1991), p. 74.

37. Jane Gross, "Where 'Boys Will Be Boys' and Adults Are Bewildered," *New York Times,* March 29, 1993.

38. Anselma Dell'Olio. "The Sexual Revolution Wasn't Our War," in Francine Klagsbrun, ed., *The First Ms. Reader* (1973), as quoted in Peter N. Carroll, *It Seemed Like Nothing Happened: The Tragedy and Promise of America in the 1970s* (New York: Holt, Rinehart and Winston, 1982), p. 25.

39. Gilder, *Men and Marriage,* p. 78.

40. Seth Faison, "Beijing Divorce Rate Soars as Society Undergoes Profound Changes," *New York Times,* August 22, 1995.

41. Rupert Wilkinson, *The Pursuit of American Character* (New York: Harper & Row, 1988), p. 75.

42. Janis Joplin, as quoted in Allen J. Matusow, *The Unraveling of America: A History of Liberalism in the 1960s* (New York: Harper & Row, 1984), p. 303.

43. Janis Joplin, as quoted in Milton Viorst, *Fire in the Streets: America in the 1960s* (New York: Simon & Schuster, 1979), p. 521.

44. Barbra Streisand, as quoted in Sally Quinn, "Who Killed Feminism?," *Washington Post,* January 19, 1992.

45. Mona Charen, A 'Sexual Harassment' Often Really Vulgar Behavior Initiated by Sexual Revolution," *Clarion-Ledger* (Jackson, MS) June 9, 1993.

46. Kathleen Barry, *Female Sexual Slavery* (Englewood Cliffs, NJ: Prentice Hall, 1979), p. 227.

47. David Gelman et al., "The Mind of the Rapist," *Newsweek,* July 23, 1990, p. 46.

48. Elizabeth Holtzman, "Rape: The Silence Is Criminal," *New York Times,* May 5, 1989.

CHAPTER 16: "I'VE GOT TO BE A MACHO MAN"

1. Billy Shehan, October 1993, as quoted in Susan Faludi, *Stiffed: The Betrayal of the American Man* (New York: William Morrow, 1999), p. 114.

2. Susan Faludi, *Backlash:* The Undeclared War Against American Women (New York: Crown, 1991), pp. 65, 69.
3. Faludi, *Stiffed,* p. 120.
4. Faludi, *Stiffed,* p. 259.
5. Faludi, *Stiffed,* pp. 34, 38.
6. James Lawrence, as quoted in Faludi, *Stiffed,* pp. 89–90. Emphasis added.
7. Faludi, *Stiffed,* p. 255.
8. Richard Matheson, *The Shrinking Man* (1956; Boston: Gregg Press, 1979).
9. Albert Einstein, as quoted in Paul Boyer, *By the Bomb's Early Light: American Thought and Culture at the Dawn of the Atomic Age* (New York: Pantheon, 1985), p. 36.
10. Ashley Montagu, *The Natural Superiority of Women* (New York: Macmillan, 1952, rev. ed., 1968), p. 41.
11. Richard Matheson, as quoted in Faludi, *Stiffed,* p. 78.
12. *The Best Years of Our Lives* (1946, directed by William Wyler, Goldwyn/RKO).
13. Richard Matheson, *Collected Stories* (Los Angeles: Dream/Press, 1989), p. xvi, as quoted in Faludi, *Stiffed,* p. 78.
14. *The Incredible Shrinking Man* (1957, directed by Jack Arnold, Universal); Faludi, *Stiffed,* p. 31.
15. John F. Kennedy, 1960 Acceptance Address, as quoted in Arthur M. Schlesinger, Jr., *A Thousand Days: John F. Kennedy in the White House* (Boston: Houghton Mifflin, 1965), p. 60.
16. Norman Mailer, *The Presidential Papers* (New York: Penguin, 1968), p. 15, as quoted in Faludi, *Stiffed,* pp. 25–26.
17. Faludi, *Stiffed,* p. 25.
18. James MacGregor Burns, *John Kennedy: A Political Profile* (New York: Harcourt Brace, 1960).
19. As quoted in William H. Chafe, *The Unfinished Journey: America since World War II* (New York: Oxford University Press, 1986), p. 333.
20. SNCC Position Paper: "Women in the Movement," in Alexander Bloom and Wini Breines, eds., *Takin' It to the Streets: A Sixties Reader* (New York: Oxford University Press, 1995), p. 47.
21. Casey Hayden and Mary King, "Sex and Caste: A Kind of Memo," in Bloom and Breines, *Takin' It to the Streets,* pp. 47–51.
22. Sara Evans, *Personal Politics: The Roots of Women's Liberation in the Civil Rights Movement and the New Left* (New York: Knopf, 1979).
23. "Redstockings Manifesto" (1969), in Bloom and Breines, *Takin' It to the Streets,* p. 486.
24. "Redstocking Manifesto."
25. Robin Morgan, "Goodbye to All That" (1970), in Bloom and Breines, *Takin' It to the Streets,* pp. 501–503.
26. "My Conviction" (1968, lyrics by Jerome Ragni and James Rado, music by Gatt MacDermott, EMI Music).
27. Morgan, "Goodbye to All That," p. 501.

28. Faludi, *Stiffed*, p. 500.
29. John D'Emilio and Estelle B. Freedman, *Intimate Matters: A History of Sexuality in America* (New York: Harper & Row, 1988), p. 311.
30. Marge Piercy, as quoted in Faludi, *Stiffed*, p. 311.
31. Mao Zedong, *Problems of War and Strategy*, ii, November 6, 1938, as quoted in *The Oxford Dictionary of Quotations* (New York: Oxford University Press, 1941, 3d., 1979), p. 328.
32. Rufus "Chaka" Walls, June 18, 1969, as quoted in Milton Viorst, *Fire in the Streets: America in the 1960s* (New York: Simon & Schuster, 1979), p. 489.
33. Evans, *Personal Politics*, p. 224.
34. Michael Bilton and Kevin Sim, *Four Hours in My Lai* (New York: Viking, 1992), p. 113.
35. Michael Bernhardt, as quoted in Faludi, *Stiffed*, p. 343.
36. John M. Del Vecchio, *The 13th Valley* (New York: Bantam, 1982), p. 103, as quoted in Susan Jeffords, *The Remasculinization of America: Gender and the Vietnam War* (Bloomington: Indiana University Press, 1989), p. 147.
37. Sophocles, *Antigone* (443 B.C.E.), lns. 756–760, in Sophocles, *The Three Theban Plays* (New York: Penguin, 1982), Robert Fagles, trans., p. 94.
38. Tim O'Brien, *The Things They Carried* (Boston: Houghton Mifflin, 1990; New York: Penguin, 1991), pp. 187, 210.
39. Faludi, *Stiffed*, p. 62.
40. Faludi, *Stiffed*, p. 13.
41. Richard Foster, as quoted in Faludi, *Stiffed*, p. 79.
42. Don Motta, as quoted in Faludi, *Stiffed*, p. 65.
43. *Network* (1976, directed by Sidney Lumet, MGM/UA).
44. Faludi, *Stiffed*, p. 37.
45. Michael Kimmel, *Manhood in America: A Cultural History* (New York: Free Press, 1996), p. 326.
46. Mailer, *Presidential Papers*, pp. 52–53, as quoted in Faludi, *Stiffed*, p. 37.
47. Kimmel, *Manhood in America*, p. 292.
48. Garry Wills, *Reagan's America: Innocents at Home* (New York: Doubleday, 1987), pp. 162–167.
49. Jeffords, *Remasculinization of America*, pp. xiv, 45, 146, 169.
50. Art Tavizon and Al Weiner, as quoted in Faludi, *Stiffed*, p. 122.
51. *First Blood* (1982, directed by Ted Kotcheff, Orion).
52. *Rambo: First Blood, Part II* (1985, directed by George Pan Cosmatos, Tri-Star).
53. Lance Morrow, "A Bloody Rite of Passage," *Time*, April 15, 1985, pp. 22–24.
54. Morrow, "Bloody Rite of Passage," p. 24.
55. Jeffords, *Remasculinization of America*, pp. 127–130; Kimmel, *Manhood in America*, p. 307.
56. Faludi, *Stiffed*, p. 31.
57. "Woman Is the Nigger of the World," 1972 (lyrics and music by John Lennon and Yoko Ono; Copyright © Ono Music, Ltd. and Northern Songs Ltd.).
58. Faludi, *Stiffed*, pp. 8–9.

59. *Saturday Night Fever* (1977, directed by John Badham, Paramount).
60. Faludi, *Stiffed,* p. 226.
61. Paul Theroux, as quoted in Kimmel, *Manhood in America,* p. 295.
62. Faludi, *Stiffed,* p. 229.
63. Kimmel, *Manhood in America,* p. 321.
64. Mona Charen, "Keeping Promises, Saving Society," *Atlanta Constitution,* June 20, 1995; Louis Sahagun, "Christian Men's Movement Taps into Identity Crisis," *Los Angeles Times,* July 6, 1995; Elizabeth Levitan Spaid, "Christian Group Aims to Reshape the Male Mold," *Christian Science Monitor,* July 5, 1995; Gayle White, "70,000 Gather in Dome to Pledge Fidelity as Promise Keepers Meet," *Atlanta Journal-Constitution,* July 1, 1995.
65. "Black Men Converge on Washington for Rally," Associated Press dispatch, October 16, 1995.
66. Desda Moss, "Theme Timely, But Organizer Is Controversial," *USA Today,* October 13, 1995.
67. Nickie McWhirter, "The Promise Keepers: Does Father Know Best?" *Detroit News,* May 2, 1995; Mark Tran, "Be a Man, for God's Sake: Try Bonding," *Guardian* (Manchester, England), November 26, 1994; Karen S. Peterson, "Stadium Rallies Draw Growing Flock," *U.S.A. Today,* March 23, 1995.
68. Faludi, *Stiffed,* p. 229.
69. Leviticus 18:22. See also Leviticus 20:13.
70. Faludi, *Stiffed,* pp. 272, 276.
71. Jerry Falwell, Brett Butler, and John Jacobs, as quoted in Kimmel, *Manhood in America,* pp. 312–314.
72. Kimmel, *Manhood in America,* p. 312.
73. Shepherd Bliss, as quoted in Kimmel, *Manhood in America,* p. 317.
74. Faludi, *Backlash,* p. 306. The words quoted are Faludi's paraphrase of Bly's argument.
75. Faludi, *Backlash,* p. 308.
76. Doug Stanton, "Inward, Ho!," *Esquire,* October 1991, pp. 113–122; Charles Gaines, "Robert Bly, Wild Thing," *Esquire,* October 1991, p. 127; Tom Daly, "Male Bonding: An Update?" *Harper's,* April 1991, pp. 38–42; Faludi, *Backlash,* p. 309.
77. Robert Bly, *Iron John: A Book About Men* (New York: Addison Wesley, 1990), pp. 86–91.
78. Kimmel, *Manhood in America,* p. 318.
79. Kimmel, *Manhood in America,* p. 317.
80. Kris Belman, as quoted in Faludi, *Stiffed,* p. 110.
81. Faludi, *Stiffed,* pp. 110–113.
82. Kevin Howard, on *The Jenny Jones Show,* April 7, 1993, as quoted in Faludi, *Stiffed,* p. 108.
83. Faludi, *Stiffed,* p. 110.
84. Faludi, *Stiffed,* p. 133.
85. Faludi, *Stiffed,* p. 114, 110.
86. Faludi, *Stiffed,* p. 317.

87. Bilton and Sim, *Four Hours in My Lai,* p. 129.

88. "Latest Disorder Has Bodybuilders Feeling Puny" (Gannett News Service), *Clarion-Ledger* (Jackson, MS), January 2, 1998.

89. "Boys Feel Pressure to be 'Big'," reported by Kevin Newman, *ABC World News Tonight,* November 15, 1999.

90. "White Rabbit" (1967, lyrics and music by Grace Slick, Irving Music, Inc. BMI).

91. "Boys Feel Pressure to Be 'Big'," *ABC World News Tonight,* November 15, 1999.

CHAPTER 17: FEARS OF OUR FATHERS, LIVING STILL

1. "The Great Mandala (The Wheel of Life)," (lyrics and music by Peter Yarrow, Mary Travers, and Albert Grossman, copyright © 1967, Pepamar Music, ASCAP).

2. Barbara Crossette, "Despite Strides, Report Says Women Still Undervalued Economically," *New York Times,* August 18, 1995.

3. "Cardinal Avers that God Is Masculine," *Boston Globe,* June 18, 1991.

4. Ari L. Goldman, "Cardinal Said God Is a Man? Not Really?" *New York Times,* June 22, 1991.

5. "Anglicans in Britain Vote to Let Women Be Priests," *New York Times,* November 12, 1992, "Catholic Bishops in U.S. Reject Policy Letter on Role of Women," *New York Times,* November 19, 1992; Richard N. Ostling, "The Second Reformation," *Time,* November 23, 1992, p. 53.

6. "Paulist's Baptisms Are Called Not Valid," *Boston Globe,* October 8, 1993; "Without a 'Father' or 'Son,' Baptisms Are Ruled Invalid," *New York Times,* October 9, 1993.

7. William J. Montalbano, "Pope Reaffirms His Stand: No Women Priests," *Los Angeles Times,* May 31, 1994; Alan Cowell, "Pope Rules Out Debate on Making Women Priests," *New York Times,* May 31, 1994; Anna Quindlen, "To the Altar," *New York Times,* June 4, 1994.

8. "A Wife's Role Is to 'Submit' Baptists Declare," *Los Angeles Times,* June 10, 1998.

9. "Pope Moves to Quell Dissent Over Ban on Female Priests," *Los Angeles Times,* July 1, 1998.

10. "Southern Baptist Convention Passes Resolution Opposing Women as Pastors," *New York Times,* June 15, 2000.

11. George Edgin Pugh, *The Biological Origin of Human Values* (New York: Basic Books, 1977), pp. 388–389.

12. Irenaus Eibl-Eibesfeldt, *The Biology of Peace and War: Men, Animals, and Aggression,* Eric Mosbacher, trans. (New York: Viking, 1979; orig. German edition, Munich: R. Piper & Co. Verlag, 1975), p. 24*n*.

13. As quoted in Ostling, "Second Reformation," p. 54.

14. Matt Friedeman, "Abortionist, Feminist, Homosexual 'Word Thieves' Tragically Effective," *Clarion-Ledger* (Jackson, MS), February 5, 1993.

15. Celestine Bohlen, "Pope Calls for End to Discrimination Against Women," *New York Times,* July 11, 1995; Suzanne Moore, "Pope on a Rope" *Guardian* (Manchester, England), July 13, 1995; Judy Mann, "A Good First Step for the Pope,"

Washington Post, July 14, 1995; Gustav Niebuhr, "To the Women of the World: An Affirmation of 'Feminine Genius,' " *New York Times,* July 16, 1995.

16. Linda Grant, "Now, About that Letter, John Paul," *Guardian* (Manchester, England), July 12, 1995.

17. Ellen Goodman, " 'People' Studies Exclude Females," *Clarion-Ledger* (Jackson, MS), June 24, 1990.

18. Steven Mufson, "Chinese Leader Presses Call for 'One Couple, One Child,' " *Washington Post,* March 21, 1995; Patrick E. Tyler, "Birth Control in China: Coercion and Evasion," *New York Times,* June 25, 1995; Jeff Newsmith, "China's Surplus of Bachelors Could Breed Chaos," *Atlanta Constitution,* February 10, 1995; Marty Singer, "Home Alone," *Chicago Tribune,* September 22, 1994.

19. *Weekend Edition* (National Public Radio), September 11, 1994.

20. As quoted in Ashley Montagu, *The Natural Superiority of Women* (New York: Macmillan, 1952, rev. ed., 1968), p. 3.

21. Christopher Smith, in Barbara Bradley, "Doomsday Predictions," *Morning Edition,* National Public Radio, December 8, 1999; http://search.npr.org/cf/cmn/cmnpd01fm.cfm?PrgDate=12/08/1999&PrgID=3

22. Ernie McBride, Sr., as quoted in Susan Faludi, *Stiffed: The Betrayal of the American Man* (New York: William Morrow, 1999), p. 68.

23. Ferdinand Lundberg and Marynia F. Farnham, *Modern Woman: The Lost Sex* (New York: Harper & Brothers, 1947).

24. Terrence Real, *I Don't Want to Talk About It: Overcoming the Secret Legacy of Male Depression* (New York: Scribner, 1997).

25. Richard Foster, as quoted in Faludi, *Stiffed,* p. 79.

26. Margaret Mead, *Male and Female: A Study of the Sexes in a Changing World* (New York: William Morrow, 1949), p. 160.

27. Mead, *Male and Female,* pp. 159–160.

28. Michael Kimmel, *Manhood in America: A Cultural History* (New York: Free Press, 1996), pp. 308–309, 314–315.

29. William F. Buckley, Jr., "The Clubhouse," in *About Men* (New York: Simon & Schuster, 1987), p. 256, as quoted in Kimmel, *Manhood in America,* p. 314.

30. George Gilder, *Men and Marriage* (Gretna, LA: Pelican, 1986), p. 82.

31. William James, "The Moral Equivalent of War" (1910), in John J. McDermott, ed., *The Writings of William James: A Comprehensive Edition* (New York: Modern Library, 1968), p. 664.

32. David D. Gilmore, *Manhood in the Making: Cultural Concepts of Masculinity* (New Haven, CT: Yale University Press, 1990), pp. 223–230.

33. Andrew Hacker, *Two Nations: Black and White, Separate, Hostile, Unequal* (New York: Scribner, 1992), pp. 29–30.

34. James, "Moral Equivalent of War," p. 669.

35. I am grateful to Dr. William D. Frazier for this insight.

36. Henry Adams, *The Education of Henry Adams* (1918; Boston: Houghton Mifflin, 1961), p. 447.

37. Arthur Miller, *Death of a Salesman* (New York: Viking Press, 1949; Penguin, 1976), p. 139.

38. William Carlos Williams, as quoted in Thomas Cahill, *The Gifts of the Jews* (New York: Nan A. Talese / Doubleday, 1998), p. ix.

39. William Shakespeare, *The Tempest,* Act II, scene 1, line 261 (spoken by Antonio).

40. Edward M. Kennedy, Eulogy for Robert F. Kennedy, June 8, 1968, in Pierre Salinger, et al., eds. *"An Honorable Profession": A Tribute to Robert F. Kennedy* (Garden City, NY: Doubleday, 1968) p. 3.

INDEX

443

CREDITS

Illustrations

PROLOGUE

Adam, digging, while Eve cares for the children, from *Speculum Humanae Salvationis.*
Musée Condé, Chantilly/Giraudon/Art Resource, New York.

CHAPTER 2

Liverpool football fans, 1977.
Wide World Photos.

San Francisco Anti-Chinese cartoon, 1882.
Caroline Buckler.

CHAPTER 3

Paleolithic cave painting from eastern Spain depicting a group of men using bows to hunt.
Museé de l'Homme/Robert Harding.

Breast Envy: "Rose of Sharon," 1938.
© Horace Bristol/CORBIS.

CHAPTER 4

Albrecht Durer, *Adam and Eve,* 1504.
Centennial Gift of Landon T. Clay, Courtesy, Museum of Fine Arts, Boston.

Going forth from Eden to Till the Soil. Carolingian Abbey of St. Martin, Tours. British Library, London, England.
Bridgeman Art Library.

Michelangelo, *Fall and Expulsion,* 1509–10. Vatican Museums and Galleries, Vatican City.
Bridgeman Art Library.

CHAPTER 5

Masaccio, *Expulsion from Eden.* Brancacci Chapel, S. Maria del Carmine, Florence.
Alinari/Art Resource, New York.

Cylinder seal from late third millennium B.C.E. Mesopotamia showing men leading and guiding a two-handled plow.
Department of Antiquities, Ashmolean Museum, Oxford, England.

God reprimanding Adam and Eve. Bronze relief on doors of the Cathedral of Hildesheim, Germany, ca. 1015.
Foto Marburg/Art Resource, New York.

CHAPTER 6

"Out of Woman" Aztec Mother of Gods.
Dumbarton Oaks Research Library and Collections, Washington, DC.

"Out of Man" Michelangelo, *The Birth of Eve,* Sistine Ceiling, 1511, Sistine Chapel, Vatican City.
Monumenti Musei e Gallerie Pontificie.

CHAPTER 7

"Venus" of Willendorf, Naturhistorisches Museum, Vienna, ca. 28,000–25,000 B.C.E.
© Ali Meyer/CORBIS.

Birth of Aphrodite, Greek relief, Ludovisi Throne. Museo Nazionale Romano delle Terme, Rome.
Alinari/Art Resource, New York.

God, Michelangelo, the Sistine Chapel in 1511.
Monumenti Musei e Gallerie Pontificie.

Bronze Zeus, Artemiisium. National Archeological Museum, Athens, ca. 460 B.C.E.
Foto Marburg/Art Resource, New York.

CHAPTER 8

Perseus severing head of Medusa, Metope from the Temple of Selinunte. Museo Archaeologico, Palermo, Italy.
Scala/Art Resource, New York.

Battle of Greeks and Amazons, from a frieze on the Mausoleum, Halikarnassos. Mid-
  4th century, B.C.E.
British Museum.

Demeter and Kore, from Thebes, Boeotia.
Louvre.

CHAPTER 9

The Women at the Tomb, from the *Rabula Gospel,* Zagba on the Euphrates, Syria, ca.
  586 C.E. Biblioteca Laurenziana, Florence, Italy.
Scala/Art Resource, New York.

Andrea della Robbia, *Madonna and Child,* late 15th century. Bargello, Florence, Italy.
Scala/Art Resource, New York.

CHAPTER 10

Master of Housebook, *Coat of Arms with the World Upside-down,* c. 1485.
Rijksprentenkabinet, Rijksmuseum, Amsterdam.

God the Father as Architect, from the *Bible Moralisee,* middle 13th century.
Osterreichische Nationalbibliothek, Vienna.

CHAPTER 11

Theodore Roosevelt poses in a studio as the mythical frontiersman, 1885.
© CORBIS.

CHAPTER 12

Christian Dior "New Look."
© Bettmann/CORBIS.

Mr. Muscle Beach 1954.
Collection of David Chapman.

CHAPTER 13

Rocky Mountain bighorn ram mounts another ram, 1981.
© W. Perry Conway/CORBIS.

Demonstrator giving the finger, 1977.
© Wally McNamee/CORBIS.

CHAPTER 14

Theodore Roosevelt as Rough Rider, painting by W. G. Read.
Library of Congress.

Adolf Hitler gives the Nazi salute at a party congress, 1934.
© Hulton-Deutsch Collection/CORBIS.

Female stumptail macaque presenting to a male.
Ernesto Rodriguez Luna.

Pat Oliphant cartoon of George Bush in drag.
© Universal Press Syndicate.

CHAPTER 15

Still from *Annie Hall,* 1977.
© Bettmann/CORBIS.

CHAPTER 16

Battle at Chu Lai, Vietnam, 1965. Photo by Kyoichi Sawada.
© Bettmann/CORBIS.

CHAPTER 17

"Eve was Framed," women's liberation demonstration in New York, 1970.
© Bettmann/CORBIS.

Lyrics

"Paper Doll"
Written by Johnny Black.
Used by permission of Edward B. Marks Music Company.

"I'm a King Bee"
Written by Slim Harpo.
© Embassy Music Corporation.
All rights reserved. Used by permission.

"Mannish Boy"
Written by Muddy Waters (McKinley Morganfield), Ellas McDaniel, and Melvin
    London.
© 1955 (Renewed 1983) Arc Music Corporation, Lonmel Music Publishing, Water-
    toons Music (BMI)/Administered by Bug Music.
All rights reserved. Used by permission.
International copyright secured.

ABOUT THE AUTHOR

Robert S. McElvaine grew up in New Jersey and was educated at Rutgers University and the State University of New York at Binghamton, from which he received his Ph.D. in history in 1974. He is the Elizabeth Chisholm Professor of Arts and Letters and Chair of the Department of History at Millsaps College in Jackson, Mississippi, where he has taught for more than twenty-five years. He is the author of six previous books: *Down and Out in the Great Depression: Letters from the Forgotten Man; The Great Depression: America, 1929–1941; The End of the Conservative Era: Liberalism After Reagan; Mario Cuomo: A Biography; What's Left?—A New Democratic Vision for America;* and *The Depression and New Deal: A History in Documents.* He is considered to be one of the foremost authorities on the era of the Great Depression.

His articles and opinion pieces appear frequently in such publications as the *New York Times, Washington Post, Los Angeles Times, Wall Street Journal,* and *Newsweek.* He has been a guest on numerous television and radio programs, including NBC's *Today, ABC World News Tonight with Peter Jennings,* National Public Radio's *All Things Considered* and *Morning Edition,* and BBC television and radio.

McElvaine has served as historical consultant for several television programs, including the seven-episode PBS series *The Great Depression.* He has received many awards for his teaching, among them a silver medal in the National Professor of the Year program of the Council for the Advancement and Support of Education. He has spent the last dozen years developing new expertise in several fields, including anthropology, human evolution, mythology, religion, ancient history, and women's history, in order to put himself in a position to offer a reinterpretation of the significance of sex in the unfolding of human history.

He and his wife, Anne, have four children. They reside in Clinton, Mississippi.